Beiträge zum
ausländischen öffentlichen Recht und Völkerrecht

Edited by

the Max Planck Society
for the Advancement of Science
represented by Prof. Dr. Armin von Bogdandy
and Prof. Dr. Anne Peters

Volume 345

Lucas Sánchez de Miquel

Legislative Remedies before Human Rights Courts

A comparative analysis

Nomos

Open Access funding provided by Max Planck Society.

The Deutsche Nationalbibliothek lists this publication in the Deutsche Nationalbibliografie; detailed bibliographic data are available on the Internet at http://dnb.d-nb.de

a.t.: Berlin, FU, Diss., 2023

Source title: Legislative Remedies in Human Rights Adjudication

1st Edition 2025

Published by
Nomos Verlagsgesellschaft mbH & Co. KG
Waldseestraße 3–5 | 76530 Baden-Baden
www.nomos.de

Production of the printed version:
Nomos Verlagsgesellschaft mbH & Co. KG
Waldseestraße 3–5 | 76530 Baden-Baden

ISBN (Print): 978-3-7560-2322-6
ISBN (ePDF): 978-3-7489-4971-8

DOI: https://doi.org/10.5771/9783748949718

Online Version
Nomos eLibrary

A mis padres

Acknowledgements

The present book is based on my doctoral thesis, defended at the Faculty of Law of the Freie Universität Berlin in November 2023. I am deeply indebted to my supervisor, Prof. Dr. Anne Peters, for her invaluable support, trust and encouragement. I would also like to thank my second supervisor, Prof. Dr. Helmut Aust, for his feedback and advice.

Special thanks also to my former colleagues at the Max Planck Institute for Comparative Public Law and International Law in Heidelberg for the constructive conversations and feedback on the thesis, particularly in the context of the 'Tuesday meetings' of Prof. Peters' team and the 'Coloquio Iberoamericano' organised by Dr. Mariela Morales. In this context, thanks also to the other doctoral candidates of the Institute for the more informal part of our time there, it was a pleasure sharing this journey with you.

This book also benefitted from research stays at the Inter-American Court of Human Rights and at the Department for the Execution of Judgments of the European Court of Human Rights, for which I also want to express my gratitude to these two institutions. At the institutional level, I also want to thank the Max Planck Society for funding my position as a Research Fellow at the Max Planck Institute and for enabling this Open Access publication. Finally, thanks to Mario Petoshati for his excellent work proof-reading and editing this book.

Para acabar, quiero dar gracias por encima de todo a mis padres, mi hermano y el resto de mi familia por su apoyo constante a lo largo de tantos años, a mis amigos por estar siempre allí a pesar de la distancia, y a Julia por acompañarme y aguantarme durante todo este trayecto.

Lucas Sánchez de Miquel

Berlin, December 2024

Inhaltsverzeichnis

List of Abbreviations

ACHR	American Convention on Human Rights
ACHPR	African Charter on Human and Peoples' Rights
ACmHPR	African Commission on Human and Peoples' Rights
ACtHPR	African Court of Human and Peoples' Rights
ACDEG	African Charter on Democracy, Elections and Governance
AHRLJ	African Human Rights Law Journal
AJICL	African Journal of International and Comparative Law
AJIL	American Journal of International Law
AJJ	American Journal of Jurisprudence
App.	Application
Art.	Article
Arts.	Articles
ARSIWA	Draft Articles on the Responsibility of States for Internationally Wrongful Acts
AU	African Union
AUILR	American University International Law Review
CAT	UN Convention Against Torture
CDDH	Steering Committee for Human Rights
CED	UN Committee on Enforced Disappearances
CEDAW	UN Convention on the Elimination of Discrimination against Women
CERD	UN Committee on the Elimination of Racial Discrimination
CESCR	UN Committee on Economic, Social and Cultural Rights
CJEU	Court of Justice of the European Union
CJTL	Columbia Journal of Transnational Law
CLR	Columbia Law Review
CoE	Council of Europe
CoM	Committee of Ministers of the Council of Europe
CRC	UN Convention on the Rights of the Child
CUP	Cambridge University Press

DR	Dominican Republic
DRC	Democratic Republic of Congo
E.g.	Exempli gratia
ECHR	European Convention on Human Rights
ECHRLR	European Convention on Human Rights Law Review
ECmHR	European Commission of Human Rights
ECtHR	European Court of Human Rights
Ed.	editor
Eds.	editors
EHRLR	European Human Rights Law Review
Et al.	et altri
Et seq.	et sequens
EU	European Union
GLJ	German Law Journal
HLR	Harvard Law Review
HRCee	UN Human Rights Committee
HRLR	Human Rights Law Review
IACmHR	Inter-American Commission of Human Rights
IACtHR	Inter-American Court of Human Rights
I.e.	Id est
ICCPR	International Covenant on Civil and Political Rights
ICESCR	International Covenant on Economic, Social and Cultural Rights
ICERD	International Convention on the Elimination of All Forms of Racial Discrimination
ICJ	International Court of Justice
ICLQ	International and Comparative Law Quarterly
ICMW	International Convention on the Protection of the Rights of All Migrant Workers and Members of Their Families
I•CON	International Journal of Constitutional Law
ICPED	International Convention for the Protection of All Persons from Enforced Disappearance
ICTY	International Criminal Tribunal for the Former Yugoslavia
ILC	International Law Commission
IJHR	International Journal of Human Rights

IJLC	International Journal of Law in Context
ISQ	International Studies Quarterly
IVF	In Vitro Fertilisation
JHRP	Journal of Human Rights Practice
JICJ	Journal of International Criminal Justice
JIDS	Journal of International Dispute Settlement
JIRD	Journal of International Relations and Development
JSAP	Journal of Small Animal Practice
JTD	Journal of Trauma and Dissociation
LCP	Law and Contemporary Problems
LGBTI	Lesbian, Gay, Bisexual, Transexual and Intersexual
LJIL	Leiden Journal of International Law
LPICT	The Law and Practice of International Courts and Tribunals
MoU	Memorandum of Understanding
MPEIPro	Max Planck Encyclopedia of International Procedural Law
MPEPIL	Max Planck Encyclopedia of Public International Law
NGO	Non-Governmental Organisation
NHRI	National Human Rights Institution
NJHR	Nordic Journal of Human Rights
NILR	Netherlands International Law Review
No.	Number
Nos.	Numbers
NQHR	Netherlands Quarterly of Human Rights
OAS	Organisation of American States
OAU	Organisation of African Unity
OJLS	Oxford Journal of Legal Studies
OUP	Oxford University Press
p.	page
pp.	pages
PACE	Parliamentary Assembly of the Council of Europe
PALU	Pan African Lawyers Union
Para.	paragraph
Paras.	paragraphs

PCIJ	Permanent Court of International Justice
SFRY	Socialist Federal Republic of Yugoslavia
TFF	Turkish Football Federation
UDHR	Universal Declaration of Human Rights
UK	United Kingdom
UN	United Nations
UNGA	United Nations General Assembly
US	United States
USD	United States Dollar
VCCR	Vienna Convention on Consular Relations
VCLT	Vienna Convention on the Law of Treaties
Vol.	volume
Vs.	versus
WILJ	Wisconsin International Law Journal
YJIL	Yale Journal of International Law
YLJ	Yale Law Journal
ZaöRV	Zeitschrift für ausländisches öffentliches Recht und Völkerrecht

Introduction

One of the main developments in the area of international adjudication during the late 20th century was the establishment of international courts and proceedings allowing individuals to lodge complaints against states for the violation of human rights norms. The traditional understanding about the consequences of judgments finding such human rights violations was that the victims were entitled to adequate reparation, usually in the form of monetary compensation. However, as the different human rights systems and the jurisprudence of the respective courts developed, it started to become clear that some infringements were of such a systemic nature that individual forms of reparation did not suffice. This gave rise to different forms of collective reparation, conceptualised as structural remedies or guarantees of non-repetition. Among those, a group of remedies that stands out due to their high degree of intrusiveness in states' sovereignty are the measures that order the reform of the domestic legal order, labelled here as legislative remedies. These remedies are the main object of analysis of this book.

One of the cornerstones of international law is the rule establishing that the infringement of treaty obligations cannot be justified on the basis of domestic laws.[1] Nevertheless, in practice, the picture looks different. In 2012, when writing about the future of international law, the late Antonio Cassesse highlighted the inconsistency between domestic legislative frameworks and international rules as one of the main problems in this regard.[2] In order to change this, he advocated in favour of an international court being in charge of determining the incompatibility of states' domestic laws with their international obligations and in that case "enjoining the state to modify its legislation forthwith".[3] Moreover, he argued that any natural or legal person with an interest in the matter should be able to trigger such proceedings and a monitoring body should supervise the implementation

1 In accordance with Art. 27 of the Vienna Convention on the Law of Treaties (VCLT).

2 Antonio Cassesse, "Towards a Moderate Monism: Could International Rules Eventually Acquire the Force to Invalidate Inconsistent National Laws?", in Antonio Cassesse (ed.), *Realizing Utopia: The Future of International Law*, Oxford: OUP, 2012, pp. 187–199, at p. 188.

3 Cassesse, "Towards Moderate Monism", 2012, p. 191.

of such reforms. This is, to some extent, a development that is already taking place before regional human rights courts, which have, over the last few decades, been slowly and rather quietly moving in that direction.[4]

Human rights violations stemming from domestic legislation (or lack thereof) are rather common before the three regional courts – the European Court of Human Rights (ECtHR), the Inter-American Court of Human Rights (IACtHR) and the African Court on Human and Peoples' Rights (ACtHPR). These infringements represent a particular challenge because if legislative issues are not adequately tackled, they are likely to give rise to numerous additional violations. For that reason, although it was not foreseen at the moment of their respective inceptions, each of these human rights courts developed their remedial practice to a point in which they began to include measures prescribing legislative reforms. These remedies have been rather common in the jurisprudence of the IACtHR since the early 2000s, while in the case law of the ECtHR, they were introduced in 2004 with the 'pilot judgment procedure' but remain highly exceptional. The ACtHPR, despite being a comparatively young court, has also increasingly adopted this remedial practice, especially during recent years when this Court's case law considerably expanded. Even though some of the most widely discussed judgments of human rights courts involve these remedial measures,[5] it is a practice that has not received much scholarly attention as a whole.

This practice is related to the expanding powers of international adjudication in general,[6] as well as to the increasing international judicialisation

4 This was also recognised by Cassesse, mentioning in this respect that the ECtHR would in principle be able to meet these conditions but failed due to do so due to its narrow interpretation of Art. 41 ECHR, while the IACtHR was doing better on that front. See Cassesse, "Towards Moderate Monism", 2012, pp. 194-198.

5 This is the case, for example, of the 'prisoners voting rights saga' before the ECtHR or the prohibition of amnesty laws by the IACtHR. On the former, see ECtHR, *Greens and M.T. vs. UK* (2010), operative para. 6 ("the respondent State must (a) bring forward (...) legislative proposals intended to amend the 1983 Act and, if appropriate, the 2002 Act in a manner which is Convention-compliant; and (b) enact the required legislation (...)"). Concerning the latter see for example IACtHR, *Gelman vs. Uruguay* (2011). The decisions on amnesty laws have on the one hand been able to end with the impunity of some perpetrators of human rights violations, but on the other hand they have also been criticised in other instances for interfering with the democratic will of the people.

6 It relates thus to the rise of 'newstyle' international courts, which follow a model of compulsory jurisdiction that has effects going far beyond the parties in dispute. See generally Karen J. Alter, *The New Terrain of International Law: Courts, Politics, Rights*, Princeton, NJ: Princeton University Press, 2014.

of national politics.[7] The rise of 'newstyle' international courts can be detected primarily at the regional level, where the tribunals in several instances reach deeply into the societies under their supervision.[8] Although it is quite common to see national laws and policies challenged on the basis of international rules and principles – not only in the field of human rights but also in other fields such as international trade or environmental law – regional human rights courts play a special role in this regard, as they are the only international courts that include binding orders to reform legislation on a consistent basis. Such remedial measures are indeed exceptional at the international level, being instead usually circumscribed to the field of constitutional adjudication, due to their high degree of intrusiveness. Thus, by issuing legislative remedies human rights courts are stretching their mandate beyond their traditional role of providing individual justice, thereby adopting a constitutional role.

It is, however, arguably still unclear in which specific type of cases the respective human rights courts order the amendment of domestic laws, as well as the concrete way in which they do so. In this regard, some authors have criticised these courts for not being sufficiently consistent and for lacking clear criteria in terms of deciding under which circumstances to order such far-reaching measures.[9] Thus, in view of the established practice of regional human rights courts ordering states under certain circumstances to amend their domestic laws, as well as the arguable inconsistency and lack of clear criteria in this regard, it is worth taking a closer look at this practice, comparatively analysing and assessing the human rights courts' approach to this issue. This is even more relevant when considering the backlash suffered by the three regional human rights courts in recent times. Some of the main points of criticism have concerned the alleged judicial activism of these bodies, going beyond what is established in the mandates of the respective Conventions, and their interference with the sovereignty of states, especially with their democratic institutions. Both of these issues

7 See for example on this point Michael C. Tolley, "Judicialization of Politics in Europe: Keeping Pace with Strasbourg", *Journal of Human Rights* 11(1), 2012, pp. 66-84.

8 Karen Alter and Lisbeth Hooghe, "Regional Dispute Settlement", in Tanja Börzel and Thomas Risse (eds.), *The Oxford Handbook of Comparative Regionalism*, Oxford: OUP, 2016, at p. 551.

9 With regard to the IACtHR, see for example Tom Antkowiak, "Remedial Approaches to Human Rights Violations: The Inter-American Court of Human Rights and Beyond", *CJTL* 46(2), 2008, pp. 351-419, at p. 383 ("While the Court's current approach in this area is uneven, it does order legislative reforms in a handful of circumstances").

are especially present in the cases in which the amendment of domestic laws is ordered by these courts.

On the other hand, two further important challenges currently faced by regional human rights protection systems relate to their effectiveness and efficiency.[10] The former challenge refers mainly to the lack of adequate protection of international rights domestically, which is one of the main goals of the human rights conventions.[11] Arguably, one way of improving effectiveness is to adopt a 'constitutional' approach in human rights adjudication, ordering states to improve the domestic implementation of rights.[12] The efficiency challenge relates to the so-called 'docket crisis', especially affecting the ECtHR, which is unable to deal in an adequate time with the high number of complaints it receives.[13] One of the reasons for the backlog is the number of 'repetitive' applications submitted to this court.[14] In this regard, ordering states to reform their domestic legislation in order to solve structural problems of incompatibility with the respective treaty can be a good way of diminishing the number of repetitive applications, improving the efficiency of the respective system by focusing on the improvement of domestic human rights protection.

Therefore, legislative measures can be considered a particularly ambivalent remedial practice. They can be very helpful in order to render the systems more efficient, tackling structural problems that can trigger many applications, and improving the internal protection of human rights, but at the same time, they can be a source of criticism for undue interference with the democratic decision-making of domestic parliaments. This book, therefore, aims to establish when and how these remedies should be included in

---

10 See generally, regarding these two concepts and its differences, Iain Cameron, "The Court and the member states: procedural aspects", in Andreas Follesdal *et al.* (eds.), *Constituting Europe*, Cambridge: CUP, 2013, pp. 25-61.

11 See Art. 1 of the ECHR, Art. 1 of the ACHR and Art. 1 of the ACHPR.

12 See on this issue Steven Greer, "Constitutionalizing Adjudication under the European Convention on Human Rights", *Oxford Journal of Legal Studies* 23(3), 2003, pp. 405-433.

13 See for example the Copenhagen Declaration (2018), in which the caseload challenge is pointed to as "a reason for serious concern". It also notes that "that further steps will need to be taken over the coming years in order to further enhance the ability of the Court to manage its caseload".

14 See Antkowiak, *CJTL* 2008, at p. 354, arguing that "flaws in [the ECtHR's] remedial framework are partially responsible for the Strasbourg Court's current crisis". The concept of 'repetitive applications' means applications directed against the same state and related to the same substantive issue (e.g., human rights violations against different persons caused by the same law).

judgments and to assess if the current approach used by the three regional human rights courts is appropriate in this regard.

I. Conceptual Clarifications

This book will mainly revolve around a concept – that of legislative remedies before human rights courts. In this regard, it is first necessary to delimit and clarify this concept. In a nutshell, the concept implies binding judicial orders to legislate following the finding of a human rights violation. The concept of legislative remedies might, however, be confusing at first glance, as one might understand that these are remedies established in legislation. Instead, these are remedies imposed by the judiciary, whereby the legislative element is to be found in their content and not in their origin. In this respect, it is useful to briefly clarify what is meant by each of the elements of "Legislative Remedies before Human Rights Courts".

1. "*Legislative ...*"

The legislative element is very important for this study, implying an obligation for the state to legislate in some way. This can take place through the amendment of a specific domestic law, but also through its repeal or the adoption of a new law. The differences between these types of legislative actions will be examined, but the term is meant to encompass all three situations. The remedial case law of regional human rights courts includes a wide array of measures, though most of them require executive action, which can consist, for example, of the payment of compensation, the restitution of property, or the publication of judgments. Some of them also require actions by the judiciary, such as the retrial of victims or the investigation into human rights violations and the prosecution and punishment of those responsible. However, human rights judgments prescribing legislative action are much rarer and carry particular problems, as will be shown later in this book.

The legislative element usually emerges very clearly from the wording of the remedial measure, but these measures can sometimes be rather vague and must be read in conjunction with the rest of the judgment in order to find that they require legislative action. This is generally the case with the remedial measures of the ECtHR, as will be explained in more detail in Chapter 3. But also some measures of the other two courts can be confusing in this regard. For example, in a case related to the territorial rights of indigenous communities, the ACtHPR prescribed the adoption of "all necessary measures, legislative, administrative or otherwise" in order to delimit and title the ancestral lands of the Ogiek people.[15] A difference with the IACtHR's remedial measures in similar cases is that here the ACtHPR refers exclusively to one indigenous community (the Ogiek), while the IACtHR usually extends such a remedy to all indigenous peoples residing in the territory of the respondent state.[16] In the latter case, this would likely need to be done through legislation. In the former case, however, the legislative nature of these measures is less clear, as demarcating and titling the territory of one particular community can in principle be done through administrative measures. In fact, the Court argued that, in this case, "the legal framework in the Respondent State already possesses legislation that can be used to effect restitution of Ogiek ancestral land".[17] Therefore, this is a measure that cannot be considered a legislative remedy *stricto senso*.

Despite this caveat, it will be shown that there are some remedial measures in which the legislative nature can be very clearly observed, while in others it is more an issue of interpretation. Thereby, this study adopts a contextual interpretation that assumes a legislative remedy when this can be inferred from the particular circumstances of the case and there is no specific indication to the contrary. In any case, it is also necessary to clarify that not every finding of a human rights court concerning the incompatibility of legislation will be examined, nor the recommendations to reform it, but only the binding judicial orders in this regard. This is where the concept of remedies comes into play.

2. "... *Remedies* ..."

In the adjudicatory context, the concept of remedies is generally understood as "the judicial relief which legal systems provide for the enforcement

15 ACtHPR, *ACmHPR vs. Kenya* (2022), operative paras. vi) and vii).

16 See for example IACtHR, *Kaliña and Lokono Peoples vs. Suriname* (2015), operative para. 14 ("the State shall take the necessary measures to establish an effective mechanism for delimiting, demarcating and titling the territories of indigenous and tribal peoples in Suriname"). See also IACtHR, *Yakye Axa vs. Paraguay* (2005), operative para. 10.

17 ACtHPR, *ACmHPR vs. Kenya* (2022), para. 96.

or defence of substantive rights".[18] This concept, however, comprises two distinct aspects: a procedural and a substantive one. The former encompasses the procedures and institutions that allow for the enforcement of rights. A remedy in this regard would consist of granting access to a judicial procedure, irrespective of the outcome. On the other hand, the substantive understanding of remedies refers precisely to the outcome of these proceedings, i.e. the specific measures ordered for redressing an infringement or preventing its recurrence. In this understanding, remedies adopt the form of secondary obligations for states, i.e. obligations that arise from the breach of a primary obligation.

In scholarship, this is sometimes also referred to as reparation, and in some instances, both terms are used interchangeably.[19] However, 'remedy' in a substantive understanding has a broader meaning than 'reparation'. According to the ILC Articles on the Responsibility of States for Internationally Wrongful Acts (ARSIWA), reparation takes the form of restitution, compensation or satisfaction. This concept thus usually comprises only the measures aimed at redressing those injured by the wrongful act. There are, however, additional secondary obligations arising from an internationally wrongful act which aim at the protection of community interests.[20] The term 'remedy', as utilised throughout this book, thus includes every secondary obligation that arises with the breach of an international norm, including – but not limited to – the obligation to provide full reparation.

This term, however, excludes the recommendations that judicial bodies make in the argumentative part of their judgments, as well as those contained in advisory opinions, as they lack the binding nature of remedial measures. Thus, only the measures included in the operative part of judgments will be taken into account, as they constitute the *res judicata* – as opposed to the statements included in the argumentative part, constituting

---

18 Chester Brown, *A Common Law of International Adjudication*, Oxford: OUP, 2007, p. 185.

19 See for example Dinah Shelton, "Righting Wrongs: Reparations in the Articles on State Responsibility", *AJIL* 96(4), 2002, pp. 833-856.

20 According to ARSIWA, cessation and guarantees of non-repetition are consequences of internationally wrongful acts separate from reparation. See André Nollkaemper, "Constitutionalization and the Unity of the Law of International Responsibility", *Indiana Journal of Global Legal Studies* 16(2), 2009, pp. 12-13 ("Indeed, the obligation of cessation, and the obligation to provide guarantees of non-repetition, have more to do with a return to legality than with reparation for injury."). He considers this shift from injury to legality as a "step toward a more public law, and indeed, constitutionally oriented, law of responsibility".

the *res interpretata*. In this respect, the status that primary obligations possess in domestic constitutional contexts is also mostly irrelevant for this study, as states are obliged to implement the remedial measures issued by an international court that has jurisdiction over them independently of this status. This is clearly the case in international human rights adjudication, as states have a concrete treaty obligation to abide by the *res judicata* of these courts' judgments against them.[21]

3. "...*before Human Rights Courts*"

Furthermore, a terminological distinction needs to be drawn between extrajudicial remedies in international law and those pertaining to the field of international adjudication. Extrajudicial remedies can be imposed "by act of the party injured, by operation of law [or] by agreements between parties".[22] They are therefore remedies that are imposed without a judicial decision expressly ordering them. A typical form of extrajudicial remedies consists in sanctioning states for their breach of international norms.[23] On the contrary, the remedies examined here are those awarded by courts, with binding character for the respondent party. This also excludes the measures contained in the decisions of quasi-judicial institutions – such as the Inter-American Commission of Human Rights (IACmHR), the African Commission on Human and Peoples' Rights (ACmHPR) or the UN human rights treaty bodies – as they lack the formal binding force of remedies.

Extrajudicial and judicial remedies are closely interlinked. The ARSIWA, for example, consists mainly of a codification of extrajudicial remedies, serving to "shape the expectations of parties to a dispute, becoming a basis for negotiations when international obligations are breached".[24] This does not, however, prevent international courts from invoking the ARSIWA in

21 Whether they have also an obligation to abide by the *res interpretata* is a more contentious issue in human rights adjudication, whereby the constitutional context would arguably come into play. See for example Davide Paris, "Allies and Counterbalances – Constitutional Courts and the European Court of Human Rights: A Comparative Perspective", *ZaöRV* 77, 2017, pp. 623-649, at p. 648, arguing that domestic constitutional courts can deviate from the *res interpretata* in the context of implementing ECtHR judgments (but not from the *res judicata*).

22 Capone, "Remedies", in *MPEPIL*, para. 1.

23 For a general overview on this topic, see Matthew Happold and Paul Eden (eds.), *Economic Sanctions and International Law*, Oxford: Hart, 2016.

24 Shelton, *AJIL* 2002, p. 833.

order to support their own decisions regarding remedies.[25] This was also the aim of the ILC, when it decided the ARSIWA "should be allowed to stand as Articles to be taken up by courts and tribunals as deemed appropriate".[26]

Moreover, the origin of extrajudicial remedies in international law can be traced back to antiquity,[27] while judicial remedies are more recent. Most authors situate their origin at the beginning of modern arbitral practice, particularly in the context of the Jay Treaty of 1794.[28] This treaty, concluded between the United States and Great Britain, provided the basis for the creation of three mixed commissions whose function was to settle issues among these states that could not be solved through negotiation. In this context, it was assumed for the first time that the remedies allowed for in international law are analogous to those of domestic law.[29] This was the approach of arbitral tribunals in the subsequent decades.[30] As the relevant treaties of that time tended not to include aspects related to the availability of specific remedies, this was left to arbitral discretion. Judicial remedies thus evolved through this arbitral jurisprudence during the 19th and early 20th centuries. Nevertheless, that practice was far from consistent, having been described as "a chaos of conflicting decisions".[31] In addition, throughout that period remedies were almost exclusively confined to the payment of damages for the violation of international agreements.[32]

This changed with the establishment of the Permanent Court of International Justice (PCIJ) in 1922. In front of this court, remedies evolved from monetary compensations to more sophisticated forms of redress. The

---

25 See generally UN Secretary General, *Responsibility of States for internationally wrongful acts: Compilation of decisions of international courts, tribunals and other bodies*, Report of the Secretary-General, UN Doc. A/74/83, 2019.

26 James Crawford, "The International Court of Justice and the Law of State Responsibility", in Christian Tams and James Sloan (eds.), *The Development of International Law by the International Court of Justice*, Oxford: OUP, 2013, pp. 70–86, at p. 81.

27 Extrajudicial remedies in antiquity took the form of war indemnities. An example in this regard are the reparations imposed by Rome over Carthage after the First Punic War. See generally Kim Oosterlink, "Reparations", in Steven N. Durlauf and Lawrence E. Blume (eds.), *The New Palgrave Dictionary of Economics*, 2nd edition, London: Palgrave Macmillan, 2008.

28 Christine Gray, *Judicial Remedies in International Law*, Oxford: OUP, 1990, p. 5.

29 Capone, "Remedies", in *MPEPIL*, para. 6.

30 Gray, *Judicial Remedies in International Law*, 1990, p. 6 ("the borrowing of remedies from municipal law was carried out unquestioningly by tribunals").

31 Gray, *Judicial Remedies in International Law*, 1990, p. 10.

32 Gray, *Judicial Remedies in International Law*, 1990, p. 12 ("the award of remedies other than damages by international arbitral tribunals is extremely unusual").

judgment of the *Factory at Chorzów* case (1927) is especially relevant in this regard, as will be observed in Chapter 2. When the International Court of Justice (ICJ) succeeded the PCIJ in 1945, it continued with the task of developing an international law of remedies, shaping and applying further measures. Thereafter, more specialised international tribunals began to emerge, such as the regional human rights courts, which will be the main object of study in this book. Each of these tribunals progressively developed its own remedial practice from the point of departure of general international law. Eventually, the three regional human rights courts began, for different reasons, to order states to reform their domestic laws, as will be seen in Chapter 3. This study will thus primarily focus on the field of international human rights adjudication, whilst also briefly analysing the issue of remedies in general international adjudication. The latter analysis will allow for an examination of the main differences between these two fields and whether legislative measures form part of a sort of 'remedial *lex specialis*'.

II. Methodological Clarifications

As previously mentioned, this book intends to offer a systematic analysis of legislative remedies before human rights courts, comparing the remedial practice of the three aforementioned human rights courts in this respect and looking at all relevant features of this remedy from different perspectives, thereby analysing both doctrinal discourses and empirical data. In order to do so, the main research questions will be: Is the reform of domestic laws a consistent remedy in international human rights adjudication? When and how is this remedy applied? What are its main features and problems? Is the approach employed by human rights courts in this respect normatively adequate?

These general questions can be divided into more specific questions that will be addressed in the respective chapters of the book. In this regard, the first part of the book will contend with the following questions: To what extent do human rights treaties affect domestic laws? How do human rights courts perform the review of legislation? Are legislative remedies part of a 'remedial *lex specialis*' of human rights courts? What was the historical process and the reasons that led the respective human rights courts to issue these types of remedies? How do they fit in the overall remedial landscape before each regional human rights court?

In turn, the second part will try to answer the following questions with the help of a case law analysis: Which type of human rights issues are being tackled through legislative remedies? Is there a common understanding among human rights courts in this regard? What degree of discretion should be afforded to the legislator in order to implement these remedial measures? What are the courts' respective approaches towards the issue of remedial deference? What are the main consequences of legislative remedies? Are legislative remedies more likely to generate non-compliance and backlash? Finally, the conclusion will briefly assess whether the previously examined remedial practice of each human rights court is adequate in light of several normative considerations.

In order to answer this array of questions, the first part of the book will build on a rather doctrinal and analytical method, while the second part will be based on an analysis of case law with a comparative approach regarding the results. With regard to the consequences of legislative remedies, the last chapter will also make use of case studies in order to focus on more concrete aspects. In this respect, the first part does not present major methodological issues; the second part, however, necessitates the clarification of some aspects. As it consists of an analysis of case law that includes all judgments containing legislative measures, a very relevant aspect is the identification of these measures. They are relatively easy to identify in the cases of the IACtHR and the ACtHPR, but with the ECtHR this looks different, as will be explained in the next section. Concerning the comparative element of the analysis, it is argued that, despite several differences in the historical development, context and practice of the three regional human rights courts, comparing their remedies seems appropriate in light of the equivalency of these remedial measures. However, some of the main differences among them should be highlighted.

1. *Identifying Legislative Measures: the Special Case of Legislative Remedies before the ECtHR*

Before both the IACtHR and the ACtHPR, the obligation to carry out a legislative reform after an infringement is a rather straightforward issue. When this is prescribed in the operative provisions of a judgment, states are obliged to legislate, and when this is not the case they are not required to do so. There are certainly cases in which states reform their legislation after a judgment of these courts without it being expressly ordered. This is however exceptional, and the link between the judgment and the reform is rather tenuous. Other potential aspects come into play, especially domestic political preferences that use international judgments as a justification that can lower the political costs of a perhaps unpopular reform.[33]

In the case of the ECtHR, the emergence of such a secondary obligation is arguably less clear. This is primarily due to the institutional architecture of the European human rights system and the role of the Committee of Ministers (CoM) in supervising the execution of judgments, as this body is able to request additional measures besides those expressly ordered in the operative part of a judgment.[34] Once the ECtHR delivers a judgment, it is transferred to the CoM (an intergovernmental body of the Council of Europe), which is in charge of supervising its execution.[35] The Department for the Execution of Judgments of the ECtHR (usually called the 'Secretariat') plays a very important role in this regard, acting as an intermediary between the respondent state and the CoM.[36] In this context, the respondent state has to deliver an Action Plan to the Secretariat specifying the measures it will take in order to comply with the judgment.[37]

Ideally, when presenting an Action Plan, states should already envisage the adoption of appropriate individual and general measures. This should include legislative reforms whenever the violation stems from a legal provision or when its legal order prevents the state from providing an effective remedy at the domestic level. In practice, however, states often depict the

---

33 The reform can thereby be defended internally as an external imposition, even if only indirect.

34 See Octavian Ichim, *Just Satisfaction under the European Convention on Human Rights*, Cambridge: CUP, 2014, p. 38 ("The Committee of Ministers has the authority to impose certain actions or even legislative adjustments"). See also Linos-Alexander Sicilianos, "The Involvement of the European Court of Human Rights in the Implementation of its Judgments: Recent Developments under Article 46 ECHR", *NQHR* 32(3), 2014, pp. 235–262, at p. 254 ("To put it otherwise, by supervising the execution of the Court's judgment, the Committee of Ministers frequently specifies (some of) the legal consequences of the violation of the Convention").

35 See generally Raffaela Kunz, "Securing the survival of the system: the legal and institutional architecture to supervise compliance with the ECtHR's judgments", in Rainer Grote, Mariela Morales and Davide Paris (eds.), *Research Handbook on Compliance in International Human Rights Law*, Edward Elgar, 2021, pp. 12-41.

36 See Basak Çalı and Anne Koch, "Foxes Guarding the Foxes? Peer Review of Human Rights Judgments by the Committee of Ministers of the Council of Europe", *HRLR* 14(2), 2014, pp. 301-325.

37 Or an Action Report in case it considers that all necessary measures have already been taken. See Rules of the Committee of Ministers for the supervision of the execution of judgments and of the terms of friendly settlements.

violation as resulting from a wrong application of the law and affecting only the victims of the case at hand. Thus, they usually limit their action plan to the payment of just satisfaction ordered by the Court.[38] This is what Hillebrecht termed "the low-hanging fruit" in compliance with human rights judgments.[39]

In such cases, the role of the Secretariat and the CoM becomes more relevant. These bodies will examine whether states – besides paying the compensation ordered by the Court – adopt the necessary individual and general measures,[40] assessing the action plans and reports and carrying out dialogue with the concerned state.[41] In practice, this means that the Secretariat, before issuing a recommendation to the CoM regarding the compliance status and whether to close the supervision proceeding, can ask for individual and general measures.[42] In order to assess the need for such measures, the Secretariat will evaluate the facts of the case and the violation established, as well as the Court's review in this regard. If the CoM then considers that general measures (such as legislative reforms) are necessary to comply with the judgment and those are not envisaged by the states, it can oblige them to modify the action plans to include such measures. However, this will ultimately depend on the political negotiations

38 See for example Alice Donald and Anne-Katrin Speck, "The European Court of Human Rights' Remedial Practice and its Impact on the Execution of Judgments", *HRLR* 19, 2019, pp. 1-35, at p. 22 ("Governments may use the absence of specific remedies as an excuse to propose the narrowest possible solution to the dysfunctions identified by the Court").

39 Courtney Hillebrecht, *Domestic Politics and International Human Rights Tribunals: The Problem of Compliance*, Cambridge: CUP, 2014, pp. 61-65.

40 See Rules of the Committee of Ministers for the supervision of the execution of judgments and of the terms of friendly settlements, Rule 6 (2) (b), establishing that the CoM will examine among others whether "general measures have been adopted, preventing new violations similar to that or those found or putting an end to continuing violations". See generally also Helen Keller and Cedric Marti, "Reconceptualizing Implementation: The Judicialization of the Execution of the European Court of Human Rights Judgments", *EJIL* 26(4), 2016, pp. 829-850.

41 It has been argued in this regard that "the Court examines and decides whether the personal interest has been affected, while the Committee of Ministers basically defends the general interest" (Ichim, *Just Satisfaction*, 2014, p. 34).

42 See Krzysztof Wojtyczek, "Judicial and Non-Judicial Elements in the Enforcement Mechanism of the European Convention on Human Rights", in Paulo Pinto de Albuquerque and Krzysztof Wojtyczek (eds.), *Judicial Power in a Globalized World*, Springer, 2019, pp. 653-672, at p. 669, noting that "[t]he determination of legal consequences is made in the form of the decision to close or not the supervision proceedings, accepting or not the measures presented by the respondent Government".

held before the CoM at an intergovernmental level, which often lead to the acceptance of such minimal compliance.[43]

Thus, it can be seen that legislative reforms as a consequence of ECtHR judgments are nothing rare, even if the Court usually abstains from prescribing them.[44] Nevertheless, whether legislative reforms are implemented or not in these types of cases will largely depend on the willingness of the respondent state's legislative or judicial authorities, or – if they lack such willingness – on the intergovernmental negotiations taking place in the execution phase before the CoM. This is different when legislative measures are included in the operative paragraphs of ECtHR's judgments, as these are the only cases in which there is no room for negotiation.[45] This is the only situation in which they can be conceptualised as legislative remedies, as here the requirement to reform domestic laws is legally binding.[46] These are, therefore, the cases that will be examined in more detail in the following chapters.

---

43 See Dia Anagnostou and Alina Mungiu-Pippidi, "Domestic Implementation of Human Rights Judgments in Europe: Legal Infrastructure and Government Effectiveness Matter", *EJIL* 35(1), 2014, pp. 205-227, at p. 212, mentioning the criticism to the CoM "for accepting minimal government action (...) as sufficient to acknowledge compliance". See also Laurence Helfer, "Redesigning the European Court of Human Rights: Embeddedness as a Deep Structural Principle of the European Human Rights Regime", *EJIL* 19(1), 2008, pp. 125-159, at p. 147, highlighting that "the Court's unwillingness to identify specific remedies (...) generated disputes within the Committee of Ministers concerning the scope of a respondent state's legal obligations".

44 Actually, after quantitatively examining the implementation of all leading judgments of the ECtHR until 2016, Stiansen finds that "approximately 25 per cent of cases require legislative changes for compliance". See Øyvind Stiansen, "Delayed but not Derailed: Legislative Compliance with European Court of Human Rights Judgments", *IJHR* 23(8), 2019, p. 1224. Sadurski even argued that "the fiction according to which, before its pilot judgments, the Strasbourg rulings dealt with specific cases, and not with the law, was just that: a fiction" (Wojciech Sadurski, "Partnering with Strasbourg: Constitutionalisation of the European Court of Human Rights, the Accession of Central and East European States to the Council of Europe, and the Idea of Pilot Judgments", *HRLR* 9(3), 2009, pp. 397- 453, at p. 421).

45 See for a more detailed explanation Chapter 3 of this book.

46 See for example Lech Garlicki, "Broniowski and After: On the Dual Nature of 'Pilot Judgments'", in Lucius Caflisch *et al.* (eds.), 2007, p. 185, explaining that one of the main features of pilot judgments is that it "constitutes not a mere recommendation but a command, at least in respect of those of its components included in the operative part of the judgment".

2. *Comparing the Three Regional Human Rights Courts*

After identifying these judgments, the remedial practices of the three regional courts will be analysed and compared. This study will thus be situated in the field of comparative international law, as it compares the approaches adopted by different regional actors with respect to international adjudication. It carries out what Roberts *et al.* term 'thick comparativism', as it compares the actual practice of courts instead of only the legal norms.[47] More concretely, it will focus on what has been labelled 'comparative regionalism' by comparing specific regional human rights systems and actors.[48]

The three regional human rights courts present notable differences in their structure and jurisdiction. This is to some extent a result of their context and historical evolution. The ECtHR was already established by 1959, followed by the IACtHR in 1979 and by the ACtHPR only in 2004. In this regard, the latter courts are part of an adjudicatory system composed of two levels, with a human rights commission accompanying the court, while in the case of the European system, the Commission was dismantled in 1998 with the entry into force of Protocol 11. This has some important implications for the jurisdiction exercised by these courts. In the case of the ECtHR, individuals can submit a complaint directly to the Court if the admissibility requirements are met. On the contrary, in the Inter-American system, individuals can only submit a complaint to the IACmHR, which will then examine the complaint and issue recommendations if it finds an infringement. Only if the state fails to comply with these recommendations will the case be transmitted to the IACtHR. This is similar to the case of the ACtHPR, with the difference being that—through an optional declaration—states can also allow individuals and NGOs to access the African Court directly.

Another important difference between these systems concerns the number of judgments issued annually by each court, which amounts to over 1000 in the case of the ECtHR, while they comprise only around twenty by both the IACtHR and the ACtHPR. Moreover, supervising compliance with the judgments is a judicial task in the case of the IACtHR, while in the European and African systems, this task is carried out by intergovernmental

47 See Anthea Roberts *et al.*, "Comparative International Law: Framing the Field", *AJIL* 109, 2015, at p. 471.

48 See generally Tanja Börzel and Thomas Risse (eds.), *The Oxford Handbook of Comparative Regionalism*, Oxford: OUP, 2016.

political bodies. All of these differences have notable effects on the remedial practice of the courts and will therefore be taken into account when analysing and comparing this practice along the rest of this book. Further differences that will be examined in this context concern the personal competence to submit an application to these courts, their advisory function, their self-understanding and their geopolitical context.

In any case, it is a fact that all three courts prescribe in some instances the reform of domestic laws, thus clearly constituting a practice that allows for comparison. In addition, the comparison of regional human rights courts has been gaining traction in scholarship during the last decade.[49] One can find general comparisons of the human rights courts in their context,[50] but also more specific ones concerning their historical evolution,[51] their approach towards specific types of cases,[52] or even their remedial intrusiveness.[53] Thus, the comparative approach seems to be adequate in this context, while taking into account the intrinsic differences among the regional human rights systems.

III. Structure and Overview

This book will be divided into two main parts, each consisting of three chapters. The first part of the book will deal with the concept of legislative remedies more generally, asking whether it constitutes a particularity of

49 Comparisons between the ECtHR and the IACtHR are the most usual in this respect, while the ACtHPR has only figured in more recent comparative analyses, due to the fact that the latter court has only started to develop its jurisprudence rather recently. See in this respect Başak Çalı, Mikael Rask Madsen and Frans Viljoen, "Comparative regional human rights regimes: Defining a research agenda", *I•CON* 16(1), 2018, pp. 128–135.

50 Laurence Burgorgue-Larsen, *Les 3 cours régionales des droits de l'homme in context: La justice qui n'allait pas de soi,* Paris: Éditions Pedone, 2020.

51 See Alexandra Huneeus and Mikael Rask Madsen, "Between universalism and regional law and politics: A comparative history of the American, European, and African human rights systems", *I•CON* 16(1), 2018, pp. 136– 160.

52 Francesco Seatzu and Simona Fanni, "A Comparative Approach to Prisoners' Rights in the European Court of Human Rights and Inter-American Court of Human Rights Jurisprudence", *Denver Journal of International Law and Policy* 44(1), 2015, pp. 21-40; Bertoni, Eduardo Andrés, "The Inter American Court of Human Rights and the European Court of Human Rights: A Dialogue on Freedom of Expression Standards", *EHRLR* 3, 2009, pp. 332-352.

53 Başak Çalı, "Explaining variation in the intrusiveness of regional human rights remedies in domestic orders", *I•CON* 16(1), 2018, pp. 214-234.

international human rights law and examining how it fits within the overall landscape of remedies, both in general international adjudication and human rights adjudication. The second part of the book will then analyse in detail the legislative remedies awarded by the three regional human rights courts, comparatively examining what type of human rights issues they are intended to tackle and if their wording allows for enough legislative room of manoeuvre, as well as the consequences of these remedies.

Chapter 1 will provide a first overview of the concept of legislative remedies, linking it to the obligations to legislate included in human rights treaties as well as to the review of legislation carried out by human rights courts. This concept will also be examined through the lens of the global constitutionalism approaches, arguing that these remedies provide for an increased constitutionalisation of human rights adjudication. In this respect, despite legislative measures being more intrusive than other remedies, it will be concluded that human rights courts are legitimated to issue them under certain circumstances.

Chapter 2 will then deal with legislative remedies in the area of general international adjudication. This is useful in order to answer the question of whether these remedies are a particularity of human rights adjudication and if they would fulfil the same function if applied by general international courts, particularly by the ICJ. In this context, the chapter explores the landscape of remedies in general international law, and how the ICJ has approached this issue. In addition, it inquires more concretely on whether legislative measures could be ordered by the ICJ, and what their remedial function would be in the context of general international law. It will conclude that although the ICJ would have the competence to order the reform of domestic laws, it should be cautious to employ it due to this court's particular function in the ecosystem of international adjudication.

Chapter 3 will then return to international human rights adjudication, situating legislative remedies in the remedial landscape of regional human rights courts. The chapter will inquire about the special nature of remedies in this field and explore whether legislative remedies are an intrinsic part of it. In addition, the evolution and the current remedial practice of human rights courts will be analysed and legislative remedies will be situated therein, before moving to the second part of the book in which the case law analysis concerning these remedial measures is carried out.

This case law analysis will start in Chapter 4 by establishing a typology of legislative remedies, dividing them into ten categories of specific human rights issues. Thereby, the chapter will examine whether legislative measures are a consistent remedy before human rights courts with respect to *when* they are employed. It will be concluded that the regional human rights courts have a common understanding of these measures, shown by the fact that most of them are awarded in order to tackle similar human rights issues, whereby the protection of vulnerable groups and fair trial rights play a paramount role. However, it will also be argued that the three courts have different priorities in this respect, as each of them has favoured the use of legislative remedies for a particular issue that the other two have not considered to be as relevant. This does moreover reflect the self-understanding of human rights courts concerning their role in their respective region.

Chapter 5 – continuing with the analysis of case law – focuses on the common nature of legislative measures with regard to *how* they are applied. The chapter will thereby analyse the wording of these measures and the issue of remedial deference towards domestic legislatures. A concept developed in this context is that of the 'margin of deliberation', implying that legislative remedies should not prevent legislatures from deliberating in order to implement them. They should be therefore sufficiently vague as to the expected outcome of the legislative reform, an issue that should be preferably decided through democratic deliberation. An exception concerns however states with authoritarian tendencies, in which the democratic conditions for this deliberation to take place are not fully present. Then, the chapter will analyse the mechanisms developed by human rights courts that relate to deference *vis-a-vis* legislatures, as well as the diverging specificity in the courts' legislative remedies, taking into account the approach developed by each human rights court in this regard.

Chapter 6 will then finally focus on the post-judgment phase, exploring the consequences of legislative remedies. First, the chapter will inquire to what extent the instances of backlash against regional human rights courts are related to their legislative measures. Then it will turn to the issue of compliance, examining if and why legislative measures are less likely to be timely implemented by states, an issue that is mainly related to domestic execution procedures. It will also be argued that, despite difficulties in its implementation, legislative remedies are able to have an impact that extends beyond the case at hand, *inter alia* by providing an opportunity structure for civil society actors to engage in strategic litigation. Finally, the question of whether and how human rights courts have reacted to the issues of backlash and non-compliance in relation to legislative remedies will also be explored in this last chapter.

Chapter 1: The Concept of Legislative Remedies

The first step to understanding and analysing legislative remedies before human rights courts is to explore the different elements surrounding this concept. As explained in the introduction, legislative remedies are binding measures issued by a judicial body that prescribes legislative reforms. This is a rather common remedy before constitutional courts, but this book will focus on international adjudication, where this remedy is much more exceptional. Although it is a fact that the three regional human rights include these types of remedial measures in some of their judgments, there are however a number of questions related to the relationship between domestic laws and international human rights law.

To what extent do human rights treaties contain obligations to legislate? Do victims of human rights violations have a secondary right to the reform of laws that contributed to the violation? How do human rights courts carry out the review of domestic laws? Who can request such a review? Can they also perform an advisory review of legislation? What is the role of legislative remedies in the constitutionalisation of human rights law? Are these remedies comparable to the ones issued by domestic constitutional courts when reviewing legislation? Why are legislative remedies considered more intrusive than other remedies of human rights courts? Are these courts legitimated to order the reform of domestic laws?

This chapter will attempt to provide an answer to these different questions, before delving into the issue of remedies in general international law and human rights law in the next chapters, where legislative remedies will be situated in their remedial context. In order to tackle all these issues, this chapter will first examine the obligations to legislate in accordance with human rights treaties, showing that legislative remedies can be conceptualised as a reiteration or concretization of primary obligations to legislate under these treaties. Then, the chapter will look at the review of domestic laws carried out by regional human rights courts, focusing on two particular issues. First, the competence to request a review of legislation will be examined, an issue that is closely related to the 'victim requirement' in human rights adjudication. Here, particular attention will be put on the innovative approach of the ACtHPR, where any individual or NGO can claim that a law is contrary to the human rights obligations of the corresponding state without the need to be qualified as a victim or to be affected by the law.

Secondly, the advisory review of legislation will be explored, as the three courts have developed different mechanisms in this regard.

Finally, the last section of the chapter will turn around legislative remedies and the constitutionalisation of human rights adjudication. It will be shown that this remedial practice contributes to an increased constitutionalisation of this regime, but at the same time, important differences persist with respect to the legislative measures issued by constitutional courts. In addition, this section will also examine the intrusiveness of these particular measures, as well as the legitimacy concerns related to them.

I. Obligations to Legislate under Human Rights Treaties

Every human rights treaty, both at the universal and the regional level, contains certain obligations for state parties to legislate. In this context, the concept of treaty obligations to legislate is understood as those provisions that require direct legislative action by states. Thus, the indirect requirements to legislate, for example in order to restrict certain rights, are not included in this analysis.[54] There are two main types of legislative human rights obligations. On the one hand, some provisions prescribe the adoption of all necessary legislative measures in order to implement the rights of the corresponding treaty in general, called here 'general obligations to legislate' (1). On the other hand, obligations to legislate that concern a concrete right or a particular human rights issue are called here 'specific obligations to legislate' (2). In the traditional distinction between negative obligations to respect and positive obligations to protect and fulfil human rights, obligations to legislate can be part of all three, depending on the concrete issue they tackle.[55] Although these are mostly positive obligations, some of the treaty provisions contain also obligations to modify or abolish

54 Such indirect obligations to legislate are typically found in provisions concerning certain political rights, such as the freedom of expression or of association, whose restriction needs to be "prescribed by law". See for example Articles 10(2) and 11(2) of the ECHR.

55 For example, specific obligations to legislate in order to protect certain vulnerable groups or to prevent or punish certain acts are clearly part of the obligation to protect, while the obligations to modify or repeal domestic laws are more related to the obligation to respect. General obligations to legislate have elements of respect, protection and fulfilment, as the line between them is not always clear. See Laurens Lavrysen, "Protection by the Law: The Positive Obligation to Develop a Legal Framework to Adequately Protect ECHR Rights", in Yves Haeck and Eva Brems (eds.),

laws that are contrary to the purpose of the corresponding treaty. In addition, human rights treaty obligations to legislate are not only those expressly provided in the treaty provisions but can also be implicit in them or be developed through the case law of the supervisory bodies (3).

This section will thus provide a general overview of the obligations to legislate included in human rights treaties and then examine its relation to legislative remedies (4). Although the following chapters focus only on the legislative measures included in judgments of the three regional human rights courts, this section will not only take into account the three regional human rights conventions but also the nine 'core' UN human rights treaties, in order to have a complete overview of these obligations.[56] There are in this respect important differences in the number of obligations to legislate included in each human rights treaty. Notably, at a regional level, the ACHR stands out with seven of these obligations, while the ECHR contains only two of them and the ACHPR just a single one. At the universal level, the human rights treaties which include the highest number of obligations to legislate are the CRC and CEDAW, with five of these obligations. The ICCPR and the CRPD include four, the ICMW, the ICERD and the ICPED three, and the ICESCR and the CAT only two.

1. General Obligations to Legislate

Obligations requiring states to legislate in order to give effect in general to the rights contained in the corresponding treaty are part of the so-called 'general measures of implementation', usually included at the beginning of each treaty.[57] These obligations imply that upon ratification, states shall make the necessary amendments in order to conform their domestic laws to the treaty provisions.[58] In this regard, the obligations to legislate are

Human Rights and Civil Liberties in the 21st Century, Dordrecht: Springer, 2014, pp. 69-130, at pp. 72-76.

56 See OHCHR, The Core International Human Rights Instruments and their monitoring bodies, available at: https://www.ohchr.org/en/professionalinterest/pages/coreinstruments.aspx.

57 See for example CRC, *General Comment No. 5: General measures of implementation of the Convention on the Rights of the Child,* 2003. See also, with respect to the ACHR, Eduardo Ferrer Mac-Gregor and Carlos Pelayo Möller, *Las Obligaciones Generales de la Convención Americana sobre Derechos Humanos*, Mexico: UNAM, 2017.

58 This does however not require the incorporation of these treaties into domestic law. See HRCee, *General Comment 31: The nature of the general legal obligation*

mostly included alongside the general obligations to respect and fulfil those rights,[59] although this is not always the case.[60] Moreover, a reservation concerning these provisions is incompatible with the treaties' object and purpose.[61]

Such general obligations to legislate can be found in five of the nine core universal human rights treaties[62] and two of the three regional human rights conventions.[63] It has to be noted, however, that sometimes these general obligations overlap with specific obligations to legislate in order to protect a concrete group, especially when the object of the treaty in question is the protection of that group.[64] Certainly, some of these provi-

---

imposed on States Parties to the Covenant (CCPR/C/21/Rev.1/Add.13), adopted on 29 March 2004, para. 13 ("States Parties are required on ratification to make such changes to domestic laws and practices as are necessary to ensure their conformity with the Covenant"). See also Paul M. Taylor, *A Commentary on the International Covenant on Civil and Political Rights*, Cambridge: CUP, 2020, p. 70. See however, concerning Art. 2(1) CAT, Gerrit Zach, "Article 2: Obligation to Prevent Torture", in Manfred Nowak, Moritz Birk, and Giuliana Monina (eds.), *The UN Convention Against Torture and its Optional Protocol: A Commentary*, 2nd ed., Oxford: OUP, 2019, pp. 72-97, at p. 81, arguing that "positive obligations of states, (...) aimed at fulfilling a certain human right by means of legislative (...) and other measures, are always relative and, therefore, subject to the principle of progressive implementation".

59 See for example Article 1 of the ACHPR ("The Member States of the Organization of African Unity parties to the present Charter shall recognize the rights, duties and freedoms enshrined in this Charter and shall undertake to adopt legislative or other measures to give effect to them").

60 For example, the ACHR includes the general obligations of respect and guarantee in its Art. 1, while Art. 2 of this Convention includes an obligation "to adopt (...) such legislative or other measures as may be necessary to give effect to those rights or freedoms".

61 HRCee, *General Comment 31: The nature of the general legal obligation imposed on States Parties to the Covenant* (CCPR/C/21/Rev.1/Add.13), adopted on 29 March 2004, at para. 5.

62 Art. 2.2 ICCPR, Art. 2(1) ICESCR, Art. 4 CRC, Art. 4(1)(a) CRPD, Art. 84 ICMW. One human rights treaty does even contain a procedural obligation specifying conditions about how states should comply with their general obligations to legislate. This is the case of Art. 4(3) CRPD, establishing that states shall "closely consult with and actively involve persons with disabilities, (...) through their representative organisations" in the implementation and development of legislative measures.

63 Art. 2 ACHR and Art. 1 ACHPR.

64 This is for example the case with Art. 2(a) CEDAW, requesting states to "embody the principle of the equality of men and women in their national constitutions or other appropriate legislation". Nevertheless, other treaties aiming at the protection of a particular group include both a general obligation to legislate and a specific one for the protection of such group. This is for example the case of the CRC, in its Arts. 3(2) and 4.

sions establish that states shall make the rights effective through legislation *or* through other measures.[65] The CESCR declared in this respect that "in many instances legislation is highly desirable and in some cases may even be indispensable".[66] Some authors have argued that these general obligations of implementation constitute an obligation of result rather than an obligation of conduct,[67] while others have stated that legislative measures are always necessary in this context, albeit sometimes not sufficient.[68]

Moreover, it can be argued that general obligations to legislate are part of customary international law.[69] In accordance with Art. 27 of the VCLT, no violations of international treaties can be justified under the basis of domestic laws. Furthermore, such a customary character can also be inferred from the PCIJ's *Advisory Opinion on the Exchange of Greek and Turkish Populations* (1925), where the PCIJ mentioned "a principle which is self-evident, according to which a State which has contracted valid international

65 See for example Art. 2(2) ICCPR. On the contrary, see Art. 2(1) ICESCR, according to which the full realisation of the rights shall be achieved "by all appropriate means, including particularly the adoption of legislative measures". See however Philip Alston and Gerard Quinn, "The Nature and Scope of States Parties' Obligations under the International Covenant on Economic, Social and Cultural Rights", *Human Rights Quarterly* 9(2), 1987, pp. 156-229, at p. 166, arguing that these obligations to legislate are different in the case of the ICCPR and the ICESCR as in the former case it is "abundantly clear that legal measures are required" while in the latter one "it is unclear whether states are required to take such action".

66 See CESCR, *General Comment 3: The Nature of States Parties' Obligations (Art. 2, Para. 1 of the Covenant)*, 14 December 1990, para. 3. See on the other hand HRCee, General Comment No. 31, para. 13, appearing to leave the door open for a change in practice instead of legislation ("Where there are inconsistencies between domestic law and the Covenant, article 2 requires that the domestic law or practice be changed to meet the standards imposed by the Covenant's substantive guarantees").

67 Anja Seibert-Fohr, "Domestic Implementation of the International Covenant on Civil and Political Rights", *Max Planck Yearbook of United Nations Law* 5, 2001, pp. 399-472, at p. 419.

68 As an effective implementation of these laws is also needed. See for example Andrea Broderick, "Article 4: General Obligations", in Ilias Bantekas et al. (eds.), *The UN Convention of the rights of Persons with Disabilities: A Commentary*, Oxford: OUP, 2018, p. 119, stating that "[w]hile the adoption of legislative measures is indispensable, obligations under Article 4(1)(b) encompass a panoply of duties that is much broader than the mere adoption of legislation". See also similarly Zach, in Manfred Nowak et al. (eds.), 2019, p. 83.

69 This was stated in the case of IACtHR, *"Juvenile Reeducation Institute" vs. Paraguay* (2004), para. 205 ("In general international law, it is a universally accepted principle of customary law that a State that has ratified a human rights treaty must make the necessary amendments to its domestic laws to ensure proper compliance with the obligations it has undertaken").

obligations is bound to make in its legislation such modifications as may be necessary to ensure the fulfilment of the obligations undertaken".[70] In the case of the ECHR, despite the absence of a general obligation to legislate in the Convention, the Court has also assumed that the general obligation to 'secure' the Convention rights under Article 1 implies an obligation to legislate for that purpose.[71] However, it has been noted that this is a customary norm that many states fail to comply with.[72]

These general obligations to legislate are a good reflection of the subsidiarity principle, according to which domestic actors are primarily responsible for the implementation of human rights treaty norms.[73] Moreover, these provisions are usually understood to have an 'accessory character', meaning that they can only be infringed in conjunction with another article of the respective treaty.[74] Nevertheless, these types of general obligations to legislate are usually a strong legal basis in order for treaty bodies or courts to request legislative reforms, as the compatibility of domestic law with the treaty in question turns into a primary obligation for state parties.[75] These general obligations have also served as a basis for courts and treaty bodies to develop further specific obligations to legislate besides those explicitly included in human rights treaties, as will be seen below.

70 PCIJ, *Exchange of Greek and Turkish Populations (Lausanne Convention VI, January 30th, 1923, Article 2)*, Series B No. 10, 21 February 1925, p. 20.

71 See ECtHR, *Maestri vs. Italy* (2004), para. 47 ("Furthermore, it follows from the Convention, and from Article 1 in particular, that in ratifying the Convention the Contracting States undertake to ensure that their domestic legislation is compatible with it"). See also Alstair Mowbray, *The Development of Positive Obligations under the European Convention on Human Rights by the European Court of Human Rights*, Oxford: Hart, 2004, at p. 225.

72 Antonio Cassesse, "Towards a Moderate Monism: Could International Rules Eventually Acquire the Force to Invalidate Inconsistent National Laws?", in Antonio Cassesse (ed.), *Realizing Utopia: The Future of International Law*, Oxford: OUP, 2012, pp. 187–199, at p. 188.

73 See Manfred Nowak, *UN Covenant on Civil and Political Rights – CCPR Commentary*, 2nd ed., Kehl am Rhein: N.P. Engel Publishers, 2005, p. 27.

74 See for example Taylor, 2020, p. 60. With regard to the CRC, see John Tobin, "Article 4: A State's General Obligation of Implementation", in John Tobin (ed.), *The UN Convention on the Rights of the Child: A Commentary*, Oxford: OUP, 2019, p. 109, arguing that this provision, "like its normative cousins from the ICESCR and ICCPR (...), is not intended to be read in isolation from the individual rights to which it applies".

75 See in this regard Taylor, 2020, pp. 77-78.

2. Specific Obligations to Legislate

Besides these general obligations to legislate, almost every human rights treaty also includes specific obligations to legislate, relating to concrete rights, groups, or acts. These provisions pertain to the so-called 'non-self-executing norms' of human rights treaties, as there is a need for states to take a certain action – in this case legislative action – in order to make them effective.[76] This section will examine the specific obligations to legislate included in human rights treaties, dividing them into four main categories: (a) obligations to legislate in order to protect specific rights, (b) obligations to legislate in order to protect specific groups, (c) obligations to legislate in order to prevent or punish certain acts, and (d) obligations to modify or abolish domestic laws.

a) *Obligations to legislate in order to protect specific rights*

There are a number of human rights treaty provisions that require states to protect certain rights by law. For example, one right that states are typically required to protect through legislation is the right to life. This is prescribed at a regional level by Art. 4 ECHR and Art. 4 ACHR, and at the universal level by Art. 6(1) ICCPR and Art. 9 ICMW.[77] This means that if states lack domestic law provisions aiming at the protection of the right to life, they will have to legislate to that effect. According to the HRCee, this implies on the one hand that states must adopt appropriate laws in order to "protect life from all reasonably foreseeable threats, including from threats emanating from private persons and entities", and on the other hand that the reasons for any deprivation of life by state authorities must be prescribed by law with sufficient precision.[78]

Other provisions aiming at the protection of specific rights are those that require states to regulate in their domestic laws the exercise of such rights. This is for example the case with Art. 27(1) CRPD, including an obligation

76 See in this regard for example CERD, *General Comment No. 35: Combating racist hate speech*, 26 September 2013, para. 13 ("As article 4 is not self-executing, States parties are required by its terms to adopt legislation to combat racist hate speech that falls within its scope").

77 The latter concerning specifically the right to life of migrant workers and their families.

78 HRCee, *General Comment 36: Article 6 (Right to Life)*, 3 September 2019, paras. 18-20.

to regulate through legislation a number of aspects concerning the right to work of persons with disabilities, such as their ability to exercise labour and trade union rights, the access to general technical and vocational training, and the promotion of their employment, both in the private and in the public sector. Besides the protection of the right to life, the ECHR only contains one other obligation to legislate, in Art. 2 of its Protocol 7, concerning the regulation of the right to appeal in criminal matters. The provision specifies that "[t]he exercise of this right, including the grounds on which it may be exercised, shall be governed by law". On the other hand, Art. 18 ACHR, which concerns the right of every person to a given name, specifies that "[t]he law shall regulate the manner in which this right shall be ensured for all".[79]

b) *Obligations to legislate in order to protect specific groups*

In addition to obliging states to legislate in order to protect certain rights, human rights treaties also seek to protect specific groups that are considered vulnerable and in need of special protection. These obligations are usually included in treaties that aim at the protection of these groups, such as CRC, CRPD and CEDAW. The protection of these groups through legislation thereby reinforces the long-term effectiveness of the treaty in question and provides a legal basis for taking additional measures.

The CRC contains several obligations to legislate aiming at the protection of children, both in general and specifically "from all forms of physical or mental violence", and "from the illicit use of narcotic drugs and psychotropic substances".[80] The CRPD includes similar protective obligations with regard to persons with disabilities, mentioning their legislative protection "from all forms of exploitation, violence and abuse".[81] CEDAW on the contrary departs from a protective approach, stipulating the state's obligation to adopt "all appropriate measures, including legislation, to ensure the full development and advancement of women",[82] and to "embody the principle of the equality of men and women in their national constitutions

79 ACHR, Art. 18.
80 CRC, Arts. 3(3), 19(1) and 33, respectively.
81 CRPD, Art. 16(1).
82 CEDAW, Art. 3. This provision is understood to provide a legal basis for requiring states to incorporate a gender perspective into their domestic laws. See in this regard Christine Chinkin, "Article 3", in Marsha A. Freeman, Christine Chinkin and Beate

or other appropriate legislation".[83] Another form of non-discrimination through law is prescribed by the ACHR, determining that "[t]he law shall recognize equal rights for children born out of wedlock and those born in wedlock".[84]

c) *Obligations to legislate in order to prevent and punish specific acts*

Most obligations to legislate under human rights treaties relate to the prevention or the punishment of certain acts. Some of these obligations are to a certain extent overlapping, such as CAT's obligation to adopt the necessary legislative measures in order "to prevent acts of torture" and CRPD's prescription for states to legislate in order "to prevent persons with disabilities (...) from being subjected to torture".[85] Similarly, the ICCPR requires to prohibit by law any type of discrimination,[86] and this is also prescribed by CEDAW regarding the discrimination of women,[87] by ICERD with respect to racial discrimination,[88] and by the CRPD concerning the discrimination on the basis of disabilities.[89] The latter provisions are in line with the general assumption that the elimination of *de jure* discrimination is a necessary prerequisite for achieving *de facto* equality.[90]

Rudolf (eds.), *The UN Convention on the Elimination of All Forms of Discrimination Against Women: A Commentary*, Oxford: OUP, 2012, pp. 101-122, at p. 108.

83 CEDAW, Art. 2. The CEDAW Committee has in this respect regularly recommended states to incorporate women's rights into their constitutions. See Andrew Byrnes, "Article 2", in Marsha A. Freeman et al. (eds.), *The UN Convention on the Elimination of All Forms of Discrimination Against Women: A Commentary*, Oxford: OUP, 2012, pp. 71–99, at p. 79.

84 Art. 17(5) ACHR.

85 CAT, Art. 2(1) and CRPD, Art. 15.

86 Article 26 ICCPR. The HRCee has also specified in this regard that "when legislation is adopted by a state party, it must comply with the requirement of article 26 that its content should not be discriminatory" (HRCee, *General Comment No. 18: Non-discrimination*, 10 November 1989, para. 12).

87 Article 2(b) CEDAW. In accordance with the CEDAW Committee, this includes the obligation to provide "appropriate remedies for women who are subjected to discrimination contrary to the Convention", which should encompass "changes in relevant laws". See CEDAW Committee, *General Recommendation No. 28 on the Core Obligations of States Parties under Article 2 of the Convention on the Elimination of All Forms of Discrimination against Women*, 16 December 2010, para. 32.

88 Article 3(d) CERD.

89 Article 27(a) CRPD.

90 See Andrea Broderick, in Ilias Bantekas et al. (eds.), 2018, p. 120.

Most of the obligations to prevent and punish specific acts through legislation are also aimed at the protection of children and other vulnerable groups.[91] For example, the ICESCR's only specific obligation to legislate establishes that children's "employment in work harmful to their morals or health or dangerous to life or likely to hamper their normal development *should be punishable by law*. States should also set age limits below which the paid employment of child labour *should be prohibited and punishable by law*".[92] A similar obligation is also included in Art. 32(2) CRC, specifying further details on this legislative duty of states.[93] In addition, the Optional Protocols to the CRC are also aiming at the protection of children by imposing a requirement to criminalize certain acts, such as the sale of children for sexual exploitation or forced labour;[94] the production, distribution, dissemination, or possession of child pornography;[95] and the recruitment or use in hostilities of persons under the age of eighteen.[96] Finally, the ICPED includes a prescription for states to "prevent and punish under its criminal law (...) the wrongful removal of children [and] the falsification, concealment or destruction of documents attesting to the true identity of [these] children".[97]

Another type of overlapping obligation can be found between the universal and the regional level. For example, both the ICCPR and the ACHR prescribe states to prohibit by law the propaganda of war and

---

91 That is the case of CRPD's obligation to "put in place effective legislation (...) to ensure that instances of exploitation, violence and abuse against persons with disabilities are identified, investigated and, where appropriate, prosecuted" (CRPD, Art. 16.5). CEDAW, on its side, requests states to adopt "all appropriate measures, including legislation, to suppress all forms of traffic in women and exploitation of prostitution of women" (CEDAW, Art. 6).

92 ICESCR, Art. 10(3) (emphasis added). These two aspects are in accordance with ILO Conventions No. 182 and 138, respectively. See Ben Saul, David Kinley and Jacqueline Mowbray, *The International Covenant on Economic, Social and Cultural Rights: Commentary, Cases, and Materials*, Oxford: OUP, 2014, pp. 837-841.

93 Actually, the CRC Committee has recommended states in several instances to "strengthen" or "amend" their laws in order to ensure that they include provisions that prohibit child labour. See Philip Alston, "Article 32: The Right to Protection from Economic Exploitation", in John Tobin (ed.), *The UN Convention on the Rights of the Child: A Commentary*, Oxford: OUP, 2019, p. 1246.

94 Optional Protocol on the Sale of Children, Child Prostitution and Child Pornography, Art. 3(1)(a).

95 Optional Protocol on the Sale of Children, Child Prostitution and Child Pornography, Art. 3(1)(c).

96 Optional Protocol on the Involvement of Children in Armed Conflict, Art. 4(2).

97 ICPED, Art. 25(1).

the incitement to discrimination, hostility or violence.[98] In contrast with Art. 4 ICERD, containing a very similar obligation, this does not need to be prohibited by criminal law,[99] but the prohibition requires some sort of sanction or punishment.[100] The HRCee actually explained that the difference between these prohibitions and other lawful limitations to the freedom of expression is precisely "that for the acts addressed in article 20, the Covenant indicates the specific response required from the State: their prohibition by law".[101]

d) *Obligations to modify or repeal domestic laws*

As it has been made evident, most obligations to legislate contained in human rights treaties concern the enactment of legislation, either to prevent or punish certain acts or to protect concrete rights or groups of persons. However, there are also some treaty obligations that refer to the modification or repeal of existing laws. This primarily concerns domestic laws that have a discriminatory effect. The ICERD includes an obligation for states to "amend, rescind or nullify any laws and regulations which have the effect of creating or perpetuating racial discrimination".[102] Additionally, both CEDAW and CRPD oblige states "to modify or abolish existing laws, regulations, customs and practices which constitute discrimination" against

98 Art. 20 ICCPR and Art. 13(5) ACHR.

99 See the different terminology used. Whereas Art. 4 ICERD requires offending speech to be "punishable by law", Art. 20 ICCPR stated it shall be "prohibited by law". See in this regard also Taylor, *ICCPR Commentary*, 2020, pp. 585-586. CERD stated that "[a]s a minimum requirement, and without prejudice to further measures, comprehensive legislation against racial discrimination, including civil and administrative law as well as criminal laws, is indispensable to combating racist hate speech effectively" (see CERD, *General Recommendation No. 35*, 2013, para. 9).

100 HRCee, *General Comment 11: Article 20 (Prohibition of Propaganda for War and Inciting National, Racial or Religious Hatred)*, 29 July 1983, para. 2. These sanctions can have a criminal, civil or administrative nature (see Taylor, *Commentary ICCPR*, 2020, p. 586).

101 HRCee, *General Comment No. 34*, para. 51.

102 CERD, Art. 2 (c). See in this regard Patrick Thornberry, *The International Convention on the Elimination of All Forms of Racial Discrimination: A Commentary*, Oxford: OUP, 2016, p. 187, stating that it is a "common practice" of the CERD to issue concrete recommendations for states to review, amend or rescind discriminatory laws.

women and persons with disabilities, respectively.[103] Finally, CEDAW includes a specific obligation of periodically reviewing protective laws "in light of scientific and technological knowledge" and amending, repealing or extending them as necessary.[104]

3. Implicit Obligations to Legislate

This section has provided an overview of the obligations to legislate expressly included in human rights treaties. However, these are not the only aspects that states need to regulate through legislation in accordance with these treaties. In this respect, there are many obligations to legislate that are implicit and that have been developed and established mainly through the case law of the respective court or treaty body. This specification of implicit obligations is in accordance with the general obligations to legislate outlined before. As states have the customary (and often also treaty-based) obligation to adjust all of their domestic laws to the corresponding human rights treaty, the supervisory bodies can concretise this mandate by indicating how it should be implemented in particular situations, thereby expanding the number of specific obligations to legislate.

This can be seen through the example of the ECHR, which—despite containing only two explicit obligations to legislate—implicitly requires legislative action in several areas. In this respect, the ECtHR has developed an important number of positive obligations linked to each Convention

---

103 CEDAW, Art. 2 (f) and CRPD, Art. 4(1)(b). According to the CRPD Committee, this obligation should encompass civil, family, criminal, labor and education laws. See CRPD Committee, *Concluding Observations on Costa Rica*, 12 May 2014, para. 8. The CEDAW Committee has taken a similar approach in this regard, while it has also encouraged states to regularly analyse the gender impact of new and existing laws, and to undertake regular reviews of legislation. See Byrnes, in Marsha A. Freeman et al. (eds.), 2012, p. 91.

104 CEDAW, Art. 11(3). It has been argued that the focus of this provision is related to the unnecessary mandatory protection of women, which would restrict their "equality of opportunity in employment by excluding them from specific jobs or tasks and by perpetuating negative stereotypes regarding their need for protection" (Frances Raday, "Article 11", in *CEDAW Commentary*, 2012, p. 302). This is the only obligation of this character in human rights treaties, as the former ones refer to the modification or abolishment of discriminatory laws only at the time of ratifying the respective Convention.

right, among them the obligations to legislate.[105] This is, for example, the case with the right to an effective domestic remedy under Art. 13 ECHR, which often has inherent legislative implications, as will be explained in Chapter 3. In addition, concerning the right to family life, the ECtHR stated for example in *Marckx vs. Belgium* (1979) that "respect for family life implies in particular (...) the existence in domestic law of legal safeguards that render possible as from the moment of birth the child's integration in his family".[106] In this context, the ECtHR has also developed an obligation to criminalize specific acts in the domestic legal framework, in order to deter human rights violations.[107] For example, in *X and Y vs. the Netherlands* (1985), dealing with the sexual abuse of mentally handicapped persons, the Court argued that "[e]ffective deterrence is indispensable in this area and it can be achieved only by criminal-law provisions".[108] Similarly, in *M.C. vs. Bulgaria* (2003), the Court argued that states "have a positive obligation inherent in Articles 3 and 8 to enact criminal-law provisions effectively punishing rape".[109]

The obligations to legislate can also evolve over time, as the respective court or treaty body interprets and develops the provisions of the corresponding treaty in light of a specific time and context. In this respect, when supervision bodies conduct an evolutionary interpretation of the corresponding treaty, they can find that certain laws are no longer compatible with it. For example, the HRCee added a new (negative) obligation to legislate in its General Comment 34 by determining that "laws that penalize the expression of opinion about historical facts are incompatible with the obligation that the Covenant imposes to State Parties".[110]

105 See generally Dimitris Xenos, *The Positive Obligations of the State under the European Convention of Human Rights*, Abingdon: Routledge, 2013.
106 ECtHR, *Marckx vs. Belgium* (1979), para. 31.
107 See in this respect Laurens Lavrysen and Natasa Mavronicola (eds.), *Coercive Human Rights: Positive Duties to Mobilise the Criminal Law under the ECHR*, London: Bloomsbury, 2020.
108 ECtHR, *X and Y vs. the Netherlands* (1985), para. 27.
109 ECtHR, *M.C. vs. Bulgaria* (2003), para. 153.
110 HRCee, *General Comment No. 34*, para. 49.

4. From Obligations to Legislate to Legislative Remedies: Is There a Victims' Right to Legislative Reforms?

The human rights obligations to legislate explored in this section are primary obligations that states need to implement when ratifying a human rights treaty. Thus, the legal order of states must be compatible with the respective treaty at the time of ratifying it and must remain compatible as long as the state remains bound by the treaty. Although the general obligation to protect human rights does not always mean that they need to be protected through law, this is the case when it is expressly mandated by a treaty or when the corresponding treaty body develops that obligation. Moreover, every time a state adopts or amends a domestic law it needs to make sure that it is compatible with its treaty obligations. If it fails to comply with these primary obligations, the supervision bodies can find a violation of the treaty and are in principle authorised to establish a secondary obligation for the concerned state to reform its domestic laws. In this respect, every legislative remedy issued by a human rights court is linked to the non-compliance of obligations to legislate, although this is not always mentioned by the courts. Both the ACtHPR and the IACtHR usually link their legislative remedies to violations of the general obligation to legislate included respectively in Art. 1 ACHPR and Art. 2 ACHR, while in the case of the ECtHR, it is most often linked to the violation of Art. 13 ECHR and the implicit positive obligations to legislate according to this provision.

As it can be observed, these obligations to legislate usually provide a sufficient legal basis for human rights courts or treaty bodies to prescribe legislative reforms. In some cases, it is precisely these obligations that trigger the finding of a treaty violation.[111] General obligations to legislate are thereby broad enough to allow for the review of domestic laws against any treaty provision, or even against the object and purpose of a treaty in general. Even if human rights violations usually originated in the application of a specific law and not in the law as such, if a legislative provision leaves no room for a rights-friendly application it becomes clear that the legislator needs to intervene. Concerning specific obligations, it is worth noting that those explicitly included in human rights instruments are only rarely triggering legislative remedies. For example, a very extended specific obligation

111 See for example Seibert-Fohr, in *Max Planck Yearbook* 2001, p. 411 ("Without the assumption of legal obligations the Committee could not have found such violations").

is that of protecting the right to life through legislation, as mentioned before. This provision has however not given rise to much jurisprudence concerning the legislative protection of this right.[112] This is most likely because the right to life is generally secured in states' criminal laws. This is also the case with other specific obligations to legislate in accordance with regional human rights treaties, such as the right to appeal in the case of the ECHR, that has not been linked to any of its legislative measures. On the other hand, as will be seen in Chapter 4, there are some categories of legislative remedies that are mirrored in the aforementioned categories of obligations to legislate. This is the case with the obligations to legislate in order to protect specific groups, or the one aiming at the prevention and punishment of certain acts.[113]

In sum, obligations to legislate are included in every human rights treaty, both explicitly and implicitly, as the adaptation of domestic laws to an international treaty has a customary character under international law. This leads to the question of whether legislative reforms are a right of victims of human rights violations or an obligation of states after committing a violation. It is different in this context for victims to have a subjective right to an amendment of the law than for states to be objectively obliged to carry out a legislative reform.[114] Victims of human rights violations have the right to an effective remedy (in the procedural sense) and reparation. These secondary rights have to be claimed primarily before domestic courts, in accordance with the subsidiarity principle. However, under most domestic jurisdictions individuals cannot request a legislative reform, nor are most domestic courts (except for constitutional courts) competent to order such reforms. From this perspective, legislative reforms do not seem to fit in the concept of secondary rights of individuals arising from human rights violations.

It is thus necessary to consider the differences between the redress of concrete victims and other remedies of human rights courts that are directed at the protection of society in general and the prevention of further vio-

112 An exception is for example the case law of the IACtHR requesting states to modify its laws related to the death penalty, that can be interpreted as dealing with the legislative protection of the right to life. For more information, see Chapter 4 of this book.

113 These are respectively mirrored in the legislative remedies aiming at the protection of vulnerable groups and in those prescribing the adequate codification of criminal offences. See Chapter 4 of this book.

114 See generally on this difference Anne Peters, *Beyond Human Rights - The Legal Status of the Individual in International Law*, Cambridge: CUP, 2016, pp. 167-193.

lations. For this reason, it seems more apt to consider legislative remedies (and guarantees of non-repetition more generally) as distinct from other remedial measures, as the main beneficiaries of such remedies are not the victims appearing before the Court. It would be therefore probably more accurate to define legislative measures included in the judgments of human rights courts as a concretization or reiteration of the obligations to legislate that can be found in human rights treaties. If states have the customary obligation to adapt their domestic legislation to the treaties that bind them, this includes the interpretation of such treaties provided by its authoritative interpreter, in this case the regional human rights courts. When these courts issue a legislative remedy, they are in fact interpreting the states' primary obligation to legislate and adapting it to a concrete situation. From this perspective, it can be argued that victims do not have the right to have the legislation amended after suffering a human rights violation, but states have an implicit obligation to amend it whenever it is found to be contrary to a human rights treaty. What human rights courts then do when issuing legislative remedies is to make these implicit obligations explicit, giving them form and substance. It is, therefore, probably more accurate to define legislative reforms as an obligation of states rather than a secondary right of victims.

In any case, the competence of human rights courts to order legislative measures seems rather clear from an international law perspective. When they find that a state has failed to comply with its primary obligation to legislate, this constitutes an internationally wrongful act that gives rise to a secondary obligation of remedying it, in this case through a legislative reform. The legal basis for the imposition of legislative remedies is thus a combination of these obligations and the remedial provisions included in human rights treaties, which will be examined in Chapter 3. However, before issuing legislative remedies human rights courts generally perform a review of the domestic laws against the standards of the respective convention. This type of judicial review is very common, going beyond the issue of legislative remedies. It will be explored in the next section.

II. The Review of Legislation by Human Rights Courts

It is common to all three regional human rights courts to review domestic laws rather often in their judgments. This is because the alleged human rights violations often stem from the application of a law, mostly through administrative acts but sometimes also through judicial decisions. Thereby, human rights courts usually extend their review to the law as such and not only to its application.[115] This type of review is generally unproblematic, being an intrinsic aspect of human rights adjudication. There are, however, two aspects related to the human rights courts' review of domestic laws that deserve closer attention.

The first aspect concerns the competence to request a review of legislation before human rights courts. In the European system, the compatibility of a law with the ECHR can be challenged in principle only by the alleged victim of a human rights violation caused by the application of that law. On the other hand, in the Inter-American system, this review can also be requested by persons other than the alleged victim, although the law needs to have been applied to an identified victim. This is different in the African system, where individuals and NGOs can request the review of legislation without identifying any concrete victim. This is a notorious development in human rights adjudication, allowing for the review of legislation *in abstracto*. It has been nevertheless generally overlooked by scholarship and will therefore be examined in this section.

Another aspect which has not received much attention but seems relevant as well concerns the possibility for human rights courts to carry out a review of legislation through advisory opinions. Here, the IACtHR is arguably the court in which this competence is most clearly crystallised, being expressly included in a provision of the ACHR. It is also the only court that has reviewed specific domestic laws through its advisory opinions, but surprisingly scarcely. The ECtHR could arguably carry out such a review through its 'new' advisory function under Protocol 16, although it has interpreted its own competences in this respect rather narrowly. Finally, whether the ACtHPR would have the competence to perform an advisory review of legislation is still rather unclear, in light of the regulation of this advisory role and its practice in this respect.

115 For example, in cases related to restrictions of the freedom of expression, association or religion, the first requirement is that the restrictive measure is taken on the basis of a domestic law. In this context, the courts review not only whether the laws in question can be qualified as such, but also if they are compatible with the relevant international standards.

1. The Competence to Request a Review of Legislation before Human Rights Courts

In general, the review of domestic laws by human rights courts is triggered by a specific action based on that law that causes an alleged human rights violation towards a concrete victim. This can be a judicial decision or an administrative act in the application of the law. This is known as legislative review *in concreto*.[116] Nevertheless, it must be noted that such a concrete review can have an abstract element, in that sometimes the object of the review is the law itself and not the specific measure of application.[117] It is, however, still a review *in concreto* because the law is reviewed in the context of its application in a specific individual case. On the contrary, legislative review *in abstracto* takes place when the compatibility of a law with human rights instruments is assessed independently of specific instances in which it was applied.[118]

The predominance of the concrete review of legislation is mainly due to the human rights courts' jurisdiction *ratione personae*, which requires alleged victimhood in order to submit a complaint. Thus, one condition for human rights courts (at least for the IACtHR and the ECtHR) to review a piece of legislation is that it must have been applied to a concrete individual in the context of an alleged violation. Through this approach, both the ECtHR and the IACtHR have reviewed the conventionality of domestic laws in numerous instances. Besides the exceptions outlined below, the review performed by these two courts is in principle always *in concreto*, based on specific instances of application of the law. If the law has not been applied to the alleged victim, these courts will generally refuse to review it. However, the ACtHPR has adopted a very different approach to this issue,

116 See for example ECtHR, *Lopes de Sousa Fernandes vs. Portugal* (2017), para. 188: "the question whether there has been a failure by the State in its regulatory duties calls for a concrete assessment of the alleged deficiencies rather than an abstract one".

117 As explained by Keller and Kühne, it is often not possible to throw a clear line between the review of an individual-concrete administrative act that applies a law and the review of the abstract-general law as such (Helen Keller and Daniela Kühne, "Zur Verfassungsgerichtsbarkeit des Europäischen Gerichtshofs für Menschenrechte", *ZaöRV* 76, 2016, p. 268). See also Janneke Gerards, "Abstract and Concrete Reasonableness Review by the European Court of Human Rights", *EHRLR* 1, 2020, pp. 218-247, defining this as an "abstract reasonableness review".

118 For a discussion on concrete and abstract review in the US, see Alec Stone Sweet and Martin Shapiro, *On Law, Politics, and Judicialization*, Oxford: OUP, 2002, at pp. 347-375.

which generally allows for a review of domestic laws even if no concrete victims are identified.

a) *The 'victim requirement' before human rights courts*

The victim requirement generally implies that the individuals or NGOs submitting a complaint to human rights courts need to be themselves the victims of the alleged human rights violation, or in any case that there needs to be at least one concrete and identifiable victim. In addition, the acts or decisions being challenged before these courts need to be related to that specific victim.[119] Thus, to claim that a domestic law is incompatible with a human rights treaty, the applicant needs to be able to prove that the law in question was applied in the context of the alleged violation. In this respect, the act causing the human rights violation is usually not the law as such, but the implementation measure directed towards the individual.[120]

The 'active' *ratione personae* competence of the ECtHR, according to Art. 34 ECHR, requires victimhood in order to submit an application to the Court.[121] In this respect, the Strasbourg Court has expressly stated in numerous cases that applicants are not allowed to complain about a provision of domestic law simply because they consider, without having been directly affected by it, that it may contravene the Convention.[122] Moreover, NGOs can generally apply to the ECtHR only if their rights as legal persons are affected, but not if the alleged violation concerns the rights of third persons or even of the organisations' members as natural persons.[123]

---

119 See for example ECtHR, *Minelli vs. Switzerland* (1983), para. 35: "The Court (...) has to give a ruling not on the Zürich legislation and practice *in abstracto* but solely on the manner in which they were applied to the applicant".

120 Thus, usually the review is focused on an individual-concrete act instead of an abstract-general act. An example of this approach can be found in the case of ECtHR, Mazurek vs. France (2000), para. 54.

121 Under Article 34 of the ECHR, the Court "may receive applications from any person, nongovernmental organisation or group of individuals *claiming to be the victim of a violation* by one of the High Contracting Parties of the rights set forth in the Convention or the Protocols thereto" (emphasis added).

122 See e.g. ECtHR, *Centre for Legal Resources on behalf of Valentin Câmpeanu vs. Romania* (2014), para. 101.

123 An exception was done in ECtHR, *Centre for Legal Resources on behalf of Valentin Câmpeanu vs. Romania* (2014) due to the "victims' vulnerability on account of their age, sex or disability, which rendered them unable to lodge a complaint on the matter with the Court" (para. 103).

The IACtHR's jurisdiction *ratione personae* represents the next step in this regard, as the Commission accepts applications from persons and organisations other than the victim of the alleged human rights violation.[124] The Court has specified in this respect that the applicants do not have to be the alleged victims, nor have the victims' authorisation to submit an application.[125] However, an indirect 'victim requirement' can also be found. In accordance with Article 35 (1) of the Rules of Procedure of the IACtHR, the Commission needs to identify the concrete victim(s) when referring a case to the Court. The Commission has therefore rejected to examine claims in which the victims were not identified or identifiable.[126]

b) *Exceptions to the victim requirement*

There are some exceptions to this victim requirement. The ECtHR has accepted under specific conditions to review a domestic law that was not applied to the individuals or NGOs submitting an application. This is for example the case with the victim's next-of-kin, whose legal standing before the ECtHR has been recognised in some cases, both on behalf of the actual

---

124 As explained in the Introduction, in the Inter-American system only states and the IACmHR have *locus standi* before the Court. Alleged victims of human rights violations cannot access the IACtHR directly but need to apply to the Commission. Therefore, when looking at the *ratione personae* jurisdiction of the IACtHR it is relevant to examine the rules of admissibility before the IACmHR. In this respect, Article 44 of the ACHR establishes that "[a]ny person or group of persons, or any nongovernmental entity legally recognized in one or more member states of the Organization, may lodge petitions with the Commission containing denunciations or complaints of violation of this Convention by a State Party".

125 See for example IACtHR, *Saramaka vs. Surinam* (2007), para. 22. As mentioned by Pasqualucci, "[t]he innovative provision allowing unrelated parties to complain of human rights violations has proven particularly effective in the Inter-American system where poverty, lack of education, and lack of legal assistance would otherwise hinder access to the enforcement organs of the regional system" (Jo M. Pasqualucci, *The Practice and Procedure of the Inter-American Court of Human Rights*, Cambridge: CUP, 2003, p. 133).

126 For example, in the case of *Ivete Jordani Demeneck vs. Brazil* the applicants claimed that the violation affected "all adult and mentally disabled persons". The Commission determined that it had no competence *ratione personae* to deal with the case because it was "a representation in the abstract, similar to an *actio popularis*". (IACmHR, *Ivete Jordani Demeneck vs. Brazil* (2012), para. 20).

victims and on their own behalf as indirect victims.[127] This concept of indirect victims is generally recognised in human rights law,[128] and it is commonly applied by the other two regional courts, too.[129]

One group of exceptions to the identification of victims by the IACmHR are the cases concerning massive or collective violations, where it has not been able to identify all victims.[130] There are, in this context, cases where the list of victims is left open even after the final judgment is handed down by the IACtHR.[131] For example, in the case of *Mapiripán vs. Colombia* (2005), concerning a massacre in which dozens of individuals were executed and thrown into a river, it was not possible to identify every direct and indirect victim. Therefore, the Court decided that all indirect victims could claim the reparations ordered in the judgment within twenty-four months after the identification of their next of kin if they proved their relationship with the deceased.[132] In addition, there are also cases in which

127 Indirect victims are those directly affected by the violation against a third person, usually a close relative. Especially in cases of death or disappearance where the state is allegedly responsible, family members have been regarded as indirect victims of violations of the right to life.

128 The UN Basic Principles and Guidelines on the Right to a Remedy and Reparation state that "the term 'victim' also includes the immediate family or dependants of the direct victim and persons who have suffered harm in intervening to assist victims in distress or to prevent victimization" (UN Basic Principles, para. 8).

129 See generally Clara Sandoval, "The Concepts of 'Injured Party' and 'Victim' of Gross Human Rights Violations in The Jurisprudence of the Inter-American Court of Human Rights: A Commentary on their Implications for Reparations", in Carla Ferstman, Mariana Goetz and Alan Stephens (eds.), *Reparations for Victims of Genocide, War Crimes and Crimes against Humanity*, Leiden: Brill, 2009, pp. 243–282, pp. 257 et seq.

130 See IACmHR, *Pueblos Mayas y miembros de las comunidades de Cristo Rey, Belluet Tree, San Ignacio, Santa Elena and Santa Famili vs. Belice* (2015), para. 27, where it allowed that victims could be identified in the future according to specific criteria. This was also accepted by the Court, for example in IACtHR, *Castro Castro Prison vs. Peru* (2006), para. 178. See however *Favela Nova Brasília vs. Brazil* (2017), paras. 35-39, where the Court refused to include additional victims because the Commission's failure to identify them previously was not justified.

131 See Sandoval, in Ferstman, Goetz and Stephens (eds.), 2009, pp. 266-272.

132 This case nevertheless turned controversial because after the payment of reparations by the state it turned out that several of those claiming to be indirect victims of the massacre had made it up, and it was argued that neither the Commission nor the Court had done enough to prevent this. See Camila Uribe and Natalia Restrepo, "Could the Inter-American Human Rights System have prevented the Existence of False Victims in the Mapiripán Case?", 23 *Revista Colombiana de Derecho Internacional*, 2013, pp. 203-234. See also Sandoval, in Ferstman, Goetz and Stephens (eds.), 2009, p. 269.

all members of a particular community – or even the community as such –are considered to be direct victims of a human rights violation.[133]

These exceptions do not, however, imply an abstract review of laws, as they mostly concern concrete acts of death or disappearance, even if the applicant is not the direct victim of that act or if the list of victims remains open. Nevertheless, this is different with respect to other exceptions to the victim requirement. This concerns especially two broad categories of cases before the ECtHR, that are labelled here as those concerning 'potential victims' and 'possible victims'. A similar concept has also been applied by the IACtHR, referring to 'self-executing laws'.

i. Potential and possible victims before the ECtHR

The concept of potential victims has been used by the ECtHR in order to refer to those individuals who run the risk of being directly affected by a law because it targets a specific category of persons that they belong to. In such cases, the Court has accepted to consider each person pertaining to the concrete category as a potential victim. This was first done in *Marckx vs. Belgium* (1979), dealing with the recognition of children born out of wedlock. The ECtHR established in this case that the Convention "entitles individuals to contend that a law violates their rights by itself, in the absence of an individual measure of implementation, if they run the risk of being directly affected by it".[134]

This approach was then developed in further cases, related to specific groups that were affected by a law because of their ethnicity, religion or sexual orientation, among others.[135] It is, therefore, a category of cases that usually relates to discriminatory laws, although the ECtHR has extended this concept beyond the usual categories of 'minorities' or 'vulnerable

133 See IACtHR, *Advisory Opinion 22/16* (2016), paras. 82 and 83; see also IACtHR, *Saramaka vs. Suriname* (2007) where all members of this indigenous community were considered victims of the human rights violations.

134 *Marckx vs. Belgium* (1979), para. 27.

135 For example, in a case of 1981 related to a law punishing homosexual acts in the UK, the Court considered that even if it was not applied to him "the maintenance in force of the impugned legislation constitutes a continuing interference with the applicant's right to respect for his private life" (*Dudgeon v. the United Kingdom* (1981), para. 41. Similarly in *Norris vs. Ireland* (1988), paras. 32-34. Concerning religion, see for example *S.A.S vs. France* (2014), para. 57.

groups'.[136] Nevertheless, an individual claiming to be a 'potential victim' needs to provide "reasonable and convincing evidence of the likelihood that a violation affecting him personally will occur; mere suspicion or conjecture is insufficient".[137]

The second category, labelled here as cases concerning 'possible victims' in order to differentiate it,[138] refers to domestic laws that provide a legal basis for the implementation of secret measures, such as surveillance measures. Here, the ECtHR has admitted claims in cases where the applicants had no means of knowing whether such implementation measures had been applied to them.[139] This allowed the ECtHR to review the legislative framework of several states in the area of secret surveillance. Thus, in the case of 'potential victims' the relevant law has not (yet) been applied to the applicants, though they run the risk of being affected by it, while 'possible victims' have no way of knowing whether they have been affected by the

136 For example, in *Michaud vs. France* (2012), the category of persons considered as potential victims were all those exercising as lawyers. The case concerned a French law obliging lawyers to report on suspicions regarding money laundering by their clients, which would violate the professional confidentiality, falling under Art. 8 ECHR. The French state objected arguing that the applicant "did not claim that the legislation in question had been applied to his detriment, but simply that he had been obliged to organise his practice accordingly and introduce special internal procedures" and that he "was in fact asking the Court to examine *in abstracto* the conformity of a domestic law with the Convention" (*Michaud vs. France* (2012), para. 49). The ECtHR however dismissed this objection considering that the applicant was among the group of people that run the risk of being directly affected by the law, as it was directed towards all French lawyers (at paras. 51-52. Similarly, in *Burden vs. UK* (2006)).

137 Schabas, *Commentary to the ECHR*, 2015, p. 743. This takes place for example in cases where a violation is likely to occur after an individual is deported to a third state (a classic example in this regard is ECtHR, *Soering vs. UK* (1989)). In these cases, the applicant can be considered a potential victim once the deportation procedure has reached a certain stage in which a concrete risk is manifested, such as in those cases where an expulsion order has already been issued.

138 The ECtHR refers to both of these categories as 'potential victims', without differentiating them.

139 The first time it used this approach was in *Klass vs. Germany* (1978), and this approach has also been applied to NGOs, that have been allowed to claim before the Court that laws allowing for secret measures directly affected their rights as legal persons (for example in *Centrum för Rättvisa vs. Sweden* (2021), at paras. 175-177).

law. In addition, 'possible victims' are usually not belonging to a specific group, contrary to 'potential victims'.[140]

ii. Self-executing laws before the IACtHR

In general, the IACtHR has adopted a similar stance to the ECtHR in terms of refusing to review domestic laws *in abstracto*, thus requiring that they were applied to the alleged victim(s) in order to examine them.[141] The IACtHR's position towards the review of domestic laws was made clear in its early years, through an advisory opinion of 1994. It was requested by the IACmHR and asked the Court among others about the legal effects of a law adopted by a state after ratifying the Convention when this law manifestly violates the obligations contained therein. The Court answered that the adoption of such a law would be contrary to the Convention, but in order to determine the consequences it distinguished between 'self-executing norms' and 'non-self-executing norms'.[142]

The Court considered that non-self-executing norms do not represent in themselves a human rights violation and therefore cannot be reviewed if they have not been applied to specific individuals.[143] With respect to self-executing norms, it stated that they trigger international responsibility without the need for them to be applied to a specific individual. The

140 See *Klass vs. Germany* (1978), para. 37 ("To that extent, the disputed legislation directly affects all users or potential users of the postal and telecommunication services in the Federal Republic of Germany").

141 In numerous cases, the IACtHR has affirmed that "[t]he purpose of the Court's contentious jurisdiction is not to review domestic laws in abstract; rather it is exercised in order to decide specific cases in which it is alleged that an act [or omission] of the State, executed against specific individuals, is contrary to the Convention". See IACtHR, *Cepeda Vargas vs. Colombia* (2010), para. 51; *Genie Lacayo vs. Nicaragua* (1995), para. 50; *Usón Ramírez vs. Venezuela* (2009), para. 154; *Cabrera García and Montiel Flores vs. Mexico* (2010), para. 207.

142 The former are laws that directly affect individuals upon their entry into force, while the latter ones "require subsequent normative measures, compliance with additional conditions, or, quite simply, implementation by state authorities" before they can affect the legal sphere of individuals (IACtHR, *Advisory Opinion 14/94*, 1994, para. 41).

143 IACtHR, *Advisory Opinion 14/94* (1994), para. 42. The Court specifically stated that "there is no provision in the Convention authorizing the Court, under its contentious jurisdiction, to determine whether a law that has not yet affected the guaranteed rights and freedoms of specific individuals is in violation of the Convention" (at para. 49).

IACtHR mentioned in this respect the example of discriminatory laws, arguing that "a norm that deprives a portion of the population of some of its rights —for example, because of race— automatically injures all the members of that race".[144] Nevertheless, this exception has not played an important role in the IACtHR's jurisprudence. Even if it declared in some judgments that a law is *per se* contrary to the Convention, these were always laws that had been applied in the context of a human rights violation.[145] It has therefore not developed the concept of potential victims to the same extent as the ECtHR.[146]

However, an evolution can be observed before the IACtHR whereby the required link between the law and the victim has been loosened to some extent.[147] This evolution is most evident if one compares two cases related to laws that were adopted or amended after the facts of the case. In *Velez Loor vs. Panama* (2010), the IACtHR considered that it could not rule on 'new' migration laws that had not been applied to the victims and the facts of the case.[148] Nine years later in *Gorigoitia vs. Argentina* (2019), the Court nevertheless accepted to review laws that were adopted after the facts of the case.[149] In this case, the IACtHR ordered Argentina to reform these laws

---

144 IACtHR, *Advisory Opinion 14/94* (1994), para. 43.

145 See for example IACtHR, *Suarez Rosero vs. Ecuador* (1997). See also the judgments concerning amnesty laws included in Chapter 4 of this book.

146 This notion of potential victims has only been applied exceptionally by the IACtHR. For example, in a case against Trinidad and Tobago where 32 individuals had been sentenced to death in accordance with a law that was found to be contrary to the Convention, the IACtHR considered all of them as victims despite the fact that only one of them had actually been executed. The Court argued in this respect that "the mere existence of the Offences Against the Person Act in itself constitutes a per se violation of that provision of the Convention" (IACtHR, *Hilaire, Constantine and Benjamin vs. Trinidad and Tobago* (2002), para. 116. See on this case Chapter 4 of this book).

147 See on this generally Pasqualucci, *The Practice and Procedure of the IACtHR*, 2002, pp. 133-134.

148 In this case, the applicants claimed not only that the migration laws applied to the victims were contrary to the Convention, but also that the reform of these laws adopted after the facts of the case had failed to remedy these incompatibilities. (IACtHR, *Velez Loor vs. Panama* (2010), para. 285).

149 This case dealt with an alleged denial of justice, because the regulation of the cassation appeal did not allow for a full review of judgments. The domestic laws governing this type of appeals had also been reformed some years after the facts of the case, but the applicants claimed that the new laws were still contrary to the ACHR. The state objected to this claim, arguing that the contested laws were not applied to the victims and thus it constituted an abstract review (IACtHR, *Gorigoitía vs. Argentina* (2019), para. 16). The Court however rejected the objection in this

adopted after the facts of the case, because its substance was the same as in those applied to the victim of the case.[150]

In sum, although some cautious steps in that direction can be observed in recent case law, the IACtHR has been deeply reluctant to review domestic laws *in abstracto*, possibly even more so than the ECtHR. This is perhaps due to the different constitutional traditions in these two regions. Abstract review is very common in European constitutionalism, where it can be requested by certain organs of the state.[151] On the other hand, American constitutionalism tends to favour concrete review.[152] This could be reflected in the fact that the ECtHR has been more flexible than the IACtHR on that front, allowing for more exceptions to its victim requirement. But in the African region, one can find a completely different situation, with no victim requirement whatsoever and with the abstract review being generally permitted.

iii. The absence of a victim requirement before the ACtHPR

The ACtHPR represents a unique case in regional human rights adjudication with respect to the abstract review of domestic norms. As it was mentioned in the introduction, in accordance with Art. 34(6) of the African Court's Protocol states can submit an optional declaration whereby they allow individuals and NGOs to apply directly to the Court, without having to lodge their claim first before the Commission. In this regard, the ACtHPR has made clear in its case law that NGOs as well as individuals can claim that the state committed a human rights violation without any sort of victim requirement. This includes also the possibility of claiming that the mere existence of a law violates human rights.

The ACtHPR's first judgment on the merits concerned an application by an individual and two NGOs alleging the unconventionality of a Tanzanian

---

case, arguing that the issue at stake was not only to review the conventionality of laws that had been applied to the applicant, but also "subsequent actions aimed at ensuring full review in cassation matters" (at para. 21).

150 IACtHR, *Gorigoitía vs. Argentina* (2019), paras. 72-74.

151 Note, however, that many constitutional courts have also the competence to perform a concrete review of laws, in the context of referrals by ordinary courts or individual applications.

152 See on how these two constitutional traditions adopted diverging forms of review Alec Stone Sweet, "Why Europe Rejected American Judicial Review: And Why It May Not Matter", *Michigan Law Review* 101(8), 2003, pp. 2744-2780.

constitutional provision prohibiting independent candidates to run for election.[153] The individual formed a political party in order to participate in the elections and the State therefore objected that he was no longer affected by this law. However, on the latter point the Court argued that

> *even if the Applicant has successfully formed a political party, he cannot be stopped from challenging the validity of the laws in question and from asserting that the same amounts to a violation of the Charter. A matter such as this cannot and must not be dealt with as though it were a personal action, and it would be inappropriate for this Court to do so. If there is a violation, it operates to the prejudice of all Tanzanians, and if the Applicants' applications succeed, the outcome inures to the benefit of all Tanzanians.*[154]

This was indeed a remarkable statement for a human rights court, apparently allowing for individuals and NGOs to challenge laws even when no specific individual was affected by them. This broad interpretation of its personal jurisdiction has been maintained by the ACtHPR in many subsequent cases. For example, the ACtHPR has found that individuals can submit 'public interest cases', aiming "to protect the interest of public at large, rather than specific private interests".[155] A clear example in this regard is *Ajavon vs. Benin* (2020). Here, the applicant requested the ACtHPR "to order the Respondent State to suspend" no less than seven domestic laws due to its incompatibility with international human rights instruments, although he was not directly affected by them, nor did he identify any concrete victim. Despite the objections by Benin, the ACtHPR accepted this complaint and went on to examine each of the contested laws, finding an incompatibility with respect to most of them. Moreover, the ACtHPR examined not only the laws that had been challenged by the applicant but some additional ones, too.[156]

---

153 ACtHPR, *Tanganyika Law Society and Legal and Human Rights Centre* vs. *Tanzania* (2013).

154 ACtHPR, *Tanganyika Law Society and Legal and Human Rights Centre* vs. *Tanzania* (2013), para. 110.

155 ACtHPR, *Suy Bi Gohore Emile vs. Côte d'Ivoire* (2020), para. 105.

156 In this respect, the applicant alleged that the Beninese Law No. 2018-34, regulating the exercise of the right to strike, was contrary to this right (para. 129). The Court found that not only the contested law, but also two further domestic laws of Benin (which had not been challenged by the applicant) in fact prohibited the right to strike, in violation of the principle of non-regression under the ICESCR (paras. 140-142). These were the Beninese laws governing respectively the public service

Several states have objected to the ACtHPR's competence to review domestic laws *in abstracto* by making reference to the material jurisdiction of the Court, which extends "to all cases and disputes submitted to it concerning the interpretation and application of the Charter, this Protocol and any other relevant Human Rights instrument ratified by the states concerned".[157] For example, the Malian government objected in one case arguing that "the Applicants' claims relate more to [the] harmonisation of national laws with the African Charter on Human and Peoples' Rights rather than to the issue of application and interpretation of the Charter and other conventions".[158] The ACtHPR has nevertheless consistently replied to such objections by determining that the compatibility of a domestic norm with the respective treaty is an issue related to its interpretation and/or application, thus comprised in its material jurisdiction.[159]

Other states have objected by making reference to the victim requirement. For example, Benin raised a number of preliminary objections to the Court's jurisdiction *ratione personae* in cases related to domestic legislation, arguing that the requirement of victim status was missing.[160] The Court has nevertheless rejected all these objections, expressly stating in this

---

and the police personnel, as in both cases the laws prevented these particular groups from exercising their right to strike.

157 Article 3(1) of the Protocol establishing the ACtHPR. Note that it is a broader provision than the ones dealing with the material jurisdiction of the other two regional human rights courts, as it includes all human rights instruments ratified by the parties, while the ECHR mentions only the Convention and the Protocols thereto, and the ACHR refers exclusively to the human rights instruments with a regional scope ratified by the parties.

158 ACtHPR, *APDF and IHRDA vs. Mali* (2018), para. 17. In another case, Benin objected to the Court's jurisdiction expressly arguing that "no provision confers on [the ACtHPR] the power to review in abstracto the conformity of domestic legislation with international conventions" (ACtHPR, Ajavon vs. Benin (2020), para. 45), and the same state has also argued that the ACtHPR "lacks jurisdiction to assess national laws conformity in accordance with international conventions" (ACtHPR, *Houngue Éric Noudehouenou vs. Benin* (2020), para. 21). In the latter case, the state even claimed that "once the Constitutional Court rules that a provision is in conformity with the Constitution, it cannot be challenged on the basis that it results in human rights violations".

159 ACtHPR, *Tanganyika Law Society and Legal and Human Rights Centre* vs. *Tanzania* (2013), para. 86. See also *APDF and IHRDA vs. Mali* (2018), para. 27, with the ACtHPR stating that the alleged incompatibility concerned rights included in the Charter and other treaties and would thus fit in the definition of Article 3(1) of the Court's Protocol.

160 In the case of ACtHPR, *XYZ vs. Benin (II)* (2020), the State raised a preliminary objection arguing that the applicant was not affected by the reform and had no

respect that Article 5(3) of the Court's Protocol, "do not require individuals or NGOs to demonstrate a personal interest in an Application in order to access the Court, especially in the case of public interest litigation".[161] The ACtHPR has recognised that this constitutes a distinctive approach, by arguing that it represents "a peculiarity of the African regional human rights system characterised by the objective nature of human rights litigation".[162] In some cases, the ACtHPR has also responded to state objections by adopting a similar position to that of the ECtHR concerning potential victims, although with a broader scope. While the ECtHR applies the notion of potential victims only to certain persons or groups that are directly targeted by the law, the ACtHPR has argued that certain laws affect all citizens, and therefore every individual of the corresponding state can challenge them before the Court.[163]

In sum, it can be observed that the ACtHPR has adopted an approach towards the review of domestic laws that is rather unusual in international adjudication. While both the ECtHR and the IACtHR generally limit the review of laws to instances in which the contested law has been applied to alleged victims, this is not the case before the ACtHPR. Despite its young age, the latter court has thus developed a particular form of adjudication that is arguably sensitive to its regional context. The ACtHPR justified this approach mentioning "the practical difficulties that ordinary African vic-

legitimate interest in it, and that this would constitute a reason of inadmissibility. See also, with a similar preliminary objection, *Ajavon vs. Benin* (2020).

161 ACtHPR, *XYZ vs. Benin (II)* (2020), para. 48. See also *Ajavon vs. Benin* (2020), para. 58, where the Court stated that "neither the Charter, nor the Protocol, nor do the Rules require that the Applicant and the victim have to be the same".

162 ACtHPR, *Ajavon vs. Benin* (2020), para. 59.

163 This is for example the case with electoral laws. In the case of ACtHPR, *XYZ vs. Benin (II)* (2020), the Court replied to Benin's objection concerning the lack of jurisdiction stating that "[c]onsidering that the Applicant himself is a citizen of the Respondent State and that the revised provisions of the electoral laws have a potential impact on his right to participate in the government of his country, it is evident that he has a direct interest in the matter" (ACtHPR, *XYZ vs. Benin (II)* (2020), para. 57). The same has also been affirmed by the ACtHPR with respect to constitutional reforms, stating that "the amendment of laws such as the constitution, which is the supreme law of the land, is of particular interest to all citizens as it has a direct or indirect bearing on their individual rights and the security and well-being of their society and country" (*XYZ vs. Benin (II)* (2020), para. 49).

tims of human rights violations may encounter in bringing their complaints before the Court".[164]

The ACtHPR is considerably less known in its region than the other two courts in their respective regions. Victims of human rights violations, due to the lack of education and legal assistance, are often prevented from knowing how to access the ACtHPR. From that perspective, the ACtHPR – mainly with the help of NGOs – is playing a role that aims to provide justice to those disenfranchised or otherwise lacking the possibilities to appear before it. It has in this context also accepted that not only laws but also specific acts of state agents can be challenged by individuals and NGOs despite not being affected by them.[165] On the other hand, this approach is not without problems concerning the subsidiary role of international human rights adjudication, especially when legislative remedies are attached to this abstract review.[166] In addition, the ACtHPR runs the risk of being flooded with applications, especially if local civil society groups or opposition parties take advantage of this approach to initiate strategic litigation against incumbent governments.[167]

164 ACtHPR, *XYZ vs. Benin (II)* (2020), para. 48. In one case it even added that "it is an estimable virtue and duty of a responsible citizen to stand for the preservation of public interest" (ACtHPR, *Houngue Éric Noudehouenou vs. Benin* (2020), paras. 27 and 38-40).

165 In ACtHPR, *Ajavon vs. Benin* (2020), the applicant accused the state of having violated the right to life when the army fired live rounds at protesters, killing dozens (para. 158). This is despite the fact that he had not been present in these protests or otherwise directly affected by the repression of protesters. The Court however examined the facts and found violations of the right to life, the prohibition of torture and the right to dignity under the ACHR, although it did not mention any specific victim in this respect (para. 174).

166 Subsidiarity, which is considered "a key principle in international law and adjudication", can be seen as requiring that domestic bodies "have first the opportunity to remedy the issue(s) and only after they have failed to do so should the supranational body step in" (see Rachel Murray and Clara Sandoval, "Balancing Specificity of Reparation Measures and States' Discretion", *JHRP* 12(1), 2020, pp. 101-124, at p. 115). Under this view, it can be problematic if a human rights courts orders preventive legislative reforms, before an actual human rights violation has taken place.

167 See in this respect James Thuo Gathii and Jacquelene Wangui Mwangi, "The African Court of Human and Peoples' Rights as an Opportunity Structure", in James Thuo Gathii (ed.), *The Performance of Africa's International Courts: Using Litigation for Political, Legal, and Social Change*, Oxford: OUP, 2020.

2. The Advisory Review of Legislation

Contentious cases are not the only instances in which regional human rights courts can review the domestic legislation of states. This can also happen through advisory proceedings. Each of the three regional human rights instruments foresees a different advisory competence for the respective court, and each court has developed a distinct practice in this regard. However, the advisory competence of all three courts has the potential of allowing them to review domestic laws of states, albeit to a different degree. It is nevertheless a potential that has remained to a large extent underdeveloped. Rather, the only court that has made use of it is the IACtHR, and only in two early instances.

The advisory competence of the ECtHR is twofold, with its 'traditional' advisory proceedings regulated in articles 47-49 ECHR on the one hand, and the 'preliminary reference' advisory proceedings that were incorporated with Protocol 16 on the other. The 'traditional' advisory role of the ECtHR – which applies to requests made by the CoM – is ill-suited for the review of domestic laws, especially due to its narrow material scope. Article 47(2) expressly excludes any hypothetical issue that the ECtHR might have to consider in the future through contentious proceedings. This is clearly the case with potentially incompatible domestic laws. In addition, the ECtHR determined that decisions about the compatibility of other instruments with the Convention would fall outside the scope of Art. 47.[168] Therefore, it does not appear feasible that the Court would engage in a review of domestic laws through this 'traditional' advisory mechanism.

On the other hand, the 'preliminary reference' advisory role introduced with Protocol 16 offers a more promising path in this respect, if the laws in question are connected to domestic judicial proceedings. Under this mechanism, the highest domestic courts can request advisory opinions from the ECtHR with respect to cases pending before them. Contrary to the Art. 47 procedure, Protocol 16 states that the Court's advisory opinions can deal not only with the interpretation of the Convention but also with its application by national authorities. The application of the ECHR takes place domestically through acts of the executive, legislative and judicial

168 In one of the advisory opinion requests by the CoM, a question was related to the compatibility the CIS Convention with the ECHR. The Court stated in this respect that reviewing this compatibility in the abstract would fall outside the scope of Art. 47 ECHR. See ECtHR, *Decision on the competence of the Court to give an advisory opinion*, 02 June 2004, para. 24.

authorities. Therefore, such acts of application of the ECHR could arguably comprise domestic laws. In this respect, a Reflection Paper issued by the ECtHR in 2013 during the process of adopting this Protocol mentioned that the concept of 'questions of principle' included in Art. 1 of Protocol 16, "could also cover cases raising an issue with regard to the compatibility with the Convention of legislation, a rule or an established interpretation of legislation by a court".[169] Therefore, it appears that this extension of the scope of review implies that domestic laws could be the subject of advisory opinions of the ECtHR.

However, looking at the advisory opinions delivered so far by the ECtHR under Protocol 16, this assumption becomes less clear.[170] Several requests have dealt with domestic laws, including cases where the domestic courts had to decide about the constitutionality of a legislative provision.[171] In these opinions, the Court came to relevant findings concerning certain requirements for domestic laws, in general, to be compatible with the Convention,[172] but it clearly distanced itself from reviewing the concrete norms at stake.[173] For example, an advisory opinion request by the French *Conseil d'État* in the course of a constitutional review of legislation asked about the discriminatory nature of a domestic provision. The ECtHR included a number of criteria for determining whether a law could be considered dis-

169 ECtHR, *Reflection Paper on the Proposal to Extend the Court's Advisory Jurisdiction*, para. 29, available at: https://www.echr.coe.int/Documents/2013_Courts_advisory_jurisdiction_ENG.pdf.

170 Until the end of 2022, the ECtHR issued five Advisory Opinions through the mechanism laid down in Protocol 16.

171 As in ECtHR, *Avisory Opinion P16-2019-001* (2020); *Advisory Opinion P16-2021-002* (2022).

172 For example, in the first advisory opinion requested by the French Cour de Cassation, the ECtHR decided that "Article 8 of the Convention requires that domestic law provide a possibility of recognition of a legal parent-child relationship with the intended mother" (ECtHR, *Advisory Opinion P16-2018-001* (2019), operative para. 1).

173 In several advisory opinions, the ECtHR stated that its role was only to issue an opinion concerning the questions posed, and that it has no jurisdiction "to evaluate the merits of the parties' views on the interpretation of domestic law" (ECtHR, *Advisory Opinion P16-2018-001* (2019), para. 25; Advisory Opinion P16-2020-002 (2022), para. 61). Moreover, in an advisory opinion requested by the Constitutional Court of Armenia in the course of a review of legislation that was in turn requested by a first-instance court, the ECtHR argued that its role was only to "inform the Constitutional Court's own interpretation of the domestic provisions relevant for the case before it" (ECtHR, *Avisory Opinion P16-2019-001* (2020), para. 50).

criminatory, but stated that "[i]t is, inter alia, in the light of these elements that the *Conseil d'État* will have to determine whether or not the difference in treatment introduced by the legislative provision being challenged in the proceedings before it satisfies the requirement of proportionality and, accordingly, whether or not this difference in treatment can be considered compatible with Article 14 taken in conjunction with Article 1 of Protocol No. 1".[174] This shows that the ECtHR has avoided reviewing the compatibility of specific provisions through its advisory procedure under Protocol 16. Therefore, although on paper this procedure appears like a venue for the ECtHR to perform an advisory review of legislation, the restrictive interpretation that the Court has adopted so far regarding its scope of review prevents it from carrying out this task.

In the case of the IACtHR, the regulation of its advisory jurisdiction under Article 64 of the ACHR contains a provision expressly determining that "[t]he Court, at the request of a member state of the Organization, may provide that state with opinions regarding the compatibility of any of its domestic laws with the aforesaid international instruments". This provision has a unique character in the international judicial landscape, with the ACHR being the only treaty that expressly allows states to ask an international judicial body for a review of their domestic laws *in abstracto.* Nevertheless, there is only one state which has made use of this provision, the country that hosts the IACtHR.

Costa Rica submitted three requests for a review of its domestic legislation between 1984 and 1991. The first of these requests asked whether a draft constitutional reform concerning the conditions for obtaining the state's nationality was compatible with several rights of the Convention.[175] The Court decided that one provision of the draft constitution would be discriminatory, as it stipulated preferential treatment for one of the spouses in cases of naturalization applicable to marriage. The following year, in 1985, Costa Rica submitted another request, this time about the compatibility of a domestic law establishing compulsory membership in an association in order to practice journalism, which the IACtHR found to be contrary to the freedom of expression.[176] Finally, the same state submitted

174 *Advisory Opinion P16-2021-002* (2022), para. 111.

175 This allowed the Court to clarify that the terms 'domestic laws' in Art. 64(2) ACHR refer to any type of legal norm, including constitutional provisions, as well as draft legislation not yet in force (IACtHR, *Advisory Opinion 4/84* (1984), paras. 14 and 29).

176 IACtHR, *Advisory Opinion 5/85* (1985), para. 85.

another request concerning a draft law in 1991, but the Court considered this request inadmissible as a case related to this law was already being reviewed by the IACmHR through the contentious procedure.[177]

Since Costa Rica's last request in 1991, states have not made further use of Article 64(2) ACHR in order to request advisory opinions about their own laws. This is somewhat surprising, as some states have been very active in requesting advisory opinions on the basis of Article 64(1) ACHR for more general issues,[178] some of them closely related to their domestic legal order.[179] What potentially prevents states from making such requests for legislative review is the quasi-binding character that the Court itself has attached to its advisory opinions.[180]

In any case, the advisory proceeding of the IACtHR under Art. 64(2) clearly allows for a legislative review through advisory opinions. Its downside however is that only governments can submit requests about their own domestic laws, and other domestic bodies or international bodies such as the IACmHR have no role under this procedure. Allowing other domestic

177 It held in this respect that the questions presented "could produce, under the guise of an advisory opinion, a determination of contentious matters not yet referred to the Court, without providing the victims with the opportunity to participate in the proceedings". (IACtHR, *Advisory Opinion 12/91* (1991), para. 28).

178 Since 2014, Colombia has requested three advisory opinions from the Court, while Panama, Costa Rica and Ecuador have requested one each. See https://corteidh.or.cr/solicitud_opiniones_consultivas.cfm.

179 For example, the Colombian government requested an advisory opinion on whether limiting presidential re-elections affects the right to political participation (see IACtHR, *Advisory Opinion 28/21* (2021)). This limitation of presidential mandates is established in the Colombian Constitution, and thus the issue could have been asked through Art. 64(2) ACHR.

180 Certainly, in the early years of its advisory practice the IACtHR stated several times that the advisory opinions lack the binding character of judgments (IACtHR, *Advisory Opinion 01/82* (1982), para. 51; IACtHR, *Advisory Opinion 15/97* (1997), para. 26). However, this perspective changed with the introduction of the doctrine of conventionality control, according to which state authorities need to apply the Inter-American standards in their domestic context (see Chapter 5 of this book). Domestic judges need to take into account the ACHR and its interpretation by the IACtHR when ruling on domestic issues, as well as legislators when drafting domestic laws. In an advisory opinion issued in 2014, the IACtHR expressly stated that "the different organs of the State must carry out the corresponding control of conformity with the Convention, based also on the considerations of the Court in exercise of its non-contentious or advisory jurisdiction" (IACtHR, *Advisory Opinion 21/14* (2014), para. 31). Thus, if the IACtHR would find a domestic law incompatible with the Convention in these advisory proceedings, the concerned state would have an obligation to amend it accordingly.

institutions, such as legislatures or high courts, or Inter-American bodies such as the IACmHR, to request advisory opinions on the compatibility of domestic laws with the ACHR would be a solution for revitalising this procedure. However, it seems highly unlikely that states would agree to a conventional reform in order to allow it. Thus, unless the Inter-American institutions do something to encourage governments to submit requests for advisory opinions under Art. 64(2) ACHR, this mechanism for the advisory review of legislation is likely to remain dormant.

Finally, whether the ACtHPR is capable of exercising some sort of legislative review through its advisory jurisdiction is still rather unclear. The relevant provision refers to the competence to "provide an opinion on any legal matter relating to the Charter or any other relevant human rights instruments".[181] In principle, this formulation is broad enough to include the review of domestic laws' compatibility with human rights instruments. In early comments about the ACtHPR's advisory jurisdiction, some authors however suggested that the Court may refuse to adopt such an interpretation, due to the resistance that African states have traditionally showed with respect to interferences in their domestic sphere.[182] Having in mind the degree of intrusiveness that the ACtHPR displayed in its contentious jurisprudence, this inference seems nevertheless outdated. In this respect, other authors have advocated in favour of a broad interpretation, arguing that "[i]n case a member state submits a request for an opinion on the compatibility of one of its own domestic laws, there simply is no unwanted intrusion in internal affairs. Denying such a request would imply an unnecessary refusal to provide a service to a state that presumably takes human rights seriously".[183] Others have even clearly affirmed that the ACtHPR's advisory jurisdiction encompasses the review of domestic laws.[184]

181 See Article 4(1) of the Protocol on the Establishment of the ACtHPR.

182 Gino J. Naldi and Konstantinos Magliveras, "Reinforcing the African System of Human Rights: The Protocol on the Establishment of a Regional Court of Human and Peoples' Rights", *NQHR* 16, 1998, p. 440 (cited in Anne Pieter van der Mei, "The Advisory Jurisdiction of the African Court on Human and Peoples' Rights", *African Human Rights Law Journal* 5(1), 2005, pp. 27-46, at p. 41).

183 Van der Mei, *AHRLJ* 2005, p. 42.

184 José Pina-Delgado, "Advisory Proceedings: African Court on Human and Peoples' Rights (ACtHPR)", in *MPEIPro*, ("States can request opinions [to the ACtHPR] on the compatibility of their domestic legislation with international human rights treaties").

With that being said, none of the requests for advisory opinions decided so far are related to any concrete domestic laws.[185] Although the ACtHPR has adopted a rather restrictive interpretation concerning the personal competence to request an advisory opinion,[186] in a case in which such a request is made by a competent body the Court would most probably accept to review domestic laws under these proceedings. This becomes clearer if one takes into account the aforementioned jurisprudence of the ACtHPR concerning the abstract review of laws in contentious proceedings. As the ACtHPR will carry out a legislative review whenever an individual or an NGO claim in contentious proceedings – without being directly affected by it – that a domestic law is contrary to the ACHPR or other instruments, it would seem logic that the same review could also be performed through an advisory proceeding. In any case, the clarification of this issue will need

185 The closest was the request made by an NGO about the compatibility of vagrancy laws with African Charter. It does not make reference to one specific law but to criminal offences that can be found in "at least 22 countries in Africa", and asks about the compatibility of these laws and about the states' "positive obligations to repeal or amend their vagrancy laws" (ACtHPR, *Advisory Opinion on the Compatibility of Vagrancy Laws with the African Charter of Human and People's Rights and other Human Rights Instruments applicable in Africa*, 2020, pp. 2 and 6). The ACtHPR admitted this request, stating with respect to the questions posed that its advisory jurisdiction comprises the assessment of "the compatibility of the matters raised in a request for an opinion with the Charter and other applicable human rights standards". It then determined that vagrancy laws are contrary to a number of provisions of the ACHPR and further instruments and highlighted that "State Parties to the Charter have a positive obligation to, inter alia, repeal or amend their vagrancy laws and related laws" (operative para. vi).

186 The ACtHPR only found that it had jurisdiction to issue three advisory opinions out of fifteen requests. The main reason for these rejections of requests made by NGOs was that the ACtHPR interpreted the concept of "any African organization recognized by the OAU" (which are the organisations that can submit requests for advisory opinions) as covering only those having a Memorandum of Understanding (MoU) with the AU, but not those with an observer status at the ACmHPR, which are the ones that can submit a contentious case to the ACtHPR if states issue a declaration under Art. 34(6) of the ACtHPR's Protocol. In this regard, the conditions for such a MoU with the AU are much stricter than those of the Commission, and this implies that most African NGOs are impeded from requesting advisory opinions to the ACtHPR. See Anthony Jones, "Form over Substance: The African Court's restrictive approach to NGO standing in the SERAP Advisory Opinion", *African Human Rights Law Journal* 17(1), 2017, pp. 320-328.

an advisory opinion request specifically related to the compatibility of a concrete law.[187]

3. From the Review of Legislation to Legislative Remedies

The review of domestic laws is very closely linked to legislative remedies in the case of both the IACtHR and the ACtHPR. These courts, when finding an incompatibility of domestic laws with the respective instrument, will generally order its reform. In the case of the ECtHR, this is different; the link is much looser, as a finding of the unconventionality of a law does usually not lead to an order to reform it. As will be explained in more detail in Chapter 3, when the ECtHR considers a domestic law incompatible with human rights standards it will find a violation, but usually portray it as limited to the specific measure of implementation of that law *vis-à-vis* the victim.[188] Despite the Court not expressly stating it, judgments where an incompatibility is found can be seen as implying the need for legislative reforms, but this is not formally binding for the state.[189] The ECtHR's main focus is to provide redress to the specific victims. When a violation is clearly stemming from a structural problem that has its origin in a domestic law, the ECtHR will recommend a reform in the argumentative part of the judgment. If the state then fails to carry out the reform and numerous repetitive cases concerning the same structural issue keep arriving, the

187 See in this respect Gathii and Mwangi, in Gathii (ed.), 2020, p. 217, arguing that the fact that not many advisory opinion requests have been submitted to the ACtHPR is "perhaps because it does not have express jurisdiction to issue advisory opinions 'about the compatibility of a State's domestic laws with the treaties within the Court's jurisdiction'".

188 See Keller and Stone Sweet, in Keller and Stone Sweet (eds.), 2008, pp. 691-692 ("The Court constructs Convention rights as general norms, which it treats as having prospective legal consequences for States. At the same time, its powers are largely limited to the rendering of individual (retrospective and particular) justice to victims of specific abuse").

189 See for example Stiansen, *IJHR* 2019, p. 1224, arguing that although "the ECtHR typically does not spell out the need to change legislation explicitly (...) where a judgment finds existing legislation to violate human rights standards, legislative changes are often needed". See also Polakiewicz, in *MPEPIL*, para. 37 ("In individual applications, when specific measures of implementation constitute the main object of an application, the ECtHR's judgments often reveal inconsistencies or *lacunae* in the underlying legislation or practices that have provoked the human rights violation in the individual case. In such cases legislative or administrative reforms are called for as a measure to prevent similar breaches of the ECHR").

ECtHR will include this as a binding obligation in the operative part, as it will be explained in more detail later in this book.

On the contrary, in the case law of the IACtHR, it is important to differentiate between the victims and the beneficiaries of remedies in a concrete case.[190] There are indeed a number of remedial measures that are not aiming at the redress of the concrete victims or injured parties, but rather at the benefit of "society as a whole", as stated by the Court in several cases.[191] Legislative reforms are typically included among these remedies.[192] Therefore, although the IACtHR adopted a rather strict interpretation of the victim requirement, generally avoiding to review laws *in abstracto*, it has not limited its remedies to the concrete victims of the case but has instead expanded the notion of beneficiaries, mostly including remedial measures of both an individual and a general nature in the same judgment. This is to some extent similar before the ACtHPR, although in this case making society as a whole the beneficiary of its remedies has arguably more to do with the absence of concrete victims in numerous cases. As it has generally allowed individuals and NGOs to challenge domestic laws *in abstracto*, it follows that often the remedial measures can only be of a general nature.

Nevertheless, it is important to note in this context that legislative remedies are often not the result of a review of concrete legislative provisions, but rather of legislative omissions. For example, most legislative remedies issued by the ECtHR concern cases in which states failed to introduce provisions in their domestic legal order allowing for the redress of certain human rights violations. Similarly, all three courts have found that some vulnerable groups lack effective legislative protection, or that specific human rights violations are not adequately criminalised under domestic law. This is closely related to the differences between negative and positive legislative remedies, which will be explained in Chapter 5. With respect to the review of legislation, this difference usually implies that in the case of positive legislative remedies human rights courts can limit its review to finding that adequate laws are missing.

190 See Sandoval, in Ferstman, Goetz and Stephens (eds.), 2009, p. 273.

191 See for example IACtHR, *Trujillo Oroza vs. Bolivia* (2002), para. 110; *La Cantuta vs. Peru* (2006), para. 162, *Arellano vs. Chile*, para. 157. See also Judith Schönsteiner, "Disuassive Measures and the Society as a Whole. A working Theory of Reparations in the Inter-American Court of Human Rights", *American University International Law Review*, 2008, pp. 127-164.

192 Other remedies directed towards 'society as a whole' are for example the training of public officials or the prosecution and punishment of the perpetrators of human rights violations.

In sum, obligations to legislate, review of legislation and legislative remedies before human rights courts are three closely connected issues. Having briefly examined the first two, the rest of this book will focus on the latter one, the remedial measures that order legislative reforms. But before analysing the concrete practice of the three regional courts in this respect in the following chapters, the final section of this chapter will briefly examine the possible constitutional nature of these remedies and the role they play in the constitutionalisation of human rights law.

III. Legislative Remedies and the Constitutionalisation of Human Rights Law

For a number of years now, legal scholars (as well as international relations scholars and political scientists, among others) have been writing about the constitutionalisation of international law.[193] While this term has been used with many connotations and examined through different lenses and approaches,[194] it refers broadly to a trend in the evolution of international law during the 20th century, where it has incorporated and adapted domestic constitutional principles, institutions and procedures.[195] This is the case not only for the 'holy trinity' of constitutional law – i.e. democracy, rule of law and human rights – but also for other constitutional principles such as proportionality,[196] subsidiarity,[197] or solidarity.[198] Moreover, international law has turned from state-centrism and bilateralism to the

---

193 See generally Jan Klabbers, Anne Peters and Geir Ulfstein (eds.), *The Constitutionalization of International Law*, Oxford: OUP, 2009. The origin of this debate can be found in the writings of several German legal scholars during the early 1990s. See for example Bruno Simma, "From Bilateralism to Community Interests in *International Law*", *Recueil des Cours de l'Academie de Droit International* 250, 1994, pp. 217-384.

194 See Antje Wiener et al., "Global constitutionalism: Human rights, democracy and the rule of law", *Global Constitutionalism* 1(1), 2012, pp. 1-15.

195 Anne Peters, "Constitutionalisation" in Jean d'Aspermont and Sahib Singh (eds.), *Concepts for International Law - Contributions to Disciplinary Thought*, Cheltenham: Edward Elgar, 2019, pp. 141-153, at p. 141. See also Anne Peters, "Fragmentation and Constitutionalization", in Anne Orford and Florian Hoffmann (eds.), *The Oxford Handbook of the Theory of International Law*, Oxford: OUP, 2016, pp. 1011–1032.

196 Anne Peters, "Proportionality as a Global Constitutional Principle", in Anthony F. Lang and Antje Wiener (eds.), *Handbook on Global Constitutionalism*, Cheltenham: Edward Elgar, 2017, pp. 248-264.

197 Paolo G. Carozza, "Subsidiarity as a Structural Principle of International Human Rights Law", *AJIL* 97(1), 2003, pp. 38-79.

virtually universal acceptance of certain norms and an increased role for individuals.[199] This debate around the constitutionalisation of international law is generally encompassed in the broader scholarly movement of global constitutionalism. According to Peters, this is a movement which "both identifies some features and functions of international law (in the interplay with domestic law) as 'constitutional' and even 'constitutionalist' (positive analysis) and seeks to provide arguments for their further development in a specific direction (normative analysis)".[200]

The constitutionalisation of international law takes place not so much on the overall level -there is no world constitution yet[201]- but rather on specific areas (both geographical and disciplinary).[202] Therefore, authors have mainly focused on issues related to the constitutionalisation of specific sub-fields of international law. This was traditionally the case for international trade law[203] and EU law,[204] and more recently also other sub-fields

198 Rüdiger Wolfrum and Chie Kojima (eds.), *Solidarity: A Structural Principle of International Law*, Heidelberg: Springer, 2010.

199 See generally Anne Peters, *Beyond Human Rights*, 2016. On that point see also Ekaterina Yahyaoui Krivenko, *Rethinking Human Rights and Global Constitutionalism: From Inclusion to Belonging*, Cambridge: CUP, 2017, p. 20 ("Any version of international constitutionalism will usually acknowledge that a constitutionalist reading of international law implies a more active role for and more attention to individuals). Challenging this perspective, Astrid Kjeldgaard-Pedersen, "Global Constitutionalism and the International Legal Personality of the Individual", *Netherlands International Law Review* 66, 2019, pp. 271–286.

200 Anne Peters, in d'Aspermont and Singh (eds.), 2019, p. 1011.

201 See however Bardo Fassbender, "The United Nations Charter as the Constitution of the International Community", *Columbia Journal of Transnational Law* 36, 1998, pp. 529–619.

202 Anne Peters, "Compensatory Constitutionalism: The Function and Potential of Fundamental International Norms and Structures", *LJIL* 19(3), 2006, pp. 579-610, at pp. 601-602.

203 See John O McGinnis and Mark L Movsesian, "The World Trade Constitution", *Harvard Law Review* 114, 2000, 511–605.

204 For a classic example, see Eric Stein, "Lawyers, Judges, and the Making of a Transnational Constitution", *AJIL* 75, 1981, pp. 01–27. See also Joseph HH Weiler, *The Constitution of Europe*, Cambridge: CUP, 1999.

such as international environmental law[205] or international criminal law.[206] International human rights law plays also a very important role in this sort of sectoral constitutionalisation. In this respect, there is an evident parallelism between international human rights treaties and constitutional codifications of fundamental rights. Despite the possible differences regarding the typology and substance of rights at these two levels, in both cases, they perform the function of setting limits to states' exercise of governmental power towards individuals within their jurisdiction.[207] One of the core features of modern constitutionalism is the focus on the protection of fundamental rights, subject to judicial review. Some authors talk even about human rights in general as a constitutional order, which comprises the international, regional and domestic layers.[208] There is also a constitutionalist logic in the relation between human rights treaties and domestic laws. The former can be seen as pertaining to a sort of 'upper track', establishing certain conditions and features of the 'lower track' norms, in this case, domestic laws. This relation can be observed in the previously examined obligations to legislate included in human rights treaties.

One of the main challenges that has been highlighted regarding the constitutionalisation of international human rights law is the lack of a judicial enforcement of these rights at the international level comparable to the one exercised by domestic constitutional courts.[209] Nevertheless, since the late 1990s clear signs of an increased constitutionalisation can be observed before regional human rights courts. These courts' role and jurisprudence is getting closer to the one of constitutional courts, and legislative remedies are arguably part of this rapprochement, as will be shown below.[210]

---

205 James R. May and Erin Daly, "Human Rights Developments in Global Environmental Constitutionalism", in James R. May and Erin Daly (eds.), *Human Rights and the Environment: Legality, Indivisibility, Dignity and Geography*, Cheltenham: Edward Elgar, 2019, pp. 93–109.

206 Andrea Birdsall and Anthony F. Lang, "The International Criminal Court and Global Constitutionalism", in Anthony F. Lang and Antje Wiener (eds.), *Handbook on Global Constitutionalism*, Cheltenham: Edward Elgar 2017, pp. 383-394.

207 Peters, *LJIL* 2006, p. 599 labels this as the "confining function". See also Stephen Gardbaum, "Human Rights as International Constitutional Rights", *EJIL* 19(4), 2008, pp. 749–768, at p. 750.

208 Wayne Sandholtz, "Human rights courts and global constitutionalism: Coordination through judicial dialogue", *Global Constitutionalism* 10(3), 2021, pp. 439-464.

209 Gardbaum, *EJIL* 2008, p. 751.

210 This part will not deal with the constitutionalisation of international organisations, which relates mostly to their internal structure and characteristics, and aspects such as transparency and participation. Although this constitutionalist perspective

1. Regional Human Rights Courts as International 'Constitutional' Courts?

The international judiciary is an important agent in the process of constitutionalisation of international law,[211] and regional human rights courts have played and continue to play a paramount role in this context. Their functions are indeed comparable to those of domestic constitutional courts at various levels. On the one hand, they are superior organs in their respective legal orders and they review the states' acts against (international) constitutional standards, which include human rights.[212] On the other hand, their aim is also to guarantee the effectiveness of their respective constitutional document (in this case human rights conventions), thereby restricting the states' sovereignty and protecting individuals against unlawful interventions.

This aim is pursued both by providing individual justice and by setting the minimum human rights standards in their respective region through authoritative interpretations.[213] Their judgments thus affect not only the relation between the individual and constitutional bodies of the state but between different constitutional organs, too.[214] The fact that these courts exercise judicial review over state acts already contributes to the international rule of law,[215] and while performing this review they expressly make use of several constitutional principles outlined above, such as subsidiarity and proportionality. Finally, the criteria used to examine the restriction of rights are also the ones used by constitutional courts.[216]

---

is also relevant for the regional human rights courts, this section will focus on the constitutional functions of these courts, and mainly on legislative remedies as a specific type of constitutional function.

211 See Anne Peters, "Are we Moving towards Constitutionalization of the World Community?", in Antonio Cassesse (ed.), *Realizing Utopia: The Future of International Law*, Oxford: OUP, 2012, pp. 118–135, at p. 119.

212 Geir Ulfstein, "Transnational Constitutional Aspects of the European Court of Human Rights", *Global Constitutionalism* 10(1), 2021, pp. 151 - 174. As Wildhaber and Greer put it, "to a large extent, the ECtHR decides broadly the same kind of issues as a domestic supreme or constitutional court, and also in largely similar ways" (Wildhaber and Greer, *HRLR* 2012, at p. 668).

213 With regard to the ECtHR, see Keller and Kühne, *ZaöRV* 2016, p. 257-259.

214 Ulfstein, *Global Consitutionalism*, 2021, p. 152.

215 Peters, *LJIL* 2006, p. 601 ("An international rule of law would probably require some form of judicial review (...) of acts of states").

216 I.e. legality, public interest, necessity and proportionality. See e.g. Keller and Kühne, *ZaöRV* 2016, p. 272.

It should be noted, however, that regional human rights courts are not substituting domestic constitutional courts but rather complementing them, as they act only in those instances in which they consider that domestic courts have failed to protect the individual and to comply with the aforementioned minimum standards, in accordance with the exhaustion of domestic remedies rule and the principle of subsidiarity.[217] There are, additionally, certain limits to the regional human rights courts' constitutional nature. The first of them concerns their lack of capacity to exercise other types of constitutional litigation, such as that concerning competence-related issues among domestic bodies or different administrative levels in federal states.[218] In the context of regional human rights protection systems, additional constitutional bodies are missing, as there is no proper legislature and executive.[219] Another main difference between regional human rights courts and domestic constitutional courts is the lack of self-enforceability of the former's judgments, which need to be implemented by domestic authorities. Instead, the judgment of a domestic constitutional court affects the validity of the concerned act immediately, without an additional step being necessary.[220] This, of course, makes an important difference with respect to the effectiveness of judgments in constitutional *vis-à-vis* regional human rights settings, and some see it as incompatible with a constitutional role.[221]

However, all three regional human rights courts have been labelled as constitutional courts of their respective regions. This is especially the case for the ECtHR, as a number of scholars have examined the constitutional

217 Keller and Kühne, *ZaöRV* 2016, p. 260. This is however sometimes also the case for domestic constitutional courts, that usually act in individual cases only when the lower courts have failed to do so in an appropriate way.

218 See Keller and Kühne, *ZaöRV* 2016, p. 270.

219 In the European human rights protection system, the closest would be the PACE and the CoM, but their functions are very different from the ones of their domestic counterparts.

220 In this respect, at a supranational level only the CJEU has afforded direct effect to is judgments.

221 Jonas Christoffersen, "Individual and Constitutional Justice: Can the Power Balance of Adjudication be Reversed?", in Jonas Christoffersen and Mikael Rask Madsen (eds.), *The European Court of Human Rights between Law and Politics*, Oxford: OUP, 2011, pp. 181–203, at p. 195.

aspects of this court.[222] This gained momentum during the late 1990s,[223] especially since the ECtHR itself defined the Convention as "a constitutional instrument of public order" in 1995,[224] and the Court turned into a permanent body with direct access for individuals in 1998. Intervening in structural issues inside states that suffer systemic deficiencies – through the introduction of the pilot judgment procedure – reinforced its constitutional role.[225] Despite this debate turning predominantly around the constitutional aspects of the ECtHR, the IACtHR has also been ascribed a constitutional character,[226] and the ACtHPR has been even labelled as a "super-constitutional court".[227] There are however some differences with respect to the constitutional character of each of these courts, as will be seen below.

a) Diverging constitutional elements of regional human rights courts

Despite the common constitutional features of regional human rights courts, each of them has arguably achieved a different degree of constitutionalisation, with diverging elements in this respect. For example, an aspect that brings the ECtHR closer to a constitutional court is the exercise of jurisdiction over all members of the international organisation it belongs

222 See *inter alia* Keller and Kühne, *ZaöRV* 2016, Ulfstein, *Global Constitutionalism* 2021. Others, such as Sadurski, have argued in this respect that the question of whether or not to consider the ECtHR as a constitutional court is largely a matter of "the yardstick used to measure constitutional character" (Wojciech Sadurski, *Constitutionalism and the Enlargement of Europe*, Oxford: OUP, 2012, at p. 44).

223 Note however that some authors already came up with this idea before the 1990s. See for example Jochen Frowein, "Der europäische Menschenrechtsschutz als Beginn einer europäischen Verfassungsrechtsprechung", *Juristische Schulung*, 1986, pp. 845-851.

224 ECtHR, *Loidizou vs. Turkey* (1996), para. 75. This claim has thereafter been repeated by the Court several times. See for a more recent instance, ECtHR, *Aliyev vs. Azerbaijan* (2018), para. 225.

225 Sadurski, *HRLR* 2009, p. 402. On the pilot judgment procedure, see Chapter 3 of this book.

226 Laurence Burgogue-Larsen, "La Corte Interamericana de Derechos Humanos como Tribunal Constitucional", in Armin von Bogdandy, Héctor Fix Fierro and Mariela Morales Antoniazzi (coords.), Ius Constitutionale Commune *en América Latina: Rasgos, Potencialidades y Desafíos* Mexico: UNAM, 2014, pp. 421-457.

227 Adem Kassie Abebe, "Taming regressive constitutional amendments: The African Court as a continental (super) constitutional court", *I•CON* 17(1), 2019, pp. 89-117, especially at p. 110.

to (the CoE). This is not the case with the IACtHR and the ACtHPR, which are only competent with regard to the member states of the OAS and the AU that have expressly accepted to be subject to these courts' jurisdiction.

In addition, individuals of all states can have direct access to the ECtHR, while this is not the case with the other two regional courts.[228] This certainly does not mean that everyone is always entitled to access the ECtHR directly, as a number of procedural and substantive conditions have to be met, but that is also the case for individual proceedings before domestic constitutional courts.[229] In the case of the IACtHR, the system consists of a twofold structure, whereby individuals can only submit their claims before the IACmHR, a quasi-judicial body. The Commission, upon receiving such a claim, tries to reach a friendly settlement among the parties, and if that fails it issues a number of recommendations in order to remedy a potential violation. Only if the state party refuses to comply with such recommendations, it will refer the case to the IACtHR. This is also the case in the African system, with the exception that individuals and NGOs can directly access the ACtHPR if states expressly accept it through an optional declaration. Thus, as a considerable amount of the proceedings in the Inter-American and African systems are taking place before a non-judicial body, a fundamental element of constitutional law (access to justice) is missing in this case.

Another distinctive constitutional element can be observed with regard to the election of judges to the ECtHR. As it occurs with most constitutional courts, judges are elected through a parliamentary body. In the case of constitutional courts, this is done through domestic parliaments, while in the case of the ECtHR through PACE, which is composed of members of the forty-seven domestic parliaments and is therefore the parliamentary body of the CoE. Each state presents a list of three potential candidates to PACE and this body decides which one will occupy the seat in the Court. On the other hand, in the case of the IACtHR and the ACtHPR, the judges are elected respectively through the General Assembly of the OAS and the Assembly of Heads of State and Government of the AU. These are bodies

228 As explained in the Introduction. See on this constitutional feature Johann Justus Vasel, *Regionaler Menschenrechtsschutz als Emanzipationsprozess*, Berlin: Duncker and Humblot, 2017, p. 183.

229 For example, the exhaustion of domestic remedies rule of the ECHR is also present in many constitutional systems, that require an individual to exhaust all ordinary judicial avenues before submitting a constitutional complaint. The same occurs with other requirements, such as the temporal limits, or the need to show that the victim has suffered a significant disadvantage.

composed of governmental representatives, thus lacking the parliamentary character of PACE.

However, an aspect in which the ECtHR's jurisprudence is less constitutionalised than the one of its Inter-American and African counterparts concerns its extensive use of declaratory judgments, in which no individual or general remedies are indicated besides the payment of a monetary compensation.[230] Constitutional courts are in this respect only rarely issuing measures of compensation, but focus mostly on other type of remedies, often those of a general nature. This is also why the introduction of the pilot judgment procedure by the ECtHR was labelled as an "emphatic expression of [the ECtHR's] constitutional turn".[231] The ECtHR did not only start to issue remedies of a constitutional nature with this procedure – an issue that will be examined below – but the selection of cases for the pilot judgment procedure can also be compared to that of constitutional courts. The latter usually deals exclusively with individual cases that have a certain 'constitutional relevance', while in the pilot judgment procedure, the ECtHR identifies cases that reflect a 'systemic problem' in a state party. Although these two concepts are not exactly the same, as the constitutional relevance often includes interpretative issues that are not giving rise to systemic problems, the selection of salient cases can be considered similar to some extent.

At the IACtHR, besides its extended use of remedial measures of a constitutional character, another distinctive constitutional feature can be found in its doctrine of conventionality control. Through this doctrine, the IACtHR mandates domestic courts and other constitutional bodies to review the compatibility of laws and administrative acts with the American Convention, as interpreted by the Court. This can be compared at a constitutional level to a form of decentralised constitutionality control, where ordinary judges can review the constitutionality of legal provisions in cases before them, against the standards developed by the corresponding constitutional court. Moreover, in domestic law-making procedures, the legislature often asks for a legal report in order to assess the constitutionality of draft laws. For this reason, it has been argued that conventionality control

230 See Chapter 3 of this book.
231 Sadusrski, *HRLR* 2009, p. 450.

"resembles more a conception of the Convention as a federal Constitution and setting the Court as a supreme court in a federal State".[232]

Finally, in the case of the ACtHPR, a particular constitutional aspect lies in the wide scope of its contentious jurisdiction, which extends not only to the interpretation and application of its constitutive treaty (as it occurs with the contentious jurisdiction of the ECtHR and the IACtHR) but also "any other relevant Human Rights instrument ratified by the States concerned".[233] According to the African Court's interpretation, this also includes the African Charter on Democracy. In this regard, it has been argued that while the ACPHR's provisions correspond to the fundamental rights provisions of domestic constitutions, the African Charter on Democracy complements it with the democratic principles usually present in those constitutions, such as the separation of powers or the minimum requirements for the amendment of constitutions.[234] Thus, the judicial review exercised by the African Court is more constitutional in the sense that it is not limited to issues of a strict human rights character, but comprises aspects of a more institutional nature.[235] In addition, the review of domestic laws *in abstracto* is also a notable constitutional feature that has been developed by the ACtHPR.[236]

b) Individual vs. constitutional justice before human rights courts

For some years now, a debate has taken place around the issue of whether human rights courts should provide individual or constitutional justice. It

---

232 See Ariel E. Dulitzky, "An Inter-American Constitutional Court? The Invention of the Conventionality Control by the Inter-American Court of Human Rights", *Texas Law Review* 50, 2015, pp. 45-93, at p. 62, comparing it to the Supremacy Clause of the U.S. Constitution, which "commands local and state judges to disregard any other conflicting rule in the laws or constitution of their State".

233 See Article 3(1) of the Protocol to the African Charter on Human and Peoples' Rights on the Establishment of the African Court on Human and Peoples' Rights. See also Adamantia Rachovitsa, "On New 'Judicial Animals': The Curious Case of an African Court with Material Jurisdiction of a Global Scope", *HRLR* 19(2), 2019, pp. 255–289.

234 Abebe, *I•CON* 2019, p. 110.

235 Abebe, *I•CON* 2019, p. 113 ("the African Court has a much wider substantive basis [than its European and Inter-American counterparts] to review the compatibility of laws (...) including not only traditional fundamental rights but also several institutional aspects").

236 See above section II.1 of this chapter.

has focused mainly on the ECtHR, as it is the human rights court that receives by far more scholarly attention.[237] In general, those in favour of the individual justice paradigm maintain that the Court should exclusively focus on redressing the individual applicants, while those advocating for the constitutionalisation of the ECtHR argue that it should be selective on the cases it decides, focusing only on those having a 'constitutional' character and increasing its use of structural remedies.[238] These normative claims appeared in the context of the 'caseload crisis' faced by the ECtHR, especially during the early 2000s, and found one of its main proponents in Luzius Wildhaber, former President of the Court. In 2002 he considered it "essential for the Court to be given the means to reduce the flow of cases so that it can concentrate on its constitutional role".[239] Ten years later, in 2012, Greer and Wildhaber still maintained that due to the backlog of cases, there were only two inevitable types of transition, either "to constitutionalisation" or to "stagnation and collapse".[240] They argued that "the Court should adjudicate the tiny fraction of the total number of applications it receives in a more 'constitutional' or principled manner", *inter alia* by interpreting the Convention "as a whole with a view to maximizing the effect of each judgment both in the respondent state and in the Council of Europe states generally".[241] It can be argued that this is precisely what the other two regional courts do, as they deal with a small number of cases and thus try to maximise the impact of every judgment.[242]

Until now the individual justice position has prevailed before the ECtHR, despite the introduction of some constitutional elements, such as the aforementioned pilot judgment procedure or the admissibility requirement of having suffered a 'significant disadvantage'.[243] Lovat and Shany mention in this respect that despite the reluctance of mandate providers to support a shift towards constitutional justice, "evidence exists that they have

237 Luzius Wildhaber, "A Constitutional Future for the European Court of Human Rights?", *Human Rights Law Journal* 23, 2002; Helfer, *EJIL* 2008, p. 127.

238 Greer and Wildhaber, *HRLR* 2012, p. 663; Steven Greer, *The European Convention on Human Rights: Achievements, Problems and Prospects*, Cambridge: CUP, 2006.

239 Wildhaber, *HRLJ* 2002, p. 161.

240 Greer and Wildhaber, *HRLR* 2012, p. 658.

241 Greer and Wildhaber, *HRLR* 2012, p. 686.

242 See on the impact of the remedial measures, Chapter 6 of this book.

243 This admissibility requirement was introduced with the entry into force of Protocol No. 14 in 2010 and has allowed the ECtHR to avoid dealing with 'minor' human rights violations, thus reducing its caseload to some extent.

implicitly acknowledged such a shift".[244] However, the backlog problem is arguably still an issue, carrying with it a considerable delay in the proceedings before the ECtHR. This is seen as a serious practical problem, as the Court is failing to comply with the standards it sets for states in terms of the right to a fair trial.[245] It is therefore likely that this debate will continue in the future, as projects to reform the European human rights protection system are still ongoing.

Furthermore, there are other authors who do not position themselves on either side of the individual vs. constitutional justice debate but argue instead in favour of a 'pluralist' conception of the ECtHR's functions. For example, Keller and Stone Sweet state that the ECtHR has a variety of functions, depending on the specific states and rights at stake. Among those functions, they expressly mention the delivery of "constitutional justice".[246] This is certainly supported by the Court's case law, mentioning already in 1978 that its task is "not only to decide cases but to elucidate, safeguard and develop the rules instituted by the Convention".[247] Similarly, Çalı identifies several functions performed by the Court, with one of them being "to trigger reform".[248] There is however a difference between triggering reform and mandating reform, especially in terms of the constitutional character of such functions. This is where legislative remedies add a substantial constitutional element to the courts' case law.

While the ECtHR has continued to deliver mostly individual justice, this is arguably different in the case of the other regional human rights courts. This can be observed on the one hand in the small number of cases they decide, especially if compared with the ECtHR. The IACtHR's and ACtHPR's case law is still limited to a yearly average of about twenty judgments, while the ECtHR delivers over 1,000 judgments each year. This is due not only to issues surrounding the structure of the Inter-American and African systems (especially the lack of direct access to the Court mentioned before) but also to a lack of resources to decide a high number of cases. As a consequence, there is necessarily some type of selection of cases, especially

244 Henry Lovat and Yuval Shany, "The European Court of Human Rights", in Yuval Shany (ed.), *Assessing the Effectiveness of International Courts*, Oxford: OUP, 2014, p. 260.

245 See Angelika Nußberger, "From High Hopes to Scepticism? Human Rights Protection and Rule of Law in Europe in an Ever More Hostile Environment", in Krieger, Nolte and Zimmermann (eds.), 2019, pp. 150-171, at p. 167.

246 Keller and Stone Sweet, in Keller and Stone Sweet (eds.), 2008, p. 703.

247 ECtHR, *Ireland vs. UK* (1978), para. 154.

248 Çalı, *EHRLR* 2008, p. 299.

before the IACmHR, which receives a considerable number of applications. In addition, both the IACtHR and the ACtHPR aim to make the most out of the few cases they decide, using their case law as a transformative tool to change social and legal realities. They thus need to look beyond the concrete victims that appear before them. This is also reflected in the wide array of remedial measures that these courts include in their judgments, which are often of a structural nature. Some examples thereof are precisely legislative remedies, which are arguably fulfilling a constitutional function.

2. Legislative Remedies as a Sign of Increased Constitutionalisation

As it was mentioned, the review of domestic legislation is rather common before human rights courts, especially with laws that have been applied in concrete cases of alleged human rights violations. The international judicial review of domestic laws is considered to be one of the main features of global constitutionalism, as it relies on that particular vision of international law and also serves to anchor this specific approach.[249] Legislative remedies however go beyond that and provide for an increased constitutionalisation of these regimes. They bring human rights adjudication closer to constitutional adjudication in its most common understanding, implying that courts can determine the consequences of the review.[250] In this context, it is quite different for an international court to find that a domestic law is incompatible with the treaty in question than to include a binding remedy ordering the reform of such law. In addition, legislative measures contribute notably to the internalisation of human rights, which is considered one of the main aims of global constitutionalism.[251] Such internalization does not take place exclusively through the incorporation of human rights standards in domestic law, as a process of 'socialization' of such standards is also necessary, but the legislative incorporation is, without a doubt, a step in that direction.

249 Başak Çalı, "International Judicial Review", in Anthony F. Lang and Antje Wiener (eds.), *Handbook on Global Constitutionalism*, Cheltenham: Edward Elgar, 2017, pp. 291-303, particularly at pp. 291 and 301.

250 There are constitutional systems in which courts are only empowered to issue declarations of incompatibility or other non-binding legislative measures, such as the UK or Canada, but these are rather the exception.

251 Çalı, in Lang and Wiener (eds.), 2017, p. 300.

When legislative remedies are included in the judgments, this makes courts transition from what is known at a constitutional level to be a weak-form judicial review of legislation to a strong-form one.[252] Although these two forms of judicial review can also have different degrees of strength or weakness, the weak-form review generally implies that decisions lack formal finality.[253] Thus, the law in question stays in force and the courts' 'declaration of incompatibility' can be overridden by the ordinary legislator.[254] This is the case for example with judicial review of legislation in the UK under the Human Rights Act, as well as in other common law states such as Canada or New Zealand. Strong review is generally understood as the ability of courts to strike down or invalidate legislation so that it can no longer be applied by the executive or the judiciary. These decisions can be overridden only through a constitutional amendment. This is the type of review performed by most European constitutional courts or by the US Supreme Court. When issuing legislative remedies, human rights courts arguably perform a review situated in the weaker scale of the strong-form. They do not limit themselves to finding an incompatibility between domestic laws and the Convention in a declaratory way, which is what they do in the absence of legislative remedies. Instead, they order the legislator to act in a specific way, with a variable degree of discretion in this regard, despite stopping short of invalidating the laws.[255] Legislative remedies are thus clearly a sign of an increased constitutionalisation of these courts.[256]

For this reason, the introduction of legislative remedies by the ECtHR through the pilot judgment procedure was seen as a constitutional step taken by that court. As Sadurski puts it, "this law-judging function of

252 See generally Mark Tushnet, "Judicial Review of Legislation", in Mark Tushnet and Peter Cane (eds.), *The Oxford Handbook of Legal Studies*, Oxford: OUP, 2005, pp. 164–182. See also Çalı, in Lang and Wiener (eds.), 2017, p. 298, mentioning the importance of the IACtHR's "expansive and detailed remedies (...) akin to strong judicial review in domestic constitutional contexts".

253 See in this regard Rosalind Dixon, "The Forms, Functions, and Varieties of Weak(ened) Judicial Review", *I•CON* 17(3), 2019, pp. 904-930.

254 The concept of weak-form judicial review was introduced by Mark Tushnet, "Alternative Forms of Judicial Review", *Michigan Law Review* 101, 2003, p. 2782.

255 See on the discretion afforded to the legislator in legislative remedies, Chapter 5. As previously explained, one fundamental difference with constitutional courts in this respect is the lack of direct effect of human rights judgments, in the sense that a law cannot be invalidated directly but requires a subsequent act by the national legislature or constitutional court.

256 See Wojciech Sadurski, "Quasi-constitutional Court of Human Rights for Europe?", *Global Constitutionalism* 10(1), 2021, pp. 175-185.

the Court makes it more obviously 'constitutional'".[257] The constitutional dimension of legislative remedies has not received that much attention in the case of the other two regional courts, probably due to the fact that legislative remedies were present since (almost) the beginning of their adjudicatory practice,[258] and because there are usually no cases with a weak-form and others with a strong-form review.[259] In this regard, no such 'constitutional turn' has taken place in the remedial practice of the IACtHR and the ACtHPR. Nevertheless, some developments of the latter courts related to its legislative remedies have also been examined through a constitutional lens. For example, the fact that the ACtHPR declared the incompatibility of constitutional provisions and even ordered to reverse constitutional amendments resulted in it being labelled as a regional "(super)constitutional court".[260] There are, however, still important differences between the legislative remedies of human rights courts and those of constitutional courts.

3. The Differences between Legislative Remedies in Constitutional and International Settings

Even though binding orders to reform legislation bring forward the constitutionalisation of human rights courts, these measures are still not equal to those commonly issued by domestic constitutional courts. Some of the main differences concern the effects of legislative remedies in the legal order of the state, the nature of these measures, and the moment of the legislative process in which they can be issued.

a) The effects on the domestic legal order

One difference that makes legislative remedies issued by regional human rights less intrusive than those of most constitutional courts is the aforementioned lack of domestic direct effects. Although they create an international obligation for states to amend their legislation, the act of giving effect

257 Sadurski, *HRLR* 2009, p. 432.

258 See Chapter 3 of this book.

259 When these courts find a law or a legislative omission to be incompatible with the respective treaty, they will generally include a legislative remedy in this respect.

260 Abebe, *I•CON* 2019, especially at p. 110.

to the decision still rests in the hands of domestic bodies. This makes an important difference, as a domestic legislative procedure still needs to take place, which includes democracy-enhancing aspects such as parliamentary debates and representative voting. On the contrary, when a constitutional court strikes down a domestic law, it usually becomes invalid from the moment the judgment is delivered. Thereby, the act of law-making takes place exclusively through the judicial decision, which can be more troublesome from a democratic perspective. In addition, legislative remedies before human rights courts usually leave a margin of discretion to the legislator. Even if this body is obliged to carry out a reform, legislative remedies vary in their specificity as to the expected outcome. Whether the margin left to the legislature in deciding the outcome of the reform is wide or narrow will also make an important difference as to its intrusiveness, an aspect that will be explored more closely in Chapter 5.

Human rights courts have, in this respect, generally refused to attempt providing their legislative measures with direct effects. For example, in the case *Ajavon vs. Benin* (2020), the applicant requested the ACtHPR "to strike down laws", but the Court rejected this request arguing that "it cannot take the place of the legislature of the Respondent State".[261] Thereby it referred to the fact that human rights judgments cannot have the effect of annulling laws, as immediately afterwards it highlighted that "it may, however, order measures with a view to repealing such laws or amending them so as to make them compliant with international human rights standards".[262]

The IACtHR nevertheless attempted to break down this barrier in its judgments concerning amnesty laws, where it declared that these laws "lack legal effects", without an additional domestic act repealing the law being necessary in this respect.[263] However, this approach presents serious theoretical and practical problems from the perspective of both domestic and international law, as the IACtHR is attributing a supranational force to its judgments that they lack domestically. In this respect, as international judgments are not self-executing, state action is an indispensable element for its enforcement.[264] In addition, the obligations to legislate under hu-

261 ACtHPR, *Ajavon vs. Benin* (2020), para. 356.

262 ACtHPR, *Ajavon vs. Benin* (2020), para. 356.

263 See for example IACtHR, *Barrios Altos vs. Peru* (2001), operative para. 4 ("Amnesty Laws No. 26479 and No. 26492 are incompatible with the [ACHR] and, consequently, lack legal effect"). See also Pasqualucci, *Practice and Procedure of the IACtHR*, 2012, p. 217, defining this as an "unprecedented step".

264 See Hillebrecht, 2014, p. 21.

man rights treaties are also state-oriented, implying that domestic action is necessary.[265] This is also shown in the concrete cases of amnesty laws, which did not become null and void domestically after the judgments of the IACtHR. Instead, a domestic procedure was initiated as a consequence of the legislative measures and the laws were repealed through an action by either the respective constitutional court or by the legislature. In sum, although legislative remedies create an (additional) international obligation for states to reform their laws, they cannot produce the reform by themselves.

b) The predominantly positive nature of legislative remedies before human rights courts

Another important difference concerns the nature of these legislative measures, whereby the measures of human rights courts can be more intrusive than those of constitutional courts. In the case of constitutional adjudication, legislative remedies are generally understood as being of a negative nature, as the assessment of the compatibility of actual laws with the constitution usually results in striking down such laws when this is not the case.[266] On the contrary, legislative remedies of human rights courts are more often than not of a positive nature, ordering legislative enactments. As a result of the obligations to legislate included in human rights treaties, it is not uncommon that a human rights violation stems from a legislative omission of the state.

As it will be explored in more detail in Chapter 5, the legislative remedies of the ECtHR are almost exclusively of a positive nature, while in the case of the IACtHR, this is more balanced but also predominantly positive and the ACtHPR is the only one ordering more often reforms of a negative nature. It has therefore been argued that the review powers of human rights courts can go beyond that of domestic constitutional courts due to the imposition of positive obligations to states, "including putting in place domestic legislative frameworks to respect rights".[267]

265 See Christina Binder, "The Prohibition of Amnesties by the Inter-American Court of Human Rights", *GLJ* 12(5), 2011, pp. 1203-1230, at p. 1216.

266 See however Allan Brewer-Carias, *Constitutional Courts as Positive Legislators*, Cambridge: CUP, 2011.

267 Çalı, in Lang and Wiener (eds.), 2017, p. 297.

c) The moment of the legislative process for issuing remedies

Another distinction concerns the moment in which the legislative measures are imposed. In several states, constitutional courts are empowered under certain circumstances to perform an *ex-ante* review of legislation in the final stages before its formal adoption. In such cases, a law can be struck down even before it enters into force. On the contrary, the legislative review carried out by human rights courts is necessarily *ex-post*, as only valid laws can produce a human rights violation.[268] Even in those 'abstract' cases outlined before, in which no violation of specific rights of an individual is required for human rights courts to intervene, the law needs to be able to produce actual effects for it to be reviewed.

The IACtHR was indeed criticised for finding that a draft law was incompatible with the Convention and ordering Guatemala to stop the procedure for its adoption. This took place in the context of the IACtHR supervising the execution of several remedial measures that prescribed the investigation of human rights violations perpetrated during Guatemala's internal armed conflict, as well as the prosecution and punishment of those responsible.[269] A legislative proposal put forward in 2019 intended to grant amnesty for every human rights violation committed during this internal conflict. In view of that, the IACtHR issued a resolution finding that this new law would have a negative and irreparable impact on the right of access to justice of the victims of these cases and that it would be *per se* contrary to the Convention, in accordance to its settled jurisprudence on amnesty laws.[270] The IACtHR therefore attached an order of provisional measures to this resolution, expressly ordering Guatemala to terminate the legislative proceedings.

268 However, as mentioned before, the advisory review of legislation carried out by some human rights courts (especially that of the IACtHR) can also take place before its adoption.

269 This conflict was one of the longest in the region, lasting from 1960 until the Peace Agreements of 1996. It confronted the armed forces of the state with Marxist guerrilla groups. As is the case with many Latin American conflicts of that time, one of the main features of the Guatemalan conflict is the high number of massacres and enforced disappearances, especially against indigenous peoples.

270 IACtHR, *Members of the Village of Chichupac and neighboring communities of the Municipality of Rabinal, Molina Theissen and 12 other Guatemalan's Cases v. Guatemala*, Provisional Measures and Monitoring Compliance with Judgment (2019), paras. 36-37. On the IACtHR's jurisprudence concerning amnesty laws, see Chapter 4 of this book.

This was criticised by one of the judges in its dissenting opinion, arguing that the draft law had not yet affected the victims' rights and that the Court would thus be prevented from intervening due to the absence of a wrongful act.[271] This would hold true if the IACtHR had found a human rights violation under its adjudicatory function, but in this case, it acted in accordance with its function of supervising compliance with previous judgments. This order therefore cannot be considered a remedy as such, but a provisional measure intended to secure the implementation of another remedy. However, it can be argued that the IACtHR entered swampy ground with this decision, as the subsidiary nature of human rights courts generally prevents them from interfering with legislative procedures, especially if domestic bodies are in principle capable of remedying the inconsistencies before the law affects individual rights. This is precisely what occurred, as the Guatemalan law did not pass the parliamentary proceedings. It remains the only instance in which a human rights court has ordered to put an end to an ongoing legislative procedure. Thus, although an *ex-ante* review is arguably better suited to prevent human rights violations, human rights courts can only act with respect to laws that produce actual effects. This is also an aspect which reduces its intrusiveness if compared with constitutional courts, that can prevent draft laws from entering into force.

4. Legislative Remedies and the Sovereignty of States

A final aspect which needs to be taken into consideration regarding the 'quasi-constitutional' dimension of legislative remedies concerns its intrusiveness upon the sovereignty of states. An added concern with respect to legislative remedies of human rights courts compared to those of constitutional courts is that they affect not only the democratic principle but also the sovereignty principle.[272] Of course, every type of review carried out by an international court implies an intrusion into the sovereign realm of states. The differences in this respect are a matter of degree, with legislative remedies arguably attaining one of the highest levels of intrusiveness. For this reason, the legitimacy of human rights courts to issue this type of remedies needs to be explored.

271 IACtHR, *Members of the Village of Chichupac and neighboring communities of the Municipality of Rabinal, Molina Theissen and 12 other Guatemalan's Cases vs. Guatemala,* Provisional Measures and Monitoring Compliance with Judgment (2019), Dissenting Opinion of Judge Vio Grossi.

272 On the issue of legislative measures and democracy, see Chapter 5 of this book.

a) The increased intrusiveness of legislative remedies

The fact that legislative remedies are not directed at the executive – who is the usual respondent body of international judgments – but at the legislature, makes them considerably more intrusive than other measures. There are fundamental differences between remedies that are directed at the executive (in the form of administrative reforms, release of prisoners, restitution of property or monetary compensation) and those directed at the legislature. First, there is a notable difference in terms of the source of authority, as legislation is directly adopted by elected representatives, while the representative component of executive acts is only indirect. Secondly, according to the rule of law and the principle of legality, acts and decisions of the executive always need to be carried out on the basis of legislation authorising them. This requirement of legislative authorisation already constrains executive discretion considerably. Therefore, the judicial review of executive decisions and concomitant remedies ordering governments to take action are generally unproblematic. In fact, in domestic settings, the constitutional review of decisions taken by the executive or lower courts is seen as "a non-controversial standard judicial function".[273] Even the strong opponents of a judicial review of legislation agree that "[c]ertainly the rule of law seems to require something like close judicial supervision of the executive".[274]

Furthermore, in most states under the regional courts' jurisdiction, the legislature is structured to allow for transparency and participation. This includes public debate and deliberation in the context of law-making, which can help to take into account a wide range of views and perspectives, thereby ensuring that the interests of different groups within society are represented in the legislative process. This is not the same in the decision-making processes of the executive branch. The domestic legislature is thus typically viewed as the key component of the democratic states' political system, and as such, the measures that override its decisions or otherwise direct its actions can be seen as a strong intrusion in the states' sovereign sphere, a type of intervention usually reserved for constitutional courts. The legislature therefore deserves a wider scope of deference, an aspect that will be explored in more detail in Chapter 5 of this book.

273 See Çalı, in Lang and Wiener (eds.), 2017, p. 292.

274 Jeremy Waldron, "The rule of law and the role of courts", *Global Constitutionalism* 10(1), 2021, pp. 91–105, at p. 91.

On the other hand, the effective protection of human rights often requires legislative interventions. Some authors have highlighted in this context the necessity of securing human rights through legislation because the protection of rights cannot exclusively depend on "administrative goodwill" or the "wide discretionary powers of particular state authorities".[275] In addition, the legislative element provides for legal certainty and stability in the protection of rights. If the protection of rights was limited to administrative measures, this would allow for an easy modification of such safeguards after a change of government. Legislative protection implies higher procedural hurdles and majority thresholds in this respect. Therefore, legislative remedies can render the protection of human rights more effective domestically, although this does not mean *per se* that international courts are legitimised to issue them.

b) The legitimacy of legislative remedies

While sovereignty has many different features and understandings, one of its main elements is self-governance. States are certainly giving up some of their self-governance prerogatives when accepting the supervision of an international court. The question then turns around the extent of this cession of sovereignty.[276] This is the well-known argument of states' consent as a source of legitimacy of international courts. It is thus relevant to examine to what extent states consented to the international review of legislation when subjecting themselves to the jurisdiction of human rights courts.

In this context, one of the main objectives of regional human rights protection systems is that of harmonising human rights protection in the different member states, with the obligations established in these treaties serving as a minimum standard in this respect.[277] One of the foundations of human rights treaties is thus to act as a framework of fundamental norms protecting certain interests and taking them away from the domestic

275 Lavrysen, "Protection by Law", 2014, p. 86.

276 Von Staden argues in this respect that "[w]here the exercise of judicial review, then, is based on such explicit delegation, it is not as such democratically deviant, as long as the terms of delegation are being observed". Andreas von Staden, "The democratic legitimacy of judicial review beyond the state: Normative subsidiarity and judicial standards of review", *I•CON* 2012, p. 1034.

277 The former President of the IACtHR, García-Sayan defined such harmonisation as a "central element" of the ACHR. See García-Sayan, *Texas Law Review*, 2011, p. 1837.

majority rule. The review of domestic laws can therefore be considered one of the main functions of human rights courts.[278] Adding this to the treaty obligations to legislate examined before, it can be argued that states have at least consented to a weak-form judicial review of legislation when subjecting themselves to the jurisdiction of human rights courts.

Concerning the strong-form review and legislative remedies, this could be seen differently. At the moment of its inception, it was certainly not foreseen that any of the three regional human rights courts would have the power to order legislative reforms. Instead, this competence has been developed through their respective judicial practice. It can thus be argued that the courts have gone "beyond what was envisaged as part of the delegation of authority".[279] However, the original consent of states still implied accepting that their legal order should conform to the respective human rights treaty, including an obligation to adapt it if this was not the case. In this respect, what human rights courts do when issuing legislative remedies can also be regarded as the concretisation of a primary obligation, as mentioned before. Moreover, tacit consent to such measures can be implied in the fact that states have – despite some exceptions – accepted them, and in some cases even encouraged courts to make use of these measures.[280]

It has to be noted moreover that there has been a shift in the past decades with respect to the traditional understanding of sovereignty. While it used to have an almost absolute character against external interference, nowadays it is generally accepted that "respect for sovereignty is being linked to respect for human rights".[281] On the basis of the principle of humanity, sovereignty thus carries with it a responsibility to protect human rights, and it can be restricted if a state fails to comply with such responsibility.[282] Peters made this argument with respect to humanitarian interventions, which affect a different element of sovereignty (mainly its external dimension) but are arguably even stronger interferences than those

278 Çalı, in Lang and Wiener (eds.), 2017, p. 297, stating that for this reason, "[i]n the field of international human rights law, the lack of a constitutional fabric argument and the lack of delegation argument are justifiably downplayed".

279 Von Staden, *I•CON* 2012, p 1034.

280 See in this respect Chapter 6 of the book, examining the issues of compliance and backlash with respect to legislative remedies.

281 Peters, *LJIL* 2006, p. 587.

282 See Peters, "Are we Moving towards Constitutionalization of the World Community?", in Cassesse (ed.), 2012, p. 130.

caused by legislative measures.[283] In this context, she claims that "sovereignty has already been relegated to the status of a second-order norm which is derived from and geared towards the protection of basic human rights, needs, interests, and security".[284] Therefore, if a state fails to guarantee the rights of its population, an external intervention can be justified. These considerations lie also at the basis of the 'responsibility to protect principle', endorsed by the UN General Assembly in 2005. Although this principle and humanitarian interventions are still controversial and have been subject to much debate (especially since the NATO-led intervention in Libya of 2011), sovereignty and human rights are nowadays clearly interconnected. In any case, this shows that the legitimacy of sovereignty-intrusive measures needs to be examined beyond the issue of consent.

As will be explained in more detail in Chapter 5, the increasing authoritarian tendencies in several states under the supervision of human rights courts makes the intrusion in their sovereign sphere by these courts more legitimate. It has also been argued with respect to the ECtHR that expanding its mandate in order to protect vulnerable or unpopular groups "can be an affirmative source of legitimacy".[285] As will be shown in Chapter 4, an important number of legislative remedies are precisely directed at the protection of such vulnerable groups. In addition, the aforementioned lack of domestic direct effects of legislative measures allows for courts to use different degrees of remedial deference when issuing them, which has also an important influence on its legitimacy. The fact that such measures allow for – or even trigger – public deliberation around a specific issue is an essential aspect to be considered in this regard, as will be explored in Chapter 5.

In sum, even if legislative remedies are highly intrusive with respect to states' sovereignty, human rights courts are arguably legitimised to issue them under specific circumstances. This legitimacy is derived from the primary obligations to legislate and the cession of sovereignty that states consented to when ratifying a human rights treaty, from the increased interlinkages between sovereignty and human rights protection, and from contextual elements concerning the balance between the degree of defer-

283 Anne Peters, "Humanity as the A and Ω of Sovereignty", *EJIL* 20(3), 2009, pp. 513–544.

284 Peters, *EJIL* 2009, p. 544.

285 Molly K. Land, "Justice as Legitimacy in the European Court of Human Rights", in Nienke Grossman et al. (eds.), *Legitimacy and International Courts*, Cambridge: CUP, 2018, pp. 83 – 113, at p. 83.

ence afforded to the domestic legislature when implementing such remedies and the democratic credentials of the state in question. The latter elements will be explored more closely with respect to the actual legislative measures of human rights courts in Chapter 5 of this book.

c) Legislative remedies and the efficiency of human rights courts

Finally, besides the effectiveness considerations concerning the protection of specific rights, there are also more pragmatic reasons for the use of legislative remedies. These have to do mainly with the caseload problems faced by human rights courts. This has been for many years now one of the main problems affecting the efficiency of the ECtHR and is also increasingly worrying for the other two regional courts.[286] One of the main consequences of this caseload crisis is the notable delay in processing applications. This leads to human rights courts failing to live up to their own standards concerning the excessive length of judicial proceedings and its effects on the right to a fair trial.[287] In addition, it has been argued with respect to the ECtHR that when it fails to provide a timely response to the complaints submitted to it, "the grievances lose their urgency, while the policies and practices they bring to the attention of the Court continue to become entrenched in their politico-legal orders".[288]

These caseload issues, especially before the ECtHR, are closely related to the so-called 'repetitive cases' (i.e., those affecting the same state and the same substantive issue) which constitute more than half of the pending applications before this Court.[289] Even if the caseload problems of the ECtHR slightly improved during the last years, especially due to more

286 In the case of the IACtHR, statistics show that by the end of 2022, 3629 petitions and cases were pending before the IACmHR, while this body refers not more than 40 cases per year to the Court. Therefore, a serious caseload problem can be found in this case before the Commission.

287 See in this context the jurisprudence included in Chapter 4 on legislative remedies concerning the excessive length of judicial proceedings.

288 Esra Demir-Gürsel, "The limits of the European Court of Human Rights vis-a-vis contestation and authoritarianism: concluding observations", in Helmut Philipp Aust and Esra Demir-Gürsel, *The European Court of Human Rights - Current Challenges in Historical Perspective*, Cheltenham: Edward Elgar, 2021, pp. 244–263, at p. 257.

289 Edith Wagner, "Repetitive Cases: European Court of Human Rights (ECtHR)", in *MPEIPro*, para. 2.

restrictive admissibility requirements and other procedural reforms, the number of repetitive cases has remained problematic.[290] This shows that while states are mostly complying with the payment of compensation and other individual measures, they are failing to solve the structural issues that lay behind human rights violations, such as adapting a deficient legislative framework. In this context, authors have found that "the docket of the Court is biased toward particularly problematic cases, where there has already been considerable resistance from the defendant state with respect to recommended policy changes".[291]

Thus, an increased use of legislative remedies could arguably contribute to a decrease in repetitive applications, as such remedies can situate the obligation to solve these structural issues in the forefront, thereby preventing additional violations caused by the application of an incompatible law or by the lack of an adequate legislative framework. The use of legislative remedies might thus be necessary for ensuring the long-term efficiency and sustainability of human rights protection systems.

Interim Conclusion: Domestic Laws in Three Stages of Human Rights Adjudication

In sum, the relation between international human rights adjudication and domestic legislation can be examined around three procedural stages. First, in the pre-judgment phase, one can find the obligations to legislate imposed by human rights treaties. As it was shown above, these obligations can be of a general or specific nature, and they can be explicit or implicit in the treaties. In addition, treaty obligations to legislate also affect the way in which legislative remedies are ascribed to remedial categories, an issue that will be explored in the next chapters. In this sense, these measures are not obligations arising *de novo* as a consequence of a human rights violation, but instead pre-existing commitments that a state has failed to live up to.

Secondly, in the judgment phase, an essential element that links treaty obligations to legislate with domestic laws is the review of legislation carried out by human rights courts. This review constitutes one of the main tasks performed by these courts and does not require extensive analysis concerning its most usual form (an alleged violation that is caused by the application of a law which is potentially incompatible with the human

290 Glas, *HRLR* 2020, p. 125.

291 Staton and Romero, *ISQ* 2019, p. 481.

rights instrument). Instead, this chapter has focused on two aspects that fall outside this traditional understanding, because they relate to situations in which the law was not applied. The first is the competence of courts to perform an abstract review of legislation under specific circumstances and the groundbreaking approach adopted by the ACtHPR in this respect. The second aspect is the advisory review of legislation, which is certainly not that closely related to the remedial part but is still important in order to examine alternative forms of review.

Thirdly, although legislative remedies are technically also included in the judgment, they concern especially the post-judgment phase, when they will need to be implemented. This implementation, as well as other consequences of legislative measures, will be examined in detail later.[292] This chapter has focused instead on the effects of legislative remedies on human rights adjudication as a whole. It has been argued in this respect that legislative remedies make an important contribution to the constitutionalisation of this regime. In this context, an aspect that authors have traditionally highlighted to clearly differentiate constitutional adjudication and human rights adjudication is that in the latter case, courts would lack the capacity to deliver binding orders directed at the legislature.[293] However, when legislative remedies are included in the judgment this difference is to some extent diluted. In addition, this chapter has also called into question other assumptions concerning the absence of constitutional features in human rights adjudication. For example, the alleged lack of competence to exercise judicial review of laws *in abstracto* has also thrown some scepticism towards the constitutionalist reading of the regional human rights courts' functions.[294] However, it has been shown that there are instances in which both the ECtHR and the IACtHR carry out such an abstract review, and that in the case law of the ACtHPR, this has become a very usual practice.

Finally, the last element related to the constitutional dimension of legislative measures concerns the intrusiveness of these measures and the legitimacy of human rights courts to order them. Although these measures can be considered especially intrusive upon the sovereignty of states, it is sustained that such sovereignty considerations are increasingly attached

292 See Chapter 6 for further discussion.

293 For example, Ulfstein, *Global Constitutionalism* 2021, p. 166, argues that the ECtHR is generally less intrusive than constitutional courts in terms of interfering with democratic decision making, because "it is up to the state to decide upon the effects of the ECtHR judgments in national law".

294 See for example Christoffersen, in Christoffersen and Madsen (eds.), 2011, p. 189.

to the effective protection of human rights. If states commit serious and systematic human rights violations as a result of their legislative framework, human rights courts supervising them are legitimised to tackle the root cause of these infringements. In addition, an indirect source of consent can be found in the obligations to legislate outlined above, as states have committed to adapt their legislative framework to the corresponding treaty. These measures can also help to ensure the efficiency of human rights protection systems in the long term. However, courts should be extremely cautious when making use of these remedial measures. On the one hand, the democratic credentials of the respondent states should be taken into account, and on the other hand, these measures should not be overly specific, in order to leave domestic legislatures a margin of deliberation. These are issues that will be assessed with respect to the remedial practice of the three courts in the second part of the book. But before that, legislative remedies will be situated in the remedial landscape of general international law (in Chapter 2) and in that of international human rights law (in Chapter 3).

Chapter 2: Legislative Remedies and General International Adjudication

The previous chapter showed that legislative reforms are ordered regularly by human rights courts and that they are related to the obligations to legislate included in human rights treaties, to the review of legislation carried out by human rights courts, and more generally also to the constitutionalisation of human rights law. However, it is unclear whether this remedial response is a particularity of human rights adjudication or if this is a common feature of international adjudication more generally. Are international courts generally authorised to order states to reform their domestic laws, or is this a consequence of the specific features of human rights adjudication? This issue will be examined in the next two chapters.

Thus, before delving into human rights adjudication, this chapter will make a brief digression and focus on remedies in general international adjudication, using the remedial practice of the ICJ as the main example in this respect.[295] In this context, the chapter inquires into two main questions. First, it asks rather generally what the landscape of remedies in general international law looks like, and how the ICJ has approached this issue. Second, it inquires more concretely whether legislative measures could be ordered by the ICJ, and what their remedial function would be in the context of general international law. In order to examine these two questions, the chapter will first put into context the award of remedies by the ICJ, together with its precedents at the PCIJ and the legal basis for this practice. Then, it will analyse the specific functions of remedies as applied by the ICJ and codified in the ARSIWA, namely those of cessation, restitution, compensation, satisfaction and non-repetition.

Thereby, the focus will be on legislative remedies, examining their presence in the ARSIWA and their potential use by the ICJ, as well as their specific function in this context. An important aspect of the overall objective of this book is to determine whether reforms of domestic law can be considered an available remedy before general international courts, and what its function would be. This will be useful to determine whether it is a

295 This does not mean that the ICJ is the only judicial forum in general international law, as this field includes also the Permanent Court of Arbitration and further arbitral tribunals.

remedy pertaining to a 'remedial *lex specialis*' in human rights adjudication. Until now, the ICJ has never explicitly ordered a reform of domestic laws in a contentious case. However, the short analysis contained in this chapter will show that the Court's jurisdiction comprises the competence to order such measures.

Although legislative reforms cannot be considered an operative remedy in general international law yet, it is possible that these remedies could be awarded by the ICJ in future cases. However, this presents specific problems concerning the function of this court. The role of the ICJ is in principle limited to solving specific disputes among states and does not comprise the review of the compatibility of domestic legal orders with international treaties, as in the case of human rights courts. In this respect, it seems rather doubtful that domestic laws would play an important role in judicial disputes among states. As will be observed below, legislative reforms could serve to operationalise other types of remedies, but it is more unlikely that they will be ordered as standalone measures of reparation or non-repetition. Another question is what such a hypothetical legislative remedy before general international courts would look like from a functional perspective. Arguably, this may be a different function than that of legislative measures before human rights courts. In order to answer this question, this chapter will examine how legislative reforms relate to each particular category of remedies.

In fact, this remedy has adopted different functions, both in the ARSIWA and in the cases in which the ICJ has dealt with legislative reforms. The ILC Commentary to the ARSIWA makes reference to legislative reforms as a remedy, but its approach is not consistent, mentioning it with respect to three distinct remedial functions. According to the ILC, legislative reforms can adopt the function of providing restitution, satisfaction and non-repetition, depending on the circumstances of the concrete case. In this respect, it seems however that the commentary is referring to different aspects of domestic legislation. When commenting on Arts. 30 and 37 (non-repetition and satisfaction), it deals with the substantive aspects of the law, by talking about legislation that allowed the breach to occur. On the other hand, in the commentary to Art. 35 (restitution), by mentioning that the enactment of the law was contrary to international law, it apparently refers to the procedural element. In addition, it is also worth highlighting that the Commentary refers almost exclusively to negative legislative reforms, as in the former case it mentions "the repeal" and in the latter "the revocation, annulment or amendment" of domestic laws. This represents also an important difference to human rights law, where positive reforms are prescribed far more often than negative ones.[296] On the other hand, in the cases before the ICJ in which legislative reforms have been discussed as a possible remedy, this has been mainly related to orders of cessation, restitution, and non-repetition, as will be shown below.

The analysis of this chapter will thus be extremely useful for the inquiry on whether legislative remedies form part of a 'remedial *lex specialis*' in human rights adjudication, an issue that will be examined more closely in the following chapter. In this respect, it will be shown that the role and function of legislative remedies is different in the field of general international law than in the field of international human rights law. Moreover, the fact that the ICJ is rather cautious with this type of remedy if compared to human rights courts reflects its self-understanding as an 'old-school' international court, with sovereignty considerations having arguably more weight in its decisions.

I. The Remedial Practice of the International Court of Justice

The award of remedies in general international adjudication cannot be understood without examining the practice of the ICJ, the main judicial body in this area. Despite attracting a lot of attention from scholarship for a long time, the ICJ's remedial practice has (until recently) remained largely outside the scope of analysis.[297] This is probably due to the fact that the ICJ has issued remedial orders only in a small minority of cases. The issue of remedies comes into play exclusively in those cases in which the ICJ finds an infringement of international obligations, and not when the Court is merely asked to clarify a concrete legal situation.[298] In the latter type

296 See Chapter 5 of this book.

297 Malcolm N. Shaw, "The International Court of Justice: A Practical Perspective", 46 *International and Comparative Law Quarterly*, 1997, p. 839 ("it is fair to say that there has been relatively little analysis of the full range of remedial powers of the Court"). Exceptions in this regard are Ian Brownlie, "Remedies in the International Court of Justice", in Vaughan Lowe and Malgosia Fitzmaurice (eds.), *Fifty Years of the International Court of Justice*, Cambridge: CUP, 1996, pp. 557-566; and especially the recent monograph of Victor Stoica, *Remedies before the International Court of Justice*, Cambridge: CUP, 2021.

298 See Juan José Quintana, *Litigation at the International Court of Justice*, Leiden: Brill Nijhoff, 2015, p. 1119, citing the distinction made by judge Gros between '*contentieux de legalité*' and '*contentieux de responsabilité*'.

of cases, judgments are declaratory, consisting essentially of "final, binding determinations of the parties' rights".[299] A typical example in this regard is a case in which the ICJ is asked to define the border between two states.[300] According to Crawford, approximately one-third of the ICJ's judgments involve state responsibility for internationally wrongful acts, while another third "involve boundaries, land or maritime delimitation" and one last third "cannot be classified".[301] Thus, most of the Court's judgments are simply declaratory, not requiring any action from the parties after the judgment has been issued.[302]

Despite it, during more than seventy-five years of judicial practice the ICJ has issued a wide array of remedial measures, although it has failed to provide a systematisation of the remedies it can award.[303] In this regard, Shaw argued that "[w]hile the substantive law to be applied by the Court is coherent and comprehensive, it is true that there remains a need to elaborate in a more sophisticated fashion a systemic range of remedies that may be provided".[304] This problem was also raised by Gray, noting that "remedies are something to be invented anew in each case".[305] This chapter aims to fill that gap by providing a systematic overview of the ICJ's remedial practice. In this respect, the remedies will be categorised with a functional approach, in accordance with the classification established in the ARSIWA, where the customary international law on remedies is codified.[306] Before engaging with each of the remedial categories and their use by the

299 Juliette McIntyre, "The Declaratory Judgment in Recent Jurisprudence of the ICJ: Conflicting Approaches to State Responsibility?", *LJIL* 29, 2016, p. 197.

300 See however Rosalyn Higgins, *Themes and Theories: selected essays, speeches and writings in international law*, Oxford: OUP, 2009, p. 901, including "the designation of a boundary line" among the remedies provided by the ICJ.

301 Crawford in Tams and Sloan (eds.), 2013, p. 85. Regarding the last category (cases which cannot be classified), Crawford mentions as examples those cases involving rivers or transboundary pollution.

302 McIntyre, *LJIL* 2016, p. 180. Note, however, that according to the ICJ in some instances the mere declaration constitutes a reparation in form of satisfaction, as will be explained below.

303 See Shaw, *ICLQ* 1997, p. 840 ("the Court itself has not as yet developed a clear pattern of applicable remedies").

304 Shaw, *ICLQ* 1997, p. 848. Along the same lines Christine Gray, *Judicial Remedies in International Law*, 1990, p. 108 ("Its [the ICJ's] treatment of remedies seems somewhat perfunctory in contrast with its approach to substantive issues").

305 Gray, *Judicial Remedies in International Law*, 1990, p. 108.

306 The ARSIWA establishes three main consequences of internationally wrongful acts, namely cessation, restitution and non-repetition; while reparation is in turn divided into restitution, compensation and satisfaction. See below section 2.

ICJ, the legal basis for the award of remedies as well as the relevant judicial precedents will be briefly examined. Thereby, the focus will be respectively on Article 36 of the Statute of the ICJ and the precedents at the PCIJ, especially the case of *Factory at Chorzów* (1927).

1. The Legal Basis for the ICJ's Remedial Competence

The legal basis for the indication of remedial measures by the ICJ is Art. 36 of its Statute, which deals with the jurisdiction of the Court and is adapted almost identically from Art. 36 of the Statute of the PCIJ.[307] This provision determines two ways of granting jurisdiction to the Court, either by so-called compromissory clauses contained "in the Charter of the United Nations or in treaties and conventions in force",[308] or through optional declarations made by state parties "in relation to any other state accepting the same obligation".[309]

Such compromissory clauses and optional declarations are usually silent on the issue of remedies, as they generally focus only on the substantive issues that the ICJ is authorised to judge upon.[310] However, Art. 36(2) of the Statute, while establishing general limits on the subject matter of the Court's jurisdiction, specifies that, among other issues, its jurisdiction comprises "the nature or extent of the reparation to be made for the breach of an international obligation".[311] This is generally understood as meaning that the ICJ has the inherent power to award any type of remedy, regardless of its character.[312] In addition, the Court has also the authority to determine the scope of its own competence, according to Art. 36(6) of its Statute and

307 Which was in turn adapted from Art. 13(2) of the Covenant of the League of Nations. With respect to the differences in the wording see Robert Kolb, *The International Court of Justice*, Oxford: Hart Publishing, 2013, p. 357.

308 Statute of the ICJ, Article 36, para. 1.

309 Statute of the ICJ, Article 36, para. 2.

310 As stated by Christian Tomuschat, "Article 36", in Andreas Zimmermann et al. (eds.), *The Statute of the International Court of Justice*, Oxford: OUP, 2019, p. 740.

311 See Kolb, 2013, pp. 359-360, arguing that the provisions contained in Art. 36(2) are also valid for Art. 36(1), precisely because their function is to give expression to these general limits in a broad sense.

312 Chittharanjan Felix Amerasinghe, *Jurisdiction of International Tribunals*, The Hague: Kluwer, 2003, p. 422. See also in this regard Tomuschat, "Article 36", p. 741.

the doctrine of '*Kompetenz-Kompetenz*'.[313] In this regard, the competence to award remedies was confirmed by the PCIJ in the case of *Factory at Chorzów* in 1927.

2. The Precedent at the PCIJ: *Factory at Chorzów*

The most fundamental judicial decision concerning the award of remedies by international courts is the judgment on the PCIJ's competence in the *Factory at Chorzów* case, which was delivered in 1927 and remains the *locus classicus* in this field.[314] It was not the first judgment in which the PCIJ awarded remedies, but in previous instances its competence to do so had not been contested.[315] The *Factory at Chorzów* case was brought by Germany against Poland, and related to the damage suffered by two German companies after Poland took possession of their factory. The PCIJ declared this seizure of property to be unlawful in its judgment on *Certain German Interests in Polish Upper Silesia* (1926).[316] Subsequently, both states started negotiations in order to determine the concrete way of remedying this violation. Failing to reach an agreement, Germany submitted an appeal before the PCIJ requesting a monetary sum in the form of compensation. Poland contested this claim arguing that the PCIJ's jurisdiction to interpret and apply the corresponding treaty did not comprise the competence to decide on "differences in regard to reparations".[317] The Court rejected this argument, stating for posterity that

313 Statute of the ICJ, Article 36, para. 6 ("In the event of a dispute as to whether the Court has jurisdiction, the matter shall be settled by the decision of the Court"). See also generally Georges Berlia, "Jurisprudence des Tribunaux Internationaux en ce qui Concerne leur Compétence", *The Hague Academy of International Law: Recueil des Cours* 88, 1955, pp. 112-160.

314 PCIJ, *Case concerning The Factory at Chorzów (Germany vs. Poland)*, Competence, PCIJ Series A. No 9, 1927. See in this respect Chester Brown, "Factory at Chorzów (Germany v Poland) (1927-1928)", in Eirik Bjorge and Cameron Miles (eds.), *Landmark Cases in Public International Law*, Oxford: Hart Publishing, 2017, pp. 61-88, referring to this case as one of "the most frequently cited judgments to have emanated from an international court or tribunal" (at p. 61).

315 For example, in the *S/S Wimbledon* case the PCIJ ordered Germany to pay a specific amount for damages in form of compensation. See PCIJ, *Case of the S.S. Wimbledon (United Kingdom et al. vs. Germany)*, PCIJ Series A. No 1, 1923, operative para. 5.

316 PCIJ, *Certain German Interests in Polish Upper Silesia (Germany vs. Poland)*, Merits, PCIJ Series A No. 7, 1926, operative para. 2(a).

317 PCIJ, *Factory at Chorzów*, Competence (1927), p. 20.

> *[i]t is a principle of international law that the breach of an engagement involves an obligation to make reparation in an adequate form. Reparation therefore is the indispensable complement of a failure to apply a convention and there is no necessity for this to be stated in the convention itself. Differences relating to reparations, which may be due by reason of failure to apply a convention, are consequently differences relating to its application.*[318]

This was the last time in which the competence of the PCIJ or the ICJ to award remedies was put into question.[319] In addition, an important number of international courts have relied on this statement – which today undoubtedly reflects customary international law – in order to declare their competence to decide on the consequences of a breach.[320] In the words of Rosalyn Higgins, "[i]t has been clear ever since the Chorzów case that (...) the existence of jurisdiction to decide the merits carries with it the legal authority to remedy any breach found".[321] On that basis, the PCIJ ordered Poland to pay "a compensation corresponding to the damage sustained" by the aforementioned companies.[322]

II. A Categorisation of Remedies in General International Law

As mentioned, the ICJ has not yet developed a clear pattern of applicable remedies. Thus, the systematisation of judicial remedies used in this

318 PCIJ, *Factory at Chorzów*, Competence (1927), p. 21. See James Crawford, *State Responsibility: The General Part*, Cambridge: CUP, 2013, p. 480, considering this passage as the "classic general statement of the consequences of an internationally wrongful act".

319 There are some cases in which the Court's competence to issue a particular type of remedy was contested, but not its authority to award remedies as such.

320 See Brown, in Bjorge and Miles (eds.), 2017, pp. 85-87, with examples of the impact of this statement in investment treaty arbitration.

321 Higgins, 2009, p. 10. See also Tomuschat, in Zimmermann *et al.*, (eds.), p. 741, arguing that "it is now firmly established that the Court is empowered to make precise determinations on reparation owed to a state victim of a breach of international law".

322 PCIJ, *Factory at Chorzów*, Merits, PCIJ Series A. No 17, 1928, p. 63. The Court did not establish the specific amount to be paid, but instead convened an "expert inquiry" under Art. 50 of its Statute in order to examine these issues (pp. 51-52). However, shortly after the PCIJ issued this judgment, the matter of the amount of compensation to be paid was solved through an agreement between the parties. See in this regard Brown, in Bjorge and Miles (eds.), 2017, p. 85.

chapter is based on the one contained in the ARSIWA. It is nowadays evident that the practice of the ICJ and the ARSIWA have mutually influenced each other, establishing a "dialectical relationship".[323] First, the ILC, while drafting the ARSIWA, derived the rules contained therein from – among other sources – the previous practice of the ICJ.[324] These provisions have then also influenced the Court's subsequent practice, as can be observed through explicit references to the ARSIWA in the ICJ's case law.[325] Crawford argued in this respect that the "symbiotic relationship between the ILC and the Court has also been significant in achieving a situation where there is now a presumption that the ILC Articles reflect international law".[326]

In the ARSIWA, the consequences of an internationally wrongful act are essentially three, consisting of the obligations of cessation, reparation and non-repetition.[327] In turn, the obligation of reparation is also tripartite and may consist of restitution, compensation and satisfaction.[328] These remedial categories will be examined along this section, starting with the primary consequence – the cessation of the unlawful conduct – and ending with the most exceptional one – the award of guarantees of non-repetition.

However, it has to be noted that this categorisation is different from the ones used by most authors when examining the remedial practice of the ICJ. Brownlie, for example, uses only three categories, consisting of

323 Crawford in Tams and Sloan (eds.), 2013, p. 75.

324 See Crawford in Tams and Sloan (eds.), 2013, p. 74 ("rules of state responsibility have been derived from cases, from practice, and from often unarticulated instantiations of general legal ideas").

325 See for example ICJ, *Gabčíkovo-Nagymaros Project (Hungary vs. Slovakia)*, ICJ Reports 7, 1997, paras. 47, 79 and 83; ICJ, *Legal Consequences of the Construction of a Wall in the Occupied Palestinian Territory*, Advisory Opinion, ICJ Reports 136, 2004, para. 140. In this respect see also Alain Pellet, "Some Remarks on the Recent Case Law of the International Court of Justice on Responsibility Issues", in Péter Kovács (ed.), *International Law: A Quiet Strength*, Budapest: Pázmány Press, 2011, p. 133 ("generally speaking, and although it does not always expressly state so, the Court applies the rules contained in the [ARSIWA], rules that are in their turn quite largely based upon the Court's own case-law").

326 Crawford in Tams and Sloan (eds.), 2013, p. 86. Along the same lines, Shelton, *AJIL* 2002, p. 834, arguing that "[t]he use and influence of the articles partly reflects the close ties between the International Law Commission (ILC) and the ICJ". See also, regarding this connection, Philippe Couvreur, *The International Court of Justice and the Effectiveness of International Law*, Brill Nijhoff, 2017, pp. 205-263.

327 ARSIWA, Arts. 30 and 31.

328 ARSIWA, Arts. 34 - 37.

declaratory judgments, damages and restitution.[329] Similarly, Brown states that "there are three forms of reparation which are generally available as remedies in international adjudication: restitution, compensation and declaratory judgments".[330] Gray adds another category, which she calls "injunctions",[331] while Amerasinghe, leaving out the category of declaratory judgments, includes "negative injunctions", "specific performance" and satisfaction.[332] Finally, Stoica includes cessation and guarantees of non-repetition in the same category and adds declaratory judgments, specific performance, restitution, compensation and satisfaction.[333] In sum, the only categories which are used by all these authors are restitution and compensation, while the ones most often ignored by them are those of cessation and guarantees of non-repetition.

In this regard, it can also be observed that several of these authors include declaratory judgments a category of remedies. One could ask in this respect whether declaratory judgments are not precisely those with an absence of remedies, as there is no secondary obligation for the respondent state arising from these judgments.[334] According to Crawford, declaratory judgments were not included in the ARSIWA because any court has the authority to make declarations on the lawfulness of a conduct, independently of its power to award remedies.[335] Certainly, declaratory judgments can form the basis of a post-judgment negotiation among states, and as they allow for flexibility in this regard states are usually satisfied with them. This marks an important difference with human rights law, where parties do not stand on an equal footing and thus leaving the issue of reparations to a negotiation among them is probably not the best solution. However, in both cases, a declaratory judgment carries with it some expectations of compliance, at least with respect to the state obligations of cessation and non-repetition. But in the absence of a binding remedy, these expectations are rather 'soft', based on the principle of good faith and reputational con-

329 Brownlie, in Lowe and Fitzmaurice (eds.), 1996, pp. 559-565.

330 Brown, 2007, p. 223. In this context, compensation and damages have the same meaning.

331 Gray, *Judicial Remedies in International Law*, 1990, pp. 77-107, especially pp. 95-96.

332 Amerasinghe, 2009, p. 177.

333 Stoica, *Remedies before the International Court of Justice*, Cambridge: CUP, 2021.

334 See below section II(4). As Kolb points out, these are decisions which are "binding but not executory". See Kolb, 2013, p. 755. On the main features of declaratory judgments see also generally Edwin Brochard, *Declaratory Judgments*, Cleveland: Banks-Baldwin, 1934, especially pp. 23-26.

335 Crawford, *State Responsibility*, 2013, p. 529.

siderations. In any case, if considered a remedy, it would be more precise to include such declaratory judgments under the category of satisfaction measures. Indeed, the Commentary to the ARSIWA specifies that such a "declaration of wrongfulness by a competent court" is "one of the most common modalities of satisfaction".[336] This was also sustained by the ICJ already in its first judgment and then confirmed in numerous subsequent cases.[337]

Finally, some authors include an additional category of remedies under the heading of "injunctions", "specific performance", or "consequential orders".[338] Such categories are however not contemplated by the ARSIWA, nor is there a clear distinction with other remedial categories, such as restitution or cessation, which also take the form of consequential orders of specific performance when applied by the ICJ. For instance, some examples mentioned under these labels are the measures prescribed in the *Tehran Hostages* judgment (1980) or the *Genocide* judgment (2007).[339] However, these orders dealt with the obligation to cease an ongoing violation, as will be explained next.

1. Cessation

The "first requirement in eliminating the consequences" of an internationally wrongful act is the adoption of measures that aim at the cessation of the infringement, or more specifically at the "discontinuance of wrongful acts or omissions".[340] This secondary obligation is considered to be "inherent in the primary obligation", and therefore acquires an 'automatic' character for cases of continuing violations.[341] Also, in contrast to restitution or satisfaction, cessation does not only aim at protecting the interests of the injured state but also those of the international community as a whole,[342]

336 See ARSIWA, Commentary to Art. 37, at para. 6.
337 See the references below, in section II(4) of this chapter.
338 Regarding the latter see Quintana 2015, pp. 1156-1167.
339 Quintana 2015, pp. 1157-1160.
340 ARSIWA, Commentary to Art. 30, para. 4; Crawford, *State Responsibility*, 2013, p. 265.
341 Robert Kolb, *The International Law of State Responsibility*, Edward Elgar, 2017, p. 149.
342 ARSIWA, Commentary to Art. 30, para. 5.

whereby its underlying principle is the protection of the rule of law.[343] It is precisely for this reason that cessation is not considered a form of reparation under the general law of state responsibility, but a separate consequence of an internationally wrongful act. However, in some instances, these types of remedies have been equated with forms of restitution[344] or satisfaction,[345] although the ICJ and the ILC confirmed that they belong to an autonomous remedial category.[346]

a) Cessation in the ICJ's case law

The ICJ has considered that the obligation to cease ongoing illegal conduct follows from the mere finding of such illegality and that an explicit order in this regard is only necessary under special circumstances.[347] There are however several judgments where such explicit orders have been included. A form of cessation was first ordered by the ICJ in the *Temple* case (1962), with the Court including in the operative part Thailand's "obligation to withdraw any military or police forces, or other guards or keepers, stationed by her at the Temple, or in its vicinity on Cambodian territory".[348]

---

343 Crawford, *State Responsibility*, 2013, pp. 459-460. In this regard, the ICJ stated that the obligation of cessation "derives both from the general obligation of each State to conduct itself in accordance with international law and from the specific obligation upon States parties to disputes before the Court" (ICJ, *Dispute regarding Navigational and Related Rights* (2009) para. 148).

344 Couvreur, 2017, at p. 233 ("In practice, therefore, the cessation of the wrongful act may correspond to a form of restitution"). See also Shelton, *AJIL* 2002, p. 836 ("Further, in some circumstances cessation and restitution can be satisfied by the same act").

345 See Shelton, *AJIL* 2002, p. 839 ("Cessation and guarantees of non-repetition were considered a form of satisfaction").

346 ICJ, *Dispute regarding Navigational and Related Rights (Costa Rica vs. Nicaragua)*, ICJ Reports 213, 2009, para. 149 ("cessation of a violation of a continuing character (...) constitute[s] a form of reparation for the injured State"). In the ARSIWA, the remedy of cessation is included in Art. 30, whereas the other forms of reparation are stated in Art. 31. See however Crawford, *State Responsibility*, 2013, p. 465, who claims (while upholding this distinction) that "[t]he result of an act of cessation may be indistinguishable from that of restitution".

347 ICJ, *Dispute regarding Navigational and Related Rights* (2009), para. 148. This reflects the aforementioned implications of declaratory judgments with respect to the obligation of cessation.

348 ICJ, *Temple of Preah Vihear (Cambodia vs. Thailand)*, ICJ Reports 6, 1962, p. 37. The Court used a similar wording in the *dispositif* of the *Land and Maritime Boundary* judgment, stating the obligation of both Cameroon and Nigeria to withdraw the

The obligation to cease the wrongful conduct may consist of both negative or positive actions by the state.[349] One form of negative action prescribed by the ICJ can be found in the *Nicaragua* judgment (1986), where the Court referred to the US' obligation "to cease and to refrain from all such acts as may constitute breaches of the foregoing legal obligations".[350] However, in most cases, an active course of action is required to cease the infringement. A prominent example in this regard is the *Tehran Hostages* case (1980), in which the ICJ stated that Iran "must immediately terminate the unlawful detention of the United States Chargé d'affaires and other diplomatic and consular staff and other United States nationals now held hostage in Iran, and must immediately release each and every one (...)".[351] The remedial order contained in the *Genocide* case (2007) consisting of the transfer of those accused of genocide to the ICTY also adopts the form of cessation. Here, the ICJ specified that this was a requirement in order to cease Serbia's continuing infringement of its obligation to punish acts of genocide.[352] Further examples of active cessation orders include the obligation to prosecute or extradite an individual,[353] or to provide consular officers access to a prisoner.[354]

---

administrative and military forces from certain areas under the sovereignty of the opposing state. See ICJ, *Land and Maritime Boundary between Cameroon and Nigeria (Cameroon vs. Nigeria: Equatorial Guinea intervening)*, ICJ Reports 303, 2002, operative para. 5 (b).

349 As stated by the France-New Zealand Arbitration Tribunal in *Rainbow Warrior (New Zealand vs. France)*, UN Reports of International Arbitral Awards, vol. XX, 1990, para. 113.

350 ICJ, *Military and Paramilitary Activities in und against Nicaragua (Nicaragua vs. United States of America)*, Merits, ICJ Reports 14, 1986, operative para. 12. The same was done in the judgment of ICJ, *Alleged Violations of Sovereign Rights and Maritime Spaces in the Caribbean Sea (Nicaragua vs. Colombia)*, General List No. 155, 21 April 2022, para. 261 (4).

351 ICJ, *Case concerning United States Diplomatic and Consular Staff in Tehran (United States of America vs. Iran)*, ICJ Reports 3, 1980, operative para. 3(a).

352 This obligation stems from Art. IV of the Convention on the Prevention and Punishment of the Crime of Genocide. See ICJ, *Application of the Convention on the Prevention and Punishment of the Crime of Genocide (Bosnia and Herzegovina vs. Serbia and Montenegro)*, ICJ Reports 43, 2007, operative para. 8.

353 The ICJ ordered Senegal to prosecute or extradite an individual, after establishing the state's responsibility for a violation of the CAT precisely for "failing to submit the case of Mr. Hissène Habré to its competent authorities for the purpose of prosecution". ICJ, *Questions relating to the Obligation to Prosecute or Extradite (Belgium vs. Senegal)*, ICJ Reports 422, 2012, operative paras. 5 and 6.

354 In the *Jadhav* judgment, the ICJ indicated that Pakistan is obliged "to inform Mr. Kulbhushan Sudhir Jadhav without further delay of his rights and to provide Indian

These examples show that, although according to the ICJ it will only order cessation under special circumstances, it is not uncommon to find such remedies in the Court's case law when the infringement has an ongoing character. Sometimes they are certainly difficult to distinguish from orders of restitution, as putting an end to the violation is also a way of restoring the *status quo ante*. Authors have therefore considered some of the aforementioned examples under the heading of restitution.[355] It is however more accurate to define them as remedial orders pertaining to the autonomous category of cessation, as they are addressing continuing violations, and their main aim is precisely to put an end to these.[356]

b) Legislative reforms as cessation

There are some cases in which the reform of domestic laws can be a way of ceasing illegal conduct. The two conditions for ordering a remedy of cessation, as stated by the arbitral tribunal in the *Rainbow Warrior* case (1990), are precisely the continuing character of the wrongful act and the maintenance in force of the infringed provision at the time when the remedy is issued.[357] In addition, an example mentioned by Crawford in this respect are those cases "where a legislative provision is maintained which is incompatible with a treaty obligation of the enacting state".[358] In such a case, the order to repeal or modify the corresponding provision would clearly constitute a measure of cessation.

A legislative reform in order to cease the violation was requested for example by Costa Rica in the case of *Certain Activities* (2015). The State included among the alleged breaches of its rights of navigation "the enactment by Nicaragua of Decree No. 079-2009 of 1 October 2009, concerning

consular officers access to him in accordance with Article 36 of the Vienna Convention on Consular Relations". See ICJ, *Jadhav (India vs. Pakistan)*, ICJ Reports 418, 2019, operative para 6.

355 See for example Brownlie in Lowe and Fitzmaurice (eds.), 1996, p. 565 ("Such orders [of restitution] were made in the Temple, Tehran Hostages and Nicaragua cases"). See also Brown, 2007, p. 196, with regard to the *Tehran Hostages* case (1980).

356 See for example ICJ, *Jadhav* (2019), para. 134, where the Court affirms that several breaches by Pakistan "constitute internationally wrongful acts of a continuing character", and that "[a]ccordignly, the Court is of the view that Pakistan is under an obligation to cease those acts".

357 France-New Zealand Arbitration Tribunal, *Rainbow Warrior* (1986), para. 573.

358 Crawford, *State Responsibility*, 2013, p. 462.

navigation on the San Juan River".[359] In consequence, one of its requests was the "repeal, by means of its own choosing, [of] those provisions of the Decree No. 079-2009 and the Regulatory Norms annexed thereto of 1 October 2009 which are contrary to Costa Rica's right of free navigation (...)".[360] Although the Court rejected this submission, considering that none of Nicaragua's breaches of international obligations were related to the application of the specific law,[361] it remains an instance in which the reform of domestic laws would have taken the form of cessation.

Furthermore, the only instance in which the ICJ expressly mentioned that a legislative reform would be necessary – although not in the form of a binding order – was the *Wall* Advisory Opinion (2004). Here, the Court stated that "Israel is under an obligation to terminate its breaches of international law; it is under an obligation to cease forthwith the works of construction of the wall (...) and *to repeal or render ineffective forthwith all legislative and regulatory acts* relating thereto".[362] In this case, Israel's legislative framework was considered to be part of the infringement, and therefore the legislative reform would clearly be a form of putting an end to it. This advisory opinion is considered "a rare example of an indirect constitutional compatibility review" between domestic laws and general international law.[363] Nevertheless, this statement cannot be considered a proper legislative remedy, as it was issued in the context of an advisory proceeding and thus lacks the binding character that remedies possess.[364]

The reform of domestic laws could thus fulfil the function of cessation in general international law, although mainly the negative aspect of such reforms (i.e., the repeal of norms that contribute to the ongoing nature of the infringement) and not the positive one (i.e., the adoption of laws in order to cease a wrongful act). In a case in which an internationally wrongful act clearly stems from legislation, it would also be in principle unproblematic for the ICJ to order such measures, although such a scenario is rather uncommon.

---

359 ICJ, *Certain Activities Carried Out by Nicaragua in the Border Area* (Costa Rica v. Nicaragua) and *Construction of a Road in Costa Rica along the San Juan River* (Nicaragua v. Costa Rica), Merits, ICJ Reports 665, 2015, para. 134.

360 ICJ, *Certain Activities* (2015), para. 137.

361 ICJ, *Certain Activities* (2015), para. 138.

362 ICJ, *Wall* Advisory Opinion (2004), operative para. 3 (B) (emphasis added).

363 Çalı, in Lang and Wiener (eds.), 2017, p. 294.

364 See on that the conceptual clarifications included in the Introduction to this book.

2. Restitution

The concept of restitution stems from Roman law and the form of redress called *restitutio in integrum*.[365] It consists of "re-establish[ing] the situation which existed before the wrongful act was committed".[366] In the aforementioned *Factory at Chorzów* case (1927), the PCIJ considered it to be the primary form of reparation in international law.[367] There are generally two main forms of restitution - material restitution and juridical restitution.[368] Material restitution refers to "the return or restoration of territory, individuals or property",[369] while juridical restitution is "the modification of a legal situation".[370] In the ICJ's case law, the latter form of restitution is found much more often than the former one.

a) Restitution in the ICJ's case law

One of the few instances in which the ICJ ordered a material restitution is the *Temple* judgment (1962), where the Court found that "Thailand is under an obligation to restore to Cambodia any objects (...) which may, since the date of the occupation of the Temple by Thailand in 1954, have been removed from the Temple or the Temple area by the Thai authorities".[371]

365 See Suzan L. Haasdijk, "The Lack of Uniformity in the Terminology of the International Law of Remedies", *LJIL* 5, 1992, pp. 245-263, especially at p. 250.

366 ARSIWA, Art. 35.

367 PCIJ, *Factory at Chorzów*, Merits, 1928, p. 47; Crawford, *State Responsibility*, 2013, p. 509. See also Chittharanjan Felix Amerasinghe, *Jurisdiction of Specific International Tribunals*, Leiden: Brill Nijhoff, 2009, p. 178, situating restitution at the top of the hierarchy of remedies.

368 Crawford, *State Responsibility*, 2013, pp. 511-512. The latter form is also called by some authors "legal restitution" (see Gray, *Judicial Remedies in International Law*, 1990, p. 590; Quintana, 2015, p. 1131).

369 Crawford, *State Responsibility*, 2013, p. 511.

370 Crawford, *State Responsibility*, 2013, p. 512. See also Jan Wouters et al., *International Law: A European Perspective*, Oxford: Hart, 2019, p. 539.

371 ICJ, *Temple of Preah Vihear* (1962), p. 37. Another similar example can be found in the *Wall* Advisory Opinion. In this case the ICJ affirmed Israel's obligation "to return the land, orchards, olive groves and other immovable property seized from any natural or legal person for purposes of construction of the wall in the Occupied Palestinian Territory". However, the alternative of compensating was also foreseen for the event that restitution "should prove to be materially impossible". ICJ, *Wall*, Advisory Opinion 2004, para. 153. As previously mentioned, this cannot be considered a remedy as such, as it lacks the binding nature.

This example shows that in practice it is often difficult to distinguish material restitution from cessation.[372] In this context, the remedy issued in the *Tehran Hostages* case (1980) consisting of the release of the US' diplomatic and consular staff could also be interpreted as a form of material restitution, as it implies the return of individuals. Nevertheless, in this case, the ICJ clearly ordered it as an obligation to cease the ongoing violation.[373]

Juridical forms of restitution, on the other hand, are included in various cases and typically consist of the annulment or modification of administrative acts or judicial decisions. Concerning the former, this type of remedy can be found for example in the *Arrest Warrant* case (2002), where the ICJ ordered Belgium to cancel an arrest warrant issued against the Congolese Foreign Minister in violation of his immunity,[374] or in the *Whaling* case (2014), where it ordered Japan to revoke all whaling permits that were granted infringing the state's international obligations.[375] In addition, more recently the ICJ ordered Colombia to amend a Presidential Decree establishing maritime areas.[376] The annulment of domestic judgments issued in violation of international norms was for example prescribed in the *Jurisdictional Immunities* case (2012), where the ICJ ordered Italy to annul the judicial decisions that were inconsistent with Germany's immunity under international law.[377]

Another specific type of juridical restitution can be found in cases concerning a violation of the Vienna Convention on Consular Relations (VCCR). In three cases – *LaGrand* (2001), *Avena* (2004), and *Jadhav* (2019) – the ICJ considered the US and Pakistan, respectively, to be responsible

372 See Crawford, *State Responsibility*, 2013, p. 512 ("Often, the result of restitution will be indistinguishable from that of cessation").

373 The wording used by the Court in this regard was "terminate the unlawful detention", which clearly situates this order under the sphere of the remedial category of cessation. See also Crawford, *State Responsibility*, 2013, p. 512.

374 ICJ, *Arrest Warrant of 11 April 2000 (Democratic Republic of the Congo v. Belgium)*, ICJ Reports 3, 2002, operative para. 3. See in this case however the separate opinion of judges Higgins, Kooijmans and Buegenthal, at paras. 88-89, disagreeing with the fact that the Court regarded this order as a form of restitution and arguing that "a call for the withdrawal of an instrument is generally perceived as relating to the cessation of continuing international wrong".

375 ICJ, *Whaling in the Antarctic (Australia v. Japan: New Zealand intervening)*, ICJ Reports 226, 2014, operative para. 7.

376 ICJ, *Alleged Violations of Sovereign Rights and Maritime Spaces in the Caribbean Sea (Nicaragua vs. Colombia)*, General List No. 155, 21 April 2022, para. 261 (6).

377 ICJ, *Jurisdictional Immunities of the State (Germany vs. Italy; Greece intervening)*, ICJ Reports 99, 2012, operative para. 4.

for the detention and conviction of foreign individuals in violation of their consular rights under Art. 36 of the VCCR. In these three cases, the ICJ ordered to "review and reconsider" the sentences issued in violation of this provision. The *LaGrand* case (2001) only referred to possible future sentences against German nationals, as the victim had already been executed by the US.[378] Hence, in this case, the remedy would not take the form of restitution but rather of a guarantee of non-repetition. However, the same was repeated some years later in the *Avena* case (2004), and here the Court also ordered the review and reconsideration of the actual decisions against the individuals affected by this infringement.[379] This type of remedial measure became thus in *Avena* a form of juridical restitution, as the review aimed at restoring the *status quo ante* of the victim by modifying a legal situation. These remedies were considered especially innovative, as they went beyond the usual approach of providing reparation to a state and moved into the realm of human rights.[380]

The *Jadhav* judgment (2019) shows that the ICJ is still willing to order these measures to remedy infringements of Art. 36 VCCR, despite the problems regarding compliance with the aforementioned judgments against the US.[381] Here, the Court abstained from issuing an order regarding prospective convictions, but it ordered to review and reconsider the sentence against Mr Jadhav.[382] In these cases, one can also see that the ICJ has generally adopted a flexible approach towards juridical restitutions, leaving at the discretion of the state the concrete modalities of giving effect to this order.[383] The form of restitution requested respectively by Mexico and

378 ICJ, *LaGrand (Germany v. United States of America)*, ICJ Reports 466, 2001, operative para. 7. See also, with respect to this case, Robert Jennings, "The LaGrand Case", *LPICT* 1, 2002, p. 13.

379 ICJ, *Avena and Other Mexican Nationals (Mexico v. United States of America)*, ICJ Reports 12, 2004, operative para. 9.

380 See Enrico Milano, "Diplomatic Protection and Human Rights before the International Court of Justice: ReFashioning Tradition?", *Netherlands Yearbook of International Law* 35, 2004, pp. 85-142, especially at p. 90 ("the remedies envisaged in its *dispositifs* go a long way in seeking to protect human rights in their substance and they represent a progressive development in the jurisprudence of the Court").

381 See Dirk Pulkowski, "Testing Compliance Theories: Towards the United States Obedience of International Law in the Avena Case", *LJIL* 19, 2006, p. 511; Andreas Paulus, "From Neglect to Defiance? The United States and International Adjudication", *EJIL* 15, 2004, p. 783.

382 ICJ, *Jadhav* (2019), operative para. 8.

383 The ICJ specified in this regard that this review and reconsideration shall be provided by the corresponding State "by means of its own choosing". ICJ, *Jadhav*

India in these cases was the annulment of the respective judgments.[384] The Court, however, did not go that far and ordered a measure of restitution based on an obligation of means (the review and reconsideration) and not of result.

b) Legislative reforms as restitution

The ILC Commentary to the ARSIWA, when examining the concept of juridical restitution as the change of a legal situation, uses the example of a "revocation, annulment or amendment of a constitutional or legislative provision enacted in violation of a rule of international law".[385] The same is also mentioned by several authors.[386] There are indeed situations in which legislative reforms could help to restore the situation that existed before the infringement of international obligations, as can be observed in the practice of the ICJ. In the cases examined in this section that contain a measure of juridical restitution, such measures consisted of the review or annulment of domestic administrative or judicial decisions. Sometimes a review or annulment of this sort is prevented by domestic provisions, establishing for example the finality of certain domestic judgments. Thus, it could be possible for the ICJ to order the reform of such laws to achieve effective restitution. Actually, in two instances the Court has recommended legislative reforms precisely for this purpose.

These two cases in which the ICJ recommended states to enact domestic laws in order to restore a legal situation are *Jurisdictional Immunities* (2012) and *Jadhav* (2019). In the latter one, dealing with a conviction in violation of the VCCR, the Court specified in the argumentative part of the judgment that Pakistan "shall take all measures to provide for effective review and reconsideration, including, if necessary, *by enacting appropriate*

(2019), operative para. 8; ICJ, *LaGrand* (2001), operative para. 7, ICJ, *Avena* (2004), operative para. 9. See for another example of juridical restitution leaving the choice of means to the state's discretion, ICJ, *Jurisdictional Immunities* (2012), para. 137.

384 ICJ, *Avena* (2004), para. 13(1)(b); ICJ, *Jadhav* (2019), para. 19(3).

385 ARSIWA, Commentary to Art. 35, para. 5.

386 Crawford, *State Responsibility*, 2013, at p. 512, mentions as an example for juridical restitution "the revocation of a provision of national law enacted in violation of international law". Gray, *Judicial Remedies in International Law*, 1990, p. 13, states that this form of reparation "involves an order by a tribunal for the repeal or alteration of a measure of the defendant's state legislature, executive or judiciary".

legislation".[387] In the former case, this was even included in the operative part of the judgment. The Court, after finding Italy responsible for violating Germany's immunity under international law, decided that Italy "must, *by enacting appropriate legislation*, or by resorting to other methods of its choosing, ensure that the decisions of its courts and those of other judicial authorities infringing the immunity which the Federal Republic of Germany enjoys under international law cease to have effect".[388]

This was the closest the ICJ has been to ordering a legislative reform, although in the end, it left the door open to "other methods". However, it can be observed that both the enactment and the annulment of domestic laws could be forms of providing restitution under general international law. Actually, in these two contentious cases in which the ICJ expressly mentioned the reform of domestic laws, this concerned the enactment of laws that would allow for either the review or the annulment of domestic judicial decisions. These are certainly special laws, related to the functioning of the domestic judicial system, and more specifically to the possibility of reviewing a *res judicata*. In this context, requesting such a legislative reform is probably the only way of ensuring compliance with the Court's orders when a review of final judgments is not foreseen in the domestic legal order. However, these legislative reforms would - as such - not fulfil the function of restitution, as the review of the domestic judgment is the concrete act that restores the victim to its *status quo ante*. Thus, the role that such reforms would play is simply that of allowing the state to comply with another remedial measure. It is even doubtful whether they could be considered a self-standing remedy in this regard.

3. Compensation

When the injury caused by an illegal conduct can no longer be reversed through restitution, general international courts may order the payment of a pecuniary sum in the form of compensation.[389] This is also the case

387 ICJ, *Jadhav* (2019), para. 146 (emphasis added).

388 ICJ, *Jurisdictional Immunities* (2012), operative para. 4 (emphasis added).

389 This was already established in the *Factory at Chorzów* case, with the PCIJ stating that "[r]estitution in kind, or, *if this is not possible*, payment of a sum corresponding to the value which a restitution in kind would bear; the award, if need be, of damages of loss sustained which would not be covered by restitution in kind or payment in place of it – such are the principles which should serve to determine the

when restitution is available but inadequate or disproportionate.[390] In this regard, the ARSIWA specifies that compensation "shall cover any financially assessable damage".[391] Hence, the appropriate remedy for non-financially assessable damage, such as moral damage to the state, would take the form of satisfaction.[392] The ILC defines this remedy as being "perhaps the most commonly sought in international practice".[393] Nevertheless, the ICJ's approach towards it has been rather restrictive, with only a handful of cases ordering compensation.[394] There are, in this regard, cases in which the Court refused to award compensation due to an insufficient link between the infringement of an international obligation and the concrete damage suffered by the state.[395]

a) Compensation in the ICJ's case law

The ICJ already awarded this form of reparation in its first contentious case, known as the *Corfu Channel* case (1949).[396] Here, the UK claimed compensation for the material damage suffered by the loss of two naval destroyers and the deaths and injuries of naval personnel. In its judgment on the merits, the ICJ determined that its competence to award compensation also implies the competence to establish the specific amount to be paid in this regard.[397] It however reserved the assessment of this amount

amount of compensation due for an act contrary to international law". PCIJ, *Factory at Chorzów Case,* Merits, (1928), p. 47 (emphasis added).

390 ARSIWA, Art. 35 (b). See generally on this point Christine Gray, "The Choice between Restitution and Compensation", *EJIL* 10(2), 1999, pp. 413-423.

391 ARSIWA, Art. 36(2).

392 Crawford, *State Responsibility*, 2013, p. 517. Nevertheless, moral damages suffered by nationals of a state that is claiming on their behalf by way of diplomatic protection take the form of compensation. See ARISWA, Commentary to Art. 36, para. 16, citing in this regard the *Lusitania* case.

393 ARSIWA, Commentary to Art. 36, para. 2.

394 See in this regard Crawford, *State Responsibility*, 2013, p. 518 ("It seems rather that the Court is averse to awarding compensation").

395 See for example ICJ, *Genocide* case (2007), para. 462. Here, the Court considered that there was no direct causal nexus between Serbia's failure to prevent genocide and the damages caused.

396 ICJ, *Corfu Channel,* Merits (1949), p. 36.

397 ICJ, *Corfu Channel,* Merits (1949), pp. 25-26. See also in this regard Hersch Lauterpacht, *The Development of International Law by the International Court*, London: Stevens and Sons Limited, 1958, pp. 203, 246-248, arguing that this case

"for further consideration".[398] Then, after entrusting the assessment of the claims brought by the UK to a group of experts, the Court validated the amount solicited by the applicant in a subsequent judgment.[399]

A measure of compensation was not issued again until the *Nicaragua* case (1986), where the Court decided that the US was under an obligation to "make reparation" to Nicaragua "for all injury caused by the breaches" of its international obligations.[400] It deferred the decision regarding the "amount of such reparation" and encouraged the parties to reach an agreement on this issue.[401] Nevertheless, before reaching an agreement Nicaragua decided to renounce its rights of action based on this case.[402] This judgment shows that the terminology used by the ICJ is not always consistent, as in that case the term 'reparation' is clearly meaning 'compensation'.[403]

Reserving the assessment of the specific amount to be paid for a later stage if the parties do not reach an agreement has been the ICJ's usual approach towards compensation. In fact, since the *Corfu Channel* case (1949) the ICJ has only determined the specific amount to be paid as compensation in three further cases, in which the parties failed to reach such an agreement. The first one is the *Diallo* case (2010), dealing with the unlawful arrest, detention and expulsion of a Guinean national by the Democratic Republic of the Congo (DRC). Here, the ICJ found in its judgment on the merits the DRC to be under the obligation "to make appropriate reparation, in the form of compensation, to the Republic of Guinea",[404] and then issued another judgment two years later determining the precise amount to be

shows the tendency of the ICJ to secure the effectiveness of the clauses conferring jurisdiction upon it.

398 ICJ, *Corfu Channel* (Merits), 1949, p. 36.

399 ICJ, *Corfu Channel (United Kingdom vs. Albania)*, Compensation, ICJ Reports 244, 1949, Annex 2 (Experts' Report).

400 ICJ, *Nicaragua* (1986), operative paras. 13 and 14.

401 ICJ, *Nicaragua* (1986), operative para. 15. See also similarly, although referring expressly to compensation, ICJ, *Gabčíkovo-Nagymaros* (1997), operative para. 2 (d).

402 Therefore, the Court discontinued the proceedings and removed the case from its list. See ICJ, *Military and Paramilitary Activities in and against Nicaragua (Nicaragua v. United States of America)*, Discontinuance, ICJ Reports 47, 1991.

403 See Haasdijk, *LJIL* 1992, pp. 249-250, arguing that the same terminological inconsistency is also reflected in the *Tehran Hostages* case (1980).

404 ICJ, *Ahmadou Sadio Diallo (Republic of Guinea v. Democratic Republic of the Congo)*, Merits, ICJ Reports 639, 2010, operative para. 7.

paid.[405] This is notably the only case in which compensation has been ordered with respect to damages suffered by an individual and not the state as such.

Another instance in which the ICJ specified the amount to be paid as compensation is the *Certain Activities* judgment (2015), dealing with the environmental damage caused by Nicaragua in Costa Rica's territory. The parties to this case did also fail to reach an agreement, and the Court issued a second judgment in 2018 assessing the amount owed to Costa Rica as a compensation for this damage.[406] This amount comprised 120,000 USD "for the impairment or loss of environmental goods and services" and 2,708.39 USD "for the restoration costs".[407] The payment of a much bigger amount was ordered in the last judgment on compensation, in the *Armed Activities* case (2022). This is due to the seriousness of the violations, related to the prohibition of the use of force and the principle of non-intervention, as well as to numerous obligations under international human rights law and international humanitarian law. There, Uganda was ordered to pay the DRC 225,000,000 USD for damage to persons, 40,000,000 USD for property damage, and 60,000,000 USD for damage related to natural resources.[408] In sum, it can be observed that the ICJ applies compensation surprisingly scarcely, and when it does it mostly leaves the content of that remedy open, allowing the parties to reach an agreement on this issue and fixing an amount only when they fail to do so.

b) Legislative reforms as compensation

Due to the exclusively pecuniary character of this remedy, it is rather difficult to think of instances in which the orders to reform domestic laws could fulfil the function of compensation. It could be possible that in some cases

405 ICJ, *Ahmadou Sadio Diallo (Republic of Guinea v. Democratic Republic of the Congo)*, Compensation, ICJ Reports 324, 2012. This included 85.000 USD in the form of non-material damage and 10.000 USD for material damage. The latter amount is surprisingly low, and the ICJ expressly rejected to include Mr. Diallo's loss of earnings during his unlawful detentions and following his unlawful expulsion (see in this respect ICJ, *Diallo* [Compensation], 2012, Declaration of judge Yusuf).

406 ICJ, *Certain Activities Carried Out by Nicaragua in the Border Area (Costa Rica v. Nicaragua)*, Compensation, ICJ Reports 226, 2018.

407 ICJ, *Certain Activities,* Compensation (2018), para. 157 (1) (a) and (b).

408 ICJ, *Armed Activites on the Territory of the Congo (Democratic Republic of the Congo v. Uganda)*, Reparations, General List No. 116, 09 February 2022.

the state would need to amend its laws in order to allow for compensation to be made, in a similar way to the aforementioned legislative reforms that would allow for the review of domestic judgments.[409] This would however be as a matter of domestic law, and the act of compensation would still be the payment of the awarded sum, not the eventual internal arrangement leading thereto. Thus, legislative reforms can hardly be conceptualised as fulfilling the function of compensation.

4. Satisfaction

The remedial category of satisfaction is aimed at redressing infringements that "cannot be made good by restitution or compensation".[410] It is however "rather exceptional", according to the ILC Commentary.[411] Its specific characteristics being less clear than the ones of the other categories, some authors have defined satisfaction very broadly, as "every performance which is extended to the aggrieved party in reparation of non-pecuniary detriments".[412] Despite being the only form of reparation that was not already recognised and applied by the PCIJ, nowadays "the availability of satisfaction is well established in international law".[413] Satisfaction can be both pecuniary and non-pecuniary, and some authors even include guarantees of non-repetition under its scope.[414] The ARSIWA contains a non-exhaustive list of modalities that satisfaction can take, including "an acknowledgement of the breach, an expression of regret, a formal apology

409 It is however less likely, as an administrative act such as the payment of a monetary sum is usually not restricted by domestic laws in the same way that the review of finals judgments is.

410 ARSIWA, Art. 37(1).

411 ARSIWA, Commentary to Art. 37, para. 1. See also Crawford, *State Responsibility*, 2013, p. 574.

412 Haasdijk, *LJIL* 1992, p. 255.

413 Crawford, *State Responsibility*, 2013, p. 507. See also in this sense *Rainbow Warrior* (1990), para. 122 ("There is a long established practice of States and international Courts and Tribunals of using satisfaction as a remedy or form of reparation").

414 See Amerasinghe, 2003, p. 418, arguing that "the most common types of satisfaction [...] may be divided into four groups: apologies, punishment of the guilty, *assurances as to the future* and pecuniary satisfaction" (emphasis added). However, the ARSIWA clearly situates guarantees of non-repetition as an autonomous remedial category in its Article 30 (b).

or another appropriate modality".[415] As will be seen in the next chapter, the scope of satisfaction is much narrower in general international adjudication than in human rights adjudication. A classic example of satisfaction in general international adjudication can be found in the *I'm Alone* case (1935), in which the arbitral tribunal resolving the dispute determined "that the United States ought formally to acknowledge its illegality, and to apologize to His Majesty's Canadian Government therefor[e]".[416]

a) Satisfaction in the ICJ's case law

The ICJ, however, has taken a different approach towards this sort of remedy. Indeed, the only type of satisfaction it has awarded has been in the form of declaratory judgments. The aforementioned *Corfu Channel* judgment (1949), awarded satisfaction this way. After declaring that the actions of the British Navy "violated the sovereignty of the People's Republic of Albania", it stated that "this declaration by the Court constitutes in itself appropriate satisfaction".[417] This form of providing satisfaction to the injured state merely by declaring the infringement of an international obligation has been confirmed in numerous subsequent judgments.[418] Such remedies are usually found in cases in which there has been no material damage, or when the damage cannot be attributed to the injuring state. Judicial declarations are however not included among the forms of satisfaction listed in the ARSIWA. According to Crawford, the reasons for this omission are that the articles were not primarily thought of as rules to be applied in formal

415 ARSIWA, Art. 37.2. There is however no hierarchy or preference in this regard (ARSIWA, Commentary to Art. 37, para. 5).

416 *S.S "I'm Alone" (Canada vs. United States of America)*, UN Reports on International Arbitral Awards, vol. III, 1935, p. 1618.

417 ICJ, *Corfu Channel*, p. 36. See also Crawford, in Tams and Sloan (eds.), 2013, p. 74, arguing that this statement constitutes a "clearly discretionary and flexible finding".

418 ICJ, *Pulp Mills on the River Uruguay (Argentina vs. Uruguay)*, ICJ Reports 14, 2010, operative para. 1; ICJ, *Certain Questions of Mutual Assistance in Criminal Matters (Djibouti vs. France)*, ICJ Reports 177, 2008, operative para. 2(a); ICJ, *Arrest Warrant* (2002), para. 31; ICJ, *Genocide* (2007), operative para. 9. See also, critical with the remedial approach in the latter case, Conor McCarthy, "Reparation for Gross Violations of Human Rights Law and International Humanitarian Law at the International Court of Justice", in Carla Ferstman et al. (eds.), *Reparations for Victims of Genocide, Crimes against Humanity and War Crimes: Systems in Place and Systems in the Making*, Brill Nijhoff, 2009, pp. 250-251.

adjudication procedures and that the authority to make declarations on the lawfulness of a conduct is independent of the power to award remedies.[419]

Certainly, the ICJ can limit its adjudicatory function to the award of judicial declarations and – although often not expressly considering it a form of satisfaction – this is indeed what it does in most cases. Nevertheless, some commentators have been critical towards this practice. Lauterpacht warned already in 1958 about the risk that "unless the rendering of declaratory judgments (...) is kept within limits, the contentious jurisdiction of the Court might be used as a means for obtaining Advisory Opinions by States".[420] Similarly, according to Tomuschat, "if the Court were confined to delivering declaratory decisions (...) its real impact in the process of conflict resolution would be greatly diminished".[421] Others however indicate that "in many instances the declaration can be sufficient to entirely resolve the dispute".[422]

If declaring a violation of international law is considered by the ICJ to be a form of satisfaction, it provides for this type of remedy in all cases concerning state responsibility, even if it does not expressly mention it. However, this also means that it is a remedial category with very limited impact, as it does not mandate any subsequent action by the infringing state. As mentioned before, it is even doubtful whether judicial declarations as such should be considered a remedy at all, as they do not give rise to any secondary obligation.

b) Legislative reforms as satisfaction

The common understanding of satisfaction in general international law comprises rather symbolic forms of providing reparation to the injured state, thus generally not including reforms of domestic law in this respect. Nevertheless, according to the ILC, there are some instances in which satisfaction can also consist of guarantees of non-repetition.[423] The example

---

419 See Crawford, *State Responsibility*, 2013, p. 529.

420 Lauterpacht, 1958, at p. 250.

421 Tomsuchat, in Zimmermann et al. (eds.), 2019, p. 740.

422 McIntyre, *LJIL* 2016, p. 181.

423 This was stated in the ARSIWA, Commentary to Art. 37, para. 5. See in this regard also Crawford, *State Responsibility*, 2013, at p. 475 ("[w]ether assurances and guarantees are a form of satisfaction caused a marked division of opinion during the drafting of Article 30(b)").

it uses with respect to this potential overlap is "the repeal of the legislation which allowed the breach to occur".[424]

Such an understanding can also be found in literature,[425] although in none of the cases in which legislative reforms were sought by the applicants or recommended by the ICJ did these correspond to a form of satisfaction. Taking into account the aforementioned restrictive approach of the ICJ towards satisfaction, which is only awarded in the form of declaratory judgments, it is rather doubtful that the Court would order legislative reforms for this purpose. Instead, if the remedial practice of the ICJ concerning satisfaction would evolve to include specific measures, it would most likely order apologies or other types of symbolic measures.

5. Guarantees of Non-Repetition

The last remedial category comprises the assurances and guarantees of non-repetition, and in contrast to the other categories it does not aim at redressing an infringement, but at preventing its recurrence. As opposed to 'assurances', 'guarantees' do not only consist of a verbal statement but require something more, such as the adoption of preventive measures.[426] The remedies of this sort have a rather exceptional character, as indicated by the words "if circumstances so require" in the ARSIWA.[427] In fact, the paragraph containing this remedial category was – according to Crawford – "the most contentious" during the process of drafting this part of the Articles.[428]

a) Guarantees of non-repetition in the ICJ's case law

The award of these remedies by the ICJ is an issue in which disagreements persist in literature. Some authors consider that the ICJ has ordered guarantees of non-repetition in a few cases, while others maintain that it has

424 ARSIWA, Commentary to Art. 30, para. 11.

425 See Haasdik, *LJIL* 1992, p. 252 ("Sometimes, however, actions as a declaration that the relevant act of the executive, legislature or judicial organs of the respondent state is a nullity in international law are classified as an aspect of satisfaction").

426 ARSIWA, Commentary to Art. 30, para. 12.

427 ARSIWA, Art. 30(b). See also ARSIWA, Commentary to Art. 30, para. 13.

428 Crawford, *State Responsibility*, 2013, pp. 469 - 470.

never done so. The cause of this controversy are the cases of *LaGrand* (2001) and *Avena* (2004). Indeed, the *LaGrand* case was the first time in which the ICJ had to deal with its competence to order guarantees of non-repetition.[429] Upon the request of such remedial measures by Germany,[430] the US declared that "the requirement of assurances of non-repetition sought in the fourth submission has no precedent in the jurisprudence of this Court and would exceed the Court's jurisdiction and authority in this case".[431] The Court rejected this view by affirming that "[w]here jurisdiction exists over a dispute on a particular matter, no separate basis for jurisdiction is required by the Court to consider the remedies a party has requested for the breach of the obligation".[432] It stated in addition that due to the seriousness of the breach – a German national had been convicted and subsequently executed by the US after a violation of his right to consular assistance in the context of his detention – an apology would not suffice.[433]

The ICJ considered however in this respect that the mere commitment expressed by the US to comply with its international obligations met Germany's request for assurances and guarantees of non-repetition.[434] It moreover specified concrete measures to be taken by the State in case it failed to comply with this commitment. As previously mentioned, it stated in the operative provisions that if German nationals should be convicted in violation of their rights under the VCCR in the future, the US "shall allow the review and reconsideration of the conviction and sentence".[435] Then, the ICJ applied exactly this same reasoning with respect to guarantees of

429 See in this regard Christian J. Tams, "Recognizing Guarantees and Assurances of Non Repetition: LaGrand and the Law of State Responsibility", *YJIL* 27, 2002, pp. 441-444. Also, the importance of this case for the law on state responsibility is reflected in the fact that the ILC decided to wait until the *LaGrand* judgment was issued in order to complete the second reading of the ARSIWA, in which guarantees of non-repetition were included as an autonomous remedy. Until then, these guarantees had been considered a form of satisfaction. See Pierre-Marie Dupuy and Cristina Hoss, "The LaGrand Case", *MPEPIL*, especially at para. 37.

430 ICJ, *LaGrand* (2001), para. 122. Germany in fact stated that "an effective remedy requires certain changes in US law and practice".

431 ICJ, *LaGrand* (2001), para. 119.

432 ICJ, *LaGrand* (2001), para. 48.

433 ICJ, *LaGrand* (2001), para. 123.

434 ICJ, *LaGrand* (2001), para. 124; operative para. 6 ("finds that this commitment must be regarded as meeting the Federal Republic of Germany's request for a general assurance of non-repetition").

435 ICJ, *LaGrand* (2001), operative para. 7.

non-repetition in the *Avena* judgment (2004), as it was dealing with the same substantive issues.[436]

Whether or not the inclusion of the aforementioned operative paragraph can be considered a guarantee of non-repetition is what causes disagreement.[437] According to Higgins, this review and reconsideration of future cases "could be viewed either as a reiteration of a primary obligation, or as a remedy for a breach".[438] Shelton affirms that it meets the "specific assurance [of non-repetition] requested by Germany".[439] Tams also considers it to be a guarantee of non-repetition, stating that "by recognizing this remedy, the [*LaGrand*] judgment seems to move away from a purely restorative approach to responsibility".[440] The Court, on its side, seems to consider that it has already ordered guarantees of non-repetition. This can be seen in the *Navigational Rights* judgment (2009), where it stated that "the Court may order, *as it has done in the past*, (...) to provide the injured State with assurances and guarantees of non-repetition".[441]

Crawford has a different view, affirming that leaving the choice of means to the discretion of the state "does not reflect the character of assurances and guarantees that the Court can award".[442] Quintana also considers that "while in LaGrand the Court did not grant a guarantee or assurance of non-repetition as a remedy, it refrained from closing the door to this form of relief being used in future cases".[443] This latter view is arguably more convincing, as the ICJ is requesting a review and reconsideration of future judgments only if the State were to fail again in complying with its primary obligation of providing consular assistance. Thus, it does not aim at a non-repetition of the violation, but at a redress after a potential repetition. Moreover, as it does not require any particular action on behalf of the state, it is doubtful whether this statement constitutes a remedy at all.

436 ICJ, *Avena* (2004), para. 150.

437 See Pellet in Kovács (ed.), 2011, at p. 129, arguing that "[t]his confusion highlights the quite artificial character of the distinction operated by the ILC Articles between, on the one side, guarantees and assurances of non-repetition (...) and on the other side, restitution".

438 See Rosalyn Higgins, "The International Court of Justice: Selected Issues of State Responsibility", in Maurizio Ragazzi (ed.), *International Responsibility Today*, Leiden: Matrinus Nijhoff, 2005, p. 278.

439 Shelton, *AJIL* 2002, p. 847.

440 Tams, *YJIL* 2002, p. 443.

441 ICJ, *Dispute regarding Navigational and Related Rights* (2009), para. 150 (emphasis added). The same was also stated in ICJ, *Pulp Mills* (2010), para. 278.

442 Crawford, *State Responsibility*, 2013, p. 477.

443 Quintana, 2015, p. 1155. On similar terms also Brown, 2007, p. 213.

There have been a number of subsequent cases in which the applicants requested specific guarantees of non-repetition but the Court refused to award them.[444] For example, in the *Armed Activities* case (2005), the ICJ considered that "the commitments assumed by Uganda under the Tripartite Agreement must be regarded as meeting the DRC's request for specific guarantees and assurances of non-repetition".[445] This approach has been followed in several instances, whereby the ICJ has usually relied on the presumption of good faith for rejecting the award of concrete guarantees of non-repetition. In several judgments, it stated that "as a general rule, there is no reason to suppose that a State whose act or conduct has been declared wrongful by the Court will repeat that act or conduct in the future".[446] Some authors have considered as "puzzling" the fact that the ICJ did not issue this type of remedy even in cases in which it would have been justified.[447] Nevertheless, there is no controversy nowadays on the fact that the ICJ does have the competence to order guarantees of non-repetition if it deems it appropriate.[448]

b) Legislative reforms as guarantees of non-repetition

Non-repetition is probably the most common function of legislative remedies in the field of human rights law.[449] In general international law, it is less clear whether legislative reforms should be conceptualised as fulfilling this role. Legislative reforms are on the one hand referred to in the Commentary to the provision of ARSIWA on guarantees of non-repetition. As

444 See for example ICJ, *Genocide* (2007), para. 466; *Pulp Mills* (2010), para. 278; *Jurisdictional Immunities* (2012), para. 138.

445 ICJ, *Armed Activites on the Territory of the Congo (Democratic Republic of the Congo v. Uganda)*, Merits, ICJ Reports 168, 2005, para. 257.

446 ICJ, *Navigational Rights*, para. 150; ICJ, *Application of the Interim Accord of 13 September 1995 (the former Yugoslav Republic of Macedonia vs. Greece)*, ICJ Reports 644, 2011, para. 168; ICJ, *Pulp Mills* (2010), para. 278. See in this regard Robert Paulson, "Compliance with Final Judgments of the International Court of Justice Since 1987", *AJIL* 98(3), 2004, pp. 434-461.

447 Crawford in Tams and Sloan (eds.), 2013, p. 82.

448 Crawford, *State Responsibility*, 2013, p. 473.

449 The UN Basic Principles and Guidelines on the Right to a Remedy and Reparation include under the heading of guarantees of non-repetition the obligation of "[r]eviewing and reforming laws contributing to or allowing gross violations of international human rights law and serious violations of international humanitarian law" (UN Basic Principles, para. 23(h)). See Chapter 3 of this book.

was mentioned in the previous section, this is done when the Commentary mentions the similarity between this remedial category and the one of satisfaction. Legislative remedies can also be found as a typical example in literature when referring to guarantees of non-repetition.[450]

In addition, in the two cases in which non-repetition was extensively discussed by the ICJ – *LaGrand* (2001) and *Avena* (2004) – both Germany and Mexico requested a reform of US law as a guarantee in this respect.[451] The Court, pointing out explicitly that it "can also hold that a domestic law has been the cause of this violation", held however that the contested law was not "inherently inconsistent" with the US' treaty obligations, as the infringement lied rather in the application of that law in the concrete case.[452] In these cases, it became clear that the ICJ can, in principle, request a legislative reform as a guarantee of non-repetition, as its competence to do so was not contested by the Respondent State nor by the Court itself. On the other hand, it seems rather doubtful that it will do so, especially taking into account the restrictive approach of the Court towards such guarantees, as shown in this section.

Interim Conclusion: The Particular Functions of Remedies in General International Adjudication as a Barrier for Legislative Measures

This chapter has provided a general overview of remedies before general international courts, as exemplified by the remedial practice of the ICJ. The first relevant observation in this regard is that this Court's remedial measures are mostly focused on achieving the cessation of internationally wrongful acts and the restitution of the injured state. Measures of compensation are also included in some – rather few – cases, while those of satisfaction have only been applied in the form of declaratory judgments. Despite some controversy in this respect, it is submitted that guarantees of non-repetition have not been ordered yet by the ICJ. Satisfaction and

450 For example, when commenting on the *inter partes* character of guarantees of non-repetition, Tams argues that "where a state is under a duty to adopt changes to its existing laws and regulations, the fiction underlying Article 59 of the ICJ Statute will become more difficult to uphold". Tams, *YJIL* 2002, p. 444.

451 ICJ, *LaGrand* (2001), para. 11(4); ICJ, *Avena* (2004), para. 12(2) ("the United States must take the steps necessary and sufficient to ensure that the provisions of its municipal law enable full effect to be given to the purposes for which the rights afforded by Article 36 are intended").

452 ICJ, *LaGrand* (2001), para. 125.

guarantees of non-repetition are thus clearly disfavoured in general international law, according to Shelton because the former "has been used in the past as a punitive measure" and the latter "anticipate[s] future breaches", while the ICJ relies on the good faith of states.[453]

In addition, most likely due to its status as the 'classical' international court per excellence, the ICJ has maintained a rather conservative approach towards the issue of remedies. It is a court that may be more hesitant to develop its jurisprudence in a way that could cause resistance by states. This is also related to its competence to adjudicate disputes, which is more dependent on instances of state consent for individual cases. By contrast, in the field of human rights adjudication, consent is given for the respective court to adjudicate alleged treaty violations by the state more generally, being therefore more difficult to withdraw.[454]

With regard to legislative remedies, two main conclusions can be drawn from this analysis. First, although the ICJ has never expressly ordered a legislative reform in one of its judgments, it would arguably have the competence to do so. This conclusion flows both from the codification of remedies included in the ARSIWA and from the practice of the Court. With respect to the latter, this chapter has shown cases where the ICJ recommended states to reform their domestic laws, as well as others in which states explicitly requested binding legislative measures. Such requests were not dismissed by the Court arguing a lack of competence. On the contrary, it even explicitly determined in the *LaGrand* judgment that a domestic law can be the cause of an internationally wrongful act, thus implying that it could prescribe a legislative reform in such a context.

However, despite having this competence, it is less clear whether it would be wise for the ICJ to exercise it. Ordering a legislative reform would not be without problems, as it interferes very strongly with the democratic element of the states' sovereignty. As shown in Chapter 1, legislation enjoys a higher democratic legitimacy than executive decrees or domestic judgments, thus causing reforms ordered by international courts to be capable of triggering resistance and even backlash.[455] In this respect, the judicial review of

453 Shelton, *AJIL* 2002, p. 844.

454 As it was mentioned before, the competence of the ICJ is based on 'compromissory clauses' included in treaties or optional declarations issued by states. While the former is similar to the competence of human rights courts, the latter leaves much more discretion for states to decide whether consent for jurisdiction is given for a concrete dispute.

455 See on the latter issue especially Chapter 6 of this book.

legislation by this Court without explicit delegation could be seen as an "usurp[ation of] power from states".[456]

Moreover, it is arguably not the function of the ICJ to ensure the compatibility of domestic laws and international instruments, but only to solve specific disputes among states. It has been argued in this context that the ICJ is "attracted by a transactional justice approach specifically tailored to address the contingencies of individual cases rather than by large-scheme purposes".[457] This is also reflected in the inter-state nature of the disputes that are submitted to this Court, which – when dealing with internal affairs of states – are more likely connected to administrative or judicial practices rather than to legislation, as the latter does generally not affect other states.[458] Although the ICJ can deal (and, in some instances, has indeed dealt) with human rights-related issues, it links the potential human rights violations to the bilateral relationship of the corresponding states and the obligations they owe each other, and not to the issue of compliance with a human rights treaty more generally. Thus, it seems that the ICJ will be cautious as to the advancement of its remedial practice on that front.

Another question which necessitates further study is the function that legislative measures would adopt in general international adjudication. If the ICJ were to include legislative remedies, they would most probably adopt the form of an order of cessation or a measure leading to juridical restitution. They would thus function as a way of ceasing the violation (for example ordering the review of a law that is directly causing an internationally wrongful act) or allowing the restoration of the legal situation that existed before the violation took place (for example, as hinted in *LaGrand*, with respect to a law that prevents courts from reviewing final domestic acts or judgments, thus impeding restitution). From a doctrinal point of view, legislative reforms could certainly also be labelled as a form of satisfaction or a guarantee of non-repetition, but the ICJ's aforementioned practice towards these sorts of remedies makes it rather doubtful that they would adopt any of these functions in its case law.

To sum up, the analysis contained in this chapter has shown that, in practice, the main function of remedies in the field of general international adjudication is putting an end to ongoing violations and providing states

456 See Çalı in Lang and Wiener (eds.), 2017, p. 295 ("In the face of a lack of explicit delegation, general international courts performing judicial review-type activities usurp power from states").

457 Zarbiyev, *JIDS* 2012, p. 259.

458 Çalı in Lang and Wiener (eds.), 2017, p. 294.

with restitution. This represents an important difference with remedies in international human rights adjudication, a field that will be examined in the next chapter. There, the use of compensation measures is especially notable, as well as the focus on guarantees of non-repetition and measures of satisfaction. Moreover, legislative remedies are not as problematic in human rights law, especially because the sovereignty of states and its democratic features can be more easily overstepped if the state in question does not respect human rights, not least because the protection of human rights is nowadays seen as an important element of this democratic principle.[459] With other international norms that are arguably less fundamental to the international legal order, sovereignty and democracy considerations are rightly taken more seriously by courts and should only be overstepped under highly exceptional circumstances. It is of course difficult to argue that some international obligations are hierarchically superior to others, but in any case, human rights have a counter-majoritarian dimension that other international rules are lacking, and this should also be taken into account when designing remedies.

---

459 See Chapter 1 of this book.

Chapter 3: The Special Nature of Remedies in International Human Rights Adjudication

The previous chapter examined the issue of legislative remedies in general international adjudication, finding that although general international courts such as the ICJ would in principle have the authority to issue such remedies, it is unlikely that they will do so having in mind their particular role and remedial practice. This is different in the case of human rights courts, which have already included legislative remedies in their judgments. Arguably, this is a consequence of the different functions of the latter courts, which are not to solve disputes among equals, but to supervise compliance with concrete treaties and determine possible infringements in an unequal relationship between states and their citizens. But perhaps there are also additional motives in this respect. This chapter will therefore focus on the question of whether remedies before human rights courts possess special functions and features, and whether legislative remedies are an intrinsic part of such specialty.

In order to answer this question, the first section of the chapter will explore the special nature of human rights remedies from an abstract perspective, while the second section will explore the remedial practice of the three regional human rights courts. This will offer an overview of the remedial landscape before each of these courts, with a particular focus on the use of legislative remedies, which will be introduced in the third section of this chapter. Such measures will be situated in the remedial context of each human rights court and some general issues will be examined in this respect, before starting with the case law analysis that will be included in the second part of this book.

I. A Remedial Lex Specialis *in International Human Rights Law?*

As examined in the previous chapter, remedies in general international law have acquired a particular shape and scope, with its basis in the PCIJ's *Factory at Chorzów* judgment and the subsequent practice of the ICJ, leading to the codification provided in the ARSIWA. From that point of departure, each sub-field of international law has developed its own law and practice on secondary obligations for the breach of primary norms.[460] This is also the case with international human rights law, a sub-field of international law that has been developing for over seventy years. In this regard, former IACtHR and ICJ judge Cançado Trinidade already argued in 2005 that international human rights law should possess an 'autonomy', in order to adapt the traditional rules and concepts of general intentional law in a way that would allow for increased protection of the individual.[461] The specialty of international human rights adjudication *vis-à-vis* general international adjudication has been extensively dealt with, although authors have mostly focused on issues of interpretation and jurisdiction, and not so much on remedies.[462] One exception in this respect is Shelton, who concludes that international human rights law "has created a mixture of remedies drawn from the traditional law on state responsibility, domestic legal systems, and the different views of judges about the role of tribunals in affording relief to victims of state abuse".[463] This is an issue closely related to the frequently discussed topic of the fragmentation of international law, as the area of remedies is one in which such fragmentation can be observed.[464]

---

460 For example, in the field of international humanitarian law see Cristián Correa, Siuchi Furuya and Clara Sandoval, Reparation for Victims of Armed Conflict, *Max Planck Trialogues on the Law of Peace and War* (vol. II), Cambridge: CUP, 2020. Regarding international trade law, see for example Chester Brown, 2007, p. 218 (arguing for instance that "'compensation' under WTO law does not have the same meaning as in general international law"); and for the field of international environmental law, see Pierre-Marie Dupuy and Jorge Viñuales, *International Environmental Law*, Cambridge: CUP, 2nd ed., 2018, at pp. 291-354.

461 Antonio Augusto Cançado Trinidade, "International Law for Humankind: Towards a New Jus Gentium", *Recueil des Cours* 316, The Hague, 2005.

462 See for example Lucius Caflisch and Antônio Augusto Cançado Trinidade, "Les conventions américaine et européenne des droits de l'homme et le droit international general", *Revue générale de droit international public* 108, 2004, pp. 5-63; Anne van Aaken and Iulia Motoc (eds.), *The European Convention on Human Rights and General International Law*, Oxford: OUP, 2018.

463 Dinah Shelton, "The Jurisprudence of Human Rights Tribunals on Remedies for Human Rights Violations", in J.F. Flauss (ed.), *International Protection of Human Rights and Victims' Rights*, Bruxelles: Bruylant, 2009, at p. 58. See also for an analysis of the specialty of human rights remedies, Frédéric Vanneste, *General International Law Before Human Rights Courts*, Antwerp: Intersentia, 2010, at pp. 504-528.

464 See ILC, *Fragmentation of international law: difficulties arising from the diversification and expansion of international law*, Report finalised by Martti Koskenniemi, 2016. See also, focusing on the perspective of the ICJ, Martti Koskenniemi and Päivi Leino, "Fragmentation of International Law? Postmodern Anxieties", LJIL 15(3), 2002, pp. 553 – 579.

This section will thus examine the special features of remedies in international human rights law from an abstract perspective, before focusing on the actual remedial practice of human rights courts and the issue of legislative remedies, examining how the courts started to include this type of remedial orders and providing a general overview of this practice. In order to analyse this issue more broadly, it is first useful to compare the main codifications concerning remedies in general international law (the ARSIWA) and human rights law (the UN Basic Principles).[465] Thereafter, the specialty of human rights remedies will be examined from functional, doctrinal and regulatory perspectives.[466]

1. The ARSIWA *vis-à-vis* the UN Basic Principles

One useful way to gain a first glimpse at the differences concerning remedies in these two fields of international law is by comparing how such remedies are codified. Remedies in general international law are codified in the ARSIWA - examined in detail in the previous chapter - while a codification of remedies in human rights law can be found in the UN Basic Principles on the Right to a Remedy and Reparation, which were adopted by the UNGA in December 2005.[467] The latter instrument represented an important development in international law, as the aspect of remedies used to belong to the sphere of inter-state responsibility, and before the Basic Principles, there was no codification of available remedies in human rights law or humanitarian law.[468] This document underwent a very long drafting

465 These are however not the only codifications in this regard. For example, the HRCee has laid down its own guidelines on the issue of remedy and reparation, which are however very similar if not identic to the UN Basic Principles. See HRCee, *Guidelines on measures of reparation under the Optional Protocol to the International Covenant on Civil and Political Rights*, 2016.

466 In this respect, it will be explored whether such specialty can flow from international human rights regulations, from the functions of remedies in this field, and from the practice of human rights courts.

467 UN Principles and Guidelines on the Right to a Remedy and Reparation for Victims of Gross Violations of International Human Rights Law and Serious Violations of International Humanitarian Law, adopted by the UN General Assembly on 16 December 2005, available at: https://www.ohchr.org/en/instrumentsmechanisms/instruments/basic-principles-and-guidelines-right-remedy-and-reparation.

468 See Theo van Boven, "Victims' Rights to a Remedy and Reparation: The New United Nations Principles and Guidelines", in Carla Ferstman et al. (eds.), *Reparations for Victims of Genocide, War Crimes and Crimes against Humanity*, Brill, 2009, p. 20.

process, where its scope was substantially expanded. Originally, its author Theo van Boven was charged with the task of conducting a study on "the right to restitution, compensation and rehabilitation for victims of gross violations of human rights and fundamental freedoms".[469] The final text, adopted sixteen years later, covers not only these three aspects but includes a rather comprehensive set of principles and guidelines, pertaining both to the procedural and the substantive dimension of the right to a remedy and reparation.

As van Boven explains, the political backing of this process came mostly from Latin American states, and to a lesser extent from Western European states.[470] This is perhaps due to the fact that the IACtHR had already developed a rather progressive remedial practice during the late 1990s and the early 2000s, as will be seen below.[471] Thus, Latin American states were already familiar with extensive remedies for human rights violations. The same goes to a lesser extent for European states, as the ECtHR also began to widen its remedial focus during that time.[472]

Although the Basic Principles are certainly not binding, as its Preamble highlights, they can be regarded as "declaratory of legal standards in the area of victims' rights".[473] Nevertheless, the issue of whether these standards match the international legal practice is still "far from settled".[474] The drafters of the Basic Principles took into account, among treaties and other documents, the previous judgments and decisions of human rights courts and treaty bodies. However, it is unclear whether the subsequent practice of these bodies continues to be reflected therein, especially due to the rapid development of their remedial jurisprudence since 2005. In any case, after the adoption of the Basic Principles, international human rights bodies have engaged more with their mandate of providing remedies to victims, even generating a "new behaviour on remedy and reparation" in accordance with these standards.[475]

---

469 Van Boven in Ferstman et al. (eds.), 2009, p. 28.

470 See van Boven in Ferstman et al. (eds.), 2009, p. 29.

471 A major shift in the remedial practice of the IACtHR took place between 1998 and 2001. See below section II. 1(b).

472 The ECtHR's first individual and general remedies (besides compensation) were also ordered in 2004, See section II. 1(a).

473 Van Boven in Ferstman et al. (eds.), 2009, p. 32.

474 Clara Sandoval, "The Legal Standing and Significance of the Basic Principles and Guidelines on the Right to a Remedy and Reparation", *ZaöRV* 78, 2018, p. 566.

475 Sandoval, *ZaöRV* 2018, p. 567.

The ARSIWA also includes a similar codification of remedies for general international law which was adopted in 2001, four years before the Basic Principles. This instrument clarifies in its Art. 33 that the obligations contained therein are intended to "be owed to another state, to several states, or to the international community as a whole".[476] Thus, individuals are in principle left out of the scope of application of the ARSIWA, whereby this provision shows that the ARSIWA "seem to recognize the need for a *lex specialis* for reparations for human rights violations".[477] Several authors have therefore advocated against the application of general international law and principles on state responsibility by human rights courts.[478]

Nevertheless, the Commentary to the ARSIWA mentions that this codification is applicable to "the whole field of the international responsibility of states, whether the obligation is owed to one or several states, to an individual or group, or to the international community as a whole".[479] In this respect, Crawford stated that the ARSIWA "are clearly conceived as applying -subject to the *lex specialis* rules- to human rights treaties".[480] Similarly, Buyse mentions that individuals "should have a right to reparation applying the ILC Articles by analogy".[481] Indeed, general international law and the ARSIWA have also been heavily influenced by the practice of

476 ARSIWA, Art. 33(1). This is notwithstanding the fact that Art. 33(2) recognises that rights arising from the international responsibility of the state "may accrue directly to any person or entity other than a State".

477 Vanneste, 2010, p. 508.

478 See for example Malcolm Evans, "State Responsibility and the ECHR", in Malgosia Fitzmaurice and Dan Sarooshi (eds.), *Issues of State Responsibility before International Judicial Institutions*, Hart, 2004, p. 159, stating that the character of the ECHR "make the international principles of State responsibility irrelevant to its operation". Similarly, Melanie Fink, "The European Court of Human Rights and State Responsibility", in Christina Binder and Konrad Lachmayer (eds.), *The European Court of Human Rights and Public International Law: Fragmentation or Unity?*, Nomos, 2014, p. 93.

479 ILC Commentary, reproduced in James Crawford, *The ILC Articles on State Responsibility: Introduction, Text and Commentaries*, Cambridge: CUP, 2002, p. 76.

480 James Crawford and Amelia Keene, "The Structure of Sate Responsibility under the European Convention on Human Rights", in Anne van Aaken and Iulia Motoc (eds.), *The European Convention on Human Rights and General International Law*, Oxford: OUP, 2018, at p. 178.

481 Antoine Buyse, "Lost and Regained? Restitution as a Remedy for Human Rights Violations in the Context of International Law", *ZaöRV* 68, 2008, pp. 129-153, at p. 135.

human rights institutions.[482] Thus, remedies in these two areas are closely connected.

As mentioned in the previous chapter, the classification of remedies provided in the ARSIWA divides the forms of reparation along the lines of restitution, compensation and satisfaction, and adds cessation and guarantees of non-repetition as separate consequences of internationally wrongful acts. On the other hand, the UN Basic Principles include five main remedial categories, labelling all of them as reparations: restitution, compensation, satisfaction, rehabilitation and guarantees of non-repetition. In this respect, one difference that stands out between the ARSIWA and the Basic Principles is that the former instrument does not include rehabilitation among its remedial categories. The main reason for this difference is precisely that the ARSIWA were intended to apply mainly for inter-state relations, and not for the relation between a state and its citizens. In this regard, a state cannot benefit from rehabilitation measures, such as medical or psychological care; these are measures specifically directed towards individual victims.

The other significant difference at play is the fact that cessation and guarantees of non-repetition are treated as legal consequences of an internationally wrongful act distinct from reparation in accordance with the ARSIWA. In the UN Basic Principles, on the other hand, cessation is included under the heading of satisfaction, and guarantees of non-repetition are considered reparatory measures and not separate consequences of a violation. The latter issue is especially surprising, as the beneficiaries of such guarantees are usually not the victims of the specific violation but rather other potential victims or society as a whole.[483] Thus, it might have been more convincing to include guarantees of non-repetition as a secondary state obligation separate from the obligation to provide reparation. The Updated Set of Principles for the Protection and Promotion of Human Rights through Action to Combat Impunity, which was adopted the same year as the UN Basic Principles, actually treat reparation and guarantees of non-repetition as two distinct issues.[484] This is most likely a better approach, as the concept of reparations is related to the redress of

482 Rober McCorquodale, "Impact on State Responsibility", in Menno T. Kamminga and Martin Scheinin (eds.), *The Impact of Human Rights Law on General International Law*, Oxford: OUP, 2009, pp. 235-254.

483 With respect to cessation, see also Shelton, 2005, p. 149, arguing that it is part of the general obligation to abide by international law and not a form of reparation.

484 UN Commission on Human Rights, *Updated Set of Principles for the Protection and Promotion of Human Rights through Action to Combat Impunity* (E/CN.4/2005/102/Add.1), 8 February 2005.

specific victims and is past-oriented, contrary to such guarantees which are future-oriented and for the benefit of society as a whole.

In sum, it can be observed that despite the differences regarding the categorisation of remedies in the ARSIWA and the UN Basic Principles, the provisions are still closely related and include rather similar secondary obligations resulting from the breach of primary ones. However, further differences can be observed when looking at the actual functions, regulations and practices concerning remedies in international human rights law.

2. The Special Function of Remedies in International Human Rights Adjudication

The most obvious difference between remedies in human rights law and those pertaining to the field of general international law is that the beneficiaries of the former remedies are generally not states but individuals. This clearly changes the purpose and function of remedies in this area. It is moreover a development that was not contemplated at the time of *Factory at Chorzów* and the early international law on remedies.[485] Thus, international human rights courts had to develop their own remedial practice departing from that of general international law but rather, adapting it to their own context and victims. In order to examine the different functions of remedies, a first look into the remedial practice of human rights courts is therefore necessary.

In this regard, a number of aspects have emerged in which remedies before human rights courts distance themselves from those before general international courts. For example, the healing purpose of remedies is much more present in the former field. This explains the aforementioned inclusion of rehabilitation as an autonomous remedial category under the UN Basic Principles and the use made by human rights courts of this type of remedy, ordering states to provide medical and psychological treatment to victims. Instead, one of the main purposes of remedies in general international law is to put an end to the internationally wrongful act. Measures of cessation are thus given more importance in this field, as was shown in the previous chapter.

485 As Dionisio Anzilotti wrote in 1906, "la conduite d'un État, toute contraire qu'elle soit au droit international, ne saurait jamais donner naissance à un droit de l'individu à la réparation du dommage souffert" (Dionisio Anzilotti, "La responsabilité internationale des Etats à raison des dommages soufferts par des étrangers", 13 *Revue Générale de Droit International Public*, 1906).

In addition, the purpose of deterrence has also a greater weight in human rights remedies. Although in human rights adjudication "[t]he goal of deterrence is intrinsically present within all remedial measures",[486] this is most clearly seen in the extended use of guarantees of non-repetition. Courts such as the ICJ are probably not too worried about repetitive cases (i.e. cases against the same state and about the same substantive issue) when designing their remedial measures. It is indeed very rare that the same inter-state dispute reaches the ICJ more than once.[487] On the contrary, repetitive violations (although suffered by different victims) are rather common before regional human rights courts, especially before the ECtHR.[488] Thus, deterrence becomes a more important element in these courts' remedial landscape, not only to prevent additional violations from taking place but also as a means of managing the various courts' caseloads. The extended use of guarantees of non-repetition in human rights adjudication is a good example of it, as they serve the purpose of preventing repetitive violations. This can also explain why legislative reforms are ordered mainly in international human rights law, and not in other areas of international adjudication.

Moreover, it is also relevant to note the subsidiary function of remedies in international human rights adjudication. As provided by the right to a remedy and reparation included in human rights treaties, the redress of human rights violations is an issue that needs to be solved primarily by domestic authorities. Only when they fail to do so can human rights courts step in. On the contrary, in general international law, the jurisdiction of courts is usually based on a treaty clause or an agreement among the parties that gives the ICJ or another international adjudicatory body the primary competence to decide over a dispute. Thus, the possibility of having access to a remedy at the domestic level does in principle not play a role before the ICJ, while it is a key aspect in the remedial practice of human rights courts. Subsidiarity comes into play during the whole procedure before human rights courts, not only in the remedial stage. In this respect, Besson

486 Cornejo, *I•CON* 2017, p. 374.

487 An exception in this regard concerns the *Jurisdictional Immunities* case, decided by the ICJ in 2012 and resubmitted by Germany in 2022 (see ICJ, *Questions of jurisdictional immunities of the State and measures of constraint against State-owned property (Germany v. Italy)*, Application Instituting Proceedings containing a Request for Provisional Measures, General List No. 183, filed in the Registry of the Court on 29 April 2022).

488 See on repetitive violations, section II.1(a) below.

identified three types of human rights subsidiarity: 'procedural subsidiarity' is the one related to the admissibility requirements, while 'substantive subsidiarity' determines the intensity of review and 'remedial subsidiarity' has to do with the choice of remedies.[489] The latter type of subsidiarity is the one most relevant for this analysis, and it is also where sharper differences among human rights courts can be found.

Subsidiarity is especially relevant before the ECtHR, where this principle has played an increasingly important role in recent decades.[490] The strict adherence to the principle of subsidiarity is, in fact, one of the main explanations for the ECtHR's remedial cautiousness, as will be explained below. The IACtHR and the ACtHPR usually include in their judgments a long list of rather specific remedies for the state to implement. This shows that, according to their understanding, if the state failed to remedy the situation in the first place and this led to the finding of a human rights violation by these courts, it is their task to indicate the specific steps that need to be taken to solve the problem. The Strasbourg Court has a different understanding of this issue, namely that even in those cases in which the victims could not obtain redress for a human rights violation at the domestic level – which in turn resulted in the finding of an infringement by the Court – the state remains primarily responsible for choosing the means for remedying it. Although the payment of a specific sum in the form of compensation is usually ordered in the ECtHR's judgments, this Court is still rather cautious with respect to other remedial orders, including them only exceptionally.[491]

In this regard, it is useful to distinguish between the negative and positive dimensions of subsidiarity. 'Negative subsidiarity' limits the intervention of the higher level (in this case, human rights courts) in favour of the lower level (the national authorities), on the grounds of the higher democratic legitimacy, the better placement and the expertise of the latter. The 'positive

489 Samantha Besson, "Subsidiarity in International Human Rights Law — What is Subsidiary about Human Rights?", *American Journal of Jurisprudence* 61 (1), 2016, pp. 69–107, at pp. 78-83.

490 In 2014, Robert Spano argued that the ECtHR had entered the "age of subsidiarity". See Robert Spano, "Universality or Diversity of Human Rights? Strasbourg in the Age of Subsidiarity", *HRLR* 14(3), 2014, pp. 487-502. Moreover, with the entry into force of Protocol 15 in 2021, the principle of subsidiarity is now part of the Preamble to the ECHR.

491 See however Besson, *AJJ* 2016, p. 83, highlighting that "[i]n recent years, remedial subsidiarity has become more and more under threat in the ECtHR's case-law, especially in the Court's struggle against the lack of enforcement of its judgments by domestic authorities".

subsidiarity' on the other hand implies the duty of the higher level to act whenever the lower level fails in its task of effectively protecting its citizens from human rights violations.[492] In a remedial context, this means to determine the concrete secondary obligations that flow from that breach.[493] In this context, the ECtHR pays arguably more attention to the so-called negative subsidiarity than to the positive one.[494] Both the IACtHR and the ACtHPR have instead a rather 'positive-subsidiarity approach' in the remedial stage of the judicial procedures. This can also be interpreted as a direct consequence of differences in the provisions that regulate the human rights courts' remedial competences, which include a subsidiary element in the case of the ECHR but not in that of the other treaties. The principle of subsidiarity makes in any case an important contribution to the specialty of remedies in human rights adjudication.

3. The Regulation of the Human Rights Courts' Remedial Competence

In general international adjudication, the main legal basis for a court to order specific remedies flows from the states' customary obligation to remedy an internationally wrongful act – as already indicated in *Factory at Chorzów*.[495] This customary nature of the obligation to remedy is, however, not so clear with respect to human rights violations. There are still a significant number of states around the world that are not subject to any sort of compulsory human rights jurisdiction and thus have no state practice in redressing its citizens after a human rights violation.[496] The legal basis for

492 See in this respect Carozza, *AJIL* 2003, pp. 44 et seq., See also Marisa Iglesias, "Subsidiarity, margin of appreciation and international adjudication within a cooperative conception of human rights", *I•CON* 15(2), 2017, p. 403.

493 See Buyse, *ZaöRV* 2008, p. 135, indicating that the "subsidiary international role entails that human rights institutions (...) can also themselves recommend or order specific reparations to be made, but only if the national level has failed to play its role".

494 This can be seen not only in its remedial practice, but also in the areas of procedural subsidiarity (with increasingly strict rules of admissibility) and the substantive subsidiarity (with the frequent use and paramount importance of the margin of appreciation).

495 The ICJ has also declared that when jurisdiction exists, no separate legal basis for remedies is necessary (ICJ, *LaGrand* (2001), para. 48).

496 See Tomuschat, *TJICL* 2002, p. 183 ("At the present time there exists no general rule of customary international law to the effect that any grave violation of human rights creates an individual reparation claim under international law"). However,

human rights courts to order specific remedies is thus to be found in the respective human rights instruments.

This section will therefore briefly examine the remedial provisions of the three regional instruments, as well as the specific legal basis for ordering legislative measures. The first human rights instrument adopted – the UDHR – provided only for the right to a remedy before domestic institutions "for acts violating the fundamental rights granted (...) by the constitution or by law".[497] As highlighted by Tomuschat, it is still unclear whether this provision implies as well a right to reparation when a primary norm of the UDHR itself has been violated.[498] Such a provision was expressly included first in the ECHR, comprising not only the right to a domestic remedy in its Art. 13 for "everyone whose rights and freedoms as set forth in this Convention are violated", but also the right to a remedy before the ECtHR itself. The procedural aspect of this remedy is contained in Art. 34 ECHR, while the substantive one is laid down in Art. 41 ECHR.[499] The latter provision is thus the main legal basis for the ECtHR to order remedies, although due to its narrow scope, the Court has interpreted other provisions broadly in order to allow for an expansion of its remedial practice, as will be seen next.

a) The ECHR's limited remedial provision

The ECHR makes only one express reference to remedies in its Art. 41, which allows the Court to afford 'just satisfaction' to the injured party if its domestic law *"allows only partial reparation to be made"*. The concept of 'just satisfaction' has been traditionally understood in a narrow sense, comprising exclusively the payment of a monetary sum. Although it could arguably be interpreted more broadly, encompassing individual measures such as the release of prisoners or the overturn of domestic judgments, it is difficult to interpret this concept as including also general measures,

---

the right of individuals to a remedy and reparation can be considered part of regional customary law in Africa, the Americas and Europe (see on human rights and regional customary law Vanneste, 2010, pp. 375-385). Actually, the IACtHR considered already in its first case on reparations that Art. 63 ACHR codifies a customary rule (IACtHR, *Velasquez Rodriguez vs. Honduras* (1989), para. 23).

497 Universal Declaration on Human Rights, Art. 8.

498 Christian Tomuschat, "Reparation for Victims of Grave Human Rights Violations", *Tulane Journal of International and Comparative Law* 10, 2002, pp. 157-184, at p. 161.

499 See on the difference between the procedural and substantive dimension of remedies the Introduction to this book.

such as the amendment of domestic laws. This is because conceptually 'just satisfaction' makes direct reference to the victims of the human rights violation, who are the addressees of such a form of reparation.[500] General measures such as legislative reforms are usually not for the benefit of the concrete victims of the violation but of other potential victims, in order to prevent them from materialising as such, or even of society in general.[501]

As a matter of fact, states were especially concerned with the possibility of the Court being able to challenge domestic laws during the drafting process of the ECHR.[502] One of the first drafts of the Convention contained a provision allowing for a wide array of remedial measures, declaring that the ECtHR "may either prescribe measures of reparation or it may require that the State concerned shall take penal or administrative action in regard to the persons responsible for the infringement, or it may demand the repeal, cancellation or amendment of the act".[503] However, this was rejected by the majority of state representatives, and the CoM instead proposed a provision suggesting that "the only form of reparations will be compensation".[504] The draft report to the CoM actually indicated that "the Court should only be permitted to give a ruling on cases of violations of the *individual* rights protected by the Convention and not of cases of violation of the Convention by legislative acts as such".[505] Thereby, the drafters "sought to create a 'sovereignty shield' that limited the Court's intrusiveness".[506]

500 In this respect, Art. 41 ECHR states that the Court shall "afford just satisfaction to the injured party". See Ichim, *Just Satisfaction,* 2014, p. 18, arguing that "[t]he Convention identifies the notion of 'just satisfaction' with the entire spectrum of reparation available to an injured party" although "[i]t normally takes the form of financial redress". See however Cassesse, "Towards Moderate Monism", 2012, arguing that Art. 41 should be interpreted differently in order to allow for extensive remedial measures, including those of a legislative nature.

501 See below section II. 3(e). See also Chapter 1 of this book.

502 See Ichim, *Just Satisfaction,* 2014, p. 11.

503 Convention for the Collective Protection of Individual Rights and Democratic Liberties by the States, Members of the Council of Europe, and for the establishment of a European Court of Human Rights to ensure observance of the Convention, Doc. INF/5/E/R, I *TP* 296–303, at pp. 300–302, Art. 13(b); cited in Schabas, *Commentary to the ECHR,* 2015, p. 830.

504 Schabas, *Commentary to the ECHR,* 2015, p. 831.

505 Preliminary Draft of the Report to the Committee of Ministers, 24 February 1950, Doc. CM/WP 1 (50) 1, A 847, III *TP* 246–79, at pp. 274–6 (emphasis in the original), cited in Schabas, *Commentary to the ECHR,* 2015, p. 831.

506 Helfer, *EJIL* 2008, p. 147.

This position prevailed to a great extent and was included in Art. 41 ECHR with the statement about providing "just satisfaction to the injured party". Therefore, due to this narrow legal basis, when the ECtHR started to include non-monetary measures in its judgments it needed to adopt an expansive interpretation of other provisions. Art. 46(1) ECHR plays the main role in this regard. This article states that "[t]he High Contracting Parties undertake to abide by the final judgment of the Court in any case to which they are parties". When the ECtHR orders the reform of domestic laws, it generally does so by relying on this provision. In this regard, the Strasbourg Court has come to sustain that Art. 46 includes an obligation to adopt the necessary individual and general measures to adequately comply with a judgment, without the need for the Court to expressly include them in its judgments.[507] Such an expansion of the legal basis was however criticised by judges dissenting to the early judgments with legislative measures,[508] and some authors also recommend a stronger legal basis for non-financial measures.[509]

Additionally, in accordance with Art. 19 ECHR, the primary function of the ECtHR is to ensure compliance with the obligations under the Convention. As legislative reforms can contribute significantly to the restoration of an ECHR-compliant status, this could also imply the competence to order

507 ECtHR, *Scozzari and Giunta vs. Italy* (2000), para. 249 ("The Court points out that by Article 46 of the Convention the High Contracting Parties undertook to abide by the final judgments of the Court in any case to which they were parties, execution being supervised by the Committee of Ministers. It follows, inter alia, that a judgment in which the Court finds a breach imposes on the respondent State a legal obligation not just to pay those concerned the sums awarded by way of just satisfaction, but also to choose, subject to supervision by the Committee of Ministers, the general and/or, if appropriate, individual measures to be adopted in their domestic legal order to put an end to the violation found by the Court and to redress so far as possible the effects").

508 See for example the partly dissenting opinion of Judge Zagrebelsky in *Hutten-Czapska v. Poland* (2006), noting "the weakness of the legal basis of the pilot-judgment procedure in its most evident aspect. I am referring to the indication in the operative provisions of the need for the State to amend its own legislation in order to solve a general problem affecting persons other than the applicant".

509 See for example Jannika Jahn, "Ruling (In)directly through Individual Measures? Effect and Legitimacy of the ECtHR's New Remedial Power", *ZaöRV* 74, 2014, p. 3 ("If the use of mandatory individual measures is to be expanded, it is hence recommended - de lege ferenda - that this power be provided with a clear legal basis so that the Court does not run the risk of losing its acceptance by the Convention states"). Similarly, Ichim, *Just Satisfaction*, 2014, pp. 255-256.

such measures,[510] and the Court has also relied on this provision in order to do so.[511] Thus, Arts. 41, 46 and 19 ECHR, when taken together, can form an annexe competence that serves as the legal basis for the ECtHR to order legislative remedies in its judgments. Former ECtHR judge Sicilianos adds in this respect Art. 32 ECHR (which reflects the principle of the *Kompetenz-Kompetenz*), and points to various resolutions of the CoM, arguing that they constitute 'subsequent practice' in the sense of Art. 31 VCLT.[512]

In sum, it can be observed that the remedial rules of the ECHR were originally rather limited, as they did not provide for other remedies besides 'just satisfaction'. Notably, the concept of *restitutio in integrum* - of crucial importance for remedies in general international law - was not included in the ECHR nor developed in the early case law of the ECtHR. This changed with the adoption of the ACHR, which includes a remedial provision allowing for remedies similar to those of general international law, including — besides the obligation to compensate victims — an additional obligation to remedy all consequences of the violation.

b) The ACHR's expansive remedial provision

The power of the IACtHR to order remedies is regulated under Art. 63(1) of the ACHR in a much broader way than that of its European counterpart.[513] This provision states the following:

> *If the Court finds that there has been a violation of a right or freedom protected by this Convention, the Court shall rule that the injured party be ensured the enjoyment of his right or freedom that was violated. It shall also rule, if appropriate, that the consequences of the measure or situation that constituted the breach of such right or freedom be remedied and that fair compensation be paid to the injured party.*[514]

The first draft of the ACHR, prepared by the Inter-American Council of Jurists in 1959, included a provision on remedies that was very similar to the

510 Sicilianos, *NQHR* 2014, p. 256; Jahn, *ZaöRV* 2014, p. 33.

511 ECtHR, *Manushaqe Puto vs. Albania* (2014), para. 105.

512 Sicilianos, *NQHR* 2014, pp. 259-260.

513 For a comparison between the remedial provisions of the ECtHR and the IACtHR, see for example Alexandra Huneeus, "Reforming the State from Afar: Structural Reform Litigation at the Human Rights Courts", *YJIL* 40(1) 2015, p. 8.

514 ACHR, Article 63(1).

one contained in the ECHR, mentioning "just compensation" as the only form of reparation "if the domestic law of the said Party allows only partial reparation to be made".[515] This was maintained in the proposal made by the IACmHR in 1968 but in the last days of negotiating the ACHR in the San José Conference of 1969, the current, far more comprehensive provision emerged and was eventually adopted.[516] As it stands, this provision offers a strong legal basis for the adoption of broad remedial measures. Although it does not specify the substance of available remedies, this has also been interpreted by the Court in a rather expansive way.

Besides the aforementioned Art. 63 ACHR, which already provides a broad mandate to issue a variety of remedies, legislative measures are supported by an additional provision. In fact, most of these orders have been directly linked to violations of the obligation to legislate contained in Art. 2 ACHR, which is considered to provide the legal basis for legislative remedies.[517] This provision establishes that

> *[T]he States Parties undertake to adopt, in accordance with their constitutional processes and the provisions of this Convention, such legislative or other measures as may be necessary to give effect to those rights or freedoms.*[518]

This general obligation to legislate finds no equivalent in the ECHR but is common in other human rights treaties, including the ACHPR.[519] The IACtHR thus often finds, in addition to other violations, that the law in question "violates *per se* Article 2 of the American Convention".[520] In such cases, the violation of Art. 2 is always found in conjunction with another human rights violation caused by the application of the law.[521] Thus, it can be observed that the ACHR contains a remedial provision that not only allows for the Court to order measures similar to those in general international law but even goes beyond that, with its general obligation to

515 Draft Convention on Human Rights, Inter-American Council of Jurists, September 1959, reproduced in the *Inter-American Yearbook of Human Rights*, 1968, p. 269.

516 Hennebel and Tigroudja, *Commentary to the ACHR*, 2022, p. 1303.

517 Novak, *Recueil des Cours* 2017, p. 162 ("The Inter-American Court is competent to order the amendment of the domestic legislation of States under Article 2 of the American Convention on Human Rights").

518 ACHR, Article 2.

519 See Chapter 1 of this book.

520 See for example IACtHR, *Suárez Rosero v Ecuador* (1997), para. 98.

521 This is due to the fact that the IACtHR cannot perform a review of legislation *in abstracto*. See in this respect Chapter 1 of this book.

legislate proving to be a solid basis for the request of legislative reforms. A similar conclusion can be reached when examining the remedial provision included in the ACHPR, which can be interpreted as being even more forward-looking than that of the ACHR.

c) The ACHPR's concise yet wide remedial provision

The ACtHPR is by far the youngest of the three regional human rights courts. The ACHPR entered into force in 1986, but it didn't foresee the creation of a court, only that of a quasi-judicial body – the ACmHPR – that was established in 1987. Moreover, out of the three main regional human rights instruments, the ACHPR is the only one that does not contain a provision on the remedies that victims are entitled to receive. For that reason, the African Commission has been cautious on that front, especially during its early practice.[522] It took almost another twenty years until the *Protocol to the ACHPR on the Establishment of an African Court on Human and Peoples' Rights* (also known as the Ouagadougou Protocol) entered into force in 2004.[523] This Protocol regulates the establishment and functioning of the ACtHPR, including a specific provision on remedies in its Art. 27, which determines that

> *If the Court finds that there has been a violation of a human or peoples' right, it shall make appropriate orders to remedy the violation, including the payment or fair compensation or reparation.*[524]

It can be observed that the drafters of the Protocol took inspiration from the American Convention, as this provision is drafted in a similar way to Art. 63 ACHR. Although it is more concise and does not include the aspects about ensuring the enjoyment of the right that was infringed, the general thrust of both provisions is almost identical. It also departs from the approach of the ECHR and clearly allows for the possibility of ordering

522 See Shelton, 2015, pp. 232-237.

523 Actually, one of the reasons for the adoption of this Protocol and the establishment of a court was the correction of this "weakness" of the ACmHPR, as it has no clear mandate to issue remedies. See Frans Viljoen, "The African Court of Human and Peoples' Rights: An Introduction", *UN Audiovisual Library*, available at: https://media.un.org/en/asset/k19/k19bku06w8.

524 Protocol to the ACHPR on the Establishment of an African Court on Human and Peoples' Rights, Article 27.

non-monetary measures. It could be even seen as going beyond the ACHR's remedial provision, as it refers to "remedy[ing] the violation" in general, and not only the consequences of it. It has been therefore considered "one of the most progressive and broadest provisions regarding reparations".[525]

Even though the main remedial provision can already be interpreted as encompassing such competence, the ACHPR includes an additional legal basis to issue legislative remedies, like its American counterpart. This is the general obligation to legislate contained in Art. 1 ACHPR, stating that state parties "shall undertake to adopt legislative or other measures to give effect to [the rights contained in the Charter]". It has been however argued that this obligation is not as strong as that of other treaties, as it talks about "giv[ing] effect" to rights, instead of "guaranteeing" or "ensuring" them.[526] By contrast, Murray claims that this provision would require states to provide constitutional protection for the rights of the ACHPR.[527]

4. The Specialty of Remedies According to Human Rights Courts

Human rights courts themselves have also commented on the specialty of their remedial approaches *vis-à-vis* those in general international adjudication. On the one hand, the point of departure for justifying the expansion of human rights courts' remedies beyond monetary measures has been the judgment of *Factory at Chorzów*. The three regional human rights courts made reference to this judgment of the PCIJ in order to sustain their competence to order such measures.[528] Furthermore, in their early judgments,

525 Christine Evans, *The Right to Reparation in International Law for Victims of Armed Conflict*, Cambridge: CUP, 2012, p. 82. This is also the view of Shelton, who argues that "[t]his provision is broader than all the current mandates of international human rights bodies to afford remedies to victims of human rights abuse" (Shelton, 2015, pp. 237-238).

526 Nsongurua J. Udombana, "Between Promise and Performance: Revisiting States' Obligations under the African Human Rights Charter", *Stanford Journal of International Law* 40, 2004, pp. 105-142, at p. 126.

527 Rachel Murray, *The African Charter on Human and Peoples' Rights: A Commentary*, Oxford: OUP, 2019, p. 19.

528 See ECHR, *Papamichalopolous v. Greece* (1995), para. 36; IACtHR, *Aloeboetoe vs. Suriname* (1993), para. 49; ACtHPR, *Rev. Christopher Mtikila vs. Tanzania* (2011), para. 27. On the IACtHR, see however Tomuschat in Tulane Journal (2002), p. 166, arguing that "the jurisprudence of the Inter-American Court is predicated on a basic misunderstanding" because "neither the Permanent Court of International Justice nor its successor, the ICJ, has ever said that states are under an obligation

human rights courts categorised the remedies that they could order along the lines of the ARSIWA.[529]

On the other hand, the remedial case law of these courts progressively departed from that in general international adjudication. This departure led to regional human rights courts themselves confirming the *lex specialis* nature of human rights adjudication. For example, the IACtHR argued in 2005 that the ACHR

> *constitutes lex specialis regarding State responsibility, in view of its special nature as an international human rights treaty vis-à-vis general international law. Therefore, attribution of international responsibility to the state, as well as the scope and effects of the acknowledgement made in the instant case, must take place in light of the Convention itself.*[530]

The ECtHR has been more flexible, arguing that it has to "determine State responsibility in conformity with the governing principles of international law, although it must remain mindful of the Convention's special character as a human rights treaty".[531] Thus, it seems that courts themselves take into account the specialty of human rights law, although such arguments are not so often found with respect to reparations, where the influence of general international law is perhaps more clearly seen.

---

to compensate their own citizens". Moreover, the IACtHR departed already in its first judgment from *Factory at Chorzów* by stating that compensation would be the "most usual" way of providing such reparation (IACtHR, *Velásquez Rodríguez v. Honduras* (1989), para. 25). On the contrary, the PCIJ affirmed in *Factory at Chorzów* that the primary form of reparation is restitution, and compensation would only come into play when restitution was no longer possible (see Chapter 2 of this book).

529 See ACtHPR, *Ernest Zongo vs. Republic of Burkina Faso* (2015), paras. 20-21, 29, specifying that under ARSIWA reparation shall take the form of restitution, compensation, and satisfaction. On the other hand, the judgment of IACtHR, *Velásquez Rodríguez v. Honduras* (1989), paras. 25 and 26, having been issued before the adoption of ARISWA, points at the elements that reparation should include, but without including satisfaction nor guarantees of non-repetition. However, some years later the Court expanded its understanding of the concept of reparation, by arguing that it is "a generic term that covers the various ways a State may make amends for the international responsibility it has incurred (restitutio in integrum, payment of compensation, satisfaction, guarantees of non-repetitions among others)". Thereby it moved much closer to the categorisation of ARSIWA, although it had still not been adopted. See IACtHR, *Loayza Tamayo v. Peru* (1998), para. 85.

530 IACtHR, *Mapiripán vs. Colombia* (2005), para. 107.

531 ECtHR, *Bankovic vs. Belgium* (2001), para. 57.

Interim Conclusion: The Progressive Specialisation of Remedies before Human Rights Courts

In sum, this section has shown that although remedies possess certain special features in human rights law if compared to general international law, this does not represent a fundamental difference. The codification of remedies provided by the ARSIWA and the UN Basic Principles are quite similar, despite some particularities in their respective categorization of remedial measures. In addition, human rights courts also initially based their remedial competences on general international law considerations, although they slowly departed from them in order to highlight the special character of human rights law. One important difference in this respect concerns the function of remedies in human rights law, especially its subsidiary role.

With respect to the legal bases for remedies included in international human rights instruments, they are also rather similar to those of a customary nature in general international law, with the exception of Art. 41 ECHR, that is narrower. In addition, both the IACtHR and the ACtHPR have a strong legal basis for ordering legislative reforms, while the ECtHR has developed such a legal basis through its extensive interpretation of Art. 46 ECHR.[532] In sum, despite some legal design differences, there is an apparent similarity between general international law and human rights law in the area of remedies. With that being said, the remedial specialty in human rights adjudication can be more clearly observed when examining the actual practice of the three courts in this respect and comparing it to that of general international courts.

II. The Remedial Practice of Human Rights Courts

In order to examine the special nature of remedies in international human rights adjudication, it becomes relevant to look at the actual practice of human rights courts. This includes the evolution of the remedial practice before each of the three regional human rights courts as well as the remedies they currently apply. This will serve to shed light not only on the special features of remedies in this area but also on the differences among these

532 This does additionally offer a "legal design explanation" for the respective court's remedial intrusiveness, which will be examined below. See Çalı, *I•CON* 2018, pp. 227-229.

courts and the role of legislative measures in this respect. Remedies before human rights courts range from very specific and intrusive injunctions to broad requirements that aim to empower domestic actors to decide how to solve certain problems within a relatively wide range of options.

In this respect, Neuman identifies three approaches that can be taken by human rights tribunals towards the issue of remedies.[533] The first approach is called the "direct remedy model" and it implies that courts can directly order a wide range of remedies. He labels the second approach as the "monitoring model", whereby the tribunal defines the remedial goal or the minimum elements of a remedy and leaves discretion to the state in order to choose among alternatives, and the third approach as the "negotiation model", implying that the tribunal will facilitate and sometimes supervise a negotiation among the interested parties in order to find the appropriate remedies. The practice of the ACtHPR and the IACtHR would in this context be closer to the 'direct remedy model', while that of the ECtHR would be rather a 'monitoring model'. However, as Neuman recognises, most human rights courts and bodies do not ascribe exclusively to one of these models but rather apply what can be seen as hybrid models. There has also been a progressive change whereby human rights courts have arguably transited from remedial models closer to that of monitoring towards that of direct remedies. In this respect, it is useful to have a look at the evolution of the remedial practice of each regional human rights court.

1. The Evolution of the Human Rights Courts' Remedial Practice

The early remedial practice of the three regional human rights courts and its evolution is particularly relevant in order to understand their respective remedial approaches. In this respect, one can find three very different situations, whereby the evolution of the geopolitical context surrounding these human rights protection systems is also important. In the case of the ECtHR, its remedial practice has been evolving very slowly for many years, from an approach that was limited to declaratory judgments to the inclusion of implicit obligations and then of individual and general remedial measures. On the other hand, the IACtHR had also a rather cautious remedial approach at the beginning, but it only lasted for a few years and then it carried out a radical transformation, to the point where

533 See Gerald L. Neuman, "Bi-Level Remedies for Human Rights Violations", *Harvard International Law Journal* 55(2), 2014, pp. 323-360.

it is now generally considered as the international court with the most progressive remedial practice. Finally, the ACtHPR directly started ordering highly intrusive measures in its first judgments. These developments will be examined more closely below.

a) The evolution of the ECtHR's remedial practice

For a long time, the ECtHR's judgments were considered "essentially declaratory".[534] In accordance with this position, the Strasbourg Court was not empowered to decide how a judgment should be implemented, nor which specific consequences flowed from the finding of a violation. Therefore, a typical outcome would be for it to declare that the finding of a violation constitutes in itself an adequate just satisfaction, although the most common remedy was (and still is) the payment of a monetary sum to the victims under the 'just satisfaction' provision.

Non-monetary remedial measures were thus avoided by the ECtHR for many years. This is clearly reflected in the case of *Marckx vs. Belgium* (1979), which has become one of the landmark cases of the ECtHR on the issue of remedies as well as on the compatibility of domestic laws and the Convention. The applicants claimed that the Belgian Civil Code of the time was discriminatory with respect to the establishment of maternal affiliation of children born out of wedlock, as well as the patrimonial rights flowing from it.[535] Despite finding that the law as such was in violation of the ECHR, the ECtHR stressed that it would be "for the respondent State, and the respondent State alone, to take the measures it considers appropriate to ensure that its domestic law is coherent and consistent".[536]

The *Marckx* case was therefore used by the ECtHR to establish a clear position concerning remedial measures. Even in cases where a domestic law as such was contrary to the convention, it was up to the state to decide whether a legislative reform would be appropriate. This remained its position towards remedies and specifically towards the reform of domestic laws

534 As for example stated in ECtHR, *Marckx vs. Belgium* (1979), para. 42.

535 ECtHR, *Marckx vs. Belgium* (1979), para. 13.

536 ECtHR, *Marckx vs. Belgium* (1979), para. 42. It suggested that its judgments should have effects beyond the concrete case "especially since the violations found stem directly from the contested provisions and not from individual measures of implementation", but left to the State the choice of means for executing its obligation to abide by the judgment.

for a long period. It often rejected requests made by victims with respect to different types of non-monetary remedial measures.[537] After some years, however, it became clear that adequate redress for victims could not always be achieved solely by means of monetary compensation measures.[538]

The first time the ECtHR deviated from this established line of jurisprudence was in *Papamichalopoulos vs. Greece (1995).* In this case, the victims suffered an unlawful expropriation which had been continuing for over twenty-five years, in violation of their right to property. The Court therefore ordered in the operative part of the judgment the return of the land within six months. However, it subsequently established that if the State should fail to provide such restitution, it would have to pay the applicants a monetary sum.[539] Although "such alternative obligations are not genuine individual measures",[540] as the option to substitute them for compensation makes them non-binding, it was a step in that direction.[541]

Another milestone for the evolution of the ECtHR's jurisprudence with regard to non-monetary measures was the case of *Scozzari and Giunta*

537 For example, in a case of 1982 in which the victims asked for the annulment of their disciplinary and criminal sanctions, the Court affirmed in its judgment that it was not "empowered" to order this (ECtHR, *Le Compte, Van Leuven and De Meyere vs. Belgium* (1982), para. 13). In another case it declared that it had no jurisdiction to request the reopening of a judicial proceeding (ECtHR, *Saidi vs. France* (1993), para. 47). When a legislative reform was sought by the victims, the Court stated that "the Convention does not empower it to accede to such a request. It reiterates that it is for the State to choose the means to be used in its domestic legal system in order to comply with the provisions of the Convention or to redress the situation that has given rise to the violation of the Convention" (ECtHR, *Yağci and Sargin vs. Turkey* (1995), para. 81).

538 See generally Costas Paraskeva, "European Court of Human Rights: From declaratory judgments to indications of specific measures", *EHRLR* 1, 2018, pp. 46-56.

539 ECtHR, *Papamichalopolous vs. Greece* (1995), operative paras. 2 and 3.

540 Ichim, *Just Satisfaction,* 2014, p. 207.

541 This approach of ordering non-monetary measures with the possibility of opting out by paying a monetary sum has been used by the ECtHR in several judgments (See for example ECtHR, *Brumarescu vs. Romania* (2001), operative paras. 1 and 2; *Ramadhi vs. Albania* (2007), operative para. 6; *Taganrog LRO vs. Russia* (2022), operative para. 13). The CoM actually specified that it is applied in "certain property cases", where states can "choose between restitution and compensation" (CoM, Supervision of the Execution of Judgments of the ECtHR, 3rd Annual Report, 2009, p. 19). However, this approach has been even employed with respect to legislative remedies (see ECtHR, *L. vs. Lithuania* (2007), operative paras. 5 and 6, ordering a legislative reform in very concrete terms, but including the alternative of paying a monetary sum). See also, criticising this approach, Ichim, *Just Satisfaction,* 2014, pp. 39-42.

vs. Italy (2000), dealing with a violation of the right to family life due to the suspension of parental rights and the insufficient contact between the applicant and her children. Here, although no concrete measures were included in the operative paragraphs, the Court first used a formula that has become very important for its remedial practice. On the basis of Art. 41 ECHR, it declared that

> *a judgment in which the Court finds a breach imposes on the respondent State a legal obligation not just to pay those concerned the sums awarded by way of just satisfaction, but also to choose, subject to supervision by the Committee of Ministers, the general and/or, if appropriate, individual measures to be adopted in their domestic legal order to put an end to the violation found by the Court and to redress so far as possible the effects.*[542]

The ECtHR thus determined for the first time that some judgments require the adoption of non-monetary measures, even if this is not expressly requested, thereby extending the scope of Art. 41 beyond the mere obligation of payment. Despite this statement, the ECtHR still held that the State "remains free to choose the means by which it will discharge its legal obligation under Article 46".[543] This changed a few years later, in 2004, when the Court started to include reparations both of an individual and general nature in its judgments.[544]

Individual non-monetary remedies were first ordered by the ECtHR in the case of *Assanidze vs Georgia (2004)*, concerning an arbitrary detention contrary to Art. 5 ECHR. Here, the Court introduced in the operative paragraphs the duty to secure "the applicant's release at the earliest possible date",[545] grounding this decision on the fact that "the violation found in the instant case does not leave any real choice as to the measures required to remedy it".[546] This approach has since been progressively expanded to further situations in which the ECtHR holds that there is only one way of redressing or even ceasing the violation.

With respect to general measures, it is important to take into account two fundamental developments that affected the European human rights

542 ECtHR, *Scozzari and Giunta vs. Italy* (2000), para. 249.

543 ECtHR, *Scozzari and Giunta vs. Italy* (2000), para. 249.

544 In the context of the ECtHR, this distinction is commonly used, whereby individual measures are those directly affecting the victims and general measures are those affecting other potential victims or society in general.

545 ECtHR, *Assanidze vs. Georgia* (2004), operative para. 14.

546 ECtHR, *Assanidze vs. Georgia* (2004), para. 202.

protection system during the 1990s, which are the main causes for the introduction of such measures.[547] The first is the enlargement of the system, with the incorporation of most of the former Eastern Bloc into the CoE. With this development, the ECtHR turned from overseeing twenty-three states relatively homogenous states in the early 1990s[548] to overseeing forty-seven states of "an unprecedented and formidable diversity".[549] Moreover, these new countries were mostly still in transition and had therefore weak institutions and democratic procedures.[550] As Sadurski puts it, "with the new arrivals into the CoE system (...) it clearly appeared that many problems were not so much due to occasionally erring courts but rather have to do with the substance of the laws themselves".[551] As a consequence, the ECtHR had to transit from "being a 'fine-tuner' of the national legal systems" to "policing the national systems in which serious violations of rights occurred".[552]

The other major development was the entry into force of Protocol 11 in 1998. This Protocol allowed individuals to have direct access to the Court. Before this, the European Commission on Human Rights acted as a gatekeeper, assessing the admissibility of cases and deciding which ones to refer to the Court, similarly to the procedure before the IACtHR and the ACtHPR.[553] Since the entry into force of Protocol 11, every individual can present a case directly before the Court under certain circumstances. This produced a huge inflow of applications at the early 2000s, concerning

547 On these developments, see among others Philip Leach, "No longer offering fine mantras to a parched child? The European Court's developing approach to remedies", in Andreas Føllesdal, Birgit Peters and Geir Ulfstein (eds.), *Constituting Europe: The European Court of Human Rights in a National, European and Global Context*, Cambridge: CUP, pp. 142-180; Huneeus, *YJIL* 2015; Sadurski, *HRLR* 2009; Helfer, *EJIL* 2008.

548 Former ECtHR judge Rudolf Bernhardt held in 1987 that "[t]he main reason for the effectiveness of the European Convention and the Court is the considerable measure of homogeneity among European states". See Rudolf Bernhardt, "Commentary: The European System", *Connecticut Journal of International Law* 2, 1987, at p. 299.

549 Sadurski, *HRLR* 2009, at p. 400.

550 See Sadurski, *HRLR* 2009, p. 410, arguing that "the less-than-ready applicants were let in – on the basis of a principle that it is better to have a troublesome country in than out".

551 Sadurski, *HRLR* 2009, pp. 413-414.

552 Sadurski, *HRLR* 2009, p. 401.

553 See generally Ed Bates, *The Evolution of the European Convention on Human Rights: From Its Inception to the Creation of a Permanent Court of Human Rights*, Oxford: OUP, 2010.

mainly 'repetitive' cases, which in turn provoked "a docket crisis of major proportions".[554]

In this context, the Steering Committee on Human Rights of the CoE (CDDH) issued a report in 2003 introducing some proposals in order to guarantee the long-term effectiveness of the system.[555] Among them, it included the possibility for the Court to identify cases with an underlying structural problem, as well as the source of this problem. However, the Court was expressly asked to abstain from indicating a corrective measure for the identified problem.[556] Shortly afterwards, the CoM also invited the Court to identify "as far as possible" the existence of a structural problem and its source,[557] while it avoided mentioning the issue of the indication of corrective measures.[558]

The reaction of the ECtHR to this recommendation came swiftly, not only identifying structural problems but going further and ordering a solution to them. Three months after the CoM Resolution, it issued the first of the so-called 'pilot judgments' in the case *Broniowski vs. Poland* (2004), dealing with property rights in the context of the transition from communist regimes to democracy.[559] The ECtHR determined that the violation in this case "originated in a widespread problem which resulted from a malfunctioning of Polish legislation and administrative practice and which has affected and remains capable of affecting a large number of persons".[560] Then, after referring to the aforementioned CoM resolution, the Court included a measure in the operative paragraphs stating that Poland "must, through appropriate legal measures and administrative practices, secure the implementation of the property right in question in respect of the

554 Helfer, *EJIL* 2008, p. 127.

555 Steering Committee for Human Rights (CDDH), Guaranteeing the long-term effectiveness of the European Court of Human Rights, CM(2003)55-Add, 8 April 2003.

556 The underlying reason for this, according to the CDDH, was the subsidiary role of the ECtHR. See CDDH, 2003, para. 14 ("The subsidiary role of the Court was underlined in that it would not be invited to indicate the corrective measures to execute a judgment").

557 Resolution Res(2004)3 of the Committee of Ministers on judgments revealing an underlying systemic problem (adopted by the Committee of Ministers on 12 May 2004, at its 114th Session).

558 However, a CoM Recommendation adopted at the same time included a general obligation for states to adopt the appropriate measures in order to solve these structural problems (Recommendation Rec(2004)6 of the Committee of Ministers to Member States on the improvement of domestic remedies, 12 May 2004).

559 For more details on this case, see Chapter 4 of this book.

560 ECtHR, *Broniowski vs. Poland* (2004), para. 189.

remaining Bug River claimants or provide them with equivalent redress in lieu".[561]

The ECtHR continued using the pilot judgment procedure in the following years, and they eventually became an important element of the Court's jurisprudence. In 2011, this procedure was formalised through its inclusion in Art. 61 the Rules of the Court, establishing two main substantive elements that all pilot judgments need to include. First, as the main condition for initiating the procedure is that the facts of the application reveal the existence of a systemic dysfunction, the Court is required to identify the "nature" of that problem. Second, the Court shall also indicate "the type of remedial measures which the Contracting Party concerned is required to take at the domestic level by virtue of the operative provisions of the judgment". [562] Therefore, some sort of remedy must be ordered whenever a pilot judgment is issued.[563] The remedial practice of the ECtHR thus suffered a notable transformation during the early 2000s. However, as will be seen below, non-monetary remedies are still highly exceptional in the Strasbourg jurisprudence. This is different with respect to the IACtHR.

b) The evolution of the IACtHR's remedial practice

The remedial practice of the IACtHR has attracted the interest of scholarship for a long time.[564] The wide array of remedial measures before that Court has been highlighted in this regard and some of them have received particular attention, such as the obligation to investigate and punish human

561 ECtHR, *Broniowski vs. Poland* (2004), operative para. 4.

562 See Rules of the ECtHR, Rule 61, para. 3. Other conditions are of a rather procedural nature, such as the duty to collect the views of the parties on the systemic problem or the requirement that the procedure is initiated either by the Court or by a member state.

563 This is further specified in another provision, establishing that if the parties reach a friendly-settlement agreement, this needs to include a declaration by the respondent state on the implementation the 'general measures' ordered in the judgment. See Rules of the ECtHR, Rule 61, para. 7.

564 See for example Fabian Novak, "The System of Reparations in the jurisprudence of the Inter-American Court of Human Rights", *The Hague Academy of International Law: Recueil des Cours* 392, 2017, pp. 9-203; Antkowiak, *CJTL* 2008; Dinah Shelton, "Reparations in the Inter-American System", in David Harris and Stephen Livingstone (eds.), *The Inter-American System of Human Rights*, Oxford: OUP, 2004, pp. 151-172.

rights violations,[565] or the orders to restitute indigenous territory.[566] In has been even argued in this regard that "[r]eparations at the Inter-American Court have radically transformed international and domestic law".[567] Part of this impact is owed to the innovative legal basis for ordering remedies that was examined before, but also to the development of the IACtHR's approach towards this issue during its early years.

The IACtHR was formally established in 1979 after the ACHR was ratified by eleven member states and entered into force in 1978. However, no contentious cases were decided by the IACtHR until about a decade later. This was due to the Inter-American Commission, to which individuals need to apply before reaching the Court, not transferring any contentious cases to the latter.[568] Thus, during its first years of existence, the IACtHR limited its judicial practice to the award of advisory opinions, which can also be requested by the state parties and other organs of the OAS.[569]

After such contentious cases started arriving before the IACtHR in the late 1980s, the Court issued its first judgment on reparations in the well-known case of *Velasquez Rodriguez vs. Honduras* (1989), dealing with enforced disappearances in Honduras. Some of the victims made a request for reparations with no less than twelve different remedies, including the prosecution of the perpetrators, public apologies and other symbolic measures.[570] The Court however took a rather narrow remedial approach in this first instance and limited itself to ordering the payment of financial compensation to the victims. This narrow approach towards remedies remained the same in the following judgments.[571] The IACtHR did not affirm, as the

565 See for example Giovanna Maria Frisso, "The Duty to Investigate Violations of the Right to Life in Armed Conflicts in the Jurisprudence of the Inter-American Court of Human Rights", 51 *Israel Law Review*, 2018, pp. 169-191.

566 Gabriela Cristina Braga Navarro, "The Struggle after the Victory: Non-compliance in the Inter-American Court of Human Rights' Jurisprudence on Indigenous Territorial Rights", *JIDS* 12, 2021, pp. 223–249.

567 Judge Elisabeth Odio Benito, "Preface", in Hennebel and Tigroudja, *Commentary to the ACHR*, 2022, p. ix.

568 According to Neuman, the reason for it was that "[t]he long-established Commission did not welcome a new Court that might impair its autonomy and undermine its prestige" (Gerald L. Neuman, "Import, Export and Regional Consent", *EJIL* 19(1), 2008, p. 103).

569 The advisory jurisdiction of the Court was nevertheless also a way for it to review domestic laws during that time. See on that Chapter 1 of this book.

570 IACtHR, *Velásquez Rodríguez v. Honduras* (1989), para. 7.

571 See Shelton, 2015, pp. 391 et seq. However, the IACmHR was at the same time taking a different approach and issuing more 'intrusive' remedies. See on that Başak Çalı,

ECtHR did at that time, that it had no competence to order non-monetary measures, but in practice, it abstained from doing so and limited itself to the "usual" remedies of compensation.[572]

This, however, started to change with the judgment on reparations in the case of *Aloebotoe v. Surinam* (1993). Here, the IACtHR departed from its previous approach and ordered non-pecuniary measures, namely the establishment of a foundation and the reopening of a school.[573] Thereafter, the use of non-pecuniary remedial measures slowly gained ground over the 'traditional' approach. In *El Amparo vs. Venezuela* (1996), the IACtHR ordered for the first time to investigate human rights violations and punish those responsible, and in *Loayza Tamayo vs. Peru* (1998) it prescribed the reinstatement of the victim in her former employment and the nullification of all legal consequences flowing from a domestic judgment.[574] Although it took some more years,[575] this rather progressive approach towards remedies eventually became the standard practice in the IACtHR's case law, especially since 2001.[576]

In this respect, one of the major advocates of non-pecuniary remedies at the IACtHR was its former president Cançado Trinidade, who illustrated his position through a number of separate opinions. For example, in a separate opinion to a judgment of 2001, he stated that

---

"Explaining variation in the intrusiveness of regional human rights remedies in domestic orders", *I•CON* 16(1), 2018, pp. 214-234, at p. 217.

572 See on the IACtHR's early remedial jurisprudence Antkowiak, *CJTL* 2008, pp. 365-368. See also Huneeus, *YJIL* 2015, pp. 8-11, explaining how the IACtHR first adopted what she calls a "declaratory model of human rights litigation", which "soon revealed its limits" due to the democratic deficits and inequalities present in the region.

573 IACtHR, *Aloeboetoe et al. v. Suriname* (1993), operative paras. 2 and 5.

574 IACtHR, *Loaza Tamayo vs. Peru* (1998), operative paras. 1 and 3. In addition, here it included for the first time remedial measures consisting in the reform of domestic laws (see below section III).

575 See in this respect Antkowiak, *CJTL* 2008, p. 370, arguing that after Loayza Tamayo the IACtHR "fell back into the comfortable remedial scheme of Velasquez-Rodriguez", avoiding to issue guarantees of non-repetition in some cases in which these would have been justified.

576 In 2001 the IACtHR issued 10 judgments on reparations, almost as many as it had issued since its inception. These judgments included a wide array of remedial measures, both of an individual and of a general nature. According to Antkowiak, "the Tribunal's current approach to redress was almost fully developed during that critical year" (Antkowiak, *CJTL* 2008, pp. 371-372).

> *"[t]he day when the work of determining the reparations due to the victims of violations of fundamental human rights were to be reduced exclusively to a simple fixing of compensations in the form of indemnizations (...) a calculating machine would suffice. The day this were to occur – which I hope will never come – the labour itself of an international tribunal of human rights would be irremediably devoid of all sense".*[577]

Trinidade's opinion demonstrates that judges' personal convictions can have an important influence on the development of human rights courts' jurisprudence and remedial practice.[578]

c) The evolution of the ACtHPR's remedial practice

Finally, due to its young age and low number of judgments, the ACtHPR's remedial practice has not evolved as much as those of the other two courts. As mentioned before, this Court became gradually operational after the entry into force of the Ouagadougou Protocol in 2004. It did take, however, some additional time until its first decision on admissibility (in 2009) and its first judgment on the merits (in 2013). Contrary to the other regional human rights courts, the ACtHPR did not start with a cautious approach towards remedies and developed this practice progressively but instead issued far-reaching remedial measures from the beginning.

The first judgment the ACtHPR decided on the merits was *Tanganyika Law Society and Legal and Human Rights Centre vs. Tanzania* (2013), dealing with the violation of electoral rights. There, the ACtHPR found the incompatibility of a provision of the Tanzanian Constitution with the ACHPR, as this provision prevented independent candidates from running for office.[579] Although the Court stated that it would reserve the issue of reparations for a subsequent judgment, it indicated in the operative part of the merits judgment that "[t]he Respondent is directed to take constitutional, legislative and all other necessary measures within a reasonable time

577 IACtHR, *"Street Children" vs. Guatemala* (2001), Separate Opinion of Judge A.A. Cançado Trindade, para. 37.

578 Se generally in this respect Gregor Maučec and Shai Dothan, "The effects of international judges' personal characteristics on their judging", *LJIL* 35, 2022, pp. 887-895.

579 For a critical view of this decision, see Alain Didier Olinga, "La première décision au fond de la Cour africaine des droits de l'homme et des peoples", *Revue des droits de l'homme* 6, 2014, pp. 1-23.

to remedy the violations (...)".[580] Thus, already in its first judgment, the ACtHPR did not hesitate to interfere with states' sovereignty to the highest extent, in the form of ordering a constitutional reform. This is probably influenced by the time in which the ACtHPR started to operate. By 2013, the international law on remedies as well as the practice of regional and global human rights bodies had evolved to a point in which ordering such intrusive measures was not uncommon.[581]

Similarly to the IACtHR in its early years, the ACtHPR used to divide the merits stage and the reparations stage of a case into two different judgments. Thereby, it generally included the remedial measures of a general nature in judgments on merits, and those of an individual nature in judgments on reparations. For example, legislative reforms are commonly found in its early judgments on the merits,[582] while some of its first judgments on reparations included not only compensatory remedies but also orders to investigate and prosecute the perpetrators of human rights violations,[583] as well as the expunging of criminal convictions from judicial records.[584] In sum, the ACtHPR did not develop its remedial practice progressively, as the other regional human rights courts did, but instead made extensive use of the available remedies already in the first opportunities it had.

2. The Current Remedial Landscape before Human Rights Courts

Having considered the evolution of the three human rights courts' remedial practices, it is also useful to have a brief outlook of the current remedial practice before each of them. There are important differences to be observed with respect not only to the intensity and intrusiveness of these remedies but also to the main reasons for each of the courts to make use of them.[585] In this regard, the general remedial landscape before each of the courts will be examined, as well as their use of specific remedial

580 ACtHPR, *Tanganyika Law Society and Legal and Human Rights Centre* vs. *Tanzania* (2013), operative para. 3.

581 Actually, the IACtHR had already ordered constitutional reforms in several cases (for example in IACtHR, *Caesar vs. Trinidad and Tobago* (2005) or in *Boyce vs. Barbados* (2007)), and even the ECtHR had recommended such reforms (as in ECtHR, *Sejdić and Finci vs. Bosnia and Herzegovina* (2009)).

582 As for example in ACtHPR, *Lohé Issa Konaté vs. Burkina Faso* (2014).

583 ACtHPR, *Ernest Zongo vs. Burkina Faso* (2015), para. 111 (x).

584 ACtHPR, *Lohé Issa Konaté vs. Burkina Faso* (2016), para. 60 (i).

585 See generally Çalı, *I•CON* 2018; Cornejo, *I•CON* 2017.

categories. This will allow not only for a comparison between the remedial practice before general international courts and human rights courts but also between the three regional human rights courts.

a) The remedial landscape before the European Court of Human Rights

In recent times, both individual and general remedial measures have found their place in the case law of the ECtHR, after it developed these remedial competences cautiously and incrementally during the last few decades. The most common approach of the Court is still to issue judgments that are essentially declaratory, frequently ordering the payment of monetary compensation. However, it is currently not rare to find non-monetary remedial measures in some judgments, although there are still no clear criteria or a consistent judicial practice as to the concrete cases in which these remedies should be included, nor to the specific substance of those measures.[586]

Several authors have examined the remedial practice of the ECtHR. For example, in 2014, former ECtHR's judge Sicilianos (writing extra-judicially) identified "more than 160 judgments" in which the ECtHR had indicated individual and/or general measures on the basis of Art. 46 ECHR.[587] This number, however, does not differentiate between judgments including these measures in the reasoning and the operative part, nor disaggregates the individual and general measures. According to this judge, "[a]n assessment of this important practice would require an analytical study", while he aimed only at giving "a brief picture" in this regard.[588]

Such an analytical study was carried out by Donald and Speck in 2019, statistically analysing all pilot and Article 46 judgments issued between 2004 and 2016. They found that during this period the ECtHR has issued 29 pilot judgments and 170 'Article 46 judgments'.[589] However, while all pilot judgments include remedial measures in the operative part, only 36 of the 170 Article 46 judgments did so, and these were mostly individual

586 See Alastair Mowbray, "An Examination of the European Court of Human Rights' Indication of Remedial Measures", *HRLR* 17, 2017, p. 478. See also Glas, *NQHR* 2016, p. 49, noting that "the Court does not elaborately reason its decision to apply the [pilot judgment] procedure".

587 Sicilianos, *NQHR* 2014, pp. 235–262.

588 Sicilianos, *NQHR* 2014, pp. 237-238.

589 Donald and Speck, *HRLR* 2019, pp. 5-6.

measures.[590] Mowbray also examined the indication of remedial measures by the ECtHR, but focusing only on those issued in the period between 2013 and 2015.[591] He finds that during these three years, the ECtHR issued only nine judgments with remedial measures in the operative part, whereby seven of them prescribed individual measures and only three general measures.[592]

It can thus be observed that most remedial measures ordered by the ECtHR are of an individual nature,[593] while those of a general nature are mostly (but not only) limited to the pilot judgment procedure.[594] Moreover, the indication of remedial measures by the ECtHR responds to two fundamental reasons. In the case of individual remedies, these are mainly included when the nature of the violation leaves no real choice as to the measures required to redress it.[595] In fact, Keller and Marti found that most of the ECtHR's individual measures are included in exceptional cases related to illegal detentions, unfair judicial proceedings or property.[596] With respect to general remedies, the main reason for its inclusion is that the violation reveals the existence of a systemic problem that can give rise to numerous well-founded applications before the ECtHR.[597] If the violation is due, for example, to a deficient legislative framework, redressing the individual victims is not enough, as the legislative malfunctioning will probably affect many other individuals who can also bring forward complaints to the ECtHR. Thus, the underlying reason has more to do with docket control than any other considerations.

590 Donald and Speck, *HRLR* 2019, p. 9.

591 Mowbray, *HRLR* 2017.

592 One of the judgments contained both individual and general remedial measures in the operative part.

593 See Donald and Speck, *HRLR* 2019, p. 9, arguing that judges "feel more comfortable to be prescriptive as regards individual measures, where the nature of the violation tends to leave no real alternative".

594 See for example ECtHR, *Lukenda vs. Slovenia* (2005); Grudić vs. Serbia (2012). See also Sicilianos, *NQHR* 2014, p. 240 ("Quasi-pilot judgments may also contain a paragraph on execution measures in their operative part").

595 See among others Jahn, *ZaöRV* 2014, p. 15; Keller and Marti, *EJIL* 2016, p. 839.

596 Keller and Marti, *EJIL* 2016, p. 842.

597 See in this regard for example Glas, *NQHR* 2016, pp. 41-70.

b) The remedial landscape before the Inter-American Court of Human Rights

The remedial practice of the IACtHR has evolved to a point at which it is probably the international court that includes the widest and most creative array of measures in its judgments.[598] Notably, in most cases the remedies are of a structural nature, going beyond the concrete victims of the human rights violation. This is one of the reasons why it is sustained that the jurisprudence of the IACtHR has acquired a transformative dimension.[599] This has been praised by some authors,[600] while others have held that the IACtHR should be more cautious, in order "not to jeopardise the entire regional human rights system with aggressive reparation judgments".[601]

This extensive remedial practice is also one of the main features which distinguishes the IACtHR from the ECtHR. Thereby, the geopolitical context in which the IACtHR has operated for the last decades is very relevant for this distinction and the remedial approach of this court. When it was established and began its judicial practice, the IACtHR was overseeing a region where military dictatorships and internal conflicts predominated, and where enforced disappearances, extrajudicial executions and torture were sadly common in many states. Moreover, the weak national courts and the fragility of some of the region's democracies resulted in a culture of impunity and a lack of effective domestic remedies.[602] This implied serious wide-scale human rights violations that could not be redressed by means of a simple monetary compensation, but required additional measures, especially in order to secure the '*nunca más*' (never again) requests of Latin

598 See Çalı, *I•CON* 2018, pp. 217-220.

599 See von Bodgandy and Urueña, *AJIL* 2020, p. 439, arguing that the IACtHR's "far-reaching orders on reparation (...) have grown to be a key component of transformative constitutionalism". See also generally Ximena Soley, "The Transformative Dimension of Inter-American Jurisprudence", in Armin von Bogdandy et al. (eds.), *Transformative Constitutionalism in Latin America*, Oxford: OUP, 2017.

600 See David L. Attanasio, "Extraordinary Reparations, Legitimacy, and the Inter-American Court", *University of Pennsylvania Journal of International Law* 37(3), 2016, p. 815.

601 Lisa J. Laplante, "Bringing effective remedies home: the inter-American human rights system, reparations, and the duty of prevention", *NQHR* 22(3), 2004, pp. 347-388, at p. 387. Similarly, Antkowiak, *CJTL* 2008, pp. 418-419.

602 See Neuman, *EJIL* 2008, at p. 101.

American societies in the aftermath of these dictatorships and civil wars.[603] Even though the situation has changed in the region and the democratic credentials of Latin American states have strongly improved during the last decades, the IACtHR is still heavily influenced by this self-understanding concerning its transformative mandate and by the lack of trust in domestic institutions, which is clearly reflected in the remedies it orders.

Another contextual reason for the remedial practice of the IACtHR is related to the number of cases it decides. While the ECtHR issues more than 1,000 judgments each year, the IACtHR nowadays delivers only around twenty judgments annually, and this number was considerably lower some years ago. Thus, as highlighted by Cavallaro and Brewer, "it remains an organ of extremely limited access for the vast majority of victims of human rights violations".[604] This is very likely one reason which explains why the IACtHR aims to amplify the impact of each case it decides, going beyond the individual applicants and triggering structural transformations.[605] One of the main ways to achieve this is through these extensive remedial orders, with its main focus on guarantees of non-repetition.

c) The remedial landscape before the African Court of Human and Peoples' Rights

Being relatively young, the ACtHPR can be said to be still developing its remedial approach. Between its first judgment on the merits in 2013 and the end of 2022, the ACtHPR has issued judgments with remedial measures in seventy-seven cases. In this regard, an exponential growth of judgments can be observed during the last years, whereby the ACtHPR has kept developing its remedial approach. As highlighted by Clooney and

603 See Çalı, *I•CON* 2018, p. 229, describing such measures as "nunca más remedies". On the 'nunca más' legacy at the IACtHR, see von Bogdandy and Urueña, *AJIL* 2020, pp. 408-413.

604 James Cavallaro and Stephanie Erin Brewer, "Reevaluating Regional Human Rights Litigation in the Twenty First Century: The Case of the Inter-American Court", *AJIL* 102(4), 2008, p. 781. The main reason put forward by the authors to explain this small number of judgments is the "meager financial and political support from the OAS" (at p. 782).

605 Cavallaro and Brewer, *AJIL* 2008, p. 795 ("considering the equally urgent situation of the hundreds or thousands of victims whose cases will never be heard by it, the Court (...) must use each case that comes before it as an opportunity to advance the broader issue underlying the litigation").

Webb, the ACtHPR is one of the few international bodies that "tend to cross-reference remedies granted by other bodies or even explain in their own jurisprudence why a remedy is appropriate for a particular violation of a right in one case but not another".[606]

In this respect, it can be observed that the ACtHPR has taken inspiration from the other regional human rights courts in the development of its remedial practice, especially from the IACtHR.[607] Despite still lacking a consolidated remedial jurisprudence, the landscape of remedies before the ACtHPR is nowadays similar to that of its Inter-American counterpart. However, the ACtHPR has been more cautious with regard to certain remedial measures, particularly those aiming at restitution and rehabilitation, while it has instead put its focus on guarantees of non-repetition. When comparing the remedial case law of these two courts in recent years, one can also observe that the array of remedies included in the inter-American case law is still wider and more diversified than in the African one.

3. A Classification of Remedies before Human Rights Courts

In order to have a closer look at the remedial landscape before regional human rights courts, their remedies will be categorised in accordance with the classification of the aforementioned UN Basic Principles, i.e., along the categories of restitution, compensation, satisfaction, rehabilitation and guarantees of non-repetition. By contrast, the ECtHR usually divides its non-monetary remedies between measures directed towards the victim (labelled individual measures) on the one hand, and towards further potential victims (general measures) on the other. Thereby, individual measures comprise restitution, rehabilitation and satisfaction, while the concept of general measures refers mostly just to guarantees of non-repetition, and compensation is treated as a separate remedy, called 'just satisfaction'. The IACtHR on the other hand uses a much closer classification to the one

606 Amal Clooney and Philippa Webb, *The Right to a Fair Trial in International Law*, Oxford: OUP, 2020, p. 59.

607 The practice of the ECtHR does also have an influence in this development, as can be observed for example with the introduction in 2020 of a 'pilot judgment procedure' before the ACtHPR, which has however not been applied yet. See in this respect Kevin Toro Sánchez, "The right to reparations in the contentious process before the African Court on Human and Peoples' Rights: A comparative analysis on account of the revised Rules of Court", *African Human Rights Law Journal* 21, 2021, pp. 812-835, at pp. 828-830.

provided in the Basic Principles, dividing the remedies it may order into six categories, namely those of restitution; rehabilitation; satisfaction; compensation; obligation to investigate, prosecute and punish; and guarantees of non-repetition.[608] Thus, it adds the measures of investigation as a distinct category from that of satisfaction, where these measures are usually included.[609]

a) Restitution

Restitution is considered the primary form of reparation in general international law, although it plays a less important role in human rights adjudication. This is due to the fact that after a human rights violation it "may be especially difficult or even impossible" to restore the victims' previous situation.[610] According to the UN Basic Principles, restitution "includes, as appropriate: restoration of liberty, enjoyment of human rights, identity, family life and citizenship, return to one's place of residence, restoration of employment and return of property".[611] As pointed out by Novak with respect to the IACtHR, human rights courts have gone beyond the approach towards restitution used in general international law, as instead of restoring a situation that existed before the violation they seek to put the victim in the hypothetical situation that would have existed if the violation had never taken place.[612] This is especially the case in situations where courts find a pattern of structural discrimination.[613]

608 See IACtHR, *Annual Report*, 2018, p. 68. Some authors use different typologies. For example, Antkowiak, *CJTL* 2008, pp. 371-386, distinguishes between "victim-centered remedies", "remedies directed to society as a whole" and "remedies directed at discrete communities".

609 However, in some cases it has also considered these measures as forms of cessation or even as guarantees of non-repetition. See Novak, *Recueil des Cours* 2017, pp. 113-114.

610 Buyse, *ZaöRV* 2008, p. 138.

611 UN Basic Principles, para. 19.

612 Novak, *Recueil des Cours* 2017, p. 80.

613 See for example IACtHR, *'Cotton Field' vs. Mexico* (2009), para. 450 ("the reparations must be designed to change this situation, so that their effect is not only of restitution, but also of rectification. In this regard, reestablishment of the same structural context of violence and discrimination is not acceptable"). See generally Elisabeth Veronika Henn, *International Human Rights Law and Structural Discrimination*, Berlin: Springer, 2021, especially at pp. 171 et seq.

In the case law of the ECtHR, measures of restitution have consisted among others in the release of prisoners,[614] the enforcement of domestic decisions,[615] the re-establishment of contact between an applicant and her daughter,[616] or the reinstatement of the victim as supreme judge.[617] Notably, it has ordered these measures only when it considered that there was no other way of remedying the violation. Similarly, the IACtHR has also ordered the release from detention,[618] the reinstatement of workers,[619] or the restoration of property[620] and family ties.[621] But it has gone beyond these rather traditional forms of restitution in human rights law, including measures such as the reforestation of indigenous territory,[622] or the restitution of nationality.[623] Moreover, the IACtHR does not take into account whether the victim can be redressed through other forms of reparation but instead includes the measures of restitution alongside the other reparatory measures.

With respect to the ACtHPR, a development concerning its approach to restitution can be observed in recent times.[624] Between 2015 and 2018, it generally avoided ordering restitution measures, especially in fair trial violations where the retrial or the release of the victims was requested. It argued that it could only order such measures under special and/or compelling circumstances and that the circumstances of these cases did not meet that threshold.[625] This argument was sustained in a consider-

614 See among others ECtHR, *Assanidze vs. Georgia* (2004); *Fatullayev vs Azerbaijan* (2010); *del Rio Prada vs. Spain* (2013).

615 ECtHR, *Ilic vs. Serbia* (2007), operative para. 3; *Kostic vs. Serbia* (2008), operative para. 3; *Pelipenko vs. Russia* (2014), operative para. 1.

616 ECtHR, *Gluhaković vs. Croatia* (2011), operative para. 3.

617 ECtHR, *Oleksandr Volkov vs. Ukraine* (2013), operative para. 9.

618 IACtHR, *Loayza Tamayo vs. Peru* (1998).

619 For example in IACtHR, *Loayza Tamayo vs. Peru* (1998); *Baena Ricardo vs. Panama* (2001).

620 For example, IACtHR, *Tibi vs. Ecuador* (2004); *Awas Tingi vs. Nicaragua* (2001); *Saramaka vs. Suriname* (2007).

621 IACtHR, *Fornerón vs. Argentina* (2012).

622 IACtHR, *Kichwa de Sarayaku vs. Ecuador* (2012).

623 IACtHR, *Ivcher Bronstein vs. Peru* (2001).

624 See on this particular issue, Misha Ariana Plagis, "The Makings of Remedies: The (R)Evolution of the African Court on Human and Peoples' Rights' Remedies Regime in Fair Trial Cases", *African Journal of International and Comparative Law* 28, 2020, pp. 45-71.

625 See for example ACtHPR, *Alex Thomas vs. Tanzania* (2015), para. 157.

able number of fair trial-related judgments against Tanzania,[626] with the ACtHPR stating that "it is not an appeal court to quash or reverse the decision of domestic courts".[627] This represented an important difference to the approach taken by the IACtHR, where restitution measures are the most usual consequence of fair trial violations. This position was therefore criticised in the literature,[628] as well as by ACtHPR's judges in separate opinions.[629]

The ACtHPR approach towards restitution started to change in late 2018 when it found in a case that the most appropriate reparation would be the retrial of the applicant,[630] and in another one that the circumstances of a fair trial violation were sufficiently serious and compelling to order the release of the victim.[631] Thereafter, orders to release or retry prisoners have become more common, although they are still far from becoming the standard practice for fair trial violations.[632] Recently, the ACtHPR has even

626 ACtHPR, *Mohamed Abubakari vs. Tanzania* (2016); *Christopher Jonas vs. Tanzania* (2017); *Kijiji Isiaga vs. Tanzania* (2018); *Thobias Mango vs. Tanzania* (2018); *Amir Ramadhani vs. Tanzania* (2018); *Anaclet Paulo vs. Tanzania* (2018); *Minani Evarist v. Tanzania* (2018); and *Armand Guehi vs. Tanzania* (2018).

627 ACtHPR, *Kijiji Isiaga vs. Tanzania* (2018), para 95. See also ACtHPR, *Ernest Francis Mtingwi vs. Malawi* (2013), paras. 14 and 15. The ACtHPR not only rejected to order the annulment of judicial decisions, but even of administrative ones. For example, it argued in a case that that it "does not have the power to rule on the requests made by the Applicant in paragraph 122 to annul the decision of the Respondent State to expel him" (ACtHPR, *Anudo Ochieng Anudo vs. Tanzania* (2018), para. 127).

628 See for example Ally Possi, "It is better that ten guilty persons escape than that one innocent suffer: the African Court on Human and Peoples' Rights and fair trial rights in Tanzania", *African Human Rights Yearbook* 1, 2017, p. 334, arguing that "the Court should not shy away from ordering concrete remedial measures such as the release of the applicant, whenever the respondent state is found to have violated some fundamental fair trial norms".

629 For example, two judges submitted dissenting opinions in the case of *Alex Thomas*, stating that they "cannot find a more 'specific and/or compelling' [reason] than that the Applicant has been in prison for about 20 years out of a 30-year prison term (...) Our view is therefore that, there is no other remedy in the circumstance other than, that the Applicant be released" (ACtHPR, *Alex Thomas v. Tanzania* (2015), Dissenting Opinion by Elsie Nwanwuri Thompson and Rafaâ Ben Achour, paras. 6-8).

630 ACtHPR, *Diocles William v. Tanzania* (2018), operative para. xi.

631 ACtHPR, *Mgosi Mwita Makungu v. Tanzania* (2018), para. 85.

632 This development in the field of restitution has been even labeled as a "(r)evolution of the remedies regime of the [ACtHPR] for violations of the right to a fair trial" (Plagis, *AJICL* 2020, p. 45). However, most judgments issued in the last few years concerned violations of the right to free legal assistance in Tanzania, and besides

stated that it "has the power to order the annulment of [a presidential] election if it deems this measure appropriate to remedy the violation found".[633] It can thus be observed that the ACtHPR's remedial jurisprudence is still in development with respect to restitution, while that of the other two human rights courts is more consolidated.

b) Compensation

As restitution is often no longer possible after a human rights violation, compensation is the remedial category mostly applied by regional human rights courts. This is also the only category explicitly mentioned in the respective human rights treaty provisions on remedies.[634] Compensation is ordered in most judgments in which the ECtHR finds a violation, as well as in almost every judgment of the IACtHR and the ACtHPR. In the latter case, an evolution of compensatory measures similar to that on restitution can be observed, as before 2018 the victims of fair trial violations were usually not afforded such measures, while since then it has become almost a standard practice for these violations.[635]

The UN Basic Principles state that compensation should be provided "for any economically assessable damage".[636] Thus, it usually comprises both material and non-material damages, covering both direct and indirect victims, but without a punitive character. Material damages usually cover direct losses and loss of profits, while non-material damages include moral damage and in the case of the IACtHR also losses for what this Court has defined as a 'harm to the project of life', i.e., to "the options that an individual may have for leading his life and achieving the goal that he sets for himself".[637] In sum, it can be observed that measures of compensation

some scarce exceptions the requests to release the victims were dismissed by the ACtHPR.

633 ACtHPR, *XYZ vs Benin (I)* (2020), para. 30.

634 See above section I.3 of this chapter.

635 Plagis, *AJICL* 2020, pp. 60-62.

636 Basic Principles, para. 20. This includes "(*a*) Physical or mental harm; (*b*) Lost opportunities, including employment, education and social benefits; (*c*) Material damages and loss of earnings, including loss of earning potential; (*d*) Moral damage; [and] (*e*) Costs required for legal or expert assistance, medicine and medical services, and psychological and social services".

637 IACtHR, *Loayza Tamayo vs. Peru* (1998), para. paras. 147-153. See also *Las Dos Erres vs. Guatemala* (2009); *Furlan vs. Argentina* (2012).

are much more common in human rights adjudication than in general international adjudication. This is also because monetary payments can make more of a difference for individual victims than for states. In order to make a difference for states, such compensatory measures would need to acquire massive proportions, which in turn can become problematic for the state that is ordered to pay them.[638]

c) Satisfaction

Satisfaction is also a particularly important remedial category with respect to human rights violations. In this regard, it can be observed that the IACtHR has made extensive use of these remedial measures, while in the case law of the other two regional courts, such instances are much rarer.[639] In general international law, satisfaction consists mainly of public apologies and acknowledgement of responsibility, although the ICJ has ordered them only in the form of declaratory judgments.[640] By contrast, human rights courts have gone beyond this traditional understanding of satisfaction.[641] For example, the IACtHR has put the focus on symbolic measures,[642] including not only apologies and acknowledgements of responsibility,[643] but also the building of monuments or public spaces in the victims' honour, or the naming of streets, schools or scholarships after them.[644] Another typical

638 See for example the problems concerning compliance with ECtHR, *Georgia vs. Russia (No. I)*, Just Satisfaction (2019), where the payment of ten million € was ordered in the form of just satisfaction.

639 See Sicilianos, *NQHR* 2014, pp. 254-255, stating that measures of restitution and guarantees of non-repetition are "well known in the European system", while those of satisfaction and rehabilitation "are rather rare".

640 See Chapter 2 of this book.

641 Moreover, in general international law the measures of satisfaction are usually only issued when restitution and compensation are not available, while in the case of human rights courts these measures are mostly complementary to the other forms of reparation.

642 As pointed by Cavallaro and Brewer, *AJIL* 2008, p. 821, "[t]he Court's issuance of symbolic reparations is a positive step insofar as it signals an awareness that its judgments will have greater impact when they receive public attention within a Country".

643 Among many other cases, see for example IACtHR, *Barrios Altos vs. Peru* (2001), *Plan de Sanchez vs. Guatemala* (2004), *La Cantuta vs. Peru* (2006).

644 As for example in IACtHR, *Mapiripán vs. Colombia* (2005) (building a monument), *Myrna Mack Chang vs. Guatemala* (2003) (naming a street); or *Molina Theissen vs. Guatemala* (2004) (naming a school).

form of satisfaction in the case law of the IACtHR is the search and delivery of the victims' remains, especially in cases of enforced disappearances or extrajudicial executions.[645]

The investigation of the facts and punishment of those responsible is also usually considered a measure of satisfaction that has great importance for human rights violations. This is also a remedy which is included quite often in the IACtHR's case law,[646] as it is closely related to the right to truth, a concept that this Court has developed and given important weight to.[647] The frequent use of these remedial measures in human rights adjudication additionally reflects the fact that domestic authorities are frequently unwilling or unable to carry out such investigations and prosecutions in the first place.[648] The ECtHR and the ACtHPR have also exceptionally ordered the investigation into human rights violations,[649] but further measures of satisfaction, such as the aforementioned symbolic measures, are absent from the jurisprudence of these two courts.[650] Besides that, all three human rights courts occasionally state that a judgment constitutes in itself a form of satisfaction, similarly to the ICJ,[651] and both the IACtHR and the ACtHPR also order in most cases the publication and circulation of the judgment or parts of it. In sum, measures of satisfaction are playing a more prominent role in the field of human rights than in general international law, although important differences between the practice of the IACtHR and that of the other two courts can be observed. While the former includes a wide array of satisfaction measures, the latter two limit them mostly to investigations into human rights violations and the publication of judgments.

---

645 Among many others in IACtHR, *Las Dos Erres vs. Guatemala* (2009), *Bámaca Velazquez vs. Guatemala* (2002).

646 For a list of cases, see Novak, *Recueil des Cours* 2017, pp. 110-113.

647 See Eduardo Ferrer Mac-Gregor, "The Right to the Truth as an Autonomous Right under the Inter-American Human Rights System", *Mexican Law Review* 9(1), pp. 121-139.

648 See Cornejo, *I•CON* 2017, pp. 390-391.

649 ECtHR, *Nihayet Arici vs. Turkey* (2012), operative para. 6; *Gasangusenov vs. Russia* (2021), operative para. 7; ACtHPR, *Ernest Zongo vs. Burkina Faso* (2015), para. 111 (x).

650 An exception in this regard are symbolic monetary awards (see Ichim, *Just Satisfaction*, 2014, pp. 141-144).

651 Actually, the IACtHR does so in every case in which it finds a violation, while the ACtHPR states this in most of its judgments and the ECtHR rather exceptionally.

d) Rehabilitation

Rehabilitation is a distinctive remedial category of human rights law. The UN Basic Principles are rather vague on this remedy, mentioning only that it "should include medical and psychological care as well as legal and social services".[652] Some authors have also considered scholarships and other measures of educational support as forms of rehabilitation.[653] Perhaps surprisingly, as one could think about rehabilitation as the cornerstone of a victim-oriented remedial approach, this is the remedial category less used by human rights courts.

The IACtHR is again the only regional human rights court that includes measures of rehabilitation consistently.[654] This usually comprises medical and psychological treatment for victims and their families, in accordance with their specific situation and needs. By contrast, the ECtHR includes measures of rehabilitation only very rarely in cases related to persons with disabilities held in detention,[655] while the ACtHPR has ordered them so far only in one judgment.[656] This scarcity of rehabilitation measures could be related to the fact that judgments of human rights courts are issued many years after the violation, with medical treatment being usually no longer necessary. The costs of the past treatment are then sometimes included in the measures of compensation. However, this reason is weaker with respect to psychological treatment, as serious human rights violations often produce trauma that requires nearly life-long treatment. Thus, both the ECtHR and the ACtHPR should probably give more weight to this type of remedial measures.

e) Guarantees of Non-Repetition

In human rights law (unlike in general international law), guarantees of non-repetition are not designed to benefit the victim (or the injured state

652 UN Basic Principles, para. 21.

653 See Novak, *Recueil des Cours* 2017, p. 89. Note however that this author does not consider rehabilitation as an independent remedial category but as a form of restitution.

654 See Shelton, 2015, pp. 394-396. For a list of cases in which rehabilitation was ordered, see also Novak, *Recueil des Cours* 2017, pp. 86-87.

655 One of these exceptional cases is ECtHR, *Sławomir Musiał vs. Poland* (2009), operative para. 4 (a).

656 ACtHPR, *Léon Mugesera vs. Rwanda* (2020), para. 177 (xvii).

in the latter case), but rather 'society as a whole'.[657] In this regard, these guarantees aim to solve structural problems that might be subjacent to the specific human rights violations.[658] Guarantees of non-repetition have gained enormous importance in the case law of the IACtHR, as these measures are one of the main elements in the 'transformative dimension' of this Court's jurisprudence.[659] The ACtHPR has also put a particular focus on such guarantees, including them in almost half of its judgments.

The UN Basic Principles mention a lot of different examples under this category,[660] but for the sake of clarity, guarantees of non-repetition can be divided into three main sub-categories: administrative reforms, legislative reforms and training for public officials. In the case law of human rights courts, these guarantees have concerned mostly legislative reforms (which will be examined in detail), but the other two sub-categories have also played an important role. Guarantees of an administrative nature concern mostly the amendment of domestic policies, practices or situations that are contrary to human rights provisions.[661] In the case law of the IACtHR,

657 See generally Schönsteiner, *AUILR* 2011. The ACtHPR has argued in this respect that guarantees of non-repetition are "not intended to repair individual prejudice but to remedy underlying causes of violation", adding however that it will also order such measures "in cases where the violation will not cease or is likely to reoccur [with respect to the same victims]" (See ACtHPR, *Andrew Ambrose @Cheusi vs. Tanzania* (2020), paras. 169-170).

658 Hennebel and Tigroudja, Commentary to the ACHR, 2022, p. 1329 ("the main objective is to remedy structural shortcomings or deficiencies, whether social, political, or legal, which are likely to contribute to the violations observed and which make it impossible to prevent them").

659 See generally Soley in von Bogdandy et al. (eds.), 2017.

660 This includes "(a) Ensuring effective civilian control of military and security forces; (b) Ensuring that all civilian and military proceedings abide by international standards of due process, fairness and impartiality; (c) Strengthening the independence of the judiciary; (d) Protecting persons in the legal, medical and health-care professions, the media and other related professions, and human rights defenders; (e) Providing, on a priority and continued basis, human rights and international humanitarian law education to all sectors of society and training for law enforcement officials as well as military and security forces; (f) Promoting the observance of codes of conduct and ethical norms, in particular international standards, by public servants, including law enforcement, correctional, media, medical, psychological, social service and military personnel, as well as by economic enterprises; (g) Promoting mechanisms for preventing and monitoring social conflicts and their resolution; and (h) Reviewing and reforming laws contributing to or allowing gross violations of international human rights law and serious violations of international humanitarian law" (UN Basic Principles, para. 23).

661 Novak, *Recueil des Cours* 2017, p. 172.

this has affected *inter alia* the improvement of detention centres,[662] or that of structural conditions in indigenous communities,[663] as well as the implementation of policies for the protection of women or human rights defenders.[664] The ECtHR and the ACtHPR have also exceptionally ordered the reform of administrative practices or the establishment of compensation schemes.[665] The education and training of public officials, on the other hand, has been only ordered by the IACtHR. These educational measures are mostly issued for public officials of a specific state institution, "such as armed forces, police, judges and prosecutors, medical personnel, penitentiary officials, among others".[666]

III. Legislative Remedies in the Case Law of Human Rights Courts

At present, each regional human rights system has reached a point in which the respective court has developed a rather consistent practice of ordering states to reform their domestic laws under certain circumstances. This is especially true in the case of the IACtHR, where ninety-nine judgments with legislative remedies can be found until the end of 2022. This represents as much as 32% of the IACtHR's judgments on reparations. The first judgment of the IACtHR with legislative remedies is *Loayza Tamayo vs. Peru* (1998). This case related to a civilian woman condemned by military courts without the possibility of appealing to ordinary justice. The domestic laws that allowed for this conviction had already been declared incompatible with the ACHR in the judgment on the merits, as they foresaw a military trial for everyone accused of treason or terrorism.[667] In the judgment on reparations, the Court ordered Peru to "adapt Decree-Laws 25,475 (Crime

662 IACtHR, *Lori Berenson vs. Peru* (2004), *Pacheco Teruel vs. Honduras* (2012).

663 This affects issues such as the lack of water or food supplies, or the access to health or education. See IACtHR, *Aloeboetoe vs. Suriname* (1993), *Yakye Axa vs. Paraguay* (2005); *Plan de Sanchez vs. Guatemala* (2004).

664 On the former, see for example IACtHR, *Cotton Field vs. Mexico* (2009). Concerning the latter, see for example IACtHR, *Luna Lopez vs. Honduras* (2013).

665 Such as in ECtHR, *Kuric and others vs. Slovenia* (2012), operative para. 9 ("Dit, à l'unanimité, que l'Etat défendeur doit (...) mettre en place un système d'indemnisation ad hoc au niveau interne"). See also ECtHR, *M.C. vs. Italy* (2013), operative para. 11. With respect to the ACtHPR, see for example *Suy Bi Gohore Emile vs. Côte d'Ivoire* (2020), ordering the state to ensure the organisation of elections to the Electoral Bureau at the local level.

666 Novak, *Recueil des Cours* 2017, p. 157.

667 See in this respect Chapter 4 of this book.

of Terrorism) and 25,659 (Crime of Treason) to conform to the American Convention on Human Rights".[668] Thereafter, the reforms of domestic laws became a rather common remedy in the Inter-American jurisprudence, particularly since 2001.[669] These have concerned a wide variety of issues, some of which have represented important developments in international human rights law.[670]

In the case of the ECtHR, this number is considerably lower but nevertheless significant. Between its first judgment with legislative remedies in 2004 and the end of 2022, this Court has ordered legislative measures in thirty-four judgments. Although this number points to a certain consistency in its practice and is higher than in the case of the ACtHPR, the exceptional nature of this remedial practice can be clearly observed when comparing it percentage-wise. While in the case of both the IACtHR and the ACtHPR legislative remedies are included in approximately one-third of the respective courts' final judgments on reparations, this is done in less than one per cent of those of the ECtHR. As mentioned before, the first judgment with legislative remedies before the ECtHR was its first pilot judgment, *Broniowski vs. Poland* (2004). Legislative remedies are, in fact, mostly included in the context of the pilot judgment procedure.[671] However, it is important to note that not all legislative remedies are issued in pilot judgments and that not all pilot judgments contain legislative remedies or even deal with domestic laws.[672] Legislative measures are mostly included by the ECtHR in cases related to property rights, inhuman conditions of

668 IACtHR, *Loayza Tamayo v. Peru* (1998), operative para. 5.

669 While until 2001 this remedy had been ordered only in the case of *Loayza Tamayo*, in that year the IACtHR included legislative measures in six judgments, thus consolidating this practice.

670 This includes for example the measures concerning the abrogation of amnesty laws, or those ordering the amendment of laws in order to recognise indigenous territory. See Chapter 4 of this book.

671 See Markus Fyrnys, "Expanding Competences by Judicial Lawmaking: The Pilot Judgment Procedure of the European Court of Human Rights", *GLJ* 12(5), 2011.

672 In order to apply the pilot judgment procedure, the ECtHR must determine the existence of "a structural or systemic problem". When explaining the difference between these two concepts, some authors have argued that the latter ones stem from "legal deficiencies" or "inadequate legislation", while "[s]tructural problems may involve situations, in which the legal mechanisms seem appropriate, but the problem concerns practice" (Jakub Czepek, "The Application of the Pilot Judgment Procedure and Other Forms of Handling Large-Scale Dysfunctions in the Case Law of the European Court of Human Rights", *International Community Law Review* 20 (2018), pp. 347–373, at pp. 352-353).

detention, and excessive length of domestic judicial proceedings, but the remedies usually concern the accessory violation of the right to an effective domestic remedy.[673]

Finally, in the case law of the ACtHPR, seventeen judgments with legislative remedies can be found until the end of 2022. Despite it being a rather low number, this is mainly due to the scarce total number of judgments issued by the ACtHPR so far.[674] It is a remedy that has become rather common in its jurisprudence, already since its first judgment on the merits in 2013.[675] The African Court has not offered a lengthy legal justification concerning its power to order the reform of domestic laws but it has instead simply assumed this competence from the beginning. Nevertheless, in some instances, this competence was contested by states. Among others, Benin submitted an objection arguing that the ACtHPR "lacks jurisdiction to assess national laws conformity in accordance with international conventions", adding that "once the Constitutional Court rules that a provision is in conformity with the Constitution, it cannot be challenged on the basis that it results in human rights violations".[676] Such objections have been consistently rejected by the Court, with the argument that Art. 3(1) of the Protocol allows it to determine the occurrence of human rights violations "including where such violations result from the application of a national law", noting in addition "that international conventions take precedence over domestic laws".[677] This section will briefly explore some general issues concerning these remedial measures, including the particular case of legislative remedies before the ECtHR, the role of human rights courts as positive or negative legislators and the function that these remedies have in human rights adjudication.

673 See generally Chapter 4 of this book.

674 However, the total number of judgments issued by the ACtHPR has been exponentially growing during the last years. While in the period of 2013-2018 it issued an average of 2,4 judgments with reparations annually, in the period of 2018-2022 this number augmented to 13 of such judgments annually on average.

675 ACtHPR, *Tanganyika Law Society and Legal and Human Rights Centre vs. Tanzania* (2013).

676 ACtHPR, *Houngue Eric Noudehouenou vs. Benin* (2020), para. 21.

677 ACtHPR, *Ajavon vs. Benin* (2020), para. 49.

1. The Special Case of Legislative Remedies before the ECtHR

As mentioned in the introduction of this book, the need for legislative action after a judgment of the ECtHR is not as straightforward as in the case of the other two regional courts, due to the role of the CoM. When supervising compliance with the ECtHR's judgments, the latter body can request additional measures besides those expressly ordered in the operative part of the judgment. This is however also highly dependent on the findings and recommendations of the court. Thus, regarding the judgments of the ECtHR and the need for legislative action, there are three possible scenarios.

In the first scenario, the judgment completely avoids discussing the necessity of a legislative reform. This is the most common situation, as the ECtHR generally abstains from indicating the consequences of a violation. In this scenario, it is rather exceptional that the CoM requires such a reform in order to close the case. Nevertheless, the state can still engage in a legislative reform *motu propio* after the judgment, for various reasons.[678] This can be done directly by legislative authorities,[679] but most commonly it is the higher courts of states that step in and take the ECtHR jurisprudence into account in order to quash legislation.[680]

678 See for example Polakiewicz, "International Law and Domestic (Municipal) Law", in *MPEPIL*, para. 37 ("Numerous judgments by the ECtHR have prompted or accelerated legislative or administrative reforms in the respondent and sometimes even in third States"). A typical motive in this respect is the avoidance of future condemnations, as highlighted by Ichim, *Just Satisfaction*, 2014, p. 35 ("Compared with its Inter-American counterpart, the [European] Court exerts significantly less leverage as to the modification of internal legislation, though one has to admit that it has an indirect influence, coupled with a rational interest of the state in preventing future condemnations").

679 See Alice Donald, "Parliaments as Compliance Partners in the European Convention on Human Rights System", in Saul, Follesdal and Ulfstein (eds.), *The International Human Rights Judiciary and National Parliaments*, Cambridge: CUP, 2017, pp. 75 – 109.

680 See generally on the role of domestic judges in the implementation of ECtHR judgments Raffaela Kunz, *Richter über internationale Gerichte? Die Rolle innerstaatlicher Gerichte bei der Umsetzung der Entscheidungen von EGMR und IAGMR*, Heidelberg: Springer, 2020. The ECtHR actually expects such intervention by domestic courts, indicates Amrei Müller, "Domestic authorities' obligations to co-develop the rights under the European Convention on Human Righs", *International Journal of Human Rights* 20(8), 2016, pp. 1058-1076, at p. 1064.

A comparative analysis of this practice in different states can be found in an edited volume by Keller and Stone Sweet.[681] They find that states "have developed procedures designed to provide legislative authorities with information and counsel on the relevance of the ECHR", including parliamentary committees and advisors that examine the conventionality of domestic laws taking into account the Court's jurisprudence.[682] More recently, Kunz showed several examples of domestic courts that "disapply or even quash laws that have been declared by the human rights courts to violate the conventions", mentioning examples of Switzerland and Germany, among others.[683] Moreover, she highlights that domestic courts do not only take into account judgments against their own states but also against other states, "in order to preventively bring the legal order in accordance with the convention standards".[684]

The second scenario takes place when the ECtHR recommends a legislative reform (with different degrees of intensity) in the reasoning of the judgment. This is done mostly in the so-called 'Article 46 judgments', which include a section under that provision that suggests the appropriate remedial measures. The Court introduces such sections with a common formula, whereby a judgment

> "*imposes on the respondent State the legal obligation not just to pay those concerned the sums awarded by way of just satisfaction pursuant to Article 41 of the Convention but also to choose, subject to supervision by the Committee of Ministers, the general and/or, if necessary, individual measures which it considers appropriate to incorporate into domestic law in order to put an end to the violation found by the Court and to redress as far as possible the effects*".[685]

In 'Article 46 judgments', this general rule is followed by an exception, indicating that "[h]owever, in certain special circumstances the Court has found it useful to indicate to a respondent State the type of measures that might be taken to put an end to the situation which has given rise to

681 Helen Keller and Alec Stone Sweet (eds.), *A Europe of Rights: The Impact of the ECHR on National Legal Systems*, Oxford: OUP, 2008.

682 Helen Keller and Alec Stone Sweet, "Assessing the Impact of the ECHR on National Legal Systems", in Keller and Stone Sweet (eds.), 2008, pp. 686-687.

683 Raffaela Kunz, "Judging International Judgments Anew? The Human Rights Courts before Domestic Courts", *EJIL* 30(4), 2019, pp. 1129–1163, at pp. 1139 – 1142.

684 Kunz, *EJIL* 2019, p. 1140.

685 As for example in ECtHR, *Ooo Informatsionnoye Agentstvo Tambov-Inform vs. Russia* (2021), para. 124.

the finding of a violation".[686] Afterwards, the recommended measure is specified. Sometimes this is done in a very broad way, stating for example that "[i]t will be for the respondent State to implement (...) such measures as it considers appropriate to secure the rights of the applicants and other persons in their position".[687] In other judgments the suggested measure is more concrete, specifying for example the legal effect that it should produce.[688] Legislative measures have played a prominent role in these judgments. Although the ECtHR usually leaves the door open to accepting other kinds of measures instead of legislative ones,[689] it is not uncommon to find judgments that are very specific as to the legislative nature of the measures recommended.[690] Some 'Article 46 judgments' also indicate the expected outcome of the legislative reform[691] or identify the concrete provisions to be amended.[692] The ECtHR has even recommended constitutional reforms in the context of 'Article 46 judgments'.[693]

686 ECtHR, *Ooo Informatsionnoye Agentstvo Tambov-Inform vs. Russia* (2021), para. 125; *Guðmundur Andri Ástráðsson v. Iceland* (2020), para. 312.

687 ECtHR, *Shlykov and others vs. Russia* (2021), para. 110.

688 See for example ECtHR, *Grabowski vs. Poland* (2015), para. 68 ("the respondent State should undertake legislative or other appropriate measures with a view to eliminating the practice which developed under section 27 of the Juvenile Act (...) and ensuring that each and every period of the deprivation of liberty of a juvenile is authorised by a specific judicial decision").

689 See for example ECtHR, *Ooo Informatsionnoye Agentstvo Tambov-Inform vs. Russia* (2021), para. 128, where the ECtHR is requesting the implementation of "appropriate legislative or jurisprudential measures (...)". In other cases, legislative measures are "preferable" but not indispensable. See in this respect ECtHR, *László Magyar vs. Hungary* (2014), para. 71; *Harackchiev and Tolumov vs. Bulgaria* (2014), para. 280.

690 See for example ECtHR, *Oleksandr Volkov vs. Ukraine* (2013), para. 200 ("These measures should include legislative reforms involving the restructuring of the institutional basis of the system"); *Katz vs. Romania* (2009), para 35 ("La Cour estime que l'Etat devrait, avant tout, prendre les measures législatives nécessaires"). See also ECtHR, *Hasan and Eylem Zengin vs. Turkey* (2007), para. 84; *Chanyev v. Ukraine* (2014), para. 35.

691 For example, in the case of *Kuzmina and others vs. Russia* (2021), para. 120, the ECtHR stated that "the Russian legal framework pertaining to the conduct of operational-search activities must be amended so as to provide for a clear and foreseeable procedure for authorisation of undercover operations, such as test purchases and operational experiments, by a judicial body providing effective guarantees against abuse". Similarly, in ECtHR, *M. and others vs. Bulgaria* (2011), para. 138.

692 See ECtHR, *Atiman vs. Turkey* (2014), para. 47 ("To that end, the Court considers that section 39 of the Regulation on the Powers and Duties of the Gendarmeries should be amended").

693 ECtHR, *Zornić vs. Bosnia and Herzegovina* (2014), para. 43; *Anchugov and Gladkov vs. Russia* (2013), para. 111.

It is, however, rather unclear whether such indications in the argumentative part of judgments are binding for states or not.[694] Formally, the operative paragraphs of the judgments are the sole part which is mandatory to implement.[695] However, some authors – and judges – have considered that when the ECtHR uses mandatory language in its reasoning, the measure spelled out this way has a binding nature.[696] In any case, the last word on the necessity to implement such measures lies again in the hands of the CoM. Although these judgments' indications form the basis of the execution process and thus limit the freedom of the state in this regard,[697] there is still room for negotiation within the CoM.[698]

This is not the case when judgments include such statements in its operative part, thus leaving no alternative for states other than implementing them.[699] In this respect, Donald and Speck, after conducting a series of interviews, highlight that a "former senior Court official ventured that

694 See for example Donald and Speck, *HRLR* 2019, p. 3, acknowledging "that the distinction between recommendatory and prescriptive judgments is contestable in view of judicial disagreement as to the precise legal effect of indicating remedial measures in the operative part as opposed to the main body of a judgment". See also Keller and Marti, *EJIL* 2016, at p. 832, recommending "to distinguish more clearly between recommendations and consequential orders and to always include the latter in the operative part of judgments".

695 See Helfer, *EJIL* 2008, p. 147 ("The remedies that the Court indicates are legally binding when they are phrased in mandatory language and appear in the operative part of the judgment").

696 Sicilianos for example argues that these Art. 46 indications range from mere recommendations to real injunctions, suggesting that this depends on the concrete wording used by the ECtHR. See Sicilianos, *NQHR* 2014, pp. 244 et seq. As to the judges, see the dissenting opinion of Judge Pinto de Albuquerque *et al.* in ECtHR, *Moreira Ferreira vs. Portugal (No. 2)* (2017), para. 17 ("The reopening clause is a key means for the execution of the Court's judgments whose legal force does not depend on whether it is inserted in the reasoning or the operative part of the judgment").

697 See Sicilianos, *NQHR* 2014, p. 245 ("Although such expressions, contained in the corpus of the judgment and not in the operative part, do not seem to create, as such, legal obligations *stricto sensu*, they denote the intention of the Court to strongly urge the respondent State to take the appropriate measures and the Committee of Ministers to exercise its supervisory function under Article 46, para. 2 in order to ensure the desirable result").

698 See Kjetil Mujezinović Larsen, "Compliance with Judgments from the European Court of Human Rights: The Court's Call for Legislative Reforms", *NJHR* 31(4), 2013, pp. 496–512.

699 This is shown for example in the provisions regulating the pilot judgment procedure, establishing that the type of remedial measures that the concerned state is required to take will be identified "by virtue of the operative provisions of the judgment" (ECtHR, Rules of the Court, Rule 61, para. 3).

where indications are in the operative part: '[T]he Committee of Ministers will feel that there is nothing to discuss. The Court has ordered it, and that's that'".[700] In sum, even though the implementation of ECtHR's recommendations to reform domestic laws in 'Article 46 judgments' will generally be requested in order to close the supervision proceedings, there is no certainty of it, as this is not always the case.

Thus, the third and most relevant scenario relates to the cases in which the Court expressly orders the reform of domestic laws, including this requirement in the operative paragraphs of the judgments. These are highly exceptional cases, but those are at the same time the only cases in which the CoM will with no doubt require the state to carry out such reforms to close the case. Nevertheless, it is also important to note in this regard that these general measures included in the operative provisions are generally rather vague as to their legislative nature.[701] The ECtHR usually avoids being too specific in these binding provisions.[702] Instead, most of them are worded in rather broad terms, and the need for legislative reforms is identified by reading the operative paragraph in conjunction with the relevant paragraphs of the judgment's reasoning. For example, in one of its first judgments with legislative remedies, the ECtHR ordered Poland to adopt "appropriate legal and/or other measures [to] secure in its domestic legal order a mechanism maintaining a fair balance between the interests

700 Donald and Speck, *HRLR* 2019, p. 23. See also Ichim, *Just Satisfaction,* 2014, pp. 219-220 ("Given that the operative provisions are binding, the state may not contest them").

701 See Lize Glas, "The Functioning of the Pilot-Judgment Procedure of the European Court of Human Rights in Practice", *NQHR* 34(1), 2016, pp. 41-70, at p. 52, noting that "the description of the measures in the operative provisions remains general; the Court does not specify which measure the State must take". For some exceptions in which the legislative nature of the remedial measures was clearly spelled out, see ECtHR, *Tunikova vs. Russia* (2021), operative para. 8 ("the respondent State must introduce, without further delay, amendments to the domestic legal and regulatory framework"); *Greens and MT vs. UK* (2010), operative para 6, establishing the obligation to "bring forward, (...) legislative proposals intended to amend the 1983 Act and, if appropriate, the 2002 Act" and to "enact the required legislation". See also ECtHR, *Grudić v. Serbia* (2012), operative para. 3, ordering the state to "implement the relevant laws in order to secure payment of the pensions and arrears in question".

702 See Ichim, *Just Satisfaction*, 2014, p. 216 ("The problem with the general measures is that they are not precise. Unlike individual measures, the Court does not indicate a course of action, but leaves the choice to the breaching state"). See on remedial specificity Chapter 5 of this book.

of landlords and the general interest of the community".[703] This statement could be seen as allowing the state to adopt non-legislative measures to solve the problem. However, when analysing the reasoning of this judgment, one can see that the ECtHR specifies that the systemic problem at stake is "the malfunctioning of Polish housing legislation".[704] As observed by Sadurski with respect to this judgment, "no amount of good will and tinkering by law-enforcers could improve the situation as long as the law remains in force".[705]

In most cases, these legislative measures are linked to a violation of Art. 13 ECHR, and prescribe the introduction of domestic remedies for specific human rights violations.[706] The idea behind this right is to provide individuals with a way of obtaining redress at the domestic level, without having to initiate a procedure before the ECtHR.[707] Until the late 2000s, this provision was considered "dormant",[708] or even "obscure".[709] However, its scope and relevance were progressively expanded due to the docket crisis of the ECtHR and its increased focus on subsidiarity.[710]

---

703 ECtHR, *Hutten Czapska vs. Poland* (2006), operative para. 4.

704 ECtHR, *Hutten Czapska vs. Poland* (2006), para. 237.

705 Sadurski, *HRLR* 2009, at p. 425. Moreover, one of the main arguments of Judge Zagrebelsky when dissenting to this measure was that, by ordering legislative remedies, the ECtHR "is entering territory belonging specifically to the realm of politics and that its indications go beyond its jurisdictional competence" (ECtHR, *Hutten Czapska vs. Poland* (2006), Dissenting Opinion of Judge Zagrebelsky).

706 Article 13 ECHR establishes that "[e]veryone whose rights and freedoms as set forth in [the] Convention are violated shall have an effective remedy before a national authority notwithstanding that the violation has been committed by persons acting in an official capacity". It is important to note that in this case the concept of domestic remedies is used in its procedural understanding, contrary to the way it is generally used along this book, which refers to its substantive understanding. See above section I(b) of this Introduction.

707 The weight given to the right to an effective remedy by the ECtHR reflects the great importance of the principle of subsidiarity in the European system of human rights protection, giving priority to the domestic level and limiting the ECtHR's interventions to those cases in which the domestic remedy was not available or ineffective. See Costas Paraskeva, "Returning the Protection of Human Rights to Where They Belong, At Home", *International Journal of Human Rights* 12(3), 2008, pp. 415-448.

708 Keller and Stone Sweet, in Keller and Stone Sweet (eds.), 2008, p. 708.

709 Helfer, *EJIL* 2008, p. 144.

710 See generally Michael Reiertsen, *Effective Domestic Remedies and the European Court of Human Rights: Applications of the European Convention on Human Rights Article 13*, Cambridge: CUP, 2022.

Several elements point to the legislative nature of measures ordering the introduction of domestic remedies. First, according to the ECtHR, such domestic remedies cannot depend on the goodwill of the state or other practical arrangements but instead need to be positively laid down and regulated in the domestic legal order. This is shown in several cases dealing with expulsion orders, in which the remedies against such orders had no automatic suspensive effect. States argued that it was sufficient for remedies to have a suspensive effect "in practice", as the domestic courts decided in almost every case to stay the deportation procedure.[711] However, the ECtHR considered that this arrangement failed to comply with Art. 13, as there was no guarantee that the authorities would comply with that practice in every case.[712] The Court stated that, in accordance with the rule of law, "the requirements of Article 13 (...) take the form of a guarantee and not of a mere statement of intent or a practical arrangement".[713]

Similarly, the ECtHR often states that the remedy shall be set up "in the national legal system",[714] and it would be difficult to imagine a domestic remedy sufficiently regulated and effective that is established only through judicial practice. This can be seen in a case related to the excessive length of judicial proceedings in Bulgaria, where the State argued that domestic judges already took into account the excessive length of criminal proceedings when sentencing. The ECtHR did not consider this to be an effective remedy because "that practice is not based on express statutory language".[715] Moreover, in several of these cases, the Court expressly determined that the structural problem "resulted from inadequate legislation",[716] that violations of Art. 13 ECHR would "require clear and specific changes in the domestic legal system",[717] or even that it would be "highly unlikely (...) that such an effective remedy can be set up without changing the domestic legislation on certain specific points".[718] Thus, as can be observed, legislative incorporation is a necessary element of an effective domestic remedy.

---

711 See for example ECtHR, *A.C. vs. Spain* (2014), para. 95; *Allanazarova v. Russia* (2017), para. 97.

712 See for example ECtHR, *Singh vs. Belgium* (2014), para. 97.

713 ECtHR, *Čonka v. Belgium* (2002), para. 83; *Gebremedhin [Gaberamadhien] vs. France* (2007), para. 66.

714 See for example ECtHR, *Gazsó vs Hungary* (2015), para. 39.

715 ECtHR, *Dimitrov and Hamanov vs. Bulgaria* (2011), para. 118.

716 ECtHR, *Lukenda vs. Slovenia* (2005), para. 93.

717 ECtHR, *Ananyev vs. Russia* (2009), para. 212.

718 ECtHR, *Burdov vs. Russia (No. 2)* (2009), para. 138.

In this context, a progressive prescriptiveness of legislative requirements can be observed before the ECtHR. What the ECtHR usually does is to mention in a first judgment the incompatibility of a law, perhaps wording it with more prescriptive terms or recommending a reform under Art. 46 in subsequent judgments related to the same law, and including it as a legislative remedy in the operative part only if the state is still failing to carry out such a reform.[719] In any case, the ECtHR's measures that will be examined in the following chapters are only those expressly included in the operative provisions of a judgment, although the reasoning will the taken into account in order to establish the legislative nature of these remedies. These are the only cases in which the need for legislative action is formally prescribed and does not depend on the will of the state nor the negotiations taking place before the CoM.

2. Human Rights Courts: Positive or Negative Legislators?

An important question concerning legislative remedies is whether human rights courts more frequently request states to either enact laws or repeal them, i.e., whether they act more as negative or positive legislators in this respect. Novak, referring to the IACtHR, argues that legislative reparations can consist of "(a) the enactment of new legislation; (b) the reform or abrogation of existing law; [and] (c) the non-enactment of new legislation incompatible with the American Convention".[720] However, it becomes apparent that the latter type is extremely rare, as in order for a law to be reviewed after an alleged human rights violation, this law needs to have been enacted in the first place. Even cases of abstract review, where the law does not need to have been applied to the victim of the case, are always dealing with laws in force and not draft laws.[721] On the other hand, it is unconvincing to put legislative reforms and derogations in the same category. Very often the legislative amendments ordered by human rights

719 See Sadurski, *HRLR* 2009, p. 428 ("When the Court has no reason to trust the State that it will get the message after a gentler, more habitual signal from the Court, it will abandon traditional subtleties and display no restraint: it will no longer disguise its condemnation of the legislation in the language of individual violation"). See also Ichim, *Just Satisfaction*, 2014, p. 219.

720 Novak, *Recueil des Cours* 2017, p. 163.

721 Advisory opinions, on the other hand, could concern the review of draft laws. See on both legislative review by human rights courts *in abstracto* and on advisory review of legislation, Chapter 1 of this book.

courts do not imply any sort of repeal. Instead, most legislative reforms ordered by human rights courts are of a positive nature, requiring the inclusion of specific elements in a domestic provision. Thus, it seems easier to divide the legislative remedies along these lines, i.e. those requesting positive legislative reforms on the one hand and those requesting negative reforms on the other.[722]

Looking a bit closer at the legislative remedies issued by human rights courts, one can observe that both the ECtHR and the IACtHR have acted more often as positive than negative legislators. This is most evident in the case law of the ECtHR, where almost all of its legislative measures have concerned the enactment of new laws instead of the amendment or repeal of existing ones. The requirement of introducing an effective domestic remedy is implemented either through the adoption of a new law regulating such a remedy or through the amendment of an existing law in order to add this regulation. Thus, in any case, the introduction of a domestic remedy represents a positive reform of domestic laws.

Positive reforms are also ordered more often by the IACtHR, although the difference between both categories is not as big as in the case of the ECtHR. The IACtHR has very often expressly ordered negative amendments in the form of a repeal of legislative provisions, such as those concerning the mandatory death penalty.[723] Ordering to strike down entire laws is rarer, although this is what was done for example in the case of amnesty laws considered contrary to the Convention.[724] However, in most cases the reforms ordered by this Court are still of a positive nature, mainly requesting the enactment of laws or provisions for the protection of vulnerable groups, or for an increased protection of fair trial rights.

This aspect is different in the case law of the ACtHPR, where negative reforms have played a more prominent role than positive ones. This is due to the fact that this court orders legislative reforms mainly when it finds a domestic provision incompatible with human rights instruments, while the other two courts focus more on legislative gaps that cause violations. For example, in cases with legislative remedies concerning political rights, the ACtHPR always requested to remove specific provisions, such as those

722 There are however a small number of legislative measures that are neutral in this respect, either because they are very vague or because they include elements of both a positive and a negative nature. See in this respect Chapter 5 of this book, with more details.

723 See for example IACtHR, *Raxcacó Reyes vs. Guatemala* (2005).

724 See for example IACtHR, *Barrios Altos vs. Peru* (2001).

prohibiting independent candidates,[725] preventing courts from reviewing an election[726] or restricting the right of association of political parties.[727] This court has also ordered to abrogate provisions of criminal codes that foresaw the mandatory imposition of the death penalty,[728] or defamation laws that contemplated imprisonment for this crime.[729] Positive reforms have also been ordered, but much more scarcely and only rather recently.[730]

In sum, one can clearly see the differences among human rights courts in this regard. While the ECtHR orders almost exclusively positive reforms of legislation and the ACtHPR negative reforms, the IACtHR stands in between, ordering both types of reforms, although slightly more often those of a positive nature.[731] This also represents a difference if compared to legislative remedies in constitutional law, which are usually of a negative nature.[732]

3. Legislative Remedies as Guarantees of Non-Repetition?

Legislative reforms ordered by human rights courts are generally considered to pertain to the category of guarantees of non-repetition. This has been stated by numerous authors, as well as by the courts themselves.[733] It is also true in most of the cases. For example, as mentioned before, one

725 ACtHPR, *Tanganyika Law Society and Legal and Human Rights Centre* vs. *Tanzania* (2013).

726 ACtHPR, *Jebra Kambole vs. Tanzania* (2020).

727 ACtHPR, *Ajavon vs. Benin* (2020).

728 ACtHPR, *Rajabu et al. vs. Tanzania (2019)*; *Amini Juma vs Tanzania* (2021).

729 ACtHPR, *Lohé Issa Konata vs. Burkina Faso* (2016).

730 For example, in 2022 the ACtHPR requested the introduction of laws to secure the right of indigenous communities to be effectively consulted (ACtHPR, *African Commission on Human and Peoples' Rights vs. Kenya* (2022)) and to ensure the higher independence of constitutional courts (ACtHPR, *Oumar Mariko vs. Mali* (2022)).

731 See in this respect Chapter 5 of this book.

732 See however Allan-Randolph Brewer Carías, *Constitutional Courts as Positive Legislators*, Cambridge: CUP, 2011.

733 For example, in the IACtHR's judgments, legislative measures are always included in a section under the heading of guarantees of non-repetition. Concerning literature, see for example Marcela Zúñiga Reyes, "Garantías de no repetición y reformas legislativas", *Revista Derecho del Estado* 46, 2020, pp. 25-55. See also, more generally, Phillip Stöckle, *Guarantees of Non-Repetition: Die Anordnung struktureller Reformen durch den Inter-Amerikanischen Gerichtshof für Menschenrechte*, Berlin: Duncker & Humblot, 2021.

of the main reasons for the ECtHR to order such measures is to create an "effect of preventing recurrence" in order to avoid the Court becoming overloaded with 'repetitive' applications.[734] The victims of human rights violations are moreover generally not the main beneficiaries of such reforms, as the law has already been applied to them and their legal situation has mostly changed due to the time that elapsed between the violation and the judgment.[735] Thus, the main aim of legislative measures is to prevent other potential victims from materialising as such.

This can be clearly seen in the legislative remedies related to the protection of vulnerable groups, where the orders to enact legislation that offers better protection are intended to prevent other members of such groups from becoming victims of a human rights violation. Legislative measures related to fair trial rights, such as those concerning judicial independence or the right to appeal, are similarly aiming to solve a structural problem that can affect several individuals other than the victims of the case. Thereby, if the procedural requirements before domestic courts are not compatible with the respective convention, the number of individuals who can be potential victims of fair trial violations is considerable. Thus, the deterrent effect of legislative remedies figures prominently in certain constellations of cases.[736]

However, there are also some instances in which legislative remedies adopt another function. This is especially the case with some forms of satisfaction. In this respect, when a domestic provision (or the lack of it) is causing a continuous human rights violation for the victim at hand, its reform could be considered a measure of cessation rather than a guarantee of non-repetition.[737] This is for example what occurs with most legislative

734 Ichim, *Just Satisfaction*, 2014, p. 253.

735 With respect to the ECtHR, this is especially the case with reparations related to conditions of detention and excessive length of judicial proceedings, where victims have mostly been transferred to another prison or cell in the former case and obtained a final judgment in the latter. But see on the contrary *Xenides-Arestis vs. Turkey* (2005), operative para. 5, ordering the State to "introduce a remedy which secures genuinely effective redress for the Convention violations identified in the instant judgment *in relation to the present applicant* as well as in respect of all similar applications pending before it" (emphasis added).

736 Actually, the protection of vulnerable groups and fair trial rights are by far the two categories of cases in which human rights courts issue legislative reparations more often. See Chapter 4 of this book.

737 See for example, with respect to the IACtHR, Attanasio, *UPJIL* 2016, pp. 840-849. See also Hennebel and Tigroudja, *Commentary to the ACHR*, 2022, p. 1305.

remedies of the ECtHR, which can be seen not only as guarantees of non-repetition but also as a direct order to cease continuing Art. 13 ECHR violations related to the lack of domestic remedies.[738] Similarly, in the case of the IACtHR, a violation of Art. 2 ACHR comes into play when the domestic legal order is not compatible with the Convention. Thus, the adaptation of domestic laws can be seen both as a cessation of such violations and as a guarantee of non-repetition at the same time.[739] Moreover, in some cases, legislative reforms are necessary to comply with the investigation of human rights violations and prosecution of those responsible, which is another form of satisfaction. This can be seen in the orders to annul amnesty laws that prevent such investigations and prosecutions.

In general, both for the IACtHR and the ACtHPR to order legislative remedies, no structural problems leading to a potential inflow of applications are necessary, in contrast to the ECtHR. Instead, it is sufficient for these courts to note that the violation in the individual case is rooted in a domestic law or the absence thereof. For that reason, they usually make no reference to other potential victims when issuing legislative remedies. Thereby, such remedies can often adopt the function of providing satisfaction, as they are requested by victims and the court focuses exclusively on that request, without taking the risk of a repeating violation into account.[740]

Besides satisfaction and guarantees of non-repetition, legislative remedies can sometimes also be ordered as a way of providing restitution to victims.[741] For example, in cases related to property rights violations where states are obliged to adopt a law allowing victims to claim such properties, this can serve to achieve the aim of restituting them. Such remedies have been issued by the IACtHR with respect to indigenous property rights, and by the ECtHR regarding property rights in the context of transition or state succession.[742] The main aim of such legislative remedies is thus to provide legal certainty as to the implementation of the state's obligation to restitute

738 The ECtHR's legislative measures most commonly order the enactment of domestic remedies after finding a violation of the right to an effective remedy under Art. 13 ECHR, thus clearly aiming at the cessation of this violation.

739 See for example Cornejo, *I•CON* 2017, p. 385, mentioning a case in which a "legislative reform was ordered (...) because the Court considered it to be a means for cessation and non-repetition in view of the background of the case".

740 See in this respect for example Shelton, 2015, p. 397, highlighting that "[t]he line between satisfaction and guarantees of non-repetition is not easy to draw".

741 See Polakiewicz, in *MPEPIL*, para. 37, arguing that measures such as legislative amendments can be regarded from a theoretical point of view "as a measure of *restitutio in integrum*".

742 See Chapter 4 of this book.

these properties, although contrary to other measures of restitution, these extend beyond the concrete victims of the case and include as beneficiary every other person that is affected by such unlawful expropriations.

Similarly, in some exceptional cases, legislative remedies have served the purpose of rehabilitation. This can be most clearly seen in the case of *Vera Rojas vs. Chile* (2021), where the IACtHR requested the continuation of the victim's medical treatment in the event of her parents' deaths or their inability to pay. In order to secure this continuation of the treatment, the IACtHR specified that Chile shall "enact a legal provision to provide legal certainty regarding compliance with this obligation".[743] Thus, it can be observed that legislative remedies can also serve to guarantee long-term compliance with other remedial measures, such as restitution or rehabilitation.

Similar to general international law, the only category of human rights remedies in which legislative reforms do not fit is that of compensation, as this category refers exclusively to monetary payments. On the other hand, legislative remedies in human rights adjudication are probably closer to guarantees of non-repetition than those in general international adjudication, where this category takes in practice more often the form of symbolic assurances of non-recurrence. However, as elucidated above, even in human rights adjudication legislative reforms can often serve purposes additional to that of non-repetition.

Interim Conclusion: The Self-Understanding of International Courts in Light of their Remedial Practice

In sum, it can be concluded that there is a remedial *lex specialis* in human rights law and that legislative remedies form part of it. Although the three human rights courts initially based their remedial practice on the general law of state responsibility, each of them slowly departed from it and nowadays it can be considered that there is an autonomous law of state responsibility for human rights violations. In practice, one of the main differences between remedies in general international adjudication and human rights adjudication lies in the fact that certain categories of remedies, such as satisfaction and guarantees of non-repetition, are rather common in the latter field while they are very rare in the former. For example, under the

743 IACtHR, *Vera Rojas vs. Chile* (2021), para. 165; operative para. 7.

ARSIWA measures of satisfaction are only to be afforded when restitution and compensation measures are unavailable. Instead, in the case law of human rights courts these are rather complementary measures that are included on top of those of restitution and compensation. In addition, measures of rehabilitation pertain exclusively to the field of human rights law. This is closely related to the special functions played by remedies in human rights adjudication, as was explained in this chapter. Moreover, human rights violations are often of such nature that restitution is no longer possible, and thus compensation becomes in practice the primary form of reparation in this area.[744] Thus, the remedial practice of human rights courts clearly shows the special nature of remedies in this field. As a consequence, the specific remedies employed by human rights courts (such as the legislative measures) should arguably not be evaluated through the prism of the general law of state responsibility, but in the context of the human rights law framework.

This chapter also explained how the remedial practice of the three courts originated and evolved, and how it currently differs. Several explanations are offered for this divergence, mainly related to the remedial legal basis included in the respective instruments, and to the historical and political context in which the three courts were created and evolved. Some of these explanations were already laid down by Çalı in an article where she examined the variation in the regional human rights courts' remedial intrusiveness. However, she concludes that another explanation is more convincing, which she calls the "legal culture explanation".[745] In accordance with this explanation, it is the "national legal cultures and shared expectations from these institutions in their regional contexts" that shape their identity and thus also their remedial practice.[746] In this regard, it is true that some constitutional courts of the Global South, such as in the Americas and Africa, have engaged in what is called 'transformative constitutionalism'.[747] This constitutional approach seeks to achieve structural changes through

744 See in this respect Buyse, *ZaöRV* 2008, pp. 137-138.

745 Çalı, *I•CON* 2018, pp. 230-232. The other two explanations refer to the legal design (i.e. the legal basis for ordering remedies) and to the cause-history (the historical context in which the courts have operated). These two explanations were examined along this chapter.

746 Çalı, *I•CON* 2018, p. 230.

747 This term was actually first employed by Klare while referring to the Constitutional Court of South Africa (see Karl E. Klare, "Legal Culture and Transformative Constitutionalism", *South African Journal of Human Rights* 14, 1998, pp. 146-188.), and it has also been used to describe the judicial practice of the Colombian Constitutional

constitutional adjudication, which is not far from the approach taken by the IACtHR and the ACtHPR. Thus, it is likely that these courts are influenced in their remedial practice by the domestic courts of their respective region. With that being said, it is most probably a combination of various factors that have led to the different remedial landscapes and approaches of the three courts.

In general, the remedial practice of courts reveals a lot about how they perceive their own role in their respective regions. In this respect, the ECtHR's main objective is to redress the individual victims that appear before it, while at the same time trying to keep states relatively satisfied with the system and preventing it from collapsing under the number of pending applications. Conversely, the IACtHR has embraced its transformative role and tries to make the most out of each case it decides in terms of achieving structural changes, without worrying too much about the states' attitude or even about compliance with its judgments. Finally, the ACtHPR appears to still be looking for its adequate place in human rights adjudication. On the one hand, it has gone beyond the ECtHR's approach, by often almost disregarding the individual aspects of the victim and focusing only on the general issues that the cases imply. On the other hand, it does usually not go as far as the IACtHR in terms of the creativity and diversity of remedial measures, being especially cautious with respect to measures of satisfaction or the training of public officials.

While the first part of this book analysed the concept of legislative remedies as well as the remedial practice of courts in both the field of general international law and human rights law, the second part will exclusively focus on the legislative measures ordered by regional human rights courts. It will do so through a case law analysis, where a typology of such measures will be established in Chapter 4, the way in which they are spelled out and the remedial deference afforded to domestic legislatures will be examined in Chapter 5 and the consequences of such measures will be explored in Chapter 6. As will be observed throughout the second part, there is a common understanding among human rights courts as to the type of human rights issues that are tackled through legislative remedies, although with different priorities in this respect. Important differences between human rights courts can also be found in terms of the specificity of such

Court (see Manuel Jose Cepeda and David Landau, *Colombian Constitutional Law*, Oxford: OUP, 2017).

measures and the room of manoeuvre left for their implementation, while its consequences are also to some extent system-dependent.

Chapter 4: A Categorisation of Legislative Remedies

The first part of this book examined legislative remedies from a conceptual perspective, situating this concept in the context of the judicial practice of both general international law and human rights law. It was shown that although legislative remedies do not exclusively belong to the field of human rights from a doctrinal perspective, they do so in practice. Even though the ICJ has, in principle, the competence to order such measures, this would prove to be more problematic than in the case of human rights courts, mainly due to the different functions of international adjudication in these two fields. Most likely due to this reason, as well as due to its legal culture as the most 'traditional' international court and the type of disputes it deals with, the ICJ seems rather hesitant to engage in such law-making tasks. On the contrary, all three regional human rights courts have over time adopted and consolidated a remedial practice that includes orders to reform domestic laws. It was therefore concluded that legislative remedies form part of a remedial *lex specialis* in human rights law, which also comprises other particular remedial features. The second part of this book will thus focus on the use of legislative remedies by human rights courts, examining when and how they are applied as well as the consequences of their use.

This chapter will establish a typology of legislative measures issued by human rights courts, categorising them and analysing the differences and commonalities among the three regional courts in this respect. It will thereby inquire into the question of what types of issues these measures intend to tackle. With this aim, the legislative remedies that have been ordered by the three regional human rights courts until the end of 2022 will be examined and divided into ten different categories, whereby several of these categories in turn contain more concrete subcategories. Each of them will be put into context and the remedial practice of each human rights court with respect to them will be explored. Most of these categories include remedial measures issued by the three regional courts, or at least two of them. This already shows that these courts have a rather common understanding regarding the purpose of legislative remedies and the type of contexts in which to apply them. However, the differences are also very important, and throughout this categorisation, it is possible to not only observe the preferences of each court when it comes to issuing legislative remedies but also to see why they have favoured some types of cases over others in this regard.

The first caveat regarding this case law analysis is that the unit of measure is not the judgments as such but the remedial measures. This is because both the IACtHR and the ACtHPR often issue judgments that include several legislative remedies relating to different topics. For example, the judgment of the ACtHPR in the case of *Ajavon vs. Benin* (2020) contains no less than five legislative measures, dealing respectively with electoral rights, fair trial rights, constitutional issues, amnesty laws, and the right to strike. This is different in the case of the ECtHR, where no judgments can be found with more than one legislative measure, due to the highly exceptional nature of these remedies in its case law. In this respect, this case law analysis will examine 193 remedial measures included in 161 judgments. In addition, it is important to note the enormous difference between the number of legislative remedies issued by the IACtHR and that of the other two regional human rights courts. While the IACtHR has issued 129 of these measures until the end of 2022, the ECtHR issued 34 and the ACtHPR only 30 until that date. It, therefore, makes sense to also have an individualised look at the practice of each regional court concerning these remedies in order to see their respective focus. Thus, the first section will categorise the legislative remedies of the three regional courts commonly. The second section will subsequently examine the intensity of the use of these particular categories separately for each court.

I. Common Categories of Legislative Remedies

There are a total of ten categories in which almost all legislative remedies issued by the three regional human rights courts can be included.[748] These are related to the protection of vulnerable groups (1), the right to a fair trial (2), the right to property (3), electoral rights (4), nationality rights (5), amnesty laws (6), death penalty (7), freedom of expression (8), constitutional issues (9) and the codification of criminal offences (10). In the following, each of them will be explored and put into context individually. The analysis of these categories of legislative remedies issued by human rights courts will start with the most transversal ones and will end with those that are more exclusive to only one or two courts.

---

748 Six of these remedies do not fit in any of the categories and were included at the end in a separate section, on 'Others'.

It is thereby worth highlighting that some measures could have been included in more than one of the categories below. For example, the cases related to the application of the death penalty are usually also related to the codification of certain criminal offences that establish capital punishment as a consequence. Also, the subcategory of measures about indigenous collective property rights could be included more broadly into the category of the protection of vulnerable people. The same goes for the measures on prisoners' voting rights, which are included in the category of electoral rights. In this respect, the more specific categories were favoured (e.g. property rights of indigenous communities) over the general ones (e.g. protection of vulnerable groups).

1. The Protection of Vulnerable Groups

The protection of groups in situation of vulnerability is one of the main purposes of the legislative measures ordered by human rights courts. This is due to the fact that vulnerability is arguably one of the foundations of human rights.[749] It is therefore a concept that has received a lot of scholarly attention in the context of regional human rights adjudication,[750] especially before the ECtHR.[751] It has been argued that vulnerability "has become more than a legal concept to the extent that it has evolved into a discourse within the broader human rights movement".[752] Although vulnerability is

749 See in this regard Peters, *ZaöRV* 2020, p. 11, pointing at the feminist origin of this explanation. See also Mikaela Heikkilä and Maija Mustaniemi-Laakso, "Vulnerability as a human rights variable: African and European developments", *African Human Rights Law Journal* 20, 2020, p. 778.

750 See for an early example, Alexander H. E. Morawa, "Vulnerability as a Concept of International Human Rights Law", *Journal of International Relations and Development* 6, 2003, pp. 139-155. See also generally Ingrid Nifosi Sutton, *The Protection of Vulnerable Groups under International Human Rights Law*, Routledge, 2017. For a more recent analysis, see Alexandra Timmer, Moritz Baumgärtel, Louis Kotzé and Lieneke Slingenberg "The potential and pitfalls of the vulnerability concept for human rights", *NQHR* 39(3), 2021, pp. 189-261.

751 Corina Heri, *Responsive Human Rights: Vulnerability, Ill-treatment and the ECtHR*, Oxford: Hart, 2021. On the Inter-American side, see Sergio García Ramírez, "Los sujetos vulnerables en la jurisprudencia 'transformadora' de la Corte Interamericana de Derechos Humanos", *Revista Mexicana de Derecho Constitucional* 41, 2019, pp. 4-34.

752 Lourdes Peroni and Alexandra Timmer "Vulnerable groups: The promise of an emerging concept in European Human Rights Convention law", *I•CON* 11(4), 2013, pp. 1056–1085, p. 190.

universal and inherent to the human condition, some groups are more vulnerable than others, due to biological, historical, or contextual reasons.[753] There are specific human rights instruments at the UN level aiming at the protection and non-discrimination of several vulnerable groups included in this category, such as children,[754] women,[755] persons with disabilities,[756] prisoners,[757] and indigenous communities.[758] Thus, it is not surprising that an important number of legislative remedies issued by regional human rights concern the protection of such groups.

As will be explained in more detail in the next chapter, the counter-majoritarian character of human rights is clearly reflected in legislative remedies, which intend to modify laws adopted by a domestic majority or otherwise put certain limits to majoritarian decision-making with the aim of protecting minorities – or as in this case, vulnerable groups.[759] This is made evident when analysing remedies directed at the protection of prisoners – one of the groups whose interests are most often neglected by majority decisions. As will be shown, most measures for the protection of vulnerable groups prescribe legislative enactments. This reflects the link

753 Vulnerability for biological reasons affects for example children and persons with disabilities, while vulnerability for historical reasons concern groups that have been historically discriminated, such as indigenous people, women or LGBTI people, and contextual reasons are for example related to persons in detention, who are controlled by and dependent on state authorities. For a more nuanced categorisation of grounds for vulnerability, see Heri, *Responsive Human Rights* 2021, pp. 31-120.

754 UN Convention on the Rights of the Child, adopted on 20 November 1989 by General Assembly resolution 44/25.

755 UN Convention on the Elimination of All Forms of Discrimination against Women, adopted on 18 December 1979 by the UN General Assembly, entered into force on 3 September 1981.

756 UN Convention on the Rights of Persons with Disabilities, adopted on 13 December 2006, entered into force on 3 May 2008.

757 United Nations Standard Minimum Rules for the Treatment of Prisoners, adopted in 1955.

758 UN Declaration on the Rights of Indigenous Peoples, adopted on 13 September 2007.

759 The main difference between these two concepts is that certain groups are not a minority from a purely numerical perspective, but still deserve special protection on account of their vulnerability. The clearest example in this regard are women.

between vulnerability and positive human rights obligations of the state,[760] whereby "legislating for the vulnerable" is a very relevant duty.[761]

Moreover, several authors have noted that human rights courts approach the issue of vulnerability not so much from an individual but from a collective perspective (i.e. focusing on vulnerable groups rather than on vulnerable individuals).[762] This is probably also why human rights courts have often issued collective measures (such as legislative ones) instead of individual measures for the protection of these groups.[763] Both the ECtHR and the IACtHR have paid a great deal of attention to vulnerable groups when issuing legislative remedies. The remedial provisions included in this category amount to 21% of the ECtHR's legislative remedies, and 20% of those of the IACtHR. On the other hand, the ACtHPR has issued only two legislative measures (i.e., 8%) that can be included in this category. In addition, the main difference among the three courts in this context lies in the concrete vulnerable groups they have focused on.

In this regard, the ECtHR's legislative remedies concerning vulnerable groups have mostly affected individuals in detention, and more particularly the absence of a domestic remedy for inhuman conditions of detention. Besides the six legislative measures related to this group,[764] the ECtHR has also issued this type of measure for the protection of persons with disabilities.[765] In all of these cases, the ECtHR found a violation of Arts. 3 and 13 of the Convention. Moreover, it found that in most cases the

760 In one of the early analyses of vulnerability and human rights adjudication, the author finds that "vulnerability, the gravity of past human rights violations, and the scope of positive protective or restorative duties of states closely interact" (Morawa, *JIRD* 2003, p. 150). On vulnerability and positive obligations, see also Dimitris Xenos, "The human rights of the vulnerable", *The International Journal of Human Rights* 13(4), 2009, pp. 591-614.

761 See Nesa Zimmermann, "Legislating for the Vulnerable? Special Duties under the European Convention on Human Rights", *Schweizerische Zeitschrift für internationales und europäisches Recht* 4/2015, pp. 539-532.

762 Heikkilä and Mustaniemi-Laakso, *AHRLJ* 2020, p. 782 ("Characteristic for both the European and African human rights bodies is that they often approach vulnerability in a primarily group-based – or identity-based – manner"). See also Xenos, *IJHR* 2009, p. 610. See however Nesa Zimmermann, 2015, p. 541, differentiating between dependency-based vulnerability, relating more to an individual, and discrimination-based vulnerability, relating rather to a group.

763 Heri, *Responsive Human Rights*, 2021, p. 142.

764 ECtHR, *Ananyev vs. Russia* (2009); *Torreggiani vs. Italy* (2013); *Varga vs. Hugary* (2015); *Neshkov vs. Bulgaria* (2015); *Sukachov vs. Ukraine* (2020), *Tomov vs. Russia* (2019).

765 ECtHR, *W.D. vs Belgium* (2016).

vulnerable group in question suffered structural human rights violations in a particular state and that there was no effective domestic remedy available for them to obtain redress before a domestic court.

Legislative remedial measures for the protection of vulnerable groups are also of particular importance in the Latin American region, due to its social context, with large segments of the population in a situation of exclusion and discrimination.[766] Human rights protection in this region is therefore often conceived as having a collective rather than an individual nature.[767] The measures of the IACtHR included in this category are predominantly related to indigenous communities, that are – particularly in this region – extremely vulnerable and have been historically disregarded. Further legislative remedies by the IACtHR concern children, detainees and women. The IACtHR usually needs to step in and order legislative reforms in these cases due to a lack of sufficient protection of vulnerable groups in the respective national legal order. Thus, like those of the ECtHR, these measures typically consist of the adoption of legal provisions that regulate concrete aspects related to these vulnerable groups and aim at their protection.

Finally, the ACtHPR has so far delivered only two judgments with legislative measures for the protection of vulnerable groups, despite the considerable amount of people in a situation of vulnerability in the African continent. As will be seen below, the legislative measures ordered by the ACtHPR have focused mostly on other issues, such as electoral rights or due process rights. Numerous cases were brought by detainees, but they primarily dealt with issues affecting the right to a fair trial, and they generally do not include structural remedies.[768] The two cases of the ACtHPR included in this section are related to the protection of women and girls in Mali; and to indigenous communities in Kenya.[769] In the following, the

766 See in this regard Soley in von Bogdandy et al. (eds.), 2017, pp. 344-346.

767 See Armin von Bogdandy, "*Ius Constitutionale Commune* en America Latina: Observations on Transformative Constitutionalism", in Armin von Bogdandy *et al.* (eds.), *Transformative Constitutionalism in Latin America: Emergence of a New Ius Commune*, Oxford: OUP, 2017, p. 34 ("A further distinctive characteristic of human rights in Latin America is the emphasis on the collective dimension of their protection. The rights protection often concerns entire groups, and judgments are drafted so that they immediately address such groups.").

768 An exception thereto are the judgments with legislative measures related to the death penalty, which also affect detainees but are examined in a separate category due to its particularities.

769 ACtHPR, *APDF and IHRDA vs. Mali* (2018); *ACmHPR vs. Kenya* (2022).

legislative remedies of the three courts aiming at the protection of each of these vulnerable groups will be examined.

a) Indigenous communities

The protection of indigenous communities has been a priority for the IACtHR for many years. This is an issue that does not significantly affect the ECtHR, as there is a comparatively low amount of indigenous peoples in the European continent.[770] This is different in the African context, with the presence of an important number of indigenous communities, but with only one judgment by the ACtHPR with legislative remedies related to this issue.[771] Thus, the most relevant remedial practice in this context comes from the IACtHR, which also served as an inspiration to the ACtHPR in its recent judgment on this issue.

Indigenous peoples are possibly the group that has been historically most discriminated in the Americas and they are, still to this day, in a situation of extreme vulnerability and exclusion.[772] It is therefore not surprising that the IACtHR, since its first judgments, has taken the task of protecting indigenous communities very seriously in its remedial practice.[773] The

770 The ECtHR has however dealt with several cases brought by the Saami community, although this jurisprudence has been criticised because the Court dismissed virtually all of these cases in the admissibility stage. See on this Peter Kovacs, "Indigenous Issues under the European Convention of Human Rights, Reflected in an Inter-American Mirror", *George Washington International Law Review* 48, 2016, pp. 781-806. See also Timo Koivurova, "Jurisprudence of the European Court of Human Rights Regarding Indigenous Peoples: Retrospect and Prospects", *International Journal on Minority and Group Rights* 18, 2011, pp. 1–37.

771 ACtHPR, *ACmHPR vs. Kenya* (2022). See on that case Ricarda Rösch, "Indigenousness and peoples' rights in the African human rights system: situating the Ogiek judgement of the African Court on Human and Peoples' Rights", *Verfassung und Recht in Übersee* 50(3), 2017, pp. 242-258.

772 See Germán Freire et al., *Indigenous Latin America in the Twenty-First Century*, Washington D.C.: World Bank, 2015, especially at pp. 57-72 with concrete data and statistics on the topic.

773 For an in-depth analysis of the case law of the IACtHR on indigenous rights, see James Anaya, *International Human Rights and Indigenous Peoples*, Austin: Kluwer, 2009, pp. 264-319. See also Tom Antkowiak, "A Dark Side of Virtue: The Inter-American Court and Reparations for Indigenous Peoples", 25 *Duke Journal of International Law*, 2015, pp. 1-80 (with a critical approach regarding the monetary remedies awarded by the Court, although not dealing with the remedies examined in this section).

Court has ordered states to legislate on a number of issues affecting these communities, whereby their right to previous and informed consent for activities that affect their territory figures prominently among them.[774] In addition, legislative measures of the IACtHR have also concerned the right of indigenous peoples to political participation,[775] as well as the recognition of their collective legal personality and their right to collective access to justice.[776] It can thus be observed that most of these cases have been related to the collective rights of indigenous communities, an issue that has been developed to a great extent by the IACtHR. In this regard, there is also an important number of legislative measures relating to the right to communal property of indigenous communities, which are however included under the category of property rights.[777]

b) Children

The other vulnerable groups included in this section have a more universal character and are spread across the three regional systems, as is the case of children.[778] However, most of the judgments with legislative measures concerning children have also been issued by the IACtHR. In seven cases against four states, this Court has ordered a reform of domestic laws to improve the protection of children. An illustrative example in this regard is the case of *'Street Children' vs. Guatemala* (2001). The victims of this

774 The IACtHR ordered in this respect both Ecuador and Suriname to adopt the necessary legislative measures to guarantee the right of indigenous communities to be previously and effectively consulted in case of activities that affect their territory (IACtHR, *Saramaka vs. Surinam* (2007), operative para. 8; *Sarayaku vs. Ecuador* (2012), operative para. 4). The same was done by the ACtHPR with respect to Kenya (ACtHPR, *ACmHPR vs. Kenya* (2022), operative para. ix).

775 In the judgment of IACtHR, *Yatama vs. Nicaragua* (2005), a remedial measure ordered to reform a specific law that impeded members of indigenous peoples to participate in electoral procedures (operative para. 11).

776 In the case of IACtHR, *Kaliña and Lokono vs. Surinam* (2015), the Court ordered to adopt legislative reforms in order to recognise the collective legal personality of indigenous communities (operative para. 13) and their collective access to justice (operative para. 15).

777 See below section I.3 of this chapter.

778 See Aoife Nolan and Ursula Kilkelly, "Children's Rights under Regional Human Rights Law - A Tale of Harmonisation?", in Carla M. Buckley *et al.* (eds.), *Towards Convergence in International Human Rights Law*, Leiden: Brill Nijhoff, 2016, pp. 296-322.

case were five homeless children who lived in an area known for having a high crime rate. At the time of the events, there was a common pattern in Guatemala of lawless actions perpetrated by state security agents against 'street children', which included threats, detentions and even homicides as a means of countering juvenile delinquency. These five children were kidnapped and murdered, and although several state agents were prosecuted for these crimes, they ended up acquitted of all charges. The IACtHR found for the first time a violation of Art. 19 ACHR, which contains the obligation of protecting children, and ordered the State to "adapt Guatemalan legislation" to this provision.[779] The other legislative remedies of the IACtHR in this respect are also mostly related to violations of Art. 19 ACHR, covering issues such as juvenile criminal justice,[780] the criminalisation of the sale of children,[781] the military recruitment of children,[782] the identification of disappeared children,[783] or the crime of statutory rape.[784]

The ACtHPR also issued a judgment with legislative remedies for the protection of girls, prescribing the amendment of Mali's Family Code due to incompatibilities related, *inter alia,* to the minimum age of marriage for girls or the obligation to eliminate traditional practices and conducts

779 IACtHR, *"Street Children" vs. Guatemala* (2001), operative para. 5. For an in-depth analysis of this case, see Mónica Feria Tina, *The Landmark Rulings of the Inter-American Court of Human Rights on the Rights of the Child,* Leiden: Martinus Nijhoff, 2008, pp. 13-32.

780 In the case of *Mendoza vs. Argentina* (2013), the IACtHR determined that "[t]he State must adapt its legal framework to the international standards for juvenile criminal justice" (operative para. 20), due to the fact that the Argentinian Criminal Code established the same sanctions for children and for adults (para. 295). See also *Vera Rojas vs. Chile* (2021), including an order to reform the laws for allowing the Children Protection Office to participate in legal proceedings on health-related issues of children.

781 This was ordered in *Fornerón and daughter vs. Argentina* (2012), operative para. 4.

782 In the case of *Vargas Areco vs. Paraguay* (2006), the Court ordered the State to "adapt its domestic legislation regarding the recruitment of minors under the age of 18 into the Paraguayan Armed Forces to applicable international standards" (operative para. 14). See also Feria Tinta, 2008, pp. 373-397.

783 IACtHR, *Molina Theissen vs. Guatemala* (2004), operative para. 8.

784 In the case of *Angulo Losada vs. Bolivia* (2022), operative para. 14, the Court ordered to amend the provision of the Bolivian Criminal Code dealing with statutory rape, as it "is based on gender traditions and stereotypes; it does not identify the particular conditions of vulnerability of the victim; it conceals power relations; and it creates a hierarchy between sexual crimes that diminishes, invisibilises and naturalises the gravity of sexual violence against children and adolescents" (para. 199).

harmful to the rights of women and children.[785] This was a very important case for the ACtHPR, as it is the first one that tackled customary practices that are present in several African societies but are clearly in violation of international women's and children's rights.[786] Finally, the ECtHR, despite having dealt extensively with children's rights,[787] focusing particularly on positive state obligations in this respect,[788] has not yet issued legislative remedies directed specifically at their protection.

c) Prisoners

As mentioned before, legislative measures for the protection of individuals in detention have played a very important role in the case law of the ECtHR.[789] Almost one-third of all the ECtHR's legislative measures are related to the protection of prisoners, whereby these cases concern generally the same systemic problem faced by states, namely the poor conditions of detention in its prisons. The ECtHR has ordered general measures aimed at solving this problem in cases against Russia, Italy, Bulgaria, Ukraine and Hungary. It can thus be observed that, with the exception of Italy, it is a problem mostly affecting states of the former Eastern Bloc.[790]

These are remedies that usually concern applicants who have been imprisoned for several years in overcrowded cells with limited personal

785 ACtHPR, *APDF and IHRDA vs. Mali* (2018), respectively at paras. 78 and 125.

786 See Tetevi Davi, "African Court on Human and Peoples' Rights Delivers Landmark Ruling on Women's Rights and the Rights of the Child in Mali", *EJIL: talk*, 27 July 2018, available at: https://www.ejiltalk.org/african-courton-human-and-peoples-rights-delivers-landmark-ruling-on-womens-rights-and-the-rights-of-the-child-in-mali/.

787 For an analysis on the ECtHR' jurisprudence on that topic, see Claire Fenton-Glynn, *Children and the European Court of Human Rights*, Oxford: OUP, 2020.

788 See on these obligations Conor O'Mahony, "Child Protection and the ECHR: Making Sense of Positive and Procedural Obligations", *International Journal of Children's Rights* 27, 2019, pp. 660-693, at pp. 664-666.

789 With respect to individual remedies, the measure that has been ordered more often by the ECtHR is the release of individuals in detention. Moreover, the only two instances in which the CoM has activated the 'infringement procedure' concern the failure of Azerbaijan and Turkey to implement these orders and release respectively Mr. Mammadov and Mr. Kavala.

790 It is however also possible to find 'Article 46 judgments' recommending of legislative reforms for the protection of prisoners against further Western states. See for example ECtHR, *J.M.B. vs. France* (2020); *Vasilescu vs. Belgium* (2014); *Bamouhammad vs. Belgium* (2015).

space,[791] but also with other deficiencies such as a lack of hot water in showers,[792] lack of access to toilets, or insalubrity in general.[793] In all cases pertaining to this category, the ECtHR decided to apply the pilot judgment procedure, justifying it on the basis of the number of previous and pending cases against the same state on the same substantive issue.[794]

In all of these cases, the Court found that the situation amounted to inhuman or degrading treatment contrary to Art. 3 ECHR.[795] However, the aspect that the legislative measures aimed to tackle was the lack of an effective domestic remedy for these violations, constituting in turn an infringement of Art. 13 ECHR.[796] The ECtHR thus usually distinguishes between two structural problems in these cases. On the one hand, the problem of the conditions of detention, which according to the Court is rather complex in nature and does not depend on a specific domestic law or the lack of it.[797] On the other hand, the problem of the absence of a

---

791 See for example ECtHR, *Ananyev vs. Russia* (2009), paras. 8-24, *Sukachov vs. Ukraine* (2020), para. 3.

792 As in ECtHR, *Torreggiani vs. Italy* (2013), paras. 8-11.

793 ECtHR, *Neshkov vs. Bulgaria* (2015), paras. 248, 253, 256. In addition, one of these judgments does not relate so much to the conditions inside prisons but to the conditions of prisoner transport in Russia, i.e. the transfers from one prison to another in trains with overcrowded carriages and unsuitable facilities for such long journeys (*Tomov vs. Russia* (2019), paras. 19-56). The Court highlighted also the exposure to extremely low temperatures as one of the main problems in this respect.

794 For example, in ECtHR, *Ananyev vs. Russia* (2009), the Court noted that since *Kalashnikov vs. Russia* (2002) it had decided more than eighty cases concerning inhuman detention conditions in Russian pre-trial remand detention centres. In *Varga vs. Hugary* (2015), para. 98, it referred only to four previous judgments decided against Hungary on that issue, but indicated that around 450 applications were still pending in this respect.

795 ECtHR, *Ananyev vs. Russia* (2009), para. 166; *Torreggiani vs. Italy* (2013), para. 79; *Varga vs. Hugary* (2015), para. 91; *Sukachov vs. Ukraine* (2020), para. 100; *Tomov vs. Russia* (2019), paras. 136, 140-142.

796 See for example ECtHR, *Ananyev vs. Russia* (2009), para. 119; *Tomov vs. Russia* (2019), paras. 155-156; *Sukachov vs. Ukraine* (2020), para. 125. Contrary to the remedies for the excessive length of proceedings or non-enforcement of domestic judgments (see section 2(b) of this chapter), where a compensatory remedy could suffice, in these cases the ECtHR qualified the existence of a preventive remedy capable of rapidly bringing the ongoing violation to an end as "indispensable" (ECtHR, *Ananyev vs. Russia* (2009), paras. 97-98).

797 For example, in *Neshkov vs. Bulgaria* (2015) the ECtHR stated that "that the problem of detention conditions did "not stem from a particular legal provision or single other cause but from a plethora of factors" (at para. 272). Similarly, in *Ananyev vs. Russia* (2009) it argued that structural problem was not "the product of a defective legal provision or regulation or a particular lacuna in Russian law" but "a

domestic remedy that can tackle the first problem is more closely related to the domestic legal framework in the concerned state.[798]

The ECtHR makes that distinction also with respect to the remedial measures. Regarding the primary problem (the conditions of detention) the Court limits itself to making some suggestions,[799] arguing that ordering specific measures in this respect would not be "appropriate to its function as an international court".[800] However, it takes a different approach regarding the secondary problem, specifying for example that this problem would "require clear and specific changes in the domestic legal system that would allow all people in the applicants' position to complain about alleged violations".[801] The ECtHR has also suggested a set of features for both preventive and compensatory remedies,[802] and highlighted in several cases the legislative nature that these domestic remedies should possess.[803] For example, in *Sukachov vs. Ukraine* (2020) the ECtHR stated that "findings under this provision [Art. 13 ECHR] require specific changes in Ukrainian legislation that will enable any person in the applicant's position to complain of a breach of Article 3 resulting from poor detention conditions and obtain adequate relief for any such breach at domestic level".[804]

Prisoners have also been regarded as deserving special protection by the IACtHR, with legislative measures directed at the improvement of deten-

---

multifaceted problem owing its existence to a large number of negative factors" (at para. 191).

798 Again, in *Neshkov vs. Bulgaria* (2015), the ECtHR argued that "the systemic problem underlying the breach of Article 13 of the Convention appears to be due chiefly to the statutory law and its interpretation by the courts" (at para. 273).

799 Legislative reforms are however included prominently among these suggestions. For example, in *Ananyev vs. Russia* (2009) the ECtHR "strongly doubt[ed] that the existing trend to use deprivation of liberty as the preventive measure of predilection can be reversed unless the relevant provisions of the Russian Code of Criminal Procedure have been amended" (at para. 202).

800 See ECtHR, *Ananyev vs. Russia* (2009), para. 194. Similarly, in *Sukachov vs. Ukraine* (2020), paras. 145-152.

801 E.g. ECtHR, *Ananyev vs. Russia* (2009), para. 212.

802 See for example ECtHR, *Ananyev vs. Russia* (2009), para. 234; *Neshkov vs. Bulgaria* (2015), paras. 281-289.

803 See for example *Neshkov vs. Bulgaria* (2015), para. 279 ("findings under this Article [13] require specific changes in the Bulgarian legal system"). In *Ananyev vs. Russia* (2009), the ECtHR did not specify any time limit for the introduction of such remedies, as it involved "the preparation of draft laws, amendments and regulations, then their enactment and implementation, together with the provision of appropriate training for the State officials concerned" (at para. 234).

804 ECtHR, *Sukachov vs. Ukraine* (2020), para. 153.

tion conditions in two states.[805] Legislative measures of the IACtHR have furthermore related to the transfer of prisoners,[806] the registration of detainees,[807] the regulation of the use of force by law enforcement officials,[808] and the imposition of corporal punishments on detainees.[809] Finally, the ACtHPR, despite having dealt extensively with complaints submitted by prisoners, has primarily focused on the fair trial aspects of their convictions and has not yet included legislative remedies related to conditions of detention or other issues concerning imprisonment in itself.

d) Women

Although women have historically suffered discrimination on a global scale, they have not figured as prominently as other vulnerable groups in the remedial practice of human rights courts.[810] There are only four cases in

805 This was ordered in the cases of IACtHR, *Pacheco Teruel vs. Honduras* (2012), operative para 3; and *Yvon Neptune vs. Haiti* (2008), operative para. 9.

806 IACtHR, *Lopez vs. Argentina* (2019), operative para. 9.

807 In the case of IACtHR, "*White Van*" *vs. Guatemala* (2001), in which the State was found to be responsible of the acts of arbitrary detention, torture and murder committed by state agents against eleven persons, the IACtHR ordered the adoption of legislative measures in order to "set up [a] register of detainees (...) guarantee its reliability and publicize it" (operative para. 4).

808 The Court ordered in IACtHR, *Montero Aranguren vs. Venezuela* (2006) to create a legal framework for the regulation of the use of force by Law Enforcement Officials (operative para. 9), after state agents entered the prison "Retén de Catia" and shot indiscriminately against the prisoners, killing sixty-three of them. Fourteen years later, in 2020, the Court issued another legislative order against Venezuela concerning the entry into prisons of military authorities carrying firearms, as the domestic provision regulating this issue "[did] not define, with the required specificity, the reasons for authorising such an action, or explain its exceptional nature or guarantee that such an intervention would be adequately regulated and supervised by civilian authorities". See IACtHR, *Olivares Muñoz vs. Venezuela* (2020), para. 173 and operative para. 8.

809 In IACtHR, *Caesar vs. Trinidad and Tobago* (2005), the Court ordered the derogation of the State's "Corporal Punishment Act", which allowed judges to order corporal punishments – carried out by the prison authorities – in addition to the deprivation of liberty (operative para. 3).

810 This is especially the case before the ECtHR, whereby its jurisprudence in this area has been criticised for adopting "a comparative approach concerned primarily with the prohibition of direct discrimination in the form of intentional distinctions in the public sphere (...) rather than a substantive approach concerned with challenging the disadvantage of traditionally disadvantaged groups" (Ivana Radacic, "Gender

which human rights courts included legislative measures for the protection and non-discrimination of women. The first legislative measure ordered by the IACtHR in this respect was related to the search for missing women. Although other judgments of the IACtHR dealt with this issue,[811] only one of them ordered a state to implement legislative reforms in this area. In the case of *Velasquez Paiz vs. Guatemala* (2015), the police did not act upon the complaint that a woman was missing, in accordance with a law which established that it could only intervene twenty-four hours after the disappearance. Hence, the IACtHR ordered Guatemala to reform this law in order to allow for an effective and immediate search for missing women.[812] The other judgment of the IACtHR included in this sub-section concerns the criminalisation of abortion in El Salvador. The victim of this case, after suffering an obstetric emergency, was reported by her doctor for the possible "perpetration of a crime", consisting of "the unlawful act of abortion".[813] She was convicted to thirty years of prison. The IACtHR found this to be disproportionate and ordered the State to amend its criminal laws in this respect.[814]

The case of *APDF and IHRDA vs. Mali* (2018) was also included in the sub-section on the protection of children, as there were specific remedies for each of these groups. Making use of the ACtHPR's expansive scope of review,[815] two NGOs submitted a complaint about the compatibility of the Malian Family Code with several provisions of the Protocol to the African Charter on Human and Peoples' Rights on the Rights of Women and the African Charter on the Rights and Welfare of the Child. The Court found that this law not only infringed several articles of the two aforementioned instruments but also of CEDAW. These incompatibilities concerned a number of issues, related to the consent for marriage, inheritance rights, and

Equality Jurisprudence of the European Court of Human Rights", *EJIL* 19(4), 2008, pp. 841-857, at p. 856).

811 For example, in the case of IACtHR, *'Cotton Field' vs. Mexico* (2009), the Court ordered a wide array of executive measures for the protection of women, such as the standardisation of investigation protocols or the establishment of a database with genetic information of disappeared women. However, no legislative measures were ordered in this regard.

812 IACtHR, *Velasquez Paiz vs. Guatemala* (2015), operative para. 17.

813 IACtHR, *Manuela vs. El Salvador* (2021), para. 286.

814 IACtHR, *Manuela vs. El Salvador* (2021), operative para. 16. It moreover requested two additional legislative amendments, concerning the regulation of medical secrecy in such instances and the issue of pre-trial detention (operative paras. 12 and 14).

815 See Chapter 1 of this book.

the obligation to eliminate traditional practices and conduct harmful to the rights of women.[816] The ACtHPR therefore ordered Mali to "amend the impugned law", as well as more generally to "harmonise its laws with the international instruments".[817]

Finally, the ECtHR ordered Russia to adopt legislative measures for the protection of women from domestic violence.[818] The Court explicitly noted that the authorities' failure to address reports of domestic violence stems from *lacunae* in its substantive and procedural laws and that in order to address these shortcomings, "the authorities must promptly revise or amend legislation to bring it into compliance with the Convention".[819] It moreover specified several substantive requirements of this legislative reform, such as the criminalisation of domestic violence, the aspects that should be covered in the definition, or issues related to the burden of proof and the protection of victims of domestic violence.[820]

e) Persons with disabilities

Although persons with disabilities probably constitute one of the most paradigmatic groups in a situation of biological vulnerability, there are only two judgments of regional human rights courts including legislative measures for their protection, in this case by the ECtHR and the IACtHR.[821] The latter case relates to the consent of persons with disabilities with respect to medical treatment. As this issue was not foreseen in the Ecuadorian laws, the State was prescribed to regulate in its legislation "the international obligation to provide support to persons with disabilities so that they are able to give their informed consent to medical treatments".[822]

In the case before the ECtHR, the judgment is also in some way related to individuals placed in detention, but deserving special treatment and protection on account of their condition as persons with disabilities. The

816 ACtHPR, *APDF and IHRDA vs. Mali* (2018), respectively at paras. 78, 95, 115, and 125.

817 ACtHPR, *APDF and IHRDA vs. Mali* (2018), para. 135 (x).

818 ECtHR, *Tunikova vs. Russia* (2021), operative para. 8.

819 ECtHR, *Tunikova vs. Russia* (2021), para. 153.

820 ECtHR, *Tunikova vs. Russia* (2021), paras. 154-157.

821 For an overview of the IACtHR' jurisprudence on that topic, see Diana Guarnizo-Peralta, "Disability rights in the Inter-American System of Human Rights: An expansive and evolving protection", *NQHR* 36(1), 2018, pp. 43-63.

822 IACtHR, *Guachalá Chimbo vs. Ecuador* (2021), operative para. 11.

facts of the case concern an individual with mental disabilities who was arrested and placed in a Belgian prison for an indeterminate period, under a law that allowed to intern persons with disabilities that were considered to represent a danger for society.[823] Arguing that the applicant had been placed for over nine years in a prison environment with no therapy adapted to his mental health condition and no prospect of reintegration, the Court found this to be in violation of Arts. 3 and 13 ECHR, as the available remedy for these types of cases was not considered effective.[824] The ECtHR, however, limited the statement of the operative part to ordering "appropriate measures to ensure that the system of internment of offenders is in conformity" with the Convention.[825] This is different to other cases related to the conditions of detention, where the introduction of an effective domestic remedy was expressly ordered. Here, the wording leaves much more discretion to the legislator in order to decide how to implement the measures; but in any case, the aforementioned law could not remain as it stood.

2. The Right to a Fair Trial

Besides the protection of vulnerable groups, the other main category in which an important number of legislative remedies can be included is that of fair trial rights. The legislative measures included in this category aim at the protection of specific procedural guarantees, and they usually consist of the amendment of specific laws that regulate judicial proceedings in order to incorporate such guarantees.[826] In addition, these remedies have not only

823 ECtHR, *W.D. vs Belgium* (2016), paras. 5-19.

824 ECtHR, *W.D. vs Belgium* (2016), paras. 116 and 155. In particular, the Court argued that the lack of suitable places in the external circuit and the lack of qualified staff in prison psychiatric wings, more than the remedy itself, were at the origin of its ineffectiveness (at para. 151).

825 ECtHR, *W.D. vs Belgium* (2016), operative para. 6.

826 Most of the fair trial-related remedies included here concern domestic laws regulating judicial proceedings, although there are also some exceptions in this regard. For example, there are cases related to due process rights in the pre-trial phase, such as in the context of criminal investigations (see IACtHR, *Favela Nova vs. Brazil* (2017)), or to the post-trial phase, such as those dealing with the implementation of judgments. See also ECtHR, *Ali Riza vs. Turkey* (2020), concerning arbitral proceedings.

affected the fair trial rights of defendants but also of victims.[827] In the case of the ECtHR, 39% of its legislative measures affect fair trial rights, while they represent 33% of those of the IACtHR and 19% in the case of the ACtHPR. There are, however, some important differences concerning the concrete elements of the right to a fair trial that each court has focused on. The legislative remedies of the ECtHR in this area are primarily concerned with the excessive length of judicial proceedings and the non-enforcement of domestic judgments, while those issued by the ACtHPR concern only judicial independence and the right to appeal. The IACtHR has focused on a wider array of fair trial-related issues in its legislative remedies, whereby the right to an independent court established by law has played a paramount role.

It is also important to highlight that certain core elements of the right to a fair trial are completely absent from the legislative remedies of human rights courts, even if these elements are often the object of disputes before them. This is for example the case with the right to counsel, the right to be present, the right to a public trial or the right to equality of arms. In particular, the legislative remedies issued by the three regional human rights courts have focused mainly on four components of the right to a fair trial. These are the right to an independent and impartial tribunal established by law (a), the excessive length of judicial proceedings (b), the right to appeal (c) and the enforcement of judgments (d). Other more exceptional legislative remedies related to the right to a fair trial have concerned means of evidence, arbitrary detentions or criminal investigations (e).

a) The right to an independent and impartial tribunal established by law

The right to an independent and impartial tribunal established by law is considered as "the essence of the rule of law and crucial to the fairness of any trial".[828] All three regional courts have issued legislative remedies in

827 For example, the IACtHR ordered several states to reform its laws on military jurisdiction in order to establish that perpetrators of human rights abuses are always prosecuted under the ordinary jurisdiction. These remedies aim mostly at protecting the rights of victims to have their human rights violations examined and judged by an independent tribunal established by law. See in this respect Clooney and Webb, 2020, p. 34 ("The right to a fair trial cannot be understood solely from the viewpoint of the defendant, even though he is the primary beneficiary of the various guarantees in international law").

828 Clooney and Webb, 2020, p. 67.

this respect. A number of them have dealt with the legislative conditions for the independence of the judiciary, affecting issues such as the stability and arbitrary dismissal of judges and prosecutors and the composition of judicial councils or constitutional courts. In addition, the IACtHR has a line of legislative remedies that focuses specifically on the extended use of the military jurisdiction and its incompatibility with the right to an ordinary judge established by law.

i) The independence of judges and prosecutors

Judicial independence is an area that has gained enormous weight in regional human rights litigation. In this context, the IACtHR has for example issued several judgments against Venezuela with legislative measures aiming to prevent the arbitrary removal of judges in this state.[829] Similarly, in recent cases, this Court has included legislative remedies related to the dismissal of provisional prosecutors and magistrates in Colombia and Peru,[830] an issue that goes hand in hand with judicial independence.[831] The IACtHR has even ordered Mexico to reform its constitution in order to guarantee the independence of another body intervening in judicial proceedings, the state's forensic services.[832]

In addition, remedies aiming to put an end to unlawful restrictions on the freedom of expression of judges are also included in this category, as these are sanctions affecting their independence. The case of *Urrutia Laubreaux vs. Chile* (2020) dealt with the sanctioning of a judge after he published an academic paper, in accordance with a domestic law that prevented judicial officials from "publishing (...) documents defending their official conduct or attacking, in any way, that of other judges".[833]

---

829 IACtHR, *Apitz Barbera vs. Venezuela* (2008), operative para. 19; *Reverón Trujillo vs. Venezuela* (2009), operative para. 10; *Chocrón Chocrón vs. Venezuela* (2011), operative para. 8. These judgments triggered a strong reaction by the State, as will be seen in Chapter 6 of this book.

830 IACtHR, *Martínez Esquivia vs. Colombia* (2020), operative para. 9 ("The State shall adjust its regulations to guarantee stability of provisional prosecutors, pursuant to paragraphs 162 and 163 of this judgment"). See also IACtHR, *Casa Nina vs. Peru* (2020), operative para. 7; *Cuya Lavi vs. Peru* (2021), operative para. 10.

831 See International Commission of Jurists, *International Principles on the Independence and Accountability of Judges, Lawyers and Prosecutors*, 2007, pp. 71-77.

832 IACtHR, *Digna Ochoa vs. Mexico* (2021).

833 IACtHR, *Urrutia Laubreaux vs. Chile* (2020), para. 133.

The IACtHR found this restriction of the freedom of expression to be too broad, noting that "regulations such as this violate not only the principle of legality but also judicial independence", and ordered Chile to "eliminate paragraph 4 of article 323 of the Organic Code of the Courts".[834] Moreover, the IACtHR has also ordered legislative reforms in order to allow for the review and overturn of judgments issued by non-independent judges, such as those issued during the Chilean military dictatorship.[835]

On the other hand, the ACtHPR's legislative remedies aiming to uphold judicial independence have been included in three judgments against Benin. These are very important cases, affecting constitutional provisions that regulate the composition of the State's Constitutional Court and Higher Judicial Council. In two of these cases, the Court found Article 115 of the Beninese Constitution, governing the composition and appointment of judges to the Constitutional Court, incompatible with the ACHPR. It specifically determined that the renewable nature of the constitutional judges' mandate would compromise its independence, in violation of Art. 26 of the ACHPR.[836] Notably, in these two cases, the remedial measures were worded quite differently. In the case of *XYZ vs. Benin (II)* (2020), the Court ordered Benin "to take all legislative and regulatory measures to guarantee the independence of the Constitutional Court, in particular with regard to the process for the renewal of their term of office".[837] In *Ajavon vs. Benin* (2020), however, the Court made a broader request for Benin "to take all necessary measures to ensure that the mandate of the judges of the Constitutional Court is marked by guarantees of independence".[838] Thus, the legislative nature and specificity of the remedial measure were diluted in this second case. But in this case, the ACtHPR found as well the law regulating the composition of the Beninese Higher Judicial Council to be contrary to the independence of the judiciary, for several reasons related to the appointment rules, the functions of this Council and the presence of members of the government in it. Thereby, it expressly ordered Benin to

834 IACtHR, *Urrutia Laubreaux vs. Chile* (2020), para. 136 and operative para. 8.

835 This was ordered in IACtHR, *Maldonado Vargas vs. Chile* (2015), operative para. 9.

836 ACtHPR, *XYZ vs. Benin (II)* (2020), paras. 68-72. ACtHPR, *Ajavon vs. Benin* (2020), para. 289. It is relevant to note that this is a different position to that held by the ECtHR, who has considered renewable terms in judicial bodies as Convention-compliant. See ECtHR, *Maktouf vs. Bosnia and Herzegovina* (2013), paras. 50–52.

837 ACtHPR, *XYZ vs. Benin (II)* (2020), operative para. xiii).

838 ACtHPR, *Ajavon vs. Benin* (2020), para. 361.

reform this law.[839] The ACtHPR ordered again the reform of the latter law in the case of *Houngue Éric Noudehouenou vs. Benin* (2022), specifying the provisions that would need to be repealed.[840]

Finally, one judgment of the ECtHR included legislative measures affecting the independence of arbitral proceedings for the settlement of football disputes in Turkey. The case concerned several disputes affecting football players and referees, which were decided before the Arbitration Committee of the Turkish Football Federation (TFF). The ECtHR found that this arbitral body did not satisfy the requirements of independence and impartiality under Art. 6 of the Convention, mainly due to its internal organisation and to the fact that "the TFF Law does not provide appropriate safeguards to protect members of the Arbitration Committee from any outside pressure".[841] It therefore prescribed the adoption of general measures to address this systemic problem, whereby a reform of the TFF Law appears to be implicitly required.[842]

ii) Restrictions to the military jurisdiction

Besides the legislative remedies dealing with judicial independence *stricto senso*, the IACtHR also has a very important line of legislative remedies aiming to secure the right to a 'competent' court. In these cases, the remedies' purpose is the limitation of the use of military courts in domestic judicial systems. This is highly relevant because the use of military jurisdiction has been traditionally very extended in the Latin American region, especially in the context of its authoritarian regimes.[843] The IACtHR has

839 ACtHPR, *Ajavon vs. Benin* (2020), paras. 309-325; operative para. xxiv (2), ordering Benin "to repeal (...) Articles 1 and 2 of Organic Law No. 2018-02 of 4 January 2018 (...) relating to the Higher Judicial Council".

840 ACtHPR, *Houngue Éric Noudehouenou vs. Benin* (2022), operative para. xvi. These specific provisions are "those that make the President of the Republic a member of the HJC and Chair of the HJC, those that entitle the President of the Republic to appoint members of the HJC, and those that make other members of the executive members of the HJC".

841 ECtHR, *Ali Riza vs. Turkey* (2020), para. 241.

842 ECtHR, *Ali Riza vs. Turkey* (2020), operative para. 5.

843 See on this issue Ivette Castañeda García, "Military justice in Latin America: a comparative analysis", in Alison Duxbury and Matthew Groves (eds.), *Military Justice in the Modern Age*, Cambridge: CUP, 2016, pp. 196-217 ("military justice has more recently been used for political and corporate ends during the years of military intervention in the political life of many Latin American countries").

taken a very firm position on that issue, ordering five states in nine cases to reform their domestic laws in order to introduce certain limitations to the use of military judicial fora.[844] In this respect, it has established that in order for a military court to exercise jurisdiction, two conditions must be met. First, the individual appearing before the court must be an active member of the military, and second, the alleged crime must be of a militaristic nature.

Some of the early cases in which the IACtHR ordered the reform of domestic laws concerned the first condition. It consisted of a series of cases against Peru, dealing with two laws that allowed civilians accused of the crimes of treason and terrorism to be judged by military courts, without the possibility of appealing to ordinary courts. The IACtHR determined that "[w]hen a military court takes jurisdiction over a matter that regular courts should hear, the individual's right to a hearing by a competent, independent and impartial tribunal previously established by law" is violated.[845] Thus, it ordered the State "to adopt the appropriate measures to amend those laws (...)".[846] The same occurred with respect to laws that allowed for retired military personnel to be judged by military courts.[847]

With regard to the second condition, an enlightening example is the four cases against Mexico concerning Art. 57 of the Mexican Code of Military Justice, which allowed military courts to judge every member of the army whenever the alleged crime was committed during service. In the case of *Radilla Pacheco vs. Mexico* (2009), the members of the military had been accused of enforced disappearance, while in the other cases they were accused of sexual assault and torture, respectively.[848] In all of these cases, military courts had exercised competence over these crimes. The Court affirmed that "military criminal jurisdiction shall have a restrictive

844 For an analysis of these cases, see Christina M. Cerna, "The Inter-American System and Military Justice", in Alison Duxbury and Matthew Groves (eds.), *Military Justice in the Modern Age*, Cambridge: CUP, 2016, pp. 325-346.

845 IACtHR, *Castillo Petruzzi vs. Peru* (1999), para. 128.

846 IACtHR, *Castillo Petruzzi vs. Peru* (1999), operative para. 14). This was later repeated in another judgment of 2004 (IACtHR, *Lori Berenson vs. Peru*, operative para. 1), and in further judgments the State was considered to be responsible of a violation of Art. 2 ACHR because of these laws, although no remedies were issued because Peru had already declared them unconstitutional (IACtHR, *Cantoral Benavides vs. Peru* (2001); *Durand and Ugarte vs. Peru* (2001); *Cesti Hurtado vs. Peru* (2001)).

847 IACtHR, *Palamara Iribarne vs. Chile* (2005), *Usón Ramirez vs. Venezuela* (2009).

848 These were the cases of IACtHR, *Rosendo Cantú vs. Mexico* (2010) and *Cabrera García and Montiel Flores vs. Mexico* (2010).

and exceptional scope and be directed toward the protection of special juridical interests, related to the tasks characteristic of the military forces" and that this jurisdiction is not the competent one "to investigate and, in its case, prosecute and punish the authors of violations of human rights".[849] The Court thus ordered Mexico in all of these cases to make this specific provision compatible with the ACHR, among other remedies.[850]

b) The right to be judged within a reasonable time

The excessive length of judicial proceedings is one of the main issues litigated before the ECtHR. The CoM stated in 2010 that it is "by far the most common issue raised in applications to the Court", thereby constituting "an immediate threat to [its] effectiveness".[851] Moreover, both the CoM and the Venice Commission have recommended states to set up domestic remedies for such undue delays.[852] It is therefore not surprising that most legislative remedies of the ECtHR relate to this issue. It is, in fact, the only human rights court that has issued legislative remedies in that respect, incorporating them in eleven judgments against seven states.[853]

849 IACtHR, *Radilla Pacheco vs. Mexico* (2009), paras. 272-273.

850 IACtHR, *Radilla Pacheco vs. Mexico* (2009), operative para. 10; *Fernandez Ortega vs. Mexico* (2010), operative para. 13; *Rosendo Cantú vs. Mexico* (2010), operative para. 12; *Cabrera Gacía and Montiel Flores vs. Mexico* (2010), operative para. 15. Similarly to the ECtHR's usual practice with respect to legislative remedies, the IACtHR also ordered to introduce a domestic remedy allowing to challenge the competence of these courts. See on these cases Eduardo Ferrer MacGregor and Fernando Silva, *Jurisdicción Militar y Derechos Humanos: El caso Radilla ante la Corte Interamericana de Derechos Humanos*, Mexico: Editorial Porrúa, 2011.

851 Recommendation CM/Rec(2010)3 of the Committee of Ministers to Member States on effective remedies for excessive length of proceedings. See also more recently Clooney and Webb, 2020, p. 390, stating that "more than half the fair trial violations confirmed by the European Court of Human Rights concerned unduly lengthy proceedings".

852 Recommendation CM/Rec(2010)3; Venice Commission, Compilation of Venice Commission Opinions and Reports Concerning Courts and Justice (2015) CDL-PI(2015)001, p. 66.

853 However, both the IACtHR and the ACtHPR have also dealt with such delays in their case law. The IACtHR found violations of Art. 8 ACHR on account of the excessive length of proceedings already in some of its first contentious cases. See for example IACtHR, *Genie Lacayo vs Nicaragua* (1997), para. 81; *Suarez Rosero vs. Ecuador* (1997), para. 73. With respect to the ACtHPR, see *Wilfred Onyango Nganya vs. Tanzania* (2016), as well as the analysis of this and similar cases included in

The facts of all cases are very similar, as they all concern one or several applicants who suffered an excessive delay in judicial proceedings, often with final judgments issued between ten and twenty years after initiating the proceedings,[854] or with final domestic judgments still pending after that time.[855] In all of these cases, the ECtHR found not only that these proceedings had been unreasonably long, constituting a violation of Art. 6 ECHR, but also that the absence of an effective domestic remedy implied a violation of Art. 13 ECHR.[856] In this context, it considered these delays a structural problem, usually concerning a specific jurisdiction.[857] For example, between 2010 and 2012 the ECtHR issued three judgments with legislative measures against Greece, concerning the excessive delays before its administrative, civil, and criminal courts, respectively.[858]

With respect to the remedial measures, the ECtHR's approach has been again to suggest possible measures in order to solve the main structural problem, i.e. the excessive delays in judicial proceedings, but at the same time to avoid specifying any binding orders in that regard.[859] However,

---

Jamil Ddamulira Mujuzi, "The African Court on Human and Peoples' Rights and its Protection of the Right to a Fair Trial", *LPICT* 16, 2017, pp. 187–223, at pp. 216-220.

854 For example, *Vassilios Athanasiou vs. Greece* (2010) concerned ten applicants that had started administrative judicial proceedings in 1994 and did not obtain a final judgment until fourteen years later (paras. 5-12). See also *Rumpf vs. Germany* (2010), where the final judgment was issued after thirteeb years (paras. 11-29).

855 See for example *Glykantzi vs. Greece* (2012).

856 ECtHR, *Lukenda vs. Slovenia* (2005), paras. 79, 86-88; *Vassilios Athanasiou vs. Greece* (2010), paras. 29, 35; *Glykantzi vs. Greece* (2012), paras. 50, 57; *Michelioudakis vs. Greece* (2012), paras. 45, 54; *Ümmühan Kaplan vs. Turkey* (2012), paras. 43, 58; *Gazsó vs Hungary* (2015), paras. 17, 21.

857 See for example *Dimitrov and Hamanov vs. Bulgaria* (2011), paras. 7-32 (on the criminal jurisdiction); *Finger vs. Bulgaria* (2011), paras. 6-34 and *Ümmühan Kaplan vs. Turkey* (2012), paras. 6-17 (on the civil jurisdiction); *Rumpf vs. Germany* (2010), paras. 11-29 (on the administrative jurisdiction); or *Gazsó vs Hungary* (2015), para. 510 (on the labour jurisdiction). In some cases, the structural problem has even concerned a narrower field of law, such as judicial proceedings related to the payment of disability benefits (ECtHR, *Lukenda vs. Slovenia* (2005)). On the other hand, sometimes the Court has also found that the excessive delays were cutting across several jurisdictions (*Vlad vs. Romania* (2013) and *Rutkowski vs. Poland* (2015)) or even across all of them (*Ümmühan Kaplan vs. Turkey* (2012)).

858 See ECtHR, *Vassilios Athanasiou vs. Greece* (2010) (on the administrative jusridiction); *Glykantzi vs. Greece* (2012) (on the civil jurisdiction) and *Michelioudakis vs. Greece* (2012) (on the criminal jurisdiction).

859 The ECtHR has stated that this structural problem "may be due to a large number of factors, of both a legal and logistical character" (ECtHR, *Dimitrov and Hamanov vs. Bulgaria* (2011), para. 115; Finger vs. Bulgaria (2011), para. 120). Thus, its suggestions

the situation is different with respect to the 'secondary' structural problem found in these cases, i.e. the lack of an effective domestic remedy to prevent and obtain redress for these delays. The ECtHR ordered in almost all of these cases to introduce such a domestic remedy in order to provide adequate relief for this situation.[860] It also stated that these remedies, in order to be considered effective, should possess certain features, such as an acceleratory and a compensatory nature.

c) The right to appeal before a higher court

The right to appeal is another aspect that has triggered several legislative measures, both by the IACtHR and the ACtHPR.[861] It was an especially important issue before the IACtHR, ordering the reform of domestic laws

have been rather broad, indicating that "comprehensive, large-scale actions of a legislative and administrative character" should be adopted (ECtHR, *Rutkowski vs. Poland* (2015), para 207).

860 ECtHR, *Vassilios Athanasiou vs. Greece* (2010), operative para. 5; *Rumpf vs. Germany* (2010), operative para. 5; *Dimitrov and Hamanov vs. Bulgaria* (2011), operative para. 6; *Finger vs. Bulgaria* (2011), operative para. 5, *Glykantzi vs. Greece* (2012), operative para. 5; *Ümmühan Kaplan vs. Turkey* (2012), operative para. 5; *Gazsó vs Hungary* (2015), operative para. 5. There are however also cases in which the ECtHR was not that straight-forward with respect to the obligations of setting up a domestic remedy. For example, in *Rutkowski vs. Poland* (2015), the State had already introduced a domestic remedy that according to the Court "at least in law, had all the features of an effective remedy" (para. 215) but had several shortcomings with respect to its interpretation and application by the judiciary (paras. 216-221). The ECtHR's remedial measure in this case stated that "the respondent State must, through appropriate legal or other measures, secure the national courts' compliance with the relevant principles under Article 6 § 1 and Article 13 of the Convention" (operative para. 6). As it can be observed, this judgment is different from other pilot judgments concerning the excessive length of judicial proceedings, as the legislative measures ordered therein affect not as much the absence of a domestic remedy (Art. 13) as the main problem of unreasonable delays (Art. 6). This is similar in the cases of *Lukenda vs. Slovenia* (2005) and *Vlad vs. Romania* (2013). In both of them, the ECtHR seemed to focus its remedial measure on the main structural problem, ordering the states to guarantee the right to be judged in a reasonable time "through appropriate legal and administrative measures" (ECtHR, *Lukenda vs. Slovenia* (2005), operative para. 5; *Vlad vs. Romania* (2013), operative para. 6).

861 The ECtHR has taken a different approach that the other two human rights courts when dealing with the right to appeal. It has interpreted this right rather narrowly, affording a wide margin of appreciation to states in the regulation of its system of appeals. See Clooney and Webb, 2020, p. 656. Notably, in the ECHR the right to appeal is not included under the fair trial provision (Art. 6 ECHR) but instead under

to allow for the appeal of judgments before higher courts in twelve cases against six different states. The first case and a prominent example in this regard is *Herrera Ulloa vs. Costa Rica* (2004). Here, the IACtHR noted that, according to the right to appeal included in Art. 8.2(h) of the ACHR, the remedies in this regard "must be effective", "accessible", and guarantee "a full review of the decision being challenged".[862] As the latter was not foreseen in the Costa Rican law, the Court ordered the State to "adjust its legal system to conform to the provisions of Article 8(2)(h)".[863] In addition, the IACtHR issued legislative remedies in three cases against Argentina because the provisions in force would not allow for the review of factual and/or evidentiary issues before a higher court.[864] Legislative remedies of the IACtHR included in this sub-category have extended beyond the appeal of judicial decisions, by ordering to regulate the possibility of appealing administrative decisions that declare a strike illegal,[865] as well as decisions of public educational institutions.[866] Despite not constituting an appeal in the formal sense, this sub-section includes also legislative measures found in two cases against Guatemala related to the right of every person sentenced to death to request an executive pardon or a commutation of the sentence.[867]

The ACtHPR has also one case in which it ordered a legislative reform related to the right to appeal. *Ajavon vs. Benin* (2019) concerned a politician and businessman from Benin who had been convicted of drug trafficking by the then newly established Anti-Economic Crimes and Terrorism Court (CRIET). The law creating CRIET was challenged mainly because it established that the proceedings before this Court would not allow for an ordinary appeal before a higher court but for a cassation appeal which does

---

a specific provision in Protocol 7, which includes however a specific obligation to legislate in order to protect this right (see Chapter 1 of this book).

862 IACtHR, *Herrera Ulloa v Costa Rica* (2004), paras. 161-165.

863 IACtHR, *Herrera Ulloa v Costa Rica* (2004), operative para. 5.

864 See IACtHR, *Mendoza vs. Argentina* (2013); *Gorigoitía vs. Argentina* (2019) and *Valle Ambrosio vs. Argentina* (2020).

865 IACtHR, *Former Employees of the Judiciary vs. Guatemala* (2021), operative para. 7.

866 IACtHR, *Pavez Pavez vs. Chile* (2022), operative para. 9.

867 See IACtHR, *Fermin Ramirez vs. Guatemala* (2005), operative para. 10; *Raxcacó Reyes vs. Gautemala* (2005), operative para. 7. As mentioned, this would not be an appeal in the legal sense because it is not taking place before a higher court but before the executive authorities. See on legislative remedies and death penalty, section I(7) of this chapter.

not consider the facts but only the formal aspects of a judgment.[868] The ACtHPR thus held that Article 19(2) of this law constituted a violation of the applicant's right to appeal,[869] and ordered in the reparations judgment Benin "to amend Sections 12 and 19(2) of Law No. 2018-13 of 2 July 2018, establishing CRIET in order to make them compliant with the provisions of Articles 3(2) of the Charter and 14(5) of the ICCPR".[870]

d) The enforcement of domestic judgments

Another sub-category of legislative measures concerning fair trial rights before the ECtHR is the one dealing with the non-enforcement of domestic judgments. The ECtHR has included legislative measures for this purpose in four judgments, against Russia, Ukraine and Moldova. They all concern cases in which the states' administrative authorities failed to implement a domestic judicial decision affording social housing or other benefits to the applicants in a reasonable time. Notably, neither the IACtHR nor the ACtHPR have dealt with this issue in their remedial case law.

The first of these cases before the ECtHR was *Burdov vs. Russia (No. 2)* (2009), concerning the non-enforcement of judgments that prescribed the payment of benefits for the Chernobyl victims.[871] The Court found that this constituted a violation of the rights to access to court and property, and – contrary to the first *Burdov* case –[872] it went on *mutu proprio* to examine

868 ACtHPR, *Ajavon vs. Benin,* (Merits, 2019), paras. 211-213.

869 ACtHPR, *Ajavon vs. Benin* (Merits, 2019), para. 215. In addition, the same law was also found to violate the right to equality before the law, because it established that the Public Prosecutor could lodge an ordinary appeal against the discharge decisions in favour of those prosecuted (para. 225).

870 ACtHPR, *Ajavon vs. Benin* (Reparations, 2019), para. 144 (vii).

871 See on this case Philip Leach, Helen Hardman and Svetlana Stephenson, "Can the European Court's Pilot Judgment Procedure Help Resolve Systemic Human Rights Violations? Burdov and the Failure to Implement Domestic Court Decisions in Russia", *HRLR* 10(2), 2010, pp. 346-359.

872 In ECtHR, *Burdov vs. Russia* (2002), the applicant claimed that despite several domestic judgments in his favour, the Russian authorities refused to pay him the benefits he was entitled to after being exposed to radioactive emission when he participated in the emergency operations in the aftermath of the Chernobyl nuclear plant disaster. The Court found that this constituted a violation of Art. 6 ECHR and Art. 1 Protocol 1 ECHR, but ordered only the payment of a monetary compensation. The State paid this sum to the applicant and argued that it had also enforced further judgments related to the payment of benefits for the Chernobyl victims (*Burdov vs. Russia (No. 2)* (2009), para. 10). This was accepted by the CoM and the case

the right to a domestic remedy under Art. 13 ECHR, finding that the remedies available in Russia for the non-enforcement of domestic judgments could not be considered effective.[873] With respect to the remedial measures, the ECtHR took a similar approach to that in most other judgments included in this analysis. It abstained from indicating specific measures to solve the structural problems but ordered states to set up a remedy "which secures adequate and sufficient redress for non-enforcement or delayed enforcement of domestic judgments".[874] The ECtHR explicitly stated in this respect that it would be "highly unlikely (...) that such an effective remedy can be set up without changing the domestic legislation on certain specific points".[875]

---

was closed. Later, Russian courts issued several additional judgments ordering the payment of default interests and compensation to Mr. Burdov for the State's failure to implement the previous decisions in a reasonable time (*Burdov vs. Russia (No. 2)* (2009), paras. 12-21). Mr. Burdov then submitted a second application before the ECtHR claiming that Russia had again failed to implement these additional judgments in due time.

873 This was because the available remedies did not have both a preventive and a compensatory nature. See *Burdov vs. Russia* (No. 2) (2009), paras. 96-117. The same violations (i.e. Arts. 6, 13 and 1 Protocol 1 ECHR) were also found in the cases of *Yuriy Nikolayevich Ivanov vs. Ukraine* (2009) and *Gerasimov vs. Russia* (2014), paras. 174 and 183. In *Olaru vs. Moldova* (2009), the introduction of a domestic remedy was ordered without previously finding a violation of Art. 13. Instead, it recalled that it had determined the Art. 13 violation in three previous cases against Moldova and it was not aware of any change in this respect (para. 58).

874 *Burdov vs. Russia* (No. 2) (2009), operative para. 6; *Olaru vs. Moldova* (2009), operative para. 4; *Yuriy Nikolayevich Ivanov vs. Ukraine* (2009), operative para. 5; *Gerasimov vs. Russia* (2014), operative para. 12.

875 *Burdov vs. Russia* (No. 2) (2009), para. 138. Here it can be seen that the ECtHR in some cases leaves a very small room of manoeuvre to states with regard to the legislative character that the domestic remedies should possess. Indeed, after this judgment Russia introduced such a remedy by reforming its domestic legislation. However, the applicants of *Gerasimov vs. Russia* (2014) were unsuccessful while attempting to make use of, as it only applied for the State's failure to enforce judgments ordering monetary payments, but not other obligations in kind (paras. 157-166). Therefore, the Court noted in this second pilot judgment against Russia concerning the same issue that "while part of the problem was successfully resolved by the first pilot judgment and the ensuing adoption of the Compensation Act (...), numerous cases which do not fall within the latter's scope" (para. 206). This led the Court to consider that the structural problem in Russia "lends itself to be resolved through an amendment of domestic legislation, as demonstrated by the positive experience of the Burdov pilot judgment" (para. 221).

The other remedies of the ECtHR included in this subcategory are also related to judgments ordering the payment of social benefits,[876] or the provision of housing and other services in kind.[877] As to the legislative origin of the structural problem, a clear difference can be observed between the two cases against Russia, in which the ECtHR stated that these problems "do not stem from a specific legal or regulatory provision or a particular lacuna in Russian law",[878] and the cases against Ukraine and Moldova, where domestic laws were identified as the source of the problem.[879]

e) Other due process rights

Finally, there are also several legislative remedies ordered by the IACtHR and the ACtHPR that aim at tackling other fair trial-related issues, not only in the strictly judicial context but also in criminal procedures more generally. For example, in the case of *Favela Nova Brasilia vs. Brazil* (2017), the IACtHR ordered Brazil to adopt legislative measures allowing victims and their families to participate in criminal investigations carried out by the police and the prosecution authorities.[880] In the case of *Oumar Mariko vs. Mali* (2022), the ACtHPR's measures prescribed the reform of the "laws governing the constitutional court", in order to allow for adversarial proceedings and the recusal of judges.[881] Further remedies included here relate

876 As in ECtHR, *Yuriy Nikolayevich Ivanov vs. Ukraine* (2009), dealing with the application of a former member of the military who had obtained a favourable domestic judgment concerning the payment of his pension.

877 See respectively ECtHR, *Olaru vs. Moldova* (2009), paras. 5-23; *Gerasimov vs. Russia* (2014), paras. 8-75.

878 ECtHR, *Burdov vs. Russia* (No. 2) (2009), para. 136; *Gerasimov vs. Russia* (2014), para. 219.

879 This is reflected most clearly in *Olaru vs. Moldova* (2009), with the Court stating that the structural problem "appears to have its origin in socially-oriented legislation (...) which bestows social housing privileges on a very wide category of persons at the expense of the local governments" (para. 54). In *Yuriy Nikolayevich Ivanov vs. Ukraine* (2009) the Court's terms were vaguer, mentioning as the source of the problem "a combination of factors, including (...) shortcomings in the national legislation" (para. 84).

880 IACtHR, *Favela Nova Brasilia vs. Brazil* (2017), operative para. 19.

881 ACtHPR, *Oumar Mariko vs. Mali* (2022), operative paras. xv and xvi.

to arbitrary detentions,[882] the use of confidential witnesses,[883] and habeas corpus rights.[884]

3. Property Rights

Property rights represent an area of debate in international human rights law. It is perhaps the only right which is included in the regional human rights instruments but neither in the ICCPR nor in the ICESCR.[885] This is due to the diverging approaches towards property rights that the Western states and those of the Eastern Bloc had at the moment of drafting these Covenants. For communist governments at that time, these rights were equated to "bourgeois trappings".[886] At the same time, Western liberal governments gave property rights a special priority precisely in order to use them as a 'weapon' against communism. The importance traditionally given to property rights in the European human rights protection system can thereby be traced to that conflict, as the ECHR was drafted in the midst of the Cold War. The drafters of the Convention embraced a rather liberal-conservative human rights perspective, avoiding the redistributionist vision of certain political forces.[887] However, the right to property was

882 A Honduran law allowed for the detention of people that were suspected to be part of the street gangs known as 'maras'. This law was challenged and its amendment was ordered by the IACtHR in the case of *Pacheco Teruel vs. Honduras* (2012), operative para. 5. See similarly IACtHR, *Tzompaxtle Tecpile vs. México* (2022), operative paras. 7 and 8.

883 In the case of IACtHR, *Norín Catrimán vs. Chile* (2014), operative para. 20, the Court ordered to reform procedural criminal laws for the means of evidence consisting in confidential witnesses to be restricted and subject to judicial control.

884 In the case of IACtHR, *Blanco Romero vs. Venezuela* (2005), the IACtHR ordered the adoption of the necessary legislative measures "in order for writs of habeas corpus to be effectively processed in cases of [en]forced disappearance" (operative para. 9).

885 See on that William Schabas, "The Omission of the Right to Property in the International Covenants", *Hague Yearbook of International Law* 4, 1991, pp. 158–159.

886 See Rosemary Foot, "The Cold War and Human Rights", in Melvyn P. Leffler and Odd Arne Westad (eds.), *The Cambridge History of the Cold War*, Cambridge: CUP, 2010, pp. 445-465.

887 See generally Marco Duranti, *The Conservative Human Rights Revolution*, Oxford: OUP, 2017.

not included in the Convention itself but was added two years later with the adoption of the first Protocol to the ECHR.[888]

Since then, this right has become a cornerstone in the case law of the ECtHR, both from an interpretative and a remedial perspective. Concerning the former, the ECtHR has interpreted the right to property rather broadly, extending its protection to all economic interests of natural and legal persons.[889] On the latter, as it will be observed, property rights are of utmost importance in the remedial jurisprudence of the ECtHR. Its first cases with legislative remedies concerned the issue of property rights in the context of transitions to democracy of former communist states.[890]

Between 2004 and 2022, the ECtHR issued eight judgments with legislative measures related to property rights against seven different states, mostly in the contexts of transitions to democracy and state succession.[891] Several of these cases are related to compensations for the confiscation of property that took place before the ECHR entered into force in these states. In this regard, the Court has affirmed repeatedly that the right to property does not imply a general obligation for states to return properties that were confiscated before the entry into force of the Convention, but when states adopt a domestic law regulating the restitution of such properties, this can be regarded as a new property right.[892] In general, three distinct sub-categories can be identified with respect to ECtHR's judgments with legislative remedies related to property rights. These are property rights in the context of transitions to democracy, usually from former communist regimes (a); property rights in the context of state succession, mainly in the Balkan region (b); and property rights in the aftermath of armed conflicts, such as the one between Turkey and Cyprus (c). Property rights have not played such an important role in the remedial practice of the other two regional courts, except for the legislative remedies concerning the collective property of indigenous peoples over their territory (d).

888 According to Schabas, the non-inclusion of the right to property in the ECHR was because "the deputies were divided on political lines, with the socialists contending that to recognize the right to property but not any other economic and social rights, such as the right to work, would send the wrong message about the substance of human rights" (Schabas, *Commentary to the ECHR*, 2015, p. 961).

889 Sabrina Praduroux, "Property and Expropriation: Two Concepts Revisited in the Light of the Case Law of the European Court of Human Rights and the European Court of Justice", *European Property Law Journal* 8(2), 2019, pp. 172–191.

890 See ECtHR, *Broniowski vs. Poland* (2004) and *Hutten-Czapska vs. Poland* (2006).

891 This represents 26% of all ECtHR's cases with legislative measures.

892 ECtHR, *Maria Atanasiu vs. Romania* (2010), paras. 135-136.

a) Property rights in the context of transitions to democracy

Most cases in which the ECtHR has dealt with transitional justice issues concern the restitution or compensation for property that was nationalised or otherwise confiscated by communist regimes.[893] As was mentioned before, this is the sub-category in which the origin of legislative remedies and also pilot judgments before the ECtHR can be found, as it was an issue that brought an enormous amount of complaints before this Court.[894] The first two cases in which the pilot judgment procedure was applied are *Broniowski vs. Poland* (2004) and *Hutten-Czapska vs. Poland* (2006). The former dealt with the State's obligation to redress or compensate individuals who, after the Soviet invasion, had been "repatriated from the 'territories beyond the Bug River' [i.e., the eastern provinces of pre-war Poland] and had to abandon their property there".[895] Poland introduced a compensation scheme, but then adopted a law in 2003 extinguishing the State's obligations towards those who had received some type of compensatory property, even though it did not correspond to the property they had abandoned.[896] The ECtHR found this to constitute a violation of Art. 1 of Protocol 1 to the ECHR, and went on to consider the effects of the Polish legislative scheme upon other potential victims.[897] It found in this respect that "the facts of the case disclose the existence, within the Polish legal order, of a shortcoming as a consequence of which a whole class of individuals have been or are still denied the peaceful enjoyment of their possessions".[898] Thus, after introducing the pilot judgment procedure, the ECtHR included a paragraph in the operative part of the judgment stating that Poland "must, through appropriate legal measures and administrative practices, secure the implementation of the property right in question in respect of the remaining Bug River claimants or provide them with equivalent redress in lieu".[899]

---

893 See generally Tom Allen and Benedict Douglas, "Closing the Door on Restitution", in Antoine Buyse and Michael Hamilton (eds.), *Transitional Jurisprudence and the ECHR: Justice, Politics and Rights*, Cambridge: CUP, 2011, pp. 208-238.

894 See Chapter 3 of this book.

895 ECtHR, *Broniowski vs. Poland* (2004), para. 11.

896 ECtHR, *Broniowski vs. Poland* (2004), para. 137.

897 ECtHR, *Broniowski vs. Poland* (2004), para. 187. The ECtHR found that this prevented the applicants' access to compensation for their properties (para. 176), and that an unjustified difference of treatment between 'Bug River claimants' was introduced with this law (para. 186).

898 ECtHR, *Broniowski vs. Poland* (2004), para. 189.

899 ECtHR, *Broniowski vs. Poland* (2004), operative para. 4.

Contrary to that judgment, where the structural problem stemmed not only from domestic laws but also from the State's administrative practice in the application of these laws, in *Hutten Czapska vs. Poland* (2006) the issue turned exclusively around the housing legislation, which left no margin for a Convention-friendly application. The system of rent control introduced by the former communist authorities in Poland resulted in legislative restrictions for landlords regarding rent increases for their dwellings.[900] After reviewing the relevant laws, the ECtHR found that the rent control scheme constituted a violation of the right to property, as in practice it was "forcing landlords to accept a level of rent which bore no relation whatsoever to the costs of maintenance of property".[901] Thus, after identifying the underlying systemic problem in this case as "the malfunctioning of Polish housing legislation",[902] the ECtHR stated in the operative part that Poland "must (...) through appropriate legal and/or other measures, secure in its domestic legal order a mechanism maintaining a fair balance between the interests of landlords and the general interest of the community".[903] Thus, although it still refrained from giving a very specific order to the legislator, the fact that such mechanism or procedure had to be "secure[d] in [the State's] domestic legal order" strongly indicates that this needed to be done through a legislative amendment.[904] In fact, the legislative nature of this remedy was criticised by some judges in separate opinions.[905]

The cases of *Maria Atanasiu vs. Romania (2010)* and *Manushaqe Puto vs. Albania* (2012) also dealt with compensations for property loss during communist regimes.[906] In both cases, the ECtHR included rather broad

900 ECtHR, *Hutten-Czapska vs. Poland* (2006), paras. 3-6, 13.

901 ECtHR, *Hutten-Czapska vs. Poland* (2006), paras. 210, 225.

902 ECtHR, *Hutten-Czapska vs. Poland* (2006), operative para. 3.

903 ECtHR, *Hutten-Czapska vs. Poland* (2006), operative para. 4. However, when commenting on the general measures, it stated that "[i]t is not for the Court to specify what would be the most appropriate way of setting up such remedial procedures or how landlords' interests in deriving profit should be balanced against the other interests at stake" (para. 239).

904 By contrast, in ECtHR, *Broniowski vs. Poland* (2004) the remedial measure was much broader, mentioning only the State's obligation to "secure the implementation of the property right" with respect to the affected individuals.

905 See ECtHR, *Hutten-Czapska vs. Poland* (2006), separate opinions of judges Zagrebelsky and Zupančič. The latter stated for example that "the Court clearly does not have, with the usual paraphernalia of constitutional law, an interest in meddling in what national legislation should or should not do".

906 The factual context of ECtHR, *Maria Atanasiu vs. Romania* (2010) is related to the nationalisation by Romania of an important number of buildings and "virtually all

remedial measures, establishing only Romania's and Albania's obligation to adopt "measures to ensure effective protection of the rights guaranteed by Article 6 § 1 of the Convention and Article 1 of Protocol No. 1, in the context of all the cases similar to the present case".[907] However, the legislative nature of these remedies can be seen in the argumentative part of the judgment, where the Court mentioned that legislative reforms were probably needed, including even "an overhaul of the legislation in order to create clear and simplified rules of procedure".[908]

b) Property rights in the context of state succession

Another important sub-category of cases with legislative measures is the one affecting property rights in the context of state succession. This is mainly related to the dissolution of the former Soviet Federal Republic of Yugoslavia (SFRY).[909] The first of these cases is *Grudić vs. Serbia* (2012), a rather particular one in this analysis, as the legislative measures were not

agricultural land" between 1949 and 1962. After the end of the communist regime, the State adopted several laws in order to redress the victims of property rights violations, through the restitution of nationalised properties or compensation when this was no longer possible. The applicants of this case claimed that they had suffered an unlawful deprivation of property and that afterwards the State had failed to restitute or compensate this loss, despite multiple domestic claims and even favourable judicial decisions in this respect (paras. 14-43). *Manushaqe Puto vs. Albania* (2012) concerned several applicants who had inherited a title over plots of land that had been however confiscated by the State or otherwise expropriated during the communist regime or even before that. Albania set up several administrative commissions in charge of determining a financial compensation for the cases in which the restoration of property was no longer possible, and these commissions had issued binding decisions requesting the payment of a financial compensation to the applicants. However, the State had failed to enforce these decisions and pay the requested sums for over ten years (ECtHR, *Manushaqe Puto vs. Albania* (2012), paras. 4-22).

907 ECtHR, *Manushaqe Puto vs. Albania* (2012), operative para. 6.

908 ECtHR, *Maria Atanasiu vs. Romania* (2010), para. 235. Similarly in *Manushaqe Puto vs. Albania* (2012), para. 110. However, as usual these concrete measures were "suggested (...) on a purely indicative basis", as "the national authorities retain full discretion in choosing (...) the general measures to be laid down in the domestic legal system" (ECtHR, *Maria Atanasiu vs. Romania* (2010), para. 236).

909 See generally on the ECtHR and state succession, Menno T. Kamminga, "Impact on State Succession in Respect of Treaties", in Menno T. Kamminga and Martin Scheinin (eds.), *The Impact of Human Rights Law on General International Law*, Oxford: OUP, 2009, pp. 99-109.

included in the context of a pilot judgment procedure and were directed towards securing restitution for the specific applicants, instead of non-repetition for further potential victims.[910]

Two further legislative measures were included in the judgment of ECtHR, *Ališić vs. Bosnia and Herzegovina, Croatia, Serbia, Slovenia and the Former Yugoslav Republic of Macedonia* (2014). This application was directed against five successor states of the SFRY and relates to the applicants' inability to withdraw 'old' currency savings from their accounts after the dissolution of this state. In the early 1990s, during an economic crisis, the SFRY restricted the withdrawal of foreign currency funds from its banks. After the State's dissolution in 1992, these funds remained frozen in some of the successor states, as they could not reach an agreement regarding the distribution of the SFRY's guarantees for those savings. In this regard, the Court observed in its Chamber judgment that both Croatia and Macedonia had repaid most or even all the 'old' foreign-currency savings, but that this was not the case for Slovenia and Serbia.[911] The ECtHR thus decided in its Chamber judgment to apply the pilot judgment procedure and included two separate measures against Serbia and Slovenia ordering each of them to "undertake all necessary measures (...) in order to allow [the applicants] and all others in their position to be paid back their 'old' foreign-currency

910 This case dealt with the Serbian Government's failure to pay the disability pensions to which the applicants were entitled. The applicants were residents of Kosovo and had been receiving disability pensions by Serbia until 2000, when Kosovo was placed under international administration. From there on the State suspended these payments, even after the applicants relocated to Serbia in 2005. In the operative paragraphs, the ECtHR stated that "the respondent Government must (...) take all appropriate measures to ensure that the competent Serbian authorities implement the relevant laws in order to secure payment of the pensions and arrears in question" (*Grudić vs. Serbia* (2012), operative para. 3). As the judgment did not talk about other pensions besides those of the applicants, it is understood that these "arrears and pensions" are only those of the applicants. Thus, in this case the legislative remedy clearly serves a function of restitution instead of non-repetition.

911 Therefore, the Court found a violation of the right to property by these two states (ECtHR, *Ališić vs. Bosnia and Herzegovina, Croatia, Serbia, Slovenia and the Former Yugoslav Republic of Macedonia* (2012), para. 74). In addition, it found that no effective remedy for claiming and potentially obtaining the repayment of the savings was available in these two states, thus constituting a violation of Art. 13 ECHR (para. 90) The Grand Chamber agreed and upheld these findings (ECtHR, *Ališić vs. Bosnia and Herzegovina, Croatia, Serbia, Slovenia and the Former Yugoslav Republic of Macedonia* (2014), paras. 125, 136).

savings".[912] In the Grand Chamber judgment, the required measures were indicated with more detail as to their legislative nature, by determining that both states "must make all necessary arrangements, *including legislative amendments* in order to allow [the applicants] and all others in their position to recover their 'old' foreign-currency savings".[913]

c) Property rights in post-conflict situations

The last sub-category of ECtHR remedies included here concerns property rights in post-conflict situations. The ECtHR has dealt with this issue in the context of several conflicts, such as the conflict in Bosnia and Herzegovina,[914] the Nagorno-Karabakh conflict,[915] as well as the Turkey-Cyprus conflict.[916] It has, however, only included legislative measures with respect to the latter one. This was done in the case of *Xenides-Arestis vs. Turkey* (2005), where the applicant alleged that Turkish military forces prevented her from accessing her property in Northern Cyprus.[917] The ECtHR found that this constituted a violation of the right to property, and noted that the violation originated in "a widespread problem affecting large numbers of people, namely the unjustified hindrance of her 'respect for her home' and 'peaceful enjoyment of her possessions' as a matter of 'TRNC' policy or practice".[918] Thus, it indicated in the operative paragraphs that the State "must introduce a remedy which

912 ECtHR, *Ališić vs. Bosnia and Herzegovina, Croatia, Serbia, Slovenia and the Former Yugoslav Republic of Macedonia* (2012), operative para. 11.

913 ECtHR, *Ališić vs. Bosnia and Herzegovina, Croatia, Serbia, Slovenia and the Former Yugoslav Republic of Macedonia* (2014), operative paras. 10 and 11 (emphasis added).

914 See generally Antoine Christian Buyse, *Post-conflict Housing Restitution: The European Human Rights Perspective with a Case Study on Bosnia and Herzegovina*, Cambridge: Intersentia, 2008.

915 See especially the two 'mirror judgments' of the ECtHR in *Chiragov vs. Armenia* (2015) and *Sargsyan vs. Azerbaijan* (2015).

916 In the case examined in this sub-section, the Court relied extensively on the reasoning applied in *Loidizou vs Turkey* (1996) and the inter-state case of *Cyprus vs. Turkey* (2001). However, in these previous judgments the Court had abstained from ordering structural remedies. See on this issue Kudret Özersay and Ayla Gürel, "Property and Human Rights in Cyprus: The European Court of Human Rights as a Platform of Political Struggle", *Middle Eastern Studies* 44(2), 2008, pp. 291-321, showing how the proceedings before the ECHR concerning property rights in the context of the Cyprus conflict were used by both parties as another arena for their political struggles.

917 ECtHR, *Xenides-Arestis vs. Turkey* (2005), para. 3.

918 ECtHR, *Xenides-Arestis vs. Turkey* (2005), para. 38.

secures genuinely effective redress for the Convention violations identified in the instant judgment in relation to the present applicant as well as in respect of all similar applications pending before it".[919]

d) Property rights of indigenous communities

With respect to the IACtHR, its only judgments with legislative measures concerning property rights are those related to the right to collective property of indigenous peoples with respect to their ancestral territories.[920] In this respect, the IACtHR has developed a specific approach towards indigenous property rights, giving them a collective dimension, as opposed to the ECtHR which deals with this issue as standard property cases.[921] The first case where this adaptation of property rights to indigenous contexts took place is *Awas Tingni vs. Nicaragua* (2001). This was considered a landmark case in international law, being "the first legally binding decision by an international tribunal to uphold the collective land and resource rights of indigenous peoples".[922] Among other issues, the IACtHR pointed in this case to "the lack of specific and effective legislation for indigenous communities to exercise their rights", and ordered Nicaragua to "adopt in its domestic law (...) an effective mechanism for delimitation, demarcation, and titling of the property of indigenous communities, in accordance with their customary law, values, customs and mores".[923] The same type of measures, ordering the adoption of legal mechanisms for indigenous communities to claim a title over their ancestral lands, have become a rather commonly utilised remedy in the IACtHR's case law related to indigenous property rights.

919 ECtHR, *Xenides-Arestis vs. Turkey* (2005), operative para. 5.

920 See generally on this issue Alejandro Fuentes, "Protection of Indigenous Peoples' Traditional Lands and Exploitation of Natural Resources: The Inter-American Court of Human Rights' Safeguards", *International Journal on Minority and Group Rights* 24(3), 2017, pp. 229-253.

921 See Elena Abrusci, "Judicial Fragmentation on Indigenous Property Rights: Causes, Consequences and Solutions", *IJHR* 21(5), 2017, pp. 550-564.

922 See James Anaya and Claudio Grossman, "The Case of Awas Tingni v. Nicaragua: A New Step in the International Law of Indigenous Peoples", *Arizona Journal of International and Comparative Law* 19(1), 2002, pp. 1-16, at p. 2.

923 IACtHR, *Awas Tingni Community vs. Nicaragua* (2001), para. 128 and operative para. 3.

It was included, *inter alia,* in three judgments against Paraguay and two against Suriname.[924] Moreover, in the remedial provisions of *Lhaka Nonhat vs. Argentina* (2020), the IACtHR added procedural requirements for the adoption of such laws. It specifically "order[ed] the State, prior to adopting the legislative and/or any other measures ordered (...), to establish actions that permit the participation of the country's indigenous peoples and/or communities (not only the victims in this case) in consultation processes in relation to such measures".[925] It should be noted, however, that in a separate opinion one of the judges criticised the use of legislative remedies in this case, arguing that these rights "do not require laws to give them effect".[926]

The ACtHPR took inspiration from this remedial case law of its Inter-American counterpart, and in 2022 ordered Kenya to adopt the necessary measures "to delimit, demarcate and title Ogiek ancestral land and to grant collective title to such land in order to ensure, with legal certainty, the Ogiek's use and enjoyment of the same".[927] However, as explained in the Introduction to this book, the main difference in this respect is that here the ACtHPR is prescribing these measures only in the benefit of one indigenous community and not for all the others inhabiting the country. This is therefore not qualified as a legislative remedy, as demarcating and titling in favour of a single community can be done through administrative measures, and it was argued that there was already a law in force that could allow for it.[928]

4. Electoral Rights

Another important category of legislative remedies is that related to electoral rights. Although the three regional courts have issued legislative remedies dealing with these rights, they have played an especially important role in the case law of the ACtHPR, with 23% of its legislative remedies

924 IACtHR, *Yakye Axa vs. Paraguay* (2005), *Sahoyamaxa vs. Paraguay* (2006), *Xákmok Kásek vs. Parguay* (2010), *Saramaka vs. Suriname* (2007), *Kaliña and Lokono vs. Surinam* (2015).

925 IACtHR, *Lhaka Nonhat vs. Argentina* (2020), para. 355.

926 See IACtHR, *Lhaka Nonhat vs. Argentina* (2020), Dissenting Opinion of Judge Sierra Porto, para. 23, stating in this respect that "rights of indigenous and tribal peoples to property demarcation, delimitation and titling – as the other rights of the indigenous population in general – are rights with direct and immediate legal effect".

927 ACtHPR, *ACmHPR vs. Kenya* (2022), operative para. iv.

928 ACtHPR, *ACmHPR vs. Kenya* (2022), para. 96.

pertaining to this field.[929] These remedies affect a number of electoral laws that were found to be incompatible with states' human rights obligations. In the case law of the other two regional courts, legislative measures concerning electoral rights are much scarcer, with only two of them issued by the IACtHR and one by the ECtHR. The two judgments of the IACtHR concern political participation and the rights of elected public officials, while the legislative remedy on electoral rights issued by the ECtHR forms part of the (in)famous UK prisoners' voting rights saga.

a) The incompatibility of electoral laws before the ACtHPR

Despite being the youngest of the three regional courts, the ACtHPR is the one that has dealt more often with electoral rights in its remedial practice, ordering several states to reform electoral laws and even constitutional provisions related to electoral issues. In accordance with its broad scope of review, the Court has not only assessed the compatibility of electoral norms with the ACHPR but also with the African Charter on Democracy and the ECOWAS Protocol on Democracy and Good Governance. Especially relevant in this respect are two cases where the Court ordered Tanzania to reform its Constitution in order to increase democratic pluralism and to allow for the judicial investigation of cases of electoral fraud.

The first of them dealt with a provision of the Constitution of Tanzania prohibiting independent candidates from running for office at all levels. This constitutional provision was found to constitute a violation of several rights under the ACHPR, including the right to political participation, the freedom of association, the right not to be discriminated against and the right to equality before the law.[930] The ACtHPR indicated in the operative provisions that "[t]he Respondent is directed to take constitutional, legislative and all other necessary measures within a reasonable time to remedy

929 In contrast, legislative remedies related to electoral rights represent a 3% of both those of the ECtHR and the IACtHR. This focus of the ACtHPR on electoral issues can be observed not only in the judgments discussed below, but also in its advisory opinions. See for example ACtHPR, *Advisory Opinion issued at the Request of the PanAfrican Lawyers Union (PALU)*, Request No. 001/2020, 16 July 2021, on the right to participate in the government of one's country in the context of an election held during a public health emergency or a pandemic.

930 ACtHPR, *Tanganyika Law Society and Legal and Human Rights Centre* vs. *Tanzania* (2013), operative paras. 1 and 2.

the violations (...)".[931] This case is presented by Gathii and Mwangi as an example of the fact that the ACtHPR "serves as a forum where opposition politicians can advance their causes", due to the structural advantages enjoyed domestically by incumbent governments, which make the task of those in the opposition extremely difficult at that level.[932]

The other case concerning electoral provisions of the Tanzanian Constitution affected its Article 41(7), establishing that "where a candidate is declared duly elected by the electoral Commission in accordance with this Article, no court shall have jurisdiction to investigate his election".[933] The ACtHPR found that this provision introduced an unjustified differentiation between litigants, thus constituting discrimination, while also violating the "right to have its case heard" (i.e., to a domestic remedy).[934] Here, it was even more specific as to the constitutional character of the remedial provision, by ordering Tanzania to "ensure that article 47(1) of the Constitution is amended and aligned with the provisions of the Charter".[935]

Another relevant judgment on this topic dealt with Ivorian Law no. 2014-335, governing the composition, organisation, duties and functioning of the State's Independent Electoral Commission. The ACtHPR found that this law (which had been challenged by an NGO) provided for an imbalance in the composition of the Electoral Commission in favour of the incumbent government, thus failing to guarantee the independence and impartiality of electoral bodies.[936] Lastly, the ACtHPR determined that Article 27 of the Charter on Political Parties of Benin infringed the freedom of association under the ACHPR because according to this provision, political parties would lose their legal status if they failed to present candidates for two parliamentary elections.[937] In the same case, the ACtHPR also found that the Electoral Code of Benin infringed the rights to freedom of association and non-discrimination by prohibiting independent candidates

931 ACtHPR, *Tanganyika Law Society and Legal and Human Rights Centre* vs. *Tanzania* (2013), operative para. 3.

932 Gathii and Mwangi, in Gathii (ed.), 2020, pp. 242-243 and 253.

933 ACtHPR, *Jebra Kambole vs. Tanzania* (2020), para. 34.

934 ACtHPR, *Jebra Kambole vs. Tanzania* (2020), operative para. vi.

935 ACtHPR, *Jebra Kambole vs. Tanzania* (2020), operative para. viii.

936 As provided by Art. 17 of the African Charter on Democracy and Art. 3 of the ECOWAS Democracy Protocol (ACtHPR, *APDH vs. Côte d'Ivoire* (2016), para. 132-135). This constituted in turn a violation of Art. 13 of the ACHPR (para. 136) as well as of the right to equal protection before the law under Art. 3(2) ACHPR (para. 151).

937 ACtHPR, *Ajavon vs. Benin* (2020), paras. 240-247, 358.

and electoral alliances, as well as the right to participate in the government of one's country because of the residency requirement for candidates, ordering its amendment.[938] Similarly, the reform of the Electoral Code of Mali was also requested in a more recent judgment.[939]

b) Prisoners' voting rights before the ECtHR

Despite the ECtHR's constant focus on conditions of detention in its case law,[940] the first case with legislative remedies affecting individuals in detention did not deal with this issue but with their voting rights.[941] This case in question, *Greens and MT vs. UK* (2010), formed part of the saga on prisoners' voting rights in this State.[942] In this case, the two applicants had attempted to register to vote but they were rejected by the authorities due to their status as convicted persons, in accordance with the British Representation of the People Act of 1983. In a succinct analysis, after finding that the 1983 Act had not been amended and the blanket voting prohibition for prisoners was still in place in the aftermath of *Hirst vs. UK* (2001), the ECtHR found a violation of Art. 3 Protocol 1 ECHR. The Court

938 ACtHPR, *Ajavon vs. Benin* (2020), paras. 198-220, 358. The same legislative remedy was also included in *XYZ vs. Benin (I)* (2020), operative para. xiv), as well as in *Houngue Eric Noudehouenou vs. Benin* (2020), operative para. xi). In these cases, it was because the Electoral Code had been adopted after a constitutional reform that been declared to be in violation of the State's human rights obligations. See below section I. 8 ("Constitutional Issues").

939 ACtHPR, *Oumar Mariko vs. Mali* (2022), operative para. xvii.

940 See above section I. 1 c).

941 There is only one judgment in which the ECtHR has included a legislative remedy dealing with electoral rights. However, it has dealt with this issue on a number of further judgments. In this respect, a notorious case is ECtHR, *Sejdić and Finci vs. Bosnia and Herzegovina* (2009), where the ECtHR found for the first time that a constitutional provision was incompatible with the Convention, although it did not order any specific remedies in this regard.

942 This issue had been dealt first with by the ECtHR in the case of *Hirst vs. UK* (2001), which received a lot of attention both in- and outside this State. See for example Sophie Briant, "Dialogue, Diplomacy and Defiance: Prisoners' Voting Rights at Home and in Strasbourg", *EHRLR* 16(3), 2011, pp. 243-252; Ed Bates, "Analysing the Prisoner Voting Saga and the British Challenge to Strasbourg", *HRLR* 14(3), 2014, pp. 503–540. See on this conflict between the ECtHR and the UK, Chapter 6 of this book.

made the legislative nature of this problem very explicit,[943] and stated that a "legislative amendment is required in order to render the electoral law compatible with the requirements of the Convention".[944] Therefore, the ECtHR included in the operative part a measure ordering the UK to "bring forward, (...) legislative proposals intended to amend the 1983 Act and, if appropriate, the 2002 Act in a manner which is Convention-compliant" as well as to "enact the required legislation".[945] This was, notably, one of the cases in which the legislative nature of the requested remedies was made more explicit by the Strasbourg Court.

c) Political participation and the rights of elected officials before the IACtHR

The IACtHR has also issued legislative remedies related to electoral rights, but it has only done so in two cases. [946] The first case, *Yatama vs Nicaragua* (2005), was also included in the section on the protection of indigenous communities, as the IACtHR included a legislative measure in order to ensure their political participation.[947] The IACtHR went nevertheless even further and, in a separate measure, ordered the reform of the State's Electoral Act, as well as the regulation of certain procedural aspects related to electoral participation that extended to the rest of the population.[948] The second case concerned Gustavo Petro, a then well-known opposition leader in Colombia who at the time of writing is the President of this State. There, the Court found that the domestic law allowing for the "disqualification

---

943 The ECtHR argued that the UK's failure "to introduce legislative proposals to put an end to the current incompatibility of the electoral law with Article 3 of Protocol No. 1 is not only an aggravating factor as regards the State's responsibility under the Convention for an existing or past state of affairs, but also represents a threat to the future effectiveness of the Convention machinery" (ECtHR, *Greens and MT vs. UK* (2010), para. 111).

944 ECtHR, *Greens and MT vs. UK* (2010), para. 112. It refrained however from indicating what the amended law should look like, as "in matters of general policy (...) opinions within a democratic society may reasonably differ" (para. 113).

945 ECtHR, *Greens and MT vs. UK* (2010), operative para. 6.

946 Nevertheless, electoral rights have also been dealt with in the IACtHR's advisory jurisprudence, such as in its advisory opinion on presidential re-elections. See IACtHR, *Indefinite Presidential Re-election in Presidential Systems in the context of the Inter-American System of Human Rights,* Advisory Opinion OC-28/21 (2021).

947 See above section I. 1 a) of this chapter.

948 IACtHR, *Yatama vs. Nicaragua* (2005), operative para. 10.

or dismissal of a democratically elected public official by an administrative authority and not by 'a conviction by a competent judge in criminal proceedings' is contrary to Article 23(2) of the Convention", and therefore ordered its reform.[949]

5. Nationality Rights

Nationality rights is also a field in which all three regional human rights courts have issued legislative remedies, although rather exceptionally.[950] Both the ECtHR and the ACtHPR have done so in one judgment, and the IACtHR in two. The American Convention is the only regional human rights treaty that includes the right to a nationality, which can be found in its Article 20. In the African system, a protocol to the ACHPR 'on the Specific Aspects of the Right to a Nationality and the Eradication of Statelessness in Africa' was adopted by the ACmHPR in 2015, while the ECtHR has usually dealt with these issues through Article 8 ECHR. The four legislative remedies included in this section affect the issue of statelessness.[951] The main difference among them is that in the case of the ECtHR, the remedy was related to statelessness in the context of state succession, while those of the IACtHR and the ACtHPR concerned the deprivation of citizenship and statelessness in the context of migration.

949 IACtHR, *Petro Urrego vs. Colombia* (2020), para. 113, operative para. 8 ("The State shall, within a reasonable time, update its domestic legal code in accordance with the parameters established in this judgment").

950 Nationality rights encompass "the right to a nationality, the right not to be arbitrarily deprived of one's nationality, the right to change one's nationality and (...) 'the right to naturalisation'". See David Owen, "On the Right to Have Nationality Rights: Statelessness, Citizenship and Human Rights", *NILR* 65, 2018, pp. 299–317, at p. 300. See also Alice Edwards, "The meaning of nationality in international law in an era of human rights", in Alice Edwards and Laura van Waas (eds.), *Nationality and Statelessness under International Law*, Cambridge: CUP, 2014, pp. 11-43.

951 See in this respect Michelle Foster and Hélène Lambert, "Statelessness as a Human Rights Issue: A Concept Whose Time Has Come", *International Journal of Refugee Law* 28(4), 2016, pp. 564–584, arguing that the landmark decisions issued by regional human rights courts reflect the current importance of statelessness as a human rights issue.

a) Statelessness in the context of state succession

Statelessness became an important issue in Europe during the 1990s, especially due to the "wave of disappearances or dissolutions of states" that took place during that time.[952] This led to the adoption of the European Convention on Nationality in 1997 and the ILC Articles on Nationality in relation to the Succession of States in 1999.[953] The ECtHR had to deal with this issue as well, for example in the case of *Kurić vs. Slovenia* (2010), which concerns the issue of nationality laws that are discriminatory in the context of state succession. This case relates to citizens of other successor states to the SFRY that were residing in Slovenia at the moment of its independence. In accordance with several laws adopted at that time, they had three months to apply for Slovenian nationality. In case they failed to do so, their names were 'erased' from the register. In consequence, a number of them became stateless. The Slovenian Constitutional Court found this to be unconstitutional, and the ECtHR ruled in its Chamber judgment that it constituted a violation of Art. 8 ECHR. It therefore included an operative provision ordering the State to adopt "appropriate general and individual measures to secure the applicants' right to a private and/or family life and effective remedies in this respect".[954] Moreover, the ECtHR stated with respect to the legislative nature of these measures that "the failure by the Slovenian legislative and administrative authorities to comply with the Constitutional Court's decisions clearly indicates the appropriate general and individual measures to be adopted in the Slovenian domestic legal order so that the violations found may be remedied: *enactment of appropriate legislation* and regulation of the situation of the individual applicants by issuing retroactive permanent residence permits".[955]

---

952 See Ineta Ziemele, "State Succession and Issues of Nationality and Statelessness", in Alice Edwards and Laura van Waas (eds.), *Nationality and Statelessness under International Law*, Cambridge: CUP, 2014, pp. 217-246, at p. 217.

953 See ILC, "Articles on Nationality of Natural Persons in relation to the Succession of States with commentaries", *Yearbook of the International Law Commission*, 1999, vol. II, Part Two, pp. 23–24; European Convention on Nationality, especially Art. 18, dealing with nationality in the context of state succession. See also Ziemele, 2014, p. 222 ("it was only after the last major wave of state successions in the 1990s that international law really made strides in elaborating standards for the regulation of nationality in this context").

954 ECtHR, *Kurić vs. Slovenia* (2010), operative para. 6.

955 ECtHR, *Kurić vs. Slovenia* (2010), para. 407 (emphasis added). Indeed, the legislative measures were implemented by Slovenia, adopting a new law on nationality

b) Deprivation of citizenship in the context of migration

The other cases included in this section have to do with the deprivation of citizenship and statelessness in the context of migration.[956] The issue of migration and human rights has been mostly discussed with respect to the ECHR,[957] as it was until recently an issue affecting more the European than the inter-American or African contexts.[958] However, a country in which this has been an issue for a long time is the Dominican Republic (DR), due to the migration flows coming from Haiti.[959] Indeed, the two cases in which the IACtHR has ordered to reform domestic laws in this area concern the

and issuing residence permits. Thereafter, the ECtHR issued its Grand Chamber judgment on this case. There, it pointed to a number of shortcomings of the enacted legislation, highlighting that under the Slovenian legal order "the whole category of the 'erased' [were] still denied compensation for the infringement of their fundamental rights" (*Kurić vs. Slovenia* (2012), para. 412). Therefore, it decided to apply the pilot judgment procedure, putting the focus on the compensatory aspect and requesting the State to set up an ad hoc compensation scheme for those 'erased' (*Kurić vs. Slovenia* (2012), operative para. 9). The question remains here whether this remedy issued by the GC can be qualified as a legislative one, as contrary to the introduction of a domestic remedy (which usually requires a legislative act) an *ad hoc* compensation scheme can be set up through administrative action. However, Slovenia introduced this compensation scheme through another legislative enactment, and in its subsequent just satisfaction judgment, the GC considered this "appropriate" and avoided including any general measures (*Kurić vs. Slovenia* (2014), paras. 138-139). In any case, the chamber judgment in *Kurić vs. Slovenia* (2010) is clearly including a legislative measure, which was indeed effective.

956 On the close links between migration and statelessness, see Sophie Nonnenmacher and Ryszard Cholewinski, "The nexus between statelessness and migration", in Alice Edwards and Laura van Waas (eds.), *Nationality and Statelessness under International Law*, Cambridge: CUP, 2014, pp. 247-263.

957 See generally Başak Çalı, Ledi Bianku and Iulia Motoc (eds.), *Migration and the European Convention on Human Rights*, Oxford: OUP, 2021. Although the ECtHR has produced important jurisprudence in this field, it has not yet included migration-related legislative remedies in its judgments. See also on the ECtHR's case law in this area David Moya and Georgios Milios (eds.), *Aliens before the European Court of Human Rights*, Leiden: Brill Nijhoff, 2021.

958 This has changed recently due to the political and social situation of Venezuela. More than 7 million people have left the country during the last years according to the UNCHR, and many Latin American states are nowadays increasingly faced with the management of migration (https://www.unhcr.org/emergencies/venezuela-situation).

959 See Eugenio Matibag and Teresa Downing-Matibag, "Sovereignty and Social Justice: The 'Haitian Problem' in the Dominican Republic", *Caribbean Quarterly* 57(2), 2011, pp. 92-117.

denial of Dominican authorities to register children born in the DR with parents in an irregular situation, thus depriving them of their access to nationality and rendering them *de facto* stateless.[960] As will be explained in Chapter 6, these remedies were the origin of a conflict between the DR and the inter-American human rights bodies.

The case of the ACtHPR included in this section is *Anudo Ochieng Anudo vs. Tanzania* (2018), dealing with the expulsion and withdrawal of the citizenship of a Tanzanian individual. When Mr. Anudo, born in Tanzania, applied for a marriage license, he was accused of misrepresenting his identity, and in consequence, his passport was confiscated and he was expelled to Kenya, a state that did not recognise him as a citizen. The ACtHPR found this to be an arbitrary deprivation of citizenship in violation of Article 15(2) UDHR, as well as an arbitrary expulsion contrary to Article 13 ICCPR.[961] When dealing with the victim's right to an effective remedy, the Court noted that in accordance with Article 10(f) of the Tanzanian Immigration Law, the decision of the Minister of Home Affairs declaring a person an "illegal immigrant" is final. After finding that this constitutes a violation of the right to be heard by a judge under Art. 7 ACHPR, the Court concluded that the aforementioned law "contains gaps in as much as it does not allow citizens by birth to exercise judicial remedy where their nationality is challenged".[962] Thus, it ordered Tanzania to "amend its legislation to provide individuals with judicial remedies in the event of dispute over their citizenship".[963]

6. Freedom of Expression

Freedom of expression is also an issue that affects the three regional courts to a similar extent.[964] In this regard, all of them have included legislative

960 These are the cases of IACtHR, *Yean and Bosco vs. Dominican Republic* (2005), operative para. 8; and *Expelled Dominicans and Haitians vs. Dominican Republic* (2014), operative paras. 19 and 20.

961 ACtHPR, *Anudo Ochieng Anudo vs. Tanzania* (2018), paras. 88 and 106.

962 ACtHPR, *Anudo Ochieng Anudo vs. Tanzania* (2018), para. 117.

963 ACtHPR, *Anudo Ochieng Anudo vs. Tanzania* (2018), operative para. viii. This was re-stated in the judgment on reparations (ACtHPR, *Anudo Ochieng Anudo vs. Tanzania* (2021), operative para. xii).

964 See for example Eduardo Andrés Bertoni, "The Inter American Court of Human Rights and the European Court of Human Rights: A Dialogue on Freedom of Expression Standards", *EHRLR* 3, 2009, pp. 332-352 (examining the impact of the

remedies related to this right in some of their judgments. A number of remedies included here concern the reform of laws that somehow impede the effective exercise of this right, such as criminal law provisions regulating the offences of libel, slander or defamation that are either too broad or disproportionate in terms of their consequences.[965] Thus, most legislative measures in this context demand negative reforms. However, a minority of legislative measures affect the right to public access to information, requesting states to enact laws that regulate this issue. Finally, a third sub-category consists of IACtHR legislative remedies relating to the freedom of expression which do not fall under the two primary sub-categories.

a) The offences of libel, slander and defamation

The IACtHR has ordered the reform of laws regulating the offences of libel, slander and defamation in four cases against Argentina, Chile and Ecuador.[966] For example, *Kimel vs. Argentina* (2008) relates to the publication of a book that expressed criticism towards the judicial authorities and a particular judge. The author was condemned for the offences of libel and slander, which were established very broadly in the Argentinian Criminal Code. Therefore, the IACtHR ordered Argentina to amend the domestic criminal laws that contain these offences, in order to "comply with the requirements of legal certainty so that, consequently, they do not to affect the exercise of the right to freedom of thought and expression".[967] The Court issued similar remedial orders in *Palamara Iribarne vs. Chile* (2005), *Palacio Urrutia vs. Ecuador* (2021) and *Baraona Bray vs. Chile* (2022).[968]

This issue was also taken up by the ACtHPR in the case of *Lohe Issa Konate vs. Burkina Faso* (2014), concerning a journalist who had been

freedom of expression case law of the ECtHR on the IACtHR's case law dealing with this topic).

965 See in this respect Jo M. Pasqualucci, "Criminal Defamation and the Evolution of the Doctrine of Freedom of Expression in International Law: Comparative Jurisprudence of the Inter-American Court of Human Rights", *Vanderbilt Journal of Transnational Law* 39, 2006, pp. 379-433.

966 See generally on the IACtHR's jurisprudence in this area Johannes Seidl, *Meinungsfreiheit in der Rechtssprechungspraxis des Interamerikanischen Gerichtshof für Menschenrechte*, Tübingen: Mohr Siebeck, 2014, especially at pp. 208-216.

967 IACtHR, *Kimel vs. Argentina* (2008), operative para. 11.

968 See IACtHR, *Palamara Iribarne vs. Chile* (2005), operative para. 13; *Palacio Urrutia vs. Ecuador* (2021); *Baraona Bray vs. Chile* (2022), operative para. 9.

convicted of defamation. Notably, in this case, the ACtHPR considered separately the violation of the freedom of expression by domestic laws *per se* and by domestic courts applying those laws.[969] With respect to the law, the ACtHPR considered that the provisions on defamation failed to meet the requirement of proportionality because they established that defamation was an offence punishable by imprisonment. The Court found that, apart from very serious and exceptional circumstances such as incitement to hatred, discrimination or violence, as well as threats or incitement to international crimes, the restriction of the freedom of expression cannot have imprisonment as a consequence.[970] Thus, it found two separate violations due to the existence of the provisions and due to the application of them by courts, and it ordered Burkina Faso to amend these provisions.[971] In a more recent case, this Court also imposed the reform of a specific provision of the Criminal Code of Benin, in order to protect the freedom of expression in the context of criticism towards judicial decisions.[972]

b) The regulation of public access to information

Access to information is also an important aspect of the freedom of expression, and it has been dealt with through legislative remedies by both the IACtHR and the ECtHR. The judgment of the IACtHR in the case of *Claude Reyes vs. Chile* (2006) concerned restrictions on public access to state-owned information. The IACtHR stated that these restrictions need to comply with certain conditions, such as being proportionate and based on a concrete law.[973] At that time there was no law in Chile regulating access to information, and therefore the Court ordered the adoption of such a law in order "to guarantee the protection of the right of access to State-held information".[974] Another relevant case in this context is *Flores Bedregal vs. Bolivia* (2022), where the IACtHR ordered the reform of Bolivia's Organic

969 ACtHPR, *Lohe Issa Konate vs. Burkina Faso* (2014), para. 124.

970 ACtHPR, *Lohe Issa Konate vs. Burkina Faso* (2014), paras. 163-165.

971 It specifically stated in the remedial order that the amendment shall repeal custodial sentences for acts of defamation and make sure that other sanctions for these acts should meet the requirements of necessity and proportionality (ACtHPR, *Lohe Issa Konate vs. Burkina Faso* (2014), operative para. 8).

972 ACtHPR, *Houngue Éric Noudehouenou vs. Benin* (2022), operative para. xvi.

973 IACtHR, *Claude Reyes vs. Chile* (2006), paras. 89-92.

974 IACtHR, *Claude Reyes vs. Chile* (2006), operative para. 7.

Law of the Armed Forces, as it established the withholding of information even when the clarification of enforced disappearances was at stake.[975]

The ECtHR has issued legislative remedies related to the freedom of expression only once, in a case related to access to information and family rights. The case concerns Serbia's failure to give information about the alleged death of the applicant's son.[976] The ECtHR noted that there were "hundreds of parents in the same situation as that of the applicant, namely, whose newborn babies had 'gone missing' following their alleged deaths in hospital wards".[977] Taking into account "the significant number of potential applicants", the Court requested Serbia to "take all appropriate measures, preferably by means of a *lex specialis* (...), to secure the establishment of a mechanism aimed at providing individual redress to all parents in a situation such as, or sufficiently similar to, the applicant's".[978]

c) Other freedom of expression-related issues

Further legislative remedies of the IACtHR related to the freedom of expression also concern the protection of journalists,[979] freedom of expression in the military,[980] and censorship. The issue of censorship was dealt with in the case of *The Last Temptation of Christ vs. Chile* (2001), related to

975 IACtHR, *Flores Bedregal vs. Bolivia* (2022), operative para. 14.

976 ECtHR, *Zorica Jovanovic vs. Serbia* (2013). A few days after he was born, while still in the hospital, the medical staff told the applicant that her son had died. However, the body was never released, the cause of death was not established through an autopsy, the applicant was not informed of when and where her son was buried, and the son's death was not officially recorded (para. 71). The applicant indeed suspected that her son was still alive and had been unlawfully given up for adoption (para. 42). The ECtHR found that these facts disclosed a violation of Art. 8 ECHR (para. 75).

977 ECtHR, *Zorica Jovanovic vs. Serbia* (2013), para. 26.

978 ECtHR, *Zorica Jovanovic vs. Serbia* (2013), para. 92 and operative para. 6 (although without expressly mentioning the preference for a *lex specialis* in the operative provision).

979 IACtHR, *Leguizamón Zaván vs. Paraguay* (2022), operative para. 12, prescribing the adoption of a law for the protection of journalists and human rights defenders from violence after exercising their right freedom of information.

980 In the case of IACtHR, *Usón Ramirez vs. Venezuela* (2009), which is also included in the category on the right to a fair trial, the State was ordered to amend a specific article of its Organic Code of Military Justice (operative para. 9). When specifying the content of the legal reform, the Court mentioned that "the State must allow for the people to exercise the democratic control over all state institutions and their

film productions and a system of previous censorship that was established in Chile's Political Constitution of 1980. In this case, named after the movie 'The Last Temptation of Christ' (as its exhibition was prohibited on the basis of this norm), the IACtHR ordered Chile to "amend its domestic law (...) in order to eliminate previous censorship".[981] Chile ended up amending its Constitution in order to comply with this judgment, which rendered it a very notorious one.

7. Amnesty Laws

Amnesty laws have gained notable importance in the field of human rights law and transitional justice.[982] This category is one of the flagships of the IACtHR, which has consistently declared the incompatibility of these laws with the Convention. Despite representing only 4% of the IACtHR's legislative remedies, those consisting in the invalidation of amnesty laws have become some of the most notorious of this Court, receiving a lot of attention in scholarship.[983] The ACtHPR took inspiration from this practice and also ordered the repeal of an amnesty law in one case due to its incompatibility with human rights obligations. On the other hand, although the ECtHR has never directly decided on the validity of an amnesty law,[984] it has generally taken a more flexible approach in cases related to this

civil servants by means of freely expressing their ideas and opinions about their performance, fearing no further repression" (para. 173).

981 IACtHR, *The Last Temptation of Christ vs. Chile* (2001), operative para. 4. In the reasoning, the Court mentioned expressly Chile's Constitution when stating that the State was failing to adapt its domestic laws to the Convention by maintaining cinematographic censorship in it (at para. 88).

982 See for example Louise Mallinder, "Can Amnesties and International Justice be Reconciled?", *International Journal of Transitional Justice* 1, 2007, pp. 208–230.

983 See Annelen Micus, *The Inter-American human rights system as a safeguard for justice in national transitions: from amnesty laws to accountability in Argentina, Chile and Peru*, Brill Nijhoff, 2015. See also Christina Binder, "The Prohibition of Amnesties by the Inter American Court of Human Rights", *GLJ* 12(5), 2011, pp. 1203-1230; Juan Pablo Perez-Leon Acevedo, "The control of the Inter-American Court of Human Rights over amnesty laws and other exemption measures: Legitimacy assessment", *LJIL* 33, 2020, pp. 667–687.

984 See however Miles Jackson, "Amnesties in Strasbourg", *Oxford Journal of Legal Studies* 38(3), 2018, p. 456, arguing that "there is a good chance that the Court will be seized of an amnesty case in the near future".

issue.[985] It has specified in this respect certain circumstances under which an amnesty law might be lawfully adopted, such as "a reconciliation process and/or a form of compensation to the victims".[986] As it will be observed, the IACtHR has also nuanced its position towards amnesty laws in its most recent cases.[987]

In general, the Latin American amnesty laws were enacted during the 1980s and 1990s, in the context of military dictatorships present at that time in the region. They were either adopted by the regime itself (the so-called 'self-amnesties') or during transitions to democracy and prevented the states from prosecuting human rights violations that were committed in a specific period. In addition, these amnesty laws were an impediment to the victims' relatives discovering the truth, as well as the victims themselves obtaining reparations. The IACtHR ordered for the first time the annulment of amnesty laws in the case of *Barrios Altos vs. Peru* (2001). It concerned two 'self-amnesty' laws, adopted in 1995 by the regime of Fujimori, which impeded holding responsible anyone who had participated in human rights violations between 1980 and 1995. The facts of the case are related to the extrajudicial execution of fifteen people by members of the Peruvian Army in 1991. When the amnesty laws entered into force, the investigation of these facts was closed by the Peruvian High Court of Justice. The IACtHR held in this case that "[s]elf-amnesty laws lead to the defenselessness of victims and perpetuate impunity; therefore, they are manifestly incompatible with the aims and spirit of the Convention", establishing thus the invalidity of

985 In *Tarbuk vs. Croatia* (2012), para. 50, the ECtHR argued that "[t]he state is justified in adopting, in the context of its criminal policy, any amnesty laws it might consider necessary, with the provision, however, that a balance is maintained between the legitimate interests of the State and the interests of individual members of the public in having the right to life protected by law". Nevertheless, in a number of cases against Turkey, the ECtHR found that the existence of amnesty provisions constituted a violation of the State's obligation to investigate acts of torture, arguing that "when an agent of the State is accused of crimes that violate Article 3 of the Convention, (...) the granting of an amnesty or pardon should not be permissible" (see ECtHR, *Yerli vs. Turkey* (2014), para. 61; *Okkali vs. Turkey* (2006), para. 78; *Terzi and Erkmen vs. Turkey* (2007), para. 34).

986 ECtHR, *Marguš vs. Croatia* (2014), para. 139.

987 See for example Perez-Leon Acevedo, *LJIL* 2020, p. 668 ("To some extent, the IACtHR has arguably 'moderated' its approach by considering and balancing competing interests in subsequent cases that involved amnesty laws").

the specific laws.[988] *Barrios Altos* soon became a leading case for the human rights jurisprudence dealing with this topic.[989]

Since then, the IACtHR has ordered this remedy in four other judgments. The case of *Almonacid Arellano vs. Chile* (2006) also dealt with 'self-amnesty',[990] while the issue in *Gomes Lund vs. Brazil* (2010) and *Gelman vs. Uruguay* (2011) were amnesty laws adopted in the context of a transition to democracy.[991] Especially in the latter case, the IACtHR's decision was criticised by a number of commentators for failing to properly consider the domestic democratic procedures, as the Uruguayan amnesty law had been validated twice through democratic referenda.[992] Finally, the case of *Mozote Massacres vs. El Salvador* (2012) dealt with an amnesty law adopted in the context of negotiations aimed at ending a non-international armed conflict. The IACtHR nuanced here its position, stating that in such a context an amnesty may be permitted, although it cannot be applied for war crimes or crimes against humanity.[993] In this case, it is also worth looking at the separate opinion of Judge Garcia-Sayán, subscribed by five of the seven judges of the IACtHR. The subscribing judges left a door open for amnesties, stating that in certain transitional situations, States may weigh "the degree of justice that can be achieved" against the aim of "tolerance

988 IACtHR, *Barrios Altos vs. Peru* (2001), para. 43, operative para. 4, finding that "Amnesty Laws No. 26479 and No. 26492 are incompatible with the [ACHR] and, consequently, lack legal effect".

989 See Pablo González Domínguez and Edward J. Pérez, "Desafíos de la Jurisprudencia de la corte interamericana de derechos Humanos sobre leyes de Amnistía en contextos de Justicia transicional", *Persona y Derecho* 80, 2019, pp. 81-106, examining the influence of *Barrios Altos* on subsequent IACtHR case law in pp. 83-88.

990 Here, the IACtHR expanded on the impossibility of granting amnesty for crimes against humanity, highlighting the irrelevance of "[t]he fact that such provisions have been adopted pursuant to domestic legislation or against it" (IACtHR, *Almonacid Arellano vs. Chile* (2006), para. 120).

991 The Court stated in this regard that the incompatibility of amnesty laws with the ACHR "does not stem from a formal question, such as its origin, but rather from the material aspect as they breach the rights enshrined in Articles 8 and 25 of the Convention" (IACtHR, *Gomes Lund vs. Brazil* (2010), para. 175).

992 See for example Roberto Gargarella, "Democracy and Rights in Gelman v. Uruguay", *AJIL Unbound*, 2015, pp. 115-119. See also Perez-Leon Acevedo, *LJIL* 2020, p. 683 ("The IACtHR should distinguish between normative provisions that lack democratic legitimacy and those that possess an important quota of democratic legitimacy").

993 IACtHR, *Mozote Massacres vs. El Salvador* (2012), paras. 285-286.

and peace".[994] These arguments were not applicable to the case at hand, but rather reflected a trend within international legal practice and scholarship to accept limited amnesties under certain conditions.[995]

Although the IACtHR has been the pioneer and the most active court in regard to amnesty laws, this issue has also been taken up by the ACtHPR, which ordered the repeal of a Beninese amnesty law. It concerned a law adopted "to grant amnesty for crimes, misdemeanors and felonies committed in the context of the legislative elections of April 2019".[996] The ACtHPR followed as well the more flexible approach and concluded that "an amnesty law is compatible with human rights only if it is accompanied by restorative measures for the benefit of the victims".[997] As this was not the case with this law, it found that Benin had violated the right to an effective remedy under Art. 7(1) of the African Charter and prescribed the repeal of this law.[998] It is interesting to compare in this respect the wording of the legislative remedies concerning amnesty laws before these two courts. While the ACtHPR ordered the State to "repeal (...) Law No. 2019 - 39 of 31 July 2019 on amnesty for criminal, tort and offences committed during the legislative elections of 28 April 2019", the IACtHR used a different formula in all its cases related to amnesty laws, by stating in the remedy that the respective laws "lack legal effect".[999] This formulation is rather surprising for an international court, and it will be examined in more detail in Chapter 5 of this book.[1000]

---

994 IACtHR, *Mozote Massacres vs. El Salvador* (2012), Separate Opinion of Judge García Sayan, paras. 37-38.

995 See in this regard Louise Mallinder, "The end of amnesty or regional overreach? Interpreting the erosion of South America's amnesty laws", *ICLQ* 65(3), 2016, pp. 645-680 ("the regional trend appears to be evolving towards a more nuanced position in which limited amnesties and alternative punishments may continue to be permissible"). See also Perez-Leon Acevedo, *LJIL* 2020, p. 683 ("The one-size-fits-all approach of the IACtHR to Latin American amnesty laws/exemption measures should be replaced with more nuanced and case-by-case approaches").

996 ACtHPR, *Ajavon vs. Benin* (2020), paras. 223 and 232.

997 ACtHPR, *Ajavon vs. Benin* (2020), paras. 234-238.

998 ACtHPR, *Ajavon vs. Benin* (2020), para. 239.

999 IACtHR, *Barrios Altos vs. Peru* (2001), operative para. 4 ("lack legal effects"); *Almonacid Arellano vs. Chile* (2006), operative para. 3 ("have no legal effects"); *Gomes Lund vs. Brazil* (2010), operative para. 3 ("lack legal effect"); *Gelman vs. Uruguay* (2011), operative para. 11 ("lacking effects"); *El Mozote Massacres vs. El Salvador* (2012), para. 296 ("lack legal effect").

1000 See in this regard Micus, 2015, pp. 158-160.

8. Mandatory Death Penalty

Unlike the European system, where the death penalty was formally abolished through Protocols 6 and 13 to the ECHR, this punishment is not *per se* incompatible with or prohibited by its American and African counterparts.[1001] The American Convention establishes several limitations regarding the application of this punishment,[1002] while the African Charter is the regional human rights treaty most permissive with the death penalty, not including any restrictions in this regard. Moreover, the ACtHPR has established that this punishment can be compatible with the right to life as long as it is provided by law and imposed after a fair trial with due process.

Thus, it is not surprising that the legislative remedies included in this section have been issued only by the IACtHR and the ACtHPR, and that the death penalty has played a less important role in the case law of the ECtHR.[1003] Indeed, the IACtHR and the ACtHPR have each included legislative remedies concerning the death penalty in four judgments. While the judgments of the former court are directed against three states (Trinidad and Tobago, Barbados and Guatemala), in the case of the latter court the

---

1001 Although Article 2(1) ECHR includes death penalty as an exception to the right to life, this was first abolished during peacetime through the adoption of Protocol 6 in 1983 and then in all circumstances through Protocol 13, adopted in 2002. See in this respect Schabas, *Commentary to the ECHR*, 2015, p. 1200, describing Protocol 13 as "the final step in full abolition". See generally also Jon Yorke, "Inhuman Punishment and Abolition of the Death Penalty in the Council of Europe", 16(1) *European Public Law*, 2010, pp. 77-103, analysing how the interpretation of Art. 3 ECHR has contributed to the dismantling of death penalty in the CoE.

1002 The ACHR (Article 4, paras. 2-6) contains some specifications in this regard. *Inter alia*, it states that capital punishment "shall not be extended to crimes to which it does not presently apply", nor "re-established in states that have abolished it", and that "every person condemned to death shall have the right to apply for amnesty, pardon or commutation of sentence". The IACtHR moreover established in an advisory opinion of 1983 that death penalty should be applied only in the "most serious common crimes" and that "certain considerations involving the person of the defendant (...) must be taken into account" (IACtHR, *Restrictions to the Death Penalty*, Advisory Opinion OC-3/83 (1983), para. 55). In addition, twelve state parties to the ACHR have ratified the 1990 Optional Protocol to abolish the death penalty. See in this respect Hennebel and Tigroudja, *Commentary to the ACHR*, 2022, pp. 182-183.

1003 The death penalty-related case law of the ECtHR concerns mostly cases of extradition to countries where death penalty is still in place. A seminal case in this regard is ECtHR, *Soering vs. UK* (1989). See also William A. Schabas, *The Abolition of the Death Penalty in International Law*, 3rd ed., Cambridge: CUP, 2003, at pp. 259-299.

four of them concern Tanzania.[1004] All of these measures are related to domestic provisions establishing the mandatory death penalty for certain crimes, such as murder or treason. This implies that the death penalty is the automatic consequence of being convicted for these crimes, without any "graduated assessment of the seriousness of the offence, so that it will bear an appropriate relation to the graduated levels of gravity of the applicable punishment".[1005]

In its first case on this topic, the IACtHR determined that the mandatory death penalty in Trinidad and Tobago treated the accused "not as individual, unique human beings, but as undifferentiated and faceless members of a mass who will be subjected to the blind application of the death penalty".[1006] The same argumentation was repeated some years later with regard to the provision of the Guatemalan Criminal Code that stipulated a mandatory death penalty for the crimes of kidnapping and abduction.[1007] In the case of Barbados, section 2 of the State's Offences Against the Person Act read: "[a]ny person convicted of murder shall be sentenced to, and suffer, death".[1008] The Court declared this provision to be "*per se* contrary to the Convention" and ordered the State, as in the other cases, to adopt "such legislative or other measures as may be necessary to ensure that the imposition of the death penalty (...) is not imposed through mandatory sentencing".[1009]

The ACtHPR used the same arguments in the case of *Ally Rajabu vs. Tanzania* (2019).[1010] The two applicants had been found guilty of murder

1004 As it can be observed, most of the IACtHR's judgments on this topic concern Caribbean common law states, a region which "remains a holdout in the steady march toward a customary international human rights norm rejecting capital punishment". See Margaret A. Burnham, "Caribbean Constitutions and the Death Penalty", in Richard Albert et al. (eds.), *The Oxford Handbook of Caribbean Constitutions*, Oxford: OUP, 2020, pp. 421-454, at p. 421.

1005 IACtHR, *Hilaire, Constantin and Benjamin vs. Trinidad and Tobago* (2002), para. 102.

1006 IACtHR, *Hilaire, Constantin and Benjamin vs. Trinidad and Tobago* (2002), para. 101.

1007 IACtHR, *Raxcacó Reyes vs. Guatemala* (2005), paras. 73-82. In addition, Guatemala had expanded death penalty to cases for which it was not foreseen when it ratified the Convention (paras. 57-66).

1008 Cited in IACtHR, *Boyce vs. Barbados* (2007), para. 49.

1009 IACtHR, *Boyce vs. Barbados* (2007), para. 72 and operative para. 7, respectively. The same was ordered in *Dacosta Cardogan vs. Barbados* (2009), operative para. 9.

1010 The aforementioned decisions of the IACtHR have not only influenced its African counterpart, but also constitutional courts, who have annulled provisions estab-

and were sentenced in accordance with section 197 of the Tanzanian Penal Code, which established the mandatory death penalty for this crime.[1011] The ACtHPR found that in the case of Tanzania death penalty was provided by law and the trial had been fair, thus in principle complying with the death penalty requirements established by this court. However, the Court determined that this provision was contrary to the Charter, due to the judges' inability to take into account the individual circumstances of those convicted.[1012] Similar to its American counterpart, the ACtHPR considered mandatory sentencing to the death penalty as arbitrary deprivations of the right to life,[1013] and ordered Tanzania "to remove the mandatory imposition of the death penalty from its penal Code as it takes away the discretion of the judicial officer".[1014] The ACtHPR then included almost identical remedies in three further judgments against Tanzania.[1015]

9. Constitutional Issues

This category is a particular one, as it deals with legislative remedies aiming not at the reform of ordinary laws but of domestic constitutions. Certainly, some remedies prescribe constitutional amendments in further cases, related to issues such as the constitutional regulation of electoral rights or fair trial rights, which are included in the corresponding sections of this chapter.[1016] However, the remedies included in this section affect issues that are of an essentially constitutional nature. It contains in this respect three cases of the IACtHR that relate to the constitutional regulations on the

---

lishing mandatory death penalty in a number of jurisdictions. See Andrew Novak, "The 'Judicial Dialogue' in Transnational Human Rights Litigation: Muruatetu & Anor v. Republic and the Abolition of the Mandatory Death Penalty in Kenya", *HRLR* 18, 2018, pp. 771–790.

1011 ACtHPR, *Ally Rajabu vs. Tanzania* (2019), para. 97.

1012 ACtHPR, *Ally Rajabu vs. Tanzania* (2019), operative para. viii.

1013 ACtHPR, *Ally Rajabu vs. Tanzania* (2019), para. 114. The ACtHPR found a violation not only of article 4 of the ACHPR (i.e. the right to life), but also of Article 1, concerning the general implementation of rights, because Tanzania had not removed this provision from its penal code after the entry into force of the Charter (para. 125).

1014 ACtHPR, *Ally Rajabu vs. Tanzania* (2019), operative para. xv (1).

1015 See ACtHPR, *Amini Juma vs. Tanzania* (2021), *Gozbert Henerico vs. Tanzania* (2022) and *Marthine Christian Msuguri vs. Tanzania* (2022).

1016 See for example ACtHPR, *Jebra Kambole vs. Tanzania* (2020), operative para. viii; ACtHPR, *XYZ vs. Benin (II)* (2020), operative para. xiii; IACtHR, *Digna Ochoa vs. Mexico* (2021).

reform of ordinary laws and another three by the ACtHPR that concern constitutional reforms.

With respect to the IACtHR, the three cases included here concern the constitutions of Trinidad and Tobago and Barbados, which contained provisions that impeded certain laws to be amended under any circumstance, making it impossible for these states to implement other legislative remedies issued by the IACtHR.[1017] Specifically, the Constitution of Trinidad and Tobago, in its section 6, precluded "individuals from challenging (...) all laws or acts carried out pursuant to any law in force in Trinidad and Tobago before 1976, the year the Constitution entered into force".[1018] The case of Barbados is very similar, as section 26 of its Constitution "prevents courts from declaring the unconstitutionality of current laws that were enacted or made before the Constitution came into force".[1019] In other judgments against these two states, the IACtHR had ordered the repeal of ordinary laws that provided respectively for corporal punishments against detainees,[1020] and for the mandatory death penalty as the consequence of certain crimes.[1021] These laws were however protected by the aforementioned constitutional clauses. The Court determined in the former case that "any provision that establishes that [Corporal Punishment] Act's immunity from challenge is likewise incompatible".[1022] In the Barbadian case, this was even more explicit, mentioning that "section 26 of the Constitution of Barbados effectively denies its citizens in general, and the alleged victims in particular, the right to seek judicial protection against violations of their right to life".[1023] The IACtHR thus ordered both states to reform their constitutions in order to allow for the amendment of ordinary laws.[1024]

1017 See generally Natalia Torres Zuñiga, "Control de Normas Constitucionales por la Corte Interamericana de Derechos Humanos", in Pablo Santolaya and Isabel Wences (eds.), *La America de los Derechos*, Madrid: CEPC, 2016, pp. 483-507, especially pp. 496-498.

1018 Cited in IACtHR, *Caesar vs. Trinidad and Tobago* (2005), para. 49(11).

1019 IACtHR, *Boyce vs. Barbados* (2007), para. 75.

1020 IACtHR, *Caesar vs. Trinidad and Tobago* (2005) operative para. 3.

1021 IACtHR, *Boyce vs. Barbados* (2007), operative para. 9.

1022 IACtHR, *Caesar vs. Trinidad and Tobago* (2005), para. 133.

1023 IACtHR, *Boyce vs. Barbados* (2007), para. 79.

1024 IACtHR, *Caesar vs. Trinidad and Tobago* (2005), operative para. 4 ("[t]he State shall amend (...) Section 6 of Trinidad and Tobago's Constitution"); *Boyce vs. Barbados* (2007), operative para. 8, ordering to "remove [the constitutional provision's] immunizing effect". The same argumentation was then repeated in the case of *Dacosta Cardogan vs. Barbados* (2009), which was also related to the

In the case of the ACtHPR, the three 'constitutional' remedies included here concern a reform of the Beninese Constitution that took place in 2019. According to the applicants of these cases, this reform was "adopted in secret, without the involvement of all sections of the Beninese society", in contravention to the principle of national consensus laid down in the African Charter on Democracy, Elections and Governance (ACDEG).[1025] In the first of these cases, the Court determined that in order to be compatible with the ACDEG, constitutional reforms need to be "preceded by a consultation of all actors and different opinions with a view to reaching national consensus or followed, if need be, by a referendum".[1026] As this was not the case with the Beninese constitutional reform, the Court found it to be in violation of Article 10(2) of the ACDEG.[1027] The ACtHPR did not stop there, but considered as well that adopting a constitutional reform without national consensus violates the right to economic, social and cultural development, included in Article 22(1) of the ACHPR, as well as the right to peace and security under Article 23(1) of the Charter.[1028] The Court repeated these arguments in two further cases against Benin.[1029] Moreover, in these three cases, the ACtHPR not only prescribed the repeal of the unconventional constitutional reform but also "all subsequent laws related to the election".[1030]

Offences against the Person Act (establishing the mandatory death penalty) and its preclusion from reform.

1025 Article 10(2) of the ACDEG establishes that "State Parties shall ensure that the process of amendment or revision of their constitution reposes on national consensus, obtained if need be, through referendum". See ACtHPR, *XYZ vs. Benin (II)* (2020), para. 5.

1026 ACtHPR, *XYZ vs. Benin (II)* (2020), para. 102.

1027 ACtHPR, *XYZ vs. Benin (II)* (2020), para. 105. In addition, the ACtHPR established that Benin had infringed the right to information under Article 9 ACHPR because the draft constitutional revision and the debates leading thereto were not publicly available to the population (paras. 119-125).

1028 ACtHPR, *XYZ vs. Benin (II)* (2020), paras. 125-128, 135-137.

1029 ACtHPR, *Ajavon vs. Benin* (2020), paras. 342-343; *Houngue Eric Noudehouenou vs. Benin* (2020), para. 66. However, contrary to the case of *XYZ vs. Benin (II)* (2020), here the Court did not find that the constitutional reform violated the rights to information, to economic, social and cultural development, nor the right to peace.

1030 ACtHPR, *Houngue Eric Noudehouenou vs. Benin* (2020), operative para. xi. In *Ajavon vs. Benin* (2020), para. 358, the ACtHPR even specified that this should be done "in any case before an election", while in *XYZ vs. Benin (II)* (2020), operative para. Xiv, it specifically ordered the repeal of "Law 2019-43 of 15 November 2019 on the Electoral Code". See Chapter 5 for a closer analysis of these orders.

10. Codification of Criminal Offences

The last category comprises remedial measures that order states to criminalise certain acts or to adapt the definition of criminal offences in their national laws. The IACtHR is the only regional human rights court that has issued legislative remedies for this purpose, but it has done so in an important number of cases. In some of them, the IACtHR ordered to legally define acts that were not contemplated by the domestic criminal codes, while in others it ordered to adapt the legal definition to international standards. The enforced disappearance of persons plays a paramount role in this regard. This crime was infamously common during the internal conflicts and authoritarian regimes that were present in Latin America in the early years of the system. In fifteen of the twenty cases included in this category, the IACtHR ordered either to codify the crime of enforced disappearance of persons or to adapt the definition of this crime to international standards.[1031] Besides enforced disappearances, the Court has also ordered states to criminalise acts of torture,[1032] as well as extrajudicial executions.[1033]

These are usually cases in which the IACtHR considers the state responsible for acts constituting *inter alia* enforced disappearance or torture and subsequently finds that these crimes are not codified or properly defined in the domestic legal order, in contravention of treaty obligations to legislate.[1034] For example, in *Trujillo Oroza vs. Bolivia* (2002), the IACtHR considered that the State stood in violation of Art. 3 of the Inter-American Convention on the Enforced Disappearance of Persons, which requires that all state parties define this conduct as a criminal offence.[1035] In addition, it stated that the lack of a legal definition hindered the criminal procedure, allowing for the

1031 The Court specified some aspects that the definition should contain. For example, it mentioned that the law should allow for a declaration of absence and presumption of death in cases of enforced disappearance (IACtHR, *Molina Theissen vs. Guatemala* (2004), operative para. 7), or that no temporal limitations should affect the prosecution of this crime (IACtHR, *Osorio Rivera vs. Peru* (2013), para. 271). This adaptation to international standards has been ordered especially against Peru, in three judgments issued between 2009 and 2016 (IACtHR, *Gomez Palomino vs. Peru* (2009), paras. 102-108; *Osorio Rivera vs. Peru* (2013), para. 206, *Tenorio Roca vs. Peru* (2016), paras. 303 and 304).

1032 IACtHR, *Heliodoro Portugal vs. Panamá* (2008), operative para. 16; *Goiburú vs. Paraguay* (2006), operative para. 14; *Deras García vs. Honduras* (2022), operative para. 13.

1033 IACtHR, *Barrios Altos vs. Peru* (2001), operative para. 5(b).

1034 On the treaty obligations to legislate, see Chapter 1 of this book.

1035 IACtHR, *Trujillo Oroza vs. Bolivia* (2002), para. 95.

impunity of perpetrators, and thus ordered the adoption of this criminal provision.[1036] With respect to the adaptation of legal definitions to international standards, the issue of prescription has also played an important role, for example in two judgments against Brazil dealing with the definition of slavery and crimes against humanity.[1037] In both of these cases, the Court ordered Brazil to amend its criminal code in order to guarantee the non-applicability of statutory limitations on these crimes. Another recent example concerns the definition of rape in the Bolivian Criminal Code. The IACtHR ordered the amendment of this provision in order to make consent the central element of the definition, instead of the requirement of violence or intimidation.[1038]

11. Others

There are finally five further legislative measures included in judgments of the IACtHR and the ACtHPR that do not fit in any of the categories examined above. Some of them are too specific, such as the ones that deal with the prohibition of in-vitro fertilisation in Costa Rica,[1039] or with impermissible restrictions to the right to strike in Benin.[1040] In other cases, they are the only ones of their nature, such as the one related to the right to

1036 IACtHR, *Trujillo Oroza vs. Bolivia* (2002), para. 97 and operative para. 2. The criminalisation of enforced disappearances as such has only been ordered again in *Gomes Lund vs. Brazil* (2010), operative para. 3.

1037 See respectively IACtHR, *Hacienda Brasil Verde vs. Brazil* (2016), operative para. 11 and *Herzog vs. Brazil* (2018), operative para. 8.

1038 IACtHR, *Angulo Losada vs. Bolivia* (2022), operative para. 13. In addition, another legislative measure in this judgment requested the codification of the crime of incest (operative para. 15).

1039 In Costa Rica, the prohibition of practicing in-vitro fertilisation (IVF) techniques was established in its domestic law. In the case of IACtHR, *Artavia Murillo vs. Costa Rica* (2012) the Court ordered the State to adopt "appropriate measures to annul the prohibition to practice IVF" (operative para. 2) and to "regulate (...) the aspects that it considers necessary for the implementation of IVF" (operative para. 3).

1040 ACtHPR, *Ajavon vs. Benin* (2020), para. 358. In this case, the applicant alleged that three articles of the Beninese Law No. 2018-34 violated the right to strike (para. 129). The Court found that not only the contested law, but also two further domestic laws of Benin prohibited the right to strike in violation of the principle of non-regression under the ICESCR (paras. 140-142).

privacy in Argentina,[1041] or the ones concerning the use of force by public officials in Ecuador and the DR.[1042]

II. Different Intensities in the Use of Legislative Remedies

The case law analysis included in this chapter has shown that there is a notoriously similar understanding among regional human rights courts with respect to the issues that should be tackled through legislative remedies. Indeed, all three regional courts have used legislative remedies with regard to six of the ten categories established in this chapter, while two of them (the IACtHR and the ACtHPR) have done so in another three categories, and there is only one category in which the legislative measures come exclusively from one court. However, notable differences among the courts can be observed when looking at the intensity with which each of them has applied legislative remedies to each category. This is reflected in the following charts:

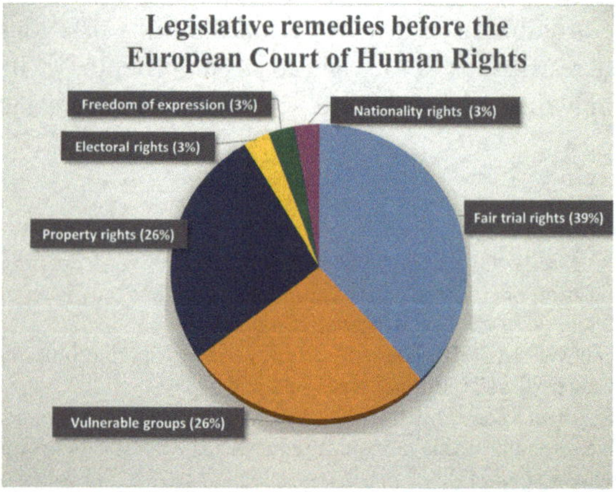

1041 See IACtHR *Fernández Prieto and Tumbeiro vs. Argentina* (2020), operative 7 ("[t]he State shall adapt its domestic law concerning the regulations that permit stopping and searching vehicles or individuals without a court order".).

1042 See respectively, IACtHR, *Casierra Quiñonez vs. Ecuador* (2022), operative para. 10; *Nadege Dorzema vs. Dominican Republic* (2012), operative para. 9. The facts of this latter case relate to the shooting of Dominican Border Patrol Officers against a truck that did not stop at a checkpoint, killing several people that were in it. The Court ordered in this regard the DR to "adapt its domestic laws on the use of force by law enforcement officials".

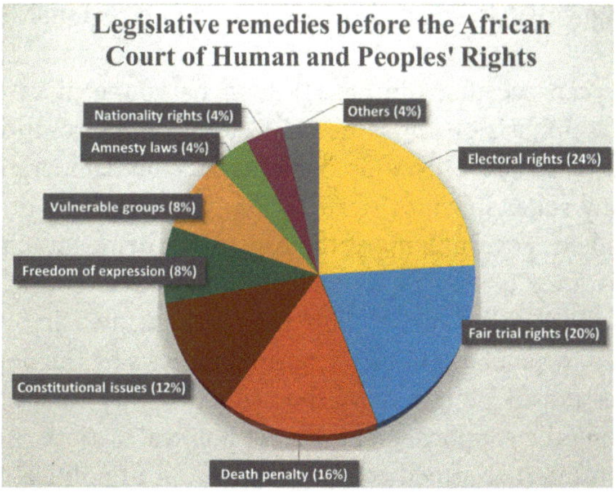

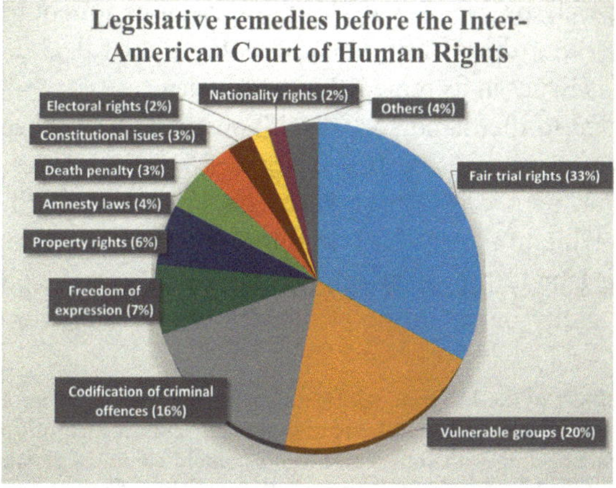

Here it becomes clear that the three courts have different priorities when it comes to the use of legislative measures. It can be observed in this respect that each regional court has favoured three categories, that comprise around two-thirds of all its respective legislative measures. Thereby, it is notable that the only category in which these remedies are frequently used by all of them is that of legislative remedies related to the right to a fair trial. It comprises 39% of the ECtHR's legislative remedies, 33% of those of the IACtHR and 20% of the ones issued by the ACtHPR. This important number of remedial measures is most probably related to the fact that fair trial is the right that is litigated more often before regional human rights courts.[1043]

Then, one can see that the ACtHPR, in its young jurisprudence, has put its main emphasis on the issue of electoral rights, comprising 24% of its legislative remedies. This is probably due to the democratic challenges affecting many states in the African region, with electoral provisions that favour incumbent governments at the expense of democratic pluralism. In addition, this issue is very rarely tackled by domestic courts, which tend to side with those in power.[1044] This has often resulted in accusations of electoral fraud, which have in turn triggered protests by the population and violent repression of protesters by the states' security forces.[1045] Electoral violence among the supporters of different political factions, military *coups d'état*, or even internal armed conflicts as a result of political struggles are also still relatively prevalent issues in the African continent.[1046] Thus, it is not surprising that the African Court devotes a great deal of attention to electoral rights issues in its remedial jurisprudence.

Issues related to the mandatory death penalty have also been important before this court, comprising 16% of its legislative measures. This is due to the fact that people who have been condemned to death in Tanzania are often applying to the ACtHPR in this respect, as this State still foresees in its criminal code the mandatory death penalty as a consequence of being found guilty of the crime of murder. Other categories have played

---

1043 With respect to the IACtHR, see for example Hennebel and Tigroudja, *Commentary to the ACHR*, 2022, p. 311, mentioning that "almost each of the four hundred judgments dealing with substantive rights contain claims of violation of Article 8 [i.e. the right to a fair trial]". However, the remedies afforded more often for fair trial violations are not legislative reforms (a rather exceptional type of remedy) but compensation and declaratory relief. See also Clooney and Webb, *The Right to a Fair Trial in International Law*, 2020, p. 832.

1044 See on this point O'Brien Kaaba, "The Challenges of Adjudicating Presidential Election Disputes in Domestic Courts in Africa", *AHRLJ* 15(2), 2015, pp. 329-354, especially at pp. 335 et seq.

1045 For example, after the elections of Benin in April 2019, allegations of fraud were raised against the State's incumbent president, due to the amendment of electoral laws in his favour shortly before the election. This caused massive protests, to which the military responded with violence against the protestors and arbitrary detentions. See Sarah Maslin Nir, "It Was a Robust Democracy. Then the New President Took Power", *The New York Times*, 4 July 2019, available at: https://www.nytimes.com/2019/07/04/world/africa/benin-protests-talon-yayi.html.

1046 On this issue, see generally Liisa Laakso, "Electoral Violence and Political Competition in Africa", in Nic Cheeseman (ed.), *The Oxford Encyclopedia of African Politics*, Oxford: OUP, 2019, pp. 552-563.

a less important role, but there is still a wide array of them. Legislative remedies related to constitutional issues comprise 12% of the total, while the remaining categories amount to 28% of the measures. However, this rest includes another five categories, making a total of eight of them. This shows that in its young jurisprudence, the ACtHPR has already opened up to use legislative remedies for a considerable variety of issues.

This is different in the case of the ECtHR, where the variety of remedial categories is more limited. Here, legislative measures have been only used with respect to six categories. This includes the aforementioned one on the right to a fair trial (39%), which is the leading one by far, followed by the legislative remedies for the protection of vulnerable people (26%) and legislative remedies for property rights (26%). The final category is especially noteworthy, as it is an area that the other regional courts have not given much weight to. As mentioned before, this importance given to the right to property by the ECtHR is probably due to its understanding of human rights, where economic liberalism can be considered an important component of its interpretation.[1047] Property rights are a good reflection of this liberal human rights tradition, especially because they often take precedence over the states' socio-economic policies. The ECtHR has also included legislative remedies related to electoral rights, nationality rights and the right of freedom of expression, but to a much lesser extent than the other three categories (3% each). In sum, the ECtHR is a court that not only limits considerably the use of legislative remedies in general but, moreover, circumscribes it mostly to very particular issues and generally avoids extending its use beyond that.

The IACtHR, on the other hand, is not only the regional court using legislative remedies more often by far, but also for a wider variety of topics. The ten categories included in this chapter all contain judgments of the IACtHR. Thereby, as is the case with the ECtHR, the IACtHR's most common category of legislative remedies is that of fair trial rights (33%), followed by the protection of vulnerable groups (20%). Unlike the ECtHR, however, the third most common category of legislative remedies before the IACtHR is the codification of criminal offences (16%). The IACtHR is alone in including legislative measures related to this issue, ordering states to codify certain crimes or adapt its definition to international standards.

1047 See Tom Allen, "Liberalism, Social Democracy and the Value of Property under the European Convention on Human Rights", *ICLQ* 59 (4), 2010, pp. 1055-1078.

This is most probably related to the importance given by the IACtHR to the issue of enforced disappearances, which were a sadly common method of repression against dissidents during Latin American military dictatorships.[1048] Most of these orders to codify criminal offences are related precisely to this crime. Therefore, in accordance with its '*nunca más*' mission, the Court puts a great focus on the adequate codification of enforced disappearances at the domestic level.[1049] This is done both with the practical purpose of ensuring that history does not repeat itself in the region and with the symbolic purpose of highlighting the relationship between this crime and the recent history of Latin America. The other remedial categories are also of considerably less weight before this Court, comprising between 2% and 7% of the total number of legislative measures issued by the IACtHR.

Interim Conclusion: A Common Understanding with Different Priorities

To conclude, the case law analysis included in this chapter has first shown the generally common understanding that human rights courts possess regarding when to make use of legislative remedies. Although the ECtHR has been more cautious than its counterparts, limiting the use of such measures to a rather narrow scope of human rights issues, this is understandable due to this court's general hesitation to innovate, especially in the remedial sphere. Thus, when the ECtHR exceptionally includes legislative remedies in a judgment, it does so mostly in fields where it has already prescribed such measures or has at least repeatedly recommended them. This contrasts with the practice of the IACtHR, where remedial innovations have traditionally been a notable feature. It is therefore not surprising that this is the court that has tackled the greatest variety of issues through its legislative measures. Nevertheless, the ACtHPR is not far behind, having included legislative measures concerning eight of the ten categories established in this chapter, despite its much more recent and limited jurisprudence. It can thus be observed that this young court is developing its remedial practice under

1048 See generally Gabriella Citroni, "The Contribution of the Inter-American Court of Human Rights and Other International Human Rights Bodies to the Struggle Against Enforced Disappearance", in Yves Haeck et al. (eds.), *The Inter-American Court of Human Rights*, Cambridge: Intersentia, 2015, pp. 379-402, especially pp. 395-398.

1049 On this 'nunca más' leitmotiv of the IACtHR, see Chapter 3 of this book.

the shadow of the IACtHR, which has been for many years a notorious example of a human rights court aiming to achieve structural transformations through its remedial measures. The ACtHPR probably wants to live up to the expectations in this regard, taking the remedial practice of its inter-American counterpart as its main source of inspiration.

In order to see this common understanding more clearly, it is also worth having a look at fields in which legislative measures have not been used by human rights courts. As it was shown, almost every legislative remedy issued by regional human rights courts fits into the ten categories outlined in this chapter.[1050] This is noteworthy because there are many other types of human rights issues dealt with frequently by the three courts, where they nevertheless avoid including legislative remedies. For example, when examining the case law guides produced by the ECtHR on the most relevant topics it deals with, one can find issues such as data protection, environment, immigration, rights of LGBTI persons, mass protests or terrorism. In none of these categories has the Strasbourg Court ever included a legislative remedy.[1051] Similarly, in the 'Journals of Jurisprudence' of the IACtHR there are also important topics not included in this chapter, and thus without legislative remedies, such as personal integrity; rights of LGBTI people; economic, social, cultural and environmental rights; or corruption and human rights.[1052]

This shows that legislative remedies are favoured by human rights courts only for specific types of human rights issues. These are probably issues that are more closely related to specific laws or legislative omissions, while

---

1050 There are five exceptions in this regard: four legislative remedies of the IACtHR and one of the ACtHPR that do not fit in these categories, which are included in section 11 ('Others').

1051 See ECtHR, *Case-law Guides by theme*, available at: https://www.echr.coe.int/Pages/home.aspx?p=caselaw/analysis/guides&c. The only category included both in the ECtHR's case law guides by theme and in this chapter is that of prisoners' rights. Besides that, the ECtHR produces also case law guides on specific articles. In this context, the only provisions to which the ECtHR attaches legislative remedies are that of the right to a fair trial (Art. 6), the right to property (Art. 1 Prot. 1), the right to free elections (Art. 3 Prot. 1), the freedom of expression (Art. 10), the prohibition of torture (Art. 3) and the right to an effective domestic remedy (Art. 13).

1052 See IACtHR, *Journals of Jurisprudence*, available at: https://www.corteidh.or.cr/publicaciones.cfm?lang=en. In this case, there are several topics which coincide with those listed in this chapter, such as judicial independence, political rights, freedom of expression, transitional justice, indigenous peoples, persons deprived of their liberty, women's human rights or children's rights.

other issues affect mostly administrative practices. On the other hand, it might also be that these are fields in which the courts consider that a stronger homogenisation among the domestic legal frameworks is necessary, while in other areas they are willing to allow for national preferences and particularities. In any case, it is shown that human rights courts have a rather common understanding of the issues that should be tackled through legislative measures.

However, despite this common understanding, the chapter has also shown that each court has different priorities concerning the use of legislative measures. This is reflected in the different intensities in the use of such measures pertaining to the respective categories. The only one where legislative remedies are employed rather intensively by the three courts is that of fair trial rights, a fundamental area of human rights litigation and a rather broad category. Another broad field is the protection of vulnerable groups, where an important number of legislative measures by the ECtHR and the IACtHR can also be found, but curiously not so much by the ACtHPR. Besides that, each court has prioritised a particular issue in this respect. This is the case of property rights before the ECtHR, electoral rights before the ACtHPR and the codification of criminal offences before the IACtHR. As it was explained above, this is probably due to the context in which these courts operate and the self-understanding they have about their respective missions and roles in their region. In this respect, electoral issues are particularly worrying in the African region, while the focus on the codification of criminal offences by the IACtHR has probably to do with its 'nunca más' mission, and the importance given to property rights by the ECtHR might be related to its more liberal self-understanding.

In sum, the systemic human rights problems with respect to which courts are willing to intervene with a high degree of intrusiveness are rather limited and common to the three regional systems, although the priorities of the courts differ to some extent. It is implied in this respect that issues which need to be tackled through legislation are systemic by nature, as they affect a large number of persons and are intrinsic to the domestic legal systems. It is mainly for this reason that courts need to act more intrusively in order to tackle such problems. The next chapter will look precisely at how intrusive regional human rights are when applying legislative remedies, by looking at the way in which such remedial measures are spelled out and how much discretion is left to the domestic legislator in order to implement them.

Chapter 5: Remedial Deference and Domestic Legislatures

The previous chapter showed that there is a common understanding among human rights courts with respect to the type of issues that trigger the use of legislative remedies, despite different priorities in this regard. In this context, such intrusive measures are usually reserved for a rather limited set of human rights issues. This intrusiveness does however not only depend on the question of *when* these measures are employed, but also on *how* this is done. This chapter will therefore focus on the different ways of employing and spelling out legislative remedies, examining in particular the question of how much deference they afford to domestic legislatures.

The concept of deference is generally used in relation to the standard of review employed by international courts when dealing with domestic decisions.[1053] There is however another (often overlooked) dimension of deference, related to the discretion afforded to domestic authorities when implementing an international judgment. I will refer to this as 'remedial deference'. Remedial deference can range from complete deference, when international courts issue judgments that are essentially declaratory and states are free to take any action in consequence, to 'zero deference' with respect to some remedies. For example, when a court specifies the sum that the state must pay as compensation, there are no alternatives other than paying that specific amount. This reflects the fact that different remedial categories offer diverging discretion in the context of their implementation. In this respect, each human rights court has developed its own approach towards remedial deference. However, the issue to be examined here is not so much the deference of the different types of remedies issued by

---

1053 For example, Fahner describes the concept of deference as "the respect that a judge gives to the findings of another institution" (see Johannes Hendrik Fahner, *Judicial Deference in International Adjudication. A Comparative Analysis*, Oxford: Hart, 2020, p. 5). Similarly, Shirlow refers in this respect to the tools used by judges to take into account the authority of other decision-makers (Esmé Shirlow, *Judging at the Interface: Deference to State Decision-Making Authority in International Adjudication*, Cambridge: CUP, 2021, p. 16). Remedial deference is arguably more closely related to the latter definition, as it does not affect a previous finding by a domestic institution but rather a future decision (the implementation of a remedial measure).

human rights courts, but rather the varying degrees of deference within the remedial category of legislative measures.

In this respect, there are many remedial categories in which the amount of deference depends on how the remedial measure is spelled out. For example, it is not the same for a court to order the state to provide human rights training to public officials than to specify the addressees of that training (such as police officers, medical personnel, etc.) or the content of it (women's rights, right to health, etc.). This is the same with respect to legislative measures, which can have different degrees of specificity. Some of them are rather vague, in the sense of prescribing only a legislative reform related to a particular topic, while others are very specific in terms of indicating the concrete provision that needs to be amended and the expected result of that reform.

This chapter will thus examine and normatively assess the specificity of legislative remedies before human rights courts. In order to carry out this normative assessment, it will first inquire about the deference that should be afforded to legislators when implementing a judgment. A concept that can be particularly useful and that will be developed in this respect is that of the 'margin of deliberation', implying that legislative remedies should not curtail the deliberative elements of domestic lawmaking procedures. In addition, the mechanisms developed by human rights courts that relate to deference *vis-à-vis* legislatures will be examined, focusing particularly on the ECtHR's margin of appreciation and the IACtHR's conventionality control. Then, the chapter will analyse the specificity of the three courts' legislative remedies, taking into account the varying nature of these measures and the approach developed by each human rights court in this regard.

I. Deference and Human Rights Remedies

The issue of deference has been extensively studied in human rights scholarship, although most of these studies focus on the deference displayed by courts at the moment of finding a human rights violation, and not so much when defining the consequences of it. It has been even argued that deference is not a very important factor in international adjudication generally, due to "[t]he limited impact of international judicial decisions, which leave States the final say on matters of domestic policy by allowing them to choose the appropriate means to comply with a judgment".[1054] This is nevertheless different when international courts include remedial measures in their judgments, as it binds states to act in a specific way. Thus, remedial deference is a very important aspect when assessing the legitimacy of such measures.[1055]

In general, human rights courts defer to domestic actors mainly for two reasons, related to their superior expertise and their higher democratic legitimacy. Fahner mentions in this context two dimensions of deference, labelled as 'epistemic deference' when it relates to the expertise concerning technical, scientific or factual issues, and 'constitutional deference' regarding the democratic legitimacy of domestic decision-makers.[1056] The latter, he argues, is especially relevant for regional human rights courts.[1057]

However, deference has to remain within boundaries to ensure the effectiveness of human rights protection systems on the ground. It has been argued in this respect that deference needs to be restrained because "it has the potential to create uncertainty and to allow an overly broad margin of appreciation within which States might be tempted to evade their international obligations".[1058] If a human rights court would be completely deferential to states, its function could be questioned. It is therefore a matter of maintaining a proper balance between the amount of discretion that state actors should possess and the effective supervision of these actors' compliance with its human rights obligations.

In this respect, the degree of deference should probably be decided on a case-by-case basis, taking into account a number of circumstances.[1059] Among them, one aspect to consider is the 'democratic pedigree' of the decision that is reviewed, which can derive from the procedure employed to adopt the decision or the democratic credentials of the decision-maker.[1060] In this context, a higher democratic pedigree of the primary decision would imply a more deferential review by the court in question. Domestic

1054 Johannes Hendrik Fahner, "The Limited Utility of Deference in International Dispute Settlement", *LPICT* 21, 2022, at p. 479.

1055 See with respect to the legitimacy of legislative remedies Chapter 1 of this book.

1056 Fahner, *Judicial Deference in International Adjudication,* 2020, pp. 149-157.

1057 Fahner, *Judicial Deference in International Adjudication,* 2020, pp. 200-202.

1058 Laurence Boisson de Chazournes and Jason Rudall, "Judicial Deference: Why Does It Matter?", *LPICT* 21, 2022, pp. 419–424, at p. 423.

1059 See generally Murray and Sandoval, *JHRP* 2020.

1060 See René Urueña, "The Democracy We Want: Standards of Review and Democratic Embeddedness at the Inter-American Court of Human Rights", in Hélène Ruiz Fabri *et al.* (eds.), *International Judicial Legitimacy*, Baden-Baden: Nomos, 2020, pp. 227-248, at p. 230.

laws adopted in the context of participatory and transparent procedures in well-functioning democracies are arguably those exhibiting the highest democratic credentials.

If the perspective switches from deference at the moment of carrying out the review to deference when designing remedies, what needs to be taken into account is especially to whom the remedy is addressed, or which is the domestic body in charge of implementing it. The democratic pedigree of domestic bodies should thereby also affect their discretion in the execution of remedial measures. Remedies addressing the legislature are particularly important in this respect. The next pages will explore whether and why legislatures deserve increased remedial deference in human rights adjudication – thereby developing the concept of a 'margin of deliberation' – as well as how the authoritarian tendencies witnessed recently in several states affect this issue.

1. An Increased Remedial Deference for Legislators

Legislative bodies play a very particular role in democratic systems and therefore possess a democratic legitimacy that is arguably higher than that of executive bodies or judicial ones. This aspect is likely the main reason for affording an increased remedial deference to legislators. Certain administrative agencies may have more expertise than legislative bodies on specific issues, but legislators can also benefit from this expertise by obtaining input from such agencies in a well-structured legislative process. In addition, another justification for affording increased deference concerns the nature of the issues legislatures deal with, which relate mostly to broad policy choices, while decisions adopted by administrative bodies are usually of a more technical nature.[1061] In the area of constitutional law, the issue of deference towards the legislature when higher courts exercise judicial review has been one of the main debates of the last decades, generating a lot of discussions at a philosophical level. These will be briefly explored next, as well as the additional complexity of translating these debates to the international level.

1061 Benedikt Pirker, "Democracy and Distrust in International Law: The Procedural Democracy Doctrine and the Standard of Review Used by International Courts and Tribunals", in Lukasz Gruszczynski and Wouter Werner (eds.) *Deference in International Courts and Tribunals*, Oxford: OUP, 2014, pp. 58–73.

a) Judicial review of legislation and parliamentary sovereignty

When examining the issue of deference towards the legislature, it is necessary to have a look at the constitutional law debate that has been going on for many decades around the judicial review of legislation (especially in its strong form) and its potential undermining of representative democracy. This debate has taken place mainly in the realm of political philosophy, and especially in the context of the UK and the US. Its origins are usually traced back to the landmark judgment of the US Supreme Court in *Marbury vs. Madison* (1803), where this Court decided that it had the competence to review acts of government and legislation against the US Constitution.

This type of judicial review then extended to many other states, especially throughout the 20th century. Some of the early critics warned against a *gouvernement des juges*, seeing the review of legislation as a reactionary move against democratic developments.[1062] On the other hand, among the early supporters of the judicial review of legislation, one can find Hans Kelsen, who argues that it is a necessary instrument for the protection of minorities.[1063] The fierce debate then continued throughout the twentieth century and has even some remnants today.[1064] It turned mainly around what Alexander Bickel has coined "the counter-majoritarian difficulty", referring to the difficulty of putting in place a system of judicial review of legislation while law-making is subject to majority decision-making.[1065]

In this philosophical battle, one of the most notorious defendants of judicial review was Ronald Dworkin, who conceived rights as 'trumps' that necessarily prevail over conflicting legislation.[1066] He argued that equality

1062 The origin of this critique can be found in Edouard Lambert, *Le Gouvernement des juges et la lutte contre la législation sociale aux États-Unis*, Paris: Giard et Cie, 1921. See also Tushnet, in Tushnet and Cane (eds.), 2005, p. 166.

1063 See Hans Kelsen, "La garantie jurisdictionnelle de la Constitution (la Justice constitutionnelle)", *Revue du Droit Public et de la Science Politique en France et à l'étranger* 45, 1928, pp. 197-257. Kelsen took part in the design of the European form of constitutional review, centralised around a specialist constitutional court. The first constitutional court of this type was established in Austria in 1920, on the basis of Kelsen's project.

1064 See for example Waldron, *Global Constitutionalism* 2021.

1065 See Alexander Bickel, *The Least Dangerous Branch: The Supreme Court at the Bar of Politics*, New Haven: Yale University Press, 2nd ed., 1986.

1066 Ronald Dworkin, "Rights as Trumps", in Jeremy Waldron (ed.), *Theories of Rights*, Oxford: OUP, 1984, at p. 153. See also Ronald Dworkin, *Taking Rights Seriously*, Cambridge, MA: Harvard UP, 1977, at pp. 194 and 269 ("A right against the Government must be a right to do something even when the majority thinks it rights should not be made dependent on whether democratic procedures take them seriously enough, as it is not possible to know whether external preferences have influenced such procedures.[1067] Similarly, Rawls stated that "in a just society (...) the rights secured by justice are not subject to political bargaining or to the calculus of social interests".[1068] Others have taken more nuanced positions, such as that of John Hart Ely, who argued in favour of reserving the judicial review of legislation for instances in which representative decision-making procedures were malfunctioning at a procedural level.[1069]

On the other side of the battlefield, one can find Jeremy Waldron, who published his famous "Core Case Against Judicial Review" in 2006. There, he argued that judges lack the elements of democratic representativeness and accountability that legislators possess, while they are equally likely to err about rights.[1070] For Waldron, it is primarily an issue of participation and representativeness, whereby the decisions taken by the legislature have always a greater participatory element and are therefore more legitimate than those of judges.[1071] This argument, however, rests on four assumptions concerning a (today perhaps utopian) well-functioning democracy committed to human rights.[1072] Fallon then replied to it by arguing that the legitimacy of judicial review lies in the fact that it contributes to the mini-

---

would be wrong to do it, and even when the majority would be worse off for having it done").

1067 Dworkin, 1977. See also Richard Bellamy, "Ronald Dworkin, *Taking Rights Seriously*", in Jacob T. Levy (ed.), *The Oxford Handbook of Classics in Contemporary Political Theory,* Oxford: OUP, 2017.

1068 John Rawls, *A Theory of Justice- Revised Edition*, Oxford: OUP, 1999, pp. 3-4.

1069 John Hart Ely, *Democracy and Distrust: A Theory of Judicial Review,* Cambridge, MA: Harvard UP, 1980.

1070 Waldron, "The Core Case Against Judicial Review", *Yale Law Journal* 115(6), 2006, pp. 1346-1406, at pp. 1372 et seq.

1071 Jeremy Waldron, "A Right-Based Critique of Constitutional Rights", *Oxford Journal of Legal Studies* 13(1), 1993, pp. 18-51, at p. 50 ("Instead of talking impersonally about 'the counter-majoritarian difficulty', we should distinguish between a court's deciding things by a majority, and lots and lots of ordinary men and women deciding things by a majority. If we do this, we will see that the question 'Who gets to participate?' always has priority over the question 'How do they decide, when they disagree?'").

1072 Waldron, *YLJ* 2006, p. 1359-1369. On the four concrete assumptions, see below section I.2.

mization of human rights violations, as the over-enforcement is preferable to the under-enforcement of rights.[1073]

Nowadays it can be observed that an overwhelming majority contends that some sort of judicial review of legislation is necessary at a constitutional level, and the debate is turning mostly around the specific forms and features that such a review should possess.[1074] Even fierce opponents such as Waldron accept that judicial review might be necessary "against legislative pathologies relating to sex, race, or religion in particular countries". [1075] In addition, judicial review of legislation is nowadays consistently established in most constitutional systems around the world, becoming especially popular in the wave of new constitutions adopted during the 1980s and 1990s.

One of the main issues that remain contested is whether constitutional courts should issue binding remedies or only some sort of recommendations, also known as 'dialogic remedies', typically found in the weak-form review.[1076] For example, Dixon defends this form of judicial review, highlighting its usefulness for so-called 'blind spots of application', where the legislature fails to take into account all possible scenarios in which a law can infringe human rights, or 'priority-driven inertia', where the legislator avoids dealing with an issue due to political motives.[1077] Others have however advocated in favour of stronger forms of review, pointing at the risks of such weak-form review and the attached remedial discretion, especially in cases concerning criminal laws, where the absence of a clear order can "produce significant individual and systemic harms".[1078]

1073 Fallon, "The Core of an Uneasy Case for Judicial Review", *Harvard Law Review*, 121 (7), 2008, pp. 1693-1736.

1074 See Tushnet, in Tushnet and Cane (eds.), 2005, p. 164 ("A residue of skepticism about the ability of judicial review as a mechanism for protecting liberal democratic rights remains (...), but the contemporary debates are over the form that judicial review should take"). See however Roberto Gargarella, *Law as a Conversation Among Equals*, Cambridge: CUP, 2022, pp. 183-201, maintaining some objections against the constitutional review of legislation.

1075 Waldron, *YLJ* 2006, p. 1352.

1076 See Kent Roach, "Dialogic remedies", *I•CON* 17(3), 2019, pp. 860–883, suggesting a two-track approach where binding remedies should be issued with respect to the individual victims and dialogic remedies for the larger systemic issues.

1077 See Dixon, *I•CON* 2019, p. 926, mentioning among these motives that the issue in question "threatens to divide a political party or legislative coalition, or undermine its support with some key group, while increasing support with others".

1078 Robert Leckey, *I•CON* 2016, p. 607.

b) The additional complexity of the international judicial review of legislation

Most of these arguments concerning the constitutional review of legislation are also applicable to the review of laws by regional human rights courts, as such a review is also mainly criticised due to its interference with domestic democratic procedures.[1079] However, some additional arguments related to the particularities of international courts have been brought up in this regard. In this respect, it has been argued that constitutional accountability mechanisms are not applicable to these courts, as it is more difficult to control them by domestic legislatures,[1080] and that international courts lack the closeness to the facts and the knowledge of national law that constitutional courts have.[1081]

Moreover, if the legislature does not agree with the constitutional review there is an option to amend the benchmark of that review (i.e. the constitution). It is usually not an easy reform procedure, as it requires high majority thresholds, but to reform the benchmark of an international review (e.g. a human rights treaty) is arguably much more difficult, as it would require all state parties to accept the amendment. For such reasons, some authors have concluded that human rights courts lack the democratic legitimacy to review domestic legislation, especially if this review is not merely declaratory but includes binding orders for a state to legislate.[1082] This is also an issue that is closely related to the critiques based on the 'judicial activism' of courts.[1083] It has been argued that the activism of an international court

1079 See Gargarella, *Law as a Conversation Among Equals,* 2022, p. 198, stating that the matter is situated at a "higher level", but "at the root the objection remains relevant".

1080 Follesdal, *Global Constitutionalism* 2021, pp. 119, 126.

1081 Bellamy, *EJIL* 2014, p. 1039; Ulfstein, *Global Constitutionalism* 2021, p. 161.

1082 See Richard Bellamy, "The Democratic Legitimacy of International Human Rights Conventions: Political Constitutionalism and the European Convention on Human Rights", *EJIL* 25(4), 2015, pp. 1019–1042, arguing that human rights courts are only legitimised to exercise weak-form judicial review of legislation. See with respect to the IACtHR, Dulitzky, *Texas Law Review* 2015, p. 67, stating that the remedial approach of the IACtHR, *inter alia* due to its power to "order national governments to amend legislation (...) is typical of a deep-integration regime such as the EU, or of a constitutional court, but not of an international human rights system".

1083 See generally Stefanie A. Lindquist and Frank B. Cross, *Measuring Judicial Activism*, Oxford: OUP, 2009.

depends precisely on the amount of deference afforded to domestic political bodies.[1084]

But courts can also have a democracy-protective role, for example when incumbent office-holders act against political rivals and attempt to hold on to power through the adoption of legislation (especially of an electoral nature) that favours them in some way.[1085] This is especially the case when parliamentary procedures and majorities are such that the party in government can reform legislation on its own. In this respect, political scientists have found that legislative processes in parliamentary systems are not only led but sometimes also carried out almost exclusively by governments.[1086] Thus, an important aspect to take into account concerns the democratic features of the law-making body in question and the legislative procedures before it, affecting issues such as transparency, participation or deliberation.[1087] This will be explored next.

2. Deference and Democratic Conditions

Much of the discussion around judicial deference *vis-a-vis* the legislature is based on the assumption of a well-functioning democracy.[1088] This can be clearly seen in Waldron's four assumptions upon which his core case

1084 Fuad Zarbiyev, "Judicial Activism in International Law—A Conceptual Framework for Analysis", *JIDS* 3(2), 2012, pp. 247-278, at p. 250 ("More precisely, judges are considered to be activist when they lack deference to political branches and pass judgment on matters which are deemed normally to be reserved to those political branches").

1085 See Cram, *ISQ* 2018, p. 479.

1086 See Sathrapally, *Beyond Disagreement*, 2012, p. 52, highlighting that "[t]he overwhelming majority of legislation is drafted and introduced by government departments", and that "[t]he government typically has control over the parliamentary timetable, as well as strong structures to ensure votes are in place where needed".

1087 For example, with respect to the ECtHR it has been argued that choices made by domestic legislatures should be afforded significant weight, but only as long as these choices are made through "genuine democratic processes and respect for the principles embodied in the ECHR as interpreted by the ECtHR" (Ulfstein, *Global Constitutionalism* 2021, p. 173).

1088 As highlighted by Kleinlein, "[d]eference is based on the assumption that domestic institutions and procedures are working as they should, in a transparent manner, allowing for participation of affected rights-holders and, generally, under conditions that are capable of generating reasonable outcomes" (Thomas Kleinlein, "The Procedural Approach of the European Court of Human Rights: Between Subsidiarity and Dynamic Evolution", *ICLQ* 68, 2019, pp. 91–110, at p. 101).

against judicial review rests. These include "(1) democratic institutions in reasonably good working order (...); (2) a set of judicial institutions, again in reasonably good order (...); (3) a commitment on the part of most members of the society and most of its officials to the idea of individual and minority rights; and (4) persisting, substantial, and good faith disagreement about rights".[1089] In this respect, it can be argued that nowadays there are many states in which these four conditions are not met, due to a recent turn towards authoritarianism.[1090] Waldron's core case was thus arguably stronger in 2006 than in 2024.

This 'authoritarian exception' has also featured in the debate around international judicial review, with some opponents of the constitutional review of legislation arguing in favour of an international review in cases concerning non-democratic states or authoritarian governments, explicitly mentioning in this respect the early case law of the IACtHR.[1091] Although at first glance this argument only seems applicable to such past situations in certain regions, it has arguably gained renewed relevance in recent times. During the last decade or so, there has been a steady tendency towards authoritarianism in states under the supervision of human rights courts, that have increasingly acquired non-democratic features.

This democratic decline has been noticeable in the three regions under review. In the European context, this eventually contributed to Russia's expulsion from the CoE, and in the cases of Turkey or Azerbaijan, this decline presents serious challenges to the ECtHR.[1092] In the Inter-American region, one can find cases such as those of Venezuela and its treaty exit, or the democratic decline in Nicaragua and El Salvador. Similar situations of authoritarianism have also been present in the African system for some

1089 Waldron, *YLJ* 2006, p. 1360. According to Waldron, "[i]n cases in which the assumptions fail, the argument against judicial review presented in this Essay does not go through" (at p. 1402).

1090 In 2019, Dixon highlighted with respect to Waldron's assumptions that "[t]he current wave of illiberal populist politics, however, has arguably threatened the stability of almost all these commitments" (Dixon, *I•CON* 2019, p. 928).

1091 Gargarella, *Law as a Conversation Among Equals*, 2022, p. 199.

1092 This is due reflected *inter alia* in Turkey's refusal to comply with the Court's orders, as it can be most clearly observed in the context of the *Kavala* case, where the ECtHR included a remedial provision ordering the release of this political prisoner. Due to the State's refusal to comply, the CoM had to activate for the second time the infringement proceedings under Art. 46(4) ECHR. The other time it made use of it, this led to a relatively fast execution of the judgment by Azerbaijan, but in this case Turkey continues to refuse releasing Mr. Kavala at the time of writing.

time, with governments such as those of Mali or Benin curtailing the democratic rights of the opposition. There is in sum what many have called a crisis of democracy at the global level.[1093] In such contexts, deferring to the domestic actors is probably not an effective strategy for human rights courts.

Actually, one of the main features of modern authoritarian regimes concerns the takeover of the domestic judiciary at the highest level, usually through the amendment of laws that regulate the composition and organisation of the high courts of the state. This allows such regimes to 'capture' these courts in order for them to decide in a way that favours the rulers' interests or otherwise legitimises the rulers' actions.[1094] If these courts exercise a constitutional review of legislation, it is much easier for such regimes to pass laws that violate human rights but are nevertheless validated by the domestic judiciary. The intervention of human rights courts with respect to such states and their domestic laws thus becomes necessary. It is, however, difficult to draw a clear line determining when the decline into authoritarianism and 'court capture' call for the intrusion of human rights courts into the legislative matters of the state.[1095] In any case, this justifies the general authority of human rights courts to intervene at the legislative level, not only with declarations of incompatibility but also with stronger remedies.

Besides this increased authoritarianism, there are further situations in which a very deferential approach by human rights courts is not convenient. Benvenisti mentions in this respect four situations reflecting "inherent flaws in the domestic democratic processes" where specific groups can be disenfranchised and lack effective judicial protection at a domestic level.[1096] These concern the cases affecting "the outsider within" (i.e. nonnationals in the country or seeking to enter it), "the outsiders without" (referring to the transnational effects of governmental decisions), foreign public governance actors, and foreign private actors. Further 'democratic failures' involve the rights of other insular minorities and disenfranchised

1093 See for example Anne Applebaum, *Twilight of Democracy: The Seductive Lure of Authoritarianism*, New York: Doubleday, 2020.

1094 See generally, with a number of examples of 'captured courts', Tom Ginsburg and Tamir Moustafa, *Rule by Law: The Politics of Courts in Authoritarian Regimes*, Cambridge: CUP, 2008.

1095 For example, the dismantling of an effective constitutional review has also occurred in states such as Poland or Hungary, where the democratic backsliding has not reached the level of Russia or Turkey.

1096 Eyal Benvenisti, "The Margin of Appreciation, Subsidiarity and Global Challenges to Democracy", *JIDS* 9, 2018, pp. 240–253, at p. 241.

groups, such as prisoners or indigenous peoples. He argued, therefore, that deference is beneficial to those who are able to participate in governance and politics, but it fails to take other people's preferences into account.[1097] Literature on both domestic and international judicial review has affirmed that in such cases the intervention of courts is justified and that the legislator's room of manoeuvre should be restrained.[1098]

In sum, a number of specific situations require human rights courts to intervene in domestic legislative arrangements. Weak-form review in the form of declarations of incompatibility is arguably insufficient. This can be seen in the example of the ECtHR, which has been issuing these declarations for a long time. Thereby, some states have consistently avoided reforming the laws that were at the source of the problem, while paying the prescribed compensation. This led to massive numbers of repetitive violations concerning the same laws, and eventually to the ECtHR starting to include legislative remedies in its judgments.[1099] However, it is argued that courts still need to take the domestic context and the democratic features of the state into account in order to decide the degree of deference to be afforded to national legislatures in this regard. This can be done through a variable 'margin of deliberation' in the context of legislative remedies.

3. A 'Margin of Deliberation'

As mentioned before, the main aspect to consider by human rights courts when applying legislative remedies is the particular role played by legislative bodies in contemporary democracies, where they act as deliberative institutions. In this context, public deliberation is one of the cornerstones of democracy and has been extensively researched in political theory.[1100] It includes many different aspects, but in a nutshell, it implies that democratic decisions should comprise a public exchange of arguments "that involves weighing and reflecting on preferences, values, and interests regarding

1097 Benvenisti, *JIDS* 2018, p. 250.

1098 At a constitutional level, see generally John Hart Ely, *Democracy and Distrust: A Theory of Judicial Review*, 1980. Referring to the ECtHR, Dothan, *When Should International Courts Intervene?*, Cambridge: CUP, 2020, p. 134.

1099 See on the evolution of the ECtHR's remedial approach in this context Chapter 3 of this book.

1100 As one of the seminal texts on deliberation and democracy, see generally Jürgen Habermas, *Between Facts and Norms*, Cambridge, MA: MIT Press, 1996.

matters of common concern".[1101] Despite some innovative mechanisms that increase the ability of citizens to engage in public deliberation by themselves, it is generally difficult for a large number of individuals to exchange arguments on an equal basis.[1102]

This is why such deliberation takes place through representatives who are elected by the citizens and form the legislative bodies. Although the ideal aim of deliberation is "to arrive at a rationally motivated consensus", as this is usually not the case, often "deliberation concludes with voting, subject to some form of majority rule".[1103] In this regard, democratic deliberation is one of the main functions of legislatures, and remedial provisions should not impede it.[1104] In accordance with the democratic principle of Habermas, "only those statutes can claim legitimacy that can meet with the assent of all citizens in a discursive process of legislation that in turn has been legally constituted".[1105] If a legislative remedy is too specific as to the expected outcome of the reform, this substantially curtails the ability of parliaments to carry out a meaningful debate and deliberation, which in turn affects the legitimacy of the outcome. In this respect, Habermas pointed elsewhere to the absence of coercion as one of the central elements of deliberation.[1106] Although legislative remedies necessarily imply some level of coercion, they should aim to promote deliberation as far as possible.

The remedial measures should therefore ideally afford the domestic legislature a 'margin of deliberation'. This is a concept closely related to the well-known margin of appreciation, a doctrine developed especially by the ECtHR which will be examined below. However, the latter is mainly related

1101 Andre Bächtiger *et al.*, "Deliberative Democracy: An Introduction", in Andre Bächtiger *et al.* (eds.), *The Oxford Handbook of Deliberative Democracy*, Oxford: OUP, 2018, pp. 1-32, at p. 2. *Inter alia*, deliberation includes mutual respect, inclusion, and equality of communicative freedom (at p. 5).

1102 See generally Robert E. Goodin, *Innovating Democracy: Democratic Theory and Practice After the Deliberative Turn*, Oxford: OUP, 2008.

1103 Joshua Cohen, "Deliberation and Democratic Legitimacy", in A. Hamlin and P. Pettit (eds.), *The Good Polity: Normative Analysis of the State*, Oxford: Blackwell, 1989, pp. 17–34, at p. 23.

1104 Certainly, deliberation does not take place exclusively before legislative bodies but in the democratic system as a whole. However, it is argued that "[f]rom almost any systemic perspective, institutions with a high level of decision-making power such as legislatures play key roles in deliberative systems" (Bächtiger *et al.*, in Bächtiger *et al.* (eds.), 2018, p. 16).

1105 Habermas, *Between Facts and Norms*, 1996, p. 110.

1106 Jürgen Habermas, *Structural Transformation of the Public Sphere*, Cambridge, MA: MIT Press, 1989, p. 202.

to the ability of domestic actors to better appreciate their national circumstances in the context of finding an infringement. The margin of deliberation is instead more closely linked to the democratic law-making procedure taking place before domestic legislatures, implying that these bodies need to be able to deliberate before implementing legislative reforms. The concept of a margin of deliberation has not been employed by legal scholarship when making reference to international judgments, instead favouring the margin of appreciation concept that already encompasses some of these democratic elements. However, the margin of appreciation refers to the state as a whole and to the general review performed by human rights courts, while the margin of deliberation as developed here refers exclusively to the legislature and the wording of legislative measures. It is thus necessary to differentiate between these two concepts, and it is argued that the concept of a margin of deliberation can be more useful than the margin of appreciation in this context.

II. The Human Rights Courts' Deference Mechanisms vis-a-vis *the Legislatures*

Human rights courts have developed particular doctrines that affect their deference *vis-à-vis* domestic actors, especially legislatures. The most well-known in this respect is the ECtHR's margin of appreciation doctrine. On the other hand, the IACtHR has been more reluctant to specify its approach towards this issue, but it can be considered to have developed a particular deference-related mechanism through its conventionality control doctrine. The ACtHPR, due to the small number of judgments issued until now, has not yet established a similar doctrine or approach towards deference.

In general, these deference mechanisms are mainly applied in the relation between human rights courts and domestic courts. However, in recent times human rights courts have also included domestic legislatures under the scope of these mechanisms, developing particular approaches towards them. For example, the ECtHR's review of laws has taken a procedural turn, where the legislative procedure followed by parliaments is examined more closely and can be more relevant than the substantial review of the norm. The IACtHR's conventionality control has also been extended to the legislative process, although the review of legislation by this Court still focuses more on the substance than the procedure.

1. The ECtHR's Margin of Appreciation Doctrine *vis-à-vis* the Legislature

The ECtHR developed its famous margin of appreciation doctrine over many years, starting with the case of *Handyside vs. UK* (1976). The basis of that doctrine can be found in the principle of subsidiarity, which usually governs the relationship between the different levels of government in federal constitutional systems and is considered to be a structural principle in international human rights law as a whole.[1107] Applying the negative dimension of subsidiarity, human rights courts need to refrain from intervening in case domestic judges are able to effectively protect the rights of individuals. Similarly, legislatures also have a primary responsibility to protect human rights, in accordance with the obligations to legislate under international treaties.[1108] In accordance with the concept of positive subsidiarity, in case legislatures or domestic courts fail to comply with these primary obligations, human rights courts would be required to step in and remedy the situation.[1109]

The margin of appreciation doctrine is a manifestation of the subsidiarity principle, and it is one of the aspects surrounding the ECtHR which has received more attention by scholarship in the last decades.[1110] States have also widely supported this deference mechanism, to the point of including it in the Preamble to the Convention through the adoption of Protocol No. 15 to the ECHR.[1111] In a nutshell, this doctrine implies that the Court will grant a wider discretion to national authorities when certain conditions are met, thereby applying an increased deference towards national policy

1107 See generally Carozza, *AJIL* 2003. The requirement of exhausting available domestic remedies, included in the three regional systems, is another manifestation of the subsidiarity principle.

1108 See on the human rights obligations to legislate Chapter 1 of this book.

1109 Eva Brems, "Positive subsidiarity and its implications for the margin of appreciation doctrine", *NQHR* 37(3), 2019, pp. 210-227.

1110 For an early analysis see Howard Charles Yourow and Eric Stein, *The Margin of Appreciation Doctrine in the Dynamics of European Human Rights Jurisprudence*, Leiden: Brill, 1995. See also Yutaka Arai-Takahashi, *The Margin of Appreciation Doctrine and the Principle of Proportionality in the Jurisprudence of the ECHR*, Cambridge: Intersentia, 2002; Andrew Legg, *The Margin of Appreciation in International Human Rights Law: Deference and Proportionality*, Oxford: OUP, 2012.

1111 The addition to the ECHR Preamble reads "that the High Contracting Parties, in accordance with the principle of subsidiarity, have the primary responsibility to secure the rights and freedoms defined in this Convention and the Protocols thereto, and that in doing so they enjoy a margin of appreciation".

choices at the expense of its own interpretation of the concerned rights.[1112] These conditions are related on the one hand to the nature of the issue at stake and the presence of a consensus among European states, and on the other hand to the democratic quality of the domestic institutions and whether they followed the appropriate procedure when adopting the act in question.

The latter has been labelled as the procedural margin of appreciation, entailing that domestic bodies will be granted a wider margin in cases where the ECtHR can assess that the acts in question have been adopted in accordance with established procedures and taking into account the Convention and the Court's case law. In this respect, a 'procedural turn' has been observed in recent years, where these considerations over the domestic procedure have gained a prominent role in international judicial review.[1113] The ECtHR has been applying this procedural review more frequently, not only with respect to the judiciary[1114] but also with regard to domestic laws and parliamentary proceedings.[1115] This procedural review has also notably affected the margin of appreciation afforded to domestic legislatures,[1116] an issue that has been considered "controversial".[1117] In this respect, Saul identified a number of cases in which the margin of appreciation is widened or limited by the Court because of parliamentary procedures, finding that "the Court is starting to develop a framework of considerations (...) that it will take into account in its assessments of parliamentary process".[1118]

1112 Sadurski, *HRLR* 2009, p. 401.

1113 See Oddný Mjöll Arnardóttir, "The 'procedural turn' under the European Convention on Human Rights and presumptions of Convention compliance", *I•CON* 15(1), 2017, pp. 09–35.

1114 For a nowadays classical example, see ECtHR, *von Hannover vs. Germany (No 2)* (2012), at paras. 124–126.

1115 One of the first cases in which this was explicitly done is ECtHR, *Animal Defenders International vs. UK* (2013).

1116 See Kleinlein, *ICLQ* 2019, p. 94 ("In a set of cases, the Court establishes a clear or at least implicit connection between the quality of parliamentary process and the breadth of the margin of appreciation").

1117 Helmut Philipp Aust, "Introduction: The European Court of Human Rights – the past in the present", in Helmut Philipp Aust and Esra Demir-Gürsel, *The European Court of Human Rights - Current Challenges in Historical Perspective*, Cheltenham: Edward Elgar, 2021, p. 3 ("First, the Court itself has recalibrated part of its case law in recent years with a growing focus on procedural review, giving member states the benefit of the doubt when their courts and – controversially so – also parliaments pay due attention to the Strasbourg case law").

1118 Matthew Saul, "The European Court of Human Rights' Margin of Appreciation and the Processes of National Parliaments", *HRLR* 15(4), 2015, 745–774, at p. 772.

However, according to Kleinlein "the content of the procedural values has remained rather vague so far".[1119] In any case, if the ECtHR is satisfied with the parliamentary proceedings, it is more likely to accept the resulting domestic law.

In this context, the ECtHR has arguably employed a thicker subsidiarity and afforded a wider margin of appreciation when dealing with domestic legislators instead of judges.[1120] For example, in the case of *SAS vs. France* (2014), it considered three aspects of national parliaments deserving a structural margin of appreciation. These are first and foremost the issue of democratic legitimacy, secondly the fact that a domestic parliament is better placed than an international court to "evaluate local needs and conditions", and thirdly that in some matters "opinions within a democratic society may reasonably differ widely".[1121] Therefore, in this case, the ECtHR expressly determined that it "has a duty to exercise a degree of restraint in its review of Convention compliance, since such review will lead it to assess a balance that has been struck by means of a democratic process within the society in question".[1122]

The ECtHR has in sum generally displayed a wide deference towards domestic actors – and especially towards legislatures – through its margin of appreciation doctrine, sometimes limiting its review to the procedural dimension of their decisions. Some authors have, therefore, warned against a potential weakening of the ECtHR's substantial review of decisions in specific situations of concern, such as those related to migration.[1123] However, the deferential approach of the ECtHR seems to be expanding, especially

See also Matthew Saul, "Shaping Legislative Processes from Strasbourg", *EJIL* 32(1), 2021, pp. 281–308.

1119 Kleinlein, *ICLQ* 2019, p. 99.

1120 Saul, *HRLR* 2015, especially at p. 772 ("It has been shown that there is a growing body of case law that supports the thesis of deeper subsidiarity in relation to parliaments"). See also Arnardóttir, *I•CON* 2017, pp. 32-33.

1121 ECtHR, *S.A.S vs. France* (2014), para. 129.

1122 ECtHR, *S.A.S vs. France* (2014), para. 154. This case has thus been considered "one striking example of the Court's restraint in carrying out a substantial review based on the quality of the domestic decision-making by the legislator" (Demir-Gürsel, in Aust and Demir-Gürsel (eds.), p. 250).

1123 See Prisca Feihle, "Asylum and immigration under the European Convention on Human Rights - an exclusive universality?", in Helmut Philipp Aust and Esra Demir-Gürsel (eds.), *The European Court of Human Rights - Current Challenges in Historical Perspective*, Cheltenham: Edward Elgar, 2021, pp. 133-157.

with respect to the so-called "good faith interpreters" of the Convention.[1124] This is in part a result of the 'Interlaken reform process' that took place during the last decade, which will be explored in the next chapter. This deference is also clearly observed with regard to the legislative measures, both in their exceptional character and in the way they are framed when included in the ECtHR's judgments, as will be shown below.

2. The IACtHR's Conventionality Control Doctrine vis-à-vis the Legislature

The doctrine of conventionality control developed by the IACtHR is (in principle) not directly linked to deference, but it still has some effects on that issue. In a nutshell, this doctrine implies – similar to constitutionality control – that domestic authorities have an obligation to review the compatibility of internal laws and decisions with the American Convention, as interpreted by the IACtHR.[1125] If the IACtHR considers that domestic actors have carried out the conventionality control adequately, it will also more likely defer to their decisions. From that point of view, this doctrine is not radically different from the procedural review exercised by the ECtHR, as the latter also considers whether the ECHR and its jurisprudence were taken into account by the domestic decision-maker.

This doctrine was first laid down by the IACtHR in the case of *Almonacid Arellano vs. Chile* (2006).[1126] There, the Court referred exclusively to the domestic judiciary, stating that this was the body in charge of carrying out the conventionality control of "domestic legal provisions which are applied to specific cases", adding that this review must also encompass the IACtHR's interpretation of the Convention.[1127] Due to this statement, the

---

1124 Başak Çalı, "Coping with Crisis: Whither the Variable Geometry in the Jurisprudence of the European Court of Human Rights", *Wisconsin International Law Journal* 35(2), 2018, pp. 237-276.

1125 See generally Yota Negishi, *Conventionality Control of Domestic Law*, Baden-Baden: Nomos, 2022.

1126 Before that, the conventionality control had already appeared in separate opinions of judge Garcia Ramirez, who thereby highlighted the 'constitutional' character of this doctrine. See for example the Separate Opinion of judge Garcia Ramirez in IACtHR, *Tibi v. Ecuador* (2004), especially in para. 3, where he compares the conventionality control assumed by the IACtHR to the constitutionality control performed by the domestic judiciary.

1127 IACtHR, *Almonacid Arellano vs. Chile* (2006), para 124.

doctrine of conventionality control has been mostly linked to the domestic judiciary, which was thought to be the actor responsible for reviewing the conventionality of domestic acts.[1128] This was also a point of critique in the early assessments of this doctrine.[1129] However, the Court clarified at a later stage that the doctrine applies to all state authorities, including the legislature.[1130]

In any case, the conventionality control doctrine has since its inception played an important part in the jurisprudence of the IACtHR, and has gained increased attention in the literature.[1131] Some authors have criticised it by arguing that it contradicts the principle of subsidiarity, as it places the ACHR on top of the domestic legal order.[1132] However, in accordance with the obligations to legislate that states commit to when ratifying a human rights treaty,[1133] they are expected to perform a review of its domestic legal order before the ratification as well as every time they adopt new laws or modify existing ones, in order to assess whether they conform with the treaty in question.[1134] One difference, however, is that the IACtHR does not just include the Convention and other treaties among the standards against which to perform such a conventionality control – it also includes its own jurisprudence. It thereby affords an *erga omnes* effect to its decisions, as well as a binding character not only to the operative paragraphs but also to

1128 IACtHR judge Ferrer MacGregor for example argued that through the conventionality control every domestic judge would turn into an inter-American judge. See IACtHR, *Cabrera García and Montiel Flores vs. Mexico* (2010), Separate Opinion of Judge Ferrer MacGregor.

1129 See Dulitzki, *Texas Law Review* 2015, p. 93 ("In fact, the conventionality control, by strengthening the judiciary vis-à-vis other branches, produces two effects: local courts become more relevant inter-American players, and the other branches lose part of the control in the relations between the country and the American Convention and Inter-American Court".).

1130 IACtHR, *Gelman vs. Uruguay*, Monitoring Compliance with Judgment, Order of the Court (2013), para. 69.

1131 See for example Pablo González-Domínguez, *The Doctrine of Conventionality Control*, Cambridge: Intersentia, 2018; Jorge Contesse, "The final word? Constitutional dialogue and the Inter-American Court of Human Rights", *I•CON* 15(2), 2017, pp. 414-435.

1132 Dulitzky, *Texas Law Review* 2015.

1133 See Chapter 1 of this book.

1134 In the inter-American system, this general obligation to legislate is provided under Article 2 ACHR.

its reasoning, contrary to what is usually the case in international human rights law.[1135]

In some cases, increased deference on behalf of the IACtHR can be observed when state authorities perform the conventionality control adequately.[1136] It is in this sense also a reflection of the subsidiarity principle, as the domestic level is given the primary responsibility of redressing the potential infringements. In this context, the doctrine has also been refined and nowadays it is clear that international regulations and jurisprudence are not given automatic primacy, as domestic laws need to be interpreted in accordance with the *pro homine* principle, giving greater weight to the interpretation that is more beneficial to the individual.[1137]

This Court seems thus to be overcoming its traditional hesitation towards deferring to national actors in the review of domestic laws. A usual justification for this approach was the lack of confidence in domestic institutions due to its "limited capacity (...) to effectively protect human rights in the region",[1138] as well as its low democratic credentials. Nevertheless, this situation has arguably changed, and nowadays most states under the supervision of the IACtHR constitute consolidated democracies with fairly effective and independent judicial systems governed by the rule of law. However, despite cautious moves in that direction, the IACtHR's approach is still far from that of the ECtHR in terms of deference to domestic legislatures. This can also be observed in the legislative measures, which are far more common and arguably also more specific in the Inter-American than in the European human rights jurisprudence, as will be explained next.

1135 Article 68(1) ACHR clearly states in this respect that "States Parties to the Convention undertake to comply with the judgment of the Court in any case *to which they are parties*" (emphasis added).

1136 See for example IACtHR, *Tenorio Roca vs. Peru* (2016), para. 231, stating that "due to a timely and correct conventionality control, in the specific case the inadequacy of the criminal definition of enforced disappearances (...) did not result in a specific element hindering the effective development of investigations" (non-official translation).

1137 See Yota Negishi, "The *pro homine* Principle's Role in Regulating the Relationship between Conventionality Control and Constitutionality Control", *EJIL* 28(2), 2017, pp. 457–481.

1138 Bernard Duhaime, "Subsidiarity in the Americas: What Room Is There for Deference in the Inter-American System?", in Lukasz Gruszczynski and Wouter Werner (eds.), *Deference in International Courts and Tribunals*, Oxford: OUP, 2014, pp. 289-315, at p. 314.

III. The Specificity of Legislative Remedies

In order to explore the deference employed by human rights courts when applying legislative remedies, it is necessary to look at the specificity of these remedial measures and examine whether they allow for public deliberation.[1139] In this respect, Donald and Speck have defined remedial specificity as "the degree of detail contained in the indication of particular non-monetary individual or general measures (...) the more specific the judgment, the less discretion remains to the state as to what remedial measure is required".[1140] While this definition refers to the indication of remedial measures in general, a slightly different understanding of remedial specificity will be employed in this context, as the required measures are already clear and consist of the reform of legislation. Thus, what will be examined is the degree of detail provided by human rights courts when ordering such reforms.

The object of this analysis are therefore the operative provisions concerning legislative reforms. The argumentative part is also relevant, as it usually includes further details on the expected outcome of these reforms. However, such recommendations included in the reasoning are in principle not formally binding for the state.[1141] This view on remedial specificity is certainly more narrow than the one employed by other authors, who also include specificity issues settled after the judgment, either by the international body in charge of supervising compliance or directly at the national level.[1142] In this respect, it is arguably a different issue when remedial specificity is included in the judgment itself than when it is decided by a supervisory body such as the CoM after a negotiation with the state or directly by the state on a voluntary basis.[1143] Therefore, these aspects will not be taken into account.

1139 See Dothan, *JIDS* 2018, p. 153 ("Deliberation is crucial for democracy to flourish. Discovering whether international courts, such as the ECHR, promote public deliberation following their judgments is a worthy challenge").

1140 Donald and Speck, *HRLR* 2019, p. 84.

1141 This is different when the remedial provisions included in the operative part specify that the reform should be implemented in accordance with specific paragraphs of the reasoning, thereby providing binding force to such paragraphs. This is for example usually the case with the remedial measures of the IACtHR, as will be seen below.

1142 Murray and Sandoval, *JHRP* 2020, p. 120.

1143 See on this point the discussion on the remedial measures of the ECtHR included in Chapter 3 of this book.

Additionally, the specificity dimension examined here mainly affects the details of the substantive outcome of the legislative reform prescribed by the respective court. Other specificity-related issues, such as the temporal deadlines concerning the adoption of the legislative reform or the obligations to report on the steps taken towards implementation will not be considered.[1144] In the former case, this is because human rights courts, despite often specifying deadlines for the implementation of remedial measures, are mostly not attaching great weight to them, as a state will be considered to have complied with the judgment even if that compliance is delayed.[1145] With respect to the specificity of obligations to report on the implementation, they are a very common feature of human rights judgments and are arguably not very intrusive, as they concern the well-accepted function of supervising compliance with such judgments. In sum, the remedial specificity dimension examined here focuses only on the degree of detail contained in legislative measures regarding their outcome.

It has been argued that the more specific a remedial order is, the more difficult it is for the state to avoid implementing it, as "the failure to comply becomes more visible with more concrete remedies".[1146] In addition, specific remedies can entail a higher sense of prescriptiveness or urgency. Staton and Romero argue in this context that "[i]t is at least plausible that vague remedies fail to persuade states that it is necessary to change their behavior".[1147] However, specificity can also bear higher costs for the supervisory bodies in case of defiance, as it will be more difficult to reach an acceptable solution in the implementation phase. When remedies are vague, a negotiation can take place between the state and the body in charge of supervising compliance, whereby some sort of middle-ground agreement can be reached. This is not the case when the remedial measure is very specific, as implementation needs to fit the measure and the space for negotiating is therefore narrower. Remedial measures thus provide the parameters within which a post-judgment negotiation will take place, and remedial vagueness can be more convenient in many cases for reaching a solution that is acceptable to both the state and the supervisory body.

1144 See on these different elements of remedial specificity Murray and Sandoval, *JHRP* 2020, p. 104. They include also a specificity dimension that concerns the indication of which domestic actors that should be involved in the implementation. This is generally implicit here, as the measures examined affect the domestic legislature.

1145 An exception in this regard are the measures of compensation, to which the payment of interests in case of delayed implementation can be attached.

1146 Staton and Romero, *ISQ* 2019, p. 480.

1147 Staton and Romero, *ISQ* 2019, p. 489.

In addition, vague remedies can be beneficial for the two main problems previously discussed concerning legislative measures. Vagueness addresses on the one hand the issue of the information deficit of human rights courts, as domestic actors can decide about the best outcome of a legislative reform based on the information they have on their domestic circumstances.[1148] On the other hand, remedial vagueness is also better suited for the democratic legitimacy issue, as it allows for debate and deliberation to take place before domestic legislative bodies, thus reaching an outcome that is more legitimate from a democratic perspective.[1149] Remedial specificity is therefore curtailing to some extent the margin of deliberation that legislatures should possess when carrying out a reform of domestic laws. If a remedial measure specifies in detail what the outcome of a legislative reform should be, there is not much room to deliberate. A margin of deliberation can even allow for a reform that goes beyond what was originally envisaged by the court. As argued elsewhere, "[i]f the supranational body sets the ceiling, this may restrict (...) broader reform".[1150] It might thus be more convenient for the respective court to set the minimum standards of the reform and to let the domestic legislator decide democratically where to go from there.

In any case, it is very relevant to examine the degree of specificity employed by human rights courts in their remedial practice. In this respect, an important element is the difference between legislative remedies of a positive and a negative nature. Remedies specifying the expected outcome of a legislative reform are mostly those of a positive nature, as in the negative ones the outcome is already implicit, consisting of a repeal of a norm. However, in the latter case, it is still important to consider whether the law or provision to be repealed is specified in the remedial measure. After analysing the varying nature of legislative remedies, this section will look into the approaches to remedial specificity employed by the three courts in their legislative measures.

1148 Staton and Romero, *ISQ* 2019, p. 489 ("Simply put, courts, certainly international courts, often do not have the kind of information necessary to match policy means to policy ends, and for that reason, they will want to depend on the information domestic actors can bring to bear. Vagueness addresses this problem").

1149 Murray and Sandoval, *JHRP* 2020, argued similarly that "[i]n selecting ambiguity, the supranational body can thereby maintain its own legitimacy by giving space to a state to decide how best it should implement" (at p. 111).

1150 Murray and Sandoval, *JHRP* 2020, p. 113.

1. The Varying Nature of Legislative Measures

As already mentioned in Chapter 1, the legislative measures ordered by human rights courts can require different actions from the domestic legislator. There are generally three possible scenarios in this regard. First, remedial measures can require the modification of existing norms in order to make them compatible with the corresponding treaty. Second, they can order the enactment of new laws for better domestic protection of human rights. Third, they can order the repeal of laws or provisions that are incompatible with the treaty. However, in the first scenario, where the courts order the amendment of existing laws, this usually consists of either the incorporation of certain elements or provisions into domestic laws or the suppression of specific elements included in these laws. Therefore, the division employed here will be between legislative remedies of a positive, negative, and neutral nature. In this respect, positive legislative remedies order the adoption of new laws or the addition of elements to existing laws, and negative legislative remedies include measures that order the repeal of entire domestic laws or specific elements of these laws, while the concept of neutral legislative remedies include those that are either vague enough to avoid specifying which action is required, or that entail both positive and negative elements.

In the categorisation of legislative remedies included in the previous chapter, it can be observed that some categories clearly comprise remedies of a negative nature, such as those concerning amnesty laws or the death penalty, while others are mostly positive, such as those on the protection of vulnerable groups or the codification of criminal offences. In the following, the specificity aspects of these three different dimensions of legislative measures will be explored, focusing thereby on the specification of a provision for the case of negative measures, the specification of an outcome for the positive ones, and the arguably higher deference included in neutral measures.

a) Negative legislative remedies and the specification of a provision

Legislative remedies of a negative nature imply the repeal of a law or an element of the relevant legislation. In terms of specificity, these can be divided among those that identify the concrete law or provision that needs to be repealed (whereby the expected outcome is precisely the repeal) and those that order broadly to repeal laws to achieve a particular objective. The latter are arguably more deferential towards the legislature, as they entail discretion to decide the elements to be removed from domestic laws in order to reach the expected outcome.

This dimension of remedial specificity does not affect the ECtHR, as this court avoids ordering legislative reforms of a negative nature. In the case of the other two courts, one can find both negative measures that identify a concrete provision and measures limited to defining an objective. Concerning the former, specifications of both laws and provisions that must be amended are relatively common in the ACtHPR's case law. This can, for example, be evidenced in the judgment of *Ajavon vs. Benin* (2020), where the African Court expressly ordered the repeal of two specific provisions and two entire laws.[1151] Moreover, there are a number of cases in which the ACtHPR identifies the law in which certain elements have to be repealed and adds the expected outcome of such suppression. For example, in four judgments it ordered Tanzania to "remove the mandatory imposition of the death penalty from its penal Code".[1152] Despite not specifying the provisions of the Tanzanian Penal Code in which this element needs to be eliminated, this indication is also narrowing the margin of deliberation.[1153]

Indicating the law or provision that needs to be repealed is also relatively common in the IACtHR's measures.[1154] For example, in the case of amnesty laws, instead of ordering more broadly to guarantee that no domestic law constitutes an obstacle to the investigation of human rights violations, the IACtHR always expressly refers to concrete laws. Nevertheless, it has

1151 ACtHPR, *Ajavon vs. Benin* (2020), operative paras. (1-4), ordering the repeal of "Article 27 paragraph 2 of Law No. 2018 - 23 (...); Articles 1 and 2 of Organic Law No. 2018-02 (...); Law No. 2019 – 39 (...); [and] Constitutional law No. 2019 – 40".

1152 ACtHPR, *Ally Rajabu vs. Tanzania* (2019); *Amini Juma vs. Tanzania* (2021); *Gozbert Henerico vs. Tanzania* (2022); *Marthine Christian Msuguri vs. Tanzania* (2022).

1153 Similarly, in ACtHPR, *Lohe Issa Konate vs. Burkina Faso* (2014) it ordered this State to "amend its legislation on defamation (...) by repealing custodial sentences for acts of defamation".

1154 See for example IACtHR, *Caesar vs. Trinidad and Tobago* (2005), operative para. 3 ("The State shall adopt, within a reasonable time, such legislative or other measures as may be necessary to abrogate the Corporal Punishment Act"); *Expelled Dominicans and Haitians vs. Dominican Republic* (2014), operative para. 18, ordering to "prevent (...) the provisions of articles 6, 8 and 11 of Law No. 169-14 from continuing to have legal effects"; *Urrutia Laubreaux vs. Chile* (2020), operative para. 8 ("The State shall eliminate paragraph 4 of article 323 of the Organic Code of the Courts").

exceptionally also prescribed the repeal of all legislative provisions related to a concrete issue. For example, in the case of *Expelled Dominicans and Haitians vs. Dominican Republic* (2014), it ordered "to annul any law or regulation of any nature, whether administrative, regulatory, legal or constitutional, (...) that establishes or results in the irregular situation of the parents (...) being used as a reason to deny Dominican nationality to those born in the territory of the Dominican Republic".[1155] The latter arguably leaves more margin, as the State has the capacity to examine and decide by itself which norms are creating the problem alluded to.

In sum, remedial measures ordering the repeal of legislation generally leave a narrow margin of deliberation to the domestic legislature. When they specify the provision or even the entire law that needs to be eliminated, there is not much room to decide otherwise domestically. Instead, when these measures limit themselves to identifying the outcome or objective of this repeal the margin is wider, but such measures are exceptions to the rule. In the latter cases, deliberation can take place before legislative bodies on how to best achieve the required objective.

b) Positive legislative remedies and the specification of an outcome

As legislative remedies of a positive nature do generally not concern existing laws, a specification of the norm is rather exceptional and takes place only in the case of a requirement to add concrete elements to a provision. This is for example taking place when human rights courts order the introduction of exceptions into criminal provisions. In these cases, the concrete provision is usually identified, and the requested exceptions are spelled out, sometimes rather vaguely and sometimes with more detail. A relatively vague measure in this respect is that of the ECtHR ordering the introduction of exceptions to the prisoner voting ban in the UK, as it only specifies that the provisions must be amended "in a manner which is Convention-compliant".[1156] Even if this can be considered to have a high degree of specificity for European standards (because it identifies the provisions to be amended), its vagueness becomes clear when comparing it with some measures of the IACtHR that order the introduction of exceptions

1155 IACtHR, *Expelled Dominicans and Haitians vs. Dominican Republic* (2014), operative para. 19.

1156 ECtHR, *Greens and MT vs. UK* (2010), operative para. 6 (a) and (b).

concerning the application of the death penalty.[1157] In other cases, human rights courts prescribe the addition of specific elements in the laws that regulate judicial proceedings.[1158]

Besides these orders to introduce exceptions, most positive measures are rather broad in this respect, and prescribe the introduction of elements into domestic legislation in general.[1159] Thus, in the case of remedial measures ordering legislative enactments, specificity depends to a great extent on the level of detail with which the expected outcome of this incorporation is spelled out. In this respect, some measures are considerably vague, ordering states to adopt measures in order to adequate their domestic legal order to a specific article of the Convention, thus leaving a wide margin of deliberation.[1160]

Most positive measures however specify the objective of these enactments, thus reducing the legislator's room for manoeuvre. Thereby, the level of detail in the specification of the outcome becomes especially relevant. For example, the measures of the ECtHR requesting to set up domestic remedies generally specify only the situation that these remedies shall tackle (such as inhuman conditions of detention or excessive length of judicial

---

1157 See for example IACtHR, *Raxcacó Reyes vs. Guatemala* (2005), operative para. 5 ("The State shall modify, within a reasonable time, Article 201 of the Penal Code in force, in order to define various specific crime categories that distinguish the different forms of kidnapping or abduction, based on their characteristics, the gravity of the facts, and the circumstances of the crime, with the corresponding provision of different punishments, proportionate to each category, and also the empowerment of the courts to individualise punishments in keeping with the specifics of the crime and the perpetrator, within the maximum and minimum limits that each crime category should include"). See also *Fermín Ramirez vs. Guatemala* (2005), operative para. 8.

1158 For example, in *Oumar Mariko vs. Mali* (2022), operative paras. xv and xvi, the ACtHPR included an obligation to "to amend the laws governing the Constitutional Court to include provisions that ensure respect for the principle of adversarial proceedings" and "to include provisions on the procedure for recusal of judges".

1159 This can be observed in the European approach concerning the introduction of domestic remedies, where the Court avoids specifying in what concrete law such remedies should be included.

1160 See for example IACtHR, *'Street Children' vs. Guatemala*, operative para. 5 ("the State of Guatemala must adopt in its domestic legislation, the legislative, administrative and any other measures that are necessary in order to adapt Guatemalan legislation to Article 19 of the Convention"); ECtHR, *Xenides-Arestis vs. Turkey* (2005), operative para. 5 ("the respondent State must introduce a remedy which secures the effective protection of the rights laid down in Article 8 of the Convention and Article 1 of Protocol No. 1 in relation to the present applicant as well as in respect of all similar applications pending before the Court").

proceedings) and the preventive and/or compensatory character they shall possess. This limits to some extent the margin of deliberation, but not completely. On the other hand, measures of the IACtHR that for example order the adoption of legislative measures "to ensure, without exception, the imprescriptibility of incipient actions for crimes against humanity and international crimes" limit to a great extent the options of the legislature, as there are not many ways of implementing it besides introducing an imprescriptibility clause in the relevant criminal provisions.

Thus, in the case of legislative incorporations, remedial specificity depends to a great extent on the expected result. In this respect, the ECtHR has usually avoided being very specific, while the IACtHR's remedies have gone along the whole range of specificity degrees, up to the level of indicating very clearly how the new provision should look like, thereby tying up the hands of the domestic legislator to a considerable extent. Finally, legislative incorporations are ordered by the ACtHPR rather scarcely, and in those exceptional cases it has stayed on an intermediate level of specificity, prescribing an outcome but in broad terms.[1161]

c) Neutral legislative remedies and the attached discretion

Finally, there is another type of legislative remedies that neither orders the introduction nor the suppression of laws or legislative elements: neutral legislative remedies. This form of remedy comes about either because the remedial measures are extremely vague or because they order an amendment in which both positive and negative elements come into play.[1162] Vagueness is a common feature of the early practice of the three courts concerning legislative remedies. For example, in its first legislative measures, the IACtHR limited itself to order the amendment of "those laws that this

1161 For example, in *Eric Houngue vs. Benin* (2022), the ACtHPR ordered to amend a specific provision of the State's Criminal Code in order to introduce an exception that broadly protects "freedom of opinion and expression in relation to criticism of judicial decisions".

1162 For example, in *Saramaka vs. Suriname* (2007), the IACtHR's legislative measure stated that "the State shall remove or amend the legal provisions that impede protection of the right to property of the members of the Saramaka people and adopt, in its domestic legislation, (...) measures as may be required to recognize, protect, guarantee and give legal effect to the right of the members of the Saramaka people to hold collective title of the territory they have traditionally used and occupied" (IACtHR, *Saramaka vs. Suriname* (2007), operative para. 7).

judgment has declared to be in violation of the [ACHR]".[1163] Similarly, the first legislative measure of the ACtHPR stated that "[t]he Respondent is directed to take constitutional, legislative and all other necessary measures within a reasonable time to remedy the violations found by the Court".[1164] The ECtHR was arguably a bit more specific than that in its early legislative measures, but it did not go into the detail of more recent judgments.[1165] This is probably due to the fact that the courts were cautiously establishing their authority to deliver this type of remedial measures, and thus intended to avoid a negative reaction on behalf of states by allowing for enough discretion in the implementation of such measures.

Vague legislative remedies can also be found in more recent judgments, but they are rather exceptional.[1166] Instead, what is more common are remedies that include an objective in broad terms and avoid specifying what kind of legislative action is needed. For example, in the case of *Casa Nina vs. Peru* (2020), one of the IACtHR's remedial measures mandated the State to "adapt its domestic laws in order to ensure job stability to provisional prosecutors". The State is thereby free to take the legislative arrangements it considers best suited to achieve this objective, whether it consists of the addition or suppression of legislative elements.

In other cases, the courts have included measures that specify the law but leave the outcome requirement very vague. For example, in *APDH vs. Côte d'Ivoire* (2016), the ACtHPR ordered to "amend Law No. 2014-335 of 18 June 2014 on the Independent Electoral Commission to make it compliant with the aforementioned instruments to which it is a party".[1167] This remedy, despite identifying the specific law to be amended, does not make clear if that reform should be of a positive or negative nature, nor

1163 IACtHR, *Castillo Petruzzi vs. Peru* (1999), operative para. 14. Similarly in *Bamaca Velasquez vs. Guatemala* (2002), operative para. 4.

1164 ACtHPR *Tanganyika Law Society and Legal and Human Rights Centre* vs. *Tanzania* (2013), operative para. 3.

1165 See for example ECtHR, *Lukenda vs. Solvenia* (2005), operative para. 5 ("the respondent State must, through appropriate legal measures and administrative practices, secure the right to a trial within a reasonable time"). In more recent judgments, the ECtHR has specified that this right needs to be protected with a domestic remedy that has a compensatory nature. See for example ECtHR, *Vlad vs. Romania* (2013), operative para. 6.

1166 See for example IACtHR, *Deras García vs. Honduras* (2022), operative para. 13.

1167 ACtHPR, *APDH vs. Côte d'Ivoire* (2016), operative para. 7.

what the precise outcome should be.[1168] Actually, in this case, Côte d'Ivoire requested an interpretation of the judgment, asking for clarification on how to implement the legislative reform. The ACtHPR rejected this request, arguing that, based on the principle of subsidiarity, it would not be its function to direct the state on how to comply with its orders.[1169]

In sum, with such vague measures, the domestic legislator has a wider margin of deliberation, as the political forces can debate on the form of implementation, democratically deciding what elements to add and/or what to eliminate from its legal order. These remedies are thus arguably better suited to tackle some of the main concerns with respect to the democratic legitimacy issues and the lack of knowledge of local circumstances. On the contrary, specifying that a concrete provision needs to be repealed or that a very detailed legislative incorporation has to be implemented restricts the capacity of parliaments to perform its constitutional function of democratic law-making, which includes meaningful deliberation on the substance of legislative reforms. This is of course especially relevant for well-functioning democracies, as this type of law-making is usually not taking place in authoritarian systems, as mentioned before.

2. The Human Rights Courts' Approaches to Remedial Specificity

Each of the three regional courts has developed its own approach to remedial specificity in the context of their legislative measures. Thereby, differences can be observed concerning the positive or negative nature of the measures as well as the degree of deference that is afforded to the domestic legislator. In this context, the ECtHR employs a very particular approach to legislative measures, which primarily consists of ordering the introduction of an effective domestic remedy for certain human rights violations. Legislative measures of a positive nature are also predominant before the IACtHR, and a typical feature of its specificity approach is the referral to the reasoning of the judgments to provide more detail to its

1168 See also ACtHPR, *APDF and IHRDA vs. Mali* (2018), where it ordered the State rather broadly to "amend the impugned law, harmonise its laws with the international instruments, and take appropriate measures to bring an end to the violations established" (at operative para. x); and *Jebra Kambole vs. Tanzania* (2020), ordering to "take all necessary constitutional and legislative measures (...) to ensure that article 41(7) of its Constitution is amended and aligned with the provisions of the Charter (at operative para. viii).

1169 See ACtHPR, *APDH vs. Côte d'Ivoire,* Interpretation of Judgment (2017).

remedies. The case of the ACtHPR is quite different, as negative reforms are prescribed more commonly than positive ones, while there are important variations in the level of specificity of its measures.

a) The European approach: prescribing the introduction of a domestic remedy

In its first judgments with legislative measures, the usual approach of the ECtHR was to spell them out rather broadly, usually mentioning only that legal measures or domestic remedies needed to be set up in order to protect a concrete right.[1170] The measures then turned gradually more specific, indicating the expected outcome in more precise terms. For example, in *Hutten Czapska vs. Poland* (2006) the ECtHR specified that legal measures must be adopted in order to "secure in its domestic legal order a mechanism maintaining a fair balance between the interests of landlords and the general interest of the community".[1171]

Starting in *Burdov (No. 2) vs. Russia* (2009), the ECtHR has predominantly used the approach of mandating the introduction of domestic remedies for a specific issue.[1172] The most common of these issues are excessive delays in domestic judicial proceedings, non-enforcement of domestic judgments, or inhuman conditions of detention, as explained in Chapter 4. Occasionally, it is specified that the remedy must have suspensive and

1170 See for example ECtHR, *Lukenda vs. Slovenia* (2005), operative para. 5.

1171 ECtHR, *Hutten-Czapska vs. Poland* (2006), operative para. 4.

1172 See ECtHR, *Burdov vs. Russia (No. 2)* (2009), operative para. 6 ("the respondent State must set up (...) an effective domestic remedy or combination of such remedies which secures adequate and sufficient redress for non-enforcement or delayed enforcement of domestic judgments").

compensatory effects,[1173] while in other cases only the compensatory aspect is mentioned,[1174] and in others, there is no specification at all.[1175]

A different approach seems to be taken in legislative remedies related to property rights, which have considerably more neutral and vague wording, referring only to the protection of the relevant rights. For example, the measure included in *Maria Atanasiu vs. Romania* (2010) mentions only that "the respondent State must take measures to ensure effective protection of the rights guaranteed by Article 6 § 1 of the Convention and Article 1 of Protocol No. 1".[1176] This type of neutral remedies constitute about a quarter of the ECtHR's legislative measures, while the rest are all of a positive nature. Notably, the ECtHR has never included a legislative remedy of a negative nature.

As mentioned in the introduction, the ECtHR indicates rather scarcely the legislative nature of its general measures in the operative part of its judgments. It is then in the argumentative part of the judgments where the need to introduce such domestic remedies through legislation is specified, sometimes with very concrete expectations as to their regulation.[1177] However, there are also some exceptions in which the need for legislative reforms is explicitly included in the remedial provision. For example, in the Chamber judgment of the case *Ališić vs. Bosnia and Herzegovina, Croatia, Serbia, Slovenia and Macedonia* (2012), the ECtHR ordered Serbia and Slovenia to "undertake all necessary measures (...) in order to allow [the applicants] and all others in their position to be paid back their 'old' for-

---

1173 This is typically the case in remedies related to conditions of detention. See ECtHR, *Sukachov vs. Ukraine* (2020), operative para. 7; *Tomov vs. Russia* (2019), operative para. 9; *Varga vs. Hungary* (2015), operative para. 9; *Neshkov vs. Bulgaria* (2015), operative para. 7 (a).

1174 This is the usual approach in cases related to the non-enforcement of domestic judgments (see for example ECtHR, *Gerasimov vs. Russia* (2014), operative para. 12) as well as in those concerning excessive delays in domestic judicial proceedings (ECtHR, *Ümmühan Kaplan vs. Turkey* (2012), operative para. 5).

1175 As for example in ECtHR, *Gaszó vs. Hungary* (2015), operative para. 5, where it only specified that the domestic remedies must be "capable of addressing, in an adequate manner, the issue of excessively long court proceedings".

1176 ECtHR, *Maria Atanasiu vs. Romania* (2010), operative para. 6. See also, with an almost identic wording, *Manushaqe Puto vs. Albania* (2012), operative para. 6.

1177 See for example ECtHR, *Sukachov vs. Ukraine* (2020), para. 153 ("The Court's findings under this provision require specific changes in Ukrainian legislation that will enable any person in the applicant's position to complain of a breach of Article 3 resulting from poor detention conditions and obtain adequate relief for any such breach at domestic level"). See also ECtHR, *Gerasimov vs. Russia* (2014), para. 221.

eign-currency savings".[1178] This is in accordance with the usual approach of avoiding to determine the legislative nature of these measures. However, the case was thereafter referred to the Grand Chamber, and it expressly added the need for legislative measures to the aforementioned remedy, by stating that both states "must make all necessary arrangements, *including legislative amendments*, in order to allow [the applicants] and all others in their position to recover their 'old' foreign-currency savings".[1179]

The 'European approach' of ordering the introduction of a domestic remedy has also been employed by the IACtHR, although rather scarcely.[1180] One of these cases is *Castañeda Gutman vs. Mexico* (2008), where the IACtHR ordered the introduction of a domestic remedy allowing individuals to challenge the constitutionality of the norms regulating the right to be elected.[1181] This is a rather surprising measure, as the possibility for individuals to challenge domestic laws before a constitutional court is generally an issue that states are free to decide, and there are many different approaches depending on the constitutional system.[1182]

The ACtHPR also adopted the 'European approach' in one case, ordering Tanzania to "amend its legislation to provide individuals with judicial remedies in the event of dispute over their citizenship".[1183] It can be seen that although this measure is similar to those of the ECtHR, ordering the introduction of a domestic remedy for a specific issue, the ACtHPR made the legislative nature very explicit, indicating that the way of setting up a domestic remedy is an amendment of legislation.[1184] In sum, the legislative remedies of the ECtHR have remained considerably broad, limiting them-

1178 ECtHR, *Ališić vs. Bosnia and Herzegovina, Croatia, Serbia, Slovenia and Macedonia* (2012), operative para. 11.

1179 ECtHR, *Ališić vs. Bosnia and Herzegovina, Croatia, Serbia, Slovenia and Macedonia* (2014), operative paras. 10 and 11 (emphasis added).

1180 See for example IACtHR, *Rosendo Cantú vs. Mexico* (2010), operative para. 13 ("The State must introduce the pertinent reforms to provide an effective remedy for contesting jurisdiction to those persons affected by the intervention of the military justice system"). See also IACtHR, *Yean and Bosco vs. Dominican Republic* (2005), operative para. 8; *Fernandez Ortega vs. Mexico* (2010), operative para. 14.

1181 IACtHR, *Castañeda Gutman vs. Mexico* (2008), operative para. 6.

1182 It is likely that the measure was ordered because Mexico was in the process of reforming its Constitution to include this possibility, and the IACtHR wanted to give an impulse to that reform by adding international pressure in this direction.

1183 ACtHPR, *Anudo Ochieng Anudo vs. Tanzania* (2018), operative para. viii).

1184 The IACtHR has also specified the requirement of reforming the laws in order to introduce such a remedy. See for example IACtHR, *Yatama vs. Nicaragua* (2005), operative para. 9 ("The State shall adopt, within a reasonable time, the necessary legislative measures to establish a simple, prompt and effective recourse to contest selves to indicating a general objective while avoiding to go into more detail.

b) The Inter-American approach: referrals to the reasoning

The IACtHR has been recognised as the court employing the highest level of remedial specificity in general.[1185] In the particular case of legislative remedies, due to the important number of them included in the IACtHR's judgments, it is possible to find a wide range of specificity degrees.[1186] Like the ECtHR, the IACtHR most often orders legislative incorporations, which constitute over half of its legislative remedies. Neutral measures represent almost a third of them, and orders to repeal legislation only amount to 18%. In terms of specificity, it is possible to find some measures that are extremely detailed as to the outcome of the legislative reform, as well as others that are very vague, and many in between these two poles.

However, an issue that is very common in the IACtHR's legislative measures is the referral to the argumentative part in order to specify certain aspects. It does so by indicating in the operative part of the judgments that the legislative reform needs to be implemented "pursuant to" one or various paragraphs of the reasoning. Although this does not always add remedial specificity,[1187] this is generally the case, especially when several

the decisions of the Supreme Electoral Council that affect human rights, such as the right to participate in government, respecting the corresponding treaty-based and legal guarantees, and derogate the norms that prevent the filing of this recourse").

1185 Murray and Sandoval, *JHRP* 2020, p. 106 ("The Inter-American Court has been recognized not only as the supranational body with the most holistic approach to reparations (...), but also as the body that has engaged the most with specificity as a particular feature of its approach to reparations").

1186 It needs to be remembered in this regard that the IACtHR has delivered twice as much legislative remedies than the other two regional courts together.

1187 For example, in IACtHR, *Former Employees of the Judiciary vs. Guatemala* (2021), the Court's remedy stated that "[t]he State shall adapt its regulations regarding the remedy, procedure and judicial competence for challenging the declaration of illegality of a strike, pursuant to paragraph 144 of this judgment" (operative para. 7). However, this paragraph of the reasoning does not contain more details concerning the content of the reform, as the formulation is identical to the one of the operative part in that respect (para. 144: "The Court notes that the violation of the right to judicial protection, with respect to the appeals filed against the declaration of illegality of the strike, was due to a lack of clarity in the regulations governing this matter. Thus, it finds it necessary to order the State, within two paragraphs are being referred to. In some instances, it even constitutes a chain of referrals. For example, in *Nadege Dorzema vs. Dominican Republic* (2012), the IACtHR ordered the State to "adapt its domestic laws on the use of force by law enforcement officials, in the terms of paragraphs 274 and 275 of this Judgment".[1188] In turn, paragraph 275 – among other requisites for the reform – stated that "[t]his legislation must include the specifications indicated in Chapter VII-1 of this Judgment". The IACtHR is thus often extending the binding nature of its remedial provisions to whole sections of its argumentation.

It has to be noted in this respect that the IACtHR also uses this approach in other remedial measures, not only in those ordering legislative reforms. In many judgments, each remedy refers to the corresponding paragraphs of the reasoning to specify how it needs to be implemented. The IACtHR thus appears to interpret that its reasoning is binding in general. In this context, the part of the reasoning that constitutes an interpretation of the Convention is afforded binding force in accordance with the aforementioned conventionality control doctrine, while the parts in which it examines the content of domestic legislation and the ways to amend it (and to implement other remedies) are made binding through these referrals of the operative provisions.

The other two courts have traditionally not included a referral to the reasoning in its remedial measures. Nevertheless, the ECtHR seems to have started using this approach in recent cases. For example, in *Tunikova vs. Russia* (2021) – related to the criminalisation of domestic violence – the ECtHR's remedy consisted of an obligation to make "amendments to the domestic legal and regulatory framework in order to bring it into line with the Court's indications in paragraphs 151-58 of the present judgment". These paragraphs then specified *inter alia* what the legal definition of domestic violence must include, the persons it should cover, issues concerning the burden of proof and the trigger of investigations in cases of domestic violence, the need for criminalisation and the type of penalties that should be attached to it.[1189] Thus, it can be seen that although in principle the remedial measure is rather broad, the referral to argumentative paragraphs in it makes it much more precise, as it attaches a binding character to what

---

years, to clearly specify or regulate, through legislative or other measures, the remedy, procedure and judicial competence for challenging the declaration of illegality of a strike").

1188 IACtHR, *Nadege Dorzema vs. Dominican Republic* (2012), operative para. 9.

1189 See ECtHR, *Tunikova vs. Russia* (2021), paras. 152-157.

in principle would constitute mere recommendations.[1190] This approach is however still highly exceptional for the ECtHR, while it is almost the rule for the IACtHR.

In sum, although the legislative measures of the IACtHR are not very specific *per se*, its consistent referrals to the reasoning provide a lot more detail and narrow down the margin of deliberation to a considerable extent. As most of its legislative measures concern incorporations or modifications, it is arguably constraining the domestic legislatures to a point that its decision-making capacities can be compromised, as the amount of legislative detail imposed by the Court entails that they can only follow the path already laid down in a judgment. It has been argued in this respect that "specificity appears to be an intrinsic element of its [the IACtHR's] legal culture".[1191]

c) The African approach: prioritising legislative incompatibilities

A particularity of ACtHPR is that it is the only human rights court that has included negative measures more frequently than positive ones in its judgments. They constitute almost half of its legislative measures, while both positive and neutral measures represent about a quarter each. Besides this focus on incompatibilities, the Court has not developed a consistent approach towards remedial specificity. Indeed, Murray and Sandoval have found that the ACtHPR varies from rather vague to much more specific remedies, thus considering it "difficult to discern a particular trend or strategy in their approach".[1192]

In the context of its focus on the incompatibility of legislation, it sometimes went considerably far in terms of extending the repeal orders to an indeterminate number of laws. For example, in multiple judgments, the ACtHPR has ordered the repeal of a specific Beninese constitutional law that implied a reform of Benin's Constitution. In the case of *Houngue*

1190 For a more lenient approach in this respect, avoiding to make reference to concrete paragraphs, see for example ECtHR, *Dimitrov and Hamanov vs. Bulgaria* (2011), operative para. 6, indicating that the State "must set up (...) an effective remedy which complies with the requirements set out in this judgment". In most legislative remedies this is even broader, stating that the remedy needs to be "in line with the Convention principles as established in the Court's case-law" (see e.g. ECtHR, *Rumpf vs Germany* (2010), operative para. 5).

1191 Murray and Sandoval, *JHRP* 2020, p. 113.

1192 Murray and Sandoval, *JHRP* 2020, p. 106.

Eric Noudehouenou vs. Benin (2020), the African Court added another measure, consisting of an obligation to repeal "all subsequent laws related to the election".[1193] In another judgment, it went even further and ordered to repeal every law adopted after this constitutional reform, although it referred to a particular one among them.[1194] These measures, despite not identifying every law to be repealed, are very specific. By referring to all laws adopted after a certain point or related to a particular issue, no margin of deliberation is left to the state.

However, such far-reaching legislative measures are rather exceptional. In general, legislative remedies before the ACtHPR do not reach the level of specificity of some of those before the IACtHR. This is despite the fact that it has taken inspiration from the latter's case law for some issues related to remedial specificity. For example, in a judgment concerning indigenous peoples' territorial rights, it specified a procedural aspect of the implementation, by stating in the remedial measure that the identification of territory must be carried out "in consultation with the Ogiek and/or their representatives".[1195] This procedural requirement was previously included by the IACtHR in some of its judgments concerning indigenous territory.[1196]

In sum, with respect to the ACtHPR, it is difficult to find a pattern of remedial specificity, as it has employed different approaches in this regard. However, a distinct feature is its focus on legislative incompatibilities and the orders to repeal legislation. This is another element that hints at the fact that this Court has adopted a more constitutional self-understanding, as the orders to repeal legislation are more common before constitutional courts than human rights courts.[1197]

1193 ACtHPR, *Houngue Eric Noudehouenou vs. Benin* (2020), operative para. xi.

1194 ACtHPR, *XYZ vs. Benin (II)* (2020), operative para. xiv ("Orders the Respondent State to take all measures to repeal Law No. 2019-40 of 1 November 2019 amending Law No. 90-032 of 11 December 1990 on the Constitution of the Republic of Benin and all subsequent laws, in particular Law 2019-43 of 15 November 2019 on the Electoral Code").

1195 ACtHPR, *ACmHPR vs. Kenya* (2022), operative para. vi).

1196 See for example IACtHR, *Sarayaku vs. Ecuador* (2012), operative para. 4.

1197 This adds to the possibility of reviewing laws *in abstracto*, that is usually a feature of constitutional courts, as discussed in Chapter 1.

Interim Conclusion: A Margin of Deliberation for Legislative Remedies

To conclude, this chapter has shown that remedial deference is a paramount element to be considered with respect to legislative remedies. In this regard, the legislature displays several features which justify it having more discretion than other bodies in the implementation of remedial measures. This has triggered a notorious debate among political philosophers with respect to the constitutional review of legislation. Especially the strong-form judicial review, which generally implies the capacity of courts to strike down legislation, has been criticised for being at odds with the democratic principle. The concepts of majority rule and deliberation are fundamental principles of democratic governance, guaranteeing that the will of the people is reflected in decision-making processes. There are nevertheless situations in which the will of the majority can lead to the discrimination of individuals or groups which are not part of that majority. In sum, the issue revolves around deciding an adequate trade-off between legitimacy and effectiveness of judgments. Thereby, one could argue that weak-form review is often not enough for an effective protection of rights.[1198]

In the case of legislative remedies before human rights courts, this problem is to some extent downplayed, as these measures lack the power to invalidate legislation, requiring instead a domestic legislative procedure in this respect. However, the specificity of such measures becomes very important in this context. In relation to this, the concept of a margin of deliberation has been developed throughout this chapter. As deliberation is considered a cornerstone of modern democracy, legislative measures should ideally spell out some general conditions or a framework into which the substance of the reform would be demarcated but leaving the legislatures a margin to deliberate in this respect. Thereby, the democratic conditions of the concerned state should also be taken into account, as the recent backsliding of democracy in many states subject to the supervision of the three regional human rights courts can result in parliamentary deliberation being a mere façade, with law-making procedures increasingly controlled by the executive and its outcome decided in non-democratic ways. In such cases affecting regimes with authoritarian tendencies, the margin of deliberation is arguably less useful.

1198 See Dixon, *I•CON* 2019, p. 930 ("Not all models of judicial weakness, therefore, will necessarily be as attractive when it comes to the effectiveness of judicial review in protecting or promoting certain democratic values").

The chapter has also examined certain deference-related mechanisms developed by the ECtHR and the IACtHR with respect to legislatures. These mechanisms are more closely related to the review of laws than to legislative remedies, but they are still relevant in this context. The ECtHR's margin of appreciation is especially important in this regard, as it has increasingly focused on the procedural aspects of domestic laws. This Court is thus taking the legislative procedures of domestic parliaments more and more into account when deciding about the compatibility of domestic laws with the Convention. It has in this respect developed different standards of review when dealing with 'good-faith' and 'bad-faith' interpreters of the ECHR.[1199] On the other hand, the IACtHR has traditionally favoured its own substantial review of laws, irrespective of domestic procedural considerations.[1200] However, with the doctrine of conventionality control, this is starting to become more nuanced, as the IACtHR has shown more deference when it found that national bodies such as legislatures performed this control adequately at the moment of adopting a law or another decision. This is nevertheless not yet consolidated in its case law, and this Court should probably apply a more deferential standard when reviewing the actions of states with fully democratic credentials, instead of maintaining the same approach it used when authoritarian regimes predominated in the region.

The same can be argued for the degree of deference displayed by this court in its legislative remedies. This deference has been evaluated taking into account the specificity of the measures with regard to the indication of the concrete law to be repealed or amended (especially in the case of negative measures) as well as the specificity concerning the expected outcome of the legislative reform (in the case of positive measures). In this respect, the IACtHR has been highly specific in many cases, by introducing referrals to its reasoning in the remedies and making these argumentative considerations binding for states in the implementation of legislative reforms. On the other hand, the ECtHR has been much more deferential in its legislative measures, mostly limiting itself to ordering the introduction of domestic remedies for a specific issue. Finally, the ACtHPR has arguably not yet developed a consistent approach to remedial specificity, as one can find legislative measures that are extremely vague and others that are very specific. However, an outstanding feature is that this court orders very often the repeal of legislative provisions, while the other two focus mostly on the enactment of domestic laws. It can thus be inferred that the ACtHPR

1199 Çalı, *Wisconsin International Law Journal*, 2018.
1200 Çalı, in Lang and Wiener (eds.), 2017, p. 300.

has adopted a more constitutional approach in this respect, as the repeal of legislation is more common before constitutional courts than before the other regional human rights courts.

In sum, remedial deference can be considered an essential aspect that human rights courts need to take into account when issuing legislative remedies. It is highly recommended that these remedies leave the states' legislature a margin of deliberation if the domestic legislative procedures are fully democratic. The specificity of remedial measures is a particularly important element in this respect. This can also affect the issues of compliance and backlash, as these are measures that are arguably more prompt to cause resistance by states. Such consequences of legislative remedies will be examined in the last chapter of the book.

Chapter 6: The Consequences of Legislative Remedies

After having examined the judicial practice of human rights courts with respect to their legislative remedies throughout the last chapters, including the typology of issues they relate to and the way they are spelled out by each court, a final aspect to consider is the post-judgment phase. What are the consequences of these remedial measures? Several judgments included in the previous analysis have been extensively commented on precisely due to their consequences, in particular because some have caused a negative reaction by states, in the form of backlash and delayed or non-compliance. It is therefore assumed that highly intrusive remedies, such as those of a legislative nature, are more likely to trigger negative consequences. Conversely, however, legislative measures can also trigger an impact that goes beyond their implementation by the state concerned, being therefore related to some forms of strategic litigation before human rights courts. These issues will be examined in the final chapter.

First, this chapter will examine the issue of whether instances of backlash against regional human rights courts are related to their legislative measures. In some of these instances, the direct link between the courts' legislative measures and the negative reaction by states can be clearly observed, as in the case of the UK and the 'prisoner voting rights saga'. In others, this relation is rather indirect, as in the restriction of access to the ACtHPR by several states. This chapter, then, will turn to the issue of compliance, examining whether and why legislative measures are less likely to be timely implemented by states. This mostly affects deficiencies in the domestic capacity to enforce international judgments, especially when the legislature must intervene.

This chapter will also argue that despite such difficulties, legislative remedies are not ready to be dismissed, as they are able to produce positive outcomes by having an impact that extends beyond the case at hand. This has in turn created an opportunity structure for civil society actors to engage in so-called strategic litigation before human rights courts, using individual cases to achieve broader transformations, such as legislative reforms. Finally, the question of how human rights courts have reacted to the issues of backlash and non-compliance in relation to legislative remedies will be explored. In this regard, such reactions can be observed in the evolving use of legislative measures on the one hand and the lowering of compliance requirements on the other. Moreover, a different situation can be observed before each of the three regional human rights courts in this respect. This is, to some extent, also related to the issues examined in the previous chapters, as the consequences of legislative remedies depend also on the specific topic to which they relate and the degree of discretion left to the legislator to implement them.

I. Legislative Remedies and Backlash Against Human Rights Courts

It is nowadays common knowledge that we live in an age of backlash against human rights on the one hand,[1201] and against international courts on the other.[1202] Thus, regional human rights courts have been particularly affected by it. Although specific instances of criticism and pushback against these courts have taken place for some time,[1203] this has gained momentum and notably increased during the last decade.[1204] Throughout this chapter, 'backlash' is used as a generic term that encompasses different forms of criticism, resistance and pushback against human rights courts. This is despite the fact that some authors have differentiated between pushback and backlash, depending on the intensity and the actors involved.[1205] However, there is no settled terminology in this regard, and the general tendency

---

1201 See for example Sanja Dragić, *Post-Backlash Human Rights Law*, Brill, 2022.

1202 See generally Courtney Hillebrecht, *Saving the International Justice Regime: Beyond Backlash against International Courts*, Cambridge: CUP, 2021. With respect to international criminal courts, see for example Joseph Powderly, "International criminal justice in an age of perpetual crisis", *LJIL* 32(1), 2019, pp. 1-11.

1203 See Mikael Rask Madsen, "The Challenging Authority of the European Court of Human Rights: From Cold War Legal Diplomacy to The Brighton Declaration and Backlash", *LCP* 79, 2016, pp. 141-178, at p. 143, mentioning the first negative reactions to the ECtHR's "expanding jurisprudence and power" in the 1980s and 1990s.

1204 See for example, Patricia Popelier, Sarah Lambrecht and Koen Lemmens (eds.), *Criticism of the European Court of Human Rights*, Cambridge: Intersentia, 2016; Marten Breuer (ed.), *Principled Resistance to ECtHR Judgments – A New Paradigm?*, Berlin: Springer, 2019; Laurence Helfer and Erik Voeten, "Walking Back Human Rights in Europe?", *EJIL* 31(3), 2020, pp. 797–827.

1205 In accordance with these authors, for example in the case of the ECtHR the resistance by states has not reached the level of backlash (or at least it had not by 2018, today they might reach a different conclusion in light of the conflict with Russia). See Mikael Rask Madsen, Pola Cebulak and Micha Wiebusch, "Backlash Against International Courts: Explaining the Forms and Patterns of Resistance to International Courts", *IJLC* 14(2), 2018, pp. 197-220, especially at pp. 207-211, nowadays is to employ 'backlash' as a catch-all concept including these various forms of resistance.[1206] This chapter will, therefore, employ this broader conception of the term 'backlash'.

Among the various current strands of critique against human rights,[1207] the one emphasising the role of democratic procedures is particularly related to legislative remedies, as it considers rights protection contrary to the will of the people. As explored in the previous chapter, this relates to the criticism against the review of legislation by courts in general, a debate held especially in the context of constitutional adjudication.[1208] The points made in this regard primarily concern the courts' lack of democratic credentials and accountability to challenge decisions taken by democratic parliaments. This is also related to the critiques pointing at an increased judicialisation of politics (the so-called '*gouvernement des juges*'), whereby a transfer of power from states' political branches (such as the legislature) to the judicial branches (notably constitutional courts and international courts) can be observed.[1209] It has been argued in this respect that "judgments involving legislative changes are likely to be particularly controversial because they challenge democratic ideals concerning majority rule and parliamentary supremacy".[1210]

Such critiques are not only made by states but also commonly found in scholarship. Waldron for example warns about the "danger that judicial

referring both to the Brighton Declaration and to the UK voting rights saga as examples of pushback not reaching the level of backlash.

1206 See for example Øyvind Stiansen and Erik Voeten, "Backlash and Judicial Restraint: Evidence from the European Court of Human Rights", *ISQ* 64(4), 2020, pp. 770-784; Mikael Rask Madsen, "From boom to backlash? The European Court of Human Rights and the transformation of Europe", in Aust and Demir-Gürsel (eds.), *The European Court of Human Rights: Current Challenges in Historical Perspective*, Cheltenham: Edward Elgar, 2021, pp. 21-42.

1207 See Anne Peters, "The Importance of Having Rights", *ZaöRV* 81(1), 2021, pp. 7-22, at pp. 16-17.

1208 See for example, with respect to the ECtHR, Koen Lemmens, "Criticising the European Court of Human Rights or Misunderstanding the Dynamics of Human Rights Protection?", in Popelier et al. (eds.), 2016, p. 37 ("Much of the critique on the Court can be seen as a disapproval of the idea that judges – be them ordinary judges, constitutional or international judges – are entitled to intervene in the legislature's affairs").

1209 On this debate, see Chapter 5 of this book.

1210 See Stiansen, *IJHR* 2019, p. 1222. See also similarly Fiona de Londras and Kanstantin Dzehtsiarou, "Mission Impossible? Addressing non-execution Through Infringement Proceedings in the European Court of Human Rights", *ICLQ* 66(2), 2017, at pp. 474 et seq.

review will tilt towards judicial sovereignty if courts begin to present themselves as pursuing a coherent program or policy, rather than just responding to particular abuses identified as such by a bill of rights – one by one, as they crop up".[1211] Especially the IACtHR has been criticised for being too activist in its remedial practice.[1212] Contesse highlights in this regard that "the Inter-American Court embraces a maximalist model of adjudication – one that leaves very little, if any, room for states to reach their own decisions".[1213] With respect to the ECtHR, Sadurski warned already in the early years of the pilot judgments procedure about the fact that "such a constitutional-style intervention of the European Court may be ineffective or, worse, counter-productive (that is, by provoking a backlash against such interference from Strasbourg)".[1214] Others have more recently advocated for an increased self-restraint on behalf of this court, stating that "Strasbourg should be cautious about enlarging its jurisdiction too far, to avoid provoking a 'damaging reaction' from the States, who might reasonably protest that the Court has (illegitimately) absorbed too much power, in relation to matters not properly within its scope".[1215]

Moreover, such intrusive remedial measures were generally not foreseen in the time in which states consented to be bound by human rights judgments but have instead been developed through the subsequent judicial practice. In an early analysis of backlash against the IACtHR, Helfer argued that when international judgments impose new or more costly obligations than those foreseen when states ratified the corresponding treaty, backlash is more likely.[1216] He labels such situations as 'overlegalization of human rights', stating that this occurs when "a treaty's augmented legalization levels require more extensive changes to national laws and practices than

1211 Waldron, *Global Constitutionalism* 2021, p. 101.

1212 See for example Ezequiel Malarino, "Judicial Activism Punitivism and Supranationalisation: Illiberal and Antidemocratic Tendencies of the Inter-American Court of Human Rights," *International Criminal Law Review* 12, 2012, pp. 665-695.

1213 Jorge Contesse, "Contestation and Deference in the Inter-American Human Rights System," *LCP* 79(2), 2016, p. 124.

1214 Sadurski, *HRLR* 2009, p. 428.

1215 Ed Bates, "Strasbourg's Integrationist Role, or the Need for Self-restraint?", *ECHRLR* 1, 2020, pp. 14-21.

1216 See Laurence R. Helfer, "Overlegalizing Human Rights: International Relations Theory and the Commonwealth Caribbean Backlash Against Human Rights Regimes", *Columbia Law Review* 102, 2002, pp. 1832-1911, at p. 1871.

was the case when the state first ratified the treaty".[1217] Legislative measures can clearly embody such 'overlegalization'.

The issue of sovereignty costs and human rights treaty ratification has been extensively explored, especially by political scientists.[1218] When such costs increase after ratification, they can trigger backlash. Hillebrecht has highlighted in this regard that measures such as legislative reforms "impose the highest cost on states".[1219] Thus, from a doctrinal perspective, there is arguably enough evidence concerning the relation between intrusive remedies such as the ones examined here and backlash against the courts issuing them. The question that remains open is whether the concrete instances of backlash experienced by regional human rights courts can be traced back to this specific remedial practice.

In this context, the backlash against human rights courts has primarily taken two forms. The first such form concerns cases of open criticism and pushback by individual states. This takes place not only in states with authoritarian or populist tendencies,[1220] but also in others with fully democratic credentials.[1221] The second form of backlash is related to collective attempts to limit the authority and competences of human rights courts. In the European system, this has taken place in the context of the institutional reform process that started at Interlaken in 2009 and later turned into a mechanism intending to limit the ECtHR's authority. At the Inter-American system, a collective form of backlash can be observed in the open letter of 2019 by five presidents of some of the most important states in the region, asking for a similar reform that would limit the IACtHR's competences and the intensity of its review. The question in this respect is whether and to which extent these forms of backlash are related to the remedial practice of the respective courts, and especially to its legislative measures, as it aligns in time with the development of this practice.

1217 Helfer, *CLR* 2002, p. 1854.

1218 See for example Emilie M. Hafner-Burton, Edward D. Mansfield and Jon C.W. Pevehouse, "Human Rights Institutions, Sovereignty Costs and Democratization", *British Journal of Political Science* 45, 2013, pp. 1-27; Oona Hathaway, "The Cost of Commitment", *Stanford Law Review* 55(5), 2003, pp. 1821-1862.

1219 Courtney Hillebrecht, *Domestic Politics and International Human Rights Tribunals: The Problem of Compliance*, Cambridge: CUP, 2014, p. 54.

1220 Such as Russia, Venezuela, or Tanzania. See, with respect to the ECtHR, Jan Petrov, "The populist challenge to the European Court of Human Rights", *I•CON* 18(2), 2020, pp. 476–508.

1221 This is for example the case of the UK. See Ed Bates, "Analysing the Prisoner Voting Saga and the British Challenge to Strasbourg", *HRLR* 14, 2014, p. 503.

1. Legislative Remedies and Individual Instances of Backlash

In recent years, there have been a number of instances of backlash by individual states against the three regional human rights courts. These will be examined with regard to its possible relation with legislative measures. It is however important to note that the intensity of such backlash is different in front of each court. In the case of the ECtHR, these have been mostly instances of resistance and criticism, whereby the position of the UK towards specific judgments of this court is especially relevant. Concerning the ACtHPR, the backlash has been probably more intense, as it has adopted the form of limiting the access of individuals and NGOs to the Court through the withdrawal of optional declarations that were issued by states in this respect. Finally, the most intensive form of backlash has arguably taken place in the Inter-American system, with several states exiting the Convention system as a whole.

a) Resisting the ECtHR

Due to the prudent application of legislative remedies by the ECtHR, this practice should not, at first glance, constitute a reason for backlash. In fact, the remedial practice of the Court is usually not listed among the main reasons that have triggered such a reaction by states.[1222] The (arguably) most contentious conflict inside the Strasbourg system, which has led to a member state's expulsion from this system, is mainly related to Russia's invasion of another CoE member state (Ukraine) in 2022. However, the disagreements and progressive distancing of the ECtHR and Russia can be traced back over a long period.[1223] This is actually the state against which the ECtHR has directed most of its legislative remedies, and some judgments concerning Russia's domestic laws have also generated resistance and

1222 See among others Mikael Rask Madsen, "Rebalancing European Human Rights: Has the Brighton Declaration Engendered a New Deal on Human Rights in Europe?", *JIDS* 9, 2018, pp. 199-222.

1223 Already after the illegal annexation of Crimea in 2014, Russia's voting rights at the PACE were suspended, among other sanctions by the CoE. Russia reacted by withholding its contribution to the CoE's budget in the following years, which in turn caused a financial crisis in this organisation, and the sanctions were eventually lifted in 2019. See generally Lauri Mälksoo and Wolfgang Benedek (eds.), *Russia and the European Court of Human Rights: The Strasbourg Effect*, Cambridge: CUP, 2017.

probably contributed to the State's discontent with the Court.[1224] Former Russian President Medvedev is quoted as stating that "we will never surrender that part of our sovereignty which would allow any international court or foreign court to render a decision changing our national legislation".[1225]

Studies on criticism towards the ECtHR in further states have also highlighted its connection to the Court's impact on domestic legislation.[1226] For example, the ECtHR has been criticised in the Netherlands for "disrespecting (...) the democratic legitimacy of national legislation".[1227] Madsen has observed in this regard that backlash may occur "when there is a clear preference for national political outcomes that clashes with developments at international institutions".[1228] There are specific instances in which this has occurred, and legislative remedies have played an important role in the negative reaction of states, despite its exceptionality. The main example in this respect concerns the 'prisoner voting rights saga', which generated strong resistance from the British government, even threatening to leave the system.[1229]

This saga has its origin in the judgment of *Hirst vs. UK (No. 2)* (2005), where the Court found that a general and indiscriminate prohibition for prisoners to vote "irrespective of the length of their sentence and irrespective of the nature or gravity of their offence and their individual circumstances", fell outside the State's margin of appreciation and constituted a violation of Article 3 Protocol 1 ECHR.[1230] With respect to remedies, it pointed out that it was for the State "to implement such measures as it considers appropriate to fulfil its obligations to secure the right to vote in

1224 In this respect, research has shown that the position of a given state towards the ECtHR depends not so much on the number of decisions against it, but rather on "a few incidental judgments" (Patricia Popelier, Sarah Lambrecht and Koen Lemmens, "Introduction", in Popelier et al. (eds.), 2016, p. 16).

1225 Cited in Aaron Matta and Armen Mazmanyan, "Russia: In Quest for a European Identity", in Popelier et al. (eds.), 2016, p. 497.

1226 See for example Michael Reiertsen, "Norway: New Constitutionalism, New Counter-Dynamics?", in Popelier et al. (eds.), 2016, p. 361.

1227 Janneke Gerards, "The Netherlands: Political Dynamics, Institutional Robustness", in Popelier et al. (eds.), 2016, p. 328.

1228 Mikael Rask Madsen, "Two-level politics and the backlash against international courts: Evidence from the politicisation of the European court of human rights", *British Journal of Politics and International Relations* 22(4), 2020, pp. 728–738.

1229 Ed Bates, "Analysing the Prisoner Voting Saga and the British Challenge to Strasbourg", *HRLR* 14(3), 2014, pp. 503-540.

1230 ECtHR, *Hirst vs. UK* (No. 2) (2005), para. 82.

compliance with this judgment".[1231] It however implicitly recommended a legislative reform, stating that it would be "leaving it *to the legislature* to decide on the choice of means for securing the rights guaranteed by Article 3 of Protocol No. 1".[1232] Five judges dissented, arguing that the Court "is not a legislator and should be careful not to assume legislative functions".[1233]

The UK refused to implement this judgment and defied the ECtHR instead.[1234] In view of this, the ECtHR subsequently introduced a very explicit order to reform the relevant domestic laws in the pilot judgment *Greens and MT vs. UK* (2010).[1235] In response, the British Parliament adopted a harsh resolution in 2011 where it expressed its refusal to implement the judgment, stating "that legislative decisions of this nature should be a matter for democratically-elected lawmakers".[1236] After a long period of tension, with the UK even threatening to leave the ECHR system, the case was closed rather problematically, with the CoM lowering its compliance requirements – as will be elucidated below.[1237]

This case of resistance is closely related to the particularities of British constitutionalism, where even the highest domestic courts have only very limited powers to challenge legislation. In fact, under the Human Rights Act of the UK, when domestic courts find legislation to be clearly incompatible with ECHR rights, Parliament remains free to decide on the consequences of such a finding. Thus, under this approach, the ECtHR displayed greater powers concerning domestic legislation than those of UK courts, and its judgment "was seen as an attack on parliamentary sovereignty".[1238] In sum, the core of this controversy was precisely the legislative nature of the measure being ordered by the ECtHR.[1239] This is therefore one of the instances in which the relation between legislative measures and backlash can be more clearly observed.

1231 ECtHR, *Hirst vs. UK* (No. 2) (2005), para. 93.

1232 See ECtHR, *Hirst vs. UK* (No. 2) (2005), para. 84 (emphasis added).

1233 ECtHR, *Hirst vs. UK* (No. 2) (2005), Joint Dissenting Opinion of Judges Wildhaber, Costa, Lorenzen, Kovler and Jebens, para. 6.

1234 See in this regard Steve Foster, "Reluctantly Restoring Rights: Responding to the Prisoner's Right to Vote", *HRLR* 9(3), 2009, pp. 489–507.

1235 ECtHR, *Greens and MT vs. UK* (2010), operative para. 6. See also, examining this judgment, Chapter 4 of this book.

1236 Cited in Bates, *HRLR* 2014, p. 513.

1237 See below section III(2) of this chapter.

1238 Angelika Nußberger, "From High Hopes to Scepticism? Human Rights Protection and Rule of Law in Europe in an Ever More Hostile Environment", in Krieger, Nolte and Zimmermann (eds.), 2019, pp. 150-171, p. 163.

1239 Bates, *HRLR* 2014, p. 530.

b) Limiting access to the ACtHPR

The remedial practice of the ACtHPR, and in particular its legislative remedies, has also been a source of conflict. Here, the recent backlash has taken the form of states limiting access to the ACtHPR by withdrawing their declarations made under Article 34(6) of the African Court's Protocol.[1240] As previously mentioned, applications to the ACtHPR can be brought only by the ACmHPR, states and African intergovernmental organisations. But as a particularity of the African system, individuals and NGOs are also allowed to apply directly before the Court if the corresponding state has consented to it through an optional declaration. At the time of writing, only ten of the thirty states under the jurisdiction of the Court submitted such a declaration, but four of them withdrew it afterwards. Rwanda withdrew its optional declaration in 2016, while Tanzania, Benin and Côte d'Ivoire did so between 2019 and 2020.[1241]

It must be noted that currently, almost all cases decided by the ACtHPR stem from these direct applications, especially by individuals.[1242] The ACmHPR has not been transmitting cases to the Court in a systematic way, as it is done by the IACmHR (or by the European Commission on Human Rights (ECmHR), before it was dismantled in 1998). Thus, authors have identified the "Commission's lack of initiative in presenting cases to the Court" as one of the main impediments that prevent the ACtHPR from dealing with more cases.[1243] Viljoen points to several reasons for this lack of initiative, including "a lack of referral criteria, deficiencies in accurately establishing (non-) implementation, and uncertainty about the

1240 See Madsen *et al.*, *IJLC* 2018, p. 210, explaining the restriction of access to an international court as a form of expressing resistance by states. See also, with respect to the African Court, Tom Daly and Micha Wiebusch, "The African Court on Human and Peoples' Rights: mapping resistance against a young court", *IJLC* 14, 2018, pp. 294– 313.

1241 For a more detailed analysis of these four withdrawals, see Sègnonna Horace Adjolohoun, "A crisis of design and judicial practice? Curbing state disengagement from the African Court on Human and Peoples' Rights", *AHRLJ* 20, 2020, pp. 1-40.

1242 See Tarisai Mutangi, "Enforcing Compliance with the Judgments of the African Court on Human and Peoples' Rights", in Aderomola Adeola (ed.), *Compliance with International Human Rights Law in Africa: Essays in Honour of Frans Viljoen*, Oxford: OUP, 2022, p. 184, explaining that by 2019 the ACtHPR had received 238 applications, twelve of which were filed by civil society organisations, and only three by the ACmHPR. The other 223 applications were filed by individuals.

1243 Allwell Uwazuruike, *Human Rights under the African Charter*, Cham: Palgrave Macmillan, 2020, at p. 171.

Commission's role, know-how and experience in presenting such cases before the Court".[1244] Thus, by withdrawing the aforementioned declarations and impeding individuals and NGOs from submitting applications, states are substantially curtailing the capacity of the ACtHPR to hear cases of alleged human rights violations.

The first state to withdraw its Article 34(6) declaration was Rwanda in March 2016. The context of this withdrawal was the procedure leading to the hearings of the case *Ingabire Victoire Umuhoza vs. Rwanda* (2017).[1245] This case dealt with the application of a Rwandan politician who had been convicted for the crime of downplaying the genocide. Notably, one of the remedies sought by the applicant in this case was the annulment of several specific sections of the Rwandan criminal code "relating to the punishment of the crime of ideology of the Genocide".[1246] As it is known, the issues concerning the Rwandan genocide remain very sensitive in this state. Thus, already in the preliminary stages of the proceedings before the ACtHPR, the Rwandan government sent a *note verbale* arguing that the State had "never envisaged that the kind of person described above [i.e., a person that denies or downplays the genocide] would ever seek and be granted a platform on the basis of the said Declaration", and that therefore it would withdraw this declaration.[1247]

However, the Rwandan government still participated in the judicial proceedings and thereby focused on the possibility of the ACtHPR including legislative measures. In fact, Rwanda objected to the Court's jurisdiction arguing that the ACtHPR is not "a legislative body which can (...) make national legislation in lieu of national legislative Assemblies".[1248] This objection was dismissed by the ACtHPR, although in the decision on the merits, it considered the law criminalising the minimisation of genocide to be compatible with the Charter, however finding its application in the con-

1244 Frans Viljoen, "Understanding and Overcoming Challenges in Accessing the African Court on Human and Peoples' Rights", *ICLQ* 67, 2018, pp. 63-98, at p. 97.

1245 See in this respect Solomon Ayele Dersso, "The Future of Human Rights and the African Human Rights System", *NJHR* 40(1), 2022, pp. 28-43, at p. 41.

1246 ACtHPR, *Ingabire Victoire Umuhoza vs. Rwanda* (2017), para. 48.

1247 Oliver Windridge, "Assessing Rwexit: the impact and implications of Rwanda's withdrawal of its article 34(6) declaration before the African Court on Human and Peoples' Rights", *African Human Rights Yearbook* 2, 2018, p. 249.

1248 ACtHPR, *Ingabire Victoire Umuhoza vs Rwanda* (2017), para. 52.

crete case disproportionate.[1249] Although Rwanda's withdrawal is probably more closely linked to the political sensitivity of the cases submitted to the ACtHPR and the nature of the victims than to remedial questions *per se*,[1250] it can be observed that the possibility of including legislative remedies also played a part in it.

Another major blow came with the decision of Tanzania (the state that hosts the ACtHPR) to withdraw its optional declaration in November 2019. The State did not offer any explanation for its withdrawal, but due to its timing, some commentators have suggested that it might be related to the case of *Ally Rajabu vs. Tanzania* (2019).[1251] In this case, the ACtHPR found that the mandatory death penalty for a sentence of murder violates the right to life, and therefore ordered a reform of the State's Criminal Code.[1252] Tanzania had also unsuccessfully objected to the ACtHPR's competence in this case, by claiming that "the Applicant does not plead violation of his rights by any of the laws of which he seeks annulment or suspension".[1253] Moreover, the Court had rendered numerous legislative remedies against Tanzania during the previous years, requesting *inter alia* the amendment of its laws on citizenship and even of the electoral rules contained in its Constitution.[1254] All of these cases had been brought to the ACtHPR directly by individuals and NGOs on the basis of the Article 34(6) Declaration. Thus, legislative remedies arguably played a more important role in this particular instance of backlash.

Then, both Benin and Côte d'Ivoire decided to withdraw their optional declarations in April 2020. In the latter case, the Ivorian notice of withdrawal mentioned that the ACtHPR's actions "not only violate the states'

1249 See ACtHPR, *Ingabire Victoire Umuhoza vs Rwanda* (2017), paras. 147 *et seq*. See also on this case Harrisson Mbori, "Ingabire Victoire Umuhoza vs Rwanda", *AJIL* 112(4), 2018, pp. 713-719.

1250 See Viljoen, *ICLQ* 2018, p. 66 ("A contributing factor to Rwanda's withdrawal may (rather) have been that the government did not foresee the submission of six cases against it, within a relatively short period, all dealing with politically sensitive matters, submitted by political opponents of the current government").

1251 Nicole Da Silva, "Individual and NGO Access to the African Court on Human and Peoples' Rights: The Latest Blow from Tanzania", *EJIL: talk!*, 16 December 2019, available at: https://www.ejiltalk.org/individual-and-ngoaccess-to-the-african-court-on-human-and-peoples-rights-the-latest-blow-from-tanzania/. See also Faix and Jamali, *NQHR* 2022, p. 66.

1252 ACtHPR, *Ally Rajabu vs. Tanzania* (2019), operative para. xv (1).

1253 ACtHPR, *Ally Rajabu vs. Tanzania* (2019), para. 62.

1254 ACtHPR, *Tanganyika Law Society and Legal and Human Rights Centre vs. Tanzania* (2013); *Anudo Ochieng Anudo* vs. Tanzania (2018).

sovereignty, but were likely to cause a disruption of its domestic legal order".[1255] In this respect, commentators have mentioned the connection to a specific order of provisional measures in which the Court ordered to suspend an arrest warrant against the former Ivorian Prime Minister.[1256] This withdrawal is therefore less related to legislative measures than those of the other states.

On the other hand, Benin's withdrawal is also closely related to an order of provisional measures, but in this case with legislative – and even constitutional – implications. This is the case of *Ajavon vs. Benin* (2020), in which the applicant (an opposition politician in exile who had already been before the ACtHPR, where he successfully challenged a Beninese law)[1257] claimed that several unrelated domestic laws, including the Constitution of Benin, would be incompatible with the State's human rights obligations.[1258] As several of these laws concerned electoral procedures, the ACtHPR issued an order of provisional measures ordering Benin to suspend the municipal elections scheduled for May 2020.[1259] This is probably what triggered the reaction of Benin.[1260] In its notice of withdrawal, the Beninese government stated that "the errors of the African Court have become a source of real

---

1255 Presse Côte d'Ivoire, "La Côte d'Ivoire retire sa déclaration de la Charte africaine des droits de l'Homme et des Peuples (Communiqué)", 29 April 2020, available at : https://www.pressecotedivoire.ci/article/5879-la-cote-divoireretire-sa-declaration-de-la-charte-africaine-des-droits-de-lhomme-et-des-peuples-communique (non-official translation).

1256 Oliver Windridge, "Under Attack? Under the Radar? Under-Appreciated? All of the Above? A Time of Reckoning for the African Court on Human and Peoples' Rights", *Opinio Iuris*, 07 Mai 2020, available at: https://opiniojuris.org/2020/05/07/under-attack-under-the-radar-under-appreciated-all-of-the-above-a-time-ofreckoning-for-the-african-court-on-human-and-peoples-rights/. ACtHPR, *Guillaume Kigbafori Soro vs. Côte d'Ivoire* (Provisional Measures), App. 012/2020, 22 April 2020, para. 42 (i).

1257 ACtHPR, *Sébastien Germain Marie Aikoué Ajavon vs. Benin* (2019).

1258 ACtHPR, *Sébastien Germain Marie Aikoué Ajavon vs. Benin* (2020).

1259 ACtHPR, *Sébastien Germain Marie Aikoué Ajavon vs. Benin,* Provisional Measures (2020).

1260 Nicole da Silva and Misha Plagis, "A Court in Crisis: African States' Increasing Resistance to Africa's Human Rights Court", *Opinio Iuris*, 19 May 2020, available at: http://opiniojuris.org/2020/05/19/a-court-in-crisis-african-states-increasing-resistance-to-africas-human-rights-court/, citing the words of the Government's spokesperson according to whom the withdrawal was necessary "in order not to jeopardize the interests of an entire nation and the duty of a government which is responsible for holding elections on time".

legal and judicial insecurity which it is the responsibility of governments to remedy".[1261]

Thus, it can be observed that the legislative measures issued by the ACtHPR played a notable role in the withdrawal of Tanzania's and Benin's optional declarations, and to a lesser extent also in that of Rwanda. In this context, it is also worth noticing that among the categories of legislative measures examined in the previous chapter, the one related to electoral rights is particularly prone to cause resistance and backlash. This is due to the sensitivity that domestic governments attach to this issue, especially when electoral laws permitting rulers to remain in power or favouring them in some other ways are ordered to be amended. This particular remedial practice of the ACtHPR is thus rather often connected to instances of backlash.[1262]

However, it is not only the concrete remedies that are important in this context but also the manner in which the ACtHPR has adopted rather flexible rules on legal standing, which allows it to review domestic legislation *in abstracto* by permitting individuals and NGOs to bring applications against laws without having been affected by them.[1263] Despite various states' objections, this type of 'abstract' applications have been accepted by the ACtHPR in numerous cases, arguing that it constitutes a particularity of the African system due to the difficulties that individuals encounter in accessing the Court.[1264] Therefore, the objective of states when withdrawing the optional declarations is probably also to avoid instances of strategic

1261 Gouvernement de la République du Benin, *Retrait du Bénin de la CADHP - Déclaration du ministre de la Justice et de la Législation*, 28 April 2020, available at : https://www.gouv.bj/actualite/635/retrait-benin-cadhp--declaration-ministre-justice-legislation/ ("les égarements de la Cour africaine sont devenus source d'une véritable insécurité juridique et judiciaire à laquelle il est de la responsabilité des gouvernants de porter remède").

1262 Some authors have also expressed criticism at the remedial practice of the ACtHPR when commenting on the withdrawals. Apollin Koagne Zouapet for example speaks of "a Court so concerned with the protection of human rights that it does not hesitate to bypass possible procedural obstacles to provide a remedy to all citizens of a country". See Apollin Koagne Zouapet, "'Victim of its commitment ... You, passerby, a tear to the proclaimed virtue': Should the epitaph of the African Court on Human and Peoples' Rights be prepared?", *EJIL: Talk!*, 05 May 2020, available at: https://www.ejiltalk.org/victim-of-its-commitment-you-passerby-a-tear-to-the-proclaimed-virtueshould-the-epitaph-of-the-african-court-on-human-and-peoples-rights-be-prepared/.

1263 See Chapter 1 of this book, examining this jurisdictional approach of the ACtHPR.

1264 See for example ACtHPR, *Ajavon vs. Benin* (2020), para. 59; ACtHPR, *XYZ vs. Benin (II)* (2020), para. 48.

litigation by NGOs aiming to challenge domestic laws even in the absence of victims.

c) Exiting the ACHR

Much like its counterparts, the IACtHR has also witnessed resistance by several states almost since its conception,[1265] and this has even reached the point in which two states have already exited the ACHR.[1266] The remedial practice of the Court has contributed to a considerable extent to this resistance and backlash. Although it had no influence on the first withdrawal from the Convention (that of Trinidad and Tobago in 1998), this was different in the second one (that of Venezuela in 2012), where several orders to reform laws affecting the domestic judiciary played an important role. Moreover, legislative measures had also a considerable influence on other conflicts between specific states and the IACtHR, such as that with the Dominican Republic in 2014 or that with Fujimori's Peru in the late 1990s.

Peru was the first state to have a major problem related to the IACtHR's remedial practice.[1267] Some of this Court's first legislative measures were directed precisely against Peru, in two cases dealing with due process rights and restrictions to the military jurisdiction.[1268] The IACtHR ordered the reform of two domestic laws which foresaw that all those accused of treason and terrorism were to be judged under the military jurisdiction.[1269] These remedies were considered "simply unacceptable" by the Peruvian government,[1270] and it withdrew the recognition of the contentious jurisdiction of

1265 See Neuman, *EJIL* 2008, p. 105. With regard to backlash and other forms of resistance towards the IACtHR, see Ximena Soley and Silvia Steininger, "Parting ways or lashing back? Withdrawals, backlash and the Inter-American Court of Human Rights", *IJLC* 14(2), 2018, pp. 237-257.

1266 Trinidad and Tobago exited the American Convention in 1998 and Venezuela in 2012.

1267 Trinidad and Tobago had already withdrawn by that time, but this was not linked to the remedies of the Court, as the first judgments on reparations against this state were issued after its withdrawal. In this case, the backlash had to do, among other issues, with provisional measures ordered by the IACtHR in cases related to the application of the death penalty.

1268 See Chapter 4 of this book. See also Cavallaro and Brewer, *AJIL* 2008, p. 789.

1269 See IACtHR, *Loayza Tamayo vs. Peru* (1998), operative para. 5; *Castillo Petruzzi vs. Peru* (1999), operative para. 14.

1270 Cited Jorge Contesse, "Resisting the Inter-American Court", *YJIL* 44(2), 2019, pp. 179-237, at p. 197.

the IACtHR in July 1999.[1271] Among its reasons for withdrawing this recognition, Peru explicitly mentioned the lack of authority of the IACtHR to order the modification of domestic laws.[1272] This withdrawal was however not accepted by the Court, arguing that the only possibility for a state is to denounce the ACHR in its entirety, which needs to be done in accordance with the established procedure.[1273] The situation could only be solved one year later with the change of government in Peru, when the authoritarian regime was substituted by a democratic one which was committed to the inter-American system. This first instance of backlash, even if it was related to the IACtHR's legislative remedies, did not prevent the Court from maintaining and even expanding this remedial practice during the following decade.

This led to the next case of major backlash towards the inter-American system, the withdrawal of Venezuela in 2012.[1274] Venezuela's backlash and eventual withdrawal from the ACHR can be attributed to several factors, among them the remedies ordered by the IACtHR against this state. Regarding legislative reforms, the IACtHR issued between 2008 and 2011 five judgments against Venezuela which included this remedy. Especially sensitive in this regard were three judgments related to the arbitrary dismissal of judges. The Court specifically ordered Venezuela to amend certain norms that considered provisional judges as "freely removable", as well as to reinstate the judges that had been ceased.[1275] This was one of the main issues that provoked Venezuela's withdrawal in 2012.[1276] Indeed, already

1271 The IACtHR can only initiate judicial proceedings against states that have expressly recognised its contentious jurisdiction through an optional declaration, in accordance with Art. 62 ACHR.

1272 Douglass Cassel, "Peru Withdraws from the Court: Will the Inter-American Human Rights System Meet the Challenge?", *Human Rights Law Journal* 20, 1999, at p. 170.

1273 See IACtHR, *Constitutional Court vs. Peru* (1999), para. 39; *Ivcher Bronstein vs. Peru* (2001), para. 40.

1274 See Alexandra Huneeus, "Venzuela's Withdrawal from the Inter-American Court", *ICONnect Blog*, 15 October 2012, available at http://www.iconnectblog.com/2012/10/venezuelas-exit-from-the-inter-american-court/. See also Soley and Steininger, *IJLC* 2018, pp. 250-252.

1275 IACtHR, *Apitz Barbera vs. Venezuela* (2008), operative para. 19; *Reverón Trujillo vs. Venezuela* (2009), operative para. 10; *Chocrón Chocrón vs. Venezuela* (2011), operative para. 8.

1276 Another main issue concerned remedies affecting domestic judgments. In the judgment of *Lopez Mendoza vs. Venezuela* (2011), the Court ordered Venezuela to overturn the conviction of the opposition leader, Leopoldo Lopez Mendoza, who in December 2008, some months after the notification of the first of the aforementioned judgments, the Supreme Court of Venezuela responded declaring this judgment of the IACtHR to be "non-executable", arguing *inter alia* that the IACtHR had issued "orders for the Legislative Branch (...) violating the sovereignty of the Venezuelan State in the organization of public powers (...) which is inadmissible".[1277] When Venezuela eventually decided to withdraw from the Convention, it expressly mentioned among other reasons the IACtHR's interference in the State's legislative practice.[1278] Venezuela's withdrawal was probably a stronger blow to the inter-American system than Trinidad and Tobago's withdrawal in 1998, due to the respective weight of these two countries in the region.[1279]

Shortly thereafter, another conflict affected the IACtHR, this time with the Constitutional Court of the Dominican Republic (DR).[1280] The origin of this conflict can be traced to legislative remedies issued by the IACtHR, in this case relating to the conformity of the Dominican nationality laws with the ACHR.[1281] Already by 2005, the IACtHR had declared these laws to be discriminatory, as they prevented children of Haitian descent from

---

had been imprisoned in violation of his due process rights, as well as to allow him to run as a candidate in the subsequent national elections. This judgment caused a major outrage in the Venezuelan Government and the State's Supreme Court declared the judgment to be "non-executable". See Judgment No. 1547 of the Supreme Court of Justice of Venezuela, 17 October 2011, operative para. 1.

1277 Supreme Court of Justice of Venezuela (Constitutional Chamber), *Judgment No. 1939*, 18 December 2008, section V (non-official translation). In this judgment, Venezuela's Supreme Court already recommended the Executive to withdraw from the Convention.

1278 See Ministry of Foreign Affairs of Venezuela, "Notificación de Denuncia" and "Fundamentación que sustenta la denuncia de la República Bolivariana de Venezuela de la Convención Americana sobre Derechos Humanos presentada a la Secretaría General de la OEA", 10 September 2012 ("la Corte Interamericana (...) violenta y malinterpreta el principio de complementariedad del sistema (...) al pretender juzgar, como lo haría un tribunal nacional, respecto a disposiciones de derecho interno").

1279 In addition, Trinidad and Tobago is part of the English-speaking countries of the Caribbean region, which have a different legal and constitutional tradition than most Latin American states and have therefore been rather separated from the inter-American system. Nowadays, Barbados is the sole English-speaking country of the Caribbean region which is subject to the jurisdiction of the IACtHR. See Helfer, *CLR* 2002.

1280 See generally Alexandra Huneeus and René Urueña, "Treaty Exit and Latin America's Constitutional Courts", *AJIL Unbound*, vol. 111, 2017, pp. 456-460.

1281 See Dinah Shelton and Alexandra Huneeus, "In re Direct Action of Unconstitutionality Initiated Against the Declaration of Acceptance of the Jurisdiction of the obtaining nationality, and ordered their reform.[1282] This triggered a strong reaction inside the DR, where Haitian immigration is a very sensitive issue. The fact that Haiti and the DR share the same island and that Haiti is one of the world's poorest countries makes many Haitians cross the border and move to the DR in search of a better future. This, in turn, is met with strong resistance in some sectors of the Dominican society. The judgment was therefore criticised by the State's secretary of foreign relations, and the DR failed to comply with the legislative measures, despite paying the monetary compensation.[1283]

In fact, the Dominican government moved in the opposite direction of the IACtHR's orders and reformed its Constitution by expressly providing that children of "illegal migrants" would not obtain Dominican nationality, taking exception to the applicable *ius soli* principle.[1284] Then, in 2014, the IACtHR issued another judgment dealing with the DR's discriminatory practice in nationality issues, ordering again the reform of several laws, including the Dominican Constitution.[1285] This judgment was again received with strong opposition by the national media and even the government.[1286] Only two months after the IACtHR had issued this judgment, the Constitutional Court of the DR declared that the instrument by which the State had

Inter-American Court of Human Rights", *AJIL*, vol. 109(4), 2015, pp. 866-872. See also Contesse, *YJIL* 2019, pp. 199-204.

1282 IACtHR, *Yean and Bosco vs. Dominican Republic* (2005). See also Chapter 4 of this book.

1283 See Cavallaro and Brewer, *AJIL* 2008, p. 790.

1284 Contesse, *YJIL* 2019, p. 200.

1285 In the case of *Dominican and Haitian Persons Expelled from the Dominican Republic vs. Dominican Republic* (2014), the IACtHR ordered, among other remedies, the "necessary measures in order to avoid that (...) the statements of articles 6, 8 and 11 of Law No 169-14 continue producing legal effects" (operative para. 18). Besides this concrete law, it also ordered the State to annul any other norm which prevented the persons born in the DR to obtain the Dominican nationality on the grounds of their parents' illegal residence, as well as to adopt the legislative ("even if necessary constitutional") measures in order to regulate an accessible inscription procedure for children born in the State's territory (operative paras. 19 and 20, respectively).

1286 See Presidency of the Dominican Republic, "El Gobierno rechaza la sentencia de la Corte Interamericana de Derechos Humanos", 23 October 2014, available at https://presidencia.gob.do/noticias/el-gobierno-dominicanorechaza-la-sentencia-de-la-corte-interamericana-de-derechos-humanos. See also further references in Soley and Steininger, *IJLC* 2018, p. 249.

accessed the ACHR was unconstitutional on procedural grounds.[1287] Nowadays the situation of the DR regarding the IACtHR is still not completely clear. The DR officially remains part of the inter-American system, as the government has not formally activated the withdrawal mechanism, but this has been the last judgment of the IACtHR against the Dominican State to date.[1288]

In sum, one can also see that legislative remedies were extremely influential in several individual instances of backlash against the IACtHR. It is thus a remedial practice that can trigger strong reactions inside the states affected by them, especially when they affect issues that are particularly sensitive and affect core aspects of the states' sovereign sphere, such as the latter issue concerning migration and nationality,[1289] or those concerning the independence of the judiciary in Venezuela.[1290] However, another question is whether these reactions are also present at a collective level, where instances of backlash have also occurred.

2. Legislative Remedies and Collective Instances of Backlash

Besides these instances of backlash by individual states against the three regional human rights courts, there is another form of backlash affecting them – called here 'collective backlash'.[1291] This takes place when several states jointly attempt to reform the respective human rights protection system in order to lessen the authority or limit the competences of courts. A typical feature of this form of backlash is the reliance on concepts such as state discretion, subsidiarity or margin of appreciation, in order to restrict

1287 Constitutional Court of the Dominican Republic, *Judgment TC/0256/14*, 04 November 2014.

1288 However, provisional measures have been issued against this state after 2014. See for example *Juan Almonte Herrera vs. Dominican Republic*, Provisional Measures (2015).

1289 Hannah Arendt mentioned already in *The Origins of Totalitarianism* that "in the sphere of international law, it had always been true that sovereignty is nowhere more absolute than in matters of 'emigration, naturalization, nationality, and expulsion'" (Hannah Arendt, *The Origins of Totalitarianism*, New York: Harvest Book 1976, p. 278.).

1290 This is because the judiciary has played a very important role in Venezuela during the last years, restricting the rights of opposition leaders to the point of imprisoning several of them, and confirming electoral results in favour of the regime after elections arguably held in contravention of international standards.

1291 See, on collective forms of backlash, Madsen et al., *IJLC* 2018, p. 198.

the intensity of the judicial review carried out by human rights courts.[1292] This can be observed in the recently concluded 'Interlaken process' at the European human rights protection system, but also in the declaration signed by five Latin American presidents in 2019, concerning the IACtHR.

a) The 'Interlaken Process' in Europe

Between 2009 and 2018, a series of inter-governmental conferences took place with the purpose of reflecting on the long-term effectiveness of the European human rights protection system.[1293] This process and the resulting institutional reforms have been known as the 'Interlaken process', due to the location of the first of these conferences in 2009.[1294] The subsequent conferences took place in Izmir (2010), Brighton (2012), Brussels (2015) and Copenhagen (2018). Each of them produced a formal declaration containing recommendations for the Court, the CoM and the member states.

The main source of concern at the background of the Interlaken process was the caseload crisis before the ECtHR, which had "reached its peak of 160,000 pending applications" some months after Interlaken.[1295] However, there was also a subjacent reason for this process, which was the growing discontent of some states with the Court's jurisprudence.[1296] In this respect, one issue put on the agenda of these conferences by "those seeking to force or persuade the Court to soften review and to grant more deference to

1292 See Hillebrecht, 2021, p. 133 ("By expanding the degree of deference that courts afford states, international justice opponents try to limit the impact that international courts have on domestic politics").

1293 See Alastair Mowbray, "The Interlaken Declaration – The Beginning of a New Era for the European Court of Human Rights?", *HRLR* 10(3), 2010, pp. 519-528; Jon Petter Rui, "The Interlaken, Izmir and Brighton Declarations: Towards a Paradigm Shift in the Strasbourg Court's Interpretation of the European Convention of Human Rights?", *NJHR* 31(1), 2013, pp. 28-54.

1294 See for example ECtHR, *The Interlaken Process and the Court*, 2016 Report to the CoM, 01 September 2016, available at: https://www.echr.coe.int/Documents/2016_Interlaken_Process_ENG.pdf.

1295 Lize Glas, "From Interlaken to Copenhagen: What Has Become of the Proposals Aiming to Reform the Functioning of the European Court of Human Rights?", *HRLR* 20, 2020, pp. 121-151, at p. 125. The main aim of the Interlaken Declaration was therefore to "to find a solution for the chronic [case] over-load". See Declaration adopted at the Interlaken Conference on the Reform of the European Court of Human Rights, 19 February 2010, available at: https://www.echr.coe.int/Documents/2010_Interlaken_FinalDeclaration_ENG.pdf.

1296 Glas, *HRLR* 2020, p. 125.

the policy preferences of governments" was the question of "whether to dismantle the components of judicial supremacy that had been established through the ECtHR's precedents".[1297]

Many authors have thus seen this process as a form of curtailing the ECtHR's authority and competences.[1298] Madsen describes it as, especially since the Brighton Conference (2012), an "institutionalized process that aimed to limit the ECtHR's power".[1299] In fact, the Brighton Declaration is often seen as a 'turning point' in this reform process, shifting from rather technical measures to improve the Court's efficiency to "a full-blown challenge to the very legitimacy and role of the ECtHR".[1300] This Declaration has even been described as aiming at "a new dawn in which the Court would play a different and more limited role",[1301] with provisions intending "to restrict the Court's scrutiny of the States' law and practice".[1302] In response to it, the ECtHR itself expressed discomfort at the idea of states dictating "how it should carry out the judicial functions conferred on it".[1303]

One of the main ways for states to limit the Court's intrusiveness and "persuade [it] to take a more state friendly position in its case law" was to focus on the principle of subsidiarity and the margin of appreciation.[1304] In almost all of these declarations, states encouraged the ECtHR to give increased prominence to these two principles,[1305] which led to their incor-

1297 Alec Stone Sweet, Wayne Sandholtz and Mads Andenas, "The Failure to Destroy the Authority of the European Court of Human Rights: 2010–2018", *LPICT* 21, 2022, pp. 244–277, at p. 246. See also Hillebrecht, 2021, p. 151 ("These reform processes questioned, at their core, the degree to which the central role of the ECtHR was to provide individual recourse or to serve as a forum for regional constitutional review").

1298 See Stone Sweet, Sandholtz and Andenas, *LPICT* 2022, p. 253 ("Through the High Level Conferences, the Court's detractors sought to revive rights minimalism"). See also Sarah Lambrecht, "Reforms to Lessen the Influence of the European Court of Human Rights: A Successful Strategy?", *European Public Law* 21(2), 2015, pp. 257-284.

1299 Madsen, *LCP* 2016, at p. 144.

1300 Oddný Mjöll Arnardóttir, "The Brighton Aftermath and the Changing Role of the European Court of Human Rights", *JIDS* 9, 2018, pp. 223–239, at p. 224.

1301 Madsen, *JIDS* 2018, p. 202.

1302 Glas, *HRLR* 2020, p. 127.

1303 High Level Conference Brighton, Speech by Sir Nicolas Bratza, President of the European Court of Human Rights (18–20 April 2012), cited in Arnardóttir, *JIDS* 2018, p. 225.

1304 Arnardóttir, *JIDS* 2018, p. 225.

1305 High Level Conference on the Future of the European Court of Human Rights, *Brighton Declaration*, 2012, paras. 11 and 12(a), available at: https://www.echr.co

poration in the Preamble of the ECHR through Protocol No. 15.[1306] The Preamble now affirms "that the High Contracting Parties, in accordance with the principle of subsidiarity, have the primary responsibility to secure the rights and freedoms defined in this Convention and the Protocols thereto, and that in doing so they enjoy a margin of appreciation". This can be seen as a mandate for the ECtHR to show an increased deference to national authorities, particularly to the domestic legislatures.[1307] Actually, according to the former ECtHR President, the message being sent with the introduction of the new Preamble is that "governments (or some of them) wish to compel the Court to exercise increased self-restraint in its scrutiny, especially when (...) national Parliaments are involved".[1308] In the words of Hillebrecht, "arguments about the degree of deference courts should afford to national authorities only thinly veil concerted efforts to attenuate the courts' impact".[1309] Thus, it can be observed that one of the aims of this reform process has been to limit to some extent the ECtHR's review of domestic laws.

Nevertheless, in these declarations states generally abstained from criticising the ECtHR's remedial approach. To the contrary, the Brighton Declaration actually "welcome[d] the continued use by the Court of proactive measures, particularly pilot judgments, to dispose of repetitive violations in an efficient manner".[1310] Moreover, this declaration seemed to favour a more constitutional approach by the ECtHR,[1311] stressing that "the Court

---

e.int/documents/2012_brighton_finaldeclaration_eng.pdf. See also *Interlaken Declaration*, Action Plan, para. 9(b), *Izmir Declaration*, Preamble, 2011, para. 5, available at: https://www.echr.coe.int/documents/2011_izmir_finaldeclaration_eng.pdf; *Brussels Declaration*, 2015, para. 7, available at: https://www.echr.coe.int/Documents/Brussels_Declaration_ENG.pdf; *Copenhagen Declaration*, 2018, para. 30, available at: https://www.echr.coe.int/Documents/Copenhagen_Declaration_ENG.pdf.

1306 See, critical with this development, Ian Cram, "Protocol 15 and Articles 10 and 11 ECHR—The Partial Triumph of Political Incumbency Post-Brighton?", *ICLQ* 67, 2018, pp. 477–503.

1307 See Lambrecht, *European Public Law* 2015, p. 273.

1308 Jean-Paul Costa, "The relationship between the European Court of Human Rights and the National Courts", *EHRLR* 3, 2013, pp. 264-274, at p. 265.

1309 Hillebrecht, 2021, p. 135.

1310 Brighton Declaration (2012), para 20 (c).

1311 See in this respect Luzius Wildhaber, "A Constitutional Future for the European Court of Human Rights", 23 *Human Rights Law Journal* 23, 2002, pp. 161-165; Luzius Wildhaber and Steven Greer, "Revisiting the Debate about 'Constitutionalising' the European Court of Human Rights", *HRLR* 12(4), 2012, pp. 655-687. See also Chapter 5 of this book.

should be in a position to focus its efforts on serious or widespread violations, systemic and structural problems (...) and hence would need to remedy fewer violations itself and consequently deliver fewer judgments".[1312] The Copenhagen Declaration (2018) mentions as well the "ineffective national implementation of the Convention that remains the principal challenge".[1313] These statements can be seen as supporting to some extent legislative remedies, which are a convenient tool for addressing systemic problems and widespread violations and can allow for a more effective implementation of the ECHR at the national level.[1314]

In sum, although on a collective level states have intended to limit the intensity of the ECtHR's review of domestic laws, they seem more supportive with respect to the Court's remedial practice in general and legislative measures in particular, as can be seen in the high-level declarations adopted between 2009 and 2018. Thus, even though the majority of the CoE member states seem to be in favour of limiting the ECtHR's scrutiny of their laws, if the Court were to find exceptionally that a specific law or the absence of it violates the Convention, they appear to support the inclusion of legislative remedies in this regard.

b) The 'Five Presidents Declaration' in the Americas

Although the IACtHR has not been subject to a process of reform similar to that concerning the ECtHR in the Interlaken process,[1315] it has also suffered a form of collective backlash from several of its most relevant member states. This occurred in 2019, when the governments of Argentina, Brazil, Colombia, Paraguay and Chile adopted a joint declaration concerning the role of the IACtHR.[1316] The attempt of these presidents sought to curtail the IACtHR's authority and to urge it to be more cautious, by expressing

1312 *Brighton Declaration* (2012), para. 33.

1313 *Copenhagen Declaration* (2018), para. 12.

1314 See generally Chapter 1 of this book.

1315 A similar reform process was however carried out with respect to the IACmHR in 2011. While it was called a process of "strengthening" the Commission, it was rather aiming at limiting several of its powers, such as that of issuing provisional measures, and the expansion of its jurisdiction more generally. See in this respect Contesse, *YJIL* 2019, pp. 209-217.

1316 See Government of Chile, *Comunicado de prensa Ministerio de Relaciones Exteriores - Ministerio de Justicia y Derechos Humanos sobre Sistema Interamericano de Derechos Humanos*, 23 April 2019, available at: https://minrel.gob.cl/comunicado

their discontent with its current practice. In this regard, the declaration used similar arguments to those employed in the European context, by underlining the principle of subsidiarity, and stating that the IACtHR should award states a "margin of appreciation for deciding about the most suitable ways for respecting rights and guarantees, in order to give weight to its own democratic procedures".[1317] This joint declaration was seen by civil society as a challenge to the Court and an attempt to undermine its authority.[1318] Some authors however argued that it could simply be regarded "as a legitimate attempt of the five signatories to clarify the limits of their consent".[1319]

Contrary to the high-level declarations of the Interlaken process, the 'Five Presidents Declaration' emphasised the issue of remedies, thereby aiming to change the IACtHR's remedial practice. The declaration highlighted in this respect the need for the IACtHR's remedies to be proportionate and to "respect the State's constitutional and legal orders".[1320] This seems to be a reference to the use of legislative remedies, being the ones that affect the domestic legal and constitutional order more directly. It is worth recalling in this context that the IACtHR's orders to reform domestic laws are much more common than those of the ECtHR. Thus, it is likely that the five presidents' attempt to undermine the IACtHR and exert its influence upon it was triggered at least partly by the remedial practice of this Court, including especially its legislative remedies. Nevertheless, this connection between legislative remedies and instances of collective backlash is still weaker than in the aforementioned individual instances of backlash.

To conclude, this section has shown that legislative remedies have been a source of negative reactions and even backlash, but there is a difference

-de-prensa-ministerio-de-relaciones-exteriores-ministerio-de/minrel/2019-0423/105105.html.

1317 Government of Chile, *Comunicado de prensa Ministerio de Relaciones Exteriores* 2019 (non-official translation).

1318 See for example Amnesty International, "Americas: The Inter-American System is Crucial for Guaranteeing Human Rights in the Region", 24 April 2019, available at: https://www.amnesty.org/en/latest/news/2019/04/americas-sistema-interamericano-fundamental-para-derechoshumanos/.

1319 Paula Baldini Miranda da Cruz, "Trackers and Trailblazers: Dynamic Interactions and Institutional Design in the Inter-American Court of Human Rights", *JIDS* 11, 2020, pp. 69-90, at p. 87.

1320 Government of Chile, *Comunicado de prensa Ministerio de Relaciones Exteriores* 2019 (non-official translation).

between states acting individually and collectively. At an individual level, legislative remedies are more likely to trigger resistance, especially when they affect sensitive issues such as electoral rights, nationality rights or the rights of prisoners. This can be seen in individual instances of backlash against all three regional courts. However, this is not the case with collective instances of backlash, that are connected to legislative remedies rather loosely. Especially when states act collectively in the framework of the international organisation to which the courts belong (as in the aforementioned example of the 'Interlaken Process' of the CoE) the remedial practice has not been among the main sources of discontent. However, the 'Interlaken Process' is the only instance of collective backlash against a human rights court from within its international organisation. Thus, it might also be that these observations stem from the particularities of the ECtHR, its rather scarce use of intrusive remedies and the wide degree of discretion left to domestic legislatures in these cases.[1321] The collective instance of backlash against the IACtHR in the form of a joint declaration by five states was more closely linked to this Court's remedial practice, but its impact was more limited, as it was not part of an institutional reform process and it was carried out by a minority of states, despite their importance in the region.

II. Legislative Remedies and Compliance

Besides the issue of backlash, the other main consequence of legislative remedies concerns the lack of timely compliance with these measures. This is to some extent also related to the previous section, as "discrete non-compliance" is sometimes also an expression of pushback by states.[1322] However, this is not always the case, especially with complex remedies such as legislative reforms.[1323] Research into backlash and compliance with the ECtHR's judgments shows that there is generally no correlation between

1321 Stiansen actually observed with respect to the ECtHR that "although the need to enact legislative changes makes for a more difficult implementation process, states are not more likely to blatantly defy such judgments" (Stiansen, *IJHR* 2019, p. 1223).

1322 Madsen et al, *IJLC* 2018, p. 209.

1323 See for example Martin Faix and Ayyoub Jamali, "Is the African Court on Human and Peoples' Rights in an Existential Crisis?", *NQHR* 40(1), 2022, pp. 56–74, at p. 60 ("However, non-compliance does not always amount to backlash (...) This is particularly evident in cases where a government pays monetary compensation to the applicant but is unwilling or unable to bring changes to the legislation").

these two issues.[1324] This section will thus explore the issue of compliance with legislative remedies. It will not examine the current state of compliance with all 193 legislative measures that were identified in this study. Instead, it will give an overview of the empirical studies on compliance with human rights judgments that differentiate the types of measures ordered by the three regional courts, focusing on legislative measures. Subsequently, possible reasons for the low rates of compliance with these measures will be explored.

1. Empirical Studies on Compliance with Legislative Remedies

Several authors have examined the issue of compliance with human rights judgments from an empirical perspective, analysing the implementation of particular remedial measures. Thereby, a difference can be observed when comparing the ECtHR and the other two human rights courts. Legislative remedies before the ECtHR have been generally considered to have positive effects on compliance, perhaps because they put the focus on a legislative gap that the state in question has failed to fill despite previous warnings by the Court.[1325] In this regard, the exceptionality of these measures comes with increased visibility and thereby makes non-compliance more costly in terms of reputation. On the contrary, in the cases of the IACtHR and the ACtHPR, legislative remedies have been found to make compliance slower and more difficult.

In this regard, Stiansen conducted a study on "legislative compliance" with ECtHR judgments, quantitatively examining the leading cases in which states carried out legislative reforms in order to execute a judgment. This study is not, however, limited to the cases in which the ECtHR explicitly ordered a legislative reform, but it includes all of the cases where the concerned state and/or the CoM considered it necessary to legislate after a judgment.[1326] The results of this statistical analysis show that "judgments

1324 Sarah Lambrecht, "Assessing the Existence of Criticism of the European Court of Human Rights", in Popelier et al. (eds.), 2016, p. 513.

1325 With respect to the practice by the ECtHR of issuing several 'warnings' before introducing a binding legislative measure, see Chapter 3 of this book.

1326 See Stiansen, *IJHR* 2019, p. 1232, explaining that in order to measure the need for legislative reforms, he included the judgments in which the state had already carried out such a reform and those in which it still needed to do so in order to comply with a judgment.

that generate a need for legislative changes are implemented at a slower rate than other judgments".[1327] Moreover, the author finds that this delayed compliance "contributes to the backlog of repetitive cases that is burdening the ECtHR".[1328] However, the picture looks different if one examines not every case where the concerned state and/or the CoM consider legislative measures to be necessary for compliance, but only those in which the ECtHR explicitly orders such legislative measures by including them in the operative paragraphs.[1329]

In a study about non-financial remedies - which comprises those of a legislative nature - Mowbray finds that those included in the operative part of judgments are executed "more swiftly than where the Article 46 indication is contained in the text of the judgment".[1330] Other authors have arrived at the same conclusion when examining compliance with pilot judgments.[1331] For example, with respect to the judgment of *Torreggiani vs. Italy* (2013), where the ECtHR included legislative measures ordering the introduction of a domestic remedy for inhuman conditions of detention, such legislative reforms were adopted only one year later.[1332] This is despite the fact that implementing legislative reforms in Italy following ECtHR judgments where this was not expressly ordered has been described as following "a slow and tortuous path".[1333] Thus, it seems that including the need for legislative reforms as a remedy in the operative part of judgments can make a difference and have a 'catalysing effect' on domestic legislative procedures.[1334]

This is probably due to the notable exceptionality of such measures, which makes them gain importance and visibility when used, thereby

---

1327 Stiansen, *IJHR* 2019, p. 1239.

1328 Stiansen, *IJHR* 2019, p. 1242. Similar findings were also made in 2013 by Larsen with respect to the cases in which the ECtHR calls for legislative reforms, whether in the reasoning or in the operative part of judgments. He arrived at the conclusion that those judgments were particularly apt for the application of the infringement proceedings under Art. 46(4) ECHR, due to their delayed compliance. See Larsen, *NJHR* 2013, pp. 496-512.

1329 See on this difference Chapter 3 of this book.

1330 Mowbray, *HRLR* 2010, p. 474.

1331 See generally Philip Leach et al., *Responding to Systemic Human Rights Violations: An Analysis of 'Pilot Judgments' of the European Court of Human Rights and their Impact at National Level*, Cambridge: Intersentia, 2010.

1332 See Federica Favuzza, "Torreggiani and Prison Overcrowding in Italy", *HRLR* 17, 2017, pp. 153–173.

1333 Leach et al, *Responding to Systemic Human Rights Violations,* 2010, p. 109.

1334 See Fyrnys, *GLJ* 2011, p. 1259.

putting more pressure on the concerned state in order to comply. In addition, the system of supervising compliance with judgments is also relevant in this respect. The CoM applies different supervision procedures depending on the seriousness of the case. Judgments containing legislative measures are always supervised under the 'enhanced procedure', where non-compliance is debated in the CoM meetings and the concerned state representative has to defend its position before the other forty-five representatives. This implies a sort of diplomatic pressure upon the state by its counterparts and can have positive effects on compliance.[1335] However, this increased pressure in the form of reputational costs applies only with respect to states that give weight to their international reputation, as can be observed in the aforementioned case of Italy, or in the process of compliance with the legislative measure included in *Rumpf vs. Germany* (2010), which was not only implemented swiftly but even welcomed by the German authorities.[1336]

With other states such as Russia, where reputational considerations do not appear to affect its action, compliance with such measures is less likely. For example, in 2019, the ECtHR highlighted that many years after the pilot judgment in *Ananyev vs. Russia* (2009), where the ECtHR ordered the introduction of a remedy for the issue of inhuman conditions of detention, no such remedies had been set up.[1337] This can also be observed in the case of Turkey and its non-compliance with the Kavala judgment even after the launch of infringement proceedings against the State and the concomitant international pressure triggered by these proceedings. Thus, the positive effects of exceptional measures in terms of reputational costs appear to affect only certain states, but not all of them.

In the case of the IACtHR, the general rate of compliance with judgments is rather low. Out of the 320 judgments on reparations issued by the IACtHR until 2022, only forty-four have been closed at the time of writ-

1335 See Lucas Sánchez de Miquel, "Supervisión de la Ejecución de Sentencias: Un Análisis Comparado de los Sistemas Europeo e Interamericano de Derechos Humanos", *Anuario de Derecho Constitucional Latinoamericano* 24, 2018, pp. 285, 297.

1336 See Andreas von Staden, *Strategies of Compliance with the European Court of Human Rights*, University of Pennsylvania Press, 2018, at pp. 175-178.

1337 See ECtHR, *Tomov vs. Russia* (2019), para. 181. The Court therefore included in this judgment another legislative measure requesting domestic remedies for the protection of detainees. See in this respect Chapter 4 of this book.

ing.[1338] One reason for this is that the IACtHR orders a wide and complex array of measures in most of its judgments. It is therefore more difficult to fully implement these judgments than for example those of the ECtHR, as most of them only require the payment of monetary compensation, which can be complied with more easily.[1339] Indeed, in the inter-American system, there are also measures that are implemented more quickly than others, without necessarily meaning that the latter ones are rejected by states.[1340] It is therefore rather common to find a situation of 'partial compliance' with the judgments of this court.[1341]

Several authors have focused on the issue, conducting empirical studies regarding compliance with the IACtHR's specific remedial measures. When analysing these studies, it becomes evident that legislative reforms are among the most difficult remedies to comply with and take the longest time to be implemented.[1342] In this regard, through a nuanced statistical analysis, Hawkins and Jacoby arrive at the conclusion that "[c]ompliance rates are lowest with court orders to amend, repeal or adopt domestic laws or judgments (7%)".[1343] Using a similar set of cases, Huneeus finds that "in over eighty cases in which it has ordered structural remedies (...) the Inter-American Court has deemed that states have fully complied in five

1338 http://www.corteidh.or.cr/cf/jurisprudencia2/casos_en_etapa_de_supervision_archivados_cumplimiento.cfm?lang=es. See von Bogdandy and Urueña, *AJIL* 2020, p. 425 with further references concerning this issue.

1339 See Neuman, *EJIL* 2008, p. 104.

1340 See Cecilia Bailliet, "Measuring Compliance with the Inter-American Court of Human Rights: The Ongoing Challenge of Judicial Independence in Latin America", *NJHR* 31, 2013, pp. 477-495.

1341 See Hawkins and Jacoby, "Partial Compliance. A Comparison of the European and the Inter-American Court of Human Rights", *Journal of International Law and International Relations* 6(1), 2010.

1342 Hillebrecht, 2014, pp. 49-50 ("For example, states are much more likely to comply with obligations around financial obligations than they are to comply with mandates requiring changes in legislation"); Damián González Salzberg, "Do States comply with the compulsory judgments of the Inter-American Court of Human Rights?", *Revista do Instituto Brasileiro de Direitos Humanos* 13, 2013, p. 108 ("Conversely, the measures ordering criminal prosecution and the amendment of domestic legislation show a much lower level of compliance"); Cavallaro and Brewer, *AJIL* 2008, p. 785 ("However, when it comes to more far-reaching measures (...) (such as (...) changing laws and practices), compliance is considerably less likely"); Huneeus, *YJIL* 2015, p. 37 ("On the other hand, the Court can order structural remedies. However, this strategy risks a lower compliance rate").

1343 Hawkins and Jacoby, *Journal of International Law and International Relations* 2010, at p. 57.

cases".[1344] Also Basch *et al.*, in their quantitative analysis of compliance, find that "remedies with the least degree of compliance are those requiring (...) legal reforms (14%)".[1345]

This also shows that when legislative measures are rather frequent, as in the case of the IACtHR, the rate of compliance with them is lower, as the increased visibility factor and the added pressure caused by the exceptional nature of such measures are not present. Reputational factors are also less likely to come into play for a concrete state when most other states of the region are in a similar situation. Moreover, supervision of compliance is carried out by the IACtHR itself, without the involvement of the OAS' political bodies. It is therefore also difficult to exercise the sort of diplomatic pressure mentioned before. Thus, among the many remedial measures included in the IACtHR's judgments, states probably tend to reach first for the 'low hanging fruit' in terms of compliance, such as the compensation measures or even the symbolic satisfaction measures.[1346]

Studies on compliance with judgments of the ACtHPR are much scarcer than in the case of the two other regional human rights courts.[1347] This is mainly due to the difficulty of obtaining up-to-date data on the implementation of the ACtHPR's judgments.[1348] In the few studies of this sort, the general state of compliance has been found to be rather poor.[1349] With

---

1344 Huneeus, *YJIL* 2015, at p. 36.

1345 Fernando Basch *et al.*, "The Effectiveness of the Inter-American System of Human Rights Protection: A Quantitative Approach to its Functioning and Compliance with its Decisions", *Sur: International Journal on Human Rights* 7, 2010, p. 18.

1346 See Hillebrecht 2014, pp. 61-65.

1347 See however the recent volume Aderomola Adeola (ed.), *Compliance with International Human Rights Law in Africa: Essays in Honour of Frans Viljoen*, Oxford: OUP, 2022.

1348 See Japhet Biegon, "Compliance Studies and the African Human Rights System", in Aderomola Adeola (ed.), 2022, p. 23 ("As a general trend across the [African] continent, recorded or official information and data on what governments are doing or have done to implement decisions of regional human rights bodies are unavailable or inaccessible"). See also Faix and Jamali, *NQHR* 2022, p. 64 ("in the vast majority of cases, it is not possible to determine the extent to which the respondent States have executed the judgments of the Court"). Similarly, Ben Kioko, "Perspective from the African Court on Human and Peoples' Rights", *JHRP* 12, 2020, pp. 163–170, at p. 168, argues that "there are challenges with providing a precise figure given the complexities involved in measuring implementation rates".

1349 See for example Victor Oluwasina Ayeni, "Implementation of the Decisions and Judgments of African Regional Human Rights Tribunals: Reflections on the Barriers to State Compliance and the Lessons Learnt", *African Journal of International and Comparative Law* 30(4), 2022, pp. 560-581.

respect to the legislative measures ordered by the ACtHPR, Kioko reported that almost none of them had been implemented by 2020.[1350] Other authors have also argued with respect to this Court that "the more politically contentious, structural and far-reaching the required measures are, the more difficult enforcement is likely to be".[1351]

In sum, it can be observed that legislative measures, when being relatively common, take more time in their implementation and are generally more difficult to comply with. On the other hand, when these measures are exceptional, as in the case of the ECtHR, they might be able to send a message of seriousness and urgency that can make compliance with them easier and swifter. However, this does not mean that all legislative measures included in ECtHR judgments are implemented without problems. Actually, these judgements are still complied with at a lower rate than most measures of economic compensation. There are several explanations for such lower rates of compliance in the case of legislative remedies.

2. The Reasons for the Low Rates of Compliance with Legislative Remedies

The first of these reasons concerns the procedure for reforming domestic laws, which is clearly more complex than the one leading to the implementation of other measures that can be solely carried out by the executive.[1352] The most common example of solely executive-driven compliance is the payment of compensation, but this is also the case with measures of rehabilitation, symbolic measures or even certain guarantees of non-repetition, such as the provision of human rights training to public officials. In the case of legislative measures, execution is likely to take more time due to the involvement of several domestic bodies.[1353] In this respect, implementation usually needs a legislative proposal by the executive, followed by a parliamentary debate (sometimes in committees and plenary sessions in different

1350 Ben Kioko, *JHRP* 2020, especially at pp. 164-168.

1351 Tarisai Mutangi, in Adeloa (ed.), 2022, p. 192.

1352 See in this respect Murray Hunt, "Enhancing Parliaments' Role in the Protection and Realisation of Human Rights", in Murray Hunt, Hayley Hooper and Paul Yowell (eds.), *Parliaments and Human Rights: Redressing the Democratic Deficit*, London: Bloomsbury, 2015, p. 470 ("Governments are not always the best champions of national parliaments, which can sometimes obstruct or slow down the implementation of a government's will").

1353 Madsen et al., *IJLC* 2018, p. 209.

chambers) and the formal adoption by the legislature,[1354] and possibly an *ex-ante* review by the domestic judiciary.[1355] This also implies more 'veto players' participating in this process, which makes implementation more difficult.[1356] In addition, wider majorities are usually necessary for its implementation, thus depending not only on the will of the government but often on an agreement with opposition parties.[1357]

Huneeus points out these differences between the executive and the legislatures in order to foresee that the latter "will be slower and less likely to implement Court orders".[1358] Stiansen, in his empirical study on legislative compliance with ECtHR judgments, finds that compliance is especially delayed in bicameral systems and states with "political divisions among veto players".[1359] Moreover, the involvement of the legislature is particularly problematic when the political will to implement a judgment is missing. In this respect, some authors have pointed to the extent to which external actors influence the legislature. For example, with respect to legislative measures concerning indigenous territory, an explanation for the low compliance rates points to the "influence of economic power within the Legislature".[1360]

It has therefore been argued that the inclusion of such remedies can be counter-productive for implementation when these measures are "perceived as overly intrusive" or unfeasible to execute.[1361] This can be seen in the aforementioned example on prisoner voting rights, where the refusal of the British Parliament to adopt the requested law was due to a disagreement "with the principle of an international court's decision 'overturning'

1354 See Stiansen, *IJHR* 2019, p. 1226.

1355 Especially domestic constitutional courts play an important role when it comes to legislative repeals, and they are not always compliance partners but can also delay or even prevent implementation. See generally Kunz, *EJIL* 2019.

1356 See Stiansen, *IJHR* 2019, p. 1227, arguing that "veto-player problems are less likely to delay implementation (...) [when] compliance only requires executive action".

1357 Huneeus, *YJIL* 2015, at p. 21, argues that human rights courts "often find themselves in the position of ordering something that their main interlocutor, the executive, cannot single-handedly accomplish", whereby "more intermediary actors mean more potential veto points".

1358 Huneeus, "Courts Resisting Courts: Lessons from the Inter-American Court's Struggle to Enforce Human Rights", *Cornell International Law Journal* 44(3), 2011, p. 517. Similarly, Anagnostou and Mungiu-Pippidi, *EJIL* 2014, p. 213.

1359 Stiansen, *IJHR* 2019, p. 1241.

1360 Navarro, *JIDS* 2021, at p. 235.

1361 See Keller and Marti, *EJIL* 2016, p. 840.

a domestic, democratically arrived at position".[1362] On the other hand, the fact that these exceptional remedial orders by the ECtHR can increase compliance can also be related to cases in which non-compliance is due to a lack of domestic capacity. As argued by Anagnostou and Mungiu-Pippidi, some states do not possess the necessary knowledge and expertise to "define the implications of [ECtHR] judgments and to formulate the most effective measures to remedy the respective violations".[1363] Thus, clear remedial orders provide states with a specific objective that needs to be achieved, and against which implementation will be measured.

In sum, the difficulty in complying with orders to reform legislation seems to relate not so much to criticism (although this aspect is not completely absent), but to the lack of appropriate internal coordination mechanisms to ensure consistent compliance.[1364] Although domestic parliaments have adopted an increasingly important role in the implementation of human rights judgments, this has been mainly done through their power to constrain the executive.[1365] There are arguably not enough established coordination procedures and instruments in place yet for a swift legislative response to judgments of human rights courts.

3. Impact beyond Compliance

Despite the low compliance rates examined before, with legislative remedies it is necessary to look further beyond this issue, also examining the impact that such measures have on the ground. In fact, while the increased possibility of backlash and the low rates of compliance are rather negative consequences of these measures, they can also have a positive impact.[1366] It has been argued in this regard that the effectiveness of human rights courts depends more on the impact of their judgments than on compliance with

1362 De Londras and Dzehtsiarou, *ICLQ* 2017, p. 474.

1363 Anagnostou and Mungiu-Pippidi, *EJIL* 2014, p. 223.

1364 Sarah Lambrecht, "Assessing the Existence of Criticism of the European Court of Human Rights", in Popelier et al. (eds.), 2016, p. 531. See on such mechanisms Dia Anagnostou and Alina Mungiu-Pippidi, *EJIL* 2014.

1365 See generally Donald in Saul et al. (eds.), 2017, examining the "parliamentary capacity to (...) monitor executive action or inaction in respect of human rights judgments".

1366 In this regard, Cavallaro and Brewer "presume that impact matters, and should matter, to regional rights bodies" (Cavallaro and Brewer, *AJIL* 2008, p. 777).

them.[1367] According to international relations scholars, such effectiveness is to a great extent linked to these courts' ability to deter human rights violations.[1368] Legislative remedies are arguably a key aspect in order to achieve this deterrence. Whether states comply with them or not is consequently of lesser importance, as these reparations are able to trigger structural changes and have a deterrent effect in and of themselves.

In recent times, a number of authors have highlighted the need to look beyond compliance in order to assess the performance and effectiveness of human rights courts.[1369] Especially with respect to the IACtHR, some authors consider that solely focusing on compliance with human rights judgments is not the best approach, as it overlooks an important dimension of such decisions.[1370] This is particularly relevant if one sees the mandate of the IACtHR as addressing systemic problems and delivering "transformative jurisprudence".[1371] Similarly, Ayeni argues with respect to the ACtHPR

1367 See for example Kal Raustiala and Anne-Marie Slaughter, "International Law, International Relations and Compliance", in Walter Carlsnaes, Thomas Risse and Beth A. Simmons, *Handbook of International Relations*, SAGE Publications, 2009, pp. 538-558, at p. 539 ("The connection between compliance and effectiveness is also neither necessary nor sufficient").

1368 See Jillienne Haglund, "Domestic Politics and the Effectiveness of Regional Human Rights Courts", *International Interactions* 46(4), 2020, pp. 551-578. See also Par Engstrom, "Introduction: Rethinking the Impact of the Inter-American Human Rights System", in Engstrom (ed.), 2019, p. 4, arguing that "[e]ffectiveness, rather than a limited focus on rule compliance, generally refers to the degree to which the international human rights institutions work to improve human rights conditions and decrease the likelihood of the repetition of abuses".

1369 See Lisa L. Martin, "Against Compliance", in Jeffrey Dunoff and Mark Pollack (eds.), *Interdisciplinary Perspectives on International Law and International Relations*, Cambridge: CUP, 2013, pp. 591-612; César Rodríguez- Garavito, "Beyond Enforcement: Assessing and Enhancing Judicial Impact", in Malcolm Langford, César Rodríguez- Garavito and Julieta Rossi (eds.), *Social Rights Judgments and the Politics of Compliance: Making It Stick*, Cambridge: CUP, 2017, pp. 79–108; Rainer Grote, Davide Paris and Mariela Morales, "Conclusion: moving beyond compliance without neglecting compliance in international human rights law", in Grote, Paris and Morales (eds.), *Research Handbook on Compliance in International Human Rights Law*, Edward Elgar 2021, pp. 510-522.

1370 See generally Par Engstrom (ed.), *The Inter-American System: Impact Beyond Compliance*, Cham: Palgrave Macmillan, 2019. See also von Bogdandy and Urueña, *AJIL* 2020, pp. 425 et seq.

1371 See Soley in von Bogdandy et al. (eds.), 2017.

that a "compliance optic (...) is too narrow to evaluate the contributions of [the African Court's] decisions to domestic human rights change".[1372]

Impact can take many different forms, whereby it generally refers to the effects of a particular judgment beyond the specific applicants. Judgments of human rights courts can have an impact on issues such as democratic change,[1373] the empowerment of specific domestic institutions,[1374] or the mobilisation of various actors.[1375] For example, at a judicial level impact can be observed when domestic courts adopt in their decisions the interpretations provided by human rights courts.[1376] In this context, one of the most visible forms of impact occurs when international judgments are able to trigger structural reforms domestically. Such an impact is caused not only by legislative remedies but also by judicial interpretations or recommendations more generally, when these result in legislative action by states. This latter form of indirect impact is typically observed in judgments of the ECtHR.[1377] On the other hand, the impact upon the legislation of states is of a more direct nature in the case of IACtHR and ACtHPR judgments, where the "nature and scope of remedies" is considered of great importance for the assessment of such impact.[1378] This direct impact of legislative measures is arguably linked to compliance with them, but there are also further forms of impact that can be generated by such measures.

1372 Victor Ayeni, "Beyond Compliance: Do Decisions of Regional Human Rights Tribunals in Africa Make a Difference?", in Aderomola Adeola (ed.), *Compliance with International Human Rights Law in Africa: Essays in Honour of Frans Viljoen*, Oxford: OUP, 2022, at p. 37.

1373 See Iulia Motoc and Ineta Ziemele (eds.), *The Impact of the ECHR on Democratic Change in Central and Eastern Europe: Judicial Perspectives*, Cambridge: CUP, 2016.

1374 See for example Oscar Parra-Vera, "Institutional Empowerment and Progressive Policy Reforms: The Impact of the Inter-American Human Rights System on Intra-State Conflicts", in Engstrom (ed.), 2019, pp. 143-166. Concerning the empowerment of specific institutions, such as NHRIs, see Tom Pegram and Nataly Herrera Rodriguez, "Bridging the Gap: National Human Rights Institutions and the Inter-American Human Rights System", in Engstrom (ed.), 2019, pp. 167-198.

1375 See generally Beth Simmons, *Mobilizing for Human Rights: International Law in Domestic Politics*, Cambridge: CUP, 2009.

1376 This is best seen in the 'conventionality control' exercised by domestic judges. See generally Pablo González-Domínguez, *The Doctrine of Conventionality Control*, Cambridge: Intesentia, 2018.

1377 See generally Helen Keller and Alec Stone Sweet (eds.), 2008.

1378 Frans Viljoen, "Impact in the African and Inter-American Human Rights Systems: A Perspective on the Possibilities and Challenges of Cross-Regional Comparison", in Engstrom (ed.), 2019, p. 310.

For example, the legislative measures issued by human rights courts also have the potential of triggering reforms in further states subject to the jurisdiction of these courts, in order to prevent adverse judgments in the future.[1379] This can be observed, for example, with the amnesty laws in Latin America. The case in which the IACtHR declared the Peruvian amnesty law to be contrary to the Convention gave legal grounds for the Supreme Court of Argentina to invalidate this state's amnesty law, thereby allowing for the prosecution of various perpetrators of human rights violations during Argentina's military dictatorship. While expressly citing the case of *Barrios Altos vs. Peru* (2001), the Argentinean Court argued that "[t]he Argentine State has assumed a series of duties under international law and, in particular, under the Inter-American legal order, with constitutional hierarchy, which have been consolidated and specified in terms of their scope and content in an evolution that clearly limits the powers of domestic law to condone or omit the prosecution of acts that involve crimes against humanity".[1380]

Another of these layers of impact beyond compliance concerns its social dimension, in the form of changing public perceptions or framing public debates around a concrete issue. For example, the first case on the merits decided by the ACtHPR, *Tanganyika Law Society and Legal and Human Rights Centre vs. Tanzania* (2013), included an order to reform the State's Constitution to allow for independent electoral candidates.[1381] This triggered the inclusion of such a provision in the Draft Constitution of Tanzania only a year later, in 2014. However, it was reported that the referendum for the approval of this Draft Constitution could not be held due to protests from opposition political parties, and thus the measure has remained in a state of non-compliance ever since.[1382] Despite this lack of compliance, the ACtHPR's judgment and its remedial orders are considered

1379 See for example Open Society Justice Initiative, *Strategic Litigation: Impacts and Insights*, 2018, p. 57, mentioning that the legislative measures included in the judgment of the IACtHR *Claude Reyes vs. Chile* (2006) triggered the adoption of right-to-information laws in five further states of the region during the following years. See also, more generally, Laurence Helfer and Erik Voeten, "International Courts as Agents of Legal Change: Evidence from LGBT Rights in Europe", *International Organization* 68(1), 2014, pp. 77 - 110.

1380 Supreme Court of Justice of Argentina, *Case of Simón, Julio Hector et al.* (Case No. 17.778), 14 June 2005 (non-official translation).

1381 ACtHPR, *Tanganyika Law Society and Legal and Human Rights Centre vs. Tanzania* (2013), operative para. 3.

1382 See Ayeni, in Adeola (ed.), 2022, p. 57.

to have had a notable impact in the region, as they triggered not only a domestic debate on this issue but also "influenced the perception of state actors across Africa on the issue of independent candidacy".[1383] In this regard, Gathii and Mwangi argue that the ACtHPR is increasingly used as a forum against incumbent governments by civil society organisations and opposition parties, and that this case shows "how filing before international courts is often a strategic decision by individuals and non-state actors as their way of organizing discontent".[1384]

Thereby, in order to take advantage of the potential impact of human rights judgments, civil society organisations have increasingly engaged in so-called 'strategic litigation' before human rights courts. One objective of such strategic litigation is precisely the inclusion of legislative measures in a judgment, especially in the African and Inter-American systems.[1385] Strategic human rights litigation is generally defined as aiming to achieve structural changes through individual applications.[1386] There are many different levels of change that litigation can lead to. For example, it can serve as a catalyst for a public discussion on a particular issue, it can contribute to the development of institutions needed to prevent the reoccurrence of violations, or it can help to shape the narrative of a specific conflict. Among them, a very important level is legal change, which has, in turn, two sides. On the one hand strategic litigation can pursue the development of (international) human rights law, as can be observed in the recent applications

---

1383 Ayeni, in Adeola (ed.), 2022, p. 70.

1384 See Gathii and Mwangi, in Gathii (ed.), 2020, pp. 248-252.

1385 This is also related to the small number of cases that reach these courts. See Cavallaro and Brewer, *AJIL* 2008, p. 770, arguing with respect to the IACtHR that "[w]ithout this broad strategic focus, supranational litigation (which affords access to only a tiny fraction of victims) will function as a lottery in which the handful of petitioners whose cases reach a court will obtain benefits not available to the vast majority of similarly situated victims".

1386 A similar concept is that of public interest litigation, which consists in using the law to advance issues of public concern. In both cases, the applicant's representatives pursue goals that go beyond the confines of the specific case and parties to it. Although it often also aims at triggering legislative reforms, public interest litigation is not limited to human rights cases with concrete victims. It is pursued in different fora and contexts, such as in environmental litigation, climate litigation or administrative litigation. Nevertheless, a human rights perspective is often used to bring about broader changes, despite the lack of concrete victims in some instances. See for example Jacqueline Peel and Hari M. Osofsky, *Climate Change Litigation: Regulatory Pathways to Cleaner Energy*, Cambridge: CUP, 2015; Guillaume Futhazar, Sandrine Maljean-Dubois and Jona Razzaque (eds.), *Biodiversity Litigation*, Oxford: OUP, 2022.

concerning climate change before the ECtHR, seeking an interpretation of the Convention that guarantees certain environmental rights at the international level.[1387] On the other hand, strategic human rights litigation can aim at the development or reform of domestic laws, thereby often seeking specific remedies in this regard.

One of the key aspects of strategic human rights litigation is precisely the request for remedies. This type of litigation is mostly carried out by specialised NGOs representing victims before human rights courts.[1388] Individual applicants are mostly interested in the remedial measures that affect them directly, while NGOs usually have a broader focus and aim to tackle issues affecting a larger number of people through representative cases.[1389] Moreover, litigation before human rights courts is a lengthy endeavour with considerable costs, which can prevent individuals in a vulnerable situation from pursuing such proceedings. NGOs are better equipped at the level of both economic resources and personal expertise. Their participation thus allows vulnerable groups such as indigenous peoples, migrants, prisoners or children to have a voice before human rights courts.[1390] It is not surprising in this regard that an important number of legislative measures have been related to the protection of such groups, as these measures are the product of strategic litigation pursued by NGOs on their behalf. In this context, the organisations intervening strategically before human rights courts often request remedies that are not directly connected to redressing the victims they represent but have a broader impact.

The role of NGOs is particularly important in the context of the Inter-American and African human rights systems. In fact, NGOs have played a key role in the Inter-American human rights system since its early days.

1387 See for example ECtHR, *KlimaSeniorinnen vs. Switzerland* (2024). See also, more generally, Cesar Rodriguez Garavito (ed.), *Litigating the Climate Emergency*, Cambridge: CUP, 2022.

1388 Other actors that are relevant in this context are the legal clinics of universities. See Sandra Carvalho and Eduardo Baker, "Experiencias de Litigio Estratégico en el Sistema Interamericano de Protección de los Derechos Humanos", *Sur: Revista Internacional de Derechos Humanos* 20, pp. 469-479.

1389 See Kate Nash, "Human Rights, Global Justice, and the Limits of Law", in Bardo Fassbender and Knut Traisbach (eds.), *The Limits of Human Rights*, Oxford, OUP, 2019, pp. 69-80, at p. 76 ("Human rights NGOs that support 'test cases' are engaged in strategic litigation intended to establish a new interpretation of legislation or to prompt new law that will steer the polity in a different direction").

1390 See for example Jérémie Gilbert, "Indigenous Peoples and Litigation: Strategies for Legal Empowerment", *JHRP* 12, 2020, pp. 301–320.

Thereby, many important human rights issues in the region "have been advanced, partially and in some instances even primarily through strategic litigation".[1391] For example, strategic litigation has been often carried out in order to secure indigenous rights in domestic legislation.[1392] The case of *Sarayaku vs. Ecuador* (2012) for instance concerned the issue of prior and informed consent by indigenous communities for activities affecting their territory. The goal of this litigation strategy was to secure prior and informed consent under the Ecuadorian legal order, but also to advance the understanding of this indigenous right more broadly.[1393]

In this case, the Sarayaku community had the support of numerous civil society organisations, both in the field of human rights and environmental law.[1394] The IACtHR adopted an interpretation of prior and informed consent in line with the indigenous community's demands, ordering the inclusion of this concept in domestic legislation.[1395] Ecuador had already complied with the remedial measures of the IACtHR concerning compensation and satisfaction in 2013, but failed to implement the legislative changes. The Sarayaku community therefore filed a claim before the Ecuadorian Constitutional Court in 2020, requesting the execution of the IACtHR's orders.[1396] This example shows that strategic litigation often extends beyond the judgment of a human rights court, in order to secure its implementation. This is also an example of impact beyond compliance, as despite the failure of the State to comply with the legislative measures ordered by the IACtHR, the Sarayaku judgment has become "by far the most visible and influential decision on Indigenous rights in the continent, and it's widely cited as a key precedent in international law".[1397]

1391 Ximena Soley, "The Crucial Role of NGOs in the Inter-American System", *AJIL Unbound* 113, 2019, pp. 355-359, at p. 357.

1392 See in this regard Gilbert, *JHRP* 2020, p. 313.

1393 The objective in this respect was to develop a substantive instead of procedural understanding of prior and informed consent, meaning that indigenous communities not only need to be consulted, but its consent needs to be expressly given in the case of projects that directly affect them. See César Rodríguez-Garavito and Carlos Andrés Baquero-Díaz, "Reframing Indigenous Rights: The Right to Consultation and the Rights of Nature and Future Generations in the Sarayaku Legal Mobilization", in Gráinne de Búrca (ed.), *Legal Mobilization for Human Rights*, Oxford: OUP, 2022.

1394 Garavito and Baquero-Díaz, in de Búrca (ed.), 2022, pp. 80-81.

1395 IACtHR, *Kichwa de Sarayaku vs. Ecuador* (2012), operative para. 4.

1396 See in this respect Garavito and Baquero-Díaz, in de Búrca (ed.), 2022.

1397 Garavito and Baquero-Díaz, in de Búrca (ed.), 2022, p. 85.

In the case of the ACtHPR, strategic litigation is also very closely related to legislative remedies. NGOs have also here been considered "essential in developing the African human rights system".[1398] This has been explored by Gathii and Mwangi, finding that especially due to this Court's permissive approach to jurisdiction, the ACtHPR constitutes an "opportunity structure" when domestic institutional spaces are closed off.[1399] As previously explained, the ACtHPR accepts complaints that are brought directly against a law, without the necessity of identifying concrete victims.[1400] NGOs have taken advantage of this and have challenged several laws before this Court.

For example, in the case of *APDH vs. Côte d'Ivoire* (2016), this NGO challenged the compatibility of the Ivorian Law providing for the composition, organisation, duties and functioning of the Independent Electoral Commission. As the organisation had not been affected by the law, individual reparations were not ordered by the ACtHPR, limiting its remedial measures to the amendment of the law in question.[1401] The aim of the NGOs was therefore strategic in the sense that it did not seek any individual benefit from litigation, but focused exclusively on legislative reforms for the benefit of society in general. In turn, this case "provided APDH with a platform to publicize the repressiveness of the Ivorian government", giving this issue increased visibility in media and civil society.[1402] Moreover, NGOs are not the only actors pursuing strategic litigation before the ACtHPR, as individuals seeking to advance specific political objectives play also an important role in this context. Makunya highlighted in this regard the importance of reparations claims made before this Court by "political activists and public interest lawyers challenging the conformity and compatibility of legislative and constitutional norms".[1403]

1398 Daly and Wiebusch, *IJLC* 2018, p. 302.

1399 Gathii and Mwangi, in Gathii (ed.), 2020.

1400 See Chapter 1 of this book. See also in this respect Gathii and Mwangi, in Gathii (ed.), 2020, pp. 223-224 ("Our basic argument is that the African Court's very permissive approach to jurisdiction, admissibility, legal standing, and rules on who bears the costs of litigation has created a body of law that provides more opportunity for filing of other similar cases").

1401 ACtHPR, *APDH vs. Côte d'Ivoire* (2016), operative para. 7.

1402 Gathii and Mwangi, in Gathii (ed.), 2020, p. 246.

1403 Trésor Muhindo Makunya, "Decisions of the African Court on Human and Peoples' Rights during 2020: Trends and Lessons", *AHRLJ* 21(2), 2021, pp. 1230-1264, at p. 1245.

Finally, NGOs have also been engaged in litigation before the ECtHR for a long time.[1404] Although the number of cases in which they participate is rather low if compared to the total number of cases before this Court, it has been argued that its "quality is high, meaning that most of these groups were very strategic about choosing to participate in cases which they believed would lead to significant changes in European law".[1405] Thus, strategic litigation is also relevant before the ECtHR, although it probably takes a different form with respect to remedies. As legislative measures are usually ordered by the ECtHR only after an important number of complaints related to a specific law or the absence of it, the strategy of NGOs is more likely related to the search for a leading case. Once the ECtHR considers that a domestic law is contrary to the Convention or that adequate domestic remedies are not in place, this can trigger numerous additional complaints by individuals who find themselves in a similar situation. If the concerned state fails to solve the structural problem and applications continue arriving, the ECtHR will likely request a legislative reform. Thus, as concrete changes are mostly achieved through repetitive cases, strategic litigation before the ECtHR usually seeks to establish a leading case that can trigger a flood of applications concerning the same issue, which can eventually lead to reforms.

In sum, this section has shown that compliance with legislative remedies is generally rather low, perhaps with the exception of those issued by the ECtHR. These low rates are due to several reasons, whereby the rather complicated process for reforming laws and the absence of domestic coordination mechanisms for legislative compliance play a prominent role. However, the section has also explained that it is necessary to look beyond compliance in order to see the impact of these remedies. This shows a different picture, with a potentially high impact at multiple levels and with several examples of actual impact, which has also led to a practice of NGOs pursuing strategic litigation before human rights courts in order to achieve *inter alia* legislative changes. Thus, despite them being able to cause backlash and diminish compliance, not every consequence of legislative remedies is negative. In this regard, before concluding this chapter, it is

1404 Some of the most active NGOs representing victims before the ECtHR and pursuing strategic litigation are the AIRE, ECCHR and the Human Rights Advocacy Centre (EHRAC). See generally Loveday Hodson, *NGOs and the Struggle for Human Rights in Europe*, Oregon: Hart Publishing, 2011.

1405 See Rachel A. Cichowski, "Civil Society and the European Court of Human Rights", in Christoffersen and Madsen (eds.), *The European Court of Human Rights*, Oxford: OUP, 2011, pp. 77-97, at pp. 95-96.

useful to have a brief look at the reaction of the three human rights courts to these negative consequences.

III. The Reaction of Human Rights Courts

The previous sections have shown, on the one hand, that there is a close relation between some instances of backlash suffered by regional human rights courts and their practice of ordering states to reform domestic laws. This is seen most clearly in examples such as the conflict between the UK and the ECtHR, the restriction of access to the ACtHPR, or the 'Five Presidents Declaration' concerning the IACtHR. On the other hand, it was shown that legislative remedies generally take more time and are more difficult to comply with than other remedial measures. Another question concerns the reaction of human rights courts to instances of backlash and non-compliance. In particular, it becomes relevant to explore whether these three courts have limited the inclusion of legislative measures in their judgments in order to prevent further potential conflicts with states, or if to the contrary they have continued as normal or even increased the use of such measures, perhaps as a display of authority.[1406] Another relevant aspect in this regard is whether they have modified the compliance requirements concerning these measures, in order not only to facilitate its implementation but also to avoid conflict with states.

Authors have observed several reactions of human rights courts to backlash, focusing particularly on those of the ECtHR. It has been argued that "[f]ollowing Brighton, the Court is noted to have started to act as if it received signals sent by state parties".[1407] In this regard, Stiansen and Voeten found an increased judicial restraint by this Court in recent years, especially in its rulings against consolidated democracies.[1408] Similarly, Çalı shows that the ECtHR increasingly applies a 'variable geometry', whereby more deference is afforded to 'good faith interpreters' and Article 18 judgments are used for "signalling the bad faith interpreters".[1409] Others have

1406 In this respect, Abebe for example mentioned with respect to the instances of backlash against the ACtHPR that "[s]imilar possibilities of backlash and experiences may in the future prod the African Court to be more prudent in sensitive cases" (Abebe, *I•CON* 2019, p. 111).

1407 Demir-Gürsel in Aust and Demir-Gürsel (eds.), pp. 248-249.

1408 Stiansen and Voeten, *ISQ* 2020, pp. 770–784.

1409 Çalı, *Wisconsin International Law Journal* 2018.

also focused on the more frequent use of subsidiarity and the margin of appreciation in the ECtHR judgments.[1410] It has been even argued that the Strasbourg Court is "walking back" on human rights.[1411] With respect to the IACtHR, it has been stated that a reaction to Venezuela's withdrawal was the adoption of "a more restrictive take on the exhaustion of local remedies and [the rejection of] cases on these grounds".[1412] However, there is not yet much research on the question of whether backlash has caused an increased remedial self-restraint by human rights courts.

1. Changes in the Use of Legislative Remedies

When examining the three courts' remedial reactions to the aforementioned instances of backlash, three different situations can be observed. With respect to the ECtHR, a decrease in the application of the pilot judgment procedure and more generally in the inclusion of operative remedies in its judgments is notable. Legislative measures were first introduced in judgments of the ECtHR in 2004, and this practice evolved cautiously through very few judgments until it was consolidated in 2009. Between 2009 and 2015, legislative measures were included in twenty-four judgments. After that, a shift can be observed, with only five judgments containing legislative measures in the period 2016-2022. It is thus evident that this remedial practice has decreased considerably in recent years.[1413] This is also the same period in which backlash against this Court has gained momentum. Of course, this does not mean that the remedial self-restraint is directly caused by the instances of backlash, but it points in that direction. This finding is moreover consistent with the other signs of self-restraint

1410 However, in a recent empirical study, Molbæk-Steensig concludes that contrary to an often-repeated assumption about an increased use of the margin of appreciation since the 'Interlaken Process' in 2010, it was applied statistically more often during the 1980s and 1990s than recently. See Helga Molbæk-Steensig, "Subsidiarity does not win cases: A mixed methods study of the relationship between margin of appreciation language and deference at the European Court of Human Rights", *LJIL* 36, 2023, at pp. 91-96.

1411 Helfer and Voeten, *EJIL* 2020.

1412 See Soley and Steininger, *IJLC* 2018, p. 252.

1413 This was also noted by Mowbray in 2017 with respect to further remedial measures, highlighting that "there has been a dramatic decline in the annual numbers of final judgments containing operative part remedial indications" (Mowbray, *HRLR* 2017, p. 460).

displayed by the ECtHR recently in the face of backlash, as mentioned before.

A similar turn, particularly regarding legislative measures, did also take place before the IACtHR. These measures had been included in an average of 40% of the IACtHR's annual judgments until 2012, when this number dropped to an average of 14% of the annual judgments between 2013 and 2019.[1414] This could be seen as a reaction to the individual instances of backlash taking place precisely at that time, particularly those of Venezuela and the DR.[1415] Actually, this shift and increased self-restraint is a remarkable development, as the remedial practice of the IACtHR has been traditionally highlighted as one of the most progressive among international courts,[1416] and was also defined in the past as being "constantly expanding".[1417] However, the instance of collective backlash seems to have triggered the oppo-

1414 Note that in the case of the IACtHR and the ACtHPR the number of judgments with legislative measures is considered on the basis of the annual percentage of judgments including such measures, while in the case of the ECtHR it is considered in terms of the absolute number of judgments with legislative measures per year. This is mainly due to the disproportion in the number of judgments issued by these courts. In this respect, the total number of annual judgments has varied a lot before the IACtHR and the ACtHPR, while before the ECtHR it has remained relatively constant. Moreover, legislative measures are included in less than 1% of the ECtHR's annual judgments, so that examining the evolution of this practice percentage-wise does not make much sense.

1415 It is precisely as of 2013, the year after Venezuela's withdrawal, when the shift in terms of ordering legislative measures can be observed. The strong emphasis put by the IACtHR on the states' obligation to perform the 'conventionality control' is also an explanation for the decreasing use of legislative remedies. In this respect, it has been argued that "when a violation of the ACHR, which is the result of a structural issue, can be prevented by an interpretation of domestic law that is 'consistent' with the jurisprudence of the Inter-American Court, through the application of conventionality control, the Inter-American Court considers that it is not necessary to indicate legislative reform measures" (Hennebel and Tigroudja, *Commentary to the ACHR*, 2022, p. 1329). On the IACtHR's conventionality control, see Chapter 5 of this book.

1416 See generally Elisabeth Lambert Abdelgawad and Kathia Martin-Chenut (eds.), *Réparer les Violations Graves et Massives des Droits de l'Homme: La Cour Interaméricaine, Pionnière et Modèle?*, Paris: Société de Législation Comparée, 2010; see also Antkowiak, *CJTL* 2008, p. 386 ("The Inter-American Court's jurisprudence has established new paradigms in international law for the redress of individuals and groups").

1417 Douglass Cassel, "The Expanding Scope and Impact of Reparations Awarded by the Inter-American Court of Human Rights", in Koen de Feyter *et al.* (eds.), *Out of The Ashes: Reparations for Gross Violations of Human Rights*, Cambridge: Intersentia, 2005, pp. 191-223.

site reaction. In 2020, the year after the 'Five Presidents Declaration', the IACtHR included legislative measures in 42% of its judgments, situating it again at a 'pre-backlash level'. In the following years, the rate was 30% (2021) and 41% (2022), clearly higher than in the period between 2013 and 2019. Thus, although the IACtHR did not officially respond to the challenge posed by this declaration, it seems that its reaction was to expand its remedial jurisprudence as a display of authority.[1418]

Finally, in the case of the ACtHPR, the withdrawals of optional declarations granting access to the Court do not appear to have caused a change in its remedial practice. Instead, the ACtHPR has consolidated this practice during the last years and has kept including legislative measures in a similar number of judgments. In this respect, a notable increase in the yearly number of judgments on reparations can be observed. While the ACtHPR issued a total of twelve judgments on reparations between 2013 and 2017, it issued sixty-five of them between 2018 and 2022. In the earlier timeframe, legislative remedies were included in 25% of these judgments, while they can be found in 24.6% of such judgments in the latter timeframe. Thus, it can be concluded that the instances of backlash experienced by the ACtHPR did not have any apparent effects on its remedial practice, at least with respect to the issue of legislative remedies.

In sum, the instances of backlash seem to have triggered a notable decrease in the use of legislative remedies by the ECtHR, while in the case of the IACtHR, such a decrease took also place after its most recent individual instances of backlash, but the subsequent collective instance of backlash appears to have triggered a move in the opposite direction, with a notable increase in its remedial practice concerning domestic laws. Finally, the various instances of backlash suffered by the ACtHPR are not appearing to have caused any reaction in terms of its use of legislative remedies.

2. Lowering of Compliance Requirements

Another type of reaction to individual instances of backlash, as well as non-compliance with legislative measures, has taken the form of lowering compliance requirements concerning these measures, thereby changing its legislative nature. As previously explained, the IACtHR is the only human

1418 See in this respect René Urueña, "Double or Nothing? The Inter-American Court of Human Rights in an Increasingly Adverse Context", *Wisconsin International Law Journal* 35(2), 2018, pp. 398.

rights court that supervises the execution of its own judgments, while this is done by a separate political body in the cases of both the ACtHPR and the ECtHR. This reaction has therefore predominantly taken place in the latter cases, whereby it is most noticeable in the European system, due to the lack of information about compliance in the African one. The CoM usually decides what is required in order to comply with a judgment of the ECtHR, as this Court most often does not give precise indications in this respect. However, in cases where the ECtHR issues a specific order, such as a legislative remedy, the CoM has accepted deviations from that order.

This can be observed most notably in the previously examined conflict between the ECtHR and the UK on prisoners' voting rights. Even after the adoption of a pilot judgment against the UK, the State failed to advance in its implementation for several years. Although the British Government introduced different legislative proposals, these were not passed by Parliament.[1419] Eventually, the State submitted an Action Plan in 2017 arguing that in view of the Parliament's opposition to passing such legislative measures, the best approach to execute these judgments would be to adopt a number of administrative measures that would allow certain prisoners to vote.[1420] These measures were accepted by the CoM, and the cases were closed in 2018.[1421] Thus, it can be observed that in view of the fact that the conflict and the lack of compliance were mainly related to the legislative nature of the measures ordered, the CoM accepted a deviation from the Court's remedies and validated executive action instead.[1422]

This acceptance of 'reduced compliance' is nevertheless problematic for two reasons. On the one hand, *Greens and MT* is one of the judgments in which the ECtHR has more clearly defined the legislative nature of the measures to be adopted. The relevant operative paragraph states that

> *the respondent State must: (a) bring forward (...) legislative proposals intended to amend the 1983 Act and, if appropriate, the 2002 Act in a manner which is Convention-compliant; and (b) enact the required*

1419 See Ergul Celiksoy, "Execution of the Judgments of the European Court of Human Rights in Prisoners' Right to Vote Cases", *HRLR* 20, 2020, pp. 555-581, especially at pp. 569-575.

1420 Essentially those on temporary license and those on home detention curfew. See Celiksoy, *HRLR* 2020, p. 572.

1421 CoM, *Resolution CM/ResDH(2018)467*, 06 December 2018.

1422 See Celiksoy, *HRLR* 2020, p. 575, arguing that "[w]hile the ECtHR considered that legislative amendment was required, the Committee of Ministers obviously did not share that assessment".

legislation within any such period as may be determined by the Committee of Ministers.[1423]

In accepting administrative measures instead of it, the CoM is arguably diminishing the Court's authority, by signalling that it will accept a deviation from the remedial provisions of the judgments even in those exceptional cases in which the Court is highly specific. On the other hand, it is not the same to have a right secured through legislation and to have it secured through administrative measures. In the latter case, the legal protection of the right is much weaker and a government can very easily modify the protective measures.[1424] Thus, securing rights through legislation is not equivalent to doing so via administrative measures, and the CoM should have had a stronger position on this issue, although it probably looked for a way out of this longstanding conflict with the UK. In any case, this shows one type of institutional reaction to backlash, which does not affect so much the remedies issued by courts but states' compliance with them.

Interim Conclusion: System-Dependent Consequences of Legislative Remedies

To conclude, this chapter has shown that the consequences of legislative remedies are different depending on which human rights court issues them. For example, although recent instances of backlash are rather common in front of the three courts, its relation to concrete legislative measures diverges in this respect. This is most probably due to the fact that domestic audiences, in particular governments and other state bodies, do not have the same expectations as to the role of each of these regional human rights courts. The understanding of these different roles is strongly influenced by the previous practice of each court, but also by the context in which they operate.

In the case of the ECtHR, the general understanding for a long time was that its judgments would perhaps include recommendations but stop short of prescribing any mandatory actions that states should carry out in order to comply with them. Ordering a legislative reform would then probably be the most unexpected outcome of a judgment under this tra-

1423 ECtHR, *Greens and MT vs. UK* (2010), operative para. 6.

1424 See on the importance of securing rights through legislation Chapter 1 of this book.

ditional understanding. This started to change with the incorporation of the former Eastern Bloc under the jurisdiction of the ECtHR and the subsequent introduction of the pilot judgment procedure. However, Western European democracies likely expected that such remedial developments would exclusively affect the newly incorporated states, as they understood that only these states had systemic deficiencies. This is what may have caused the instance of backlash concerning the UK, as the expectations of the State were that ECtHR's role was perhaps to 'fine-tune' its domestic arrangements, but in no case to go as far as ordering a reform of its laws. Such expectation was even stronger on a topic such as its electoral norms, which is understood to be one of the fields in which the sovereign power of a state is reflected. These unfulfilled expectations can explain the backlash of the UK, but also the criticism of other states such as Switzerland or the Netherlands against this Court. However, this is arguably not the case for the majority of states under the ECtHR's jurisdiction, as can be observed by the support given to its remedial practice in the context of the 'Interlaken Process'.

The expectations of states are different in the case of the IACtHR. Driven by its '*nunca más*' mission, the understanding of this court's role since its very early years has comprised its capacity to interfere with states' sovereignty at the highest extent, *inter alia* by ordering structural reforms. It is probably for this reason that the individual instances of backlash against this court are not so much connected to its capacity to order legislative reforms *per se*, but to the specific content of these prescribed reforms. In this respect, states were probably not expecting that the IACtHR would be a 'fine-tuning' court avoiding intrusiveness. Instead, extensive remedial orders were part of the IACtHR's practice almost from the beginning, and at that time the regional context was arguably one that required such intrusive interventions, due to the lack of states' willingness and capacity to carry out the necessary reforms by themselves. However, times have changed and nowadays most Latin American states have turned into rather robust democracies highly capable of responding to human rights violations. This is probably a reason for the instance of collective backlash against this court, in which the governments of five of the strongest states in the region attempted to change this traditional understanding of the IACtHR's role and bring it closer to that of its European counterpart.

States' expectations are also at the core of the instances of backlash against the ACtHPR. Although this court included legislative remedies already in its first judgment on the merits, this practice (as well as the

ACtHPR's case law) developed rather slowly and did not gain consistency until about 2019. In this respect, States were probably not expecting a very intrusive court when they submitted their optional declarations granting individuals and NGOs direct access to the ACtHPR, which was mostly made in the early 2010s.[1425] They were especially not expecting issues such as the abstract review of legislation, a competence that has not been adopted by any other international court and that became evident only in recent years.[1426] This can be observed in some of the states' objections to the African Court's competence.[1427] Thus, by noticing that almost every case decided by the ACtHPR was submitted to it directly by individuals or NGOs, states probably found that restricting access by withdrawing the optional declarations was an effective way of curtailing the Court's expanding authority.

Besides the issue of backlash, the other main consequence of legislative remedies, which relates to (non-)compliance with such measures, is also system-dependent. One can see in this respect that the exceptional nature of such measures in the European system can have positive effects on compliance, as these measures have increased visibility and are thereby able to put additional pressure and generate reputational costs. However, it needs to be noted that this increased compliance is observed only when comparing it to the legislative measures ordered by the other two regional courts. If one compares it with other measures of the ECtHR, it becomes clear that financial compensation is more easily implemented. This is also the case before the other two human rights courts, where legislative remedies are among the measures that take the longest to be executed. This is mainly related to institutional and technical aspects of the implementation process, such as the absence of adequate mechanisms to coordinate the different bodies involved in legislative reforms or the increased amount of 'veto players' in the legislative procedure.

1425 As argued by Gathii and Mwangi, "although the African Court was designed in a manner protective of the sovereignty of African states, the manner in which litigants have used it indicates that the constraints the states designed may not always work in the ways they anticipated". Gathii and Mwangi, in Gathii (ed.), 2020, p. 253).

1426 See Chapter 1 of this book.

1427 See for example the state objection in the case of ACtHPR, *Ingabire Victoire Umuhoza vs Rwanda* (2017), para. 52 ("[The ACtHPR is not] "a legislative body which can (...) make national legislation in lieu of national legislative Assemblies").

In addition, legislative measures have also the most notable intrinsic impact in the European system, where they allow the Court to get rid of repetitive cases concerning the same law. This holds true for the other two systems as well, but there the number of repetitive cases and backlog in general is not as problematic as in the European system. In fact, although the number of pending judgments before the ECtHR has decreased in recent years (mainly due to the restriction of admissibility criteria),[1428] the "high number of repetitive applications has remained problematic".[1429] Besides this intrinsic impact on the system itself, legislative remedies can also produce effects on third states, that sometimes carry out their own legislative reforms in order to avoid adverse judgments. Other forms of impact include those on the social level, by triggering certain debates or empowering actors or social movements that push for reform. In this regard, when a court orders a legislative reform, civil society can articulate its demands around compliance with an international judgment that is binding for the state. Moreover, both the European and the inter-American systems allow for third-party interventions in the process of supervising compliance with judgments, so that civil society and NGOs can also give their views on the adequacy of the reform in question. This also implies that even a vague remedy that allows for deliberation at the domestic level can thereafter be re-evaluated at the international level in order to assess the content of the reform. As it was shown, specialised NGOs have taken advantage of this and engaged in strategic litigation before regional human rights courts aiming precisely at legislative reforms in concrete states.

Finally, there are also notable variations in the reaction of human rights courts to these consequences. In this respect, the most evident reaction has taken place in the European system. The ECtHR has not only notably reduced the inclusion of legislative remedies in the face of backlash, but the CoM has even lowered the compliance requirements regarding some of these measures previously ordered by the Court, thereby changing its legislative nature. On the other hand, the IACtHR seems to have initially diminished its use of legislative remedies shortly after several individual instances of backlash, but then increased it when several states collectively questioned this practice. Before the ACtHPR, the inclusion of legislative measures has remained rather constant despite the notable increase in the number of judgments decided by this Court in the last years. Thus, its

1428 See Dinah Shelton, "Significantly Disadvantaged? Shrinking Access to the European Court of Human Rights", *HRLR* 16(2), 2016, pp. 303–322.

1429 Glas, *HRLR* 2020, p. 125.

remedial practice does not seem to have been affected by these negative consequences.

Concluding Remarks

As has been shown throughout this book, legislative remedies are a relatively common instrument before human rights courts, especially if one leaves the usual Eurocentric perspective aside. Arguably, it is also a type of remedy that deserves more attention. In this regard, the book has made a number of relevant findings concerning this remedy, which will be summarised below. In addition, this concluding part will offer a brief normative assessment of the human rights courts' approach to this remedial practice, which consists of ordering states to reform their domestic laws. It will be argued that an increased constitutionalisation of human rights adjudication might be necessary in this context, not in the sense of admitting only a small number of applications that raise structural issues, but in that of intervening at a structural level whenever this is necessary. On the other hand, such structural interventions (*inter alia* in the form of legislative remedies) should not be too specific, as domestic legislatures must retain a margin of deliberation. In this context, the ECtHR is probably falling short on the former issues, while the IACtHR is going too far on the latter one and the ACtHPR is probably achieving the best balance in this regard.

I. Main Findings

Chapter 1 of this book provided a first overview of the concept of legislative remedies. It explored the relationship between human rights courts and domestic laws around three different stages, taking into account the primary obligations to legislate under human rights treaties, the review of legislation carried out by human rights courts and their remedial orders in this respect. It found that legislative remedies can be to some extent considered a concretisation of these primary obligations to legislate. These obligations are both customary (in particular the general obligations to legislate) and treaty-based (especially the specific obligations to legislate). In addition, the first chapter highlighted some important developments in the international human rights review of legislation, concerning in particular the competence to exercise this review *in abstracto*. A notable innovation in this context can be observed before the ACtHPR, which has consistently accepted to review the compatibility of laws without the need to identify a victim to whom the law was applied. On the contrary, both the ECtHR and the IACtHR generally review only laws that were actually applied and thereby caused an alleged human rights violation, despite some exceptions in this respect. Another potential way of reviewing laws *in abstracto* relates to the advisory competence of human rights courts, but it was shown that it is a potential that has remained largely unused. Finally, the chapter argued that legislative remedies make an important contribution to the constitutionalisation of human rights adjudication, assuming a role that is usually reserved for constitutional courts, and that human rights courts are legitimised to order such sovereignty-intrusive measures under certain circumstances. The latter is due to the increased interconnectedness between sovereignty and human rights protection and to the (at least implicit) consent of states to this practice.

The first part of this book made also a comparison between remedies in general international adjudication and human rights adjudication, in order to show that those pertaining to the latter field possess a special nature and that legislative remedies form an intrinsic part of this specialty. In this respect, although the regulation and codification of remedies are not fundamentally different in both areas of international law, in practice human rights courts have progressively departed from the approach taken by the PCIJ and by the ICJ, which was examined in Chapter 2. Notably, the increasing focus of human rights courts – especially the IACtHR and the ACtHPR – on satisfaction and guarantees of non-repetition is not mirrored in the jurisprudence of the ICJ, where measures of cessation and restitution prevail. The use of legislative measures is also part of this particularity of human rights adjudication. Although the ICJ has never ordered a legislative reform, it was argued in light of the cases in which this Court has dealt with domestic laws that if it would do so this would probably adopt a different function than guaranteeing non-repetition. Thus, it can be concluded that there is a 'remedial *lex specialis*' in human rights law and, therefore, remedies before human rights courts should not be assessed under the logic of the general law of state responsibility.

In addition to comparing remedies in these two fields of international law, it was also useful to compare in Chapter 3 the remedial landscape before each regional human rights court, and the evolution of their respective practice in this regard. The most notable differences are related to the remedial self-restraint of the ECtHR on the one hand and the remedial activism of the IACtHR on the other, whereby the ACtHPR has also tended towards the approach of its American counterpart. These differences between courts can be attributed to the remedial legal basis included in the respective instruments, as well as the historical and political context in which the three courts were created and evolved.

An observation concerning these contextual explanations is that international courts situated in the Global South, such as the IACtHR and the ACtHPR, are generally less worried about stepping outside the traditional boundaries of international adjudication and intruding on the sovereignty of states with their remedies. On the contrary, those situated in the Global North, such as the ECtHR, are considerably more restrained in this respect. In the case of the ICJ, the different geographical origin of its judges can lead to some sort of compromise on this issue, whereby remedies end up being not as intrusive as that of the Global South courts (such as the IACtHR) but more than those of the Global North (such as the ECtHR). This is also mirrored at the domestic adjudicatory level.[1430] For example, a number of constitutional courts in the Global South have adopted a transformative approach that aims at changing social structures through individual cases, thereby issuing remedies that step well into the political realm.[1431] This has not taken place to the same extent before constitutional courts of the Global North.

This difference might be due to the fact that these regions of the Global South have had more recent experiences of authoritarianism, and perhaps these regional courts have an increased mistrust towards domestic politicians and institutions. In any case, regional courts in the Global South have developed a particular understanding of international adjudication, and this is reflected in their remedial practice. However, this is not without problems, as states in the Global South, due to the history of intrusions in their sovereign sphere by foreign states and international institutions (especially those of a financial nature) are more zealous to protect their sovereignty against such outside interventions. Therefore, the remedial practice of human rights courts has also been the cause of resistance and even backlash on behalf of states, an issue that was examined in chapter 6 of this book.

1430 Being therefore related to what Çalı termed as the 'legal culture explanation' for the variation in the intrusiveness of remedies. See Çalı, *I•CON* 2018, pp. 214-234.

1431 See generally Philipp Dann, Michael Riegner and Maxim Bönnemann (eds.), *The Global South and Comparative Constitutional Law*, Oxford: OUP, 2023; Daniel Bonilla Maldonado (ed.), *Constitutionalism of the Global South*, Cambridge: CUP, 2013.

In general, the second part of the book turned around the actual practice of regional human rights courts with respect to legislative remedies. This was done through an analysis of case law in which all legislative measures issued by human rights courts were identified, grouped, and analysed. First, Chapter 4 divided these remedies into ten categories, related to the specific human rights issues they deal with. This showed that the three courts have a common understanding of such measures, as most of them were issued to tackle the same problems in different regions, especially those related to fair trial rights and to some extent also to the protection of vulnerable groups. However, the three courts have also different priorities in this regard, as shown by the fact that each of them has afforded increased attention to a particular issue in the context of its legislative remedies. This is the case of property rights before the ECtHR, electoral rights before the ACtHPR, and the codification of criminal offences (especially enforced disappearances) before the IACtHR. Arguably, these priorities are also a good reflection of the self-understanding of each regional court with respect to its particular mission, with the strong 'nunca más' element at the IACtHR, the role of the ACtHPR as a democracy defender and the liberal human rights approach of the ECtHR.

Then, Chapter 5 focused on the wording of these measures. This chapter also examined the question of the amount of deference that should be afforded by human rights courts to domestic legislatures, concluding that a 'margin of deliberation' is necessary in this respect. This implies that legislative bodies should be able to deliberate before implementing such remedies, which is in turn mainly related to the specificity of the remedial measures and the room of manoeuvre available for its implementation. If legislative remedies are too specific as to the outcome of the required reform, there is not much room for deliberation before the domestic legislature. In this regard, it was shown that in general, the IACtHR has employed a high degree of remedial specificity in these cases, while the legislative measures of the ECtHR are considerably vague and those of the ACtHPR lay in between.

Finally, Chapter 6 dealt with the consequences of legislative measures. These consequences are mainly related to the issues of (non-)compliance and backlash. It was shown that concrete legislative remedies contributed to or were even the main cause of backlash by some individual states in the three regional systems. In addition, these measures take the longest to be implemented, although this is mostly related to a lack of effective domestic coordination mechanisms for the implementation judgments that involve the legislature. However, these remedies are also able to produce a notable impact, not only by catalysing reforms but also by triggering social debates around certain issues or empowering specific actors, such as specialised NGOs that have engaged in strategic litigation before regional human rights courts aiming precisely at the reform of legislation on concrete issues.

In sum, it can be concluded that legislative remedies have a high degree of consistency and commonality in international human rights adjudication, especially with respect to the issue of when they are employed and the type of consequences they trigger. The three courts have consolidated their remedial practice, and legislative measures clearly form part of it. However, the answer to this question becomes more nuanced if one does not focus on when, but on how legislative measures are applied. In that context, each court has developed a distinct approach regarding the wording and specificity of such measures, as well as the frequency of their use. It is thus also necessary to briefly assess the practice of the three regional courts in this respect.

II. Nomative Assessment

The first element of this assessment concerns the general competence of these courts to order legislative reforms. Nowadays there should be no doubts about the existence of this competence. This remedial practice has been consolidated separately in each regional system, and even if it was not part of the original cession of state sovereignty to these courts, it can be considered that in view of this consolidated jurisprudence states have acquiesced to it. Despite the aforementioned instances of resistance and non-compliance with such orders, governments of state parties have not collectively attempted to modify this practice.[1432] Thus, it can be concluded that despite some individual objections to it, the majority of states have consented to the competence of human rights courts to order legislative reforms.

Moreover, from an international law perspective, it has been clear since the *Factory at Chorzów* judgment of 1927 that the competence of a court to

1432 As shown in Chapter 5, the arguably only instance of collective backlash against the IACtHR was the 'Five Presidents Declaration', and this affected only five of the twenty states subject to the jurisdiction of this Court, while in the case of the ECtHR, the state parties actually supported this remedial practice in the context of the 'Interlaken Process'.

decide the outcome of a case implies a competence to establish the appropriate remedies in this regard. As shown in Chapter 2, even a traditional international court such as the ICJ, whose role is generally to solve disputes among states and not to examine more broadly the compatibility of a domestic legal order with a treaty, would be competent to order legislative reforms. In the case of human rights courts, which were precisely set up to ensure that states live up to their international human rights commitments *inter alia* through legislation, their competence in that respect becomes more evident.

This is shown in the fact that every human rights treaty includes not only specific obligations to legislate in order to protect concrete rights or groups or to prevent or punish certain acts, but also general obligations to legislate in order to ensure that the state parties' domestic legal order conforms to the treaty and ensures the protection of the rights contained therein, as shown in Chapter 1. Even if there are human rights treaties that do not expressly include such a general obligation to legislate – such as the ECHR – this is considered to constitute a customary obligation under international law. Thus, if domestic laws are incompatible with the states' human rights obligations, or if states are failing to provide adequate protection of such rights due to the absence of laws, they are obliged to reform their legal order. What courts are doing in this respect can be regarded as a reiteration and concretisation of a primary human rights obligation of states.

One could therefore even ask if in such cases a human rights violation against a concrete victim needs to take place for a court to intervene and order a legislative reform. Despite some exceptions, this is the position taken both by the ECtHR and the IACtHR, due to the rules concerning its personal and material jurisdiction, which include a 'victim requirement' in order to submit cases before them. However, as examined in Chapter 1, the ACtHPR has adopted a different view on what constitutes a notable development in human rights adjudication. This court does not require the existence of a concrete victim and has admitted a number of complaints that concerned exclusively a domestic law or a legislative provision, without identifying any individual affected by it, often including legislative remedies in the context of such cases.

Although this may seem surprising for a human rights court, it does make sense due to the aforementioned conceptualisation of legislative remedies. If they are not viewed as secondary obligations that arise from the infringement of a primary obligation, being therefore inextricably linked to this infringement, but rather as a reiteration or concretisation of the primary obligation, their link to a violation and a concrete victim is not a *conditio sine qua non* but can be dispensed with. In sum, the African Court is taking a novel approach to the issue of domestic laws' conformity with human rights obligations that can arguably be useful to prevent violations from occurring in the first place, providing this court with an undoubtedly stronger constitutional character.

The other two regional courts are more constrained in this respect through their strict procedural rules on jurisdiction, but loosening them and adopting a similar approach could be a promising option in order to follow the path of constitutionalisation. Nevertheless, this would not be without problems. If any individual could claim that laws are contrary to the respective convention without being affected by them, the most obvious risk is that courts would be flooded with such complaints, especially because the rule on the exhaustion of domestic remedies would be difficult to apply. In this regard, for an individual or an NGO to be empowered to bring a claim against the constitutionality of a legislative provision *in abstracto* at the domestic level is very rare. Usually, this competence is reserved to specific institutional bodies, such as parliamentary groups or ombudsmen. Thus, human rights courts would find themselves in a situation where the exhaustion of domestic remedies could not be required, as no such remedies are available. This is to some extent also occurring in the cases concerning an abstract review of legislation before the ACtHPR. When states objected to the admissibility of such cases claiming that the applicant had not exhausted domestic remedies, the ACtHPR dismissed the objections arguing that no remedies were available for an individual to challenge a domestic law.[1433]

Another aspect of this assessment concerns the use that each regional human rights court has made of its competence to issue legislative remedies. It is argued in this respect that whenever the courts find that the domestic legal order of states is incompatible with the corresponding treaty, they should order a reform of the concerned laws to make it compatible. However, despite constituting binding orders that prescribe these reforms, legislative remedies should be broad enough to leave the domestic legislature a margin of deliberation. This concept was developed in Chapter 5 of this book, and it implies that the legislature should have a certain amount of discretion to implement the legislative measures imposed by human rights courts. This is mainly due to the democratic legitimacy of the procedure

1433 See ACtHPR, *Lohé Issa Konaté vs. Burkina Faso* (2014), paras. 108-114.

and decisions adopted by legislative bodies, which is higher than that of the domestic executive or judiciary. In this respect, democratic deliberation is arguably a cornerstone of modern democracies, and it takes place to a considerable extent before legislative bodies. Thus, legislative remedies before human rights courts should afford a margin for legislatures to deliberate and democratically decide the concrete outcome of the requested reform. This can be done through remedial vagueness, by prescribing a legislative reform but avoiding to specify in detail how the new provision should be drafted, as explained in Chapter 5.

Of course, it is also possible that states could abuse the vagueness of legislative remedies, carrying out a reform that is not in line with the jurisprudence of the human rights court in question. This is to some extent related to the democratic decline witnessed in some states recently, as these are arguably more likely to abuse the lack of specificity. Therefore, it is argued that remedial specificity should be dependent on the respondent state in question, also because democratic deliberation is less likely to take place in states with authoritarian tendencies, as examined also in Chapter 5. In the case of other states, good faith in the implementation of judgments should arguably be presumed, and democratic deliberation should not be curtailed due to the potential of abuse regarding vague legislative remedies.

In this respect, it can be argued that the IACtHR has often been too specific in its legislative remedies. There are a number of judgments in which this court prescribed the concrete elements to be included in a legislative amendment, detailing as well how such elements should be regulated. The domestic implementation of such orders then turns into a sort of automatic task. No deliberation can take place because the judgment is to a great extent already drafting the new law, and implementing such judgments then simply consists in transposing these prescriptions into domestic norms. This has arguably been a source of backlash, as shown in Chapter 6.[1434] A higher degree of remedial deference would thus be probably convenient in this context. The IACtHR has even attempted to completely bypass the domestic legislature by determining that some laws "lack legal effect".[1435] Deciding on the domestic validity of laws is however clearly outside its

1434 As stated by Cavallaro and Brewer, the fact that the IACtHR is "instructing states not only to undertake general tasks, but also to carry them out in a specific way (...) can provoke hostile reactions by both states and the general public". See Cavallaro and Brewer, *AJIL* 2008, p. 824.

1435 See for example IACtHR, *Barrios Altos vs. Peru* (2001), operative para. 4.

sphere of competences. In general, only constitutional courts are empowered to deprive a legislative provision of legal effects domestically.

In addition, precisely because legislative remedies before constitutional courts are generally negative – prescribing the repeal of legislation – the deliberative element is not that relevant. If a law or a provision simply needs to be repealed, there is not much to be debated. The deliberation will take place at a later stage, when the legislature adopts a new law to replace the one that was declared unconstitutional. However, legislative remedies before the ECtHR and the IACtHR are usually of a positive nature, prescribing the adoption of new laws or the inclusion of specific elements into existing laws. Thus, the margin of deliberation becomes much more relevant for such positive legislative measures.

In the case of the ACtHPR this is different, being the only court that orders mostly legislative reforms of a negative nature. In addition, when this court included legislative reforms of a positive nature, it generally worded them broadly enough to allow for domestic deliberation. Thus, it can be concluded that in principle the ACtHPR's practice in this respect conforms to the normative considerations outlined above. While it prescribes legislative reforms in all cases in which it finds an incompatibility, it generally allows for a margin of deliberation for its implementation. It is nevertheless a jurisprudence that arguably lacks the consolidation and consistency of the other two regional courts' case law. Despite having issued a similar number of legislative measures than that of the ECtHR, this has been done in a much shorter period of time. Moreover, as shown in Chapter 3, the remedial practice of the ACtHPR has been changing in recent years, when it has been dealing with a higher number of cases. One can in sum consider that this court, though still in the process of consolidating its remedial jurisprudence, is going in the right direction.

The ECtHR can also be considered to have acted in a sufficiently deferent way when issuing legislative remedies. It has worded such remedies very vaguely, usually limiting itself to prescribing the introduction of an effective remedy in the domestic legal order for a particular issue. Nevertheless, it can also be argued that this court is not making use of legislative remedies in enough cases. Despite finding relatively often that domestic norms are incompatible with the ECHR, legislative reforms are ordered extremely rarely. Upon reaching such findings, it usually orders the payment of monetary compensation and leaves the decision on whether to take additional measures in the hands of the concerned state. States then generally limit themselves to paying compensation and perhaps taking an individual measure concerning the victim – such as a retrial or release from prison – but avoid taking any structural measures in this regard. This, in turn, provokes that numerous repetitive cases concerning the same law are submitted to the ECtHR by additional victims, eventually leading to the serious backlog crisis that has been taking place in the European system for a number of years now. The ECtHR will only after several judgments concerning the same law recommend its reform in the reasoning of the judgment. But even then, the reform still depends on the negotiations taking place before the CoM, as such recommendations included in the reasoning are not formally binding. An actual order in this respect – included in the operative paragraphs of the judgments – will be introduced only after a number of attempts to solve the issue through these softer ways, in conjunction with a lack of cooperation on behalf of the state.

The mechanism which was intended to solve this problem – the pilot judgment procedure – has arguably failed to live up to the expectations. This is mainly due to its highly exceptional character and the scarcity of instances in which it has been applied. Its use has even decreased in recent years, with only four pilot judgments issued between 2017 and 2022. Moreover, there has been a lack of engagement and cooperation by states to solve their structural deficits.[1436] If the ECtHR aims to be more sustainable and efficient in the long term with respect to its management of cases, it would have to increase the use of legislative remedies, thereby potentially reducing the number of repetitive cases and being able to deliver judgments in a timely manner.[1437]

In sum, the argument in this respect is that the ECtHR is being overly cautious about states' concerns, even when dealing with authoritarian laws or institutions.[1438] While it is true that the preservation of the CoE system "may at times and on certain matters require the integration of their laws and policies, [and] at other times necessitating the recognition of their difference and autonomy",[1439] the ECtHR is arguably paying much more

1436 See generally Leach *et al.*, 2010.

1437 This was also one of the recommendations made by Antonio Cassesse, arguing that "the Court should, after finding that a breach of the Convention has occurred on account of an inconsistent national law, enjoin the responsible state to change that law", which could be done with a different interpretation of Art. 41 ECHR. Cassesse, "Towards Moderate Monism", in Cassesse (ed.), 2012, p. 197.

1438 See in this respect Demir-Gürsel in Aust and Demir-Gürsel (eds.), 2021, p. 257.

1439 Esra Demir-Gürsel, "For the sake of unity: the drafting history of the European Convention on Human Rights and its current relevance", in Aust and Demir-Gürsel (eds.), 2021, pp. 109-132.

attention to the second aspect than the first one. Nevertheless, when it includes such remedies, it generally provides the domestic legislatures with enough margin to deliberate with regard to its implementation. In the case law of the IACtHR one can find the opposite scenario, where it includes legislative measures in an adequate number of cases but is too specific in the wording of such measures, curtailing the discretion that legislative bodies should possess. The ACtHPR is arguably maintaining the best balance in this respect, issuing legislative remedies when they are necessary but without being overly intrusive in its remedial specificity. Although its case law is still being consolidated in this regard, it seems that the older courts could learn something from the newer court.

Going back to the beginning of this book, when Cassesse advocated for international courts with the power to prescribe reforms of domestic legislation in cases of incompatibility with international obligations, he wrote that putting such measures into effect "could only be predicated on a dramatic change in the domestic and international ethos—a process which is likely to occur only over many decades", and that "any progress may only occur within regional groupings".[1440] Indeed, a decade later there has been some progress in that direction within regional human rights protection systems, where courts have developed a consistent practice of prescribing legislative reforms. This is certainly a practice that needs to be refined, and additional measures should be put into place (especially at the domestic level) to ensure the compatibility of domestic laws and human rights treaties. In any case, however, international courts are progressing in the direction envisaged back then – this progress is not likely to stop any time soon.

1440 Cassesse, "Towards Moderate Monism", in Cassesse (ed.), 2012, pp. 192, 199.

Bibliography

van Aaken, Anne and Motoc, Iulia (eds.), *The European Convention on Human Rights and General International Law*, Oxford: OUP, 2018.

Abebe, Adem Kassie, "Taming regressive constitutional amendments: The African Court as a continental (super) constitutional court", *International Journal of Constitutional Law* 17(1), 2019, pp. 89-117.

Abrusci, Elena, "Judicial Fragmentation on Indigenous Property Rights: Causes, Consequences and Solutions", *International Journal of Human Rights* 21(5), 2017, pp. 550-564.

Acosta, Diego and Freier, Luisa, "Regional Migration Management in South America", in Anna Triandafyllidou (ed.), *Handbook of Migration and Globalisation, Cheltenham*: Edward Elgar, 2018, pp. 69-85.

Adeola, Aderomola (ed.), *Compliance with International Human Rights Law in Africa: Essays in Honour of Frans Viljoen*, Oxford: OUP, 2022.

Adjolohoun, Sègnonna Horace, "A crisis of design and judicial practice? Curbing state disengagement from the African Court on Human and Peoples' Rights", *African Human Rights Law Journal* 20, 2020, pp. 1-40.

Albertson Fineman, Martha, "The Vulnerable Subject: Anchoring Equality in the Human Condition", *Yale Journal of Law and Feminism* 20(1), 2008, pp. 1-23.

Allen, Tom, "Liberalism, Social Democracy and the Value of Property under the European Convention on Human Rights", *International and Comparative Law Quarterly* 59 (4), 2010, pp. 1055-1078.

Allen Tom and Douglas, Benedict, "Closing the Door on Restitution", in Antoine Buyse and Michael Hamilton (eds.), *Transitional Jurisprudence and the ECHR: Justice, Politics and Rights*, Cambridge: CUP, 2011, pp. 208-238.

Alston, Philip, "Article 32: The Right to Protection from Economic Exploitation", in John Tobin (ed.), *The UN Convention on the Rights of the Child: A Commentary*, Oxford: OUP, 2019, pp. 1225-1272.

Alston, Philip and Quinn, Gerard, "The Nature and Scope of States Parties' Obligations under the International Covenant on Economic, Social and Cultural Rights", *Human Rights Quarterly* 9(2), 1987, pp. 156-229.

Alter, Karen J., *The New Terrain of International Law: Courts, Politics, Rights*, Princeton, NJ: Princeton University Press, 2014.

Alter, Karen J. and Hooghe, Lisbeth, "Regional Dispute Settlement", in Tanja Börzel and Thomas Risse (eds.), *The Oxford Handbook of Comparative Regionalism*, Oxford: OUP, 2016, pp. 538–558.

Amerasinghe, Chittharanjan Felix, *Jurisdiction of International Tribunals*, The Hague: Kluwer, 2003.

Amerasinghe, Chittharanjan Felix, *Jurisdiction of Specific International Tribunals*, Leiden: Brill Nijhoff, 2009.

Anagnostou, Dia and Mungiu-Pippidi, Alina, "Domestic Implementation of Human Rights Judgments in Europe: Legal Infrastructure and Government Effectiveness Matter", *European Journal of International Law* 35(1), 2014, pp. 205-227.

Anaya, James and Grossman, Claudio, "The Case of Awas Tingni v. Nicaragua: A New Step in the International Law of Indigenous Peoples", *Arizona Journal of International and Comparative Law* 19(1), 2002, pp. 1-16.

Anaya, James, *International Human Rights and Indigenous Peoples*, Austin: Kluwer, 2009.

Antkowiak, Tom, "Remedial Approaches to Human Rights Violations: The Inter-American Court of Human Rights and Beyond", *Columbia Journal of Transnational Law* 46(2), 2008, pp. 351-419.

Antkowiak, Tom, "A Dark Side of Virtue: The Inter-American Court and Reparations for Indigenous Peoples", *Duke Journal of International Law* 25, 2015, pp. 1-80.

Anzilotti, Dionisio, "La responsabilité internationale des Etats à raison des dommages soufferts par des étrangers", *Revue Générale de Droit International Public* 13, 1906.

Applebaum, Anne, *Twilight of Democracy: The Seductive Lure of Authoritarianism*, New York: Doubleday, 2020.

Attanasio, David, "Extraordinary Reparations, Legitimacy, and the Inter-American Court", *University of Pennsylvania Journal of International Law* 37(3), 2016, pp. 813-871.

Arai-Takahashi, Yutaka, *The Margin of Appreciation Doctrine and the Principle of Proportionality in the Jurisprudence of the ECHR*, Cambridge: Intersentia, 2002.

Arendt, Hannah, *The Origins of Totalitarianism*, Oregon: Harvest Book, 1976.

Arnardóttir, Oddný Mjöll, "The 'procedural turn' under the European Convention on Human Rights and presumptions of Convention compliance", *International Journal of Constitutional Law* 15(1), 2017, pp. 9–35.

Arnardóttir, Oddný Mjöll, "The Brighton Aftermath and the Changing Role of the European Court of Human Rights", *Journal of International Dispute Settlement* 9, 2018, pp. 223–239.

Aust, Helmut Philipp, "Introduction: The European Court of Human Rights – the past in the present", in Helmut Philipp Aust and Esra Demir-Gürsel (eds.), *The European Court of Human Rights - Current Challenges in Historical Perspective*, Cheltenham: Edward Elgar, 2021, pp. 1-19.

Ayeni, Victor Oluwasina, "Beyond Compliance: Do Decisions of Regional Human Rights Tribunals in Africa Make a Difference?", in Aderomola Adeola (ed.), *Compliance with International Human Rights Law in Africa: Essays in Honour of Frans Viljoen*, Oxford: OUP, 2022, pp. 35-71.

Ayeni, Victor Oluwasina, "Implementation of the Decisions and Judgments of African Regional Human Rights Tribunals: Reflections on the Barriers to State Compliance and the Lessons Learnt", *African Journal of International and Comparative Law* 30(4), 2022, pp. 560-581.

Baldini, Paula and da Cruz, Miranda, "Trackers and Trailblazers: Dynamic Interactions and Institutional Design in the Inter-American Court of Human Rights", *Journal of International Dispute Settlement* 11, 2020, pp. 69-90.

Bailliet, Cecilia, "Measuring Compliance with the Inter-American Court of Human Rights: The Ongoing Challenge of Judicial Independence in Latin America", *Nordic Journal of Human Rights* 31, 2013, pp. 477-495.

Basch, Fernando *et al.*, "The Effectiveness of the Inter-American System of Human Rights Protection: A Quantitative Approach to its Functioning and Compliance with its Decisions", *Sur: International Journal on Human Rights* 7(12), 2010, pp. 8-35.

Bates, Ed, *The Evolution of the European Convention on Human Rights: From Its Inception to the Creation of a Permanent Court of Human Rights,* Oxford: OUP, 2010.

Bates, Ed, "Analysing the Prisoner Voting Saga and the British Challenge to Strasbourg", *Human Rights Law Review* 14(3), 2014, pp. 503–540.

Bates, Ed, "Strasbourg's Integrationist Role, or the Need for Self-restraint?", *European Convention of Human Rights Law Review* 1, 2020, pp. 14-21.

Bächtiger, Andre *et al.*, "Deliberative Democracy: An Introduction", in Andre Bächtiger *et al.* (eds.), *The Oxford Handbook of Deliberative Democracy*, Oxford: OUP, 2018, pp. 1-32.

Bellamy, Richard, "The Democratic Legitimacy of International Human Rights Conventions: Political Constitutionalism and the European Convention on Human Rights", *European Journal of International Law* 25(4), 2015, pp. 1019–1042.

Bellamy, Richard, "Ronald Dworkin, *Taking Rights Seriously*", in Jacob T. Levy (ed.), *The Oxford Handbook of Classics in Contemporary Political Theory,* Oxford: OUP, 2017.

Benvenisti, Eyal, "The Margin of Appreciation, Subsidiarity and Global Challenges to Democracy", *Journal of International Dispute Settlement* 9, 2018, pp. 240–253.

Berlia, Georges, "Jurisprudence des Tribunaux Internationaux en ce qui Concerne leur Compétence", *The Hague Academy of International Law: Recueil des Cours* 88, 1955, pp. 112-160.

Bernhardt, Rudolf, "Commentary: The European System", *Connecticut Journal of International Law* 2, 1987, pp. 299-301.

Bertoni, Eduardo Andrés, "The Inter American Court of Human Rights and the European Court of Human Rights: A Dialogue on Freedom of Expression Standards", *European Human Rights Law Review* 3, 2009, pp. 332-352.

Besson, Samantha, "Subsidiarity in International Human Rights Law — What is Subsidiary about Human Rights?", *American Journal of Jurisprudence* 61(1), 2016, pp. 69–107.

Bickel, Alexander, *The Least Dangerous Branch: The Supreme Court at the Bar of Politics*, New Haven: Yale University Press, 2nd ed., 1986.

Biegon, Japhet, "Compliance Studies and the African Human Rights System", in Aderomola Adeola (ed.), *Compliance with International Human Rights Law in Africa: Essays in Honour of Frans Viljoen*, Oxford: OUP, 2022, pp. 10-34.

Binder, Christina, "The Prohibition of Amnesties by the Inter American Court of Human Rights", *German Law Journal* 12(5), 2011, pp. 1203–1230.

Birdsall, Andrea and Lang, Anthony F., "The International Criminal Court and Global Constitutionalism", in Anthony F. Lang and Antje Wiener (eds.), *Handbook on Global Constitutionalism*, Cheltenham: Edward Elgar, 2017, pp. 383-394.

von Bogdandy, Armin, "*Ius Constitutionale Commune* en America Latina: Observations on Transformative Constitutionalism", in Armin von Bogdandy *et al.* (eds.), *Transformative Constitutionalism in Latin America: Emergence of a New Ius Commune*, Oxford: OUP, 2017, pp. 27-48.

von Bogdandy, Armin and Urueña, René, "International Transformative Constitutionalism in Latin America", *American Journal of International Law* 114(3), 2020, pp. 403–442.

Boisson de Chazournes, Laurence and Rudall, Jason, "Judicial Deference: Why Does It Matter?", *The Law and Practice of International Courts and Tribunals* 21, 2022, pp. 419–424.

Bonilla Maldonado, Daniel (ed.), *Constitutionalism of the Global South,* Cambridge: CUP, 2013.

Börzel, Tanja and Risse, Thomas (eds.), *The Oxford Handbook of Comparative Regionalism*, Oxford: OUP, 2016.

van Boven, Theo, "Victims' Rights to a Remedy and Reparation: The New United Nations Principles and Guidelines", in Carla Ferstman and Mariana Goetz (eds.), *Reparations for Victims of Genocide, War Crimes and Crimes against Humanity*, Leiden: Brill Nijhoff, 2009, pp. 15–37.

Braga Navarro, Gabriela Cristina, "The Struggle after the Victory: Non-compliance in the Inter-American Court of Human Rights' Jurisprudence on Indigenous Territorial Rights", *Journal of International Dispute Settlement* 12, 2021, pp. 223–249.

Brems, Eva, "Positive subsidiarity and its implications for the margin of appreciation doctrine", *Netherlands Quarterly of Human Rights* 37(3), 2019, pp. 210-227.

Breuer, Marten (ed.), *Principled Resistance to ECtHR Judgments – A New Paradigm?*, Berlin: Springer, 2019.

Brewer-Carias, Allan Randolph, *Constitutional Courts as Positive Legislators: A Comparative Law Study*, Cambridge: CUP, 2011.

Briant, Sophie, "Dialogue, Diplomacy and Defiance: Prisoners' Voting Rights at Home and in Strasbourg", *European Human Rights Law Review* 16(3), 2011, pp. 243-252.

Brochard, Edwin, *Declaratory Judgments*, Cleveland: Banks-Baldwin, 1934.

Broderick, Andrea, "Article 4: General Obligations", in Ilias Bantekas et al. (eds.), *The UN Convention of the rights of Persons with Disabilities: A Commentary*, Oxford: OUP, 2018, pp. 106-139.

Brown, Chester, *A Common Law of International Adjudication*, Oxford: OUP, 2007.

Brown, Chester, "Factory at Chorzów (Germany v Poland) (1927-1928)", in Eirik Bjorge and Cameron Miles (eds.), *Landmark Cases in Public International Law*, Oxford: Hart, 2017, pp. 61-88.

Brownlie, Ian, "Remedies in the International Court of Justice", in Vaughan Lowe and Malgosia (eds.), *Fifty Years of the International Court of Justice*, Cambridge: CUP, 1996, pp. 557-566.

Burgogue-Larsen, Laurence, "La Corte Interamericana de Derechos Humanos como Tribunal Constitucional", in Armin von Bogdandy, Héctor Fix Fierro and Mariela Morales Antoniazzi (coords.), Ius Constitutionale Commune *en América Latina: Rasgos, Potencialidades y Desafíos,* Mexico: UNAM, 2014, pp. 421-457.

Burgorgue-Larsen, Laurence, *Les 3 cours régionales des droits de l'homme in context: La justice qui n'allait pas de soi,* Paris: Éditions Pedone, 2020.

Burnham, Margaret A., "Caribbean Constitutions and the Death Penalty", in Richard Albert *et al.* (eds.), *The Oxford Handbook of Caribbean Constitutions*, Oxford: OUP, 2020, pp. 421454.

Buyse, Antoine, *Post-conflict Housing Restitution: The European Human Rights Perspective with a Case Study on Bosnia and Herzegovina*, Cambridge: Intersentia, 2008.

Buyse, Antoine, "Lost and Regained? Restitution as a Remedy for Human Rights Violations in the Context of International Law", *Zeitschrift für ausländisches öffentliches Recht und Völkerrecht* 68, 2008, pp. 129-153.

Byrnes, Andrew, "Article 2", in Marsha A. Freeman *et al.* (eds.), *The UN Convention on the Elimination of All Forms of Discrimination Against Women: A Commentary*, Oxford: OUP, 2012, pp. 71–99.

Caflisch, Lucius and Cançado Trinidade, Antônio Augusto, "Les conventions américaine et européenne des droits de l'homme et le droit international general", *Revue générale de droit international public* 108, 2004, pp. 5-63.

Cameron, Iain, "The Court and the member states: procedural aspects", in Andreas Føllesdal, Birgit Peters and Geir Ulfstein (eds.), *Constituting Europe: The European Court of Human Rights in a National, European and Global Context*, Cambridge: CUP, 2013, pp. 25-61.

Cançado Trinidade, Antonio Augusto, "International Law for Humankind: Towards a New Jus Gentium", *The Hague Academy of International Law: Recueil des Cours* 316, 2005.

Carozza, Paolo, "Subsidiarity as a Structural Principle of International Human Rights Law", *American Journal of International Law* 97(1), 2003, pp. 38-79.

Carvalho, Sandra and Baker, Eduardo "Experiencias de Litigio Estratégico en el Sistema Interamericano de Protección de los Derechos Humanos", *Sur: Revista Internacional de Derechos Humanos* 20, pp. 469-479.

Cassel, Douglass, "Peru Withdraws from the Court: Will the Inter-American Human Rights System Meet the Challenge?", *Human Rights Law Journal* 20, 1999, pp. 167-175.

Cassel, Douglass, "The Expanding Scope and Impact of Reparations Awarded by the Inter-American Court of Human Rights", in Koen de Feyter *et al.* (eds.), *Out of The Ashes: Reparations for Gross Violations of Human Rights*, Cambridge: Intersentia, 2005, pp. 191-223.

Cassesse, Antonio, "Towards a Moderate Monism: Could International Rules Eventually Acquire the Force to Invalidate Inconsistent National Laws?", in Antonio Cassesse (ed.), *Realizing Utopia: The Future of International Law*, Oxford: OUP, 2012, pp. 187–199.

Castañeda García, Ivette, "Military justice in Latin America: a comparative analysis", in Alison Duxbury and Matthew Groves (eds.), *Military Justice in the Modern Age*, Cambridge: CUP, 2016, pp. 196-217.

Cavallaro, James and Brewer, Stephanie Erin, "Re-evaluating Regional Human Rights Litigation in the Twenty-First Century: The Case of the Inter-American Court", *American Journal of International Law* 102(4), 2008, pp. 768–827.

Celiksoy, Ergul, "Execution of the Judgments of the European Court of Human Rights in Prisoners' Right to Vote Cases", *Human Rights Law Review* 20, 2020, pp. 555-581.

Cepeda, Manuel Jose and Landau, David, *Colombian Constitutional Law*, Oxford: OUP, 2017.

Cerna, Christina M., "The Inter-American System and Military Justice", in Alison Duxbury and Matthew Groves (eds.), *Military Justice in the Modern Age*, Cambridge: CUP, 2016, pp. 325-346.

Chinkin, Christine, "Article 3", in Marsha A. Freeman *et al.* (eds.), *The UN Convention on the Elimination of All Forms of Discrimination Against Women: A Commentary*, Oxford: OUP, 2012, pp. 101-122.

Christoffersen, Jonas, "Individual and Constitutional Justice: Can the Power Balance of Adjudication be Reversed?", in Jonas Christoffersen and Mikael Rask Madsen (eds.), *The European Court of Human Rights between Law and Politics*, Oxford: OUP, 2011, pp. 181–203.

Cichowski, Rachel A., "Civil Society and the European Court of Human Rights", in Jonas Christoffersen and Mikael Rask Madsen (eds.), *The European Court of Human Rights between Law and Politics*, Oxford: OUP, 2011, pp. 77-97.

Citroni, Gabriella "The Contribution of the Inter-American Court of Human Rights and Other International Human Rights Bodies to the Struggle Against Enforced Disappearance", in Yves Haeck *et al.* (eds.), *The Inter-American Court of Human Rights*, Cambridge: Intersentia, 2015, pp. 379-402.

Clooney, Amal and Webb, Philippa, *The Right to a Fair Trial in International Law*, Oxford: OUP, 2020.

Cohen, Joshua, "Deliberation and Democratic Legitimacy", in Alan Hamlin and Philipe Pettit (eds.), *The Good Polity: Normative Analysis of the State*, Oxford: Blackwell, 1989, pp. 17–34.

Contesse, Jorge, "Contestation and Deference in the Inter-American Human Rights System", *Law and Contemporary Problems* 79(2), 2016, pp. 123-145.

Contesse, Jorge, "The final word? Constitutional dialogue and the Inter-American Court of Human Rights", *International Journal of Constitutional Law* 15(2), 2017, pp. 414-435.

Contesse, Jorge, "Resisting the Inter-American Court", *Yale Journal of International Law* 44(2), 2019, pp. 179-237.

Cornejo Chavez, Leiry, "New remedial responses in the practice of regional human rights courts: Purposes beyond compensation", *International Journal of Constitutional Law* 15(2), 2017, pp. 372–392.

Correa, Cristián, Furuya, Siuchi and Sandoval, Clara, "Reparation for Victims of Armed Conflict", *Max Planck Trialogues on the Law of Peace and War (vol. II)*, Cambridge: CUP, 2020.

Costa, Jean-Paul, "The relationship between the European Court of Human Rights and the National Courts", *European Human Rights Law Review* 3, 2013, pp. 264-274.

Couvreur, Philippe, *The International Court of Justice and the Effectiveness of International Law*, Leiden: Brill Nijhoff, 2017.

Cram, Ian, "Protocol 15 and Articles 10 and 11 ECHR—The Partial Triumph of Political Incumbency Post-Brighton?", *International and Comparative Law Quarterly* 67, 2018, pp. 477–503.

Crawford, James, *The ILC Articles on State Responsibility: Introduction, Text and Commentaries*, Cambridge: CUP, 2002.

Crawford, James, "The International Court of Justice and the Law of State Responsibility", in Christian Tams and James Sloan (eds.), *The Development of International Law by the International Court of Justice*, Oxford: OUP, 2013, pp. 70–86.

Crawford, James, *State Responsibility: The General Part*, Cambridge: CUP, 2013.

Crawford, James and Keene, Amelia, "The Structure of Sate Responsibility under the European Convention on Human Rights", in Anne van Aaken and Iulia Motoc (eds.), *The European Convention on Human Rights and General International Law*, Oxford: OUP, 2018, pp. 178–198.

Czepek, Jakub, "The Application of the Pilot Judgment Procedure and Other Forms of Handling Large-Scale Dysfunctions in the Case Law of the European Court of Human Rights", *International Community Law Review* 20, 2018, pp. 347–373.

Çalı, Başak, "The Purposes of the European Human Rights System: One or Many?", *European Human Rights Law Review* 3, 2008, pp. 299-306.

Çalı, Başak and Koch, Anne, "Foxes Guarding the Foxes? Peer Review of Human Rights Judgments by the Committee of Ministers of the Council of Europe", *Human Rights Law Review* 14(2), 2014, pp. 301-325.

Çalı, Başak, "International Judicial Review", in Anthony F. Lang and Antje Wiener (eds.), *Handbook on Global Constitutionalism*, Cheltenham: Edward Elgar, 2017, pp. 291-303.

Çalı, Başak, Madsen, Mikael Rask and Viljoen, Frans, "Comparative regional human rights regimes: Defining a research agenda", *International Journal of Constitutional Law* 16(1), 2018, pp. 128–135.

Çalı, Başak, "Explaining variation in the intrusiveness of regional human rights remedies in domestic orders", *International Journal of Constitutional Law* 16(1), 2018, pp. 214-234.

Çalı, Başak, "Coping with Crisis: Whither the Variable Geometry in the Jurisprudence of the European Court of Human Rights", *Wisconsin International Law Journal* 35(2), 2018, pp. 237–276.

Çalı, Başak, Bianku, Ledi and Motoc, Iulia (eds.), *Migration and the European Convention on Human Rights*, Oxford: OUP, 2021.

Daly, Tom and Wiebusch, Micha, "The African Court on Human and Peoples' Rights: mapping resistance against a young court", *International Journal of Law in Context* 14, 2018, pp. 294–313.

Dann, Philipp, Riegner, Michael and Bönnemann, Maxim (eds.), *The Global South and Comparative Constitutional Law*, Oxford: OUP, 2023.

De Londras, Fiona and Dzehtsiarou, Kanstantin, "Mission Impossible? Addressing non-execution Through Infringement Proceedings in the European Court of Human Rights", *International and Comparative Law Quarterly* 66(2), 2017, pp. 467–490.

Demir-Gürsel, Esra, "For the sake of unity: the drafting history of the European Convention on Human Rights and its current relevance", in Helmut Philipp Aust and Esra Demir-Gürsel (eds.), *The European Court of Human Rights - Current Challenges in Historical Perspective*, Cheltenham: Edward Elgar,, 2021, pp. 109-132.

Demir-Gürsel, Esra, "The limits of the European Court of Human Rights vis-a-vis contestation and authoritarianism: concluding observations", in Helmut Philipp Aust and Esra Demir-Gürsel (eds.), *The European Court of Human Rights - Current Challenges in Historical Perspective*, Cheltenham: Edward Elgar, 2021, pp. 244–263.

Dersso, Ayele, "The Future of Human Rights and the African Human Rights System", *Nordic Journal of Human Rights* 40(1), 2022, pp. 28-43.

Dixon, Rosalind, "The Forms, Functions, and Varieties of Weak(ened) Judicial Review", *International Journal of Constitutional Law* 17(3), 2019, pp. 904-930.

Donald, Alice, "Parliaments as Compliance Partners in the European Convention on Human Rights System", in Matthew Saul, Andreas Follesdal and Geir Ulfstein (eds.), *The International Human Rights Judiciary and National Parliaments*, Oxford: OUP, 2017, pp. 75-109.

Donald, Alice and Speck, Anne-Katrin, "The European Court of Human Rights' Remedial Practice and its Impact on the Execution of Judgments", *Human Rights Law Review* 19, 2019, pp. 1-35.

Dothan, Shai, *International Judicial Review: When Should International Courts Intervene?*, Cambridge: CUP, 2020.

Dragić, Sanja, *Post-Backlash Human Rights Law*, Leiden: Brill Nijhoff, 2022.

Duhaime, Bernard, "Subsidiarity in the Americas: What Room is there for Deference in the Inter-American System?", in Lukasz Gruszczynski and Wouter Werner (eds.), *Deference in International Courts and Tribunals*, Oxford: OUP, 2014, pp. 289-315.

Dulitzky, Ariel E., "An Inter-American Constitutional Court? The Invention of the Conventionality Control by the Inter-American Court of Human Rights", *Texas Law Review* 50, 2015, pp. 45-93.

Dupuy, Pierre-Marie and Viñuales, Jorge, *International Environmental Law*, Cambridge: CUP, 2nd ed., 2018.

Duranti, Marco, *The Conservative Human Rights Revolution: European Identity, Transnational Politics, and the Origins of the European Convention*, Oxford: OUP, 2017.

Dworkin, Ronald, *Taking Rights Seriously*, Cambridge, MA: Harvard University Press, 1977.

Dworkin, Ronald, "Rights as Trumps", in Jeremy Waldron (ed.), *Theories of Rights*, Oxford: OUP, 1984.

Edwards, Alice, "The meaning of nationality in international law in an era of human rights", in Alice Edwards and Laura van Waas (eds.), *Nationality and Statelessness under International Law*, Cambridge: CUP, 2014, pp. 11-43.

Ely, John Hart, *Democracy and Distrust: A Theory of Judicial Review*, Cambridge, MA: Harvard University Press, 1980.

Enabulele, Amos, "Incompatibility of national law with the African Charter on Human and Peoples' Rights: Does the African Court on Human and Peoples' Rights have the final say?", *African Human Rights Law Journal* 16, 2016, pp. 1-28.

Engstrom, Par (ed.), *The Inter-American System: Impact Beyond Compliance*, Cham: Palgrave Macmillan, 2019.

Evans, Christine, *The Right to Reparation in International Law for Victims of Armed Conflict*, Cambridge: CUP, 2012.

Evans, Malcolm, "State Responsibility and the European Convention on Human Rights", in Malgosia Fitzmaurice and Dan Sarooshi (eds.), *Issues of State Responsibility before International Judicial Institutions*, Oxford: Hart, 2004, pp. 139–160.

Fahner, Johannes Hendrik, *Judicial Deference in International Adjudication. A Comparative Analysis*, Oxford: Hart, 2020.

Fahner, Johannes Hendrik, "The Limited Utility of Deference in International Dispute Settlement", *The Law and Practice of International Courts and Tribunals* 21, 2022, pp. 467– 479.

Fallon, Richard, "The Core of an Uneasy Case for Judicial Review", *Harvard Law Review* 121(7), 2008, pp. 1693-1736.

Fassbender, Bardo, "The United Nations Charter as the Constitution of the International Community", *Columbia Journal of Transnational Law* 36, 1998, pp. 529–619.

Faix, Martin and Jamali, Ayyoub, "Is the African Court on Human and Peoples' Rights in an Existential Crisis?", *Netherlands Quarterly of Human Rights* 40(1), 2022, pp. 56–74.

Favuzza, Federica, "Torreggiani and Prison Overcrowding in Italy", *Human Rights Law Review* 17, 2017, pp. 153–173.

Feihle, Prisca, "Asylum and immigration under the European Convention on Human Rights - an exclusive universality?", in Helmut Philipp Aust and Esra Demir-Gürsel (eds.), *The European Court of Human Rights - Current Challenges in Historical Perspective*, Cheltenham: Edward Elgar, 2021, pp. 133-157.

Fenton-Glynn, Claire, *Children and the European Court of Human Rights*, Oxford: OUP, 2020.

Feria Tina, Mónica, *The Landmark Rulings of the Inter-American Court of Human Rights on the Rights of the Child*, Leiden: Martinus Nijhoff, 2008, pp. 13-32.

Ferrer Mac-Gregor, Eduardo, "The Right to the Truth as an Autonomous Right under the Inter-American Human Rights System", *Mexican Law Review* 9(1), pp. 121-139.

Ferrer MacGregor, Eduardo and Silva, Fernando, *Jurisdicción Militar y Derechos Humanos: El caso Radilla ante la Corte Interamericana de Derechos Humanos*, Mexico: Editorial Porrúa, 2011.

Ferrer MacGregor, Eduardo and Pelayo Möller, Carlos, *Las Obligaciones Generales de la Convención Americana sobre Derechos Humanos*, Mexico: UNAM, 2017.

Fink, Melanie, "The European Court of Human Rights and State Responsibility", in Christina Binder and Konrad Lachmayer (eds.), *The European Court of Human Rights and Public International Law: Fragmentation or Unity?*, Baden-Baden: Nomos, 2014, pp. 93-118.

Follesdal, Andreas, "International Human Rights Courts and the (International) Rule of Law: Part of the solution, part of the problem, or both?", *Global Constitutionalism* 10(1), 2021, pp. 118-138.

Foot, Rosemary, "The Cold War and Human Rights", in Melvyn P. Leffler and Odd Arne Westad (eds.), *The Cambridge History of the Cold War*, Cambridge: CUP, 2010, pp. 445-465.

Foster Michelle and Lambert, Hélène, "Statelessness as a Human Rights Issue: A Concept Whose Time Has Come", *International Journal of Refugee Law* 28(4), 2016, pp. 564–584.

Foster, Steve, "Reluctantly Restoring Rights: Responding to the Prisoner's Right to Vote", *Human Rights Law Review* 9(3), 2009, pp. 489–507.

Frisso, Giovanna Maria, "The Duty to Investigate Violations of the Right to Life in Armed Conflicts in the Jurisprudence of the Inter-American Court of Human Rights", 51 *Israel Law Review*, 2018, pp. 169-191.

Freire, Germán *et al.*, *Indigenous Latin America in the Twenty-First Century*, Washington D.C.: World Bank, 2015.

Frowein, Jochen, "Der europäische Menschenrechtsschutz als Beginn einer europäischen Verfassungsrechtsprechung", *Juristische Schulung*, 1986, pp. 845-851.

Fuentes, Alejandro, "Protection of Indigenous Peoples' Traditional Lands and Exploitation of Natural Resources: The Inter-American Court of Human Rights' Safeguards", *International Journal on Minority and Group Rights* 24(3), 2017, pp. 229-253.

Futhazar, Guillaume, Maljean-Dubois, Sandrine and Razzaque, Jona (eds.), *Biodiversity Litigation*, Oxford: OUP, 2022.

Fyrnys, Markus, "Expanding Competences by Judicial Lawmaking: The Pilot Judgment Procedure of the European Court of Human Rights", *German Law Journal* 12(5), 2011, pp. 1231-1260.

García Ramírez, Sergio, "Los sujetos vulnerables en la jurisprudencia 'transformadora' de la Corte Interamericana de Derechos Humanos", *Revista Mexicana de Derecho Constitucional* 41, 2019, pp. 4-34.

García-Sayán, Diego, "The Inter-American Court and Constitutionalism in Latin America", *Texas Law Review* 89(7), 2011, pp. 1835-1862.

Gardbaum, Stephen, "Human Rights as International Constitutional Rights", *European Journal of International Law* 19(4), 2008, pp. 749–768.

Gargarella, Roberto, "Democracy and Rights in Gelman v. Uruguay", *AJIL Unbound* 109, 2015, pp. 115-119.

Gargarella, Roberto, *Law as a Conversation Among Equals*, Cambridge: CUP, 2022.

Garlicki, Lech, "Broniowski and After: On the Dual Nature of 'Pilot Judgments'", in Lucius Caflisch *et al.* (eds.), *Human Rights – Strasbourg Views. Liber Amicorum Luzius Wildhaber*, Kehl am Rhein: Engel Verlag, 2007, pp. 177-192.

Gathii, James Thuo and Mwangi, Jacquelene Wangui, "The African Court on Human and Peoples' Rights as an Opportunity Structure", in James Thuo Gathii (ed.), *The Performance of Africa's International Courts: Using Litigation for Political, Legal, and Social Change*, Oxford: OUP, 2020, pp. 211-253.

Gerards, Janneke, "The Netherlands: Political Dynamics, Institutional Robustness", in Patricia Popelier *et al.* (eds.), *Criticism of the European Court of Human Rights*, Cambridge: Intersentia, 2016, pp. 327-360.

Gerards, Janneke, "Abstract and Concrete Reasonableness Review by the European Court of Human Rights", *European Convention on Human Rights Law Review* 1, 2020, pp. 218-247.

Gilbert, Jérémie, "Indigenous Peoples and Litigation: Strategies for Legal Empowerment", *Journal of Human Rights Practice* 12, 2020, pp. 301–320.

Ginsburg, Tom and Moustafa, Tamir, *Rule by Law: The Politics of Courts in Authoritarian Regimes*, Cambridge: CUP, 2008.

Glas, Lize, "The Functioning of the Pilot-Judgment Procedure of the European Court of Human Rights in Practice", *Netherlands Quarterly of Human Rights* 34(1), 2016, pp. 41-70.

Glas, Lize, "From Interlaken to Copenhagen: What Has Become of the Proposals Aiming to Reform the Functioning of the European Court of Human Rights?", *Human Rights Law Review* 20, 2020, pp. 121 151.

González Domínguez, Pablo, *The Doctrine of Conventionality Control*, Cambridge: Intesentia, 2018.

González Domínguez, Pablo and Pérez, Edward J., "Desafíos de la Jurisprudencia de la Corte Interamericana de Derechos Humanos sobre Leyes de Amnistía en Contextos de Justicia Transicional", *Persona y Derecho* 80, 2019, pp. 81-106.

González Salzberg, Damián, "Do States comply with the compulsory judgments of the Inter-American Court of Human Rights?", *Revista do Instituto Brasileiro de Direitos Humanos* 13, 2013, pp. 93-114.

Goodin, Robert E., *Innovating Democracy: Democratic Theory and Practice After the Deliberative Turn*, Oxford: OUP, 2008.

Gray, Christine, *Judicial Remedies in International Law*, Oxford: OUP, 1990.

Greer, Steven, "Constitutionalizing Adjudication under the European Convention on Human Rights", *Oxford Journal of Legal Studies* 23(3), 2003, pp. 405-433.

Greer, Steven, *The European Convention on Human Rights: Achievements, Problems and Prospects*, Cambridge: CUP, 2006.

Grote, Rainer, Paris, Davide and Morales, Mariela, "Conclusion: moving beyond compliance without neglecting compliance in international human rights law", in Rainer Grote, Davide Paris and Mariela Morales (eds.), *Research Handbook on Compliance in International Human Rights Law*, Cheltenham: Edward Elgar, 2021, pp. 510-522.

Guarnizo-Peralta, Diana, "Disability rights in the Inter-American System of Human Rights: An expansive and evolving protection", *Netherlands Quarterly of Human Rights* 36(1), 2018, pp. 43-63.

Habermas, Jürgen, *Structural Transformation of the Public Sphere*, Cambridge, MA: MIT Press, 1989.

Habermas, Jürgen, *Between Facts and Norms*, Cambridge, MA: MIT Press, 1996.

Haasdijk, Suzan L., "The Lack of Uniformity in the Terminology of the International Law of Remedies", *Leiden Journal of International Law* 5, 1992, pp. 245-263.

Hafner-Burton, Emilie, Mansfield, Edward D. and Pevehouse, Jon C.W., "Human Rights Institutions, Sovereignty Costs and Democratization", *British Journal of Political Science* 45, 2013, pp. 1-27.

Haglund, Jillienne, "Domestic Politics and the Effectiveness of Regional Human Rights Courts", *International Interactions* 46(4), 2020, pp. 551-578.

Happold, Matthew and Eden, Paul (eds.), *Economic Sanctions and International Law*, Oxford: Hart, 2016.

Hathaway, Oona, "The Cost of Commitment", *Stanford Law Review* 55(5), 2003, pp. 1821-1862.

Hawkins, Darren and Jacoby, Wade, "Partial Compliance. A Comparison of the European and the Inter-American Court of Human Rights", *Journal of International Law and International Relations* 6(1), 2010, pp. 35-85.

Heikkilà, Mikaela and Mustaniemi-Laakso, Maija, "Vulnerability as a human rights variable: African and European developments", *African Human Rights Law Journal* 20, 2020, p. 777-798.

Helfer, Laurence, "Overlegalizing Human Rights: International Relations Theory and the Commonwealth Caribbean Backlash Against Human Rights Regimes", *Columbia Law Review* 102, 2002, pp. 1832-1911.

Helfer, Laurence, "Redesigning the European Court of Human Rights: Embeddedness as a Deep Structural Principle of the European Human Rights Regime", *European Journal of International Law* 19(1), 2008, pp. 125-159.

Helfer, Laurence and Voeten, Erik, "International Courts as Agents of Legal Change: Evidence from LGBT Rights in Europe", *International Organization* 68(1), 2014, pp. 77-110.

Helfer, Laurence and Voeten, Erik, "Walking Back Human Rights in Europe?", *European Journal of International Law* 31(3), 2020, pp. 797–827.

Heri, Corina, *Responsive Human Rights: Vulnerability, Ill-treatment and the ECtHR*, Oxford: Hart, 2021.

Henn, Elisabeth Veronika, *International Human Rights Law and Structural Discrimination*, Berlin: Springer, 2021.

Hennebel, Ludovic and Tigroudja, Hélène, *The American Convention on Human Rights: A Commentary*, Oxford: OUP, 2022.

Higgins, Rosalyn, "The International Court of Justice: Selected Issues of State Responsibility", in Maurizio Ragazzi (ed.), *International Responsibility Today*, Leiden: Matrinus Nijhoff, 2005, pp. 271–286.

Higgins, Rosalyn, *Themes and Theories: selected essays, speeches and writings in international law*, Oxford: OUP, 2009.

Hillebrecht, Courtney, *Domestic Politics and International Human Rights Tribunals: The Problem of Compliance*, Cambridge: CUP, 2014.

Hillebrecht, Courtney, *Saving the International Justice Regime: Beyond Backlash against International Courts*, Cambridge: CUP, 2021.

Hodson, Loveday, *NGOs and the Struggle for Human Rights in Europe*, Oxford: Hart, 2011.

Huneeus, "Courts Resisting Courts: Lessons from the Inter-American Court's Struggle to Enforce Human Rights", *Cornell International Law Journal* 44(3), 2011, pp. 493-533.

Huneeus, Alexandra, "Reforming the State from Afar: Structural Reform Litigation at the Human Rights Courts", *Yale Journal of International Law* 40(1), 2015, pp. 1-40.

Huneeus, Alexandra and Urueña, René, "Treaty Exit and Latin America's Constitutional Courts", *AJIL Unbound* 111, 2017, pp. 456-460.

Huneeus, Alexandra and Madsen, Mikael Rask "Between universalism and regional law and politics: A comparative history of the American, European, and African human rights systems", *International Journal of Constitutional Law* 16(1), 2018, pp. 136–160

Hunt, Murray, "Enhancing Parliaments' Role in the Protection and Realisation of Human Rights", in Murray Hunt, Hayley Hooper and Paul Yowell (eds.), *Parliaments and Human Rights: Redressing the Democratic Deficit*, London: Bloomsbury, 2015, pp. 469-484.

Ichim, *Just Satisfaction under the European Convention on Human Rights*, Cambridge: CUP, 2014.

Iglesias, Marisa, "Subsidiarity, margin of appreciation and international adjudication within a cooperative conception of human rights", *International Journal of Constitutional Law* 15(2), 2017, pp. 393–413.

Jackson, Miles, "Amnesties in Strasbourg", *Oxford Journal of Legal Studies* 38(3), 2018, pp. 451–474.

Jahn, Jannika, "Ruling (In)directly through Individual Measures? Effect and Legitimacy of the ECtHR's New Remedial Power", *Zeitschrift für ausländisches öffentliches Recht und Völkerrecht* 74, 2014, pp. 1-40.

Jennings, Robert, "The LaGrand Case", *Law and Practice of International Courts and Tribunals* 1(1), 2002, pp. 13-54.

Jones, Anthony, "Form over Substance: The African Court's restrictive approach to NGO standing in the SERAP Advisory Opinion", *African Human Rights Law Journal* 17(1), 2017, pp. 320-328.

Kaaba, O'Brien, "The Challenges of Adjudicating Presidential Election Disputes in Domestic Courts in Africa", *African Human Rights Law Journal* 15(2), 2015, pp. 329-354.

Kamminga, Menno T., "Impact on State Succession in Respect of Treaties", in Menno T. Kamminga and Martin Scheinin (eds.), *The Impact of Human Rights Law on General International Law*, Oxford: OUP, 2009, pp. 99-109.

Katona, Nóra, "Article 4. Obligation to Criminalize Torture", in Manfred Nowak *et al.* (eds.), *The United Nations Convention Against Torture and its Optional Protocol. A Commentary*, 2nd ed., Oxford: OUP, 2019, pp. 176-193.

Keller, Helen and Stone Sweet, Alec (eds.), *A Europe of Rights: The Impact of the ECHR on National Legal Systems,* Oxford: OUP, 2008.

Keller, Helen and Marti, Cedric, "Reconceptualizing Implementation: The Judicialization of the Execution of the European Court of Human Rights Judgments", *European Journal of International Law* 26(4), 2016, pp. 829-850.

Keller, Helen and Kühne, Daniela, "Zur Verfassungsgerichtsbarkeit des Europäischen Gerichtshofs für Menschenrechte", *Zeitschrift für ausländisches öffentliches Recht und Völkerrecht* 76, 2016, pp. 245-307.

Kelsen, Hans, "La garantie jurisdictionnelle de la Constitution (la Justice constitutionnelle)", *Revue du Droit Public et de la Science Politique en France et à l'étranger* 45, 1928, pp. 197-257.

Kjeldgaard-Pedersen, Astrid, "Global Constitutionalism and the International Legal Personality of the Individual", *Netherlands International Law Review* 66, 2019, pp. 271–286.

Kioko, Ben, "Perspective from the African Court on Human and Peoples' Rights", *Journal of Human Rights Practice* 12, 2020, pp. 163–170.

Klabbers, Jan, Peters, Anne and Ulfstein, Geir (eds.), *The Constitutionalization of International Law*, Oxford: OUP, 2009.

Klare, Karl E., "Legal Culture and Transformative Constitutionalism", *South African Journal of Human Rights* 14, 1998, pp. 146-188.

Kleinlein, Thomas, "The Procedural Approach of the European Court of Human Rights: Between Subsidiarity and Dynamic Evolution", *International and Comparative Law Quarterly* 68(1), 2019, pp. 91-110.

Koivurova, Timo, "Jurisprudence of the European Court of Human Rights Regarding Indigenous Peoples: Retrospect and Prospects", *International Journal on Minority and Group Rights* 18, 2011, pp. 1–37.

Kolb, Robert, *The International Court of Justice*, Oxford: Hart, 2013.

Kolb, Robert, *The International Law of State Responsibility*, Cheltenham: Edward Elgar, 2017.

Koskenniemi, Martti and Leino, Päivi, "Fragmentation of International Law? Postmodern Anxieties", *Leiden Journal of International Law* 15(3), 2002, pp. 553-579.

Kovacs, Peter, "Indigenous Issues under the European Convention of Human Rights, Reflected in an Inter-American Mirror", *George Washington International Law Review* 48, 2016, pp. 781-806.

Kunz, Raffaela, "Judging International Judgments Anew? The Human Rights Courts before Domestic Courts", *European Journal of International Law* 30(4), 2019, pp. 1129–1163.

Kunz, Raffaela, *Richter über internationale Gerichte? Die Rolle innerstaatlicher Gerichte bei der Umsetzung der Entscheidungen von EGMR und IAGMR*, Heidelberg: Springer, 2020.

Kunz, Raffaela, "Securing the survival of the system: the legal and institutional architecture to supervise compliance with the ECtHR's judgments", in Rainer Grote, Mariela Morales and Davide Paris (eds.), *Research Handbook on Compliance in International Human Rights Law*, Cheltenham: Edward Elgar, 2021, pp. 12-41.

Laakso, Liisa, "Electoral Violence and Political Competition in Africa", in Nic Cheeseman (ed.), *The Oxford Encyclopedia of African Politics*, Oxford: OUP, 2019, pp. 552-563.

Lambert, Edouard, *Le Gouvernement des juges et la lutte contre la législation sociale aux États-Unis*, Paris: Giard et Cie, 1921.

Lambert Abdelgawad, Elisabeth and Martin-Chenut, Kathia (eds.), *Réparer les Violations Graves et Massives des Droits de l'Homme: La Cour Interaméricaine, Pionnière et Modèle?*, Paris: Société de Législation Comparée, 2010.

Lambrecht, Sarah, "Reforms to Lessen the Influence of the European Court of Human Rights: A Successful Strategy?", *European Public Law* 21(2), 2015, pp. 257-284.

Lambrecht, Sarah, "Assessing the Existence of Criticism of the European Court of Human Rights", in Patricia Popelier *et al.* (eds.), *Criticism of the European Court of Human Rights*, Cambridge: Intersentia, 2016, pp. 505-555.

Land, Molly K., "Justice as Legitimacy in the European Court of Human Rights", in Nienke Grossman *et al.* (eds.), *Legitimacy and International Courts*, Cambridge: CUP, 2018, pp. 83-113.

Laplante, Lisa, "Bringing effective remedies home: the inter-American human rights system, reparations, and the duty of prevention", *Netherlands Quarterly of Human Rights* 22(3), 2004, pp. 347-388.

Lauterpacht, Hersch, *The Development of International Law by the International Court*, London: Stevens and Sons Limited, 1958.

Lavrysen, Laurens, "Protection by the Law: The Positive Obligation to Develop a Legal Framework to Adequately Protect ECHR Rights", in Yves Haeck and Eva Brems (eds.), *Human Rights and Civil Liberties in the 21st Century*, Dordrecht: Springer, 2014, pp. 69-130.

Lavrysen, Laurens and Mavronicola, Natasa (eds.), *Coercive Human Rights: Positive Duties to Mobilise the Criminal Law under the ECHR*, London: Bloomsbury, 2020.

Leach, Philip, "No longer offering fine mantras to a parched child? The European Court's developing approach to remedies", in Andreas Føllesdal, Birgit Peters and Geir Ulfstein (eds.), *Constituting Europe: The European Court of Human Rights in a National, European and Global Context*, Cambridge: CUP, 2013, pp. 142-180.

Leach, Philip, Hardman, Helen and Stephenson, Svetlana, "Can the European Court's Pilot Judgment Procedure Help Resolve Systemic Human Rights Violations? Burdov and the Failure to Implement Domestic Court Decisions in Russia", *Human Rights Law Review* 10(2), 2010, pp. 346-359.

Leach, Philip *et al.*, *Responding to Systemic Human Rights Violations: An Analysis of 'Pilot Judgments' of the European Court of Human Rights and their Impact at National Level*, Cambridge: Intersentia, 2010.

Leckey, Robert, "The Harms of Remedial Discretion", *International Journal of Constitutional Law* 14(3), 2016, pp. 584–607.

Legg, Andrew, *The Margin of Appreciation in International Human Rights Law: Deference and Proportionality*, Oxford: OUP, 2012.

Lemmens, Koen, "Criticising the European Court of Human Rights or Misunderstanding the Dynamics of Human Rights Protection?", in Patricia Popelier *et al.* (eds.), *Criticism of the European Court of Human Rights*, Cambridge: Intersentia, 2016, pp. 13-40.

Lindquist, Stefanie A. and Cross, Frank B., *Measuring Judicial Activism*, Oxford: OUP, 2009.

Lovat, Henry and Shany, Yuval, "The European Court of Human Rights", in Yuval Shany (ed.), *Assessing the Effectiveness of International Courts*, Oxford: OUP, 2014, pp. 253–276.

Madsen, Mikael Rask, "The Challenging Authority of the European Court of Human Rights: From Cold War Legal Diplomacy to The Brighton Declaration and Backlash", *Law and Contemporary Problems* 79, 2016, pp. 141-178.

Madsen, Mikael Rask, "Rebalancing European Human Rights: Has the Brighton Declaration Engendered a New Deal on Human Rights in Europe?", *Journal of International Dispute Settlement* 9, 2018, pp. 199-222.

Madsen, Mikael Rask, Cebulak, Pola and Wiebusch, Micha, "Backlash Against International Courts: Explaining the Forms and Patterns of Resistance to International Courts", *International Journal of Law in Context* 14(2), 2018, pp. 197-220.

Madsen, Mikael Rask, "Two-level politics and the backlash against international courts: Evidence from the politicisation of the European court of human rights", *British Journal of Politics and International Relations* 22(4), 2020, pp. 728–738.

Madsen, Mikael Rask, "From boom to backlash? The European Court of Human Rights and the transformation of Europe", in Helmut Philipp Aust and Esra Demir-Gürsel (eds.), *The European Court of Human Rights: Current Challenges in Historical Perspective*, Cheltenham: Edward Elgar, 2021, pp. 21-42.

Malarino, Ezequiel, "Judicial Activism, Punitivism and Supranationalisation: Illiberal and Antidemocratic Tendencies of the Inter-American Court of Human Rights", *International Criminal Law Review* 12, 2012, pp. 665-695.

Mallinder, Louise, "Can Amnesties and International Justice be Reconciled?", *International Journal of Transitional Justice* 1, 2007, pp. 208–230.

Mallinder, Louise, "The end of amnesty or regional overreach? Interpreting the erosion of South America's amnesty laws", *International and Comparative Law Quarterly* 65(3), 2016, pp. 645-680.

Matibag, Eugenio and Downing-Matibag, Teresa, "Sovereignty and Social Justice: The 'Haitian Problem' in the Dominican Republic", *Caribbean Quarterly* 57(2), 2011, pp. 92-117.

Matta, Aaron and Mazmanyan, Armen, "Russia: In Quest for a European Identity", in Patricia Popelier *et al.* (eds.), *Criticism of the European Court of Human Rights*, Cambridge: Intersentia, 2016, pp. 481-504.

Martin, Lisa L., "Against Compliance", in Jeffrey Dunoff and Mark Pollack (eds.), *Interdisciplinary Perspectives on International Law and International Relations*, Cambridge: CUP, 2013, pp. 591-612.

Mbori, Harrisson, "Ingabire Victoire Umuhoza vs. Rwanda", *American Journal of International Law* 112(4), 2018, pp. 713-719.

Maučec, Gregor and Dothan, Shai, "The effects of international judges' personal characteristics on their judging", *Leiden Journal of International Law* 35(4), 2022, pp. 887-895.

May, James R. and Daly, Erin, "Human rights developments in global environmental constitutionalism", in James R. May and Erin Daly (eds.), *Human rights and the environment: legality, indivisibility, dignity and geography*, Cheltenham: Edward Elgar, 2019, pp. 93–109.

Mälksoo, Lauri and Benedek, Wolfgang (eds.), *Russia and the European Court of Human Rights: The Strasbourg Effect*, Cambridge: CUP, 2017.

McCarthy, Conor, "Reparation for Gross Violations of Human Rights Law and International Humanitarian Law at the International Court of Justice", in Carla Ferstman and Mariana Goetz (eds.), *Reparations for Victims of Genocide, Crimes against Humanity and War Crimes: Systems in Place and Systems in the Making*, Leiden: Brill Nijhoff, 2009, pp. 350–378.

McCorquodale, Robert, "Impact on State Responsibility", in Menno T. Kamminga and Martin Scheinin (eds.), *The Impact of Human Rights Law on General International Law*, Oxford: OUP, 2009, pp. 235-254.

McGinnis, John O. and Movsesian, Mark L., "The World Trade Constitution", *Harvard Law Review* 114, 2000, pp. 511–605.

McIntyre, Juliette, "The Declaratory Judgment in Recent Jurisprudence of the ICJ: Conflicting Approaches to State Responsibility?", *Leiden Journal of International Law* 29(1), 2016, pp. 177–195.

van der Mei, Anne Pieter, "The Advisory Jurisdiction of the African Court on Human and Peoples' Rights", *African Human Rights Law Journal* 5(1), 2005, pp. 27-46.

Micus, Annelen, *The Inter-American human rights system as a safeguard for justice in national transitions: from amnesty laws to accountability in Argentina, Chile and Peru*, Leiden: Brill Nijhoff, 2015.

Milano, Enrico, "Diplomatic Protection and Human Rights before the International Court of Justice: Re-Fashioning Tradition?", *Netherlands Yearbook of International Law* 35, 2004, pp. 85-142.

Molbæk-Steensig, Helga, "Subsidiarity does not win cases: A mixed methods study of the relationship between margin of appreciation language and deference at the European Court of Human Rights", *Leiden Journal of International Law* 36(1), 2023, pp. 83-107.

Morawa, Alexander H. E., "Vulnerability as a Concept of International Human Rights Law", *Journal of International Relations and Development* 6, 2003, pp. 139-155.

Motoc, Iulia and Ziemele, Ineta (eds.), *The Impact of the ECHR on Democratic Change in Central and Eastern Europe: Judicial Perspectives*, Cambridge: CUP, 2016.

Mowbray, Alstair, *The Development of Positive Obligations under the European Convention on Human Rights by the European Court of Human Rights*, Oxford: Hart, 2004.

Mowbray, Alastair, "The Interlaken Declaration - The Beginning of a New Era for the European Court of Human Rights?", *Human Rights Law Review* 10(3), 2010, pp. 519-528.

Mowbray, Alastair, "An Examination of the European Court of Human Rights' Indication of Remedial Measures", *Human Rights Law Review* 17, 2017, pp. 451-478.

Moya, David and Milios, Georgios (eds.), *Aliens before the European Court of Human Rights*, Leiden: Brill Nijhoff, 2021.

Muhindo Makunya, Trésor, "Decisions of the African Court on Human and Peoples' Rights during 2020: Trends and Lessons", *African Human Rights Law Journal* 21(2), 2021, pp. 1230-1264.

Mujezinovic Larsen, Kjetil "Compliance with Judgments from the European Court of Human Rights: The Court's Call for Legislative Reforms", *Nordic Journal of Human Rights* 31(4), 2013, pp. 496-512.

Mujuzi, Jamil Ddamulira, "The African Court on Human and Peoples' Rights and its Protection of the Right to a Fair Trial", *The Law and Practice of International Courts and Tribunals* 16, 2017, pp. 187–223.

Murray, Rachel, *The African Charter on Human and Peoples' Rights: A Commentary*, Oxford: OUP, 2019.

Murray, Rachel and Sandoval, Clara, "Balancing Specificity of Reparation Measures and States' Discretion", *Journal of Human Rights Practice* 12(1), 2020, pp. 101-124.

Mutangi, Tarisai "Enforcing Compliance with the Judgments of the African Court on Human and Peoples' Rights: Prospects and Challenges", in Aderomola Adeola (ed.), *Compliance with International Human Rights Law in Africa: Essays in Honour of Frans Viljoen*, Oxford: OUP, 2022, pp. 183-231.

Müller, Amrei, "Domestic authorities' obligations to co-develop the rights under the European Convention on Human Rights", *International Journal of Human Rights* 20(8), 2016, pp. 1058-1076.

Nash, Kate, "Human Rights, Global Justice, and the Limits of Law", in Bardo Fassbender and Knut Traisbach (eds.), *The Limits of Human Rights*, Oxford, OUP, 2019, pp. 69-80.

Negishi, Yota, "The *Pro Homine* Principle's Role in Regulating the Relationship between Conventionality Control and Constitutionality Control", *European Journal of International Law* 28(2), 2017, pp. 457–481.

Negishi, Yota, *Conventionality Control of Domestic Law*, Baden-Baden: Nomos, 2022.

Neuman, Gerald L., "Import, Export and Regional Consent in the Inter-American Court of Human Rights", *European Journal of International Law* 19(1), 2008, pp. 101–123.

Neuman, Gerald L., "Bi-Level Remedies for Human Rights Violations", *Harvard International Law Journal* 55(2), 2014, pp. 323-360.

Nifosi-Sutton, Ingrid, *The Protection of Vulnerable Groups under International Human Rights Law*, Abingdon: Routledge, 2017.

Nolan, Aoife and Kilkelly, Ursula, "Children's Rights under Regional Human Rights Law - A Tale of Harmonisation?", in Carla M. Buckley *et al.* (eds.), *Towards Convergence in International Human Rights Law*, Leiden: Brill Nijhoff, 2016, pp. 296-322.

Nollkaemper, André, "Constitutionalization and the Unity of the Law of International Responsibility", *Indiana Journal of Global Legal Studies* 16(2), 2009, pp. 535–563.

Nonnenmacher, Sophie and Cholewinski, Ryszard, "The nexus between statelessness and migration", in Alice Edwards and Laura van Waas (eds.), *Nationality and Statelessness under International Law*, Cambridge: CUP, 2014, pp. 247-263.

Novak, Andrew, "The 'Judicial Dialogue' in Transnational Human Rights Litigation: Muruatetu & Anor v. Republic and the Abolition of the Mandatory Death Penalty in Kenya", *Human Rights Law Review* 18, 2018, pp. 771–790.

Novak, Fabian, "The System of Reparations in the jurisprudence of the Inter-American Court of Human Rights", *The Hague Academy of International Law: Recueil des Cours* 392, 2017, pp. 9-203.

Nowak, Manfred, *UN Covenant on Civil and Political Rights - CCPR Commentary*, 2nd ed., Kehl am Rhein: N.P. Engel Publishers, 2005.

Nußberger, Angelika, "From High Hopes to Scepticism? Human Rights Protection and Rule of Law in Europe in an Ever More Hostile Environment", in Heike Krieger, Georg Nolte and Andreas Zimmermann (eds.), *The International Rule of Law: Rise or Decline?,* Oxford: OUP, 2019, pp. 150-171.

O'Mahony, Conor, "Child Protection and the ECHR: Making Sense of Positive and Procedural Obligations", *International Journal of Children's Rights* 27, 2019, pp. 660-693.

Olinga, Alain Didier, "La première décision au fond de la Cour africaine des droits de l'homme et des peoples", *Revue des droits de l'homme* 6, 2014, pp. 1-23.

Oosterlink, Kim, "Reparations", in Steven N. Durlauf and Lawrence E. Blume (eds.), *The New Palgrave Dictionary of Economics*, 2nd ed., London: Palgrave Macmillan, 2008.

Owen, David, "On the Right to Have Nationality Rights: Statelessness, Citizenship and Human Rights", *Netherlands International Law Review* 65, 2018, pp. 299–317.

Özersay, Kudret and Gürel, Ayla, "Property and Human Rights in Cyprus: The European Court of Human Rights as a Platform of Political Struggle", *Middle Eastern Studies* 44(2), 2008, pp. 291-321.

Paraskeva, Costas, "Returning the Protection of Human Rights to Where They Belong, At Home", *International Journal of Human Rights* 12(3), 2008, p. 415-448.

Paraskeva, Costas, "European Court of Human Rights: From declaratory judgments to indications of specific measures", *European Human Rights Law Review* 1, 2018, pp. 46-56.

Paris, Davide, "Allies and Counterbalances - Constitutional Courts and the European Court of Human Rights: A Comparative Perspective", *Zeitschrift fur auslandisches öffentliches Recht und Völkerrecht* 77, 2017, pp. 623-649.

Parra-Vera, Oscar, "Institutional Empowerment and Progressive Policy Reforms: The Impact of the Inter-American Human Rights System on Intra-State Conflicts", in Par Engstrom (ed.), *The Inter-American System: Impact Beyond Compliance*, Cham: Palgrave Macmillan, 2019, pp. 143-166.

Pasqualucci, Jo M, *The Practice and Procedure of the Inter-American Court of Human Rights*, Cambridge: CUP, 2003.

Pasqualucci, Jo M., "Criminal Defamation and the Evolution of the Doctrine of Freedom of Expression in International Law: Comparative Jurisprudence of the Inter-American Court of Human Rights", *Vanderbilt Journal of Transnational Law* 39, 2006, pp. 379-433.

Pasqualucci, Jo M., *The Practice and Procedure of the Inter-American Court of Human Rights*, 2nd ed., Oxford: OUP, 2012.

Paulson, Robert, "Compliance with Final Judgments of the International Court of Justice Since 1987", *American Journal of International Law* 98(3), 2004, pp. 434-461.

Paulus, Andreas, "From Neglect to Defiance? The United States and International Adjudication", *European Journal of International Law* 15, 2004, pp. 783–812.

Peel, Jacqueline and Osofsky, Hari M., *Climate Change Litigation: Regulatory Pathways to Cleaner Energy*, Cambridge: CUP, 2015.

Pegram, Tom and Herrera Rodriguez, Nataly, "Bridging the Gap: National Human Rights Institutions and the Inter-American Human Rights System", in Par Engstrom (ed.), *The Inter-American System: Impact Beyond Compliance*, Cham: Palgrave Macmillan, 2019, pp. 167-198.

Pellet, Alain, "Some Remarks on the Recent Case Law of the International Court of Justice on Responsibility Issues", in Péter Kovács (ed.), *International Law: A Quiet Strength*, Budapest: Pázmány Press, 2011, pp. 111-134.

Perez-Leon-Acevedo, Juan Pablo, "The control of the Inter-American Court of Human Rights over amnesty laws and other exemption measures: Legitimacy assessment", *Leiden Journal of International Law* 33, 2020, pp. 667–687.

Peters, Anne, "Compensatory Constitutionalism: The Function and Potential of Fundamental International Norms and Structures", *Leiden Journal of International Law* 19(3), 2006, pp. 579-610.

Peters, Anne, "Humanity as the A and Ω of Sovereignty", *European Journal of International Law* 20(3), 2009, pp. 513-544.

Peters, Anne, "Are we Moving towards Constitutionalization of the World Community?", in Antonio Cassesse (ed.), *Realizing Utopia: The Future of International Law*, Oxford: OUP, 2012, pp. 118–135.

Peters, Anne, *Beyond Human Rights - The Legal Status of the Individual in International Law*, Cambridge: CUP, 2016.

Peters, Anne, "Fragmentation and Constitutionalization", in Anne Orford and Florian Hoffmann (eds.), *The Oxford Handbook of the Theory of International Law*, Oxford: OUP, 2016, pp. 1011–1032.

Peters, Anne, "Proportionality as a Global Constitutional Principle", in Anthony F. Lang and Antje Wiener (eds.), *Handbook on Global Constitutionalism*, Cheltenham: Edward Elgar, 2017, pp. 248-264.

Peters, Anne, "Constitutionalisation", in Jean d'Aspermont and Sahib Singh (eds.), *Concepts for International Law - Contributions to Disciplinary Thought*, Cheltenham: Edward Elgar, 2019, pp. 141-153.

Peters, Anne, "The Importance of Having Rights", *Zeitschrift für ausländisches öffentliches Recht und Völkerrecht* 81(1), 2021, pp. 7-22.

Petrov, Jan, "The populist challenge to the European Court of Human Rights", *International Journal of Constitutional Law* 18(2), 2020, pp. 476–508.

Piacentini, Isabela, *La Réparation dans la Jurisprudence de la Cour Interaméricaine des Droits de l'Homme*, Paris: Université Panthéon-Assas, 2013.

Pirker, Benedikt, "Democracy and Distrust in International Law: The Procedural Democracy Doctrine and the Standard of Review Used by International Courts and Tribunals", in Lukasz Gruszczynski and Wouter Werner (eds.) *Deference in International Courts and Tribunals*, Oxford: OUP, 2014, pp. 58–73.

Plagis, Misha Ariana, "The Makings of Remedies: The (R)Evolution of the African Court on Human and Peoples' Rights' Remedies Regime in Fair Trial Cases", *African Journal of International and Comparative Law* 28, 2020, pp. 45-71.

Possi, Ally, "It is better that ten guilty persons escape than that one innocent suffer: the African Court on Human and Peoples' Rights and fair trial rights in Tanzania", *African Human Rights Yearbook* 1, 2017, pp. 311-336.

Popelier, Patricia, Lambrecht, Sarah and Lemmens, Koen, (eds.), *Criticism of the European Court of Human Rights*, Cambridge: Intersentia, 2016.

Popelier, Patricia, Lambrecht, Sarah and Lemmens, Koen, "Introduction", in Patricia Popelier *et al.* (eds.), *Criticism of the European Court of Human Rights*, Cambridge: Intersentia, 2016, pp. 3-22.

Powderly, Joseph, "International criminal justice in an age of perpetual crisis", *Leiden Journal of International Law* 32(1), 2019, pp. 1-11.

Praduroux, Sabrina, "Property and Expropriation: Two Concepts Revisited in the Light of the Case Law of the European Court of Human Rights and the European Court of Justice", *European Property Law Journal* 8(2), 2019, pp. 172–191.

Pulkowski, Dirk, "Testing Compliance Theories: Towards the United States Obedience of International Law in the Avena Case", *Leiden Journal of International Law* 19(2), 2006, pp. 511–554.

Quintana, Juan José, *Litigation at the International Court of Justice*, Leiden: Brill Nijhoff, 2015.

Rachovitsa, Adamantia, "On New 'Judicial Animals': The Curious Case of an African Court with Material Jurisdiction of a Global Scope", *Human Rights Law Review* 19(2), 2019, pp. 255–289.

Radacic, Ivana, "Gender Equality Jurisprudence of the European Court of Human Rights", *European Journal of International Law* 19(4), 2008, pp. 841-857.

Raday, Frances, "Article 11", in Marsha A. Freeman *et al.* (eds.), *The UN Convention on the Elimination of All Forms of Discrimination Against Women: A Commentary*, Oxford: OUP, 2012, pp. 279- 310.

Raustiala Kal and Slaughter, Anne-Marie, "International Law, International Relations and Compliance", in Walter Carlsnaes, Thomas Risse and Beth A. Simmons (eds.), *Handbook of International Relations*, London: SAGE Publications, 2009, pp. 538-558.

Rawls, John, *A Theory of Justice - Revised Edition*, Oxford: OUP, 1999.

Reiertsen, Michael, "Norway: New Constitutionalism, New Counter-Dynamics?", in Particia Popelier *et al.* (eds.), *Criticism of the European Court of Human Rights*, Cambridge: Intersentia, 2016, pp. 361-384.

Reiertsen, Michael, *Effective Domestic Remedies and the European Court of Human Rights: Applications of the European Convention on Human Rights Article 13*, Cambridge: CUP, 2022.

Roach, Kent, "Dialogic Remedies", *International Journal of Constitutional Law* 17(3), 2019, pp. 860–883.

Roberts, Anthea *et al.*, "Comparative International Law: Framing the Field", *American Journal of International Law* 109, 2015, pp. 467-474.

Rodríguez-Garavito, César, "Beyond Enforcement: Assessing and Enhancing Judicial Impact", in Malcolm Langford, César Rodríguez-Garavito and Julieta Rossi (eds.), *Social Rights Judgments and the Politics of Compliance: Making It Stick*, Cambridge: CUP, 2017, pp. 79–108.

Rodríguez-Garavito, César and Baquero-Díaz, Carlos Andrés, "Reframing Indigenous Rights: The Right to Consultation and the Rights of Nature and Future Generations in the Sarayaku Legal Mobilization", in Gráinne de Búrca (ed.), *Legal Mobilization for Human Rights*, Oxford: OUP, 2022, pp. 73-88.

Rodríguez Garavito, César (ed.), *Litigating the Climate Emergency: How Human Rights, Courts, and Legal Mobilization Can Bolster Climate Action*, Cambridge: CUP, 2022.

Rösch, Ricarda, "Indigenousness and peoples' rights in the African human rights system: situating the Ogiek judgement of the African Court on Human and Peoples' Rights", *Verfassung und Recht in Übersee* 50(3), 2017, pp. 242-258.

Rui, Jon Petter, "The Interlaken, Izmir and Brighton Declarations: Towards a Paradigm Shift in the Strasbourg Court's Interpretation of the European Convention of Human Rights?", *Nordic Journal of Human Rights* 31(1), 2013, pp. 28-54.

Sadurski, Wojciech, "Partnering with Strasbourg: Constitutionalisation of the European Court of Human Rights, the Accession of Central and East European States to the Council of Europe, and the Idea of Pilot Judgments", *Human Rights Law Review* 9(3), 2009, pp. 397-453.

Sadurski, Wojciech, *Constitutionalism and the Enlargement of Europe*, Oxford: OUP, 2012.

Sadurski Wojciech, "Quasi-constitutional Court of Human Rights for Europe?", *Global Constitutionalism* 10(1), 2021, pp. 175-185.

Sánchez de Miquel, Lucas, "Supervisión de la Ejecución de Sentencias: Un Análisis Comparado de los Sistemas Europeo e Interamericano de Derechos Humanos", *Anuario de Derecho Constitucional Latinoamericano* 24, 2018, pp. 275-309.

Sandholtz, Wayne, "Human rights courts and global constitutionalism: Coordination through judicial dialogue", *Global Constitutionalism* 10(3), 2021, pp. 439-464.

Sandoval, Clara, "The Concepts of 'Injured Party' and 'Victim' of Gross Human Rights Violations in The Jurisprudence of the Inter-American Court of Human Rights: A Commentary on their Implications for Reparations", in Carla Ferstman and Mariana Goetz (eds.), *Reparations for Victims of Genocide, War Crimes and Crimes against Humanity*, Leiden: Brill Nijhoff, 2009, pp. 243–282.

Sandoval, Clara, "The Legal Standing and Significance of the Basic Principles and Guidelines on the Right to a Remedy and Reparation", *Zeitschrift für ausländisches öffentliches Recht und Völkerrecht* 78, 2018.

Sathanapally, Aruna, *Beyond Disagreement: Open Remedies in Human Rights Adjudication*, Oxford: OUP, 2012.

Saul, Ben, David, Kinley, David and Mowbray, Jacqueline, *The International Covenant on Economic, Social and Cultural Rights: Commentary, Cases, and Materials*, Oxford: OUP, 2014.

Saul, Matthew, "The European Court of Human Rights' Margin of Appreciation and the Processes of National Parliaments", *Human Rights Law Review* 15(4), 2015, pp. 745–774.

Saul, Matthew, "Shaping Legislative Processes from Strasbourg", *European Journal of International Law* 32(1), 2021, pp. 281–308.

Schabas, William A., "The Omission of the Right to Property in the International Covenants", *Hague Yearbook of International Law* 4, 1991, pp. 135-160.

Schabas, William A., *The Abolition of the Death Penalty in International Law*, 3rd ed., Cambridge: CUP, 2003.

Schabas, William A., *The European Convention on Human Rights: A Commentary*, Oxford: OUP, 2015.

Schönsteiner, Judith, "Dissuasive Measures and the 'Society as a Whole': A Working Theory of Reparations in the Inter-American Court of Human Rights", *American University International Law Review* 23(1), 2011, pp. 127-164.

Seatzu, Francesco and Fanni, Simona, "A Comparative Approach to Prisoners' Rights in the European Court of Human Rights and Inter-American Court of Human Rights Jurisprudence", *Denver Journal of International Law and Policy* 44(1), 2015, pp. 21-40.

Seibert-Fohr, Anja, "Domestic Implementation of the International Covenant on Civil and Political Rights", *Max Planck Yearbook of United Nations Law* 5, 2001, pp. 399-472.

Seidl, Johannes, *Meinungsfreiheit in der Rechtssprechungspraxis des Interamerikanischen Gerichtshof für Menschenrechte*, Tübingen: Mohr Siebeck, 2014.

Shaw, Malcolm N., "The International Court of Justice: A Practical Perspective", *International and Comparative Law Quarterly* 46(4), 1997, pp. 831-865.

Shelton, Dinah, "Righting Wrongs: Reparations in the Articles on State Responsibility", *American Journal of International Law* 96(4), 2002, pp. 833-856.

Shelton, Dinah, "Reparations in the Inter-American System", in David Harris and Stephen Livingstone (eds.), *The Inter-American System of Human Rights,* Oxford: OUP, 2004, pp. 151-172.

Shelton, Dinah, "The Jurisprudence of Human Rights Tribunals on Remedies for Human Rights Violations", in Jean-François Flauss (ed.), *International Protection of Human Rights and Victims' Rights*, Bruxelles: Bruylant, 2009, pp. 57-75.

Shelton, Dinah and Huneeus, Alexandra, "In re Direct Action of Unconstitutionality Initiated Against the Declaration of Acceptance of the Jurisdiction of the Inter-American Court of Human Rights", *American Journal of International Law* 109(4), 2015, pp. 866-872.

Shelton, Dinah, *Remedies in International Human Rights Law*, 3rd ed., Oxford: OUP, 2015.

Shelton, Dinah, “Significantly Disadvantaged? Shrinking Access to the European Court of Human Rights” *Human Rights Law Review* 16(2), 2016, pp. 303–322.

Shirlow, Esmé, *Judging at the Interface: Deference to State Decision-Making Authority in International Adjudication*, Cambridge: CUP, 2021.

Sicilianos, Linos Alexander, “The Involvement of the European Court of Human Rights in the Implementation of its Judgments: Recent Developments under Article 46 ECHR”, *Netherlands Quarterly of Human Rights* 32(3), 2014, pp. 235–262.

Simma, Bruno, “From Bilateralism to Community Interests in *International Law*”, *Recueil des Cours de l'Academie de Droit International* 250, 1994, pp. 217-384.

Simmons, Beth, *Mobilizing for Human Rights: International Law in Domestic Politics*, Cambridge: CUP, 2009.

Soley, Ximena, “The Transformative Dimension of the Inter-American Jurisprudence”, in Armin von Bogdandy *et al.* (eds.), *Transformative Constitutionalism in Latin America: Emergence of a New Ius Commune*, Oxford: OUP, 2017, pp. 337-357.

Soley, Ximena and Steininger, Silvia, “Parting ways or lashing back? Withdrawals, backlash and the Inter-American Court of Human Rights”, *International Journal of Law in Context* 14(2), 2018, pp. 237-257.

Soley, Ximena, “The Crucial Role of NGOs in the Inter-American System”, *AJIL Unbound* 113, 2019, pp. 355-359.

Spano, Robert, “Universality or Diversity of Human Rights? Strasbourg in the Age of Subsidiarity,” *Human Rights Law Review* 14, 2014, pp. 487-502.

Staton, Jeffrey and Romero, Alexia, “Rational Remedies: The Role of Opinion Clarity in the Inter-American Human Rights System”, *International Studies Quarterly* 63, 2019, pp. 477–491.

Stein, Eric, “Lawyers, Judges, and the Making of a Transnational Constitution”, *American Journal of International Law* 75, 1981, pp. 1–27.

Stiansen, Øyvind, “Delayed but not Derailed: Legislative Compliance with European Court of Human Rights Judgments”, *International Journal of Human Rights* 23(8), 2019, pp. 1221-1247.

Stiansen, Øyvind and Voeten, Erik, “Backlash and Judicial Restraint: Evidence from the European Court of Human Rights”, *International Studies Quarterly* 64(4), 2020, pp. 770-784.

Stoica, Victor, *Remedies before the International Court of Justice*, Cambridge: CUP, 2021.

Stone Sweet, Alec and Shapiro, Martin, *On Law, Politics, and Judicialization*, Oxford: OUP, 2002.

Stone Sweet, Alec, “Why Europe Rejected American Judicial Review: And Why It May Not Matter”, *Michigan Law Review* 101(8), 2003, pp. 2744-2780.

Stone Sweet, Alec, Sandholtz, Wayne and Andenas, Mads, “The Failure to Destroy the Authority of the European Court of Human Rights: 2010–2018”, *The Law and Practice of International Courts and Tribunals* 21, 2022, pp. 244–277.

Stöckle, Phillip, *Guarantees of Non-Repetition: Die Anordnung struktureller Reformen durch den Inter-Amerikanischen Gerichtshof für Menschenrechte*, Berlin: Duncker & Humblot, 2021.

Tams, Christian J., "Recognizing Guarantees and Assurances of Non Repetition: LaGrand and the Law of State Responsibility", *Yale Journal of International Law* 27, 2002, pp. 441-444.

Taylor, Paul M., *A Commentary on the International Covenant on Civil and Political Rights*, Cambridge: CUP, 2020.

Thornberry, Patrick, *The International Convention on the Elimination of All Forms of Racial Discrimination: A Commentary*, Oxford: OUP, 2016.

Timmer, Alexandra, Baumgärtel, Moritz, Kotzé, Louis and Slingenberg, Lieneke, "The potential and pitfalls of the vulnerability concept for human rights", *Netherlands Quarterly of Human Rights* 39(3), 2021, pp. 189-261.

Tobin, John, "Article 4. A State's General Obligation of Implementation", in John Tobin (ed.) *The UN Convention on the Rights of the Child: A Commentary*, Oxford: OUP, 2019, pp. 108-158.

Tolley, Michael C., "Judicialization of Politics in Europe: Keeping Pace with Strasbourg", *Journal of Human Rights* 11(1), 2012, pp. 66-84.

Tomuschat, Christian, "Reparation for Victims of Grave Human Rights Violations", *Tulane Journal of International and Comparative Law* 10, 2002, pp. 157-184.

Tomuschat, Christian, "Article 36", in Andreas Zimmermann *et al.* (eds.), *The Statute of the International Court of Justice: A Commentary*, 3rd ed., Oxford: OUP, 2019, pp. 712-798.

Toro Sánchez, Kevin, "The right to reparations in the contentious process before the African Court on Human and Peoples' Rights: A comparative analysis on account of the revised Rules of Court", *African Human Rights Law Journal* 21, 2021, pp. 812-835.

Torres Zuñiga, Natalia, "Control dc Normas Constitucionales por la Corte Interamericana de Derechos Humanos", in Pablo Santolaya and Isabel Wences (eds.), *La América de los Derechos*, Madrid: CEPC, 2016, pp. 483-507.

Tushnet, Mark, "Alternative Forms of Judicial Review", *Michigan Law Review* 101, 2003, pp. 2781-2802.

Tushnet, Mark, "Judicial Review of Legislation", in Mark Tushnet and Peter Cane (eds.), *The Oxford Handbook of Legal Studies*, Oxford: OUP, 2005, pp. 164–182.

Udombana, Nsongurua J., "Between Promise and Performance: Revisiting States' Obligations under the African Human Rights Charter", *Stanford Journal of International Law* 40, 2004, pp. 105-142.

Ulfstein, Geir, "Transnational Constitutional Aspects of the European Court of Human Rights", *Global Constitutionalism* 10(1), 2021, pp. 151-174.

Uribe Sanabria, Camila and Restrepo Ortiz, Natalia, "Could the Inter-American Human Rights System have prevented the Existence of False Victims in the Mapiripán Case?", *Revista Colombiana de Derecho Internacional* 23, 2013, pp. 203-234.

Urueña, René, "Double or Nothing? The Inter-American Court of Human Rights in an Increasingly Adverse Context", *Wisconsin International Law Journal* 35(2), 2018, pp. 398-425.

Urueña, René, "The Democracy We Want: Standards of Review and Democratic Embeddedness at the Inter-American Court of Human Rights", in Hélène Ruiz Fabri *et al.* (eds.), *International Judicial Legitimacy*, Baden-Baden: Nomos, 2020, pp. 227-248.

Uwazuruike, Allwell, *Human Rights under the African Charter*, Cham: Palgrave Macmillan, 2020.

Vanneste, Frédéric, *General International Law Before Human Rights Courts*, Cambridge: Intersentia, 2010.

Vasel, Johann Justus, *Regionaler Menschenrechtsschutz als Emanzipationsprozess*, Berlin: Duncker and Humblot, 2017.

Viljoen, Frans, "Understanding and Overcoming Challenges in Accessing the African Court on Human and Peoples' Rights", *International and Comparative Law Quarterly* 67, 2018, pp. 63-98.

Viljoen, Frans, "Impact in the African and Inter-American Human Rights Systems: A Perspective on the Possibilities and Challenges of Cross-Regional Comparison", in Par Engstrom (ed.), *The Inter-American System: Impact Beyond Compliance*, Cham: Palgrave Macmillan, 2019, pp. 303-326.

von Staden, Andreas, "The democratic legitimacy of judicial review beyond the state: Normative subsidiarity and judicial standards of review", *International Journal of Constitutional Law* 10(4), 2012, pp. 1023–1049.

von Staden, Andreas, *Strategies of Compliance with the European Court of Human Rights*, Philadelphia: University of Pennsylvania Press, 2018.

Waldron, Jeremy, "A Right-Based Critique of Constitutional Rights", *Oxford Journal of Legal Studies* 13(1), 1993, pp. 18-51.

Waldron, Jeremy, "The Core Case Against Judicial Review", *Yale Law Journal* 115(6), 2006, pp. 1346-1406.

Waldron, Jeremy, "The Rule of Law and the Role of Courts", *Global Constitutionalism* 10(1), 2021, pp. 91–105.

Wiener, Antje *et al.*, "Global constitutionalism: Human rights, Democracy and the Rule of Law", *Global Constitutionalism* 1(1), 2012, pp. 1-15.

Weiler, Joseph H.H, *The Constitution of Europe*, Cambridge: CUP, 1999.

Wildhaber, Luzius, "A Constitutional Future for the European Court of Human Rights?", *Human Rights Law Journal* 23, 2002, pp. 161-165.

Wildhaber, Luzius and Greer, Steven, "Revisiting the Debate about 'Constitutionalising' the European Court of Human Rights", *Human Rights Law Review* 12(4), 2012, pp. 655-687.

Windridge, Oliver, "Assessing Rwexit: the impact and implications of Rwanda's withdrawal of its article 34(6)-declaration before the African Court on Human and Peoples' Rights", *African Human Rights Yearbook* 2, 2018, pp. 243-258.

Wojtyczek, Krzysztof, "Judicial and Non-Judicial Elements in the Enforcement Mechanism of the European Convention on Human Rights", in Paulo Pinto de Albuquerque and Krzysztof Wojtyczek (eds.), *Judicial Power in a Globalized World*, Berlin: Springer, 2019, pp. 653-672.

Wolfrum, Rüdiger and Kojima, Chie (eds.), *Solidarity: A Structural Principle of International Law*, Heidelberg: Springer, 2010.

Wouters, Jan *et al.*, *International Law: A European Perspective*, Oxford: Hart, 2019.

Xenos, Dimitris, "The human rights of the vulnerable", *International Journal of Human Rights* 13(4), 2009, pp. 591-614.

Xenos, Dimitris, *The Positive Obligations of the State under the European Convention of Human Rights*, Abingdon: Routledge, 2013.

Yahyaoui Krivenko, Ekaterina, *Rethinking Human Rights and Global Constitutionalism: from Inclusion to Belonging*, Cambridge: CUP, 2017.

Yorke, Jon, "Inhuman Punishment and Abolition of the Death Penalty in the Council of Europe", *European Public Law* 16(1), 2010, pp. 77-103.

Yourow, Howard Charles and Stein, Eric, *The Margin of Appreciation Doctrine in the Dynamics of European Human Rights Jurisprudence*, Leiden: Brill Nijhoff, 1995.

Zach, Gerrit, "Article 2: Obligation to Prevent Torture", in Manfred Nowak *et al.* (eds.), *The United Nations Convention Against Torture and its Optional Protocol. A Commentary*, 2nd ed., Oxford: OUP, 2019, pp. 72-97.

Zarbiyev, Fuad, "Judicial Activism in International Law—A Conceptual Framework for Analysis", *Journal of International Dispute Settlement* 3(2), 2012, pp. 247-278.

Ziemele, Ineta, "State Succession and Issues of Nationality and Statelessness", in Alice Edwards and Laura van Waas (eds.), *Nationality and Statelessness under International Law*, Cambridge: CUP, 2014, pp. 217-246.

Zimmermann, Nesa, "Legislating for the Vulnerable? Special Duties under the European Convention on Human Rights", *Swiss Review of International and European Law* 25(4), 2015, pp. 539-562.

Zúñiga Reyes, Marcela, "Garantías de no repetición y reformas legislativas", *Revista Derecho del Estado* 46, 2020, pp. 25-55.

BLOGPOSTS AND ENCYCLOPEDIA ENTRIES

Capone, Francesca, "Remedies", in *Max Planck Encyclopedia of Public International Law*, available at: https://opil.ouplaw.com/display/10.1093/law:epil/9780199231690/law9780199231690-e1089.

Da Silva, Nicole, "Individual and NGO Access to the African Court on Human and Peoples' Rights: The Latest Blow from Tanzania", *EJIL: talk!*, 16 December 2019, available at: https://www.ejiltalk.org/individual-and-ngo-access-to-the-african-court-on-human-andpeoples-rights-the-latest-blow-from-tanzania/.

Da Silva, Nicole and Plagis, Misha, "A Court in Crisis: African States' Increasing Resistance to Africa's Human Rights Court", *Opinio Iuris*, 19 May 2020, available at: http://opiniojuris.org/2020/05/19/a-court-in-crisis-african-states-increasing-resistance-toafricas-human-rights-court/.

Davi, Tetevi, "African Court on Human and Peoples' Rights Delivers Landmark Ruling on Women's Rights and the Rights of the Child in Mali", *EJIL: talk*, 27 July 2018, available at: https://www.ejiltalk.org/african-court-on-human-and-peoples-rights-delivers-landmarkruling-on-womens-rights-and-the-rights-of-the-child-in-mali/.

Dupuy, Pierre-Marie and Hoss, Cristina, "The LaGrand Case", in *Max Planck Encyclopedia of Public International Law*, available at: https://opil.ouplaw.com/display/10.1093/law:epil/9780199231690/law-9780199231690-e155.

Huneeus, Alexandra, "Venzuela's Withdrawal from the Inter-American Court", *ICONnect Blog*, 15 October 2012, available at http://www.iconnectblog.com/2012/10/venezuelas-exitfrom-the-inter-american-court/.

Pina-Delgado, José, "Advisory Proceedings: African Court on Human and Peoples' Rights (ACtHPR)", *Max Planck Encyclopedia of International Procedural Law* (MPEiPro), available on: https://opil.ouplaw.com/view/10.1093/law-mpeipro/e3635.013.3635/lawmpeipro-e3635.

Polakiewicz, Jörg, "International Law and Domestic (Municipal) Law, Law and Decisions of International Organizations and Courts", *Max Planck Encyclopedia of Public International Law*, available at: https://opil.ouplaw.com/display/10.1093/law:epil/9780199231690/law9780199231690-e1057.

Wagner, Edith, "Repetitive Cases: European Court of Human Rights (ECtHR)", in *Max Planck Encyclopedia of International Procedural Law*, available at: https://opil.ouplaw.com/display/10.1093/law-mpeipro/e3696.013.3696/law-mpeipro-e3696.

Windridge, Oliver, "Under Attack? Under the Radar? Under-Appreciated? All of the Above? A Time of Reckoning for the African Court on Human and Peoples' Rights", *Opinio Iuris*, 07 Mai 2020, available at: https://opiniojuris.org/2020/05/07/under-attack-under-the-radarunder-appreciated-all-of-the-above-a-time-of-reckoning-for-the-african-court-on-human-andpeoples-rights/.

Zouapet, Apollin Koagne, "'Victim of its commitment ... You, passerby, a tear to the proclaimed virtue': Should the epitaph of the African Court on Human and Peoples' Rights be prepared?", *EJIL: Talk!*, 05 May 2020, available at: https://www.ejiltalk.org/victim-of-itscommitment-you-passerby-a-tear-to-the-proclaimed-virtue-should-the-epitaph-of-the-africancourt-on-human-and-peoples-rights-be-prepared/.

ONLINE RESOURCES

IACtHR, *"Cases Filed by the Monitoring Compliance with Judgment"* [sic], available at: https://www.corteidh.or.cr/casos_en_supervision_por_pais_archivados.cfm?lang=en.

UNCHR, *Emergency Appeal - Venezuela Situation*, available at: https://www.unhcr.org/emergencies/venezuela-situation.

Viljoen, Frans, "The African Court on Human and Peoples' Rights: An Introduction", *UN Audiovisual Library*, available at: https://media.un.org/en/asset/k19/k19bku06w8.

Ministry of Foreign Affairs of Venezuela, *"Notificación de Denuncia"* and "*Fundamentación que sustenta la denuncia de la República Bolivariana de Venezuela de la Convención Americana sobre Derechos Humanos presentada a la Secretaría General de la OEA*", 10 September 2012, available at: https://www.oas.org/dil/esp/Nota_Republica_Bolivariana_de_Venezuela_al_SG_OEA.PDF.

Presidency of the Dominican Republic, *"El Gobierno rechaza la sentencia de la Corte Interamericana de Derechos Humanos"*, 23 October 2014, available at https://presidencia.gob.do/noticias/el-gobierno-dominicano-rechaza-la-sentencia-de-la-corteinteramericana-de-derechos-humanos.

Open Society Justice Initiative, *Strategic Litigation: Impacts and Insights*, 2018, available at: https://www.justiceinitiative.org/publications/strategic-litigation-impacts-insights-globalexperience.

Government of Chile, *Comunicado de prensa Ministerio de Relaciones Exteriores - Ministerio de Justicia y Derechos Humanos sobre Sistema Interamericano de Derechos Humanos*, 23 April 2019, available at: https://minrel.gob.cl/comunicado-de-prensaministerio-de-relaciones-exteriores-ministerio-de/minrel/2019-04-23/105105.html.

Amnesty International, *"Americas: The Inter-American System is Crucial for Guaranteeing Human Rights in the Region"*, 24 April 2019, available at: https://www.amnesty.org/en/latest/news/2019/04/americas-sistema-interamericanofundamental-para-derechos-humanos/.

Maslin Nir, Sarah, "It Was a Robust Democracy. Then the New President Took Power", *The New York Times*, 4 July 2019, available at: https://www.nytimes.com/2019/07/04/world/africa/benin-protests-talon-yayi.html.

Gouvernement de la République du Benin, *Retrait du Bénin de la CADHP - Déclaration du ministre de la Justice et de la Législation*, 28 April 2020, available at : https://www.gouv.bj/actualite/635/retrait-benin-cadhp---declaration-ministre-justicelegislation/.

Presse Côte d'Ivoire, *"La Côte d'Ivoire retire sa déclaration de la Charte africaine des droits de l'Homme et des Peuples (Communiqué)"*, 29 April 2020, available at: https://www.pressecotedivoire.ci/article/5879-la-cote-divoire-retire-sa-declaration-de-lacharte-africaine-des-droits-de-lhomme-et-des-peuples-communique.

List of Sources

A. Treaties

UNGA, *Universal Declaration of Human Rights*, adopted by General Assembly Resolution 217 A(III) of 10 December 1948.

CoE, *European Convention for the Protection of Human Rights and Fundamental Freedoms*, 4 November 1950, entered into force on 3 September 1953.

UN, *Vienna Convention on Consular Relations*, 24 April 1963, entered into force on 19 March 1967.

UNGA, *International Covenant on Civil and Political Rights*, 16 December 1966, entered into force on 23 March 1976, UN Treaty Series 999, p. 171.

UNGA, *International Covenant on Economic, Social and Cultural Rights*, 16 December 1966, entered into force on 3 January 1976, UN Treaty Series 993, p. 3.

UN, *Vienna Convention on the Law of Treaties*, adopted on 23 May 1969, entered into force on 27 January 1980, UN Treaty Series 1155, p. 331.

OAS, *American Convention on Human Rights*, 22 November 1969, entered into force on 18 July 1978.

UNGA, *Convention on the Elimination of All Forms of Discrimination against Women*, 18 December 1979, entered into force on 3 September 1981, UN Treaty Series 1249, p. 13.

OAU, *African Charter on Human and Peoples' Rights ('Banjul Charter')*, 27 June 1981, entered into force on 21 October 1986.

UNGA, *Convention on the Rights of the Child*, 20 November 1989, entered into force on 2 September 1990, UN Treaty Series 1577, p. 3.

OAU, *African Charter on the Rights and Welfare of the Child*, 11 July 1990, entered into force on 29 November 1999.

UNGA, *International Convention on the Protection of the Rights of All Migrant Workers and Members of Their Families*, 18 December 1990, entered into force on 1 July 2003 (A/RES/45/158).

CoE, *European Convention on Nationality*, 6 November 1997, entered into force on 1 March 2000.

UNGA, *Convention on the Rights of Persons with Disabilities*, adopted on 13 December 2006, entered into force on 3 May 2008, A/RES/61/106, Annex I.

AU, *African Charter on Democracy, Elections and Governance*, adopted by the eighth ordinary session of the Assembly, held in Addis Ababa, Ethiopia, on 30 January 2007.

B. Judical Decisions

1. Permanent Court of International Justice

a)Judgments

PCIJ, *Case of the S.S. Wimbledon (United Kingdom et al. vs. Germany)*, PCIJ Series A. No 1, Judgment of 17 August 1923.

PCIJ, *Certain German Interests in Polish Upper Silesia (Germany vs. Poland)*, Merits, PCIJ Series A No. 7, Judgment of 25 May 1926.

PCIJ, *Case concerning The Factory at Chorzów (Germany vs. Poland)*, Competence, PCIJ Series A. No 9, Judgment of 26 July 1927.

PCIJ, *Case concerning the Factory at Chorzów (Germany vs. Poland)*, Merits, PCIJ Series A.No 17, Judgment of 13 September 1928.

b)Advisory Opinions

PCIJ, *Exchange of Greek and Turkish Populations (Lausanne Convention VI, January 30th, 1923, Article 2)*, PCIJ Series B No. 10, Advisory Opinion of 21 February 1925.

2. International Court of Justice

a)Judgments

ICJ, *Corfu Channel Case (United Kingdom vs. Albania)*, Merits, ICJ Reports 1949, p. 4, Judgment of 9 April 1949.

ICJ, *Corfu Channel Case (United Kingdom vs. Albania)*, Compensation, ICJ Reports 1949, p. 244, Judgment of 15 December 1949.

ICJ, *Case concerning the Temple of Preah Vihear (Cambodia vs. Thailand)*, Merits, ICJ Reports 1962, p. 6, Judgment of 15 June 1962.

ICJ, *Case concerning United States Diplomatic and Consular Staff in Tehran (United States of America vs. Iran)*, ICJ Reports 1980, p. 3, Judgment of 24 May 1980.

ICJ, *Case concerning* the *Military and Paramilitary Activities in und against Nicaragua (Nicaragua vs. United States of America)*, Merits, ICJ Reports 1986, p. 14, Judgment of 27 June 1986.

ICJ, *Case concerning the Gabčíkovo-Nagymaros Project (Hungary vs. Slovakia)*, ICJ Reports 1997, p. 7, Judgment of 25 September 1997.

ICJ, *LaGrand Case (Germany v. United States of America)*, ICJ Reports 2001, p. 466, Judgment of 27 June 2001.

ICJ, *Case concerning the Arrest Warrant of 11 April 2000 (Democratic Republic of the Congo v. Belgium)*, ICJ Reports 2002, p. 3, Judgment of 14 February 2002.

ICJ, *Case concerning the Land and Maritime Boundary between Cameroon and Nigeria (Cameroon vs. Nigeria: Equatorial Guinea intervening)*, ICJ Reports 2002, p. 303, Judgment of 10 October 2002.

ICJ, *Case concerning Avena and Other Mexican Nationals (Mexico v. United States of America)*, ICJ Reports 2004, p. 12, Judgment of 31 March 2004.

ICJ, *Case concerning Armed Activities on the Territory of the Congo (Democratic Republic of the Congo v. Uganda)*, Merits, ICJ Reports 2005, p. 168, 19 December 2005.

ICJ, *Case concerning the Application of the Convention on the Prevention and Punishment of the Crime of Genocide (Bosnia and Herzegovina vs. Serbia and Montenegro)*, ICJ Reports 2007, p. 43, Judgment of 26 February 2007.

ICJ, *Case concerning Certain Questions of Mutual Assistance in Criminal Matters (Djibouti vs. France)*, ICJ Reports 2008, p. 177, Judgment of 4 June 2008.

ICJ, *Dispute regarding Navigational and Related Rights (Costa Rica vs. Nicaragua)*, ICJ Reports 2009, p. 213, Judgment of 13 July 2009.

ICJ, *Case concerning Pulp Mills on the River Uruguay (Argentina vs. Uruguay)*, ICJ Reports 2010, p. 14, Judgment of 20 April 2010.

ICJ, *Case concerning Ahmadou Sadio Diallo (Republic of Guinea v. Democratic Republic of the Congo)*, Merits, ICJ Reports 2010, p. 639, Judgment of 30 November 2010.

ICJ, *Case concerning the Application of the Interim Accord of 13 September 1995 (the former Yugoslav Republic of Macedonia vs. Greece)*, ICJ Reports 2011, p. 644, Judgment of 5 December 2011.

ICJ, *Jurisdictional Immunities of the State (Germany vs. Italy; Greece intervening)*, ICJ Reports 2012, p. 99, Judgment of 3 February 2012.

ICJ, *Questions relating to the Obligation to Prosecute or Extradite (Belgium vs. Senegal)*, ICJ Reports 422, Judgment of 20 July 2012.

ICJ, *Case concerning Ahmadou Sadio Diallo (Republic of Guinea v. Democratic Republic of the Congo)*, Compensation, ICJ Reports 2012, p. 324, Judgment of 19 June 2012.

ICJ, *Whaling in the Antarctic (Australia v. Japan: New Zealand intervening)*, ICJ Reports 2014, p. 226, Judgment of 31 March 2014.

ICJ, *Certain Activities Carried Out by Nicaragua in the Border Area (Costa Rica v. Nicaragua)* and *Construction of a Road in Costa Rica along the San Juan River (Nicaragua v. Costa Rica)*, Merits, ICJ Reports 2015, p. 665, Judgment of 16 December 2015.

ICJ, *Certain Activities Carried Out by Nicaragua in the Border Area (Costa Rica v. Nicaragua)*, Compensation, ICJ Reports 2018, p. 226, Judgment of 2 February 2018.

ICJ, *Jadhav Case (India vs. Pakistan)*, ICJ Reports 2019, p. 418, Judgment of 17 July 2019.

ICJ, *Case concerning Armed Activities on the Territory of the Congo (Democratic Republic of the Congo v. Uganda)*, Reparations, General List No. 116, Judgment of 09 February 2022.

ICJ, *Alleged Violations of Sovereign Rights and Maritime Spaces in the Caribbean Sea (Nicaragua vs. Colombia)*, General List No. 155, Judgment of 21 April 2022.

b)Advisory Opinions

ICJ, *Legal Consequences of the Construction of a Wall in the Occupied Palestinian Territory*, ICJ Reports 2004, p. 136, Advisory Opinion of 9 July 2004.

c)Orders

ICJ, *Case concerning the Military and Paramilitary Activities in and against Nicaragua (Nicaragua v. United States of America)*, Discontinuance, ICJ Reports 1991, p. 47, Order of 26 September 1991.

ICJ, *Questions of jurisdictional immunities of the State and measures of constraint against State-owned property (Germany v. Italy)*, Application Instituting Proceedings containing a Request for Provisional Measures, General List No. 183, filed in the Registry of the Court on 29 April 2022.

3. Inter-American Court of Human Rights

a)Judgments

IACtHR, *Case of Velásquez Rodríguez vs. Honduras*, Reparations and Costs, Judgment of 21 July 1989, Series C No. 7 [cited as: IACtHR, *Velásquez Rodríguez v. Honduras* (1989)].

IACtHR, *Case of Aloeboetoe et al. vs. Suriname*, Reparations and Costs, Judgment of 10 September 1993, Series C No. 15 [cited as: IACtHR, *Aloeboetoe vs. Suriname* (1993)].

IACtHR, *Case of Genie Lacayo vs. Nicaragua*, Preliminary Objections, Judgment of 27 January 1995, Series C No. 21 [cited as: IACtHR, *Genie Lacayo vs. Nicaragua* (1995)].

IACtHR, *Case of El Amparo v. Venezuela*, Reparations and Costs, Judgment of 14 September 1996, Series C No. 28 [cited as: IACtHR, *El Amparo vs. Venezuela* (1996)].

IACtHR, *Case of Genie Lacayo vs. Nicaragua*, Merits, Reparations and Costs, Judgment of 29 January 1997, Series C No. 30 [cited as: IACtHR, *Genie Lacayo vs. Nicaragua* (1997)].

IACtHR, *Case of Suárez Rosero vs. Ecuador*, Merits, Judgment of 12 November 1997, Series C No. 35 [cited as: IACtHR, *Suárez Rosero vs. Ecuador* (1997)].

IACtHR, *Case of Loayza Tamayo vs. Peru*, Reparations and Costs, Judgment of 27 November 1998, Series C No. 42 [cited as: IACtHR, *Loayza Tamayo vs. Peru* (1998)].

IACtHR, *Case of Castillo Petruzzi et al. vs. Peru*, Merits, Reparations and Costs, Judgment of 30 May 1999, Series C No. 52 [cited as: IACtHR, *Castillo Petruzzi vs. Peru* (1999)].

IACtHR, *Case of the Constitutional Court vs. Peru*, Competence, Judgment of 24 September 1999, Series C No. 55 [cited as: IACtHR, *Constitutional Court vs. Peru* (1999)].

IACtHR, *Case of Baena Ricardo et al. vs. Panama*, Merits, Reparations and Costs, Judgment of 02 February 2001, Series C No. 72 [cited as: IACtHR, *Baena Ricardo vs. Panama* (2001)].

IACtHR, *Case of 'The Last Temptation of Christ' (Olmedo Bustos et al.) vs. Chile*, Merits, Reparations and Costs, Judgment of 5 February 2001. Series C No. 73 [cited as: IACtHR, *The Last Temptation of Christ vs. Chile* (2001)].

IACtHR, *Case of Ivcher Bronstein vs. Peru*, Merits, Reparations and Costs, Judgment of 6 February 2001, Series C No. 74 [cited as: IACtHR, *Ivcher Bronstein vs. Peru* (2001)].

IACtHR, *Case of the 'White Van' (Paniagua Morales et al.) vs. Guatemala*, Reparations and Costs, Judgment of 25 May 2001, Series C No. 76 [cited as: IACtHR, *'White Van' vs. Guatemala* (2001)].

IACtHR, *Case of the 'Street Children' (Villagrán Morales et al.) vs. Guatemala*, Reparations and Costs, Judgment of 26 May 2001, Series C No. 77 [cited as: IACtHR, *'Street Children' vs. Guatemala* (2001)].

IACtHR, *Case of Cesti Hurtado vs. Peru*, Reparations and Costs, Judgment of 31 May 2001, Series C No. 78 [cited as: IACtHR, *Cesti Hurtado vs. Peru* (2001)].

IACtHR, *Case of the Mayagna (Sumo) Awas Tingni Community vs. Nicaragua*, Merits, Reparations and Costs, Judgment of 31 August 2001, Series C No. 79 [cited as: IACtHR, *Awas Tingi vs. Nicaragua* (2001)].

IACtHR, *Case of Barrios Altos vs. Peru*, Reparations and Costs, Judgment of 30 November 2001, Series C No. 87 [cited as: IACtHR, *Barrios Altos vs. Peru* (2001)].

IACtHR, *Case of Cantoral Benavides vs. Peru*, Reparations and Costs, Judgment of 3 December 2001, Series C No. 88 [cited as: IACtHR, *Cantoral Benavides vs. Peru* (2001)].

IACtHR, *Case of Durand and Ugarte vs. Peru*. Reparations and Costs, Judgment of 3 December 2001, Series C No. 89 [cited as: IACtHR, *Durand and Ugarte vs. Peru* (2001)].

IACtHR, *Case of Bámaca Velásquez vs. Guatemala*, Reparations and Costs, Judgment of 22 February 2002, Series C No. 91 [cited as: IACtHR, *Bámaca Velasquez vs. Guatemala* (2002)].

IACtHR, *Case of Trujillo Oroza vs. Bolivia*, Reparations and Costs, Judgment of 27 February 2002, Series C No. 92 [cited as: *Trujillo Oroza v. Bolivia* (2002)].

IACtHR, *Case of Hilaire, Constantine and Benjamin et al. vs. Trinidad and Tobago*, Merits, Reparations and Costs, Judgment of 21 June 2002, Series C No. 94 [cited as: IACtHR, *Hilaire, Constantin and Benjamin vs. Trinidad and Tobago* (2002)].

IACtHR, *Case of Myrna Mack Chang vs. Guatemala*, Merits, Reparations and Costs, Judgment of 25 November 2003, Series C No. 101 [cited as: IACtHR, *Myrna Mack Chang vs. Guatemala* (2003)].

IACtHR, *Case of Herrera Ulloa vs. Costa Rica*, Preliminary Objections, Merits, Reparations and Costs, Judgment of 2 July 2004, Series C No. 107 [cited as: IACtHR, *Herrera Ulloa v Costa Rica* (2004)].

IACtHR, *Case of Molina Theissen vs. Guatemala*, Reparations and Costs, Judgment of 03 July 2004, Series C No. 108 [cited as: IACtHR, *Molina Theissen vs. Guatemala* (2004)].

IACtHR, *Case of the 'Juvenile Reeducation Institute' vs. Paraguay*, Preliminary Objections, Merits, Reparations and Costs, Judgment of 2 September 2004, Series C No. 112 [cited as: IACtHR, *'Juvenile Reeducation Institute' vs. Paraguay* (2004)].

IACtHR, *Case of Tibi vs. Ecuador*, Preliminary Objections, Merits, Reparations and Costs, Judgment of 07 September 2004, Series C No. 114 [cited as: IACtHR, *Tibi vs. Ecuador* (2004)].

IACtHR, *Case of the Plan de Sánchez Massacre vs. Guatemala*, Reparations, Judgment of 19 November 2004, Series C No. 116 [cited as: IACtHR, *Plan de Sanchez vs. Guatemala* (2004)].

IACtHR, *Case of Lori Berenson Mejía vs. Peru*, Merits, Reparations and Costs, Judgment of 25 November 2004, Series C No. 119 [cited as: IACtHR, *Lori Berenson vs. Peru* (2004)].

IACtHR, *Case of Caesar vs. Trinidad and Tobago*, Merits, Reparations and Costs, Judgment of 11 March 2005, Series C No. 123 [cited as: IACtHR, *Caesar vs. Trinidad and Tobago* (2005)].

IACtHR, *Case of the Yakye Axa Indigenous Community vs. Paraguay*, Merits, Reparations and Costs, Judgment of 17 June 2005, Series C No. 125 [cited as: IACtHR, *Yakye Axa vs. Paraguay* (2005)].

IACtHR, *Case of Fermín Ramírez vs. Guatemala*, Merits, Reparations and Costs, Judgment of 20 June 2005, Series C No. 126 [cited as: IACtHR, *Fermin Ramirez vs. Guatemala* (2005)].

IACtHR, *Case of Yatama vs. Nicaragua*, Preliminary Objections, Merits, Reparations and Costs, Judgment of 23 June 2005, Series C No. 127 [cited as: IACtHR, *Yatama vs. Nicaragua* (2005)].

IACtHR, *Case of the Girls Yean and Bosco vs. Dominican Republic*, Preliminary Objections, Merits, Reparations and Costs, Judgment of 8 September 2005, Series C No. 130 [cited as: IACtHR, *Yean and Bosco vs. Dominican Republic* (2005)].

IACtHR, *Case of Raxcacó Reyes vs. Guatemala*, Merits, Reparations and Costs, Judgment of 15 September 2005, Series C No. 133 [cited as: IACtHR, *Raxcacó Reyes vs. Guatemala* (2005)].

IACtHR, *Case of the Mapiripán Massacre vs. Colombia*, Merits, Reparations and Costs, Judgment of 15 September 2005, Series C No. 134 [cited as: IACtHR, *Mapiripán vs. Colombia* (2005)].

IACtHR, *Case of Palamara Iribarne vs. Chile*, Merits, Reparations and Costs, Judgment of 22 November 2005, Series C No. 135 [cited as: IACtHR, *Palamara Iribarne vs. Chile* (2005)].

IACtHR, *Case of Gómez Palomino vs. Peru*, Merits, Reparations and Costs, Judgment of 22 November 2005, Series C No. 136 [cited as: IACtHR, *Gomez Palomino vs. Peru* (2005)].

IACtHR, *Case of Blanco Romero et al. vs. Venezuela*, Merits, Reparations and Costs, Judgment of 28 November 2005, Series C No. 138 [cited as: IACtHR, *Blanco Romero vs. Venezuela* (2005)].

IACtHR, *Case of the Sawhoyamaxa Indigenous Community vs. Paraguay*, Merits, Reparations and Costs, Judgment of 29 March 2006, Series C No. 146 [cited as: IACtHR, *Sahoyamaxa vs. Paraguay* (2006)].

IACtHR, *Case of Montero Aranguren et al. (Detention Center of Catia) vs. Venezuela*, Preliminary Objection, Merits, Reparations and Costs, Judgment of 5 July 2006, Series C No. 150 [cited as: IACtHR, *Montero Aranguren vs. Venezuela* (2006)].

IACtHR, *Case of Claude Reyes et al. vs. Chile*, Merits, Reparations and Costs, Judgment of 19 September 2006, Series C No. 151 [cited as: IACtHR, *Claude Reyes vs. Chile* (2006)].

IACtHR, *Case of Goiburú et al. vs. Paraguay*, Merits, Reparations and Costs, Judgment of 22 September 2006, Series C No. 153 [cited as: IACtHR, *Goiburú vs. Paraguay* (2006)].

IACtHR, *Case of Vargas Areco vs. Paraguay*, Merits, Reparations and Costs, Judgment of 26 September 2006, Series C No. 155 [cited as: IACtHR, *Vargas Areco vs. Paraguay* (2006)].

IACtHR, *Case of Almonacid Arellano et al. vs. Chile*, Preliminary Objections, Merits, Reparations and Costs, Judgment of 26 September 2006, Series C No. 154 [cited as: IACtHR, *Almonacid Arellano vs. Chile* (2006)].

IACtHR, *Case of La Cantuta vs. Peru*, Merits, Reparations and Costs, Judgment of 29 November 2006, Series C No. 162 [cited as: IACtHR, *La Cantuta vs. Peru* (2006)].

IACtHR, *Case of the Miguel Castro Castro Prison vs. Peru*, Merits, Reparations and Costs, Judgment of 25 November 2006, Series C No. 160 [cited as: IACtHR, *Castro Castro Prison vs. Peru* (2006)].

IACtHR, *Case of Boyce et al. v. Barbados*. Preliminary Objection, Merits, Reparations and Costs, Judgment of 20 November 2007, Series C No. 169 [cited as: IACtHR, *Boyce vs. Barbados* (2007)].

IACtHR, *Case of the Saramaka People vs. Suriname*, Preliminary Objections, Merits, Reparations, and Costs, Judgment of 28 November 2007, Series C No. 172 [cited as: IACtHR, *Saramaka vs. Suriname* (2007)].

IACtHR, *Case of Kimel vs. Argentina*, Merits, Reparations and Costs, Judgment of 2 May 2008, Series C No. 177 [cited as: IACtHR, *Kimel vs. Argentina* (2008)].

IACtHR, *Case of Yvon Neptune vs. Haiti*, Merits, Reparations and Costs, Judgment of 6 May 2008, Series C No. 180 [cited as: IACtHR, *Yvon Neptune vs. Haiti* (2008)].

IACtHR, *Case of Apitz Barbera et al. ('First Court of Administrative Disputes') vs. Venezuela*, Preliminary Objection, Merits, Reparations and Costs, Judgment of 5 August 2008, Series C No. 182 [cited as: IACtHR, *Apitz Barbera vs. Venezuela* (2008)].

IACtHR, *Case of Castañeda Gutman vs. Mexico*, Preliminary Objections, Merits, Reparations and Costs, Judgment of 6 August 2008, Series C No. 184 [cited as: IACtHR, *Castañeda Gutman vs. Mexico* (2008)].

IACtHR, *Case of Heliodoro Portugal vs. Panama*, Preliminary Objections, Merits, Reparations and Costs, Judgment of 12 August 2008, Series C No. 186 [cited as: IACtHR, *Heliodoro Portugal vs. Panamá* (2008)].

IACtHR, *Case of Reverón Trujillo vs. Venezuela*, Preliminary Objection, Merits, Reparations and Costs, Judgment of 30 June 2009, Series C No. 197 [cited as: IACtHR, *Reverón Trujillo vs. Venezuela* (2009)].

IACtHR, *Case of DaCosta Cadogan v. Barbados*. Preliminary Objections, Merits, Reparations and Costs, Judgment of 24 September 2009, Series C No. 204 [cited as: IACtHR, *Cardogan vs. Barbados* (2009)].

IACtHR, *Case of González et al. ('Cotton Field') vs. Mexico*, Preliminary Objection, Merits, Reparations and Costs, Judgment of 16 November 2009, Series C No. 205 [cited as: IACtHR, *'Cotton Field' vs. Mexico* (2009)].

IACtHR, *Case of Usón Ramírez v. Venezuela*, Preliminary Objection, Merits, Reparations and Costs, Judgment of 20 November 2009, Series C No. 207 [cited as IACtHR, *Usón Ramírez vs. Venezuela* (2009)].

IACtHR, *Case of Radilla Pacheco vs. Mexico*, Preliminary Objections, Merits, Reparations and Costs, Judgment of 23 November 2009, Series C No. 209 [cited as: IACtHR, *Radilla Pacheco vs. Mexico* (2009)].

IACtHR, *Case of the Las Dos Erres Massacre vs. Guatemala*, Preliminary Objection, Merits, Reparations and Costs, Judgment of 24 November 2009, Series C No. 211 [cited as: IACtHR, *Las Dos Erres vs. Guatemala* (2009)].

IACtHR, *Case of Cepeda Vargas v. Colombia*, Preliminary Objections, Merits, Reparations and Costs, Judgment of 26 May 2010, Series C No. 213 [cited as: IACtHR, *Cepeda Vargas vs. Colombia* (2010)].

IACtHR, *Case of Fernández Ortega et al. v. Mexico*, Preliminary Objection, Merits, Reparations and Costs, Judgment of 30 August 2010, Series C No. 215 [cited as: IACtHR, *Fernandez Ortega vs. Mexico* (2010)].

IACtHR, *Case of the Xákmok Kásek Indigenous Community v. Paraguay*, Merits, Reparations and Costs, Judgment of 24 August 2010, Series C No. 214 [cited as: IACtHR, *Xákmok Kásek vs. Paraguay* (2010)].

IACtHR, *Case of Rosendo Cantú et al. v. Mexico*, Preliminary Objection, Merits, Reparations and Costs, Judgment of 31 August 2010, Series C No. 216 [cited as: IACtHR, *Rosendo Cantú vs. Mexico* (2010)].

IACtHR, *Case of Vélez Loor v. Panama*, Preliminary Objections, Merits, Reparations and Costs, Judgment of 23 November 2010, Series C No. 218 [cited as: IACtHR, *Velez Loor vs. Panama* (2010)].

IACtHR, *Case of Gomes Lund et al. ('Guerrilha do Araguaia') v. Brazil*, Preliminary Objections, Merits, Reparations and Costs, Judgment of 24 November 2010, Series C No. 219 [cited as: IACtHR, *Gomes Lund vs. Brasil* (2010)].

IACtHR, *Case of Cabrera García and Montiel Flores v. Mexico*, Preliminary Objection, Merits, Reparations and Costs, Judgment of 26 November 2010, Series C No. 220 [cited as: IACtHR, *Cabrera García and Montiel Flores vs. Mexico* (2010)].

IACtHR, *Case of Gelman v. Uruguay*, Merits and Reparations, Judgment of 24 February 2011, Series C No. 221 [cited as: IACtHR, *Gelman v. Uruguay* (2011)].

IACtHR, *Case of Chocrón Chocrón v. Venezuela*, Preliminary Objection, Merits, Reparations and Costs, Judgment of 1 July 2011, Series C No. 227 [cited as: IACtHR, *Chocrón Chocrón vs. Venezuela* (2011)].

IACtHR, *Case of López Mendoza v. Venezuela*, Merits, Reparations and Costs, Judgment of 1 September 2011, Series C No. 233 [cited as: IACtHR, *Lopez Mendoza vs. Venezuela* (2011)].

IACtHR, *Case of Fornerón and daughter vs. Argentina*, Merits, Reparations and Costs, Judgment of 27 April 2012, Series C No. 242 [cited as: IACtHR, *Fornerón vs. Argentina* (2012)].

IACtHR, *Case of Pacheco Teruel et al. vs. Honduras*, Merits, Reparations and Costs, Judgment of 27 April 2012, Series C No. 241 [cited as: IACtHR, *Pacheco Teruel vs. Honduras* (2012)].

IACtHR, *Case of Kichwa Indigenous People of Sarayaku vs. Ecuador*, Merits and Reparations, Judgment of 27 June 2012, Series C No. 245 [cited as: IACtHR, *Sarayaku vs. Ecuador* (2012)].

IACtHR, *Case of Furlan and family vs. Argentina*, Preliminary Objections, Merits, Reparations and Costs, Judgment of 31 August 2012, Series C No. 246 [cited as: IACtHR, *Furlan vs. Argentina* (2012)].

IACtHR, *Case of Nadege Dorzema et al. v. Dominican Republic*, Merits, Reparations and Costs, Judgment of 24 October 2012, Series C No. 251 [cited as: IACtHR, *Nadege Dorzema vs. Dominican Republic* (2012)].

IACtHR, *Case of the Massacres of El Mozote and surrounding areas v. El Salvador*, Merits, Reparations and Costs, Judgment of 25 October 2012, Series C No. 252 [cited as: IACtHR, *Mozote Massacres vs. El Salvador* (2012)].

IACtHR, *Case of Artavia Murillo et al. (In Vitro Fertilization) v. Costa Rica*, Preliminary Objections, Merits, Reparations and Costs, Judgment of 28 November 2012. Series C No. 257 [cited as: IACtHR, *Artavia Murillo vs. Costa Rica* (2012)].

IACtHR, *Case of Mendoza et al. v. Argentina*, Preliminary Objections, Merits and Reparations, Judgment of 14 May 2013, Series C No. 260 [cited as: IACtHR, *Mendoza vs. Argentina* (2013)].

IACtHR, *Case of Luna López vs. Honduras*, Merits, Reparations and Costs, Judgment of 10 October 2013, Series C No. 269 [cited as: IACtHR, *Luna López vs. Honduras* (2013)].

IACtHR, *Case of Osorio Rivera and family members v. Peru*, Preliminary Objections, Merits, Reparations and Costs, Judgment of 26 November 2013, Series C No. 274 [cited as: IACtHR, *Osorio Rivera vs. Peru* (2013)].

IACtHR, *Case of Norín Catrimán et al. (Leaders, Members and Activist of the Mapuche Indigenous People) v. Chile*, Merits, Reparations and Costs, Judgment of 29 May 2014, Series C No. 279 [cited as: IACtHR, *Norín Catrimán vs. Chile* (2014)].

IACtHR, *Case of expelled Dominicans and Haitians v. Dominican Republic*, Preliminary Objections, Merits, Reparations and Costs, Judgment of 28 August 2014, Series C No. 282 [cited as: IACtHR, *Expelled Dominicans and Haitians vs. Dominican Republic* (2014)].

IACtHR, *Case of Maldonado Vargas et al. v. Chile*, Merits, Reparations and Costs, Judgment of 2 September 2015, Series C No. 300 [cited as: IACtHR, *Maldonado Vargas vs. Chile* (2015)].

IACtHR, *Case of Velásquez Paiz et al. v. Guatemala*, Preliminary Objections, Merits, Reparations and Costs, Judgment of 19 November 2015, Series C No. 307 [cited as: IACtHR, *Velasquez Paiz vs. Guatemala* (2015)].

IACtHR, *Case of the Kaliña and Lokono Peoples v. Suriname*, Merits, Reparations and Costs, Judgment of 25 November 2015, Series C No. 309 [cited as: IACtHR, *Kaliña and Lokono vs. Surinam* (2015)].

IACtHR, *Case of Tenorio Roca et al. v. Peru*, Preliminary Objections, Merits, Reparations and Costs, Judgment of 22 June 2016, Series C No. 314 [cited as: IACtHR, *Tenorio Roca vs. Peru* (2016)].

IACtHR, *Case of the Hacienda Brasil Verde Workers v. Brazil*, Preliminary Objections, Merits, Reparations and Costs, Judgment of 20 October 2016, Series C No. 318 [cited as: IACtHR, *Hacienda Brasil Verde vs. Brazil* (2016)].

IACtHR, *Case of Favela Nova Brasília vs. Brazil*, Preliminary Objections, Merits, Reparations and Costs, Judgment of 16 February 2017, Series C No. 333 [cited as: IACtHR, *Favela Nova Brasília vs. Brazil* (2017)].

IACtHR, *Case of Lagos del Campo vs. Peru*, Preliminary Objections, Merits, Reparations and Costs, Judgment of 31 August 2017, Series C No. 340 [cited as: IACtHR, *Lagos del Campo vs. Peru* (2017)].

IACtHR, *Case of Herzog et al. v. Brazil*, Preliminary Objections, Merits, Reparations and Costs, Judgment of 15 March 2018, Series C No. 353 [cited as: IACtHR, *Herzog vs. Brazil* (2018)].

IACtHR, *Case of Gorigoitía v. Argentina*, Preliminary Objection, Merits, Reparations and Costs, Judgment of 2 September 2019, Series C No. 382 [cited as: IACtHR, *Gorigoitía vs. Argentina* (2019)].

IACtHR, *Case of Lopez et al. v. Argentina*, Preliminary Objections, Merits, Reparations and Costs, Judgment of 25 November 2019, Series C No. 396 [cited as: IACtHR, *Lopez vs. Argentina* (2019)].

IACtHR, *Case of the Indigenous Communities of the Lhaka Nonhat Association (Our Land) v. Argentina*, Merits, Reparations and Costs, Judgment of 6 February 2020, Series C No. 400 [cited as: IACtHR, *Lhaka Nonhat vs. Argentina* (2020)].

IACtHR, *Case of Petro Urrego v. Colombia*, Preliminary Objections, Merits, Reparations and Costs, Judgment of 8 July 2020, Series C No. 406 [cited as: IACtHR, *Petro Urrego vs. Colombia* (2020)].

IACtHR, *Case of Valle Ambrosio et al. v. Argentina*, Merits and Reparations, Judgment of 20 July 2020, Series C No. 408 [cited as: IACtHR, *Valle Ambrosio vs. Argentina* (2020)].

IACtHR, *Case of Urrutia Laubreaux v. Chile*, Preliminary Objections, Merits, Reparations and Costs, Judgment of 27 August 2020, Series C No. 409 [cited as: IACtHR, *Urrutia Laubreaux vs. Chile* (2020)].

IACtHR, *Case of Fernández Prieto and Tumbeiro v. Argentina*, Merits and Reparations, Judgment of 1 September 2020, Series C No. 411 [cited as: IACtHR, *Fernández Prieto and Tumbeiro vs. Argentina* (2020)].

IACtHR, *Case of Martínez Esquivia v. Colombia*, Preliminary Objections, Merits and Reparations, Judgment of 6 October 2020, Series C No. 412 [cited as: IACtHR, *Martínez Esquivia vs. Colombia* (2020)].

IACtHR, *Case of Casa Nina v. Peru*, Preliminary Objections, Merits, Reparations and Costs, Judgment of 24 November 2020, Series C No. 419 [cited as: IACtHR, *Casa Nina vs. Peru* (2020)].

IACtHR, *Case of Guachalá Chimbo et al. v. Ecuador*, Merits, Reparations and Costs, Judgment of 26 March 2021, Series C No. 423 [cited as: IACtHR, *Guachalá Chimbo vs. Ecuador* (2021)].

IACtHR, *Case of Cuya Lavy et al. v. Peru*, Preliminary Objections, Merits, Reparations and Costs, Judgment of 28 September 2021, Series C No. 438 [cited as: IACtHR, *Cuya Lavi vs. Peru* (2021)].

IACtHR, *Case of Vera Rojas et al. v. Chile*, Preliminary Objections, Merits, Reparations and Costs, Judgment of 1 October 2021, Series C No. 439 [cited as: IACtHR, *Vera Rojas vs. Chile* (2021)].

IACtHR, *Case of Manuela et al. v. El Salvador*, Preliminary Objections, Merits, Reparations and Costs, Judgment of 2 November 2021, Series C No. 441 [cited as: IACtHR, *Manuela vs. El Salvador* (2021)].

IACtHR, *Case of Former Employees of the Judiciary v. Guatemala*, Preliminary Objections, Merits and Reparations, Judgment of 17 November 2021, Series C No. 445 [cited as: IACtHR, *Former Employees of the Judiciary vs. Guatemala* (2021)].

IACtHR, *Case of Palacio Urrutia et al. v. Ecuador*, Merits, Reparations and Costs, Judgment of 24 November 2021, Series C No. 446 [cited as: IACtHR, *Palacio Urrutia vs. Ecuador* (2021)].

IACtHR, *Case of Digna Ochoa et al. v. Mexico*, Preliminary Objections, Merits, Reparations and Costs, Judgment of 25 November 2021, Series C No. 447 [cited as: IACtHR, *Digna Ochoa vs. Mexico* (2021)].

IACtHR, *Case of Pavez Pavez v. Chile*, Merits, Reparations and Costs, Judgment of 4 February 2022, Series C No. 449 [cited as: IACtHR, *Pavez Pavez vs. Chile* (2022)].

IACtHR, *Case of Casierra Quiñonez et al. v. Ecuador*, Preliminary Objection, Merits, Reparations and Costs, Judgment of 11 May 2022, Series C No. 450 [cited as: IACtHR, *Casierra Quiñonez vs. Ecuador* (2022)].

IACtHR, *Case of Deras García et al. v. Honduras*, Merits, Reparations and Costs, Judgment of 25 August 2022, Series C No. 462 [cited as: IACtHR, *Deras García vs. Honduras* (2022)].

IACtHR, *Case of Flores Bedregal et al. v. Bolivia*, Preliminary Objections, Merits, Reparations and Costs, Judgment of 17 October 2022, Series C No. 467 [cited as: IACtHR, *Flores Bedregal vs. Bolivia* (2022)].

IACtHR, *Case of Tzompaxtle Tecpile et al. v. Mexico*, Preliminary Objection, Merits, Reparations and Costs, Judgment of 7 November 2022, Series C No. 470 [cited as: IACtHR, *Tzompaxtle Tecpile vs. México* (2022)].

IACtHR, *Case of Leguizamón Zaván et al. v. Paraguay*, Merits, Reparations and Costs, Judgment of 15 November 2022, Series C No. 473 [cited as: IACtHR, *Leguizamón Zaván vs. Paraguay* (2022)].

IACtHR, *Case of Angulo Losada v. Bolivia*, Preliminary Objections, Merits and Reparations, Judgment of 18 November 2022, Series C No. 475 [cited as: IACtHR, *Angulo Losada vs. Bolivia* (2022)].

b) Advisory Opinions

IACtHR, 'Other treaties' subject to the consultative jurisdiction of the Court (Art. 64 American Convention on Human Rights), Advisory Opinion OC-1/82, 24 September 1982, Series A No. 1 [cited as IACtHR, Advisory Opinion 01/82 (1982)].

IACtHR, *Restrictions to the Death Penalty (Arts. 4(2) and 4(4) American Convention on Human Rights)*, Advisory Opinion OC-3/83, 8 September 1983, Series A No. 3 [cited as: IACtHR, *Advisory Opinion 3/83* (1983)].

IACtHR, *Proposed Amendments of the Naturalization Provisions of the Constitution of Costa Rica*, Advisory Opinion OC-4/84, 19 January 1984, Series A No. 4 [cited as IACtHR, *Advisory Opinion* 4/84 (1984)].

IACtHR, *Compulsory Membership in an Association prescribed by law for the Practice of Journalism (Arts. 13 and 29 American Convention on Human Rights,* Advisory Opinion OC5/85, 13 November 1985, Series A No. 5 [cited as IACtHR, *Advisory Opinion 5/85* (1985)].

IACtHR, *Compatibility of Draft Legislation with Article 8(2)(h) of the American Convention on Human Rights,* Advisory Opinion OC-12/91, 6 December 1991, Series A No. 12 [cited as IACtHR, *Advisory Opinion 12/91* (1991)].

IACtHR, *International Responsibility for the Promulgation and Enforcement of Laws in Violation of the Convention (Arts. 1 and 2 of the American Convention on Human Rights)*, Advisory Opinion OC-14/94, 9 December 1994, Series A No. 14 [cited as: IACtHR, *Advisory Opinion 14/94* (1994)].

IACtHR, *Reports of the Inter-American Commission on Human Rights (Art. 51 of the American Convention on Human Rights)*, Advisory Opinion OC-15/97, 14 November 1997, Series A No. 15 [cited as IACtHR, *Advisory Opinion 15/97* (1997)].

IACtHR, *Rights and guarantees of children in the context of migration and/or in need of international protection*, Advisory Opinion OC-21/14, 19 August 2014, Series A No. 21 [cited as IACtHR, *Advisory Opinion 21/14* (2014)].

IACtHR, *Entitlement of legal entities to hold rights under the Inter-American Human Rights System (Interpretation and scope of Article 1(2), in relation to Articles 1(2), 8, 11(2), 13, 16, 21, 24, 25, 29, 30, 44, 46 and 62(3) of the American Convention on Human Rights, as well as of Article 8(1)(A) and (B) of the Protocol of San Salvador)*, Advisory Opinion OC-22/16, 26 February 2016, Series A No. 22 [cited as: IACtHR, *Advisory Opinion 22/16* (2016)].

IACtHR, *Indefinite Presidential Re-election in Presidential Systems in the context of the Inter-American System of Human Rights (Interpretation and scope of Articles 1, 23, 24 and 32 of the American Convention on Human Rights, XX of the American Declaration of the Rights and Duties of Man, 3(d) of the Charter of the Organization of American States and of the Inter-American Democratic Charter)*, Advisory Opinion OC-28/21, 7 June 2021, Series A No. 28 [cited as: IACtHR, *Advisory Opinion 28/21* (2021)].

c) Orders

IACtHR, *Case of Gelman v. Uruguay*, Monitoring Compliance with Judgment, Order of the Inter-American Court of Human Rights of 20 March 2013 [cited as: IACtHR, *Gelman vs. Uruguay*, Monitoring Compliance with Judgment (2013)].

IACtHR, *Matter of Juan Almonte Herrera et al. regarding Dominican Republic*, Provisional Measures, Order of the Inter-American Court of Human Rights of 13 November 2015 [cited as: IACtHR, *Juan Almonte Herrera vs. Dominican Republic*, Provisional Measures (2015)].

IACtHR, *Case of the Members of the Village of Chichupac and neighboring communities of the Municipality of Rabinal, Case of Molina Theissen and 12 other Guatemalan's Cases v. Guatemala*, Provisional Measures and Monitoring Compliance with Judgment, Order of the Inter-American Court of Human Rights of 12 March 2019 [cited as: IACtHR, *Members of the Village of Chichupac and neighboring communities of the Municipality of Rabinal, Molina Theissen and 12 other Guatemalan's Cases vs. Guatemala,* Provisional Measures and Monitoring Compliance with Judgment (2019)].

4. European Court of Human Rights

a)Judgments

ECtHR, Application no. 5493/72, *Case of Handyside vs. United Kingdom,* Merits, Plenary, 7 December 1976 [cited as: ECtHR, *Handyside vs. UK* (1976)].

ECtHR, Application no. 5310/71, *Case of Ireland v. the United Kingdom*, Merits and Just Satisfaction, Plenary, 18 January 1978 [cited as: ECtHR, *Ireland vs. UK* (1978)].

ECtHR, Application no. 5029/71, *Case of Klass and others v. Germany*, Merits, Plenary, 6 September 1978 [cited as: ECtHR, *Klass vs. Germany* (1978)].

ECtHR, Application no. 6833/74, *Case of Marckx vs. Belgium*, Merits and Just Satisfaction, Plenary, 13 June 1979 [cited as: ECtHR, *Marckx vs. Belgium* (1979)].

ECtHR, Application no. 7525/76, *Case of Dudgeon v. the United Kingdom*, Merits, Plenary, 22 October 1981 [cited as: ECtHR, *Dudgeon v. the United Kingdom* (1981)].

ECtHR, Applications nos. 6878/75 and 7238/75, *Case of Le Compte, Van Leuven and De Meyere vs. Belgium (Article 50)*, Just Satisfaction, Chamber, 18 October 1982 [cited as: ECtHR, *Le Compte, Van Leuven and De Meyere vs. Belgium* (1982)].

ECtHR, Application no. 8660/79, *Case of Minelli v. Switzerland*, Merits and Just Satisfaction, Chamber, 25 March 1983 [cited as: ECtHR, *Minelli v. Switzerland* (1983)].

ECtHR, Application no. 8978/80, *Case of X and Y vs. the Netherlands*, Merits and Just Satisfaction, Chamber, 26 March 1985 [cited as: ECtHR, *X and Y vs. the Netherlands* (1985)].

ECtHR, Application no. 10581/83, Case of *Norris vs. Ireland,* Merits and Just Satisfaction, Plenary, 26 October 1988 [cited as: ECtHR, *Norris vs. Ireland* (1988)].

ECtHR, Application no. 14038/88, Case of *Soering vs. UK,* Merits and Just Satisfaction, Plenary, 07 July 1989 [cited as: ECtHR, *Soering vs. UK* (1989)].

ECtHR, Application no. 14647/89, *Case of Saïdi v. France*, Merits and Just Satisfaction, Chamber, 20 September 1993 [cited as: ECtHR, *Saïdi vs. France* (1993)].

ECtHR, Applications nos. 16419/90 and 16426/90, *Case of Yağci and Sargin vs. Turkey*, Merits and Just Satisfaction, Chamber, 08 June 1995 [cited as: ECtHR, *Yağci and Sargin vs. Turkey* (1995)].

ECtHR, Application no. 14556/89, Case of *Papamichalopolous v.* Greece *(Article 50)*, Just Satisfaction, Chamber, 31 October 1995 [cited as: ECHR, *Papamichalopolous v. Greece* (1995)].

ECtHR, Application no. 15318/89, Case of *Loidizou vs Turkey,* Merits, Chamber, 18 December 1996 [cited as: ECtHR, *Loidizou vs Turkey* (1996)].

ECtHR, Application no. 34406/97, *Case of Mazurek vs. France,* Merits and Just Satisfaction, Third Section, 1 February 2000 [cited as: ECtHR, *Mazurek vs. France* (2000)].

ECtHR, Applications nos. 39221/98 and 41963/98, *Case of Scozzari and Giunta vs. Italy*, Merits and Just Satisfaction, Grand Chamber, 13 July 2000 [cited as: ECtHR, *Scozzari and Giunta vs. Italy* (2000)].

ECtHR, Application no. 28342/95, *Case of Brumărescu v. Romania*, Just Satisfaction, Grand Chamber, 23 January 2001 [cited as: ECtHR, *Brumărescu vs. Romania* (2001)].

ECtHR, Application no. 25781/94, *Case of Cyprus vs. Turkey,* Merits, Grand Chamber, 10 May 2001 [cited as: ECtHR, *Cyprus vs. Turkey* (2001)].

ECtHR, Application no. 40787/98, *Case of Hirst vs. UK,* Merits and Just Satisfaction, Third Section, 24 July 2001 [cited as: ECtHR, *Hirst vs. UK* (2001)].

ECtHR, Application no. 51564/99, *Case of Čonka v. Belgium*, Merits and Just Satisfaction, Third Section, 5 February 2002 [cited as: ECtHR, *Čonka v. Belgium* (2002)].

ECtHR, Application no. 47095/99, *Case of Kalashnikov vs. Russia,* Merits and Just Satisfaction, Third Section, 15 July 2002 [cited as: ECtHR, *Kalashnikov vs. Russia* (2002)].

ECtHR, Application no. 39272/98, *Case of M.C. vs. Bulgaria*, Merits and Just Satisfaction, First Section, 4 December 2003 [cited as: ECtHR, *M.C. vs. Bulgaria* (2003)].

ECtHR, Application no. 71503/01, *Case of Assanidze vs. Georgia,* Merits and Just Satisfaction, Grand Chamber, 08 April 2004 [cited as: ECtHR, *Assanidze vs. Georgia* (2004)].

ECtHR, Application no. 39748/98, *Case of Maestri vs. Italy*, Merits and Just Satisfaction, Grand Chamber, 17 February 2004 [cited as: ECtHR, *Maestri vs. Italy* (2004)].

ECtHR, Application no. 31443/96, *Case of Broniowski vs. Poland,* Merits, Grand Chamber, 22 June 2004 [cited as: ECtHR, *Broniowski vs. Poland* (2004)].

ECtHR, Application no. 23032/02, *Case of Lukenda vs. Slovenia,* Merits and Just Satisfaction, Third Section, 6 October 2005 [cited as: ECtHR, *Lukenda vs. Slovenia* (2005)].

ECtHR, Application no. 74025/01, Case of *Hirst vs. UK (No. 2)*, Merits and Just Satisfaction, Grand Chamber, 6 October 2005 [cited as: ECtHR, *Hirst vs. UK (No. 2)* (2005)].

ECtHR, Application no. 46347/99, *Case of Xenides-Arestis vs. Turkey,* Merits, Third Section, 22 December 2005 [cited as: ECtHR, *Xenides-Arestis vs. Turkey* (2005)].

ECtHR, Application no. 35014/97, Case of *Hutten-Czapska v. Poland,* Merits and Just Satisfaction, Grand Chamber, 19 June 2006 [cited as: ECtHR, *Hutten-Czapska v. Poland* (2006)].

ECtHR, Application no. 52067/99, *Case of Okkali vs. Turkey,* Merits and Just Satisfaction, Second Section, 17 October 2006 [cited as: ECtHR, *Okkali vs. Turkey* (2006)].

ECtHR, Application no. 13378/05, *Case of Burden and Burden vs. UK,* Merits and Just Satisfaction, Fourth Section, 12 December 2006 [cited as: ECtHR, *Burden vs. UK* (2006)].

ECtHR, Application no. 25389/05, *Case of Gebremedhin [Gaberamadhien] vs. France,* Merits and Just Satisfaction, Second Section, 26 April 2007 [cited as: ECtHR, *Gebremedhin [Gaberamadhien] vs. France* (2007)].

ECtHR, Application no. 30132/04, Case of *Ilic vs. Serbia,* Merits and Just Satisfaction, Second Section, 09 October 2007 [cited as: ECtHR, *Ilic vs. Serbia* (2007)].

ECtHR, Application no. 1448/04, *Case of Hasan and Eylem Zengin vs. Turkey,* Merits and Just Satisfaction, Second Section, 9 October 2007 [cited as: ECtHR, *Hasan and Eylem Zengin vs. Turkey* (2007)].

ECtHR, Application no. 38222/02, *Case of Ramadhi and others vs. Albania,* Merits and Just Satisfaction, Fourth Section, 13 November 2007 [cited as: ECtHR, *Ramadhi vs. Albania* (2007)].

ECtHR, Application no. 31300/05, Case of *Terzi and Erkmen vs. Turkey,* Merits and Just Satisfaction, Second Section, 28 July 2009 [cited as: ECtHR, *Terzi and Erkmen vs. Turkey* (2007)].

ECtHR, Application no. 41760/04, Case of *Kostic vs. Serbia,* Merits and Just Satisfaction, Second Section, 25 November 2011 [cited as: ECtHR, *Kostic vs. Serbia* (2008)].

ECtHR, Application no. 27527/03, *Case of L. vs. Lithuania,* Merits and Just Satisfaction, Second Section, 11 September 2007 [cited as: ECtHR, *L. vs. Lithuania* (2007)].

ECtHR, Application no. 33509/04, *Case of Burdov vs. Russia (No. 2),* Merits and Just Satisfaction, First Section, 15 January 2009 [cited as: ECtHR, *Burdov vs. Russia (No. 2)* (2009)].

ECtHR, Application no. 28300/06, *Case of Sławomir Musiał v. Poland,* Merits and Just Satisfaction, Fourth Section, 20 January 2009 [cited as: ECtHR, *Sławomir Musiał* v. Poland (2009)].

ECtHR, Application no. 29739/03, *Case of Katz vs. Romania,* Merits and Just Satisfaction, Third Section, 20 January 2009 [cited as: ECtHR, *Katz vs. Romania* (2009)].

ECtHR, Applications nos. 476/07, 22539/05, 17911/08 and 13136/07, *Case of Olaru and others vs. Moldova,* Merits, Fourth Section, 28 July 2009 [cited as: ECtHR, *Olaru vs. Moldova* (2009)].

ECtHR, Application no. 20292/04, *Case of Ananyev vs. Russia,* Merits and Just Satisfaction, First Section, 30 July 2009 [cited as: ECtHR, *Ananyev vs. Russia* (2009)].

ECtHR, Application no. 40450/04, *Case of Yuriy Nikolayevich Ivanov vs. Ukraine,* Merits and Just Satisfaction, Fifth Section, 15 October 2009 [cited as: ECtHR, *Yuriy Nikolayevich Ivanov vs. Ukraine* (2009)].

ECtHR, Applications nos. 27996/06 and 34836/06, *Case of Sejdić and Finci v. Bosnia and Herzegovina*, Merits and Just Satisfaction, Grand Chamber, 22 December 2009 [cited as: ECtHR, *Sejdić and Finci vs. Bosnia and Herzegovina* (2009)].

ECtHR, Application No. 40984/07, Case of *Fatullayev vs. Azerbaijan,* Merits and Just Satisfaction, First Section, 22 April 2010 [cited as: ECtHR, *Fatullayev vs. Azerbaijan* (2010)].

ECtHR, Application no. 26828/06, Case of *Kurić and others vs. Slovenia,* Merits, Third Section, 13 July 2010 [cited as: ECtHR, *Kurić vs. Slovenia* (2010)].

ECtHR, Application no. 46344/06, *Case of Rumpf vs. Germany,* Merits and Just Satisfaction, Fifth Section, 2 September 2010 [cited as: ECtHR, *Rumpf vs. Germany* (2010)].

ECtHR, Applications nos. 30767/05 and 33800/06, Case of *Maria Atanasiu and others vs. Romania,* Merits and Just Satisfaction, Third Section, 12 October 2010 [cited as: ECtHR, *Maria Atanasiu vs. Romania* (2010)].

ECtHR, Applications nos. 60041/08 and 60054/08, *Case of Greens and M.T. vs. the United Kingdom,* Merits and Just Satisfaction, Fourth Section, 23 November 2010 [cited as: ECtHR, *Greens and MT vs. UK* (2010)].

ECtHR, Application no. 50973/08, *Case of Vassilios Athanasiou vs. Greece,* Merits and Just Satisfaction, First Section, 21 December 2010 [cited as: ECtHR, *Vassilios Athanasiou vs. Greece* (2010)].

ECtHR, Application No. 21188/09, Case of *Gluhaković vs. Croatia,* Merits and Just Satisfaction, First Section, 12 April 2011 [cited as: ECtHR, *Gluhaković vs. Croatia* (2011)].

ECtHR, Applications nos. 48059/06 and 2708/09, *Case of Dimitrov and Hamanov vs. Bulgaria,* Merits and Just Satisfaction, Fourth Section, 10 May 2011 [cited as: ECtHR, *Dimitrov and Hamanov vs. Bulgaria* (2011)].

ECtHR, Application no. 37346/05, *Case of Finger vs. Bulgaria,* Merits and Just Satisfaction, Fourth Section, 10 May 2011 [cited as: ECtHR, *Finger vs. Bulgaria* (2011)].

ECtHR, Application no. 41416/08, *Case of M. and others vs. Bulgaria,* Merits and Just Satisfaction, Fourth Section, 26 July 2011 [cited as: ECtHR, *M. vs. Bulgaria* (2011)].

ECtHR, Applications nos. 40660/08 and 60641/08, *Case of Von Hannover vs. Germany (No. 2),* Merits and Just Satisfaction, Grand Chamber, 7 February 2012 [cited as: ECtHR, *Von Hannover vs. Germany (No 2)* (2012)].

ECtHR, Application no. 24240/07, *Case of Ümmühan Kaplan vs. Turkey,* Merits and Just Satisfaction, Second Section, 20 March 2012 [cited as: ECtHR, *Ümmühan Kaplan vs. Turkey* (2012)].

ECtHR, Application no. 54447/10, *Case of Michelioudakis vs. Greece,* Merits and Just Satisfaction, First Section, 3 April 2012 [cited as: ECtHR, *Michelioudakis vs. Greece* (2012)].

ECtHR, Application no. 31925/08, *Case of Grudić v. Serbia*, Merits and Just Satisfaction, Second Section, 17 April 2012 [cited as: ECtHR, *Grudić v. Serbia* (2012)].

ECtHR, Application no. 26828/06, *Case of Kurić and others vs. Slovenia,* Merits and Just Satisfaction, Grand Chamber, 26 June 2012 [cited as: ECtHR, *Kurić vs. Slovenia* (2012)].

ECtHR, Applications nos. 604/07, 43628/07, 46684/07 and 34770/09, *Case of Manushaqe Puto and others vs. Albania,* Merits and Just Satisfaction, Fourth Section, 31 July 2012 [cited as: ECtHR, *Manushaqe Puto vs. Albania* (2012)].

ECtHR, Application no. 33210/11, *Case of Singh and others vs. Belgium,* Merits and Just Satisfaction, Second Section, 2 October 2012 [cited as: ECtHR, *Singh vs. Belgium* (2012)].

ECtHR, Applications nos. 24604/04 and 16855/05, *Case of Nihayet Arıcı and others vs. Turkey,* Merits and Just Satisfaction, Second Section, 23 October 2012 [cited as: ECtHR, *Nihayet Arıcı vs. Turkey* (2012)].

ECtHR, Application no. 40150/09, *Case of Glykantzi vs. Greece,* Merits and Just Satisfaction, First Section, 30 October 2012 [cited as: ECtHR, *Glykantzi vs. Greece* (2012)].

ECtHR, Application no. 60642/08, *Case of Ališić and others vs. Bosnia and Herzegovina, Croatia, Serbia, Slovenia and the Former Yugoslav Republic of Macedonia,* Merits and Just Satisfaction, Fourth Section, 6 November 2012 [cited as: ECtHR, *Ališić vs. Bosnia and Herzegovina, Croatia, Serbia, Slovenia and the Former Yugoslav Republic of Macedonia* (2012)].

ECtHR, Application no. 12323/11, *Case of Michaud vs. France,* Merits and Just Satisfaction, Fifth Section, 6 December 2012 [cited as: ECtHR, *Michaud vs. France* (2012)].

ECtHR, Application no. 31360/10, *Case of Tarbuk vs. Croatia,* Merits and Just Satisfaction, First Section, 11 December 2012 [cited as: ECtHR, *Tarbuk vs. Croatia* (2012)].

ECtHR, Applications nos. 43517/09, 46882/09, 55400/09, 57875/09, 61535/09, 35315/10 and 37818/10, *Case of Torreggiani and others vs. Italy,* Merits and Just Satisfaction, Second Section, 8 January 2013 [cited as: ECtHR, *Torreggiani vs. Italy* (2013)].

ECtHR, Application no. 21722/11, *Case of Oleksandr Volkov vs. Ukraine,* Merits, Fifth Section, 09 January 2013 [cited as: ECtHR, *Volkov vs. Ukraine* (2013)].

ECtHR, Application no. 21794/08, *Case of Zorica Jovanovic vs. Serbia,* Merits and Just Satisfaction, Second Section, 26 March 2013 [cited as: ECtHR, *Zorica Jovanovic vs. Serbia* (2013)].

ECtHR, Application no. 48876/08, *Case of Animal Defenders International v. United Kingdom,* Merits and Just Satisfaction, Grand Chamber, 22 April 2013 [cited as: ECtHR, *Animal Defenders International v. UK* (2013)].

ECtHR, Applications nos. 11157/04 and 15162/05, *Case of Anchugov and Gladkov vs. Russia,* Merits and Just Satisfaction, First Section, 4 July 2013 [cited as: ECtHR, *Anchugov and Gladkov vs. Russia* (2013)].

ECtHR, Applications nos. 2312/08 and 34179/08, *Case of Maktouf and Damjanović v. Bosnia and Herzegovina,* Merits and Just Satisfaction, Grand Chamber, 18 July 2013 [cited as: ECtHR, *Maktouf vs. Bosnia and Herzegovina* (2013)].

ECtHR, Application no. 5376/11, *Case of M.C. and others vs. Italy,* Merits, Second Section, 3 September 2013 [cited as: ECtHR, *M.C. vs. Italy* (2013)].

ECtHR, Application no. 42750/09, *Case of del Rio Prada vs. Spain,* Merits and Just Satisfaction, Grand Chamber, 21 October 2013 [cited as: ECtHR, *del Rio Prada vs. Spain* (2013)].

ECtHR, Applications nos. 40756/06, 41508/07 and 50806/07, *Case of Vlad and others vs. Romania,* Merits and Just Satisfaction, Third Section, 26 November 2013 [cited as: ECtHR, *Vlad vs. Romania* (2013)].

ECtHR, Application no. 69037/10, *Case of Pelipenko vs. Russia,* Just Satisfaction, First Section, 16 January 2014 [cited as: ECtHR, *Pelipenko vs. Russia* (2014)].

ECtHR, Application no. 26828/06, *Case of Kurić vs. Slovenia,* Just Satisfaction, Grand Chamber, 12 March 2014 [cited as: ECtHR, *Kurić vs. Slovenia* (Just Satisfaction) (2014)].

ECtHR, Application no. 6528/11, *Case of A.C. and others vs Spain,* Merits and Just Satisfaction, Third Section, 22 April 2014 [cited as: ECtHR, *A.C. vs Spain* (2014)].

ECtHR, Application no. 73593/10, *Case of László Magyar v. Hungary,* Merits and Just Satisfaction, Second Section, 20 May 2014 [cited as: ECtHR, *László Magyar v. Hungary* (2014)].

ECtHR, Application no. 4455/10, *Case of Marguš v. Croatia,* Merits and Just Satisfaction, Grand Chamber, 27 May 2014 [cited as: ECtHR, *Marguš v. Croatia* (2014)].

ECtHR, Applications nos. 29920/05, 3553/06, 18876/10, 61186/10, 21176/11, 36112/11, 36426/11, 40841/11, 45381/11, 55929/11, 60822/11, *Case of Gerasimov and others vs. Russia,* Merits and Just Satisfaction, First Section, 1 July 2014 [cited as: ECtHR, *Gerasimov vs. Russia* (2014)].

ECtHR, Application no. 43835/11, *Case of S.A.S vs. France,* Merits and Just Satisfaction, Grand Chamber, 01 July 2014 [cited as: ECtHR, *S.A.S vs. France* (2014)].

ECtHR, Application no. 59177/10, *Case of Yerli vs. Turkey,* Merits and Just Satisfaction, Second Section, 8 July 2014 [cited as: ECtHR, *Yerli vs. Turkey* (2014)].

ECtHR, Applications nos. 15018/11 and 61199/12, *Case of Harackchiev and Tolumov vs. Bulgaria,* Merits and Just Satisfaction, Fourth Section, 8 July 2014 [cited as: ECtHR, *Harackchiev and Tolumov vs. Bulgaria* (2014)].

ECtHR, Application no. 3681/06, *Case of Zornić vs. Bosnia and Herzegovina,* Merits and Just Satisfaction, Fourth Section, 15 July 2014 [cited as: ECtHR, *Zornić vs. Bosnia and Herzegovina* (2014)].

ECtHR, Application no. 60642/08, *Case of Ališić vs. Bosnia and Herzegovina, Croatia, Serbia, Slovenia and the Former Yugoslav Republic of Macedonia,* Merits and Just Satisfaction, Grand Chamber, 16 July 2014 [cited as: ECtHR, *Ališić vs. Bosnia and Herzegovina, Croatia, Serbia, Slovenia and the Former Yugoslav Republic of Macedonia* (2014)].

ECtHR, Application no. 47848/08, *Case of Centre for Legal Resources on behalf of Valentin Câmpeanu vs. Romania,* Merits and Just Satisfaction, Grand Chamber, 17 July 2014 [cited as: ECtHR, *Centre for Legal Resources on behalf of Valentin Câmpeanu vs. Romania* (2014)].

ECtHR, Application no. 62279/09, *Case of Atiman vs. Turkey,* Merits and Just Satisfaction, Second Section, 23 September 2014 [cited as: ECtHR, *Atiman vs. Turkey* (2014)].

ECtHR, Application no. 46193/13, *Case of Chanyev v. Ukraine,* Merits and Just Satisfaction, Fifth Section, 9 October 2014 [cited as: ECtHR, *Chanyev v. Ukraine* (2014)].

ECtHR, Applications nos. 604/07, 43628/07, 46684/07 and 34770/09, *Case of Manushaqe Puto vs. Albania*, Revision, Fourth Section, 4 November 2014 [cited as: ECtHR, *Manushaqe Puto vs. Albania* (2014)].

ECtHR, Application no. 64682/12, *Case of Vasilescu vs. Belgium,* Merits and Just Satisfaction, Second Section, 25 November 2014 [cited as: ECtHR, *Vasilescu vs. Belgium* (2014)].

ECtHR, Applications nos. 36925/10, 21487/12, 72893/12, 73196/12, 77718/12 and 9717/13, *Case of Neshkov and others vs. Bulgaria,* Merits and Just Satisfaction, Fourth Section, 27 January 2015 [cited as: ECtHR, *Neshkov vs. Bulgaria* (2015)].

ECtHR, Application nos. 14097/12, 45135/12, 73712/12, 34001/13, 44055/13, and 64586/13, *Case of Varga and others vs. Hugary,* Merits and Just Satisfaction, Second Section, 10 March 2015 [cited as: ECtHR, *Varga vs. Hugary* (2015)].

ECtHR, Application no. 46043/14, *Case of Lambert and others vs. France,* Merits and Just Satisfaction, Grand Chamber, 5 June 2015 [cited as: ECtHR, *Lambert vs. France* (2015)].

ECtHR, Application no. 13216/05, *Case of Chiragov and others vs. Armenia,* Merits, Grand Chamber, 16 June 2015 [cited as: ECtHR, *Chiragov vs. Armenia* (2015)].

ECtHR, Application no. 40167/06, *Case of Sargsyan vs. Azerbaijan,* Merits, Grand Chamber, 16 June 2015 [cited as: ECtHR, *Sargsyan vs. Azerbaijan* (2015)].

ECtHR, Application no. 57722/12, *Case of Grabowski vs. Poland,* Merits and Just Satisfaction, Fourth Section, 30 June 2015 [cited as: ECtHR, *Grabowski vs. Poland* (2015)].

ECtHR, Applications nos. 72287/10, 13927/11 and 46187/11, *Case of Rutkowski vs. Poland,* Merits and Just Satisfaction, Fourth Section, 7 July 2015 [cited as: ECtHR, *Rutkowski vs. Poland* (2015)].

ECtHR, Application no. 48322/12, *Case of Gazsó vs Hungary,* Merits and Just Satisfaction, Second Section, 16 July 2015 [cited as: ECtHR, *Gazsó vs Hungary* (2015)].

ECtHR, Application no. 47687/13, *Case of Bamouhammad vs. Belgium,* Merits and Just Satisfaction, Second Section, 17 November 2015 [cited as: ECtHR, *Bamouhammad vs. Belgium* (2015)].

ECtHR, Application no. 73548/13, *Case of W.D. vs Belgium,* Merits and Just Satisfaction, Second Section, 6 September 2016 [cited as: ECtHR, *W.D. vs Belgium* (2016)].

ECtHR, Application no. 46721/15, *Case of Allanazarova v. Russia,* Merits and Just Satisfaction, Third Section, 14 February 2017 [cited as: ECtHR, *Allanazarova v. Russia* (2017)].

ECtHR, Application no. 19867/12, *Case of Moreira Ferreira v. Portugal (No. 2)*, Merits, Grand Chamber, 11 July 2017 [cited as: ECtHR, *Moreira Ferreira vs. Portugal (No. 2)* (2017)].

ECtHR, Application no. 56080/13, *Case of Lopes de Sousa Fernandes v. Portugal,* Merits and Just Satisfaction, Grand Chamber, 19 December 2017 [cited as: ECtHR, *Lopes de Sousa Fernandes v. Portugal* (2017)].

ECtHR, Applications nos. 68762/14 and 71200/14, *Case of Aliyev v. Azerbaijan*, Merits and Just Satisfaction, Fifth Section, 20 September 2018 [cited as: ECtHR, *Aliyev v. Azerbaijan* (2018)].

ECtHR, Application no. 13255/07, *Case of Georgia vs. Russia (I),* Just Satisfaction, Grand Chamber, 31 January 2019 [cited as: ECtHR, *Georgia vs. Russia (I)* (2019)].

ECtHR, Applications nos. 18255/10 and 5 others, Case of *Tomov and others vs. Russia,* Merits and Just Satisfaction, Third Section, 9 April 2019 [cited as: ECtHR, *Tomov vs. Russia* (2019)].

ECtHR, Applications nos. 30226/10 and 4 others, *Case of Ali Riza and others vs. Turkey,* Merits and Just Satisfaction, Second Section, 28 January 2020 [cited as: ECtHR, *Ali Riza vs. Turkey* (2020)].

ECtHR, Application no. 14057/17, *Case of Sukachov vs. Ukraine,* Merits and Just Satisfaction, Fifth Section, 30 January 2020 [cited as: ECtHR, *Sukachov vs. Ukraine* (2020)].

ECtHR, Application no. 9671/15 and 31 others, *Case of J.M.B. and others vs. France,* Merits and Just Satisfaction, Fifth Section, 30 January 2020 [cited as: ECtHR, *J.M.B. vs. France* (2020)].

ECtHR, Application no. 26374/18, *Case of Guðmundur Andri Ástráðsson v. Iceland,* Merits and Just Satisfaction, Grand Chamber, 1 December 2020 [cited as: ECtHR, *Guðmundur Andri Ástráðsson vs. Iceland* (2020)].

ECtHR, Applications nos. 78638/11 and 3 others, Case of *Shlykov and others vs. Russia,* Merits and Just Satisfaction, Third Section, 19 January 2021 [cited as: ECtHR, *Shlykov vs. Russia* (2021)].

ECtHR, Application no. 78019/17, *Case of Gasangusenov vs. Russia,* Merits and Just Satisfaction, Third Section, 30 March 2021 [cited as: ECtHR, *Gasangusenov vs. Russia* (2021)].

ECtHR, Applications nos. 66152/14 and 8 others, *Case of Kuzmina and others vs. Russia,* Merits and Just Satisfaction, Third Section, 20 April 2021 [cited as: ECtHR, *Kuzmina vs. Russia* (2021)].

ECtHR, Application no. 43351/12, *Case of OOO Informatsionnoye Agentstvo Tambov-Inform v. Russia,* Merits and Just Satisfaction, Third Section, 18 May 2021 [cited as: ECtHR, *OOO Informatsionnoye Agentstvo Tambov-Inform v. Russia* (2021)].

ECtHR, Application no. 35252/08, *Case of Centrum för Rättvisa vs. Sweden,* Merits and Just Satisfaction, Grand Chamber, 25 May 2021 [ECtHR, *Centrum för Rättvisa vs. Sweden* (2021)].

ECtHR, Applications nos. 55974/16 and 3 others, *Case of Tunikova and others vs. Russia,* Merits and Just Satisfaction, Third Section, 14 December 2021 [cited as: ECtHR, *Tunikova vs. Russia* (2021)].

ECtHR, Applications nos. 32401/10 and 19 others, *Case of Taganrog LRO and others vs. Russia,* Merits and Just Satisfaction, Third Section, 7 June 2022 [cited as: ECtHR, *Taganrog LRO vs. Russia* (2022)].

ECtHR, Application no. 53600/20, *Case of Verein KlimaSeniorinnen Schweiz and others vs. Switzerland,* Merits and Just Satisfaction, Grand Chamber, 09 April 2024 [cited as: ECtHR, *KlimaSeniorinnen vs. Switzerland* (2024)].

b) Advisory Opinions

ECtHR, *Decision on the competence of the Court to give an advisory opinion*, Grand Chamber, 02 June 2004.

ECtHR, *Advisory Opinion concerning the recognition in domestic law of a legal parent-child relationship between a child born through a gestational surrogacy arrangement abroad and the intended mother*, requested by the French Court of Cassation (Request no. P16-2018001), 10 April 2019 [cited as: ECtHR, *Advisory Opinion P16-2018-001* (2019)].

ECtHR, *Advisory Opinion concerning the use of the "blanket reference" or "legislation by reference" technique in the definition of an offence and the standards of comparison between the criminal law in force at the time of the commission of the offence and the amended criminal law,* requested by the Armenian Constitutional Court (Request no. P16-2019-001), 29 May 2020 [cited as: ECtHR, *Advisory Opinion P16-2019-001* (2020)].

ECtHR, *Advisory opinion on the difference in treatment between landowners' associations "having a recognised existence on the date of the creation of an approved municipal hunters' association" and landowners' associations set up after that date,* requested by the French Conseil d'État (Request no. P16-2021-002), 13 July 2022 [cited as: ECtHR, *Advisory Opinion P16-2021-002* (2022)].

ECtHR, *Advisory opinion concerning impeachment legislation*, requested by the Supreme Administrative Court of Lithuania (Request P16-2020-002), 08 April 2022 [cited as: *ECtHR, Advisory Opinion P16-2020-002* (2022).

c) Admissibility Decisions

ECtHR, Application no. 52207/99, *Case of Banković and others vs. Belgium and others,* Decision, Grand Chamber, 12 December 2001 [cited as: ECtHR, *Banković vs. Belgium* (2001)].

ECtHR, Application no. 66274/09, *Case of Ligue de musulmans de Suisse and others v. Switzerland,* Decision, Second Section, 28 June 2011 [cited as: ECtHR, *Ligue de musulmans de Suisse v. Switzerland* (2011)].

5. African Court of Human and Peoples' Rights

a)Judgments

ACtHPR, Application 011/2011, *Case of Rev. Christopher Mtikila vs. United Republic of Tanzania,* Reparations, 30 September 2011 [cited as: ACtHPR, *Rev. Christopher Mtikila vs. Tanzania* (2011)].

ACtHPR, Application 001/2013, *Case of Ernest Francis Mtingwi vs. Republic of Malawi,* Jurisdiction, 15 March 2013 [cited as: ACtHPR, *Ernest Francis Mtingwi vs. Malawi* (2013)].

ACtHPR, Application 009/2011, *Case of The Tanganyika Law Society and Legal and Human Rights Centre vs. United Republic of Tanzania*, Merits, 14 June 2013 [cited as: ACtHPR, *Tanganyika Law Society and Legal and Human Rights Centre vs. Tanzania* (2013)].

ACtHPR, Application 004/2013, *Case of Lohé Issa Konaté vs. Burkina Faso*, Merits, 5 December 2014 [cited as: ACtHPR, *Lohé Issa Konaté vs. Burkina Faso* (2014)].

ACtHPR, Application 013/2011, *Case of the beneficiaries of the late Norbert - Zongo Abdoulaye Nikiema alias Ablasse, Ernest Zongo and Blaise IIboudo vs. Burkina Faso*, Reparations, 05 June 2015 [cited as: ACtHPR, *Ernest Zongo vs. Republic of Burkina Faso* (2015)].

ACtHPR, Application 005/2013, *Case of Alex Thomas vs. United Republic of Tanzania*, Merits, 20 November 2015 [cited as: ACtHPR, *Alex Thomas vs. Tanzania* (2015)].

ACtHPR, Application 006/2013, *Case of Wilfred Onyango and others vs. United Republic of Tanzania*, Merits, 18 March 2016 [cited as: ACtHPR, *Wilfred Onyango Nganya vs. Tanzania* (2016)].

ACtHPR, Application 004/2013, *Case of Lohé Issa Konaté vs. Burkina Faso*, Reparations, 3 June 2016 [cited as: ACtHPR, *Lohé Issa Konaté vs. Burkina Faso* (2016)].

ACtHPR, Application 007/2013, *Case of Mohamed Abubakari vs. United Republic of Tanzania*, Merits, 3 June 2016 [cited as: ACtHPR, *Mohamed Abubakari vs. Tanzania* (2016)].

ACtHPR, Application 001/2014, *Case of Actions pour la Protection des Droits de l'Homme (APDH) vs. Republic of Côte d'Ivoire*, Merits, 18 November 2016 [cited as: ACtHPR, *APDH vs. Côte d'Ivoire* (2016)].

ACtHPR, Application 011/2015, *Case of Christopher Jonas vs. United Republic of Tanzania,* Merits, 28 September 2017 [cited as: ACtHPR, *Christopher Jonas vs. Tanzania* (2017)].

ACtHPR, Application No. 003/2017 for Interpretation of the Judgment of 18 November 2016 in the Matter of *Actions pour la Protection des Droits de l'Homme (APDH) vs. Côte d'Ivoire* (2016), 28 September 2017 [cited as: ACtHPR, *APDH vs. Côte d'Ivoire,* Interpretation of Judgment (2017)].

ACtHPR, Application 003/2014, *Case of Ingabire Victoire Umuhoza vs. Republic of Rwanda*, Merits, 24 November 2017 [cited as: ACtHPR, *Ingabire Victoire Umuhoza vs. Rwanda* (2017)].

ACtHPR, Application 001/2015, *Case of Armand Guehi vs. United Republic of Tanzania*, Merits and Reparations, 18 March 2018 [cited as: ACtHPR, *Armand Guehi vs. Tanzania* (2018)].

ACtHPR, Application 032/2015, *Case of Kijiji Isiaga vs. United Republic of Tanzania*, Merits, 21 March 2018 [cited as: ACtHPR, *Kijiji Isiaga vs. Tanzania* (2018)].

ACtHPR, Application 012/2015, *Case of Anudo Ochieng Anudo vs. United Republic of Tanzania*, Merits, 22 March 2018 [cited as: ACtHPR, *Anudo Ochieng Anudo vs. Tanzania* (2018)].

ACtHPR, Application 046/2016, *Case of APDF and IHRDA vs. Republic of Mali*, Merits and Reparations, 11 May 2018 [cited as: ACtHPR, *APDF and IHRDA vs. Mali* (2018)].

ACtHPR, Application 005/2015, *Case of Thobias Mango and another vs. United Republic of Tanzania*, Merits, 11 May 2018 [cited as: ACtHPR, *Thobias Mango vs. Tanzania* (2018)].

ACtHPR, Application 010/2015, *Case of Amir Ramadhani vs. United Republic of Tanzania*, Merits, 11 May 2018 [cited as: ACtHPR, *Amir Ramadhani vs. Tanzania* (2018)].

ACtHPR, Application 020/2016, *Case of Anaclet Paulo vs. United Republic of Tanzania*, Merits and Reparations, 11 May 2018 [cited as: *ACtHPR, Anaclet Paulo vs. Tanzania* (2018)].

ACtHPR, Application 027/2015, *Case of Minani Evarist vs. United Republic of Tanzania*, Merits and Reparations, 21 September 2018 [cited as: ACtHPR, *Minani Evarist vs. Tanzania* (2018)].

ACtHPR, Application 016/2016, *Case of Diocles William vs. United Republic of Tanzania*, Merits and Reparations, 21 September 2018 [cited as: ACtHPR, *Diocles William vs. Tanzania* (2018)].

ACtHPR, Application 006/2016, *Case of Mgosi Mwita Makungu vs. United Republic of Tanzania*, Merits, 7 December 2018 [cited as: ACtHPR, *Mgosi Mwita Makungu vs. Tanzania* (2018)].

ACtHPR, Application 013/2017, *Case of Sébastien Germain Marie Aikoué Ajavon vs. Republic of Benin*, Merits, 29 March 2019 [cited as: ACtHPR, *Ajavon vs. Benin*, (Merits, 2019)].

ACtHPR, Application 007/2015, *Case of Ally Rajabu and others vs. United Republic of Tanzania*, Merits and Reparations, 28 November 2019 [cited as: ACtHPR, *Ally Rajabu vs. Tanzania* (2019)].

ACtHPR, Application 013/2017, *Case of Sébastien Germain Marie Aikoué Ajavon vs. Republic of Benin*, Reparations, 28 November 2019 [cited as: ACtHPR, *Ajavon vs. Benin* (Reparations, 2019)].

ACtHPR, Application 012/2020, *Case of Guillaume Kigbafori Soro and 19 others vss Republic of Côte d'Ivoire*, Provisional Measures, 22 April 2020 [cited as: ACtHPR, *Guillaume Kigbafori Soro vs. Côte d'Ivoire*, Provisional Measures (2020)].

ACtHPR, Application 004/2015, *Case of Andrew Ambrose @Cheusi vs. United Republic of Tanzania*, Merits and Reparations, 26 June 2020 [cited as: ACtHPR, *Andrew Ambrose @Cheusi vs. Tanzania* (2020)].

ACtHPR, Application 044/2019, *Case of Suy Bi Gohore Emile and 8 others vs. Côte d'Ivoire*, Merits and Reparations, 15 July 2020 [cited as ACtHPR, *Suy Bi Gohore Emile vs. Côte d'Ivoire* (2020)].

ACtHPR, Application 018/2018, *Case of Jebra Kambole vs. United Republic of Tanzania*, Merits and Reparations, 15 July 2020 [cited as: ACtHPR, *Jebra Kambole vs. Tanzania* (2020)].

ACtHPR, Application 011/2015, *Case of Christopher Jonas vs. United Republic of Tanzania*, Reparations, 25 September 2020 [cited as: ACtHPR, *Christopher Jonas vs. Tanzania* (2020)].

ACtHPR, Application 059/2019, *Case of XYZ vs. Republic of Benin*, Merits and Reparations, 27 November 2020 [cited as: ACtHPR, *XYZ vs. Benin (I)* (2020)].

ACtHPR, Application 010/2020, *Case of XYZ vs. Republic of Benin*, Merits and Reparations, 27 November 2020 [cited as: ACtHPR, *XYZ vs. Benin (II)* (2020)].

ACtHPR, Application 012/2017, *Case of Prof. Lèon Mugesera vs Republic of Rwanda*, Merits and Reparations, 27 November 2020 [cited as: ACtHPR, *Lèon Mugesera vs. Rwanda* (2020)].

ACtHPR, Application 062/2019, *Case of Sébastien Germain Marie Aikoué Ajavon vs. Republic of Benin*, Merits and Reparations, 04 December 2020 [cited as: ACtHPR, *Ajavon vs. Benin* (2020)].

ACtHPR, Application 003/2020, *Case of Houngue Eric Noudehouenou vs. Republic of Benin,* Merits and Reparations, 4 December 2020 [cited as: ACtHPR, *Houngue Eric Noudehouenou vs. Benin* (2020)].

ACtHPR, Application 024/2016, *Case of Amini Juma vs. United Republic of Tanzania*, Merits and Reparations, 30 September 2021 [cited as: ACtHPR, *Amini Juma vs. Tanzania* (2021)].

ACtHPR, Application 012/2015, *Case of Anudo Ochieng Anudo vs. United Republic of Tanzania*, Reparations, 2 December 2021 [cited as: ACtHPR, *Anudo Ochieng Anudo vs. Tanzania* (2021)].

ACtHPR, Application 056/2016, *Case of Gozbert Henerico vs. United Republic of Tanzania,* Merits and Reparations, 10 January 2022 [cited as: ACtHPR, *Gozbert Henerico vs. Tanzania* (2022)].

ACtHPR, Application 029/2018, *Case of Oumar Mariko vs. Republic of Mali*, Merits and Reparations, 24 March 2022 [cited as: ACtHPR, *Oumar Mariko vs. Mali* (2022)].

ACtHPR, Application 006/2012, *Case of the African Commission on Human and Peoples' Rights vs. Republic of Kenya*, Reparations, 23 June 2022 [cited as: ACtHPR, *ACmHPR vs. Kenya* (2022)].

ACtHPR, Application 052/2016, *Case of Marthine Christian @ Msuguri vs. United Republic of Tanzania,* Merits and Reparations, 1 December 2022 [cited as: ACtHPR, *Marthine Christian Msuguri vs. Tanzania* (2022)].

ACtHPR, Application 028/2020, *Case of Houngue Eric Noudehouenou vs. Republic of Benin,* Merits and Reparations, 1 December 2022 [cited as: ACtHPR, *Houngue Éric N.oudehouenou vs. Benin* (2022)].

b) Advisory Opinions

ACtHPR, Advisory Opinion No 001/2018, *On the compatibility of Vagrancy Laws with the African Charter on Human and Peoples' Rights and other human rights instruments applicable in Africa*, requested by Pan African Lawyers Union (PALU), 04 December 2020 [cited as: ACtHPR, *Advisory Opinion 001/2018* (2020)].

ACtHPR, Advisory Opinion No 001/2020, *On the right to participate in the government of one's country in the context of an election held during a public health emergency or a pandemic, such as the Covid-19 crisis*, requested by Pan African Lawyers Union (PALU), 16 July 2021 [cited as: ACtHPR, *Advisory Opinion No 001/2020* (2021)].

6. Domestic Courts

US Supreme Court, *Marbury vs. Madison,* 5 U.S. 137, 1803.

Supreme Court of Justice of Venezuela (Constitutional Chamber), *Judgment No. 1939*, 18 December 2008, section V.

Supreme Court of Justice of Venezuela, *Judgment No. 1547*, 17 October 2011.

Constitutional Court of the Dominican Republic, *Judgment TC/0256/14*, 04 November 2014.

7. Arbitral Aawards

S.S "I'm Alone" (Canada vs. United States of America), UN Reports on International Arbitral Awards, vol. III, 1935, p. 1618.

Rainbow Warrior (New Zealand vs. France), UN Reports of International Arbitral Awards, vol. XX, 30 April 1990.

C. Other Sources

1. Organization of American States

Inter-American Council of Jurists, *Draft Convention on Human Rights*, September 1959, reproduced in Inter-American Yearbook of Human Rights, 1968.

IACmHR, Report No. 79/12, Petition 342-07, Admissibility, *Ivete Jordani Demeneck et al. vs. Brazil*, 8 November 2012 [cited as IACmHR, *Ivete Jordani Demeneck vs. Brazil* (2012)].

IACmHR, Report No. 64/15, Petition 633-04, Admissibility, *Mayan Peoples and Members of the Cristo Rey, Belluet Tree, San Ignacio, Santa Elena and Santa Familia Communities vs. Belize*, 27 October 2015 [cited as: IACmHR, *Mayan Peoples v. Belize* (2015)].

IACtHR, *Annual Report*, 2018, available at: https://www.corteidh.or.cr/sitios/informes/docs/ENG/eng_2018.pdf.

IACtHR, Journals of Jurisprudence, available at: https://www.corteidh.or.cr/publicacio nes.cfm?lang=en.

2. Council of Europe

ECtHR, *Rules of the Court*, as amended on 23 June 2023, available at: https://www.echr .coe.int/documents/rules_court_eng.pdf.

CoE, Steering Committee for Human Rights (CDDH), *Guaranteeing the long-term effectiveness of the European Court of Human Rights*, CM (2003)55-Add, 8 April 2003.

ECtHR, *Reflection Paper on the Proposal to Extend the Court's Advisory Jurisdiction*, available at: https://www.echr.coe.int/Documents/2013_Courts_advisory_jurisdictio n_ENG.pdf.

CoE, Venice Commission, *Compilation of Venice Commission Opinions and Reports Concerning Courts and Justice* (2015) CDL-PI (2015)001, 66.

ECtHR, *Case-law Guides by theme*, available at: https://www.echr.coe.int/Pages/home. aspx?p=caselaw/analysis/guides&c.

CoE, *Declaration adopted at the Interlaken Conference on the Reform of the European Court of Human Rights*, 19 February 2010, available at: https://www.echr.coe.int/Doc uments/2010_Interlaken_FinalDeclaration_ENG.pdf.

CoE, High Level Conference on the Future of the European Court of Human Rights, *Brighton Declaration*, 2012, available at: https://www.echr.coe.int/documents/2012_b righton_finaldeclaration_eng.pdf.

CoE, *Izmir Declaration*, 2011, available at:

https://www.echr.coe.int/documents/2011_izmir_finaldeclaration_eng.pdf;

CoE, *Brussels Declaration*, 2015, available at:

https://www.echr.coe.int/Documents/Brussels_Declaration_ENG.pdf;

ECtHR, *The Interlaken Process and the Court*, 2016 Report to the CoM, 01 September 2016, available at: https://www.echr.coe.int/Documents/2016_Interlaken_Process_E NG.pdf.

CoE, *Copenhagen Declaration*, 2018, available at: https://www.echr.coe.int/Documents /Copenhagen_Declaration_ENG.pdf.

a) Committee of Ministers of the CoE

CoM, *Resolution Res(2004)3 on judgments revealing an underlying systemic problem*, adopted by the Committee of Ministers on 12 May 2004, at its 114th Session.

CoM, *Recommendation Rec(2004)6 of the Committee of Ministers to Member States on the improvement of domestic remedies*, adopted by the Committee of Ministers on 12 May 2004, at its 114th Session.

CoM, Supervision of Execution of Judgments of the ECtHR, *3rd Annual Report*, 2009.

CoM, *Recommendation CM/Rec(2010)3 of the Committee of Ministers to Member States on effective remedies for excessive length of proceedings*, adopted on 24 February 2010 at the 1077th meeting of the Ministers' Deputies.

CoM, *Rules of the Committee of Ministers for the supervision of the execution of judgments and of the terms of friendly settlements*, adopted by the Committee of Ministers on 10 May 2006 at the 964 the meeting of the Ministers' Deputies and amended on 18 January 2017 at the 1275 the meeting of the Ministers' Deputies.

CoM, Resolution CM/ResDH(2018)467, Execution of the judgments of the European Court of Human Rights, *Case of Hirst vs. the United Kingdom (No. 2) and 4 other cases*, adopted by the Committee of Ministers on 6 December 2018 at the 1331st meeting of the Ministers' Deputies.

3. African Union

OAU, *Protocol to the African Charter on Human and Peoples' Rights on the Establishment of an African Court on Human and Peoples' Rights*, 10 June 1998, entered into force on 25 January 2004.

AU, *Protocol to the African Charter on Human and Peoples' Rights on the Rights of Women in Africa*, 11 July 2003.

4. United Nations

UN, *Statute of the International Court of Justice*, 18 April 1946.

UNGA, *United Nations Standard Minimum Rules for the Treatment of Prisoners* (A/RES/70/175), adopted on 30 August 1955.

UNGA, *Optional Protocol on the Sale of Children, Child Prostitution and Child Pornography*, A/RES/54/263, 25 May 2000, entered into force on 18 January 2002.

UNGA, *Optional Protocol on the Involvement of Children in Armed Conflict*, A/RES/54/263, 25 May 2000, entered into force on 12 February 2002.

UN Commission on Human Rights, *Updated Set of Principles for the Protection and Promotion of Human Rights through Action to Combat Impunity* (E/CN.4/2005/102/Add.1), 8 February 2005.

UNGA, *Principles and Guidelines on the Right to a Remedy and Reparation for Victims of Gross Violations of International Human Rights Law and Serious Violations of International Humanitarian Law*, adopted by the UNGA Resolution 60/147, 16 December 2005.

UNGA, *United Nations Declaration on the Rights of Indigenous Peoples* (A/RES/61/295), adopted on 2 October 2007.

UN HRCee, *Guidelines on measures of reparation under the Optional Protocol to the International Covenant on Civil and Political Rights* (CCPR/C/158), 30 November 2016.

UN Secretary General, *Responsibility of States for internationally wrongful acts: Compilation of decisions of international courts, tribunals and other bodies*, Report of the Secretary General, UN Doc. A/74/83, 2019.

a) UN Human Rights Treaty Bodies

i) General Comments

HRCee, *General Comment 11: Article 20 (Prohibition of Propaganda for War and Inciting National, Racial or Religious Hatred)*, adopted at the 19th Session of the Human Rights Committee, 29 July 1983.

HRCee, *General Comment No. 18: Non-discrimination*, adopted at the 37th Session of the Human Rights Committee, 10 November 1989.

CESCR, *General Comment 3: The Nature of States Parties' Obligations (Art. 2, Para. 1 of the Covenant)*, adopted at the 5th Session of the Committee on Economic, Social and Cultural Rights, 14 December 1990.

CRC Commitee, *General Comment No. 5: General measures of implementation of the Convention on the Rights of the Child*, adopted by the Committee on the Rights of the Child at its 34th session, 27 November 2003.

HRCee, *General Comment 31: The nature of the general legal obligation imposed on States Parties to the Covenant* (CCPR/C/21/Rev.1/Add.13), adopted at the 80th Session of the Human Rights Committee, 29 March 2004.

CEDAW Committee, *General Recommendation No. 28 on the Core Obligations of States Parties under Article 2 of the Convention on the Elimination of All Forms of Discrimination against Women* (CEDAW/C/GC/28), adopted by the Committee at its 47th Session, 16 December 2010.

HRCee, *General Comment No. 34: Article 19, Freedoms of opinion and expression* (CCPR/C/GC/34), adopted at the adopted at the 102nd Session of the Human Rights Committee, 12 September 2011.

CERD, *General Recommendation No. 35: Combating racist hate speech* (CERD/C/GC/35), adopted by the Committee on the Elimination of Racial Discrimination at its 83rd session, 26 September 2013.

HRCee, *General Comment No. 36: Article 6 (Right to Life)* (CCPR/C/GC/36), adopted at the 124th Session of the Human Rights Committee, 3 September 2019.

ii) Observations

CRPD Committee, *Concluding Observations on the Initial Report of Costa Rica* (CRPD/C/CRI/CO/1), 12 May 2014.

b) UN International Law Commission

ILC, "Articles on Nationality of Natural Persons in relation to the Succession of States with commentaries", *Yearbook of the International Law Commission*, 1999, vol. II, Part Two, pp. 23–24.

ILC, *Draft Articles on Responsibility of States for Internationally Wrongful Acts*, November 2001.

ILC, *Fragmentation of international law: difficulties arising from the diversification and expansion of international law*, Report finalized by Martti Koskenniemi, 2016.

5. Others

League of Nations, *Covenant of the League of Nations*, 28 April 1919, available at: https://libraryresources.unog.ch/ld.php?content_id=32971179.

International Commission of Jurists, *International Principles on the Independence and Accountability of Judges, Lawyers and Prosecutors – A Practitioners Guide*, 2007, Practitioners Guide No. 1, available at: https://www.icj.org/no-1-international-principles-onthe-independence-and-accountability-of-judges-lawyers-and-prosecutors/.

ECOWAS, *Protocol on Democracy and Good Governance* (A/SP1/12/01), 21 December 2001.